OXFORD STUDIES IN ROMAN SOCIETY AND LAW

General Editors

OXFORD STUDIES IN ROMAN SOCIETY AND LAW

The aim of this monograph series is to create an interdisciplinary forum devoted to the interaction between legal history and ancient history, in the context of the study of Roman law. Focusing on the relationship of law to society, the volumes will cover the most significant periods of Roman law (up to the death of Justinian in 565) so as to provide a balanced view of growth, decline, and resurgence. Most importantly, the series will provoke general debate over the extent to which legal rules should be examined in light of the society which produced them in order to understand their purpose and efficacy.

Medicine and the Law under the Roman Empire

Edited by

CLAIRE BUBB

and

MICHAEL PEACHIN

OXFORD
UNIVERSITY PRESS

OXFORD
UNIVERSITY PRESS

Great Clarendon Street, Oxford, OX2 6DP,
United Kingdom

Oxford University Press is a department of the University of Oxford.
It furthers the University's objective of excellence in research, scholarship,
and education by publishing worldwide. Oxford is a registered trade mark of
Oxford University Press in the UK and in certain other countries

Published in the United States of America by Oxford University Press
198 Madison Avenue, New York, NY 10016, United States of America

British Library Cataloguing in Publication Data
Data available

Library of Congress Control Number: 2023932989

ISBN 978–0–19–289861–6

DOI: 10.1093/oso/9780192898616.001.0001

Contents

Acknowledgments

This volume stems from a conference held at New York University on October 4–5, 2019. We would like to thank the NYU Classics Department and the Institute for the Study of the Ancient World for their support of that conference, especially Marc LeBlanc and Nancy Smith-Amer for their skillful logistical work and Roger Bagnall for his early input. We are extremely grateful to everyone who participated for an enriching two days of presentations and discussion, all of which helped shape the volume's final form. We are obliged also to all of our wonderful contributors and owe a particular debt to Ulrike Babusiaux, Alice König, and Joseph Howley for working flexibly with us to navigate some of the curve balls the pandemic threw at the completion of this volume. We would similarly like to thank our editor, Charlotte Loveridge, our interim editor, Karen Raith, our project editor, Alexander Hardie-Forsyth, our project manager, Thomas Deva, and the series editors, Tom McGinn and Paul Du Plessis, for their patience and continued faith in this project despite pandemic delays, and for all of their and their teams' hard work along the way. A penultimate expression of gratitude comes from Peachin, who wishes to acknowledge the Institute for Advanced Study in Princeton; membership there during the 2020–2021 academic year greatly facilitated his work on this project. Finally, we want to thank Brill Publishers for permitting the article by Luis Salas, which appeared in an earlier form as Chapter 5 ("It is Difficult Not to Write Anatomy: Galen on Erasistratus and the Arteries") in his book, *Cutting Words—Polemical Dimensions of Galen's Anatomical Experiments* (Leiden, New York, and Cologne: Brill, 2021), to be revisited in this volume.

List of Contributors

Ulrike Babusiaux, Universität Zürich

Claire Bubb, New York University

Anna Dolganov, Austrian Academy of Sciences

Kendra Eshleman, Boston College

Bruce W. Frier, University of Michigan

Joseph Howley, Columbia University

Alice König, University of St. Andrews

Michael Peachin, New York University

Caroline Petit, University of Warwick and Humboldt-Universität zu Berlin

Matthew Roller, Johns Hopkins University

Luis Alejandro Salas, Washington University in St. Louis

Michael Trapp, King's College London

James Uden, Boston University

Abbreviations and Cited Editions of the Galenic Corpus Used in the Volume

We have collected here a complete list of Galenic works cited across this volume, including their abbreviation, their full title in English and Latin, and the bibliographical details and abbreviations of any editions referred to. This is neither a complete list of the Galenic corpus, nor a complete list of editions of the works mentioned, but it will be sufficient to allow a reader unfamiliar with Galen to navigate the citations in this volume. In addition to any editions listed here, we have always, where available, cited the pagination from the Kühn edition (K), which is standard in most later editions and translations: C. G. Kühn, ed., *Claudii Galeni Opera Omnia* (Leipzig: C. Cnobloch, 1821–1833) (re-issued, Cambridge: Cambridge University Press, 2011). The abbreviations and titles here largely follow those in the appendices to the Cambridge Galen Translation series, which also offer a comprehensive list of editions and translations. For ancient authors other than Galen, we follow the abbreviations in S. Hornblower, A. Spawforth, and E. Eidinow, eds., *Oxford Classical Dictionary* (4th ed.) (Oxford: Oxford University Press, 2012).

*indicates a work that is generally considered to be pseudo-Galenic.

AA	*On Anatomical Procedures* (*De anatomicis administrationibus*) G = I. Garofalo, *Galenus: Anatomicarum Administrationum Libri qui Supersunt Novem. Earundem Interpretation Arabica Hunaino Isaaci Filio Ascripta* (Naples: Brill, 1986–2000).
Aff.Pec.Dig.	*On the Affections and Errors of the Soul* (*De propriorum animi cuiuslibet affectuum et peccatorum dignotione et curatione*)
Ant.	*Antidotes* (*De antidotis*)
Art.Sang.	*Whether Blood Is Naturally Contained in the Arteries* (*An in arteriis natura sanguis contineatur*) F-W = D. J. Furley and J. S. Wilkie, *Galen on Respiration and the Arteries* (Princeton, NJ: Princeton University Press, 1984).
Comp.Med.Gen.	*The Composition of Drugs According to Kind* (*De compositione medicamentorum per genera*)
Cons.	*Customary Practices* (*De consuetudinibus*) *CMG Suppl.* III = I. M. Schmutte, ed., and F. Pfaff, trans., *Galeni De consuetudinibus*. Corpus Medicorum Graecorum Supplementum III (Leipzig: Teubner, 1941).
CP	*Antecedent Causes* (*De causis procatarcticis*) H = R. J. Hankinson, *Galen on Antecedent Causes* (Cambridge: Cambridge University Press, 1998).

Cris.	*On Crises* (*De crisibus*) Alex. = B. Alexanderson, *Peri Kriseon Galenos*. Studia Graeca et Latina Gothoburgensia, 23 (Stockholm: Almquist & Wiksell, 1967).
Di.Dec.	*Critical Days* (*De diebus decretoriis*)
Diff.Puls.	*The Distinct Types of Pulse* (*De differentiis pulsuum*)
Dig.Puls.	*The Discernment of the Pulse* (*De diagnoscendis pulsibus*)
Hipp.Epid.II	*Commentary on Hippocrates'* Epidemics II (*In Hippocratis Epidemiarum librum II*) *CMG Suppl.Or.* V 2 = U. Vagelpohl and S. Swain, eds. and trans., *Galeni In Hippocratis Epidemiarum Librum II Commentariorum I–VI*. Corpus Medicorum Graecorum, Supplementum Orientale V 2 (Berlin: De Gruyter, 2016).
Hipp.Epid.III	*Commentary on Hippocrates'* Epidemics III (*In Hippocratis Epidemiarum librum III*) *CMG* V 10,2,1 = E. Wenkebach, ed., *Galeni In Hippocratis Epidemiarum Libr. III Comm. III*. Corpus Medicorum Graecorum V 10,2,1 (Leipzig: Teubner, 1936).
Hipp.Epid.VI	*Commentary on Hippocrates'* Epidemics VI (*In Hippocratis Epidemiarum librum VI*) *CMG* V 10,2,2 = E. Wenkebach, ed., and F. Pfaff, trans., *Galeni In Hippocratis Epidemiarum Libr. VI Comm. I–VI et Comm. VI–VIII*. Corpus Medicorum Graecorum V 10,2,2 (Berlin: Teubner, 1956).
Hipp.Prog.	*Commentary on Hippocrates'* Prognostic (*In Hippocratis Prognosticum*) *CMG* V 9,2 = H. Diels, J. Mewaldt, and J. Heeg, eds., *Galeni In Hippocratis Prorrheticum I commentaria III, De comate secundum Hippocratem, In Hippocratis Prognosticum commentaria III* (Leipzig and Berlin: Teubner, 1915).
Hipp.Prorrh.	*Commentary on Hippocrates'* Prorrhetics (*In Hippocratis De praedictionibus*) *CMG* V 9,2 = Diels, Mewaldt, and Heeg, *Galeni* (1915) (see above, under *Hipp.Prog.*).
HNH	*Commentary on Hippocrates'* Nature of Man (*In Hippocratis De natura hominis*) *CMG* V 9,1 = J. Mewaldt, G. Helmreich, and J. Westenberger, eds., *Galeni In Hippocratis De natura hominis Comm. III, In Hippocratis De vitcu acutorum Comm. IV, De diaeta Hippocratis in Morbis Acutis*. Corpus Medicorum Graecorum V 9,1 (Leipzig and Berlin: Teubner, 1914).
HVA	*Commentary on Hippocrates'* Regimen in Acute Diseases (*In Hippocratis De acutorum morborum vitcu*) *CMG* V 9,1 = Mewaldt et al., *Galeni* (1914) (see above, under *HNH*).
Indol.	*Avoiding Distress* (*De indolentia*) BJP = V. Boudon-Millot, J. Jouanna, and A. Pietrobelli, *Galien. Tome IV. Ne pas se chagriner* (Paris: Belles Lettres, 2010).

Inst.Log.	*Introduction to Logic* (*Institutio Logica*) Kalbfleisch = K. Kalbfleisch, *Galeni institutio logica* (Leipzig: Teubner, 1896).
Lib.Prop.	*On My Own Books* (*De libris propriis*) B-M = V. Boudon-Millot, *Galien. Tome I. Introduction Générale, Sur l'Ordre de ses Propres Livres, Sur ses Propres Livres, Que l'Excellent Médecin est Aussi Philosophe* (Paris: Belles Lettres, 2007).
Loc.Aff.	*On Affected Places* (*De locis affectis*)
MM	*On the Method of Healing* (*De methodo medendi*)
Nat.Fac.	*On Natural Faculties* (*De naturalibus facultatibus*) *SM* = J. Marquardt, I. von Müller, and G. Helmreich, *Claudii Galeni Pergameni Scripta Minora* (Leipzig: Teubner, 1884–1893).
Opt.Med.	*That the Best Doctor Is Also a Philosopher* (*Quod optimus medicus sit quoque philosophus*) B-M = Boudon-Millot, *Galien* (2007) (see above, under *Lib.Prop.*). *SM* = Marquardt et al., *Scripta Minora* (1884–1893) (see above, under *Nat.Fac.*).
Opt.Med.Cogn.	*On Recognizing the Best Physician* (*De optimo medico cognoscendo*) *CMG Suppl.Or.* IV = A. Z. Iskandar, *Galeni De optimo medico cognoscendo.* Corpus Medicorum Graecorum, Supplementum Orientale IV (Berlin: Akademie Verlag, 1988).
Ord.Lib.Prop.	*On the Order of My Own Books* (*De ordine librorum propriorum*) B-M = Boudon-Millot, *Galien* (2007) (see above, under *Lib.Prop.*).
PHP	*On the Opinions of Hippocrates and Plato* (*De placitis Hippocratis et Platonis*) *CMG* V 4,1,2 = P. De Lacy, *Galeni De placitis Hippocratis et Platonis.* Corpus Medicorum Graecorum V 4,1,2 (Berlin: Akademie Verlag, 2005).
Praen.	*On Prognosis* (*De praenotione ad Epigenem*) *CMG* V 8,1 = V. Nutton, *Galeni De praecognitione.* Corpus Medicorum Graecorum V 8,1 (Berlin: Akademie Verlag, 1979).
Protr.	*Exhortation to Study the Arts* (*Protrepticus*) B = V. Boudon, *Galien. Tome II. Exhortation à l'Étude de la Médecine. Art Médical* (Paris: Belles Lettres, 2002).
Sem.	*On Semen* (*De semine*) *CMG* V 3,1 = P. De Lacy, *Galeni De semine.* Corpus Medicorum Graecorum V 3,1 (Berlin: Akademie Verlag, 1992).
SMT	*The Capacities [and Mixtures] of Simple Drugs* (*De simplicium medicamentorum [temperamentis ac] facultatibus*)
**Ther.Pamph.*	*Theriac, to Pamphilianus* (*De theriaca ad Pamphilianum*) B-M = V. Boudon-Millot, *Galien. Tome X. Thériaque à Pamphilianos* (Paris: Belles Lettres, 2021).
**Ther.Pis.*	*Theriac, to Piso* (*De theriaca ad Pisonem*) B-M = V. Boudon-Millot, *Galien. Tome VI. Thériaque à Pison* (Paris: Belles Lettres, 2016).

Thras.	*Thrasybulus* (*Thrasybulus sive Utrum medicinae sit an gymnasticae hygiene*)
Ut.Diss.	*The Anatomy of the Uterus* (*De uteri dissectione*) *CMG* V 2,1 = D. Nickel, *Galeni De uteri dissectione*. Corpus Medicorum Graecorum V 2,1 (Berlin: Akademie Verlag, 1971).
Ut.Resp.	*On the Function of Breathing* (*De utilitate respirationis*) F-W = Furley and Wilkie, *Galen on Respiration* (1984) (see above under *Art.Sang.*).
Ven.Sect.Er.	*On Venesection Against Erasistratus* (*De venae sectione adversus Erasistratum*)
Ven.Sect.Er.Rom.	*On Venesection Against the Erasistrateans at Rome* (*De venae sectione adversus Erasistrateos Romae degentes*)

PART I

INTRODUCTION

Setting Medicine and Law Apart, Together

Claire Bubb and Michael Peachin

This volume draws the fields of medicine and law, as these existed during the early imperial period of Rome, into conversation with one another. Now, the mere fact that a self-conscious juxtaposition of these two fields in their ancient manifestations has never been seriously attempted might alone warrant the undertaking. That said, it can indeed be argued that there are truly compelling reasons for launching precisely such a project.[1]

We begin with the fact that each of our enterprises was crowned by a resplendent intellectual effort, which manifested itself in a voluminous literature. Here lay the terrain of two rarified and exquisitely trained elites. Just as vital, however, were the pragmatic real-world incarnations of these disciplines, where society's big and little fish alike might thrive. One goal in the pages that follow will thus be to imagine the cerebral and the more workaday facets of each discipline as integral

A note to the reader: There are a number of issues or topics that are discussed in various places throughout this volume—for example, the matter of professionalism in a Roman context. Rather than pepper our footnotes too heavily with cross-references, we steer the reader to our index, which will serve as the primary comprehensive guide to discussion of such matters.

[1] The only work known to us which attempts earnestly to study these two fields jointly is Herberger, *Dogmatik* (1981). Herberger focuses on a particular theoretical approach, Dogmatism, that happens to appear in each of our fields, and he traces this phenomenon from antiquity to the nineteenth century. Thus, the chapters of his book relevant to antiquity draw only one connection between medicine and law, namely, their common engagement with Dogmatism. However, see also Mendelson, "Aspects" (2002), where causation in medicine and law is examined comparatively. In a different vein, Below, *Der Artzt* (1953), studies the regulation of doctors, and their practice of medicine, by the jurists; he thus offers a concentrated study of a medically relevant set of legal questions, rather than anything like the joint study we are concerned with here. We would like to draw attention, though, to Elizabeth Rawson's comment at the start of a chapter on medicine qua intellectual pursuit: "It is interesting to contrast the way in which Greek influence was exercised in this most Greek of all subjects [i.e., medicine], with the way it affected the most Roman, law" (Rawson, *Intellectual Life* (1985) 171). In other words, Rawson appears to sense affinities, which might cause one to single out, and then compare, medicine and law as intellectual pursuits. Rawson's comment also shines a spotlight on an elephant in the room, so to speak: namely, the quintessential Greekness of elite medicine and the unambiguous Latinity of Roman jurisprudence during the high imperial period. However, as the arguments presented in this introduction—and, indeed, those resulting from the volume as a unity—will hopefully convey, the practitioners of these arts were nevertheless operating in the same broader social-political-cultural world and were subject to the pulls of that environment in notably similar ways. Cf. also the comments of Uden, below, p. 218.

Claire Bubb and Michael Peachin, *Setting Medicine and Law Apart, Together* In: *Medicine and the Law under the Roman Empire.* Edited by: Claire Bubb and Michael Peachin, Oxford University Press. © Claire Bubb and Michael Peachin 2023. DOI: 10.1093/oso/9780192898616.003.0001

parts of an original whole—even if the concentration will indeed be on the elite practitioners of these fields.[2] This logic of amalgamation will take a further step. The argument will be that both of these arts, in *all* of their manifestations, were thoroughly bound up in a broad matrix of social, political, cultural, and intellectual concerns, which will have served substantially to shape these occupations themselves, and to do so through and through. Then, finally, we will also want to suggest that a particular set of defining characteristics, which becomes discernible with respect to both medicine and law, serves on the one hand to join these two occupations as a fairly distinct pair, while it simultaneously works to isolate them as a duo, in certain regards, from most other brands of specialized expertise. Thus, by juxtaposing law and medicine in all of these ways, we hope to encourage the kind of broad and more nuanced vision of these two areas themselves—as well as of the wider nexus of specialized expertise under the Roman Empire altogether—which has been gaining significant traction in recent times.[3]

Ultimately, however, one all-encompassing concern lurks here. The issue can be suggested via two questions. First, in the broadest terms possible, and especially if we move beyond the purely utilitarian, what kinds—and we mean expressly any and every kind—of *work* were the fields of law and medicine expected to perform in that now faraway world of ancient Rome? Second, how might the sundry wants of the ancient community with regard to these fields have served to shape the very nature of medical and legal expertise in those times—and indeed, of medicine and law altogether? What, in other words, and in the most all-encompassing sense possible, was the place of a science like medicine or law in the thoughts, desires, and perceived needs of the ancient Roman community, and how did all of that, in turn, potentially influence the substance of these fields of endeavor? We will not be able to address these issues comprehensively, or even too terribly closely; however, we do very much hope that the present volume will encourage further thought in these directions.

So as to set the stage for our discussion, we will now present two figures who typically would not be expected to cross paths—or, in any case, they would not be expected to do so in the arena of modern scholarship. Each of these individuals reaped towering acclaim in the second century CE because of his engagement in an expert pursuit. One fashioned an identity for himself as doctor, the other as jurist.

[2] With regard to the less eminent lawyers, one might now begin with: Jones, "Juristes romains dans l'orient grec" (2007); Lehne-Gstreinthaler, "Jurists in the Shadows" (2016); Dolganov, "*Nutricula causidicorum*" (2020). Of course, the relevant entries in Kunkel, *Juristen* (1967/2001) are still to be consulted. For the parallel group of medical practitioners—a wide and diverse population—see, Nutton, "Healers" (1992) and *Ancient Medicine* (2013) 254–278, as well as the epigraphic evidence collected in Samama, *Les médecins* (2003) and Alonso Alonso, *Médicos* (2018).

[3] We note with enthusiasm that this sort of attention to the cultural contexts of technical or scientific knowledge in the classical world more broadly has burgeoned in recent decades, with studies like, for example, Barton, *Power and Knowledge* (1994); Tuplin and Rihll, *Science and Mathematics* (2002); Gill, Whitmarsh, and Wilkins, *Galen and the World of Knowledge* (2009); Lehoux, *What Did the Romans Know?* (2012); Berrey, *Hellenistic Science at Court* (2017).

The first man, though a true VIP in his own time and place, will hardly be a staple in the scholarly diets of our readers. We speak of Herakleitos, son of Herakleitos, grandson of Oreios, a most exalted gentleman at Lycian Rhodiapolis, who plays the starring role in a group of inscribed texts from that burgh.[4] Here was an individual of extraordinary accomplishment in two facets of the medical arts. We read that, at Athens, the Epicurean philosophers and the guild of theater artists had celebrated Herakleitos during games, and that in the estimation of these groups, he was, "the number one doctor, and author, and poet of the medicinal and philosophical arts, of all time, whom they recorded in writing as being the Homer of doctorly poems, and they sang the praise of his books and poems, and placed these in the imperial libraries."[5] Another of the stones from this dossier offers an epigram composed by his townsmen, wherein Herakleitos is celebrated as "doctor and hegemon of song."[6] We further discover that the city council, the people's assembly, and the board of elders at Rhodiapolis honored Herakleitos by setting up a gilt portrait of him, which was paired with a statue of the deity Paideia. Even more, he was allegedly celebrated in similar fashion at Alexandria, Rhodes, and Athens—three of the most important intellectual hubs of the time.[7] In short, Herakleitos was a genius at turning medicine into an art form. However, and just as the Epicureans and the thymelic synod at Athens had remarked, this man was not merely a superlative litterateur; he was also, at least in their estimation, the best practicing physician ever. Nor was he simply a wonderfully talented doctor; for in his medical practice, Herakleitos had apparently refused ever to charge a patient for the services he rendered.[8] That is to say, this doctor was also a medical philanthropist, another of the qualities trumpeted by his townsmen at Rhodiapolis.[9] Indeed, it was Herakleitos who, above and

[4] For what follows, see the evidence as collected and interpreted by İplikçioğlu, "Heraklit von Rhodiapolis" (2014). This epigraphic dossier consists of: (1) the dedication of an altar of Asklepios and Hygeia in honor of Herakleitos (*TAM* II 910 = *CIG* III 4315 = *IGRR* III 733 = *SEG* 27, 937 = İplikçioğlu 233–242 = *SEG* 64, 1409); (2) a more recently discovered Rhodiapolitan decree honoring Herakleitos (İplikçioğlu 232–234 = *SEG* 64, 1410); (3) a likewise recently discovered epigram inscribed by his compatriots to honor this man (İplikçioğlu 243–245 = *SEG* 64, 1411); (4) a dedicatory inscription for Herakleitos' temple of Asklepios and Hygeia (*TAM* II 906 = *IGRR* III 732 = İplikçioğlu 232 + İplikçioğlu 242); (5) Herakleitos' dedication of the statues of the deities for the interior of this temple (İplikçioğlu 242–243). Note also now Yalvaç, "Herakleitos of Rhodiapolis" (2022) 1–3, offering a new restoration of another inscription from Rhodiapolis, *TAM* II 911; the suggested restoration would give us another version of the fourth text just listed.

[5] İplikçioğlu, "Heraklit von Rhodiapolis" (2014) 233, lines 7–11: *ὃν ἐτείμησαν καὶ οἱ Ἀθήνησιν Ἐπικούρειοι φιλόσοφοι κ[αὶ ἡ ἱερὰ θυμελικὴ]/σύν[ο]δος ἐν ἀγῶνι ἰσελαστικῷ πρῶτον ἀπ' αἰῶνος ἰατρὸν καὶ συνγραφέ[α καὶ ποιητὴν]/ἔργων ἰατρικῆς καὶ φιλοσοφίας, ὃν ἀνέργαψαν ἰατρικῶν ποιημάτων Ὅμη[ρον εἶναι]/ἐπαινέσαντες αὐτοῦ τὰ συν[γρ]άμματα καὶ ποιήματα καὶ ἀποθέμεν[οι ἐν ταῖς]/ἱερωτάταις βιβλιοθήκαις.* On other "new Homers" see Schmitz, *Bildung und Macht* (1997) 46–47 n. 25.

[6] İplikçioğlu, "Heraklit von Rhodiapolis" (2014) 243, lines 2–4: *Ἡράκλειτον/ἰητρόν, ἀοι/δῆς ἡγεμονῆα.*

[7] İplikçioğlu, "Heraklit von Rhodiapolis" (2014) 231, lines 7–9, and 233, lines 4–6.

[8] İplikçioğlu, "Heraklit von Rhodiapolis" (2014) 231, line 17, and 233, lines 11–12.

[9] Another doctor, C. Stertinius Xenophon, was not at all so generous with his services. On him see below, pp. 26–28.

beyond his gratis doctoring, had financed the town's temple of the healing gods Asklepios and Hygieia, where he served in a life-long tenure as chief priest. That shrine was generously adorned with statues of its two deities, again at Herakleitos' expense.[10] And on top, even, of all this, the man donated copies of the complete corpus of his writings, some sixty books overall, to this temple and to the Rhodiapolitan town library, "gifts thus being given to wise doctors"; the corpus of writing was likewise donated to the libraries in Alexandria, Rhodes, and Athens.[11] And lastly, Herakleitos financed medical games at Rhodiapolis in honor of Asklepios, to the tune of nearly 15,000 *denarii*.[12] The Homer of medical poetry, hegemon of song, philosopher, renowned intellectual at Athens, Rhodes, and Alexandria, whose many books were on offer at the libraries in those cities, and in two libraries at Rhodiapolis, the top practicing physician of all time, who did not stoop to charging for his doctoring, teacher of doctors via his writings on medicine, donor of the temple of Asklepios and Hygeia at Rhodiapolis, life-long priest of these two deities, and patron of medical games honoring the doctor god—such a man was our Herakleitos.

Now, despite any hyperbole or generic formulae that might lurk in the texts commemorating him, Herakleitos was no doubt a rather impressive character.[13] In the present context, though, it is the distinct concatenation of remarkable traits and efforts that should draw our attention. Herakleitos was, of course, a member of the gentry at Rhodiapolis; but additionally, in his primary (it seems) chosen field of endeavor, medicine, he was at once a prodigiously productive author and a peerless practitioner.[14] Clearly, this man had ascended to the pinnacle of the socio-political and intellectual world in his own place of origin, as well as throughout the eastern portions of the Roman Empire. But just as clearly, what gained him much of the socio-political capital he surely cherished, and which is so elaborately dished up by the stones proudly sprinkled around Rhodiapolis, were his avowedly incomparable (and, n.b., thoroughly intertwined) talents as a practicing doctor and as the author of prose and poetry on medicine and philosophy.

Not long at all after Herakleitos will have reached his acme, an even greater career, which likewise banked decidedly on skill and fame as a specialized expert,

[10] İplikçioğlu, "Heraklit von Rhodiapolis" (2014) 231, lines 17–19, 232, 233, lines 12–13, and 243.

[11] İplikçioğlu, "Heraklit von Rhodiapolis" (2014) 231, lines 19–21 (with mention of Alexandria, Rhodes, Athens), 233, lines 13–15 (with the books going to the temple and the library in Rhodiapolis, but no mention of the other three towns), and 243, lines 12–15, including the expression *δωρήματα δόντα/ἰητροῖσι σοφοῖς*. For some remarks on local public libraries, like this one at Rhodiapolis, see Neudecker, "Aspekte öffentlicher Bibliotheken" (2004) 302–308.

[12] İplikçioğlu, "Heraklit von Rhodiapolis" (2014) 231, lines 23–4, and 223, lines 15–16.

[13] It is worth noting that the Rhodiapolitan epigram celebrating Herakleitos, given the letter forms of this inscription, will have been set up some 200 years after the man's lifetime. In short, his reputation was not only great in his own day, but quite durable. See İplikçioğlu, "Heraklit von Rhodiapolis" (2014) 244.

[14] Note the comments by König and Peachin below (pp. 162–164) as to Vitruvius' requirement that a truly expert architect possess both practical and learned skill in his field.

would accrue to a native of Hadrumetum in Africa proconsularis. L. Octavius Cornelius P. Salvius Iulianus Aemilianus, or more simply Julian, was making a name for himself as both a top-tier governmental official and as the empire's foremost jurisprudent. The list of offices he attained is truly impressive: quaestor to the emperor Hadrian, tribune of the plebs, praetor, prefect of the treasury, consul, pontifex, curator of the public buildings at Rome, governor of lower Germany, governor of nearer Spain, proconsul of Africa, and close associate of the emperors Hadrian, Antoninus Pius, and Lucius Verus. Here was one of the most preeminent statesmen of the day.[15] But then, at Pupput, not far at all from his native Hadrumetum, Julian was commemorated by the town fathers, who ordered that a statue of him be set up in the center of their city. The inscription on the stone base supporting that effigy pointedly accentuates a particular development in this man's life: Julian's salary, when he served the emperor Hadrian as quaestor, was—exceptionally—doubled "on account of his utterly outstanding learning."[16] What the town fathers at Pupput allude to is the fact that Julian was recognized as arguably the premier legal mind of his day; and, as it would later turn out, he was to enjoy a reputation as one of the greatest Roman jurisconsults ever.[17] In short, we must recognize, as did Hadrian, and as did the folks at Pupput, that Julian's stellar accomplishments in the legal realm were decidedly part and parcel of his socio-political standing altogether—and, conversely, that his overall stature will have contributed variously to his preeminence as a jurist.[18] The whole edifice of this man's life, in other words, leaned heavily upon a foundation cemented by intellectual achievement, which itself was manifested not only by Julian's pragmatic legal interventions (e.g., as member of the imperial *consilium*, or surely in his role as provincial governor), but especially via a remarkable corpus

[15] For Julian's life and career, see *PIR*² S 136, or Bund, "Salvius Iulianus" (1976). See also the splendid "Note di prosopografia e bibliografia" by G. De Cristofaro, contained in a CD Rom (pp. 65–78 of the CD) which is appended to Casavola, *Giuristi adrianei* (2011). And for an overview of Julian's literary oeuvre, see Liebs, "Jurisprudenz" (1997) 101–105.

[16] *CIL* VIII 24094 = *ILS* 8973 lines 3–5: *cui divos Hadrianus soli / salarium quaesturae duplicavit / propter insignem doctrinam*. For reassurance that the *doctrina* involved here is legal, see Liebs, *Hofjuristen* (2010) 37; also Eck, "Senatorisches Leben" (2012) 177; and on the fact that this salary increase was indeed a highly unusual gift by an emperor, and not idle puffery on the part of the town fathers at Pupput, see Millar, *Emperor* (1977) 491.

[17] Looking back from his perch in the sixth century CE, the emperor Justinian marked him as, "the greatest author of the science of jurisprudence" and "a man of the very greatest authority." See: Iust. C. 3.33.15.1 (a. 530) (*summum auctorem iuris scientiae*) and 4.5.10.1 (a. 530) (*summae auctoritatis hominem*).

[18] Kunkel, *Juristen* (1967/2001) 123–124, for example, notes Pomponius' description, in his *Enchiridion*, of several jurists: Proculus, Caelius Sabinus, and C. Cassius Longinus. In each case, Pomponius connects the *auctoritas* that accrues to the man from his juristic *doctrina* inextricably with his broader socio-political cachet. And, indeed, Kunkel cites Jacques Cujas, who expressly made the point (à propos of what Pomponius says about Longinus) long ago (in his *De origine iuris et iuris auctoribus ex Enchridio Pomponii*, in *Opera II*, Frankfurt 1623): *accedit ad doctrinam commendatio ex potentia* ("there accrues to his learning a boost from his overall power") (we borrow the quotation from Kunkel). On all of this during the republican period, see Mantovani, "*Iuris scientia* e *honores*" (1997). See also below, n. 49.

of juristic writing.[19] This African gentleman, and the lawyerly brilliance that helped to establish his ascendancy, in toto, emphatically recalls the situation of our Rhodiapolitan doctor.

These two life stories confront us with quite a lot to unpack. Let us perhaps begin at the top, so to speak—that is, with the writing to which men like Herakleitos and Julian so ardently devoted themselves. Literary production of this kind is, of course, what now can most readily be grasped of these two sciences as they operated in antiquity. And indeed, our individual worries about the nature of these literatures (medical on Bubb's part, legal for Peachin) generated several early conversations, which led to a conference at New York University in the early fall of 2019 and now, ultimately, to the pages offered here. In any case, we begin with literature.

Now, it is crucial to realize that both the writings of the doctors and those of the lawyers have typically been perceived, at least by modern scholars, as belonging to the body of so-called technical literature—on the face of it, a widespread production of unaffected "how-to" manuals.[20] However, this kind of writing, as a class, has for some years been undergoing a significant reassessment. The most fundamental conclusion of this discussion is that ancient technical prose literature, as a whole, was both produced and consumed qua literature—i.e., that this kind of writing was, in some way, or ways, aesthetic, or artistic, or intellectually oriented, and not mulishly utilitarian.[21] Didactic verse is likewise being envisioned through precisely such a recalibrated lens.[22] We are thus confronted with a challenge: if our two bodies of writing do indeed belong to this particular sector of ancient literary production, how do they fit in generally with the other technical books? That is to say, how might our perception of medical and legal writing change, if we begin to

[19] Julian served often, it would seem, on the imperial *consilia*, where his legal acumen must constantly have come into play in the regulation of real-world situations; and he was the man chosen by Hadrian to consolidate the praetor's edict, a watershed event in the history of Roman law and legal scholarship. Cf. Crook, *Consilium Principis* (1955) 182, or Amarelli, *Consilia principum* (1983) 168 n. 81. As for the preeminence of his literary output, note, e.g., Schulz, *Geschichte* (1961) 117, "Die Digesten des Salvius Iulianus sind die großartigste literarische Leistung der römischen Jurisprudenz; sie beherrscht sichtlich die Rechtswissenschaft bis zum Ende des Prinzipats."

[20] See, e.g., von Albrecht, *Roman Literature* (1997), who presents both the writers on law and Celsus (qua author on medicine, though he is an atypical specimen—cf. below, p. 29) under the rubric "Technical and Educational Authors."

[21] See, e.g., Formisano, *Tecnica* (2001); Asper, *Wissenschaftstexte* (2007); Fögen, *Wissen* (2009); Taub and Doody, *Authorial Voices* (2009); Asper and Kanthak, *Writing Science* (2013). Also important is König and Woolf, *Authority and Expertise* (2017).

[22] For example, the *Theriaca* by Nicander of Colophon, a poet, priest, and doctor (n.b., not unlike our Herakleitos), offers just under 1,000 lines of hexameter verse about poisonous animals; and a recent edition and commentary raises precisely some of the issues we are referring to. See Overduin, *Nicander* (2015) 1–2, who writes, "The poem's reception in modern criticism has been dominated by two main objections: its lack of literary merit as a poem, and its lack of practical usefulness as a handbook on snakebites. . . . My study aims to provide a picture of the *Theriaca* as a poem with its own literary merits." Note also Taub, "Explaining a Volcano" (2009), on the pseudo-Vergilian *Aetna*. Broadly on Latin didactic verse, Volk, *Poetics* (2002).

think of this oeuvre as "literature"; and then, what exactly might the consequences be if we do that?

First, let us consider the justification for classing (say) Galen or Ulpian with other authors of technical "handbooks." As it happens, we have a provocative indication of one nuclear intellectual family to which our fields, and hence their literatures, were imagined as belonging. A. Cornelius Celsus' *Artes* looks to have been an attempt to sketch the forms of, let us say, technical or pragmatic knowledge or expertise most essentially required by any gentleman worth his salt. Such a fellow, at least to Celsus' mind, ought to have been conversant in these areas: medicine, agriculture, rhetoric, military science, philosophy, and, perhaps, law.[23] So, were we to cast our lot with Celsus, then the disciplines of (and thus the literatures about) agriculture, rhetoric, military science, and philosophy will have been the siblings of our two.[24] On this view of things, other forms of literature—history, for example—become something more like cousins, at some degree of remove. Be that all as it may, insofar as we really do consider the corpora on medicine and law as properly classed among some group of (roughly speaking) technical or pragmatic writings (though in fact, there is not much point in any attempt to establish an absolutely fixed group), then we must equally presume that much of what is now being said about ancient technical literature, in toto, can and should likewise be said, to one extent or another, about legal or medical literature. What, then, is the situation regarding our two corpora of writing?

[23] The various contents of this encyclopedia (if indeed we should call it that) are attested to by uneven evidence. Without dilating on the details—which can be found in the cited sources below—we note that law is by far the least secure member of this list. As a result, some include law: Wellmann, "Cornelius" (1900) 1273–1276; Kappelmacher, *Untersuchungen* (1918) esp. 1–18; von Albrecht, *Roman Literature* (1997) 1239; Sallmann, "Celsus" (2006). Others recommend caution in this regard: Schulze, *Celsus* (2001) 7, 13–17; Sconocchia, "Medicina romana" (2002) 332. And yet others are minded to exclude law: Barwick, "Zu den Schriften" (1948); Krenkel, "Zu den *Artes*" (1959), though he does consider it, with skepticism, in "A. Cornelius Celsus" (1973); Serbat, *Celse* (1995) xi–xiv; Gautherie, *Celse* (2017) 37–39.

[24] Celsus was hardly the only person, of course, to envision something along the lines of an intellectual canon, "technical" or otherwise. Varro's *Disciplinae*, to name another example, rounded up the *artes liberales* thus: grammar, dialectic, rhetoric, geometry, arithmetic, astronomy, music, medicine, and architecture. See: Ritschl, *Opuscula* (1877) 352–402; Hadot, *Arts libéraux* (1984) 57–58, 156–190; or, briefly, von Albrecht, *Roman Literature* (1997) 596. Or, one might think of Velleius Paterculus, who offers an excursus on (roughly speaking) cultural history, in which he includes the following *professiones*: tragedy, comedy, philosophy, oratory, history, poetry, to which he adds, as a kind of brief appendix (albeit with no detail whatsoever), grammarians, potters, painters, and sculptors (Vell. 1.16–17.4); for comment on this passage, see Noé, "Gli excursus" (1982) and Russo, "The literary *excursus*" (2008). As for the *artes liberales*, these were also tallied in the juristic literature thus: philosophy, grammar, rhetoric, geometry/land surveying, law, medicine, architecture; on this, see Visky, *Geistige Arbeit* (1977). Galen, too, has suggestions about the matter (*Protr.* 14 (I.39K = 117 B)): medicine, rhetoric, music, geometry, arithmetic, logic, astronomy, grammar, and law. Cf. also König and Peachin, below (p. 163), for Vitruvius' roundup of the disciplinary competence expected of any truly expert architect, viz.: draftsmanship, geometry, optics, arithmetic, history, philosophy, physiology, music, mathematics, medicine, law, astronomy. And, for a reckoning altogether of the "greatest and most outstanding things which wise men spend their lives pursuing," as proposed by Q. Caecilius Metellus (*cos.* 206 BCE), see Plin. *HN* 7.139.

Ancient medical literature was traditionally conceived of as, in the first place, a body of lore which could instruct the practicing doctor when he was faced with the task of healing patients—as such, very much a technical genre of writing. Indeed, until the middle of the nineteenth century, ancient medical texts were largely in the hands of the medical community, who continued to look to those aged books for practical wisdom. The current standard edition of Galen's writing, for example—by far the largest trove of medical writing to survive from antiquity—dates to the 1820s and was edited by a doctor for the benefit of medical students.[25] When it did fall to the hands of Classicists, beginning in the early twentieth century, ancient medicine remained a highly specialized field, linked to the rest of Classical literature mainly through its ties to philosophy. All in all, medical literature was both envisioned and treated as a phenomenon isolated from the rest of the Classics, and indeed as somehow distinct even from its brethren technical treatises.[26] As the last millennium waned, however, scholarship on medical literature was rather on the forefront of the growing awareness that much ancient technical literature was indeed both produced and consumed in what could be labeled a more aesthetic sense, viz., as a form of writing that we could feel comfortable calling literature.[27] To argue the subject at length here, then, would be largely to knock on an open door.

In the realm of ancient legal writing the situation is arguably more complex.[28] To begin with, we must first and foremost never lose sight of two absolutely crucial facts. First, the lion's share of extant writing about law has been transmitted to us via the monstrous congeries that is Justinian's *Digest*. In other words, we simply do not possess anything like proper texts of original books—we have no lawyerly equivalent to the oeuvre of Galen.[29] Rather, we must grapple with a kind of Monte Testaccio, which one can scavenge for bits and pieces, so as then to puzzle together the vague lineaments of the originals.[30] Thus, discussing these books as written

[25] Kühn, *Opera Omnia* (1821–1833); for the history of the edition, see Nutton, "Kühn" (2002).

[26] On legal literature having long been perceived similarly, see below, n. 61.

[27] Reardon, *Courants littéraires* (1971) notably included an entire half-chapter dedicated to Galen, though considering him mostly in the light of a philosopher, while the preface of Nutton, *Prognosis* (1979) argues that Galen, in this semi-autobiographical work, ought to be considered a "master of all the techniques of literary composition" (p. 63). Appreciation of the literary aspects of Galen's more purely medical texts has grown in the following decades, with Petit, *Rhétorique de la Providence* (2018) offering a recent example of the progress in this direction. The same trend is visible across medical literature beyond Galen; see, e.g., Jouanna, "Rhétorique et médecine" (1984); Pigeaud and Pigeaud, *Textes médicaux latins* (2000); and Cross, *Hippocratic Oratory* (2018).

[28] Indeed, it should be noted that the writings of the jurists have not played much of a role at all in the ongoing reassessment of technical literature. One exception, which indicates the rule, is Harries, "*Iurisperiti*" (2017).

[29] Gaius' *Institutes*, the one nearly complete text that we do have, pales utterly by comparison with the remaining corpus of Galen's writing. Nor is it anything like representative of the body of Roman legal writing.

[30] Until very recently, the original works of the Roman jurists were to be read, insofar as this is at all possible, via Lenel, *Palingenesia* (1889/2000), or also, for the earlier practitioners of this art, in Bremer, *Iurisprudentiae antehadrianae* (1896–1901). Now, however, a long-term project, currently headed up

artifacts is a precarious undertaking. Second, and equally important, is the fact that the remnants of those originals have been preserved primarily in the form of a codification (Justinian's *Digest*), whose plainly stated purpose was precisely to serve as *the* font of substantive law for the community, and whose influence on all subsequent legal thinking has been enormous. This has often led to a kind of reflexive and tacit, though also sweeping, conflation of an original body of writing which was, to a notable extent, *about* law, with what we would think of as *the* binding statutory law itself. Now, while this view of things is by no means entirely wrong, it is also not entirely accurate.[31] In fine, then, while the substantive law and the juristic literature of the high imperial period are easily perceived as effectively one and the same, it is important to recognize that, ultimately, and most accurately, when one reads the *Digest*, one is contemplating the now sparse disiecta membra of an originally vast and privately produced literature *about* law—yet which could, given the right circumstances, serve precisely as the substantive law. With all of this in mind, let us now contemplate what presently can, with any confidence, be said about Roman legal literature.

The departure point for any analysis must be that, indeed, readings of the extant corpus of Roman legal writing by modern scholars have long been preponderantly utilitarian. That is to say, one investigates this stuff so as to discover what the substance of the law on this, that, or the other matter was, all the while operating with a latent assumption that the regulation of the matters in question is what these texts were first and foremost created *for*. Again, there is nothing at all necessarily wrong with such an approach. For when all is said and done, the written oeuvre of the jurists could very well function as a vast bundle of proffered rules for the conduct of affairs; and, to be sure, the jurists themselves were hardly divorced from, or blind to, the realities of their world—nor, conversely, did the denizens of that real world disregard the work of the jurists.[32] That all said, some

by Aldo Schiavone, and published by L'Erma di Bretschneider, the *Scriptores iuris Romani*, is producing volumes devoted to the literary oeuvre of individual jurists, with each volume including a text, a translation into Italian, and a commentary. And precisely as the editor of the series says, "Si tratta di una novità assoluta nel panorama della storiografia giuridica e sul mondo antico." See Ferrary, Schiavone, and Stolfi, *Scriptores iuris Romani I* (2018) VII. See also the brief restatement of the matter by Schiavone, "Singularity and Impersonality" (2022) 3–11.

[31] With regard to this issue of the law, as it was created by jurists, and this especially via their writing, one might begin with the compressed but fecund sketch by Liebs, "Jurisprudenz" (1997) 97–99; however, the bibliography on jurists' law is not small. The most essential parameters of the matter now being adumbrated are nicely summed up by, e.g., Schiller, *Roman Law* (1978) 269, "The role of the jurists in the development of the Roman law of the classical epoch is of primary importance, directly or indirectly affecting all phases of the evolution of the law.... Technically, the contribution of the jurists has been said not to have the character of a formal source of the law, though the opposite view has been advanced. Nevertheless, jurists' law constitutes the major element in the totality of the private law of the classical period."

[32] So, to name but one example, the relationships between this body of writing about the law and the real world economy have attracted significant attention. The precise extent and nature of the relationships between the two territories can be discussed; however, that there are relationships is beyond

scholars have indeed drawn attention to the cracks in what can seem to be an unbroken legalistic façade. A splendid example of this is to be found in an article by Bruce Frier. In this piece, Frier tackles an instance of some Roman jurisprudents seemingly attempting to connect their casuistry, which is often terrifically self-involved, to the real world—i.e., to fit high-minded legal theory and quotidian legal practice together. This brings Frier to consider the more artistic side of the literature about law, and thus to ask what this brand of writing might have been for—i.e., what work, altogether, the jurists' literary oeuvre was meant to perform. So as not to miss the nuance of his argument, it is worth quoting him at some length (we have added emphasis):[33]

> *It is not difficult to locate areas in which the Roman jurists apparently elaborate law as an "art form".* . . . The discussions in these texts frequently do smell of the midnight lamp. . . . *At issue here is the "inner" nature of juristic casuistry, above all its degree of flexibility in reaching out to embrace analytical alternatives in order to promote the overall social adequacy of Roman law. The difficult task is to obtain a model that properly balances the internal dynamics of Roman jurisprudence (law as an "art form") against the external demands placed upon it (law as a social subsystem).* . . . [T]o what extent can the law that the jurists created, considered as an entirity or on a rule-by-rule basis, be regarded as actually socially adequate for its time and place? . . . Or to put the question much more broadly: *"What good did Roman law do the Romans?" On this broader level, the "historicization" of Roman law remains still almost entirely a matter of guesswork.*

In short, and crucially for the present context, Frier lucidly points out that, to some degree, the original generation of writing about Roman law was not invariably a purely practical, pragmatic, or utilitarian affair. This stuff was not universally produced with only one thing in mind, namely, to regulate events on a daily basis in Roman courts of law, and thereby to stabilize, by making them more predictable, the quotidian workings of society. Rather, writing about Roman law was, in some part, an artistic confection—or, to put it slightly differently, these jurists were oftentimes producing a type of writing that we might feel comfortable classifying as "literature."

That said, and just as Frier points out, the Roman juristic literature, in its aspect as a literary phenomenon, has traditionally suffered from conspicuous neglect.[34]

dispute. See, e.g., Kehoe, *Law and the Rural Economy* (2007); Lo Cascio and Mantovani, *Diritto romano e economia* (2018); Candy, "Parallel developments" (2020). Note also the essays in Aubert and Sirks, Speculum iuris (2002).

[33] Frier, "Why Did the Jurists Change Roman Law?" (1994) 144–145.

[34] Almost half a century ago, Millar, *Emperor* (1977) 94 hit this nail directly on its head: "The works of the classical jurists of this period, which were later to be excerpted and collated for the *Digest* of Justinian, were not written as 'law codes' but as private scholarly works. . . . I know of no really

Now to be sure, the ties to philosophy or rhetoric have not been missed.[35] The same goes for connections with antiquarian and grammatical writing.[36] However, we simply have not had any proper attempt to envision Roman legal writing as a form of literature which might have been fabricated, in some way or ways, like (say) the literature devoted to philosophy, or like any of the other types of (say) technical literature. Just recently, however, Dario Mantovani has finally begun to put thinking along these lines on a better footing. He has shown us, in a grand leap forward, that we must be prepared to read a text produced by a Roman jurisprudent as a piece of literature, as an aesthetic production, and, in particular, as a form of writing with affinities especially to historical or philosophical texts.[37] The corollary is that legal literature, on the face of it, ought to have been both intended by its authors and understood by its readers to function, in some way or ways, as did most any, or all, of the other branches of technical literature—or, let us say, as did the various writings that might have been classed as being part of a group that could be called the *artes liberales*. There is surely a great deal still to be done in this regard; but, with this push from Mantovani, we are now on the way.[38]

So, given everything that has just been said, it would seem that we can safely assume ancient writings about medicine and law to have been, at least in some significant part, aesthetic productions. Perhaps we should think of them, following Celsus, as closely associated with their kin in the fields of agriculture, military science, rhetoric, and philosophy. Antiquarian, grammatical, and historical writing (at the very least) should also be stirred into the mix. But be that all as it may, there would appear to be one grand underlying truth here. When a man sat down in antiquity to compose a text about medicine or law, the goals he envisioned for that project will not have been simply and purely utilitarian. Authors of medical texts were not writing with one and only one thought in mind, namely, to tell practicing doctors how to practice. Roughly the same goes for the jurisprudents. These men are hardly likely to have thought that they were merely fixing up

illuminating study of the works of the classical jurists considered as scholarly literature of the period." For the suggestion that the juristic literature should be examined as literature, see Peachin, "Jurists and the Law" (2001) 118–120.

[35] On philosophy, Giltaij, "Greek Philosophy" (2016) 197 (citing earlier bibliography) remarks that the philosophical elements discovered in the writings of the jurisprudents are generally thought to have been, "employed more or less in a scientific sense, to define, elucidate and enhance existing legal notions... [t]he degree to which the influence of Greek philosophy went beyond that remains problematic." As for rhetoric, one might nowadays begin with Babusiaux, *Papinians* Quaestiones (2011). Note also her forthcoming article, "Römische Rechtsrhetorik."

[36] See Lehne-Gstreinthaler, Iurisperiti et oratores (2019) 315–329, with earlier bibliography.

[37] Mantovani, *Les jurists* (2018). Cf. also his brief restatement of the matter, Mantovani, "Aspects of the Critical Edition" (2022) 258–260.

[38] Also, the essays by Massimo Brutti, Emanuele Stolfi, Andrea Lovato, and Luigi Raggi in Nasti and Schiavone, *Jurists and Legal Science* (2022) now provide an absolutely splendid picture of the paths long trod by Romanist scholarship, and which have tended to obscure the ways in which the individual jurists shaped their original writings. Indeed, this whole volume, which means to complement the *Scriptores iuris Romani* project (above n. 30), and working in concert with Mantovani's *Les jurists* (2018), is creating a watershed moment in the history of the study of Roman law.

binding statutes, which would then invariably be received as such, thereupon to be inexorably implemented in the courts.

This broad realization has consequences, thus bringing us to a series of other issues which will be tackled in this book. For if substantial concerns aside from, or beyond, workaday practicalities were implicated in the writing about medicine and law, then we must ask: what were those concerns, and what roles might they have played in shaping the very *substance* of medicine or law as the one or the other eventually appeared in its written form?

The question just posed draws our attention to the matter of rhetoric in legal and medical writing, mentioned briefly already. Rhetoric is plainly wrapped up with the aesthetic or artistic aspect of our two bodies of writing, and there will be plenty more to say about the issue in the pages that follow. For the moment, however, let us adumbrate another issue of crucial significance, which is closely intertwined with eloquence.

One should never lose sight of the fact that the rhetorical or aesthetic side of any given piece of ancient writing was highly likely to have been punctiliously tailored, so as to serve the purposes of the intense agonism which infected ancient society to its very core. Thus, Julian and Herakleitos were not commemorated *merely* as *accomplished* writers. Rather, the one soared to a kind of stratosphere as the Homer (no less!) of medical poetry, while the other was forever treasured as the greatest author of all on legal science. In short, good was not good enough; absolute best was always better. We glimpse this mentality through the eyes of Claudius Mamertinus, when he gazes back upon earlier times, and pines for the venerable "science of civil law, which catapulted the Manilii, the Scaevolas, the Servii to the very pinnacle of grandeur," or through those of Galen, who relishes the "mighty reputation . . . and great name" that followed from his own successful career.[39] Celebrated intellectualism, in other words, was part and parcel of the overall image as an especially great man, and was contested tooth and nail.[40] This issue of a pervasive penchant for one-upmanship will also be handled in the pages to come. Suffice it to say, at this point, that the elegance and grace with which one might infuse one's writing was hardly a matter of mere art for art's sake. For in the world fashioned by Roman antiquity's elite writers, and these will include those who composed on medicine and law, the pen might indeed function nearly like a sword.[41]

This issue of agonism also serves to transport us from the heights of bookish elegance to the more prosaic manifestations of law and medicine; for here, in

[39] *Pan. Lat.* III (XI) 20.1: *iuris civilis scientia, quae Manilios Scaevolas Servios in amplissium gradum dignitatis evexit* (delivered in 362 CE); Galen *Praen.* 5 (XIV.625K = *CMG* V 8,1 94) (*πολλὴ δόξα . . . καὶ μέγα τοὔνομα Γαληνοῦ*).

[40] In this regard, note Eck, "Senatorisches Leben" (2022a). See also: Jones, "Culture in the Careers of Eastern Senators" (2005)—though, n.b., he is chary of allowing culture too much influence over the rise of easterners to the rank of senator; and Salomies, "Redner und Senatoren" (2005).

[41] Champlin, "Aselius Sabinus" (2017) 186 nicely distills our point: "Lively cultural discussion at Rome veered easily into combat sport."

doctors' "offices" and in courtrooms, the same kind of competitive rivalry that infected much of the literature was likewise relentlessly on display. But now, another element is added to the equation. For when either medicine or law popped up in the forum, emulous strife between the actors suddenly became a species of cherished public entertainment.[42] Indeed, the deeply practical nature of each endeavor meant that the stakes of such encounters could literally be life-or-death for the unfortunate patient or litigant in question, adding further zest for the audience and increasing the potential glory or humiliation for the expert participants.[43]

For this competitive urge in the realm of medicine, we can look to the testimony of Galen, who found tremendous success as a practicing doctor (not to mention the time to write prodigiously on medicine) in Rome over the course of the second century CE, as well as to the numerous inscriptions from cities praising their local doctors, similar to those erected for Herakleitos.[44] It is clear from these that medical practice was an unremittingly competitive and public affair. Treatment of patients was habitually performed before a critical audience. A doctor and his patient did not enjoy the private, confidential relationship that is so carefully protected in today's world—nor does it seem that either would have particularly desired it. Quite the contrary, a patient, particularly a rich, influential, and urban one, would crowd his bedside with onlookers, both medical and otherwise, in the hopes that competition would lead to the best treatment.[45] Galen describes sick-rooms packed with doctors jockeying for control of the case and non-medical friends and family interjecting their opinions: the arguments were heated—tears and brawls were not unheard of—and reputations were made and broken by the patients' outcomes.[46] While life and death were on the line at the bedside, heightening the stakes, the eristic, performative mood spilled well beyond the

[42] For a sense of the wider background, against which spectacular medicine and law might be placed, one might think of the various skilled practitioners who competed in the context of festivals. On this, see Chaniotis, "Festivals and Contests" (2011) 21–26, listing championships in: athletics; drama; music; equestrian disciplines; dance; sculpting; medicine; philology; among sophists, and rhapsodes; and also in beauty. Moreover, Chaniotis stresses the social prestige that accrued to the victors in these competitions (p. 26). Note also Vitr. *De arch.* 10.16.3, who describes a public presentation at Rhodes by the architect Callias of Arados. Callias demonstrated his model of a contraption that would snatch up threatening siege machines. The Rhodians were so impressed by this lecture that they replaced their former publicly supported architect, Diognetus, with Callias.

[43] Galen himself recognizes the affinities between our two fields in this regard: at *Di.Dec.* 1.1 (IX.772K), he compares the sufferer of an illness to being in just as bad a state of fear as those being judged on a capital charge in the courts and, at *Hipp.Prog.* 3.6 (XVIIIb.231K = *CMG* V 9,2 329), he explains that the term κρίσις in illness (i.e., crisis or turning point) is a transference from the κρίσις in the courts (i.e., judgment, turning point in the case).

[44] For the inscriptions, see Samama, *Les médecins* (2003).

[45] See, for example, Galen *Praen.* 2 (XIV.609K = *CMG* V 8,1 78), where Eudemus "gathers the best of the doctors in the city" to determine his treatment; cf. 8 (XIV.641–642K = *CMG* V 8,1 110), where Boethus does the same for his wife.

[46] Galen's *On Prognosis* offers many relevant anecdotes; for a broader survey and analysis of bedside interactions in Galen, see Mattern, *Galen* (2008). For a broader inquiry into the patient/healer relationship beyond Galen, see Israelowich, *Patients and Healers* (2015).

realm of practical treatment: highly rhetorical medical lectures, heated medical debates (complete with heckling audience), judged medical competitions, and even public demonstrations of dissection and vivisection in support of medical theories were all a part of the cosmos of erudite entertainment available to those who enjoyed frequenting the courts or the packed performances of the sophists. Indeed, Aelius Aristides, the famous orator who was also a notorious invalid, sees the cross-over potential and offers rhetorical performances from his sickbed in between medical consultations.[47] In short, even when not engaged in patient care, a Roman doctor of Herakleitos' or Galen's level (that is, one with a sufficiently elevated social standing to work *pro bono*, or to be able to produce literature) would have had repeatedly to prove his intellectual chops against his rivals in public. And all this, as we have remarked above, also had a profound impact on the literature, where, with a conscious eye to outdoing their rivals, learned doctors supplemented drier, pragmatic treatises in their oeuvres with carefully crafted productions (like Herakleitos' poetry), with rhetorically charged polemics (like much of Galen's corpus), and even with esoteric scholarly editions of the work of previous doctors, which might seem more at home in the library of Alexandria than in a doctor's surgery.

The world of law functioned similarly. To begin, one need look no further than the *ius controversum*, i.e., the many gray areas, where different jurists held different opinions on matters of law, where these divergent positions were contested tooth and nail, and where personal *auctoritas* was the factor that often could carry the day.[48] Obviously, points of what might be substantive law were at stake here, and thus, the most cogent *legal* argument mattered. However, hand-in-hand with the legal conundrum per se went the authority of the man promoting his interpretation; and, let us not forget that this fellow's *auctoritas* qua legal expert, precisely as we saw with Julian, was thoroughly intertwined with his status otherwise.[49] Thus, prevailing in a tussle over a point of law must often have involved consequences that went well beyond anyone's worries about fixing the

[47] Aristid. *Or.* 47.64; on the window that Aristides gives to the social history of medicine in his day, see Israelowich, *Society, Medicine, and Religion* (2012) 37–135.

[48] This *ius controversum* is a topic with a very large bibliography. However, see especially: Bretone, "*Ius controversum*" (2008), or Marotta and Stolfi, Ius controversum (2012). Cf. also Moatti, *Birth of Critical Thinking* (2015) 195–197, placing this into a larger intellectual context. The crux of the matter (though with regard specifically to juristic *responsa*, on which see immediately below) was put nicely long ago by Leonhard, "Iurisprudentia" (1918) 1163: "Wurde im Einzelfall dem befragten Juristen das Gutachten eines anderen mitgeteilt, dem er beizupflichten nicht geneigt war, so war es Gebot der Wahrung der eigenen Autorität, die eigene Ansicht schärfer zu begründen, um die fremde nicht gebilligte Ansicht wirksam zu bekämpfen." This all said, due caution is necessary. Thus, see the comments in Frier's contribution to this volume regarding the ways in which the jurists, despite all of their wrangling, did indeed find ways to cooperate, so as to inject some level of stability into the substantive law.

[49] See above, n. 18. Also on this point, see briefly Lehne, "Die Stellung" (2014) 239–240, and earlier, Mantovani, "*Iuris scientia* e *honores*" (1997) 670–676. Broadly on *auctoritas*, see now David and Hurlet, *L'*auctoritas (2020), and especially the articles of Mantovani and Schiavone in that volume.

legal issue so that it might be predictable, and equally well past the mere satisfaction which might accrue to the jurist recognized as being right. Indeed, the entire place in the world of the man engaged in such a dispute hung, to no insignificant degree, in the balance.

As for the matter presently under consideration, it is crucial to realize that these lawyerly scuffles, while they surely surfaced in many a piece of writing about law, appear also to have spilled out of the books and into the open. Aulus Gellius, for example, recalls putting his reading aside one day, and loping down to the forum. There, he discovered lively debate in the many *stationes ius publice docentium et respondentium* (i.e., the "offices" where jurisprudents both taught law and gave legal advice to interested parties) as to whether a serving quaestor could be summoned before a praetor. Gellius quickly fetched his copy of Varro's *Antiquitates rerum humanarum*, read an apposite passage from that tome to the assembled crowd, and thereby managed to settle the matter.[50] The important point for us is that these stations, just like the doctors' rendezvous, seem to have been places where an audience could gather, so as to gawk at, heckle, or cheer on the experts contentiously displaying their prowess.[51] The law courts themselves were probably more raucous yet. Here, barristers, advising jurists, litigants, witnesses, judges, and large audiences, with claques potentially working for both sides in the dispute, all gathered together for a rollicking good time.[52] And one emperor, Caracalla, can even be suspected of hijacking some litigants and their legal troubles so as to get up a nice entertainment for his traveling entourage.[53]

In sum, then, doctors and lawyers alike contended vehemently with each other in their writings; but, the very same urge to contend spilled over into the most obviously pragmatic spheres of their arts. At stake for the doctor or lawyer was *auctoritas* and, hence, *dignitas*, both in the field itself and in society overall. Thus, courts of law and medical treatments were turned into arenas where the practitioners of these arts could plume themselves—and do so, in no small part, by assailing their colleagues. And all of this, in the courtroom or at the bedside, regularly offered merriment to a fascinated and rabid audience. Indeed, at some

[50] Gell. *NA* 13.13.

[51] For legal disputation in apparently public locales, note Cic. *Top.* 14.56, with mention of the debates that occurred when legal responses were offered (*in respondendo disputationes*), and at *Top.* 17.66, where Cicero remarks that jurists, not unlike philosophers and orators, will profit from studying previous arguments when it comes to tussling about their legal consultations: *licebit igitur diligenter argumentorum cognitis locis non modo oratoribus et philosophis, sed iuris etiam peritis copiose de consultationibus suis disputare.* Scaevola, to name a further example of this phenomenon, is recorded to have responded in the negative to a question about a matter of inheritance, and then to have articulated his position in disputing the issue (*in disputando adiecebat*): Paul (1 *ad Vitell.*) D. 28.2.19. Ultimately, however, we are not at all well informed about this phenomenon, with much remaining speculative. See Tuori, "A Place for Jurists?" (2010). Note also that Frier (below p. 178) wonders how sharp such debates may have been.

[52] For a full treatment of this phenomenon, though centered on Rome itself, see Bablitz, *Actors and Audience* (2007).

[53] See Williams, "Caracalla and the Rhetoricians" (1974).

point, one might even begin to wonder whether the dispositions of the doctors and lawyers guided them more toward healing patients and resolving legal strife or, rather, in the direction of their own diverse wants.[54] Since a universally valid answer to this question will hardly be forthcoming, perhaps we might best suppose that inclinations gravitated between these two poles.

Let us now attempt to tally all that we have thus far portrayed. First, certain members of elite society chose to dress themselves in the mantle of the medical arts or of jurisprudence and might consequently devote themselves to writing on the subject.[55] This writing, however, was neither invariably nor purely utilitarian, but also entailed a whole range of concerns, some social, some political, some artistic, or intellectual—and all of this routinely revolved, to some degree, around the self-representation of the artist. Moreover, such literature could easily tilt toward polemic, given that reputations, and thus life courses, were at stake.[56] Then, the elite doctors and lawyers, along with others who specialized as did they, but were of a lesser social caliber, also went out into the world and practiced law or medicine. Here, too, *aemulatio* was ever present. And finally, the bickering and jostling for position which marked the courts and the doctors' rounds functioned simultaneously as giddy diversion for substantial audiences.

Against such a background, we offer a fundamental proposition. It is our contention that, when all is said and done, not one single part of this intricate pastiche can be properly understood if that part is isolated from the others. The chief object of all that is contained between the covers of the present book, then, is to move scholarly thought about ancient law and medicine precisely in the direction of comprehending all of this, with respect to both of these fields, as an organic whole.[57]

[54] Indeed, Galen, channeling just such a mentality, accuses some of his contemporaries of sticking to medical views that they know or suspect are mistaken simply for reputational concerns; see *MM* 1.7 (X.58K); *Aff.Pec.Dig.* 2.2–3 (V.63, 69K).

[55] Of course, the social and cultural environment in the Roman world was such that the elites involving themselves in these two fields were drawn from largely different pools—though, see the comments on some potential "dualizers" at the end of this chapter. By and large, a Roman gentleman would not find it proper to become a doctor, nor would his Greek counterpart feel much at home in Roman law. Our point, however, is that in choosing to specialize in these fields at an elite level, these people, despite their various differences, were aiming at precisely similar goals.

[56] Though, again, note the comments in Frier's chapter below as to intermittent cooperation among the lawyers.

[57] Our point, in effect, is now forcefully put by Schiavone, "Jurists and Legal Science" (2022) 10. Talking of the "authorality" of the jurists, he notes that this phenomenon is "... revealed in the network of connections linking the profile of each author to an environment, to a time, to a world and a circulation of ideas; to a general view of his duties and his role, and of those of the science he cultivates; to a peculiar relationship with political power: all elements that determine and condition even the most technical choices—their axis and their specific curvature, we might say—in a subtle but always decipherable interplay between knowledge merely received and new knowledge personally produced." He then goes on to point to "... the historical importance of a set of disciplinary devices and the ontological apparatus underlying them, which otherwise were destined to appear—as they have often done and continue to do today in many respects—as structures outside of time, almost as if the social

That said, a return to the issue posed at the very outset now seems apposite: Why should we have chosen to isolate these two disciplines in particular? The concatenation of factors just outlined provides the key. For this precise group of factors, which characterizes coequally medicine and law, and hence surely binds the two disciplines, in a certain sense and to some degree concurrently isolates them; and it isolates them, as a distinct pair, from pretty well all of the other *artes liberales*. Therefore, if we are to grasp either of these fields through and through, it seems that we should somehow come to grips with this situation—or at the very least, we should remain ever alive to it. A few words devoted to this matter will not be out of place.

In order that we might adhere to Roman imperial thinking in this regard, let us first recall the lists of *artes*, or *disciplinae*, or *professiones* in which one or both of our fields were included (see above, n. 24): (1) medicine and perhaps law, together with agriculture, military science, rhetoric, and philosophy (Celsus); (2) medicine, together with grammar, dialectic, rhetoric, geometry, arithmetic, astronomy, music, and architecture (Varro); (3) medicine and law, together with draftsmanship, geometry, optics, arithmetic, history, philosophy, physiology, music, mathematics, and astronomy (Vitruvius); (4) medicine and law, together with philosophy, grammar, rhetoric, geometry/land surveying, and architecture (Visky on the legal authors); (5) medicine and law, together with rhetoric, music, geometry, arithmetic, logic, astronomy, and grammar (Galen). Now, against the background laid out above, and with the added assistance of these ancient groupings, it seems that we might propose the following. Medicine and law are quite obviously akin to some of these fields, with philosophy and rhetoric being, on the face of it, the closest relatives.[58] These latter likewise enjoyed extensive catalogues of luminous writing, as well as a deep-rooted agonism, both in highbrow print and in the raucous forum. Renown of a potent sort was equally here something to be coveted, and stored up. And yet, neither of these disciplines could boast quite the utilitarian aura which both law and medicine had about them. Rhetoric and philosophy are thus not precisely the siblings of law and medicine, but they plainly must be apprehended as something like first cousins to our disciplines. Then, one would also want to think about history. This area, too, was a branch of learning that could boast a vast and prestigious literature; and, likewise, this literature lent itself to intense rivalries among the worthy gentlemen who had penned the stuff.[59] That said, history seems not to have generated quite the sorts of cutthroat public spectacles that law or medicine supplied. Well-attended recitals

metaphysics that founded them was not—as it is—only the result of a historically determined cultural operation, but proved to be truly an archetypal system over and above history: a fallacy from which we have not yet completely escaped."

[58] Both of these disciplines are therefore treated in this volume; and, hence, we refer the reader to the essays included here, especially in Parts IV and V.

[59] Excellent on this, overall, is Marincola, *Authority and Tradition* (1997).

there were, to be sure; however, the "in-your-face" scrappiness that so characterized the surgery and the courtroom seems generally not to have been dragged onto the stage by the historians.[60] And, of course, the utilitarian aspect is not quite the same. As for all of the other occupations trotted out above, the point is really not worth belaboring: these are all second cousins, at best, to law or medicine. Therefore, it does indeed seem that medicine and law were, on the one hand, and in a manner worthy of note, isolated as a duo from the various other pursuits with which they were, in antiquity, associated; and, on the other hand, precisely the characteristics which gave rise to this isolation were shared by our two disciplines.[61] Indeed, it was a yet vague awareness of this which inspired the editors of the present volume to get to work.

What has just been said, however, leaves us still brushing up against a thorny, yet arguably *the* pivotal, question: What, exactly, are we to take away from all of this? We have indicated throughout this introductory essay that an all-encompassing apprehension of ancient engagement with medicine and law seems to us imperative. Let us accentuate that point as we now move toward concluding our prefatory remarks.

So, the ultimate consequences generated by our setting of medicine and law apart, yet together, can profitably be introduced by a figure independent of either field, namely, Cornelius Tacitus. The entry on this man in the latest edition of the *Oxford Classical Dictionary* begins thus: "Tacitus, Roman historian." *Was* he that? Should we fasten the monochromatic label "historian" on this person? Indeed, what might Tacitus himself have thought about his own appearance in this important book of reference? Obviously, the *Annales* and the *Historiae* weigh heavily whenever the man's name crops up. That said, the younger Pliny, for example, was well aware of his friend's standing as an orator. He describes the trial of Marius Priscus (for malfeasance in governing Africa), which was a truly momentous public happening.[62] After Salvius Liberalis harangued the crowd in defense of Priscus, Tacitus responded, to Pliny's taste, "with resounding eloquence, and, in the defining trait of his oratory, majestically."[63] And, of course, he who so famously and magnificently had prosecuted Priscus was also a highly

[60] For all of this, see Chaniotis, *Historie und Historiker* (1988) 368–389.

[61] With respect to the sometimes-perceived intellectual isolation of the actual substance of legal science, see: Schiavone, "Sapere giuridico e identità" (2003) 65–66; and, Schiavone, *Invention of Law* (2012) 38: "In general, in the mirror held up by the educated, the philosophers, the historians, and the erudite men of Latin culture, legal matters were perceived as a distant world—an isolation that was both its greatness and its downfall." And as Dieter Nörr abundantly demonstrated, the law and its practitioners suffered some rather withering criticism (which may, perhaps, have worked to augment any latent sense of intellectual remoteness—or, alternatively, may in some part have resulted from it): Nörr, *Rechtskritik* (1974). And, on similar visions of medical literature, see above, p. 10.

[62] There had been a delay in the proceedings, and thus, Tacitus would speak at a subsequent meeting of the senate—a session, in Pliny's words (*Ep.* 2.11.10), *cuius ipse conspectus augustissimus fuit*.

[63] Plin. *Ep.* 2.11.17: *respondit Cornelius Tacitus eloquentissime et, quod eximium orationi eius inest, σεμνῶς*.

respected author on the subject of oratory (the *Dialogus de oratoribus*). Tacitus, in other words, was well regarded as both a practicing and an intellectually engaged orator. Beyond that, this same Tacitus was equally a biographer (the *De vita Iulii Agricolae*); and an ethnographer (the *De origine et situ Germanorum*). There is yet more to the man. We happen to possess an inscription which is just about certainly Tacitus' tombstone.[64] Following Géza Alföldy's interpretation of this relic, Tacitus himself wished to be remembered, at least so far as the extant portion of his epitaph takes us, as: *consul, XVvir sacris faciundis, Xvir stlitibus iudicandis, tribunus militum, quaestor Augusti, tribunus plebis*, and *praetor*. The extant portion of the inscription describes only the earlier stages of a senatorial career; and, the tally of governmental positions will have continued. That, however, is precisely the point. Tacitus' epitaph gives every indication of having been a perfectly typical senatorial tombstone. The implication, which in the present context then matters, is that this man's achievements as historian, orator, biographer, or ethnographer were almost certainly *not* mentioned in his own summation of his own life.[65] What are we to make of that?

Let us then fantasize, and imagine Tacitus reading the *Oxford Classical Dictionary* entry on himself. Would he have been pleased, or instead, quite puzzled, to find himself so monochromatically memorialized as, "Tacitus, Roman historian?" What of all his other talents in the liberal arts? What of his magnificent career in public service? Our point should be plain. The true Tacitus was a package much more substantial than "Roman historian." Dylan Sailor, in a remarkable book on Tacitus, begins precisely from the epitaph, and lucidly cuts to the quick of the issue:[66]

> . . . [the inscription] does remind us that his [Tacitus'] books were only part of a life made up of countless interactions with other people: appearances at the bar, epistolary exchanges with associates, literary recitations exciting or tedious, eulogies delivered, rituals performed, circus games attended, funerals planned. Interwoven with his other social acts was his publication of several short works and two long works of narrative history. Time has ensured that these are the social acts we can still access directly; the rest are simply gone. This book is the result of an attempt to take seriously the reminder this inscription offers, that Tacitus' writing was part of a life. More specifically, it explores ways in which his

[64] See Alföldy, "Bricht der Schweigsame sein Schweigen?" (1995) and *CIL*^{2} VI 41106. For an incorporation of the information from this inscription into Tacitus' life story altogether, see Birley, "The Life and Death of Cornelius Tacitus" (2000).

[65] As Eck, "Senatorisches Leben" (2022a) 8 points out, "Doch die Inschriften schweigen über alle Tätigkeiten von Senatoren, die über den politisch-administrativ-militärischen Bereich hinausgegangen sind." See the following pages in this article, however, for more on the issue of the intellectual side of senatorial life as it appeared epigraphically; in short, from about the time of Marcus Aurelius on, we have a bit of epigraphic evidence for the intellectual talents of senators, though still not on tombstones.

[66] Sailor, *Writing and Empire* (2008) 2.

historiographical work interacts with, interprets, and manages the relations between his political biography, his literary career, and his social self.

We want to suggest that this kind of approach should be applied not only to historians and historiography, but also to doctors and lawyers, medicine and law, and, indeed, universally to reconstructions of the lives and occupations of any ancient persons who chose to involve themselves in any form of expertise, and especially when that engagement came to include writing.[67]

What has just been said, however, confronts us with a last interesting and noteworthy aspect of this foray into correlating medicine and law. The issue is this. Our doctors and lawyers, precisely *unlike* Tacitus, and resoundingly *unlike* the idealized intellectual "all-rounder" (to be profiled by König and Peachin below), can easily appear to have confined themselves, more often than not, to their one particular area of expertise. They tended, especially the sub-elite, but also many of those who were more prominent, neither to practice in nor to write about other fields of knowledge.[68] Now, a fixation of this sort on one specialty is perhaps foreseeable, given the extensive learning required for each pursuit and the profound care that men like our Herakleitos and Julian put into fashioning their socio-intellectual personae. However, devotion to only one field of expertise was not an unbreakable norm. Indeed, one can isolate examples of adepts in medicine or law who, in one way or another, could lay claim (or appear to have done so) to more than one area of talent. We feel that it is well worth corralling some exemplary persons of this sort briefly. For these instances of versatility, even if they were ultimately comparatively few, and even if the exact depth and breadth of the sundry talents accumulated by such individuals remain perforce slightly obscure, nonetheless teach us to be wary when we talk of expertise, or specialization, or professionalism in the ancient Roman context.

So, with respect to the lawyers, one must be attuned to men of the elite who might have written in areas beyond law, as well as to those, upper-class or not, who were arguably expert in law and in some other field (or fields), yet possibly did not write.[69] We begin with L. Coelius Antipater, who is described, like Tacitus, as "Roman historian" in the *Oxford Classical Dictionary*. However, Antipater was also a reputed orator and jurisconsult. We know full well that he wrote history: but

[67] The recent cluster of biographies of Galen, for example, are an excellent step in this direction, i.e., Boudon-Millot, *Galien de Pergame* (2012); Mattern, *Prince of Medicine* (2013); and Nutton, *Galen* (2020), the last of which particularly aims to ground the *contents* of his intellectual work within the broader context of his life, that is "to show how all the varied aspects of his life and work fit together" (p. 2).

[68] One thing, though, should be pointed out immediately. The fragmentary condition of the writings of the jurists makes determining the character of any given book by one of these men quite precarious. This is a caveat to be held firmly in mind; and it will concern us momentarily.

[69] N.b.: We are not going to worry directly here about the various individuals known both for their talents as advocates (forensic oratory) and for their juristic skill—men like, e.g., L. Licinus Crassus (on whom, see Lehne-Gstreinthaler, Iurisperiti et oratores (2019) 141–144).

did he write in either of his other fields? We do not know. Be that all as it may, the important point in the present context is that Antipater's interests in the law, however far these may have extended, did not preclude him from developing expertise (which was recognized and acknowledged) in other fields of endeavor.[70] He, though, was active before the rise of the, let us say, real (or, "professional") jurists and, therefore, should perhaps not constitute much of a worry.[71] L. Cincius, however, lived during the Augustan period, and presents us with a case not unlike that of Antipater.[72] Cincius can be labeled as "Fachjurist," more plainly as "Jurist," or, in contrast, can be classed as "grammarian and antiquarian."[73] Regardless of any label that might be affixed to this man, he is known to have written the following: *De fastis, De comitiis, De consulum potestate, De re militari, Mystagogica, De verbis priscis, De officio iurisconsulti*.[74] What, then, shall we call Cincius? And how shall we describe his area of expertise? Indeed, should we be asking, or trying to answer, these questions altogether? Then, there is the case of L. Volusius Maecianus. Here is a man who was singled out by Marcus Aurelius and Lucius Verus for his expertise (*peritia*) in the civil law, and who wrote variously about clear-cut legal subjects.[75] He also, however, produced a book on the subject of metrology, which Detlef Liebs has called "eine Gelegenheitsarbeit für den jungen Mark Aurel."[76] What are we to think of such a confection? Was this indeed part of Maecianus' juristic oeuvre? Or, had he perhaps moved beyond the bounds of this field, so as to assert himself in another area of technical knowhow?[77] We might wonder similarly about the three jurists, each of whom wrote a book *De re militari*: P. Taruttienus Paternus, Arrius Menander, and Aemilius Macer.[78] For the last of these, we now have the outstanding account by Sergio Alessandrì, who sees clearly the bundle of problems that we must confront in dealing with such a piece of writing, produced by such an author. In particular, he evinces some concern regarding Macer's level of expertise in things

[70] For fuller consideration of Antipater, and his three areas of expertise, see Peachin, "Lehne-Gstreinthaler" (2021) 651–652.

[71] We are thinking here of Frier, *Rise of the Roman Jurists* (1985); and we thus place the "professionalization" of jurisprudence in the Ciceronian age.

[72] We use Cincius as representative. Several other individuals, who will not be discussed here, raise similar issues. For these, see Lehne-Gstreinthaler, Iurisperiti et oratores (2019) 319–329, a section of her discussion entitled "Die Antiquare und Grammatiker."

[73] Respectively: Lendle, "Giuffre" (1976) 775; Lehne-Gstreinthaler, Iurisperiti et oratores (2019) 316; Rawson, *Intellectual Life* (1985) 247. And then, there is Leonhard, "Iurisprudentia" (1918) 1165, who says explicitly that Cincius was *not* a jurist.

[74] Best on Cincius now is Lehne-Gstreinthaler, Iurisperiti et oratores (2019) 315–319.

[75] Marcus and Lucius Verus: Ulp. (10 *ad legem Iuliam et Papiam*) D. 37.14.17. Plainly legal writings of Maecianus: *De iudiciis publicis, Quaestionum de fideicommissis, Ex lege Rhodia*, on which, Liebs, "Jurisprudenz" (1997) 131–133.

[76] Liebs, "Jurisprudenz" (1997) 132.

[77] On Maecianus' *Distributio, item vocabula ac notae partium in rebus, pecunia aere numerate, pondere, mensura*, see Cuomo, "Measures for an emperor" (2007).

[78] On them, Liebs, "Jurisprudenz" (1997) 136–138, 214–216. The classic account of juristic writing on the military is Giuffrè, *La letteratura* (1974).

military, and moves ever so slightly in the direction of categorizing this *De re militari* as more an administrative, than a legal, piece of writing.[79] Finally, towards the far end of our timeframe, we hear of one M. Caecilius Novatillianus (fl. mid-third cent. CE). He is commemorated by the *ordo* at Beneventum, probably his town of origin, as their patron, and as "distinguished orator and poet" (*orator et poeta inlustris*).[80] But in Tarraco, where that local *ordo* celebrated him because of his activities there as judicial legate (*legatus iuridicus*), the compliments have shifted somewhat. In this Spanish venue, poetry and oratory have vanished altogether, with Novatillianus now remembered as "most abstinent, most just, most learned" (*abstinentissimus iustissimus disertissimus*).[81] Since he is being complimented specifically with respect to his function as judicial legate, we are perhaps warranted in assuming that the adjective *disertissimus* means to amplify Novatillianus' learnedness in the law, be that knowledge imagined or real.[82] If we may make this assumption, then here was a man who was thought to be skilled as orator, poet, and jurist. Did he write in all three fields? Did he write in any of these fields? Surely, at least as a poet, he will have put something onto paper.

As for the doctors, our own Herakleitos has already made it clear that expertise in, and writing on, philosophy could fuse seamlessly with a medical persona.[83] Consider also Sextus Empiricus, who survives today only as a philosophical author, but who was a doctor as well and wrote at least one medical text.[84] Galen, too, not only presented himself as equally adept in medicine and philosophy, but argued that, in fact, one could not be a truly worthy physician without also being a consummate philosopher, trained in all the branches, "logical, natural, and ethical."[85] His written output mirrors these convictions: philosophical books comprise a large fraction of his oeuvre and they are not limited merely to the more

[79] Alessandrì, *Aemilius Macer* (2020) 11: "Apparentemente distante dal privilegiato ambito di indagine del giurista, cioè l'apparato amministrativo imperiale, si presenta, infine, il *de re militari*, tanto che potrebbe avvertirsi come singolare il fatto che Macro si sia addentrato nello studio della materia senza possedere una particolare esperienza militare. Anche in questo caso, però, occorre tener conto del contesto storico in cui Macro vive ed opera, dal momento che a partire dal principato dei Severi si assiste a un graduale processo di militarizzazione dell'amministrazione imperiale, che avrebbe di lì a poco determinato la dissoluzione di ciò che era rimasto del sistema magistratuale. La giurisprudenza severiana avvertì la necessità di raccogliere in modo organico le disposizioni relative all'ordinamento dei militari, che si erano andate a sovrapporsi nel tempo, in modo da enucleare principi generali di facile applicazione."

[80] *CIL* IX 1571 and 1572 = *ILS* 2939.

[81] *CIL* II^2/14, 973.

[82] N.b., however: Christol, *Essai* (1986) 152 connects this adjective to Novatillianus' oratorical skill, as per the Beneventum inscription; nor was this man admitted by Kunkel, *Juristen* (1967/2001) as a jurist.

[83] See above, p. 5.

[84] Sextus mentions at *M.* 1.61 that he wrote "treatises" (ὑπομνήμασιν) on the Empiricist sect of medicine, which may or may not be identical to the "treatises on medicine" that he mentions at *M.* 7.202 (ἰατρικοῖς ὑπομνήμασι); see Bailey, *Sextus Empiricus* (2002) 86–99, who indicates that Sextus was not the only Empiricist doctor with a foot in both disciplines.

[85] Galen *Opt.Med.* 3.8 (I.60–61K = 291 B-M) (τό τε λογικὸν καὶ τὸ φυσικὸν καὶ τὸ ἠθικόν).

medically relevant aspects of the field, but range from technical and extensive treatises on logic to broadly accessible tracts of moral philosophy.[86] Indeed, his mean-spirited observation that this double specialization is no easy task, and that "the majority by far of those who study both medicine and philosophy succeed in neither," suggests that this dual approach was far from uncommon; further, his added comment that many who attempted to master both fields failed to succeed because "they did not remain at their studies, but turned instead towards politics" suggests just the same sort of multi-faceted, intellectual-political careers that we see among the jurists (e.g., Julian).[87] Though philosophy appears to have been the most typical companion of medical expertise, it was by no means the only other intellectual arena into which our doctors strayed.[88] Hermogenes of Smyrna, for example, had very broad interests.[89] The fields to which he devoted himself included medicine, various kinds of history (local, universal, military), philology, geography, and more. Nor were these interests passive: Hermogenes produced seventy-two books in the field of medicine, but also seventeen or eighteen works on historical topics, more about Homer, several books on city foundations, and the list goes on. Moving on, Lucian scoffs at a certain Callimorphus, an army doctor, but also author of a *History of the Parthian War*. Indeed, Lucian reveals the man to have claimed that it was perfectly natural (*οἰκεῖον*) for a doctor to write history—because Asclepius was the son of Apollo, and Apollo was chief of the muses and overlord of all *paideia*.[90] Christopher Jones takes this Callimorphus to be a real person (not an invention of Lucian's), and adduces two other doctors, Statilius Crito and Oribasius of Pergamum, who both wrote history, the former having described Trajan's Dacian wars, the latter Julian's ill-fated Persian expedition.[91] Thus, despite Lucian's slap, medicine and history could indeed go hand in hand. Then, an intense focus on, or specialization in, verse was not beyond the reach of the medical expert. Galen devotes considerable time and ink to the study of Old Comedy and enjoys alluding to a range of poets beyond just the inevitable Homer.[92] Though his was largely an antiquarian or aesthetic interest, some of his peers took a more active role. A second-century inscription at Athens contains a poem

[86] On the comparative emphasis on philosophy in Galen's corpus, see Bubb, this volume, pp. 198–199; for his own list of his philosophical works, see *Lib.Prop.* 14–19 (XIX.39–48K = 164–173 B-M).

[87] Galen *Ord.Lib.Prop.* 4.6 (XIX.59–60K = 100 B-M) (*πολὺ πλῆθος ἀνθρώπων ἀσκούντων ἰατρικήν τε καὶ φιλοσοφίαν ἐν οὐδετέρᾳ κατορθοῦσιν… οὐ κατέμειναν ἐν ταῖς ἀσκήσεσιν ἀλλ' ἐπὶ τὰς πολιτικὰς πράξεις ἀπετράποντο*).

[88] Beyond the figures mentioned here, the epigraphic record reveals numerous other doctors who also styled themselves philosophers; see Samama, *Les médecins* (2003), nos. 231, 334, 389, 433, 478, 481.

[89] See Chaniotis, *Historie und Historiker* (1988) 327–328.

[90] Lucian *Hist. conscr.* 16.

[91] Jones, *Culture and Society* (1986) 63–64; for Statilius, see *PIR*[2] S 823; for Oribasius, *PLRE* I Oribasius.

[92] For Galen's studies of comedy, see *Lib.Prop.* 20.1 (XIX.48K = 173 B-M); for a prime example of his engagement with other poets, see the *Protrepticus* (*Protr.*), in which he cites or alludes to Homer, Euripides, Sophocles, Pindar, Sappho, and Archilochus; see also De Lacy, "Galen and the Greek Poets" (1966) and Nutton, "Galen's Library" (2009) 30–32.

on medical decorum honoring Serapion, "p[oet, … doctor], and Stoic philosopher;" and, while the content and the context of the inscription make it plausible that the restored title of "doctor" is an accurate one, Plutarch—a friend of this Serapion—introduces him as "Serapion the poet."[93] Medicine, then, if he did indeed specialize in it, was not the first, but the second or even third string to his bow. A few centuries earlier, at Corinth, one Thrasippos is more briefly and unambiguously, but no less grandiosely, memorialized as "poet and doctor, second to none of the Greeks."[94] And then, of course, the curious genre of medical poetry surely deserves mention here, though whether or not it should be classified for our purposes as distinct from the rest of medical literature is debatable.[95] Multiple examples of this genre survive in both Greek and Latin, and Galen also attests to a range of other pharmacological poets whose work is lost.[96] And let us not forget that our own Herakleitos, that "Homer of medical poetry," deserves a spot in this group as well.

Finally, there are two cases known to us (and n.b., only these two) in which one and the same man seems potentially to have united both of our fields. The first is C. Stertinius Xenophon. Best known as the imperial physician allegedly responsible for poisoning Claudius, he preceded this dubious claim to fame with an illustrious career, of which Fergus Millar formulated a lucid portrait:[97]

> … Stertinius Xenophon from Cos, who exhibits all the main characteristics of the class of men we are concerned with: eminence in a branch of learning, personal attachment to the court, a secretarial function there, public honours in Rome, and an unbroken role in his native city. He is perhaps first attested as an ambassador from Cos in AD 23, when the rights of asylum of the temples in many Greek cities were defended in Rome. Later he was in practice as a doctor in Rome. When Claudius, possibly before he became emperor, wished to appoint

[93] Samama, *Les médecins* (2003) no. 22 (π[οιητὴν …]/[ἰατρὸν καὶ φι]λόσοφον Στωικ[όν]); Plut. *Pyth. Or.* 396D (ὁ ποιητὴς Σαραπίων); for more on Serapion, see Flacelière, "Le Poète Stoïcien Serapion" (1951) and Bowersock, *Greek Sophists* (1969) 67–68.

[94] Samama, *Les médecins* (2003), no. 28 (ποιητάν τε καὶ ἰητῆρα … /οὐθενὸς Ἑλλάνων δεύτερον). Further, Lougovaya, "*Medici Docti*" (2019) analyses a series of verse inscriptions dedicated to or by doctors and suggests that they reflect the broad cultural aspirations of these doctors, if not their own poetical output; see also Samama, *Les médecins* (2003) 77–78.

[95] Of course, the poetry that Thrasippos produced may also have been medical in nature, but we do not need to automatically assume this: certainly, there is no reason to assume as much for Serapion's verses, which Plutarch implies were about philosophy (*Mor.* 396F, 402F); indeed, the two lines attributed to a Serapion in Stobaeus (III.10.2), if we can believe them to be his, are not medical at all. Galen *Comp.Med.Gen.* 5.10 (XIII.820K) (cf. *Ant.* 1.5 (XIV.32K)) indicates that pharmacological poetry was often composed in verse for the pragmatic reason that the meter assured more accurate transmission and encouraged easier memorization, rather than on any aesthetic or literary grounds; see, though, above, n. 22, as well as Hautala, "Addresses to the Reader" (2014) for studies of the genre, including a defense of its literary aspirations.

[96] See the examples discussed in Hautala, "Addresses to the Reader" (2014); for Galen's references, see Vogt, "Lehrdichtung im Urteil Galens" (2005) 53–54.

[97] Millar, *Emperor* (1977) 85–86. See also the comprehensive account of Stertinus' life and career in Buraselis, "Kos between Hellenism and Rome" (2000) 66–110.

> him as his own doctor, he rejected the normal salary of 250,000 *sesterces*, saying that he earned 600,000 in private practice (which he proved by pointing to his houses in the city). So Claudius appointed both himself and his brother at 500,000.... His honours and functions rapidly extended. An inscription from Calymnus on Cos honours him as Chief Doctor (*archiatros*) of the Divine Emperors, and in charge of *apokrimata* (legal decisions?) in Greek, tribune, *praefectus fabrum*, as having received military decorations at the British triumph—and also as benefactor (*euergetês*) of his city, High Priest of the Gods, High Priest of the Emperor for life, and of Asclepius, Hygia and Epione; another inscription from Cos lengthens the list of priesthoods. By now he was a prominent public figure. In 53 Claudius made a speech in the senate asking for a grant of immunity from taxation for Cos: "It should be granted to Xenophon's entreaties that the people of Cos, free of all tribute, should devote themselves to their island, sacred and in the service of their god [Asclepius] alone." Claudius' patronage was ill-rewarded, for in the following year Xenophon is said to have assisted in poisoning him.

The broad similarities to a man like our Herakleitos are patent. In the present context, however, we would like to draw particular attention to Millar's query as to whether one of his posts might have involved Stertinius in the composition of legal decisions. One inscription labels Stertinius ἐπὶ τῶν ἀποκριμάτων, while another has him as ἐπὶ τῶν Ἑλληνικῶν ἀποκριμάτων.[98] Now, the exact nature of this position at the emperor's side is not crystal clear. While the term *apokrimata* came to be associated with rescripts (*subscriptiones*)—imperial responses that were drafted, and perhaps even formulated, by important jurists—there is no firm attestation of it being used with this meaning in Stertinius' day.[99] Thus, it is conceivable that his responses were somehow legal in nature and that responsibility for them could imply a certain level of legal literacy; but, it is equally plausible that Stertinius was simply in charge of fashioning the imperial responses to various types of embassies from the Hellenophone east, more on the model of, or somehow in conjunction with, the office of the *ab epistulis*.[100] In any case, if the former view has any substance to it, then might we suspect Stertinius to have

[98] For all of the evidence on this man, including the two inscriptions referred to, see *PIR*² S 913.

[99] On the development of the term *apokrimata*, see Millar, *Emperor* (1977) 226 and 243. Also Mason, *Greek Terms* (1974) 24 and 126: "ἀπόκριμα, though it strictly means *responsum*, refers primarily to written replies.... The secretary ἐπὶ ἀποκριμάτων [viz., Stertinius] will have been chiefly concerned with the administration of written *rescripta*." But, as Mason points out just prior to this statement, "... a *rescript* may embody a judicial decision or *decretum*, or conversely a decision of the emperor which might be appropriately termed a *constitutio* might subsequently be published and proclaimed, and hence be viewed as an edict." In short, the terminology, Greek and Latin alike, is less than crystal clear. With regard to the parties responsible for the formulation of imperial subscriptions, and citing earlier literature on the matter, see Peachin, "Weitere Gedanken" (2015).

[100] Taking the latter kind of stance are: Cuq, "Mémoire sur le *Consilium principis*" (1884) 392–394, who suggests the connection with the *ab epistulis*; G. Lafaye (*IGRR* IV 1086 [1927]); and Hirschfeld, *Die*

accumulated expertise in the law, aside from his obvious chops in medicine? Ultimately, there can be no certainty. However, whatever kind of responses this doctor might have been responsible for creating, it seems absolutely safe to suppose a significant level of scholarly expertise in an area that was not medicine—for even if Stertinius operated in the office of the *ab epistulis*, a certain level of scholarly cultural achievement, aside from medicine, will have been de rigeur. Next is C. Calpurnius Asclaepiades. On his tombstone, his wife, Veronia Chelidon, commemorates him as *medicus*, and as having been recognized by the tip-top men for his learning and rectitude (*studiorum et morum causa probatus a viris clarissimis*).[101] Then, however, she also tells the world that her husband had been an *assessor* to Roman magistrates in several provinces, including Asia. Typically, these assessors provided legal advice to the magistrates they served.[102] Asclaepiades is furthermore said to have held a position involving oversight of the selection of jurors—*custodiar(ius* ?) [*tabellar(um)* ?] *in urna iudicum*. Thus, Veronia's husband can appear to have had talent in both medicine and the law. This has caused some consternation among historians of the law. After suggesting that Asclaepiades perhaps gave expert medical advice to magistrates during trials, Hermann Hitzig left the matter of legal expertise ultimately undecided.[103] Wolfgang Kunkel was likewise perturbed, and so, in reproducing the text of the inscription, printed, "*medicus* (!)," and suggested that Asclaepiades provided a generalized, rather than a specifically legal, kind of advice to the magistrates he served.[104] On the other hand, those who view Asclaepiades through the lens of medicine, or simply as an intellectual, appear to see him as exclusively a doctor.[105]

What Stertinius Xenophon, Calpurnius Asclaepiades, and all of the other figures in this catalogue of multi-taskers seem to us to suggest is that law and medicine, though particular in all the various ways that we have highlighted in this introduction, were nevertheless equal members in the capacious array of intellectual pursuits through which an elite member of the Roman Empire might burnish his reputation. The apparent majority of doctors and lawyers chose to specialize exclusively. However, a not insignificant group found it desirable, whatever the motive(s) may have been, to diversify into another pursuit, or pursuits. And so,

kaiserlichen Verwaltungsbeamten[2] (1905) 323 n. 1. Pflaum, *Les carrières* (1960–1961) I, 41–44 renders the position into Latin as (*procurator*) *ad responsa Graeca*, and does not propose any connection with the office of the *ab epistulis*; and at III, 1020, he puts Stertinius, along with Ti. Claudius Balbillus and Dionysius Alexandrinus, under the heading (*procurator*) *ad legationes et ad responsa Graeca*. Buraselis, "Kos between Hellenism and Rome" (2000) 70, 73 similarly glosses the position as *ad responsa Graeca*. Klaus Wachtel, in his *PIR* entry on Stertinius (cf. above, n. 98) does not offer interpretation of this post.

[101] *CIL* XI 3943 = *ILS* 7789.

[102] See, e.g., *TLL* II.4, 874, or Berger, *Encyclopedic Dictionary* (1953) 351.

[103] Hitzig, *De assessoribus* (1891) 82–83.

[104] Kunkel, *Juristen* (1967/2001) 331 n. 697. Nor does Kunkel list this man among his jurists.

[105] For example: Mattern, "Physicians and the Roman Imperial Aristocracy" (1999) 4–5; Bowie, "Greek Culture in Arrian's Bithynia" (2014) 42.

this group of people must be taken into account when we ponder what it may have meant to be a doctor or a lawyer in this period of time.

Ultimately, then, rather than leading us to any neat conclusions, the sum total of all that has been discussed here brings us instead to a broad vista of more questions to be asked, and perhaps eventually answered. We highlight but a few. First, as Calpurnius Asclaepiades pushes us to wonder: how do we even recognize ancient doctors and lawyers? For instance, what precisely should we do with someone like Cornelius Celsus, who surely must be admitted to have accumulated significant medical expertise in writing the portion of his *Artes* that dealt with medicine, yet has usually not been counted as, quite, a doctor?[106] To pose such questions will have significant implications for issues like specialization, expertise, professionalism—or, to take this all one modest step further, for how one valorized and weaponized, relative to each other, the harvests of time devoted to *otium* and *negotium*.[107] Then, and relatedly, once one has satisfactorily identified a doctor or a lawyer, how ought he (or, in the rare case, she) be evaluated vis-à-vis his or her abilities in the field of choice?[108] This potentially extends any such inquiry even further, namely, to something as fundamental as distinguishing between what was "accurate" or "true" and that which was "inaccurate," "false," or, just generally, untrustworthy. In other words, by what standards of expertise did one identify the person who could be relied upon as the teller of truth, or the source of accuracy, with respect to some field of knowledge? What role, precisely, did learning, versus (say) social standing or rhetorical skill, play in such a matter?[109] And where, and how, in all of this, did notions of morality fit in? Or again, what are we to make of the stark cultural segregation implicit in our two

[106] The view that Celsus was indeed a practicing doctor, mostly rejected in later twentieth-century scholarship, was put back on the table by Schulze, *Aulus Cornelius Celsus* (1999). The debate, however, remains open and is probably impossible to settle definitively—especially given precisely the types of questions we are raising here; cf. Gautherie, *Celse* (2017) 42–45. In short, if we choose to take Celsus as a "doctor," the capacious nature of his writing must lead us to include him in our list of multi-taskers above and to ask: was he equally a rhetor and a farmer, etc.? Or was he simply a doctor with wide interests, who was, in Gautherie's formulation of the issue, "à la fois un spécialiste dans un domaine et un encyclopédiste éclairé" (45)? Either answer is eminently interesting.

[107] The pendant to all that we have been discussing, for many a member of the early imperial elite, was indeed much time and effort devoted to *negotium*, i.e., a "career" in government service. As for expertise or professionalism there, the bottom line is that a satisfactory level of competence in various fields was gained by doing, rather than by any form of regularized and/or regulated job-specific training. In sum, Eck, "Professionalität" (2022b) 54: "Das Grundprinzip der von Stufe zu Stufe akkumulierten Erfahrung in einem weiten Sinn findet sich dort (i.e., in the "cursus inscriptions") fast überall. Somit muß diese Form der Bewältigung der öffentlichen Aufgaben damals als sachadäquat angesehen worden sein." So, then, take Salvius Julianus: Shall we conclude that his *otium*-time (when he produced, among other things, the 90-book *Digesta*) was more professionalized than was his *negotium*-time (when he served as, e.g., Hadrian's *quaestor*, or as *praefectus aerarii Saturni*)? Our question, ultimately, is: What would Julian have thought or said about this?

[108] We note that Galen was motivated by precisely this question to write his *On Choosing the Best Physician*. For the evidence concerning female physicians in antiquity, see Flemming, *Roman Women* (2000) 35–42 and Appendix 2.

[109] On issues of this kind, see Meyer, "Evidence and Argument" (2016). The essays in König and Woolf, *Authority and Expertise* (2017) have also provided a great deal of insight in this direction.

fields, with medicine a decidedly Greek endeavor and law, at least with respect to its creation and development, a Roman one?[110] Here our attention to the imperial period comes more closely into focus. It is precisely in the earlier imperial period that both of our fields see a shift. Jurisprudence becomes a more defined endeavor, with more clearly delineated (even "professionalized") specialists. Medicine, in its turn, takes a discrete leap forward in social acceptance: where Cato, Pliny, and even Celsus see Greek physicians as othered inferiors, doctors—though remaining, especially in their upper tiers, a largely Greek or Hellenized population—become steadily more integrated into elite society and eligible for increasing levels of prestige as the decades roll on.[111] Meanwhile, as Gellius reminds us, jurists—like the rest of the Roman elite—were ever more tightly implicated in Hellenocentric cultural and educational expectations. How, then, do our fields relate to the complex cultural currents at play in this period?[112] How does this sort of cultural predetermination shape the choices of a Julian or a Herakleitos or a Galen? And what does it all mean for someone like our Calpurnius Asclaepiades, if indeed he turned his hand to both medicine and law? In short, we would like to suggest that by thinking in terms such as these, the very *substance* of any and every kind of engagement with a field like medicine or law will want some degree of reevaluation. Thus, roughly as Sailor does with Tacitus and his historical writing, we need to ask just how far, and in what ways, Galen's lifelong project of comprehending and constructing "Galen the doctor," both for himself and for others, will have inflected the very *substance* of medicine, both as it appeared in the pages of his books and as it was manifested in his practice of this art. The same goes for any author of any given book on the law. In sum, once we have thought about individual devotees of medicine or law, and how the range of things that mattered to them, in aggregate, might have affected their own engagements (equally in writing and in practice) with these disciplines, we must then return to the medical and legal sciences themselves, so as to wonder just how *their* essences, in toto, might have been shaped by the diverse wants and needs of the men who made them.[113] For let us never forget: these enterprises, law and

[110] In this context, we might simply take note of an intriguing matter of diction. There is no one simple word for "jurist" or "lawyer" in either Latin or Greek—nothing akin to the comparatively straightforward labels of *medicus* or ἰατρός for our doctors. Is this of significance? And if it is, what might the implications be? Given the present state of our own knowledge, we hesitate to venture guesses. As to the various labels applied to those skilled in the law, see Lehne-Gstreinthaler, Iurisperiti et oratores (2019) 11–14, 367–370.

[111] See the extensive discussion of this shift in Israelowich, *Society, Medicine, and Religion* (2012) 57–62 and *Patients and Healers* (2015) 17–31.

[112] The topic of Greco-Roman relations in the culture of this period is a vast one. One might start with Swain, *Hellenism and Empire* (1996); Schmitz, *Bildung and Macht* (1997); Goldhill, *Being Greek under Rome* (2001); Borg, *Paideia* (2004).

[113] In line with what we are suggesting here, Harris, "Contagion" (2021) now argues that the near universal failure of antiquity's elite physicians to recognize certain diseases as contagious (despite the fact that "lay" people understood this full well) was due to the doctors' "professional arrogance, coupled with exaggerated respect for the writings of the Hippocratics and others" (p. 26).

medicine, were crafted by frail human beings living in particular times and circumstances, and did not spring organically from the earth's soil. Medicine and law are cultural artifacts, not natural phenomena.[114]

None of the questions just spelled out receive anything like comprehensive treatment in this volume; and, perhaps, there cannot ever be anything like a static, or final, or synthetic vision of matters such as these. We hope, however, by juxtaposing these two fields and their mutual affinities, to offer a beginning. Accordingly, we have structured the volume as follows.

We begin from the observation, which was amply demonstrated by our original poster boys, Herakleitos and Julian, and which we have repeatedly emphasized throughout this introduction, that there are three elements which in unison thoroughly affected pretty well everything about Roman imperial-age medicine and law: (1) competition, including the frequent desire to entertain; (2) expertise (often specialized) and its construction(s); and (3) the rhetorical education had by all the elite. We have thus built the volume around these three matters, with a part focused on each, and each part itself consisting of four essays: an introduction that grounds the part's topic in Roman society more broadly; a pair of case studies in law and medicine, respectively; and a response that moves towards a synthesis and new directions.

The first such part ("Selling the Subject-Matter: When Science, Competition, and Entertainment Commingle") starts, so to speak, in the street, where competition and performance drove the shape of medicine and law as they were practiced. Matthew Roller provides a general introduction, addressing the never-ending social, political, and intellectual competition that was fundamentally characteristic of the lives of most members of the elite; he emphasizes that competition was implicit in every public display of learning in this period, equally on paper and in the open air of public spaces. Anna Dolganov and Luis Salas then provide case studies of specific moments of competition in each field, performed, as they could be, with great popularity and unpredictable results in front of a live audience. Kendra Eshleman thereupon draws these two papers together, by once again zooming out to their broader social contexts, focusing on the audiences who gave witness to these competitions.

The next part ("Over-Shooting the Subject-Matter: When Pragmatism and Expertise Collide") shifts towards the literature produced in these two fields, recognizing that we are dealing with two areas dominated by highly specialized expertise. These papers together examine how elite doctors and lawyers navigated the competitive and performative world considered in the previous section, while

[114] A quotation borrowed from Rosen, *Law as Culture* (2006) xi, nails the issue, albeit in a slightly arch manner. Writing of law as an undertaking thoroughly embedded in the culture of those who produced that law, he offers this sentiment: "If you think that you can think about a thing, inextricably attached to something else, without thinking of the thing it is attached to, then you have a legal mind" (this is a quotation which Rosen attributes to Thomas R. Powell).

simultaneously forwarding the pragmatic utility of their enterprises. Alice König first collaborates with us here to explore how we ought to understand ancient expertise and the degree to which anything like the modern concept of "professionalization" existed, a debated topic for antiquity and one essential especially to our understanding of the intersection between the utilitarian and the literary in our chosen fields. Bruce Frier and Claire Bubb move to the specifics, scrutinizing moments when jurists and doctors step beyond the purely practical in their fields of expertise, with Frier introducing the element of intermittent collegiality, as opposed to a never-ending tug-of-war, among the lawyers. James Uden closes out this section with a reflection on the boundaries between "experts" and "intellectuals" and, thus, the ways in which these specialists were received by society more broadly.

With the next part ("Positioning the Subject-Matter: When Rhetoric and Science Converge"), our gaze moves in the direction of the all-pervasive role of rhetoric, and a question roughly of this sort: what happens when a field of intellectual engagement, which is seemingly utilitarian in nature, begins to take the shape of a more aesthetic thing? After an introduction that broadly situates both fields vis-à-vis rhetoric—the field upon which all higher education was based, and which thus informed nearly everything done by members of the educated class—Ulrike Babusiaux and Caroline Petit provide analyses of the ways in which consideration of the rhetorical underpinnings of these fields can illuminate their broader purposes. Joseph Howley then joins us in responding to these observations, examining how rhetoric itself, a field with its own specialized experts, stands in relation to our pair.

Finally, Michael Trapp provides a conclusion for the entire volume, reflecting on how the practice of philosophy does and does not participate in the phenomena, as a whole, that the volume has raised with regard to medicine and law. Philosophy is the subject that comes closest to meeting the same criteria that seem so unique to medicine and law, and this analysis therefore serves to crystalize the differences that unite this pair, as well as the ways in which they are both inextricably part and parcel of the larger world that created them.[115]

Bibliography

Alessandrì, *Aemilius Macer* (2020) = S. Alessandrì, *Aemilius Macer. De officio praesidis. Ad legem XX hereditatium. De re militari. De appellationibus* (Rome: Bretschneider, 2020).

[115] A final admonishment to the reader. While volumes such as this typically prefer articles of nearly equal lengths, we have preferred to loosen the reins in this respect. We hope that the gain in interest more than offsets the loss in terms of symmetry.

Alföldy, 'Bricht der Schweigsame sein Schweigen?' (1995) = G. Alföldy, 'Bricht der Schweigsame sein Schweigen?' *Mitteilungen des Deutschen Archäologischen Instituts (Römische Abteilung)* 102 (1995) 252–268.

Alonso Alonso, *Médicos* (2018) = M. Á. Alonso Alonso, *Los médicos en las inscripciones latinas de Italia (siglos II a.C.-III d.C.). Aspectos sociales y profesionales* (Santander: Ediciones Universidad Cantabria, 2018).

Amarelli, *Consilia principum* (1983) = F. Amarelli, *Consilia principum* (Naples: Jovene, 1983).

Asper, *Wissenschaftstexte* (2007) = M. Asper, *Griechische Wissenschaftstexte. Formen, Funktionen, Differenzierungsgeschichten* (Stuttgart: Franz Steiner, 2007).

Asper and Kanthak, *Writing Science* (2013) = M. Asper and A.-M. Kanthak, eds., *Writing Science: Medical and Mathematical Authorship in Ancient Greece* (Berlin: De Gruyter, 2013).

Aubert and Sirks, Speculum iuris (2002) = J.-J. Aubert and B. Sirks, eds., Speculum iuris*: Roman Law as a Reflection of Social and Economic Life in Antiquity* (Ann Arbor: University of Michigan Press, 2002).

Bablitz, *Actors and Audience* (2007) = L. Bablitz, *Actors and Audience in the Roman Courtroom* (London and New York: Routledge, 2007).

Babusiaux, *Papinians* Quaestiones (2011) = U. Babusiaux, *Papinians* Quaestiones. *Zur rhetorischen Methode eines spätklassischen Juristen* (Munich: C. H. Beck, 2011).

Babusiaux, 'Römische Rechtsrhetorik' (forthcoming) = U. Babusiaux, 'Römische Rechtsrhetorik,' in K. Gräfin von Schlieffen, ed., *Handbuch Juristische Rhetorik* (Berlin: De Gruyter, forthcoming).

Bailey, *Sextus Empiricus* (2002) = A. Bailey, *Sextus Empiricus and Pyrrhonean Scepticism* (Oxford: Clarendon, 2002).

Barton, *Power and Knowledge* (1994) = T. Barton, *Power and Knowledge: Astrology, Physiognomics, and Medicine in the Roman Empire* (Ann Arbor: University of Michigan Press, 1994).

Barwick, 'Zu den Schriften' (1948) = K. Barwick, 'Zu den Schriften des Cornelius Celsus und des alten Cato,' *Würzburger Jahrbücher für die Altertumswissenschaft* 3 (1948) 117–132.

Below, *Der Artzt* (1953) = K.-H. Below, *Der Artzt im römischen Recht* (Munich: C. H. Beck, 1953).

Berger, *Encyclopedic Dictionary* (1953) = A. Berger, *Encyclopedic Dictionary of Roman Law* (Philadelphia: The American Philosophical Society, 1953).

Berrey, *Hellenistic Science at Court* (2017) = M. Berrey, *Hellenistic Science at Court* (Berlin: De Gruyter, 2017).

Birley, 'The Life and Death of Cornelius Tacitus' (2000) = A. R. Birley, 'The Life and Death of Cornelius Tacitus,' *Historia* 49 (2000) 230–247.

Borg, *Paideia* (2004) = B. Borg, ed., *Paideia: The World of the Second Sophistic* (Berlin and New York: De Gruyter, 2004).

Boudon-Millot, *Galien de Pergame* (2012) = V. Boudon-Millot, *Galien de Pergame. Un Médecin Grec à Rome* (Paris: Belles Lettres, 2012).

Bowersock, *Greek Sophists* (1969) = G. Bowersock, *Greek Sophists in the Roman Empire* (Oxford: Clarendon, 1969).

Bowie, 'Greek Culture in Arrian's Bithynia' (2014) = E. L. Bowie, 'Greek Culture in Arrian's Bithynia,' *Ktèma: civilisations de l'Orient, de la Grèce et de Rome antiques* 39 (2014) 37–49.

Bremer, *Iurisprudentiae antehadrianae* (1896–1901) = F. P. Bremer, *Iurisprudentiae antehadrianae quae supersunt* (Leipzig: Teubner, 1896–1901, repr. 1985).

Bretone, '*Ius controversum*' (2008) = M. Bretone, '*Ius controversum* nella giurisprudenza classica,' *Atti della Accademia Nazionale dei Lincei, Classe di Scienze Morali, Storiche e Filologiche, Memorie* 9,23 (2008) 755–879.

Bund, 'Salvius Iulianus' (1976) = E. Bund, 'Salvius Iulianus, Leben und Werk,' in *Aufstieg und Niedergang der Römischen Welt* II.15 (Berlin and New York: De Gruyter, 1976) 408–454.

Buraselis, 'Kos between Hellenism and Rome' (2000) = K. Buraselis, 'Kos between Hellenism and Rome: Studies on the Political, Institutional and Social History of Kos from ca. the Middle Second Century B.C. until Late Antiquity,' *Transactions of the American Philosophical Society* 90.4 (2000) 1–189.

Candy, 'Parallel developments' (2020) = P. Candy, 'Parallel Developments in Roman Law and Maritime Trade during the Late Republic and Early Principate,' *Journal of Roman Archaeology* 33 (2020) 53–72.

Casavola, *Giuristi adrianei*² (2011) = F. Casavola, *Giuristi adrianei*² (Rome: Bretschneider, 2011).

Champlin, 'Asellius Sabinus' (2017) = E. Champlin, 'Asellius Sabinus: Culture, Wit, and Power in the Golden Age of Gastronomy,' *Ancient Society* 47 (2017) 159–196.

Chaniotis, *Historie und Historiker* (1988) = A. Chaniotis, *Historie und Historiker in den griechischen Inschriften. Epigraphische Beiträge zur griechischen Historiographie* (Stuttgart: Franz Steiner, 1988).

Chaniotis, 'Festivals and Contests' (2011) 21–26 = A. Chaniotis, 'Festivals and Contests in the Greek World,' in A. Hermary and B. Jaeger, eds., *Thesaurus cultus et rituum antiquorum VII. Festivals and Contests* (Los Angeles: J. Paul Getty Museum, 2011) 1–43, 160–172.

Christol, *Essai* (1986) = M. Christol, *Essai sur l'évolution des carrières sénatoriales dans la 2ᵉ moitié du IIIᵉ s. ap. J.-C.* (Paris: Nouvelles Éditions Latines, 1986).

Crook, *Consilium Principis* (1955) = J. A. Crook, *Consilium Principis. Imperial Councils and Counsellors from Augustus to Diocletian* (Cambridge: Cambridge University Press, 1955).

Cross, *Hippocratic Oratory* (2018) = J. Cross, *Hippocratic Oratory: The Poetics of Early Greek Medical Prose* (London and New York: Routledge, 2018).

Cuomo, 'Measures for an Emperor' (2007) = S. Cuomo, 'Measures for an Emperor: Volusius Maecianus' Monetary Pamphlet for Marcus Aurelius,' in J. König and T. Whitmarsh, eds., *Ordering Knowledge in the Roman Empire* (Cambridge: Cambridge University Press, 2007) 206–228.

Cuq, 'Mémoire sur le *Consilium principis*' (1884) = E. Cuq, 'Mémoire sur le *Consilium principis* d'Auguste à Dioclétien,' in *Mémoires présentés par divers savants à l'Académie des inscriptions et belles-lettres de l'Institut de France. Première série, Sujets divers d'érudition* 9 (1884) 311–504.

David and Hurlet, *L'*auctoritas (2020) = J.-M. David and F. Hurlet, eds., *L'*auctoritas *à Rome. Une notion constitutive de la culture politique* (Bordeaux: Ausonius, 2020).

De Lacy, 'Galen and the Greek Poets' (1966) = P. De Lacy, 'Galen and the Greek Poets,' *Greek, Roman, and Byzantine Studies* 7.3 (1966) 259–266.

Dolganov, '*Nutricula causidicorum*' (2020) = A. Dolganov, '*Nutricula causidicorum*. Legal Practitioners in Roman North Africa,' in K. Czajkowski, B. Eckhardt, and M. Strothmann, eds., *Law in the Roman Provinces* (Oxford: Oxford University Press, 2020) 358–416.

Eck, 'Senatorisches Leben' (2022a) = W. Eck, 'Senatorisches Leben jenseits von Politik, Militär und Administration: die öffentliche Repräsentation der intellektuellen Seite der Führungsschicht,' in id., *Gesellschaft und Administration im römischen Reich*, ed. A. Kolb (Berlin and Boston: De Gruyter, 2022) 3–17 = id., in M. van Ackeren and J. Opsomer, eds., *Selbstbetrachtungen und Selbstdarstellungen. Der Philosoph Marc Aurel im interdisziplinären Licht* (Wiesbaden: Reichert, 2012) 169–186.

Eck, 'Professionalität' (2022b) = W. Eck, 'Professionalität als Element der politisch-administrativen und militärischen Führung. Ein Vergleich zwischen der Hohen Kaiserzeit und dem 4. Jahrhundert n.Chr.,' in id., *Gesellschaft und Administration im römischen Reich*, ed., A. Kolb (Berlin and Boston: De Gruyter, 2022) 47–63 = id., in P. Eich, S. Schmidt-Hofner, and C. Wieland, eds., *Der wiederkehrende Leviathan: Staatlichkeit und Staatswerdung in Späntike und Früher Neuzeit* (Heidelberg: Universitätsverlag Winter, 2011) 97–115.

Ferrary, Schiavone, Stolfi, *Scriptores iuris Romani I* (2018) = J.-L. Ferrary, A. Schiavone, and E. Stolfi, eds., *Quintus Mucius Scaevola Opera. Scriptores iuris Romani 1* (Rome: Bretschneider, 2018).

Flacelière, 'Le Poète Stoïcien Serapion' (1951) = R. Flacelière, 'Le Poète Stoïcien Serapion d'Athènes, Ami de Plutarque,' *Revue des Études Grecques* 64 (1951) 325–327.

Flemming, *Roman Women* (2000) = R. Flemming, *Medicine and the Making of Roman Women: Gender, Nature, and Authority from Celsus to Galen* (Oxford: Oxford University Press, 2000).

Fögen, *Wissen* (2009) = T. Fögen, *Wissen, Kommunikation und Selbstdarstellung. Zur Struktur und Charakteristik römischer Fachtexte der frühen Kaiserzeit* (Munich: C. H. Beck, 2009).

Formisano, *Tecnica* (2001) = M. Formisano, *Tecnica e scrittura. Le letterature tecnico-scientifiche nello spazio letterario tardolatino* (Rome: Carocci, 2001).

Frier, *Rise of the Roman Jurists* (1985) = B. W. Frier, *The Rise of the Roman Jurists. Studies in Cicero's 'Pro Caecina'* (Princeton: Princeton University Press, 1985).

Frier, 'Why Did the Jurists Change Roman Law?' (1994) = B. W. Frier, 'Why Did the Jurists Change Roman Law? Bees and Lawyers Revisited,' *Index. International Survey of Roman Law. Quaderni camerti di studi romanistici* 22 (1994) 135–149.

Gautherie, *Celse* (2017) = A. Gautherie, *Rhétorique et Thérapeutique dans le* De Medicina *de Celse* (Turnhout: Brepols, 2017).

Gill, Whitmarsh, and Wilkins, *Galen and the World of Knowledge* (2009) = C. Gill, T. Whitmarsh, and J. Wilkins, eds., *Galen and the World of Knowledge* (Cambridge: Cambridge University Press, 2009).

Giltaij, 'Greek Philosophy' (2016) = J. Giltaij, 'Greek Philosophy and Classical Roman Law,' in P. J. du Plessis, C. Ando, and K. Tuori, eds., *The Oxford Handbook of Roman Law and Society* (Oxford: Oxford University Press, 2016) 188–199.

Giuffrè, *La letteratura* (1974) = V. Giuffrè, *La letteratura* 'de re militari.' *Appunti per una storia degli ordinamenti militari* (Naples: Jovene, 1974).

Goldhill, *Being Greek under Rome* (2001) = S. Goldhill, ed., *Being Greek under Rome: Cultural Identity, the Second Sophistic, and the Development of Empire* (Cambridge: Cambridge University Press, 2001).

Hadot, *Arts libéraux* (1984) = I. Hadot, *Arts libéraux et philosophe dans la pensée antique* (Paris: Brepols, 1984).

Harries, '*Iurisperiti*' (2017) = J. Harries, '*Iurisperiti*: Men Skilled in Law,' in König and Woolf (2017) 83–106.

Harris, 'Contagion' (2021) = W. V. Harris, 'Contagion in Ancient Thinking about Disease,' *Mediterraneo antico. Economie società culture* 24 (2021) 11–26.

Hautala, 'Addresses to the Reader' (2014) = S. Hautala, '"As a Matter of Fact, This Is Not Difficult to Understand!": The Addresses to the Reader in Greek and Latin Pharmacological Poetry,' in B. Maire, ed., *'Greek' and 'Roman' in Latin Medical Texts: Studies in Cultural Change and Exchange in Ancient Medicine* (Leiden: Brill, 2014) 183–200.

Herberger, *Dogmatik* (1981) = M. Herberger, *Dogmatik. Zur Geschichte von Begriff und Methode in Medizin und Jurisprudenz* (Frankfurt: Klostermann, 1981).

Hirschfeld, *Die kaiserlichen Verwaltungsbeamten*^{2} (1905) = O. Hirschfeld, *Die kaiserlichen Verwaltungsbeaten bis auf Diocletian*^{2} (Berlin: Weidmann, 1905, repr. 1963).

Hitzig, *De assessoribus* (1891) = H. F. Hitzig, *De magistratuum et judicum Romanorum assessoribus* (Bern: Typis Caroli Staempflii, 1891).

İplikçioğlu, 'Heraklit von Rhodiapolis' (2014) = B. İplikçioğlu, 'Heraklit von Rhodiapolis, ein gefeierter Artzt der traianischen Zeit,' in J. Fischer, ed., *Der Beitrag Kleinasiens zur Kultur- und Geistesgeschichte der griechisch-römischen Antike. Akten des Internationalen Kolloquiums Wien, 3.-5. November 2010* (Vienna: Österreichische Akademie der Wissenschaften, 2014) 231–256.

Israelowich, *Society, Medicine, and Religion* (2012) = I. Israelowich, *Society, Medicine, and Religion in the Sacred Tales of Aelius Aristides* (Leiden and Boston: Brill, 2012).

Israelowich, *Patients and Healers* (2015) = I. Israelowich, *Patients and Healers in the High Roman Empire* (Baltimore: Johns Hopkins University Press, 2015).

Jones, *Culture and Society* (1986) = C. P. Jones, *Culture and Society in Lucian* (Cambridge, MA and London: Harvard University Press, 1986).

Jones, 'Culture in the Careers of Eastern Senators' (2005) = C. P. Jones, 'Culture in the Careers of Eastern Senators,' in W. Eck and M. Heil, eds., Senatores populi Romani. *Realität und mediale Präsentation einer Führungsschicht* (Stuttgart: Franz Steiner, 2005) 263–270.

Jones, 'Juristes romains dans l'orient grec' (2007) = C. Jones, 'Juristes romains dans l'orient grec,' *Comptes Rendus de l'Académie des Inscriptions* 151 (2007) 1331–1359.

Jouanna, 'Rhétorique et médecine' (1984) = J. Jouanna, 'Rhétorique et médecine dans la Collection hippocratique. Contribution à l'histoire de la rhétorique au ve siècle,' *Revue des Études Grecques* 97 (1984) 26–44.

Kant, *Critik* (1781) = I. Kant, *Critik der reinen Vernunft* (Riga: Johann Friedrich Hartknoch, 1781).

Kappelmacher, *Untersuchungen* (1918) = A. Kappelmacher, *Untersuchungen zur Enzyklopädie des A. Cornelius Celsus* (Vienna: W. Braumüller, 1918).

Kehoe, *Law and the Rural Economy* (2007) = D. Kehoe, *Law and the Rural Economy in the Roman Empire* (Ann Arbor: University of Michigan Press, 2007).

König and Woolf, *Authority and Expertise* (2017) = J. König and G. Woolf, eds., *Authority and Expertise in Ancient Scientific Culture* (Cambridge: Cambridge University Press, 2017).

Krenkel, 'Zu den *Artes*' (1959) = W. A. Krenkel, 'Zu den *Artes* des Celsus,' *Philologus* 103 (1959) 114–129.

Krenkel, 'A. Cornelius Celsus' (1973) = W. A. Krenkel, 'A. Cornelius Celsus,' in *Argentea Aetas. In memoriam Entii V. Marmorale* (Genoa: Università di Genova, Istituto di filologia classica e medievale, 1973) 17–28.

Kühn, *Opera Omnia* (1821–1833) = C. G. Kühn, ed., *Claudii Galeni Opera Omnia* (Leipzig: C. Cnobloch, 1821–1833) [re-issued, Cambridge: Cambridge University Press, 2011].

Kunkel, *Juristen* (1967/2001) = W. Kunkel, *Die Römischen Juristen. Herkunft und soziale Stellung* (Cologne, Weimar, and Vienna: Böhlau, 2001) [repr. of the 2nd 1967 ed., with an important forward by D. Liebs].

Lehne, 'Die Stellung' (2014) = C. Lehne, 'Die Stellung der Juristen im Formularverfahren,' *Zeitschrift der Savigny-Stiftung für Rechtsgeschichte, Römische Abteilung* 131 (2014) 216–312.

Lehne-Gstreinthaler, 'Jurists in the Shadows' (2016) = C. Lehne-Gstreinthaler, "Jurists in the Shadows': The Everyday Business of the Jurists of Cicero's Time,' in P. du Plessis, ed., *Cicero's Law. Rethinking Roman Law of the Late Republic* (Edinburgh: Edinburgh University Press, 2016) 88–99.

Lehne-Gstreinthaler, Iurisperiti et oratores (2019) = C. Lehne-Gstreinthaler, Iurisperiti et oratores. *Eine Studie zu den römischen Juristen der Republik* (Vienna, Cologne, and Weimar: Böhlau, 2019).

Lehoux, *What Did the Romans Know?* (2012) = D. Lehoux, *What Did the Romans Know? An Inquiry into Science and Worldmaking* (Chicago: University of Chicago Press, 2012).

Lendle, 'Giuffrè' (1976) = O. Lendle, review of Giuffrè, *La letteratura* (1974) in *Gnomon* 48 (1976) 774–778.

Lenel, *Palingenesia* (1889/2000) = O. Lenel, *Palingenesia iuris civilis* (Aalen: Scientia Verlag 2000) [originally Leipzig 1889, revised ed. Graz 1960, repr. Aalen 2000].

Leonhard, 'Iurisprudentia' (1918) = R. Leonhard, 'Iurisprudentia,' *Realencyclopaedie der classischen Altertumswissenschaft* X,1 (Stuttgart: J. B. Metzler, 1918) 1159–1200.

Liebs, 'Jurisprudenz' (1997) = D. Liebs, 'Jurisprudenz,' in K. Sallmann, ed., *Handbuch der lateinischen Literatur der Antike. Bd. 4. Die Literatur des Umbruchs: von der römischen zur christlichen Literatur; 117–284 n. Chr.* (Munich: C. H. Beck, 1997) 83–217.

Liebs, *Hofjuristen* (2010) = D. Liebs, *Hofjuristen der römischen Kaiser bis Justinian* (Munich: Bayerische Akademie der Wissenschaften, 2010).

Lo Cascio and Mantovani, *Diritto romano e economia* (2018) = E. Lo Cascio and D. Mantovani, eds., *Diritto romano e economia. Due modi di pensare e organizzare il mondo (nei primi tre secoli dell'Impero)* (Pavia: Pavia University Press, 2018).

Lougovaya, '*Medici Docti*' (2019) = J. Lougovaya, '*Medici Docti* in Verse Inscriptions,' *Archiv für Papyrusforschung* 40 (2019) 139–159.

Mantovani, '*Iuris scientia* e *honores*' (1997) = D. Mantovani, '*Iuris scientia* e *honores.* Contributo allo studio dei fattori sociali nella formazione giurisprudenziale del diritto romano (III-I sec. A.C.),' in *Nozione formazione e interpretazione del diritto dall' età romana alle esperienze moderne. Ricerche dedicate al Professor Filippo Gallo I* (Naples: Jovene, 1997) 617–680.

Mantovani, *Les jurists* (2018) = D. Mantovani, *Les jurists écrivains de la Rome antique. Les oeuvres des jurists comme littérature* (Paris: Belles Lettres, 2018).

Mantovani, 'Aspects of the Critical Edition' (2022) = D. Mantovani, 'Aspects of the Critical Edition of Roman Juristic Works. The Example of Ulpian's *De officio proconsulis,*' in Nasti and Schiavone, eds., *Jurists and Legal Science* (London and New York: Routledge, 2022) 235–260.

Marincola, *Authority and Tradition* (1997) = J. Marincola, *Authority and Tradition in Ancient Historiography* (Cambridge: Cambridge University Press, 1997).

Marotta and Stolfi, Ius controversum (2012) = V. Marotta and E. Stolfi, eds., Ius controversum *e processo tra tarda repubblica ed età dei Severi* (Rome: Bretschneider, 2012).

Mason, *Greek Terms* (1974) = H. J. Mason, *Greek Terms for Roman Institutions. A Lexicon and Analysis* (Toronto: Hakkert, 1974).

Mattern, 'Physicians and the Roman Imperial Aristocracy' (1999) = S. Mattern, 'Physicians and the Roman Imperial Aristocracy: The Patronage of Therapeutics,' *Bulletin of the History of Medicine* 73 (1999) 1–18.

Mattern, *Galen* (2008) = S. Mattern, *Galen and the Rhetoric of Healing* (Baltimore: Johns Hopkins University Press, 2008).

Mattern, *Prince of Medicine* (2013) = S. P. Mattern, *The Prince of Medicine. Galen in the Roman Empire* (Oxford: Oxford University Press, 2013).

Mendelson, 'Aspects' (2002) = D. Mendelson, 'Aspects of Causation in Hippocratic Medicine and Roman Law of Delict,' in I. Freckelton and D. Mendelson, eds., *Causation in Law and Medicine* (London: Taylor & Francis, 2002) 58–77.

Meyer, 'Evidence and Argument' (2016) = E. Meyer, 'Evidence and Argument: The Truth of Prestige and its Performance,' in P. J. du Plessis, C. Ando, and K. Tuori, eds., *The Oxford Handbook of Roman Law and Society* (Oxford: Oxford University Press, 2016) 270–282.

Millar, *Emperor* (1977) = F. Millar, *The Emperor in the Roman World* (Ithaca and London: Cornell University Press, 1977).

Moatti, *Birth of Critical Thinking* (2015) = C. Moatti, *The Birth of Critical Thinking in Republican Rome* (Cambridge: Cambridge University Press, 2015). Translation by J. Lloyd of *La Raison de Rome. Naisance de l'esprit critique à la fin de la République* (Paris: Editions du Seuil, 1997).

Nasti and Schiavone, *Jurists and Legal Science* (2022) = F. Nasti and A. Schiavone, eds., *Jurists and Legal Science in the History of Roman Law* (London and New York: Routledge, 2022).

Neudecker, 'Aspekte öffentlicher Bibliotheken' (2004) = R. Neudecker, 'Aspekte öffentlicher Bibliotheken in der Kaiserzeit,' in B. E. Borg, ed., *Paideia: The World of the Second Sophistic* (Berlin and New York: De Gruyter, 2004) 293–313.

Noé, 'Gli excursus' (1982) = E. Noé, 'Gli excursus letterari dei Velleio Patercolo,' *Clio* 18 (1982) 511–523.

Norr, *Rechtskritik* (1974) = D. Nörr, *Rechtskritik in der römischen Antike* (Munich: Bayerischen Akademie der Wissenschaften, 1974).

Nutton, *Prognosis* (1979) = V. Nutton, *Galen: On Prognosis. CMG V. 8. 1* (Berlin: Akademie-Verlag, 1979).

Nutton, 'Healers' (1992) = V. Nutton, 'Healers in the Medical Market Place: Towards a Social History of Graeco-Roman Medicine,' in A. Wear, ed., *Medicine in Society: Historical Essays* (Cambridge: Cambridge University Press, 1992) 15–58.

Nutton, 'Kühn' (2002) = V. Nutton, 'In Defense of Kühn,' in id., ed., *The Unknown Galen. Bulletin of the Institute of Classical Studies. Supplement 77* (London: Institute of Classical Studies, 2002) 1–7.

Nutton, 'Galen's Library' (2009) = V. Nutton, 'Galen's Library,' in C. Gill, T. Whitmarsh, and J. Wilkins, eds., *Galen and the World of Knowledge* (Cambridge: Cambridge University Press, 2009) 19–34.

Nutton, *Ancient Medicine* (2013) = V. Nutton, *Ancient Medicine*, second ed. (London and New York: Routledge, 2013).

Nutton, *Galen* (2020) = V. Nutton, *Galen: A Thinking Doctor in Imperial Rome* (London and New York: Taylor & Francis, 2020).

Overduin, *Nicander* (2015) = F. Overduin, *Nicander of Colophon's* Theriaca. *A Literary Commentary* (Leiden: Brill, 2015).

Peachin, 'Jurists and the Law' (2001) = M. Peachin, 'Jurists and the Law in the Early Roman Empire,' in L. de Blois, ed., *Administration, Prosopography and Appointment Policies in the Roman Empire* (Amsterdam: J. C. Gieben, 2001) 109–120.

Peachin, 'Weitere Gedanken' (2015) = M. Peachin, 'Weitere Gedanken zum Prozess des Verfassens kaiserlicher Reskripte,' in U. Babusiaux and A. Kolb, eds., *Das Recht der 'Soldatenkaiser.' Rechtliche Stabilität in Zeiten politischen Umbruchs?* (Berlin, Munich, and Boston: De Gruyter, 2015) 211–224.

Peachin, 'Lehne-Gstreinthaler' (2021) = M. Peachin, review of Lehne-Gstreinthaler, Iurisperiti et oratores (2019), in *Zeitschrift der Savigny-Stiftung für Rechtsgeschichte, Roman. Abt.* 138 (2021) 643–652.

Petit, *Rhétorique de la Providence* (2018) = C. Petit, *Galien de Pergame ou la rhétorique de la Providence: médecine, littérature et pouvoir à Rome* (Leiden and Boston: Brill, 2018).

Pflaum, *Les carrières* (1960–1961) = H.-G. Pflaum, *Les carrières procuratoriennes équestres sous le Haut-Empire romain* (Paris: Imprimerie nationale, 1960–1961).

Pigeaud and Pigeaud, *Textes médicaux latins* (2000) = A. Pigeaud and J. Pigeaud, eds., *Les textes médicaux latins comme littérature* (Nantes: Institut universitaire de France, Université de Nantes, 2000).

Rawson, *Intellectual Life* (1985) = E. Rawson, *Intellectual Life in the Late Roman Republic* (London: Duckworth, 1985).

Reardon, *Courants littéraires* (1971) = B. P. Reardon, *Courants littéraires grecs des IIe et IIIe siècles après J.-C.* (Paris: Belles Lettres, 1971).

Ritschl, *Opuscula* (1877) = F. Ritschl, *Opuscula philologica. Volumen III: Ad litteras Latinas spectantia* (Leipzig: Teubner, 1877).

Rosen, *Law as Culture* (2006) = L. Rosen, *Law as Culture. An Invitation* (Princeton: Princeton University Press, 2006).

Russo, 'The literary *excursus*' (2008) = F. Russo, 'The Literary *excursus* of Velleius Paterculus and the Exaltation of the Italic Contribution to the Grandeur of Rome,' *Florentia Illiberitana. Revista de estudios de la antigüedad clásica* 19 (2008) 293–312.

Sailor, *Writing and Empire* (2008) = D. Sailor, *Writing and Empire in Tacitus* (Cambridge: Cambridge University Press, 2008).

Sallmann, 'Celsus' (2006) = K. Sallmann, 'Cornelius Celsus, A.,' in *Brill's New Pauly* (2006) [https://referenceworks-brillonline-com.proxy.library.nyu.edu/entries/brill-s-new-pauly/celsus-ii-e229920?s.num=0&s.f.s2_parent=s.f.book.brill-s-new-pauly&s.q=Cornelius+Celsus#e229990].

Salomies, 'Redner und Senatoren' (2005) = O. Salomies, 'Redner und Senatoren. Eloquenz als Standeskultur (1.-3. Jh. n. Chr.),' in W. Eck and M. Heil, eds., Senatores populi Romani. *Realität und mediale Präsentation einer Führungsschicht* (Stuttgart: Franz Steiner, 2005) 229–262.

Samama, *Les médecins* (2003) = É. Samama, *Les médecins dans le monde grec. Sources épigraphiques sur la naissance d'un corps médical* (Geneva: Librairie Droz, 2003).

Schiavone, 'Sapere giuridico e identità' (2003) = A. Schiavone, 'Sapere giuridico e identità romana. Un'interpretazione,' in M. Citroni, ed., *Memoria e identità. La cultura romana costruisce la sua imagine* (Florence: Università degli Studi di Firenze, 2003) 61–79.

Schiavone, *Invention of Law* (2012) = A. Schiavone, *The Invention of Law in the West* (Cambridge, MA: Belknap Press of Harvard University Press, 2012).

Schiavone, 'Singularity and Impersonality' (2022) = A. Schiavone, 'Singularity and Impersonality in the Thought of Roman Jurists,' in Nasti and Schiavone, eds., *Jurists and Legal Science* (London and New York: Routledge, 2022) 3–11.

Schiller, *Roman Law* (1978) = A. A. Schiller, *Roman Law. Mechanisms of Development* (The Hague, Paris, and New York: Mouton, 1978).

Schmitz, *Bildung und Macht* (1997) = T. Schmitz, *Bildung und Macht: zur sozialen und politischen Funktion der zweiten Sophistik in der griechischen Welt der Kaiserzeit* (Munich: C. H. Beck, 1997).

Schulz, *Geschichte* (1961) = F. Schulz, *Geschichte der römischen Rechtswissenschaft* (Weimar: Hermann Böhlaus Nachfolger, 1961).

Schulze, *Aulus Cornelius Celsus* (1999) = C. Schulze, *Aulus Cornelius Celsus—Artzt oder Laie: Autor, Konzept und Adressaten der* De medicina libri octo (Trier: WVT Wissenschaflicher Verlag Trier, 1999).

Schulze, *Celsus* (2001) = C. Schulze, *Celsus* (Hildesheim, Zurich, and New York: G. Olms, 2001).

Sconocchia, 'Medicina romana' (2002) = S. Sconocchia, 'Medicina romana e greca di prima età imperiale,' in C. Santini, ed., *Letteratura scientifica e tecnica di Grecia e Roma* (Rome: Carucci, 2002) 316–362.

Serbat, *Celse* (1995) = G. Serbat, *Celse. De la medicine* (Paris: Belles Lettres, 1995).

Swain, *Hellenism and Empire* (1996) = S. Swain, *Hellenism and Empire: Language, Classicism, and Power in the Greek World AD 50–250* (Oxford: Clarendon, 1996).

Taub, 'Explaining a Volcano' (2009) = L. Taub, 'Explaining a Volcano Naturally: *Aetna* and the Choice of Poetry,' in Taub and Doody, eds., *Authorial Voices* (Trier: WVT Wissenschaftlicher Verlag, 2009) 125–141.

Taub and Doody, *Authorial Voices* (2009) = L. C. Taub and A. Doody, eds., *Authorial Voices in Greco-Roman Technical Writing* (Trier: WVT Wissenschaftlicher Verlag, 2009).

Tuori, 'A Place for the Jurists?' (2010) = K. Tuori, 'A Place for the Jurists in the Spaces of Justice?' in F. de Angelis, ed., *Spaces of Justice in the Roman World* (Leiden and Boston: Brill, 2010) 43–65.

Tuplin and Rihll, *Science and Mathematics* (2002) = C. J. Tuplin and T. E. Rihll, eds., *Science and Mathematics in Ancient Greek Culture* (Oxford: Oxford University Press, 2002).

Visky, *Geistige Arbeit* (1977) = K. Visky, *Geistige Arbeit und die 'artes liberales' in den Quellen des römischen Rechts* (Budapest: Akadémiai Kiadó, 1977).

Vogt, 'Lehrdichtung im Urteil Galens' (2005) = S. Vogt, '"...er schrieb in Versen, und er tat recht daran": Lehrdichtung im Urteil Galens,' in T. Fögen, ed., *Antike Fachtexte = Ancient Technical Texts* (Berlin: De Gruyter, 2005) 51–78.

Volk, *Poetics* (2002) = K. Volk, *The Poetics of Latin Didactic: Lucretius, Vergil, Ovid, Manilius* (Oxford: Oxford University Press, 2002).

von Albrecht, *Roman Literature* (1997) = M. von Albrecht, *A History of Roman Literature. From Livius Andronicus to Boethius* (Leiden, New York, and Cologne: Brill, 1997).

Wellmann, 'Cornelius' (1900) = M. Wellmann, 'Cornelius Nr. 82,' in *Realenzyklopaedie der classischen Altertumswissenschaft* IV, 1 (Stuttgart: J. B. Metzler, 1900) 1273–1276.

Williams, 'Caracalla and the Rhetoricians' (1974) = W. Williams, 'Caracalla and the Rhetoricians. A Note on the *cognitio de Goharienis*,' *Latomus* 33 (1974) 663–667.

Yalvaç, 'Herakleitos of Rhodiapolis' (2022) = U. Yalvaç, 'Herakleitos of Rhodiapolis: *Addenda et Corrigenda* to *TAM* II 911,' *Libri: Journal of Epigraphy, Reviews and Translations* 7 (2022) 1–3.

PART II

SELLING THE SUBJECT-MATTER

When Science, Competition, and Entertainment Commingle

Introduction

Competition in the Roman Empire—Structure, Characteristics, and New Arenas

Matthew Roller

Scholars have long ascribed to Roman aristocrats, especially in the republican period, the habit of competing with one another for political, social, and economic advantage. This competitive habit has been thought to be most visible in the canvassing for election to public office, as multiple candidates for a given magistracy put themselves forward before the people and sought to secure the votes that would install them, in preference to other candidates, in the position desired. Aristocratic competition was hardly limited to elections, however: magistrates, once installed, sought to outdo one another in carrying out the duties of office and exploiting the opportunities it afforded, and to dominate the monumental space of the city in commemorating their achievements. Much work has been done in recent decades, especially by Germanophone scholars, to articulate and characterize the arenas and stakes of competitive activity among republican aristocrats. Less scholarly attention has been paid to the question of competition in the imperial age. Did aristocrats still compete once popular elections for public office had ceased, and once the traditional forms of monumental public display had come to be monopolized by the emperor and his regime? Not in the same way, or in all the same arenas, to be sure. However, closer attention to other, and in some cases new, areas of aristocratic activity and interest in this period reveal beyond doubt that this group's competitive impulses persisted undiminished, though changed, and furthermore that the arenas, modes, and stakes of competition were constantly evolving. The specific questions pertaining to the current volume are to consider how and to what extent medicine and law in particular constitute

I thank Claire Bubb and Michael Peachin for organizing the "Medicine and the Law" conference at New York University in October 2019, and inviting me to develop initial thoughts on this topic there, in conversation with the other conferees. Five doctoral students at Johns Hopkins University—Richard Buckley-Gorman, Juan Dopico, Giacomo Loi, Connor Sedlacek, and Kathryn Stutz—participated in a graduate seminar I led in Fall 2019 on "Competition in the early Roman empire," where we collectively developed and worked out many ideas. Finally, I thank Claire and Michael again, along with Karl Hölkeskamp and Elke Stein-Hölkeskamp, for their detailed comments, corrections, and bibliographic suggestions at several stages of this chapter's development.

Matthew Roller, *Introduction: Competition in the Roman Empire—Structure, Characteristics, and New Arenas* In: *Medicine and the Law under the Roman Empire*. Edited by: Claire Bubb and Michael Peachin, Oxford University Press.
 DOI: 10.1093/oso/9780192898616.003.0002

arenas of aristocratic competition in the imperial age; and, if they are indeed competitive arenas, what the characteristics and dynamics of these competitions are.

Georg Simmel and Competition Theory

Since the nineteenth century, social theorists have understood "competition" to be a specific form of social struggle.[1] Individuals or groups may vie for control of scarce resources, i.e. goods (tangible or intangible) whose supply is insufficient to satisfy all parties who want or need them. For Max Weber, competition is a distinctively "peaceful" and "regulated" form of such struggle, since it has rules and abjures physical violence.[2] Georg Simmel, in a particularly influential articulation, develops the ideas of non-violence and regulation in a specific direction. For Simmel, competition is a *mediated* form of struggle in which the resources sought by the contestants do not lie directly within their own power to obtain. Rather, the power to award victory and bestow the desired prizes or resources lies with a "third party" (which Simmel calls a *dritte Instanz*)—a judge or other figure, individual or corporate, that stands apart from the struggling contestants, evaluates their performances relative to one another and in light of the norms and regulations governing the conduct of the competition, and on that basis awards the victory or prize to one (or a subset) of the competitors. Simmel furthermore distinguishes "competition" from direct, unmediated "conflict" where the contestants struggle directly with one another, and the resources or prize sought can be secured directly by whichever party prevails (e.g. seized by force in warfare). However, conflict and competition so defined are not absolutely exclusive, and a given struggle may display each form in different respects, or transition from one form to the other over time.[3]

Simmel developed this theory in the context of the industrialized, global society of the turn of the twentieth century, and he adduces examples ranging from the

[1] See Ulf, 'Competition' (2011) for an account, beginning in the late eighteenth century, of "competition" as an economic and social phenomenon, especially as applied to the study of ancient Greece; also Nullmeier, 'Wettbewerbskulturen' (2002) 157–160 for Jacob Burckhardt's views about the Greek *agon;* and Jessen, 'Konkurrenz' (2014) 10–18 for approaches to "competition" in various academic disciplines since the early twentieth century.

[2] Weber, *Wirtschaft* (1956) 20–21; English tr. in Roth and Wittich, *Weber* (1978) 38–40.

[3] Simmel, *Soziologie* (1992 (1908)) 323–347; English tr. in Wolff and Bendix, *Simmel* (1955) 57–85. Here I cite the argument as presented in Simmel's 1908 book *Soziologie*, slightly expanded and developed from a 1903 essay entitled 'Soziologie der Konkurrenz' (= Simmel, *Aufsätze* (1989 (1903)) 221–245). For a modern assessment, and on the development of Simmel's thought, see Werron, 'Direkte' (2010) and Werron, 'Konstruktion' (2011). I seek here to maintain Simmel's own semantic distinctions, wherein the general category of contention is *Kampf* ("struggle"), and its species are direct/unmediated *Konflikt* ("conflict") and indirect/mediated *Konkurrenz* or *Wettbewerb* ("competition"). See Werron, 'Direkte' (2010) 302–307 for these terms, and 312–316 for modern examples of how conflict and competition can coexist, collide, or evolve into one another.

medieval period to his own day. Social scientists and historians, especially in Germany, have subsequently developed this and other theories of competition and employed them to analyze a range of historical and contemporary struggles. Ancient Mediterranean societies are among those to which Simmelian analysis has been applied, with adjustments for the premodern context.[4] Specific scholars and approaches will be discussed below; for now let us simply observe a few familiar Roman social and political practices that answer well to Simmel's articulation of "competition": popular elections in the Republic, whose competitive dynamics were noted earlier; musical or poetic or athletic contests, where a duly appointed judge or panel of judges determines the relative merit of the prize seekers within the framework of the norms of the competition; and trials carried out in law courts, where a judge or panel of judges determines which one of the two litigants' cases will prevail in consideration of law, justice, expediency, and other values that are pertinent in judicial settings. The "scarce resources" in these cases are the available offices, which are fewer than the candidates; the single crown awarded to the athlete or artist deemed best in each category of competition; the single verdict that can favor only one litigant and advocate; and, of course, the prestige—intangible but very real—that accrues to the victors in all these arenas, which is perhaps the scarcest and most valuable resource of all.

Simmel and subsequent theorists are also concerned with the social effects of competition. As a form of struggle, it entails that people are at odds, and in this respect has a socially disintegrative force. But it also has powerfully integrative effects. Those who enter into a given competition subject themselves to the accepted practices and norms that govern that competition. Hence the competitors carry out their struggle within a framework of opportunities and constraints that they themselves, the "third party" judges, and society at large generally accept as valid. Furthermore, as Simmel stresses, the fact that competitors seek the favor of the third party, the judges who they hope will grant them the prize, entails that competitors will, if possible, solicitously court those judges, show and declare that their values and aims align with the judges' own, and stress that they collectively share the broader community's core values and interests—while also, of course, rubbishing their rivals and declaring these rivals' values antithetical to those of the judges and community at large. Thus competition involves significant efforts by competitors to build community and create solidarity with certain individuals and

[4] General collections on competition in contemporary and past societies include Starbatty et al., *Kultur* (2012); Tauschek, *Kulturen* (2013); Jessen, *Konkurrenz* (2014); and Kirchhoff, *Konkurrenz* (2015). For competition in ancient Rome in particular, see the edited collection of Hölkeskamp and Beck, *Verlierer* (2019), and the monographic studies by Künzer, *Kulturen* (2016) and Stein-Hölkeskamp, *Unterschiede* (2019). Anglophone scholarship on ancient Mediterranean competition is sparser and more empirical: the only broad investigations I know are two edited collections, Fisher and Van Wees, *Competition* (2011) and Damon and Pieper, *Eris* (2019), neither of which systematically engages the existing theory or prior scholarship on competition.

groups, even as they also cultivate and accentuate social rifts with other individuals and groups.[5]

In thinking about the dynamics of competition in the Roman world, I find it helpful to supplement Simmel's framework with certain aspects of "field theory," which has long had a place in the social sciences and has been widely popularized in the past generation by Pierre Bourdieu. A "field" is a domain of specialized social activity that has come to develop practices, norms, training or acculturation, and even institutions specific to itself, and thereby attains a degree of autonomy from the larger world (though it can and does feel pressure and influence from forces beyond itself). A "field" so conceived is fundamentally relational: social actors take positions and make moves within a network of forces or power relations that exist among the actors; these forces, along with the actors themselves, constitute the field as such. These actors seek advantage for themselves relative to other actors by accumulating forms of "capital" (essentially forms of recognition, whether tangible or intangible) that are often distinctive to the field in question. Indeed, simply to "be in" a "field" so understood—to take a position, and to act within its network of power relations—is automatically to be engaged in struggle with other actors to accumulate capital. For the "game" (as Bourdieu often calls it) is set up to require struggle and opposition, which are, as it were, conditions of entry. As examples of fields, Bourdieu in various works discusses the modern practices of politics, musical composition, literary production, painting, and the standard academic disciplines, among others. This framing of "field" is helpful not least because it clarifies exactly how, and on what, those who participate in a given competition agree and disagree: they operate as actors within a field that has its distinctive norms, practices, acculturation, and institutions, and they pursue whatever form of capital has currency there; thus, precisely in struggling with one another, they are all objectively invested in the perpetuation of the field as such.[6] In other ways too, as we shall see, the characteristics of "fields" just described will prove helpful for understanding the structure and dynamics of Roman aristocratic competition.

Bourdieu has been criticized, however, for evidently conceiving of "fields" in general on the template of modern elite professions—as activities in which actors participate almost exclusively, for which they have received extensive training, and

[5] Simmel himself speaks much more about the socially integrative effects of competition than the disintegrative effects: Simmel, *Soziologie* (1992 (1908)) 325–329, 341–345 = Wolff and Bendix, *Simmel* (1955) 58–63, 76–80, and *passim*. On these effects in modern societies see Imbusch, 'Konkurrenz' (2015) (esp. 216–220 on Weber and Simmel; also 233–234), with further bibliography. Regarding Rome, see Hölkeskamp, 'Konkurrenz' (2014) *passim*; Nebelin, 'Aristokratische Konkurrenz' (2014) 153–158 (an interesting attempt to articulate precisely the points on which republican aristocrats had to agree in order to enter into competition for public office); and Künzer, *Kulturen* (2016) 64–65.

[6] Most aspects of "field theory" as Bourdieu presents it can be found in Bourdieu, 'Cultural' (1993 (1983)) and Bourdieu, 'Political' (1991 (1981)). See also Hilgers and Mangez, 'Introduction' (2015) for a helpful general summary, and Lahire, 'Limits' (2015) 66–72 on Bourdieu's articulation of "field" in relation to his sociological predecessors.

which can provide at least some of these actors with a living. The relatively high level of autonomy from the larger world that such fields display, and the all-consuming, exclusive focus they tend to demand of their practitioners, are not characteristic of all domains of specialized activity even in the modern world, let alone in premodern societies.[7] In particular, these features do not characterize well the various domains of aristocratic activity in the Roman world, which tend to overlap and to display lower levels of autonomy, institutionalization, and specific acculturation; furthermore, Roman aristocrats rarely devoted themselves to one such activity exclusively, and normally participated in many such activities simultaneously (see below on "generalists" vs. "specialists"). To avoid the risk of importing connotations inappropriate for a Roman setting, then, in this chapter I generally avoid the term "field"—even while accepting for ancient Rome a number of the characteristics Bourdieu connects with this term—and prefer less-marked terms such as "domain," "area," and "arena." I particularly favor "arena" not only for its distinctively Roman resonances, but also because Pliny the Younger authorizes precisely this metaphorical usage when he refers to one of his own favorite competitive domains—the centumviral court, where he argued many cases and built a formidable reputation for legal advocacy and oratory—as "my arena."[8]

Scholarly Approaches to Roman Aristocratic Competition

As noted earlier, scholarly discussion of aristocratic competition in the Roman world has focused particularly on the republican period, and on arenas of competition in which the "third party" judge is the *populus Romanus*, however defined and constituted. As scholars have demonstrated over the past several decades, the republican aristocracy relentlessly cultivated a political culture of visibility, of being "known"—*nobilis*—to the people. This aristocratic quest for public visibility was pursued across a variety of distinct domains: in standing for elective magistracies that the people, marshaled in its voting tribes and centuries, held the power

[7] For a critique of Bourdieu's (implicit) conceptualization of "fields" as modern professions, see Lahire, 'Limits' (2015), esp. 72–75 for a range of (modern) activities for which Bourdieu's articulation seems too strong. Lahire himself uses terms like "universe," "function," and "logic" to label the more general category of somewhat specialized, somewhat autonomous activities, and restricts "field" to the most specialized and autonomous ones (e.g. p. 72).

[8] For Pliny's metaphor see *Ep.* 6.12.2: *itaque Bittio Prisco, quantum plurimum potuero, praestabo, praesertim in harena mea, hoc est apud centumviros* ("And so, I will do all I can for Bittius Priscus, especially in my own arena, that is to say, the centumviral court"). One could literalize the metaphor by analyzing the actual Roman arena, i.e. the sandy floor of the amphitheater that is the venue for gladiatorial combat, as an "arena" of competition characterized by a degree of autonomy, specific acculturation, and institutionalization, and where—notwithstanding the direct combat between the contestants—the prizes sought are awarded by third-party judges. But that is beyond the scope of this chapter.

to bestow or withhold; as office holders addressing the people and seeking their approval on matters of political significance; in great public processions like triumphs and funerals; in being donors and patrons of buildings, monuments, games, and so on; and as advocates pleading cases in civil or criminal trials and seeking to impress the *corona*, the gallery of public observers, who assembled to watch the trial. Furthermore, all such activity tended to be staged in the quintessentially public spaces of the republican city: the *forum*, *comitium*, *sacra via*, capitol, and *campus martius*. The *populus Romanus*, variously constituted as the judge or evaluator of such aristocratic performances, held considerable power to confer prestige and political advancement upon the individuals it favored, and withhold it from those it disfavored. K.-J. Hölkeskamp has been particularly influential in expounding and articulating this culture of aristocratic publicity and visibility in the republican period; he has also analyzed the competitive dynamics of this political culture with great theoretical sophistication.[9]

Yet this is not the whole story: even in the Republic, other competitions existed for other prizes that lay in the power of other "third parties" to bestow. It was well and good for an advocate to impress the *corona* with his oratory during a trial. But he lost the case unless he persuaded the actual, officially designated judges of the case, the *iudices*, to vote for the verdict he sought. This "third party," consisting of senators and/or equestrians in varying combinations over time, was an elite, not popular, group—often, indeed, with its own internal rifts and divergent interests—and had to be courted in a manner quite different from a popular group. Likewise, oratory within the senate conferred great prestige and power upon speakers who could persuade other senators to support their proposals in preference to the proposals of others. Here the "third party" judges consisted exclusively of other senators—senators who at other moments stepped into the role of orators themselves, seeking to persuade their peers and being subjected in their own turn to these peers' "third party" adjudication.[10] Finally, by the last century of the Republic, literary and intellectual activities of various sorts, as well as dimensions of consumption and lifestyle more broadly, emerged as competitive

[9] E.g. Hölkeskamp, *Senatus* (2004) chs. 5, 6, 8; Hölkeskamp, *Libera* (2017) chs. 3, 5; Hölkeskamp, *Roman* (2020) chs. 3, 4; all with further bibliography. (Most of these chapters are updated and expanded versions of earlier publications; here I cite only the most recent version.) For the competitive dimension see Nebelin, 'Aristokratische Konkurrenz' (2014); Hölkeskamp, *Reconstructing* (2010) ch. 7; Hölkeskamp, *Libera* (2017) ch. 5; and—above all, and now fundamental—Hölkeskamp, 'Konkurrenz' (2014). For a less theorized, somewhat different account of aristocratic competition in the era of the first Punic war, see Bleckmann, *Nobilität* (2002) 225–243.

[10] The "double role" of senators relative to senatorial oratory and debate—where individual senators had to switch frequently between the roles of competitor and "third party" judge—is noted by Künzer, *Kulturen* (2016) 56. It is a feature of other aristocratic competitive arenas as well: see Roller, 'Amicable' (2018) for the younger Pliny as a participant in the imperial culture of literary recitation, who sometimes gives recitations of his own work before a public judging audience, sometimes attends and judges the recitations of others, and sometimes even judges the behavior of other attendees/judges at such events.

arenas for aristocrats. The readership or audience that could confer honor and prestige upon a poet, philosopher, owner of a grand house, connoisseur of art objects, or impresario of spectacular dinner parties (*convivia*) was a broader group of educated, higher-status Romans—hardly the *populus Romanus* as a whole, but also not just senators and equestrians.

Yet these and other arenas in which the judging "third party" was *not* the *populus Romanus* have received far less attention in recent years than those in which the people *did* play that role. This attention differential can perhaps be imputed to the "democracy debate" of the 1980s–2000s—the scholarly controversy spurred by Fergus Millar's thesis that the Roman Republic could be styled a "democracy" on account of the *populus Romanus*' supposed sovereignty in choosing magistrates and passing legislation. This thesis directed concerted attention to the activities of "the people" and the roles they played in their interactions with the aristocratic ruling class.[11] Scholars who regarded Millar's thesis as over-strong advanced various criticisms and objections, including the counter-thesis that the people's role in the state is better conceptualized as a "third party" judging role for competitions among aristocrats—a view that ascribes considerably less political agency and initiative to the *populus Romanus* than Millar's thesis does.[12] In any case, the focus of discussion has been on the people's role relative to the activities of government. Our purposes, however, require us to reverse the telescope and look through the other end: if we start with the question of aristocratic competition more broadly, our field of view quickly widens out to include not only those public, political arenas in which the people serve as third-party judges, but many further and multifarious arenas in which other groups and individuals serve as judges. Much scope remains for studying such arenas, even in the republican period.[13]

If we look beyond the republican period and into the imperial age, we find that scholarly engagement with questions of aristocratic competition, of any type and in any arena, is scarcer still—and the scholarship that exists is difficult to locate, being scattered in article- or chapter-length explorations of particular topics or problems. We can, however, glean a rough overview of the landscape. A valuable article by Frédéric Hurlet on the culture of publicity in the Augustan age underscores this period's continuities with the late Republic. He stresses, however, innovations like the increasing importance of the *princeps* himself as a "third party" judge of aristocratic performances, and the emergence of the imperial court

[11] Millar, *Crowd* (1998) 208–226 (and ch. 8 *passim*); this book gathers and recapitulates arguments Millar had been making since the 1980s.

[12] Extended responses to and critiques of Millar's argument include Mouritsen, *Plebs* (2001) 13–17; Morstein-Marx, *Oratory* (2004) 6–23; and Hölkeskamp, *Reconstructing* (2010) 1–11 (and *passim* in all cases). Hölkeskamp, *Roman* (2020) 16–18 provides a very compact summary of the whole "democracy debate."

[13] Elke Stein-Hölkeskamp has explored productively in this area; more on her work below.

and its courtiers—those individuals who are close to the *princeps* in various capacities, and carry out their activities inside the *princeps*' house—as an arena of political competition with distinctively "secret," rather than public and visible, dynamics.[14] Looking beyond the Augustan age, over the course of the Julio-Claudian period the selection of magistrates and the passage of legislation shifted out of the control of popular assemblies, and certain criminal courts shifted out of public jurisdiction, all into the administration of the Senate and/or the *princeps*. Thus the role of the *populus Romanus* as "third party" judge in key arenas of aristocratic competition declined significantly. Yet these arenas of competition persisted, in new guises or with new "third party" judges, during the first and second centuries CE. Aristocrats still competed to obtain magistracies or offices, and in the military commands and other roles that followed from office holding, albeit via elections held within the senate and in light of explicit concessions, endorsements, or outright adlection into office by the emperor. Hence those who sought public office now competed for the favor of a small group of senatorial peers and/or the favor of the emperor himself. (Indeed, competitors in these and other arenas can often be seen to seek favor from several distinct "third parties" simultaneously, each with its own interests and agendas and its own prizes to bestow, and each requiring cultivation in different ways.) Competition in oratory and eloquence persisted and indeed thrived—especially in the courts, though trials offered fewer large public audiences overall than in the past; and within the senate, which beyond its longstanding function as a deliberative body gained several criminal jurisdictions and the capacity to function as a court. Competition among aristocrats for public visibility and approval via public monuments also continued, though primarily in the towns of Italy and in the provinces, and no longer in the public spaces of the city of Rome, where the monumental landscape had largely come to be reserved for the imperial family and its close associates.[15] Relatively little scholarly work has been done on these developments from a "competition" perspective. However, in a 2011 article I survey some of this territory with all brevity; and an important recent book by Isabelle Künzer examines these developments (and more) in much greater depth from a Simmelian perspective, albeit within a narrow time frame—the early Trajanic period, as portrayed in the works of Pliny and Tacitus.[16]

[14] Hurlet, 'Concurrence' (2012); also Nebelin, 'Aristokratische Konkurrenz' (2014) 164–166. Eck, 'Senator' (2005) 8–9 discusses early imperial inscriptions asserting the commemorand/honorand's proximity to or favored standing with the emperor.

[15] On senatorial monuments in the Augustan age, see Eck, 'Senatorial' (1984), esp. 139–145; also Eck, 'Emperor' (2010) for the early empire more generally.

[16] Roller, 'Speaking' (2011) 199–215; also Klingenberg, 'Zwischen' (2019) on elections and senatorial status in the early empire. Künzer, *Kulturen* (2016) 47–96 (her ch. 2) is invaluable on these questions and on the state of scholarship; in pp. 99–291 (her ch. 3) she examines many of these arenas in much greater depth for her selected period.

In addition, arenas of literary, intellectual, and "lifestyle" competition burgeoned in the early imperial age, and the attention they receive in early imperial texts increased dramatically. These arenas, as noted earlier, first emerged in the republican period, and even then stood largely outside the overtly "political" arenas spotlighted by the "democracy debate." Elke Stein-Hölkeskamp has pioneered the investigation of these arenas: in a series of articles published over two decades, recently augmented by a monographic study, she has examined how aristocratic dining practices, sartorial choices, domestic architecture and decoration, collecting and connoisseurship, and literary activity were transformed into competitive activities by late republican and early imperial aristocrats, and how such activities became mechanisms for manufacturing and perpetuating social distinctions that articulated hierarchies within the aristocracy and differentiated aristocrats from non-aristocrats. She also shows that such activities were sometimes positioned as a kind of counter-discourse to the competition for public honors embedded in the dominant political culture of publicity.[17] I myself have explored, in several articles, the arenas of competition in eloquence and literary activity that become prominent in the early imperial age, though without employing the Simmelian theoretical framework adopted here.[18] For all such competitions, small and elite audiences of cognoscenti, and even audiences of one (say, the emperor, a provincial governor, or the "single judge" in many civil trials) were of great importance as "third party" judges, while large public audiences were generally less attainable and in many cases less relevant than in the republican period—though by no means non-existent.

Many key topics remain inadequately explored, or entirely unaddressed. For example, no scholarship, to my knowledge, discusses from a "competition" perspective the fact that early imperial aristocrats continued to assume major military commands (subject to the emperor's approval).[19] For the successful, these commands might lead to great visibility and glory, public honors such as the *ornamenta triumphalia*, and subsequent lofty appointments in imperial administration—or to political oblivion and even death, if such success was

[17] Stein-Hölkeskamp, *Unterschiede* (2019)—the monographic study—constitutes her most detailed and complete statement; that book's bibliography lists her prior contributions. Her theoretical apparatus includes both Simmel and Bourdieu, the latter especially for his work on social status and distinction, to which her own title nods. On the fascinating case of L. Licinius Lucullus as a pathbreaking figure in "lifestyle" competition (among other arenas), see Lundgreen, 'Lucullus' (2019). For aristocratic villa culture as an arena of competition, see Platts, 'Keeping up' (2011).

[18] See Roller, 'Amicable' (2018) on recitation as a competitive arena; Roller, 'Centumviral' (2019) on the emergence of the centumviral court a major domain of advocacy in the early empire, thanks to its continuing use of large jury panels and (at least sometimes) its ability to attract a large *corona*; and Roller, 'Losing' (2019) on Asinius Pollio's role in establishing recitation and declamation as arenas of competition in the Augustan age.

[19] Geisthardt, *Zwischen* (2015) (esp. ch. 4) discusses in valuable detail a group of high-ranking military commanders at the time of the civil wars of 68–69 CE, including their relationships with one another and with the several emperors and pretenders of this period. His perspective, however, is not specifically that of "competition."

deemed to threaten the emperor's position. To what extent, then, could the emperor himself become entangled in broader aristocratic contests for status and distinction? Nor are the dynamics of competition even limited to human agents strictly speaking: J. E. Lendon has shown how the great Greek cities of the Roman empire, fully anthropomorphized, competed for preeminence and glory, with their ambassadors appealing to one another or to imperial authorities to be adjudged superior to rival cities, and seeking to receive the associated honors and resources. Lendon's extraordinarily stimulating demonstration adumbrates the rewards attending a deeper study of this topic.[20] Overall, then, the landscape of aristocratic competition in the first two centuries of the empire was fractured, multiplex, and kaleidoscopic; it is simply less systematizable and comprehensible, and perhaps for that reason alone less studied, than in the republican period—especially absent a single galvanizing, focusing question like the "democracy debate."

A noteworthy feature of aristocratic competition under the empire is the tendency—to judge from surviving texts—for individuals to pursue distinction in "technical" areas that require specialist knowledge and skills. Any mastery so acquired was displayed via speaking or writing, often (if not always) in more or less polemical language and in agonistic settings. Sophistic disputation is perhaps the most visible and, to date, best studied arena for such competition. Maud Gleason, in her pathbreaking book *Making Men*, memorably conjures the drama of rival sophists clashing in public, with their verbal acrobatics and flamboyant displays of mastery (real or feigned) across many fields of knowledge—always seeking to outstrip their rivals in the judgment of other specialists, of the lay audience of spectators gathered around, and of the broader reading audience of the texts in which these clashes are described.[21] Other studies have analyzed the polemical language in specialist texts of this period, and discussed the public-facing character of the clashes between rival experts in some technical field who each seek, largely through rhetorical display, to persuade the onlookers and readers to deem them preeminent over their opponent(s).[22] This brings us back to the topic of the present volume. For regarding the "technical" areas of law and

[20] Lendon, *Empire* (1997) 73–78.

[21] Gleason, *Making* (1995), esp. 131–158; also König, 'Competitiveness' (2011) on competitiveness among sophists as presented in Philostratus' *Lives of the Sophists*; and Howley, *Gellius* (2018) 204–252 on the success of the sophist Favorinus in his public encounters with various challengers and detractors, as described and judged by Aulus Gellius standing as a "third party" to these encounters. Whitmarsh, *Second Sophistic* (2005) 37–40 briefly discusses sophistic competition in general. Bourdieu, 'Cultural' (1993 (1983)) 48–52 offers stimulating reflections on small expert audiences vs. larger "lay" audiences as judges of performances by actors in any given "field."

[22] See e.g. Zadorojnyi, 'Competition' (2019) on the representations of sophistic disputation in Pollux's *Onomasticon*, as well as Pollux's own competitive polemics; also Rosen, 'Paradoxes' (2019) on competitive displays of medical virtuosity as described in the Hippocratic corpus, and the evaluation of those displays by other physicians, the spectating public, the patient, and the readers of the text. See n. 32 below for more on medical competition.

medicine, the contributions of Luis Salas and Anna Dolganov that follow abundantly document the spectacularity, the polemics directed against rivals, and the quest to be judged preeminent that attend medical displays such as prognoses and vivisections, on the one hand, and legal processes carried out in the courts of Rome and the provinces on the other hand.

General Questions

As a summary of the approaches described above, and to lay out a "competition-aware" framework for approaching the subsequent contributions in this volume, I would like to offer the following set of questions. These will, I hope, be helpful for analyzing competition in any arena and in any phase of Roman society; and therefore, *a fortiori*, helpful for the current analysis of law and medicine as competitive arenas in the imperial age.

1. How are arenas of competitive activity—their boundaries, norms, and conventional practices—determined, and who determines them? For example, in the courts, what actions are defined as crimes, and what disputes are granted standing to be tried in a court constituted to receive them? How and by whom are such decisions made?
2. Where does competition end and conflict begin? When and how does mediated, indirect struggle, in any given case, potentially turn into unmediated, direct struggle between the contending parties—or vice versa?
3. How does a would-be competitor enter an arena of competition? What, if any, are the eligibility or selection criteria for a given arena, and how (and by whom) are these criteria determined and enforced if necessary?[23]
4. Who is/are the judge(s) in a given competition, and why? That is, what individuals or groups are instituted as the "third party (/ies)" (per Simmel) empowered to determine the victor and to confer the prize that the competitors seek, and how are they so instituted? For example, many civil cases at Rome were adjudicated by an individual acting as judge (the *unus iudex*), whom the contending parties themselves chose and agreed upon. Meanwhile, in the criminal trials (the *quaestiones*) of the late Republic, as well as in the centumviral court of the late Republic and early imperial age, the panel of judges was drawn from the *album* of persons who were deemed qualified and eligible to serve in such a role—but the property and rank criteria for being included in the *album* shifted frequently over time.

[23] On conditions of entry into various "fields," see Bourdieu, 'Cultural' (1993 (1983)) 41–43; and Bourdieu, 'Political' (1991 (1981)) 175–180.

5. On what basis does the judging "third party" evaluate the performances it observes, in coming to the decision to award the victory, prize, resources, etc. to one competitor or another? What standards of performance, or alignment with norms of the specific arena or values of the broader community, are appealed to by the competitors and/or upheld by the judges in determining the victor? While the judges obviously have preexisting views and inclinations, once the competition is under way the competitors will seek, if possible, to persuade them to deem this or that aspect more important than another—according to how they estimate their own relative strengths and weaknesses, and how they can present these as aligning with what they deem to be the interests and values of the judges and community at large. The potential for cheating or corruption arises in this connection—efforts by competitors to bribe the judges, or otherwise to gain "unfair" advantage by transgressing the norms or accepted practices of the given arena.
6. To what extent do competitors seek to define or configure an arena of competition to their own advantage? Countless inscriptions and other texts, from all periods, attest individuals claiming to be the first or best or only person to achieve some particular feat: superlative language like *primus/πρῶτος*, *unus/μόνος*, *optimus*, *maximus*, and *nemo ante me*, directed at the reader as "third party" judge, are the lexical smoking guns of a competitive situation, as scholars have long noted. How and to what extent do such claims of priority function to define a competitive arena, challenge others to enter the implied contest, and appeal to the reader/listener/observer (as "third party" judge) to affirm the validity of the claim?[24]
7. How do winners respond to the outcome? While they will no doubt crow that their victory resulted from superior performance within the norms and accepted practices of the particular arena and in alignment with the values of the community, they may also seek to cement their preeminence by tilting the playing field and raising barriers against would-be rivals—say, in the case of elections, by reducing their frequency or the number of offices available, imposing novel eligibility restrictions, and so on.[25]

[24] On superlative language in inscriptions see Alföldy, 'Rolle' (1986 (1980)); also Wiseman, 'Competition' (1985) 3–10; Damon and Pieper, 'Introduction' (2019) 14–15; and Mattern, *Galen* (2008) 82–83. Bourdieu, 'Cultural' (1993 (1983)) 42–43, 58–61 argues that any new entrant into a field, simply by taking up a position, thereby causes a reconfiguration and adjustment of all the relations of power connecting the other actors within the field. On such a view, my question here points to an inevitable dynamic: the terms and stakes of competition necessarily change, to some extent, whenever a new competitor joins in.

[25] Bourdieu, 'Cultural' (1993 (1983)) 59–60 observes a generational dynamic wherein the most recognized, best-capitalized, typically older actors in a field seek in various ways to eternalize their own preeminence, as well as the state of the field in which they achieved that preeminence. Meanwhile, less

8. How do losers respond to the outcome? They may simply accept defeat, as seems typically to have happened in republican-era elections: as Hölkeskamp and others have stressed, such acceptance must be understood in the context of annual tenure of office and annual elections, whereby all the prizes are made available again next year to be competed for anew.[26] If winners, once in power, earnestly sought to remain there indefinitely and stifle future challenges (per question 7 above), losers would be less likely to accept defeat. Alternatively, losers may reject their loss, alleging that the winners cheated, the judges were biased or bribed, and so on—in short, challenging the integrity of the process of administering and judging the competition.[27] In addition, competitors who lose, or potential competitors who deem their prospects for victory slim, may seek to shift the boundaries of the arena, or abandon the competition altogether and shift to (or carve out) a different arena that better suits their strengths and increases their chances of success in the future—returning us to question 6 above. This response may provide a key to understanding how arenas of competition emerge and develop over time, including in the early imperial age: the assessment by some competitors or would-be competitors that traditional aristocratic honors were less available or beneficial than previously spurs efforts to define new competitive arenas—domains of activity that they regard, under prevailing social and political circumstances, as offering better prospects for accumulating the social capital and for manufacturing the social distinctions they seek.[28]
9. And finally: to what extent does victory or defeat in a given competition "spill over" into other competitions, such that the symbolic or cultural capital that a contestant gains or loses in one competition impacts his

recognized, poorly capitalized, typically younger actors seek to shift the symbolic order so as to improve their own chances to accumulate capital and become better recognized in their own turn (also Hilgers and Mangez, 'Introduction' (2015) 11–12).

[26] E.g. Hölkeskamp, *Libera* (2017) 139–140, 148 discusses aspects of the electoral process that appear designed to augment the perceived legitimacy and acceptability of the outcome for the losers. Also Pina Polo, 'Veteres' (2012) surveys subsequent careers of defeated candidates, and discusses the varied responses of defeated candidates to their loss (79–82).

[27] Simmel, *Soziologie* (1992 (1908)) 343 = Wolff and Bendix, *Simmel* (1955) 78–79 charmingly suggests that the vanquished party in a competition, having been subject to exactly the same chances as the victor, can blame only his own inadequacy for his loss. Of course, some losers look for *anything* on which to blame their loss, precisely to avoid acknowledging their own inadequacy: see e.g. Hölkeskamp, 'Konkurrenz' (2014) 37, 44–45, and the 2020 US presidential election.

[28] For new competitive strategies and arenas in the early empire, see Stein-Hölkeskamp, 'Aussteigen' (2019); (in brief) Hölkeskamp, 'Verlierer' (2019) 21; Roller, 'Amicable' (2018); Roller, 'Centumviral' (2019); and Roller, 'Losing' (2019) (per n. 18). In general on "losers" in aristocratic competition, see Hölkeskamp and Beck, *Verlierer* (2019). An interesting nineteenth-century French example is given by Bourdieu, 'Cultural' (1993 (1983)) 70.

> chances in an entirely different arena?[29] A longstanding debate about aristocratic "specialization" during the republican period—whether a successful public career could be based on notable success in one particular area of aristocratic endeavor (e.g. exclusively or primarily oratorical virtuosity, or military success, or legal expertise, or patronal activity)—has tended to be answered, cautiously, in the negative: that is, a fully realized republican aristocrat was required to be a "generalist" and display at least a modicum of capability across a range of relevant endeavors, and that outstanding achievement in just one area generally could not substitute for, or easily be converted into, success in another area, or success overall.[30] The first two centuries of the imperial period, however, witnessed enormous growth in imperial administration, leading *inter alia* to the development of the "equestrian" career pathway, falling within the emperor's administrative sphere, to accompany the traditional (but evolved) "senatorial" career pathway. It is easy to imagine that this new world also entailed shifts in the specific capabilities required of administrators. For this era, the same question about aristocratic "specialization" has tended to be answered, cautiously, in the affirmative: that it *was* possible, at least to some extent and in specific cases, for aristocrats who gained particular visibility and reputation in a "technical" area like jurisprudence or rhetoric (though not only these) to convert this narrow preeminence into broader career opportunities within imperial administration.[31]

Returning to the topic of the current volume, then, we must ask whether and to what extent a Roman of the imperial age who attained prominence specifically as a physician or legal expert could parlay that prominence into political or social

[29] On the extent to which an actor can redeploy capital gained in one arena of competition to another arena, or can cash out one arena's capital for another's so as to move into that new arena with an advantageous position, see Bourdieu, *Outline* (1977 (1972)) 171–183 (on "symbolic capital"), with Hilgers and Mangez, 'Introduction' (2015) 19–20.

[30] On the norm of being a "generalist" in the republican period, see David, 'L'éloquence' (2011). He identifies very few possible exceptions, and in particular rules out forensic pleading as a "specialist" path to distinction in this period. Rosillo López, 'Common' (2010) 287–288 makes a congruent argument: she contends that being merely a middling orator in the late Republic did not harm one's public career chances, provided one performed well in other arenas. Beck, 'Rolle' (2008) 119–123 presents Scipio Africanus as an anomalous case of a "specialist" in the sphere of military command, whose consular career was owed almost exclusively to that specialization. See also Van der Blom, *Oratory* (2016) 46–66 on "routes to political success" aside from oratory for republican aristocrats; and Walter, 'Karrierespezialisten' (2011) for a broader overview.

[31] For a cautious "negative," however, see Eck, 'Spezialisierung' (2001) 21–23 (and *passim*), who contends that provincial governors of the imperial age appear overall to be "generalists" in the republican mold: they seldom display any particular "specialization" themselves, but rather lean on lower-ranking specialists (in law and the like) to provide expertise—specialists who, he says, did not enter into leading positions themselves. Yet Jones, 'Culture' (2005) discusses cases of senators and equestrians from the East who appear to have owed their advancement into higher political and administrative posts precisely to their renown as rhetors or jurists. Hölkeskamp, *Libera* (2017) 108–115 discusses in general the emergence of aristocratic "specialization" in the imperial age.

success more broadly: into a presence in the imperial court, say, or in the *consilium* of a governor or emperor, and thence into further prestigious and lucrative posts such as high magistracies and promagistracies, legateships, prefectures, and the like. Can cultural and social capital gained in these "specialist" competitive arenas in fact be converted into advantageous positions in other arenas of competition? Galen's career (*PIR*^{2} G 24) offers one example of a possible trajectory. Born into a propertied family in Pergamon, he obtained such renown from his medical demonstrations and writings, both at home and later in Rome, that he gained entry to the imperial court, and intimacy with Marcus Aurelius and subsequent emperors. This is a remarkable social achievement, to be sure. However, Galen evidently never held any public office or administrative post whose responsibilities went beyond the ambit of the medical, philosophical, and literary engagements for which he was famous.[32] The career of the Severan jurist Ulpian (*PIR*^{2} D 169) offers a contrast. Ulpian, whose writings on a great range of legal matters are known thanks to their heavy excerpting in the *Digest* of Justinian, was a well-born Tyrian who came to Rome and eventually held a series of prominent posts in the imperial service: *a libellis*, *praefectus annonae*, praetorian prefect (in which post he was murdered), and member of Severus Alexander's *consilium*. While his legal expertise was recognized by contemporaries, there seems no reason to think that this recognition *led* to his having the distinguished administrative career he enjoyed, or that his specific expertise provided a currency he could "convert" into these high posts. Rather, his juristic writing is probably better seen as an instance of aristocratic literary activity, on par with writing historiography, poetry, or philosophical works. Dario Mantovani has recently argued that juristic writing, which modern scholars commonly deem "technical" and therefore non- or sub-literary, did not suffer from any such devaluation compared to other forms of writing in the eyes of imperial Romans, notwithstanding its intentionally modest level of rhetorical elaboration.[33] On this view, producing texts in this genre is simply another manifestation of the status-enhancing literary production in which Roman aristocrats had been engaging for several centuries—one of many arenas of aristocratic competition in which success could add luster to a traditional "generalist" profile. Thus Ulpian's specialist legal expertise does not seem to have had a determinative impact on his

[32] For a sketch of Galen's career in Rome and the imperial court, see Mattern, 'Physicians' (1999) 12–13. For competitive dynamics among imperial physicians, see Mattern, 'Physicians' (1999) *passim*, and Mattern, *Galen* (2008) ch. 3. Generally speaking, physicians in the Roman imperial world manifested a wide range of geographical and social origins. Some from lower-status backgrounds, thanks to their virtuosity, attained equestrian status and held equestrian offices in Rome (Mattern, 'Physicians' (1999) 6–7)—but these represent only the tiniest fraction of all physicians. I thank Claire Bubb for corrections, comments, and references regarding medical competition and Galen.

[33] Mantovani, *Les Juristes* (2018) ch. 1, esp. 23–29 on the ways in which the (modern) category "literature" has been applied to the diverse forms of Roman writing, and how juristic writing may be situated relative to these various frames. Peachin, 'Jurists' (2001) 118–120 already suggests that juristic writing was possibly regarded as just another form of aristocratic writing.

career as a courtier and high administrator, though it can't have hurt. Meanwhile, Galen's medical expertise did gain him extraordinary advancement into the imperial court, but evidently it did not open doors to opportunities lying clearly beyond that expertise.

In this chapter I have tried to present the broader cultural context of aristocratic competition against which the competitive activities of medical and legal experts in the imperial age might be considered. Indeed, the issue of competitiveness and agonism lurks nearly everywhere in this volume, starting with the introduction by Bubb and Peachin, and continuing through the essays on both the quotidian and the more elevated manifestations of medicine and law. At this point, however, let us turn to two essays that foreground the arresting manifestations of competitiveness that characterized so many public appearances by ancient physicians and lawyers.

Bibliography

Alföldy, 'Rolle' (1986 (1980)) = G. Alföldy, 'Die Rolle des Einzelnen in der Gesellschaft des römischen Kaiserreiches,' in G. Alföldy, *Die römische Gesellschaft: ausgewählte Beiträge* (Stuttgart: Franz Steiner Verlag, 1986) 334–377. (Originally published as *Sitzungsberichte der Heidelberger Akademie der Wissenschaften, Philosophisch-historische Klasse*, Jahrgang 1980, 8. Abhandlung.)

Beck, 'Rolle' (2008) = H. Beck, 'Die Rolle des Adeligen: Prominenz und aristokratische Herrschaft in der römischen Republik,' in H. Beck et al., eds., *Die Macht der Wenigen. Aristokratische Herrschaftspraxis, Kommunikation und 'edler' Lebensstil in Antike und früher Neuzeit* (Munich: Oldenbourg, 2008) 101–123.

Bleckmann, *Nobilität* (2002) = B. Bleckmann, *Die römische Nobilität im ersten Punischen Krieg. Untersuchungen zur aristokratischen Konkurrenz in der Republik* (Berlin: Akademie Verlag, 2002).

Blösel and Hölkeskamp, *Militia* (2011) = W. Blösel and K.-J. Hölkeskamp, eds., *Von der militia equestris zur militia urbana: Prominenzrolle und Karrierefelder im antiken Rom* (Stuttgart: Franz Steiner Verlag, 2011).

Bourdieu, *Outline* (1977 (1972)) = P. Bourdieu, *Outline of a Theory of Practice*, tr. R. Nice (Cambridge: Cambridge University Press, 1977). (Originally published as P. Bourdieu, *Esquisse d'une théorie de la pratique* (Geneva: Librairie Droz, 1972).)

Bourdieu, 'Political' (1991 (1981)) = P. Bourdieu, 'Political representation: elements for a theory of the political field,' trs. G. Raymond and M. Adamson, in P. Bourdieu, *Language and Symbolic Power*, ed. J. Thompson (Cambridge, MA: Harvard University Press, 1991) 171–202. (Originally published as P. Bourdieu, 'La représentation politique. Éléments pour une théorie du champ politique,' *Actes de la recherche en sciences sociales* 36–7 (1981) 3–24.)

Bourdieu, 'Cultural' (1993 (1983)) = P. Bourdieu, 'The field of cultural production, or: the economic world reversed,' tr. R. Nice, in P. Bourdieu, *The Field of Cultural*

Production, ed. R. Johnson (New York: Columbia University Press, 1993) 29–73. (Originally published, in this same English translation, in *Poetics* 12 (1983) 311–356.)

Damon and Pieper, 'Introduction' (2019) = C. Damon and C. Pieper, 'Introduction,' in Damon and Pieper, *Eris* (2019) 1–25.

Damon and Pieper, *Eris* (2019) = C. Damon and C. Pieper, eds., *Eris vs. Aemulatio: Valuing Competition in Classical Antiquity* (Leiden: Brill, 2019).

David, 'L'éloquence' (2011) = J.-M. David, 'L'éloquence judiciaire entre compétence aristocratique et spécialization carriériste,' in Blösel and Hölkeskamp, *Militia* (2011) 157–173.

De Blois, *Administration* (2001) = L. De Blois, ed., *Administration, Prosopography and Appointment Policies in the Roman Empire* (Amsterdam: J. C. Gieben, 2001).

Eck, 'Senatorial' (1984) = W. Eck, 'Senatorial self-representation: developments in the Augustan age,' in E. Segal and F. Millar, eds., *Caesar Augustus: Seven Aspects* (Oxford: Clarendon Press, 1984) 129–167.

Eck, 'Spezialisierung' (2001) = W. Eck, 'Spezialisierung in der staatlichen Administration des römischen Reiches in der hohen Kaiserzeit,' in De Blois, *Administration* (2001) 1–23.

Eck, 'Senator' (2005) = W. Eck, 'Der Senator und die Öffentlichkeit—oder: wie beeindruckt man das Publikum?' in Eck and Heil, *Senatores* (2005) 1–18.

Eck, 'Emperor' (2010) = W. Eck, 'Emperor and senatorial aristocracy in competition for public space,' in C. Noreña and B. Ewald, eds., *The Emperor and Rome: Space, Representation, and Ritual* (Cambridge: Cambridge University Press, 2010) 89–110.

Eck and Heil, *Senatores* (2005) = W. Eck and M. Heil, eds., *Senatores Populi Romani: Realität und mediale Präsentation einer Führungsschicht* (Stuttgart: Franz Steiner Verlag, 2005).

Fisher and Van Wees, *Competition* (2011) = N. Fisher and H. Van Wees, eds., *Competition in the Ancient World* (Swansea: Classical Press of Wales, 2011).

Geisthardt, *Zwischen* (2015) = J. Geisthardt, *Zwischen Princeps und Res Publica: Tacitus, Plinius, und die senatorische Selbstdarstellung in der hohen Kaiserzeit* (Stuttgart: Franz Steiner Verlag, 2015).

Gleason, *Making* (1995) = M. Gleason, *Making Men: Sophists and Self-Presentation in Ancient Rome* (Princeton: Princeton University Press, 1995).

Hilgers and Mangez, *Bourdieu's* (2015) = M. Hilgers and E. Mangez, eds., *Bourdieu's Theory of Social Fields: Concepts and Applications* (New York: Routledge, 2015).

Hilgers and Mangez, 'Introduction' (2015) = M. Hilgers and E. Mangez, 'Introduction to Pierre Bourdieu's theory of social fields,' in Hilgers and Mangez, *Bourdieu's* (2015) 1–36.

Hölkeskamp, *Senatus* (2004) = K.-J. Hölkeskamp, *Senatus Populusque Romanus. Die politische Kultur der Republik–Dimensionen und Deutungen* (Stuttgart: Franz Steiner Verlag, 2004).

Hölkeskamp, *Reconstructing* (2010) = K.-J. Hölkeskamp, *Reconstructing the Roman Republic: An Ancient Political Culture and Modern Research* (Princeton: Princeton University Press, 2010).

Hölkeskamp, 'Konkurrenz' (2014) = K.-J. Hölkeskamp, 'Konkurrenz als sozialer Handlungsmodus—Positionen und Perspektiven der historischen Forschung,' in Jessen, *Konkurrenz* (2014) 33–57.

Hölkeskamp, *Libera* (2017) = K.-J. Hölkeskamp, *Libera Res Publica. Die politische Kultur des antiken Rom—Positionen und Perspektiven* (Stuttgart: Franz Steiner Verlag, 2017).

Hölkeskamp, 'Verlierer' (2019) = K.-J. Hölkeskamp, 'Verlierer in der 'Konkurrenz unter Anwesenden': Agonalität in der politischen Kultur der römischen Republik,' in Hölkeskamp and Beck, *Verlierer* (2019) 11–29.

Hölkeskamp, *Roman* (2020) = K.-J. Hölkeskamp, *Roman Republican Reflections. Studies in Politics, Power, and Pageantry* (Stuttgart: Franz Steiner Verlag, 2020).

Hölkeskamp and Beck, *Verlierer* (2019) = K.-J. Hölkeskamp and H. Beck, eds., *Verlierer und Aussteiger in der 'Konkurrenz unter Anwesenden': Agonalität in der politischen Kultur des antiken Rom* (Stuttgart: Franz Steiner Verlag, 2019).

Howley, *Gellius* (2018) = J. Howley, *Aulus Gellius and Roman Reading Culture: Text, Presence, and Imperial Knowledge in the* Noctes Atticae (Cambridge: Cambridge University Press, 2018).

Hurlet, 'Concurrence' (2012) = F. Hurlet, 'Concurrence gentilice et arbitrage impérial. Les pratiques politiques de l'aristocratie augustéenne,' *Politica Antica* 2 (2012) 33–54.

Imbusch, 'Konkurrenz' (2015) = P. Imbusch, 'Konkurrenz—Ordnungsprinzip zwischen Integration und Disintegration,' in Kirchhoff, *Konkurrenz* (2015) 215–239.

Jessen, 'Konkurrenz' (2014) = R. Jessen, 'Konkurrenz in der Geschichte—Einleitung,' in Jessen, *Konkurrenz* (2014) 7–32.

Jessen, *Konkurrenz* (2014) = R. Jessen, ed., *Konkurrenz in der Geschichte. Praktiken—Werte—Institutionalisierungen* (Frankfurt: Campus Verlag, 2014).

Jones, 'Culture' (2005) = C. Jones, 'Culture in the careers of eastern senators,' in Eck and Heil, *Senatores* (2005) 263–270.

Kirchhoff, *Konkurrenz* (2015) = T. Kirchoff, ed., *Konkurrenz: historische, strukturelle und normative Perspektiven* (Bielefeld: Transcript Verlag, 2015).

Klingenberg, 'Zwischen' (2019) = A. Klingenberg, 'Zwischen republikanischer Tradition und kaiserzeitlichen Realität: der soziale Abstieg von Senatoren und die senatorischen Rollenbilder im frühen Prinzipat,' in Hölkeskamp and Beck, *Verlierer* (2019) 207–224.

König, 'Competitiveness' (2011) = J. König, 'Competitiveness and anti-competitiveness in Philostratus' *Lives of the Sophists*,' in Fisher and Van Wees, *Competition* (2011) 279–300.

Künzer, *Kulturen* (2016) = I. Künzer, *Kulturen der Konkurrenz. Untersuchungen zu einem senatorischen Interaktionsmodus an der Wende vom ersten zum zweiten Jahrhundert n. Chr.* (Bonn: Dr. Rudolf Habelt GmbH, 2016).

Lahire, 'Limits' (2015) = B. Lahire, 'The limits of the field: elements for a theory of the social differentiation of activities,' in Hilgers and Mangez, *Bourdieu's* (2015) 62–101.

Lendon, *Empire* (1997) = J. E. Lendon, *Empire of Honour: The Art of Government in the Roman World* (Oxford: Oxford University Press, 1997).

Lundgreen, 'Lucullus' (2019) = C. Lundgreen, 'Lucullus und die politische Kultur der römischen Republik: Konkurrenz und Distinktion zwischen Feldherren, Feinschmeckern und Fischteichbesitzern,' in Hölkeskamp and Beck, *Verlierer* (2019) 81–126.

Mantovani, *Juristes* (2018) = D. Mantovani, *Les juristes écrivains de la Rome antique: les oeuvres des juristes comme littérature* (Paris: Belles Lettres, 2018).

Mattern, 'Physicians' (1999) = S. Mattern, 'Physicians and the Roman imperial aristocracy: the patronage of therapeutics,' *Bulletin of the History of Medicine* 73 (1999) 1–18.

Mattern, *Galen* (2008) = S. Mattern, *Galen and the Rhetoric of Healing* (Baltimore: Johns Hopkins University Press, 2008).

Millar, *Crowd* (1998) = F. Millar, *The Crowd in Rome in the Late Republic* (Ann Arbor: University of Michigan Press, 1998).

Morstein-Marx, *Oratory* (2004) = R. Morstein-Marx, *Mass Oratory and Political Power in the Late Roman Republic* (Cambridge: Cambridge University Press, 2004).

Mouritsen, *Plebs* (2001) = H. Mouritsen, *Plebs and Politics in the Late Roman Republic* (Cambridge: Cambridge University Press, 2001).

Nebelin, 'Aristokratische Konkurrenz' (2014) = M. Nebelin, 'Aristokratische Konkurrenz in der römischen Republik. Möglichkeiten—Soziale Schließung—Transformation,' in Jessen, *Konkurrenz* (2014) 141–174.

Nullmeier, 'Wettbewerbskulturen' (2002) = F. Nullmeier, 'Wettbewerbskulturen,' in M. Müller et al., eds., *Der Sinn der Politik: kulturwissenschaftliche Politikanalysen* (Konstanz: UVK, 2002) 157–175.

Peachin, 'Jurists' (2001) = M. Peachin, 'Jurists and the law in the early Roman Empire,' in L. De Blois, ed., *Administration, Prosopography and Appointment Policies in the Roman Empire* (Amsterdam: J. C. Gieben, 2001) 109–120.

Pina Polo, 'Veteres' (2012) = F. Pina Polo, '*Veteres candidati:* losers in the elections in republican Rome,' in F. Marco Simón et al., eds., *Vae victis! perdadores in el mundo antiguo* (Barcelona: Collecció Instrumenta, 2012) 63–82.

Platts, 'Keeping up' (2011) = H. Platts, 'Keeping up with the Joneses: competitive display within the Roman villa landscape, 100 BC–AD 200,' in Fisher and Van Wees, *Competition* (2011) 239–277.

Roller, 'Speaking' (2011) = M. Roller, 'To whom am I speaking? The changing venues of competitive eloquence in the early empire,' in Blösel and Hölkeskamp, *Militia* (2011) 197–221.

Roller, 'Amicable' (2018) = M. Roller, 'Amicable and hostile exchange in the culture of recitation,' in A. König and C. Whitton, eds., *Roman Literature under Nerva, Trajan, and Hadrian: Literary Interactions, AD 96–138* (Cambridge: Cambridge University Press, 2018) 183–207.

Roller, 'Centumviral' (2019) = M. Roller, 'The rise of the centumviral court in the Augustan age: an alternative arena of aristocratic competition,' in K. Morrell et al., eds., *The Alternative Augustan Age* (Oxford: Oxford University Press, 2019) 266–281.

Roller, 'Losing' (2019) = M. Roller, 'Losing to Cicero: Asinius Pollio and the emergence of new arenas of competitive eloquence under Augustus,' in Hölkeskamp and Beck, *Verlierer* (2019) 189–205.

Rosen, 'Paradoxes' (2019) = R. Rosen, 'Paradoxes and anxieties of competition in Hippocratic medicine,' in Damon and Pieper, *Eris* (2019) 152–173.

Rosillo López, 'Common' (2010) = C. Rosillo López, 'The common (*mediocris*) orator of the late Republic: the Scribonii Curiones,' in C. Steel and H. Van der Blom, eds., *Community and Communication: Oratory and Politics in Republican Rome* (Oxford: Oxford University Press, 2010) 287–298.

Roth and Wittich, *Weber* (1978) = G. Roth and C. Wittich, eds., *Max Weber, Economy and Society: An Outline of Interpretive Sociology* (Berkeley: University of California Press, 1978).

Simmel, *Aufsätze* (1989 (1903)) = G. Simmel, *Aufsätze und Abhandlungen 1901–1908* (= *Gesamtausgabe*, vol. 7), ed. O. Rammstedt (Frankfurt: Suhrkamp, 1989).

Simmel, *Soziologie* (1992 (1908)) = G. Simmel, *Soziologie: Untersuchungen über die Formen der Vergesellschaftung* (= *Gesamtausgabe*, vol. 11), ed. O. Rammstedt (Frankfurt: Suhrkamp, 1992).

Starbatty et al., *Kultur* (2012) = J. Starbatty et al., eds. *Kultur des Wettbewerbs: Wettbewerb der Kulturen* (Stuttgart: Franz Steiner Verlag, 2012).

Stein-Hölkeskamp, 'Aussteigen' (2019) = E. Stein-Hölkeskamp, 'Aussteigen, Absteigen, Umsteigen? Die Entwicklung konkurrierender Felder der Distinktion von der späten Republik zum frühen Prinzipat,' in Hölkeskamp and Beck, *Verlierer* (2019) 168–188.

Stein-Hölkeskamp, *Unterschiede* (2019) = E. Stein-Hölkeskamp, *Die feinen Unterschiede: Kultur, Kunst und Konsum im antiken Rom* (Berlin: de Gruyter, 2019).

Tauschek, *Kulturen* (2013) = M. Tauschek, ed., *Kulturen des Wettbewerbs—Formationen kompetitiver Logiken* (Münster: Waxmann, 2013).

Ulf, 'Competition' (2011) = C. Ulf, 'Competition in Greece,' in Fisher and Van Wees, *Competition* (2011) 85–111.

Van der Blom, *Oratory* (2016) = H. Van der Blom, *Oratory and Political Career in the Late Roman Republic* (Oxford: Oxford University Press, 2016).

Walter, 'Karrierespezialisten' (2011) = U. Walter, 'Von integralen Aristokraten zum Karrierespezialisten? Versuch einer Bilanz,' in Blösel and Hölkeskamp, *Militia* (2011) 223–237.

Weber, *Wirtschaft* (1956) = M. Weber, *Wirtschaft und Gesellschaft: Grundriss der verstehenden Soziologie* (Tübingen: Mohr, 1956).

Werron, 'Direkte' (2010) = T. Werron, 'Direkte Konflikte, indirekte Konkurrenzen: Unterscheidung und Vergleich zweier Formen des Kampfes,' *Zeitschrift für Soziologie* 39 (2010) 302–318.

Werron, 'Konstruktion' (2011) = T. Werron, 'Zur sozialen Konstruktion moderner Konkurrenzen. Das Publkum in der "Soziologie der Konkurrenz",' in H. Tyrell et al., eds., *Georg Simmels große 'Soziologie': eine kritische Sichtung nach hundert Jahren* (Bielefeld: Transcript Verlag, 2011) 227–258.

Whitmarsh, *Second Sophistic* (2005) = T. Whitmarsh, *The Second Sophistic* (= *Greece & Rome* new surveys in the Classics, v. 35) (Cambridge: Cambridge University Press, 2005).

Wiseman, 'Competition' (1985) = T. P. Wiseman, 'Competition and co-operation,' in T. P. Wiseman, ed., *Roman Political Life, 90 B.C.–A.D. 69* (Exeter: University of Exeter Press, 1985) 3–19.

Wolff and Bendix, *Simmel* (1955) = K. Wolff and R. Bendix, trs. *Georg Simmel: Conflict and The Web of Group-Affiliations* (Glencoe, IL: The Free Press, 1955).

Zadorojnyi, 'Competition' (2019) = A. Zadorojnyi, 'Competition and competitiveness in Pollux's *Onomasticon*,' in Damon and Pieper, *Eris* (2019) 324–342.

Law as Competitive Performance

Performative Aspects of the Legal Process in Roman Imperial Courts

Anna Dolganov

Let me begin with a famous court case from republican Rome, the so-called *causa Curiana* of 92 BCE. The case concerned the inheritance of a wealthy man named Marcus Coponius, who had written a will in which he appointed an as yet unborn son as his heir, naming his friend Manius Curius as a pupillary substitute. When Coponius died childless, his friend Curius entered upon the inheritance. The nearest male relative who was due to inherit on intestacy proceeded to contest the will as invalid. The dispute came before the court of the *centumviri*—a panel of judges appointed from the wealthiest property classes at Rome. The case of Curius was argued by the senator Lucius Licinius Crassus, a leading orator and political figure. The case of Coponius' family was argued by the senator Quintus Mucius Scaevola, a legal expert and similarly illustrious Roman politician. Both arguments were recorded and circulated at Rome, where several decades later they were still available to Cicero, who tells us the whole story.[1]

The enduring celebrity of the *causa Curiana* in Roman aristocratic circles highlights the centrality of legal practice in Roman political culture and its importance as a prestige activity of the elite. In the Roman tradition, the forum and its courts were synonymous with public life, a place where Roman statesmen practiced forensic oratory and served as judicial magistrates, advisors, and judges, while young men apprenticed themselves to senior statesmen, eventually making their own début pleading court cases.[2] Forensic activity was integral to the Roman

The author would like to thank the Austrian Science Fund (FWF) for financing the project on Roman court proceedings (P-31021) within the framework of which this article was researched and written. Warm thanks are due to Prof. Claudio Gallazzi and Prof. Rosario Pintaudi for organizing the author's visits to the papyrus collections of the Università degli Studi di Milano and the Biblioteca Laurenziana, to the staff of the Biblioteca Laurenziana for sending high-resolution digital images, and to the staff of the Bodleian Library for facilitating the author's examination of the relevant papyri. Finally, many thanks to Michael Peachin and Claire Bubb for exemplary curation of this project, from the initial conference to the final volume.

[1] See Liebs, *Vor den Richtern Roms* (2007) 45–52 and 198–205 for sources and bibliography.

[2] On the forensic culture of the Roman Republic, see Frier, *The Rise of the Roman Jurists* (1985) 42–196 and Powell and Patterson, *Cicero the Advocate* (2004) 1–52.

Anna Dolganov, *Law as Competitive Performance: Performative Aspects of the Legal Process in Roman Imperial Courts* In: *Medicine and the Law under the Roman Empire*. Edited by: Claire Bubb and Michael Peachin, Oxford University Press.
 DOI: 10.1093/oso/9780192898616.003.0003

system of patronage, in which influential men were traditionally expected to provide legal representation and advice to their clients and friends.[3] The role of the courts as a domain of elite competition developed in step with the professionalization of oratory and jurisprudence, a process that began in the late Republic and gained momentum under the Principate within the expanding sphere of Roman civil administration.[4] In the time of Pliny the Younger, the centumviral court of the *causa Curiana* had become an even more prominent forum for elite Romans to engage in competitive rhetorical display and distinguish themselves in their pursuit of prestigious public careers.[5]

So much is well known and has been the subject of numerous studies, including the work of several contributors to this volume. Less well charted is the development of forensic culture in the Roman provinces, where Roman forms of legal practice are attested at the assizes of governors.[6] These were copiously attended public events held in provincial cities every year, where the governor's judicial activity served to broadcast the rational and beneficial nature of Roman rule, as well as the Roman state's monopoly of legitimate violence, conveyed through grisly penal spectacles.[7] The function of assizes as a theater of imperial power amplified the performative dimension of legal practice. For the orators arguing cases before the governor and his circle, an impressive performance could contribute to the progress of careers and lead to administrative appointments or

[3] See David, *Le patronat judiciaire* (1992) with the remarks of Frier, 'Review of David' (1994) and Alexander, 'Oratory, rhetoric and politics' (2007) 101–105.

[4] See Burnand, 'The advocate as a professional' (2004); Frier, *The Rise of Roman Jurists* (1985) 269–288; and Dolganov, '*Nutricula causidicorum*' (2020) 379–386. On the rising importance of forensic activity as a means of political advancement in the late Republic, see Wiseman, *New Men in the Roman Senate* (1971) 178–181 and Harris, *War and Imperialism* (1979) 257; see Cic. *Comment. pet.* 2: *nominis novitatem dicendi gloria maxime sublevabis* ("you will mitigate the newness of your name most of all by the glory of your public speaking"). This development coincided with the ebbing of Roman military conquest in the later second century BCE. Forensic oratory from the late Republic onwards fulfils a number of sociological criteria for a professionalized field (e.g. curriculum of specialized training, adherence to an abstraction-based knowledge system, institutional organization, and eventually credentialization and Verbeamtung) and merits discussion from this perspective. Further signs of professionalization include the production of technical literature and the emergence of a class of experts—including the so-called sophists of the imperial Greek East, see Schmitz, 'Professionals of *paideia*?' (2017). For an overview of sociological definitions of professionalization, see Abbott, *System of Professions* (1988) 1–32 and more recently Webley, 'The sociology of legal professions' (2020) 221–223.

[5] On the flourishing field of forensic oratory in high imperial Rome, see Bablitz, *Actors and Audience* (2007) 141–158; Crook, *Legal Advocacy* (1995) 172–197; Dominik, 'Tacitus and Pliny' (2007); and Balbo, 'Roman oratory and power' (2017). On the centumviral court, see Bablitz, *Actors and Audience* (2007) 61–70. Its public prestige is illustrated by Pliny's description of massive audiences attending the trial of Attia Viriola in *Ep.* 6.33.

[6] On the employment of Roman forms of legal practice in provincial courts, see Crook, *Legal Advocacy* (1995) 58–69 and Dolganov, '*Nutricula causidicorum*' (2020). This is apparent in the late empire; see Humfress, *Orthodoxy and the Courts* (2007) 29–134.

[7] On the Roman assize system, see Burton, 'Proconsuls, assizes' (1975) and Haensch, 'Zur Konventsordnung' (1997). On Roman penal spectacles, see Coleman, 'Fatal charades' (1990) and Shaw, 'Judicial nightmares' (2003). On the function of judicial violence in premodern states, see Foucault, *Surveiller et punir* (1975) 9–83.

promotion to the equestrian civil service.[8] In the course of the Principate, rhetorical training and Roman-style forensic activity were widely adopted by provincial elites and became a cornerstone of urban life and civil careers throughout the empire.[9]

In this chapter, I will explore the ramifications of the Roman model of legal practice as a form of elite competition and social performance for the legal process itself. How did the performative aspects of Roman judicial administration impact the legal process in Roman courts? How did the status of legal practitioners, some of whom belonged to the provincial officeholding class or the immediate entourage of the governor, affect the dynamics and outcomes of trials? For the city of Rome and most regions of the empire, the available evidence offers little direct insight into these questions. Consequently, I will pose them to a rich corpus of papyri from Roman Egypt, where numerous transcripts of court hearings have survived. Since Roman governors received many more requests for hearings than could be conducted in person, it will be important to consider whether the selection of cases for adjudication bore any relation to the spectacularization of justice by Roman tribunals.[10]

My analysis will begin with Cicero's descriptions of judicial hearings before Roman governors in Sicily and Asia in the first century BCE. I will continue with six court cases from Roman Egypt spanning the first three centuries of the Principate and conclude with judicial proceedings before the emperor Caracalla in the early third century. Emended and updated texts and translations of the six papyri are provided in the Appendix. Accordingly, I do not include the Greek of these documents in the body of the paper. My discussion will focus on forensic orators, whose activity is most directly documented in records of Roman court proceedings.[11]

[8] See my analysis of careers in the African epigraphic evidence in Dolganov, '*Nutricula causidicorum*' (2020), with careers of *advocati fisci* listed at 407–411. On orators and legal experts in eastern provincial inscriptions see, respectively, Puech, *Orateurs et sophistes* (2002) and Jones, 'Juristes romains' (2007).

[9] See Lendon, *That Tyrant, Persuasion* (2022) on the high empire and Heath, *Menander* (2004) and Humfress, *Orthodoxy and the Courts* (2007) on the late empire.

[10] See the well-known papyrus documenting the submission of at least 1,804 petitions to the prefect of Egypt at a single assize in the early third century, see *P.Yale* I 61 (Arsinoite, *ca.* 208–210 CE)—although not all petitioners requested hearings, see Kelly, *Petitions and Litigation* (2011) 86–91.

[11] Whereas the real-time activity of orators is recorded in the proceedings, the work of legal experts and judicial advisors is typically subsumed under general statements that the governor "has consulted" them (*σκεψάμενος*); see e.g. *P.Ryl.* II 75 col. ii (unknown location, 134 CE) ll. 27–29. These categories of legal practitioners were by no means entirely distinct, since practitioners of forensic oratory could serve as judicial advisors and judges, while legal experts could also plead as advocates, see e.g. Plin. *Ep.* 1.20.12: *frequenter egi, frequenter iudicavi, frequenter in consilio fui* ("I often pleaded cases, I often adjudicated cases, I often served as an advisor to magistrates") and the high-profile orator and legal expert from Gerasa described by Philo of Byblos *FgrHist* 790 F 34.

Performing Roman Justice in Sicily in the Late Republic

In his prosecution of Gaius Verres for corruption (*repetundae*) as governor of Sicily in the 70s BCE, Cicero describes a number of trials taking place at Roman assizes.[12] Some are criminal cases that fell under the governor's jurisdiction, while others are civil lawsuits that the governor could instruct and delegate to judges or choose to adjudicate himself.[13] In line with the charge of *repetundae*, nearly all cases recounted by Cicero involve wealthy Sicilian defendants who are subjected to extortion and abuse. While Cicero is by no means an unbiased source on these events, the courtroom scenarios he describes were aimed at an experienced Roman jury and included circumstantial information confirmed by witnesses.[14] They may therefore be regarded as plausible, if tendentious, portrayals of judicial proceedings at the court of a Roman governor in the late Republic.

Cicero gives a particularly detailed account of the criminal trial of Sopater, a Sicilian from Halyciae, who had been accused of an unspecified capital crime and acquitted by the previous governor Gaius Licinius Sacerdos.[15] Sopater's opponents proceeded to file the same charges with the new governor Verres, who accepted the case for a second trial.[16] All litigants and witnesses were summoned to the provincial capital of Syracuse, where the case was heard by Verres according to Roman procedure, with an advisory council (*consilium*) of Roman citizens from the region (*in consilio habebat homines honestos e conventu Syracusano* ("on his advisory panel he had upstanding men from the district of Syracuse"), II 2.70). The same men had advised Sacerdos when Sopater was acquitted. Sopater's defence was led by a Roman knight named Q. Minucius, a tax-farmer and businessman (*negotiator*) at Syracuse. Cicero refers to Minucius as a *patronus*

[12] The main trial-narratives are: Philodamus of Lampsacus: II 1.63–86; Dio of Halaesa: II 1.27–28, II 2.19–24; Sosippus and Philocrates of Agyrium: II 2.25–27; Heraclius of Syracuse: II 2.35–52; Epicrates of Bidis: II 2.53–65; Heraclius of Centuripa: II 2.66–67; Sopater of Halyciae: II 2.68–81; Sthenius of Thermae: II 2.82–118; II 3.18 and 3.41. For commentary, see Gildenhard, *Cicero, Against Verres* (2011) and Schwameis, *Cicero, De praetura Siciliensi* (2019).

[13] On the criminal jurisdiction of governors, see Ermann, '*Ius Gladii*' (2001) and the list of public crimes in *SB* XII 10929 (133–137 CE) with Jördens, 'Eine kaiserliche Konstitution' (2011) and Laffi, *In greco per i Greci* (2013) 71–74. In republican Sicily, procedures for remitting or delegating cases and appointing judges were outined in the so-called *lex Rupilia* embedded in the governor's provincial edict; see Cic. *Verr.* II 2.32. It is clear, however, that governors had discretionary power to adjudicate any case. According to Cicero, Verres routinely delegated cases in which he was not personally interested (*ex lege Rupilia sortitio nulla, nisi cum nihil intererat istius* ("there was no selection of judges according to the *lex Rupilia*, unless the case was of no interest to that man"), II 2.34) but selected cases that offered opportunities for financial gain for adjudication by himself or his agents.

[14] Cicero's elisions and manipulations are numerous; for example, the crime of Sopater (II 2.68–82) is never specified nor the prosecutor identified. For readings against the grain of Cicero's rhetoric in the Verrines, see Steel, 'Being economical with the truth' (2004) and Stone, 'Gaius Verres troubleshooter' (2018). On the prosecution of Verres as part of a political struggle involving the Pompeians and their Sicilian *clientela*, see Brunt, 'Patronage and politics' (1980) and Morrell, *Pompey, Cato* (2017) 24–54.

[15] See Cic. *Verr.* II 2.68–81 with Schwameis, *Cicero, De praetura Siciliensi* (2019) 315–341.

[16] Cicero elides on what grounds the same case was brought to court; possibly, the accusers brought new evidence or claimed that the previous verdict had been unduly influenced by a friendly *consilium*.

(II 2.74), the traditional Roman term for a member of the elite who furnished legal representation to his friends and dependents. Whether *patronus* signifies a true patronage relationship or more narrowly refers to Minucius' role as a forensic advocate remains unclear.[17] According to Cicero, Verres had received large bribes from the prosecution and decided to convict the defendant (II 2.70). On the day of the trial, he dismissed one of the senior advisors, a Roman knight named M. Petilius, appointing him as a judge in a private legal dispute (II 2.71). This was allegedly a ploy to precipitate the exodus of other members of the *consilium* who had previously acquitted Sopater. These men expressed their obligation to serve as Petilius' advisors and as advocates of both parties in the trial.[18] As the council dispersed, Minucius was surprised to learn that he was still expected to plead the case (II 2.72):

> *Respondet, "Ad quos?"*
>
> *"Ad me", inquit, "si tibi idoneus videor qui de homine Siculo ac Graeculo iudicem."*
>
> *"Idoneus es", inquit, "sed pervellem adessent ii qui adfuerant antea causamque cognorant."*
>
> *"Die", inquit; "illi adesse non possunt."*
>
> *"Nam hercule", inquit Minucius, "me quoque Petilius ut sibi in consilio adessem rogavit", et simul a subselliis abire coepit.*
>
> "Before whom?" said Minucius.
>
> "Before me!" answered Verres, "if I seem to you competent to adjudicate a case involving a mere Sicilian Greek."
>
> "You are competent," said Minucius, "but I would very much like those councillors to be present who were here before and have heard the case on a previous occasion."
>
> "On this day they cannot attend," said Verres.
>
> "In truth, Petilius asked me to serve on his *consilium* as well!" said Minucius and immediately began to depart from the benches.

With Minucius gone, the rest of Sopater's Roman friends and *advocati* departed as well, leaving only the Sicilians. Verres proceeded to question Sopater without legal

[17] On the semantics of *patronus*, see Neuhauser, *Patronus und Orator* (1958). On the difficulty of determining whether *patronus* in a judicial setting signifies patronage relations, see Prag, 'Provincials, patrons' (2013). And note Lehne-Gstreinthaler, Iurisperiti et oratores (2019) 373–380.

[18] Cicero seems to insinuate that Petilius saw through Verres' plan but could not refuse serving as *iudex* once his friends were free to join him; this implies that a Roman judge could expect to be assisted by a Roman *consilium* of his choice and suggests hierarchical dynamics and ties of friendship and patronage binding the individuals in question.

defence and condemned him with a *consilium* composed of members of his own entourage.

In this and other trials in the *Verrines*, it is a consistent pattern that legal practitioners (advocates and judicial advisors) are Roman citizens—either members of the governor's personal staff or Romans from the local *conventus civium Romanorum*. The latter are mainly *negotiatores* or *publicani* of Italian origin, with a few references to wealthy provincials granted Roman citizenship.[19] The involvement of Roman legal practitioners is independent of the status of the litigants, who are predominantly Greek provincials. For example: in the inheritance case of Dio of Halaesa, who is assisted by a Roman *patronus*, a Roman *negotiator* leads the prosecution (II 2.22).[20] When criminal charges are brought against Sthenius of Thermae, the accuser is a Roman *negotiator* (II 2.94). The criminal trial of Philodamus of Lampsacus in Asia features Roman *publicani* and *negotiatores* on the governor's *consilium* and a Roman *negotiator* prosecuting the case (II 1.73–74). Similarly, Sopater's trial involves Roman *negotiatores* on Verres' *consilium* and the *negotiator* Minucius leading the defence. The participation of Roman citizens is characterized by Cicero as an indispensable element of the legal process: as soon as Petilius is appointed *iudex*, there is no question that other Romans must serve on his *consilium* and as advocates in the trial; as soon as Verres' council of Roman *honesti homines* departs, it is inconceivable that a man of Minucius' rank proceed to plead the case.[21] Despite the continued presence of Sopater's Sicilian friends and advisors, the absence of Roman *advocati* is equated by Cicero with the lack of any legal defence (*reus autem sine patrono atque advocatis* ("moreover, a defendant without a defense advocate or other legal assistants"), II 2.74); the agency of the Sicilians is thereby erased completely.

Cicero's trial narratives thus consistently depict legal practice at the court of the governor as an exclusive activity, dominated by Roman citizens from the provincial civic and business elite. While Cicero's highly rhetorical account does not necessarily indicate formal restrictions on provincial access to Roman tribunals, it does reflect a strong Roman notion of *patrocinium* in the legal sphere, whereby the status of advocates was expected to be commensurate with that of the presiding

[19] Such as Pompeius Chlorus, the *patronus* of Dio of Halaesa, see II 2.23. See further Brunt, 'Patronage and politics' (1980) 274–275.

[20] The status of the *advocati* assisting Heraclius of Syracuse (II 2.38) is not specified. That *sine advocatis* denotes the absence of Roman advocates at Sopater's trial (II 2.74), in spite of Sicilians being present, may indicate that Heraclius' *advocati* were Roman as well. Cicero notes Heraclius' lack of a *patronus* (*eum praeter Marcellos patronum, quem suo iure adire aut appellare posset, habere neminem* ("he had no patron, aside from the Marcelli, whom he was within his rights to approach or call upon for assistance"), II 2.36) a term clearly reserved for Romans.

[21] This was a matter of *ius* and *dignitas*: *Minucius, qui Syracusis sic negotiaretur ut sui iuris dignitatisque meminisset... causam sese dimisso atque ablegato consilio defensurum negavit* ("Minucius, who did business at Syracuse while remaining mindful of his rank and rights... said that he would not defend the case since the advisory council had been dismissed and disbanded"), II 2.73.

official.[22] The departure of members of Verres' *consilium* to participate in Petilius' trial reinforces the impression of a rotating pool of elite Roman legal actors, who took turns exercising different courtroom roles in trials before the governor and other Roman judges.

Alongside a regular cast of Roman actors in the governor's courtroom, Cicero refers to crowds of provincial spectators witnessing and reacting to the proceedings. As described by Cicero, provincial audiences scrutinize Verres' every move, from the composition of his *consilium*, to the procedures he employs to appoint judges, to the emotions he displays during the hearing.[23] In the case of Heraclius of Syracuse, Verres and his advisors are concerned that irregular selection of judges and condemnation of an absent litigant will incite public opprobrium.[24] The conviction of Sopater takes place in the forum of Syracuse amid a massive confluence of spectators (*conventus maximus*, II 2.74) who wait with baited breath for the outcome of the trial (*summum silentium, summa exspectatio* ("there was the utmost silence and the utmost anticipation"), ibid.). Rattled by the departure of Minucius, Verres appears "feverish with doubt" (*aestuabat dubitatione*) and paces back and forth, so that "all who were present could perceive" his conflicting emotions (*ut omnes qui aderant intellegere possent*, ibid.).[25] His hasty interrogation and verdict are delivered "before the eyes of the entire province" (*in ore atque in oculis provinciae*, II 2.81).[26] While Cicero's rhetorical aims are clear, his emphasis on audiences as active and discerning interpreters of the performative semantics of Roman trials corresponds to the evidence of other sources.[27]

The judicial process itself is described by Cicero in theatrical terms. With its initial cast of characters, Sopater's trial is poised to be the second acquittal of a

[22] Schwameis, *Cicero, De praetura Siciliensi* (2019) 317 ("Die Abwesenheit eines römischen Anwalts und römischer *advocati*, derentwegen V. besorgt gewesen sei (§ 73 f.), war rechtlich gesehen irrelevant") seems to miss this point. The prevalence of Roman prosecutors in criminal trials in the Verrines may have a formal explanation: it is possible that a Roman *accusator* was necessary for non-citizens to pursue public crimes through the court of the governor, as was the case in the *quaestiones* at Rome, on which see Lintott, 'Legal procedure' (2004).

[23] On the *consilium*, see e.g. II 2.74; on the appointment of judges, see e.g. II 2.37–42, 2.77 and 2.127; on the emotions, see e.g. II 2.55 and 2.73.

[24] *multo etiam rem turpiorem fore et iniquiorem visum iri* ("the case was going to be much more disgraceful, and would appear much more unfair"), II 2.42.

[25] *itaque aestuabat dubitatione, versabat se utramque in partem non solum mente, verum etiam corpore, ut omnes qui aderant intellegere possent in animo eius metum cum cupiditate pugnare* ("and so he stewed in doubt, turning this way and that, not only in his mind, but even physically, so that all who were present could perceive that fear and greed were battling with each other in his thoughts"), II 2.74.

[26] Cicero often personifies "the province" as a collective plaintiff that gathers evidence and delivers testimony against its abuser (see e.g. II 2.113, 117, and 139 and II 3.64). Evoking the setting of Verres' alleged judicial crimes, Cicero's collection of evidence against Verres likewise takes place in the forum of Syracuse amid a large public gathering (*in foro summa hominum frequentia*, 2.2.189) accompanied by shouts from the crowd (*clamare omnes ex conventu*, 2.2.188).

[27] On the active role of audiences, see Bablitz, *Actors and Audience* (2007) 120–140 and Hall, 'Roman judges' (2017). Graphic descriptions of trials in a late Roman schooltext illustrate how, from a young age, inhabitants of the Roman empire were trained to parse the semantics of Roman adjudication, see Dionisotti, 'From Ausonius' schooldays' (1982).

respectable provincial, unjustly persecuted by his enemies and defended by an eminent Roman *patronus*. This, at any rate, is the judicial narrative that the advocate Minucius expects to be upheld in court (II 2.70). When the original *consilium* disperses, however, the dominant narrative shifts to that of the prosecution: a criminal investigation of a "mere Sicilian Greek" previously acquitted under questionable circumstances (II 2.72). The departure of Minucius transforms the trial into yet another kind of spectacle: a certain conviction conducted without legal defence (II 2.74). A similar scenario is recounted by Cicero at Lampsacus, where the civic magistrate Philodamus and his son are tried and executed for killing a Roman *lictor* from a neighboring province. The trial is presided over by two governors and prosecuted by a Roman businessman to whom the city itself is indebted; with no Roman or Greek daring to take on the defence, conviction inevitably follows (II 1.72–74). As described by Cicero, Philodamus' trial for the murder of a Roman official appears to have been intentionally conducted in a peremptory fashion, as a progression toward an inescapable verdict. Familiar from the high empire, such trials employed judicial violence to terrorize viewers and allign their perspective with that of the Roman tribunal.[28] But this Kafkaesque scenario was apparently not the sort of spectacle Verres had envisioned. According to Cicero, it was crucial for the legitimacy of his reversal of Sopater's acquittal for it to appear to result from investigation and debate; hence, Verres perceived Minucius' withdrawal from the defence as sabotage of his carefully orchestrated judicial scenario (II 2.73–74). The plausibility of Cicero's accounts of these trials, tendentious as they may be, presupposes general awareness of the performative nature of Roman adjudication.

Minucius' refusal to plead in Sopater's defence is suggestive of what was at stake for high-profile legal practitioners at Roman assizes. According to Cicero, Minucius recuses himself from his client's inevitable conviction as detrimental to his own reputation. Precisely why is not explained: possibly, Minucius felt that the trial made a mockery of his role in Sopater's earlier acquittal; if *patronus* is to be taken literally, Minucius may have been concerned about losing social and economic capital through his perceived inability to defend the interests of his clients; if *patronus* is meant in a narrower sense, he may have been specifically concerned with his standing as a forensic orator.[29] Either way, the episode establishes a direct connection between Minucius' status and public reputation and his success in the courtroom. While Cicero does not identify the prosecutor, other trial narratives lead us to expect that the *negotiator* Minucius faced off against someone with a similar social profile.[30] In this respect, Minucius' desire to

[28] On judicial violence effecting non-identification between the viewer and the victim, see Grig, 'Torture and truth' (2002) with references to further literature.

[29] On the ambiguity of *patronus* in a judicial context, see the literature cited in n. 17.

[30] See my discussion of the profile of legal practitioners in the Verrines at nn. 19–22. Cicero's elision of the prosecutor's identity may provide indirect evidence of his elevated status.

avoid defeat may imply a competitive dynamic, whereby one orator's loss was perceived to be his opponent's gain. It is generally clear from Cicero that participation in the governor's judicial activity was an important context for the brokering of political and economic influence. Accordingly, Cicero notes that Minucius sought to withdraw from Sopater's trial without antagonizing Verres and jeopardizing his own business interests.[31] Elsewhere, he mentions Minucius being passed over by Verres in the allotment of tax-farming contracts (II 3.148–151), which suggests that their courtroom encounter had negative consequences for Minucius' financial affairs. By contrast, Cicero repeatedly states that Verres promoted those who acted as prosecutors at his behest.[32]

While taking Cicero's rhetorical agenda into account, his trial narratives suggest that the trials conducted by republican governors were widely understood to be highly performative public events, mediated by elite legal practitioners drawn from the governor's staff and the provincial *conventus* of Roman citizens. From Cicero's descriptions, it appears that such trials were strongly influenced by the interpersonal dynamics between the governor and the legal actors in question. For the latter, the importance of performing in court extended beyond the concrete legal case to their own public image and political and economic ambitions. The orchestrated spectacle of Sopater's criminal trial and Minucius' abandonment of his client to avoid disgrace in the courtroom—events to which Minucius himself testified in the proceedings against Verres[33]—offer a powerful illustration of the sociopolitical importance attached to forensic activity among Roman colonial elites in the empire of the late Republic, in line with cultural models imported from Rome.

Performing Roman Justice in Egypt under the Principate

During the first two centuries of the Principate, literary and documentary sources attest to a process that may be described as the globalization of Roman forensic culture among the civic elites of the empire.[34] Compared to the age of Cicero, this process was no longer limited to colonial elites but encompassed provincial elites of local origin, whose wealth and participation in the empire's political structures often earned them and their families Roman citizenship. As legal practice grew in importance for imperial careers, Roman assizes functioned as a prestigious public stage for ambitious men to pursue fame and promotion by

[31] *Minucius, qui Syracusis sic negotiaretur ut sui iuris dignitatisque meminisset, et qui sciret se ita in provincia rem augere oportere ut ne quid de libertate deperderet* ("Minucius, who did business at Syracuse while remaining mindful of his rank and rights, and who understood that it was best to increase his wealth in the province in such a fashion as not to lose any portion of his freedom"), II 2.73.

[32] See e.g. II 2.94 (Pacilius, *egens* implying prospective rewards), II 2.22 and 90–91 (Naevius Turpio) and II 2.108 and 3 *passim* (Apronius).

[33] As implied by II 2.69 and 80.

[34] See my discussion in Dolganov, '*Nutricula causidicorum*' (2020).

displaying their skill as orators and judicial advisors. Just as the historian Appian of Alexandria achieved an equestrian career by progressing from Alexandrian magistracies to pleading fiscal cases at Rome, the African rhetorician Apuleius made a name for himself as a forensic orator at the court of the *proconsul* of Africa.[35] The epigraphic record offers numerous examples of imperial careers propelled by rhetorical skill and success in the courts.[36]

Courts operating as a venue for elite competition had obviously significant implications for the legal process. While epigraphic, literary, and legal sources offer few glimpses into the courtrooms of the empire, we possess a large papyrological corpus of court transcripts from Roman Egypt that attest to distinctly Roman forms of legal practice, with advocates pleading cases before officials, judicial councillors advising them, and legal experts pronouncing on questions of law.[37] In instances where the full nomenclature of legal practitioners is provided, they are consistently revealed to be Roman citizens and members of the officeholding class of Alexandria.[38] The recurrence of names suggests, furthermore, that there was a circle of elite orators and legal experts who followed the governor on his assize tour of the province.[39]

In what follows, I will analyze a series of court cases from Roman Egypt that show forensic orators in action at the court of the governor (and other Roman tribunals) and assess the impact of their rhetorical performance on the dynamics of the legal process. Existing research on this material has not been attentive to the status of legal practitioners or the performative context of the hearings. It has been assumed, for example, that the court protocols show advocates of modest skill operating at lower levels of society in the Egyptian hinterland.[40] This is hardly an accurate assessment of the hearings that took place before the Roman governor of

[35] For Appian's career, see *PIR*² A 943 with App. *Praef.* 15 and Fronto *Ep. ad Ant. Pium* 9.2. Apuleius' activity as a forensic orator at the court of the proconsul is evidenced by his ability to recommend Pontianus for his apprenticeship in oratory (*tirocinium orationis*), see *Apol.* 94; further on Apuleius' career, see August. *Ep.*138 with Dolganov, '*Nutricula causidicorum*' (2020) 375–377.

[36] One of many instances is a municipal councillor of a small coastal city in the province of Mauretania, who "by virtue of his studies in his early youth" (*beneficio studiorum prima aetate iuventutis*) was appointed to the *advocatio fisci* in Baetica; his forensic victories later earned him an appointment as *defensor populi* at Rome, see *CIL* VIII 9249 (Rusguniae, early 3c. CE) = Dolganov, '*Nutricula causidicorum*' (2020) appendix E 6.

[37] On Roman court proceedings as a documentary genre, see Coles, *Reports of Proceedings* (1966) and Palme, 'Roman litigation' (2014).

[38] This is discussed at length in Dolganov, *Administration of Justice* (forthcoming). For an example, see *SB* XVI 12749 = *P.Daris* 2 = *P.Strasb.* IV 179 (Arsinoe, 176–179 CE), a judicial record from an Arsinoite assize featuring an Alexandrian advocate with Roman citizenship and a series of Alexandrian officials on the prefect's *consilium*. Evidently, all were traveling on the assize tour.

[39] Ties between legal practitioners (both orators and legal experts) and imperial tribunals evolved into a statutory affiliation, documented from the late second century onwards, see Dolganov, '*Nutricula causidicorum*' (2020) 379–388 and Jones, *The Later Roman Empire* (1964) I 470–522.

[40] See Crook, *Legal Advocacy* (1995) 7: "[papyri] constitute day-to-day, bread-and-butter accounts of very ordinary litigation below the level of the metropolitan 'great and grand'" and 158: "Cicero would have regarded the standards of advocacy as low, and Gallus would have regarded those of jurisprudence as equally so." See also Heath, 'Practical advocacy' (2004) 64: "the papyri do not come

Egypt. The judicial records are, as a general rule, heavily abbreviated, with entire speeches often reduced to one-sentence summaries, but their concise formulation by no means implies that the advocates in question possessed moderate rhetorical capabilities.[41] On the contrary, any sign of rhetorical artifice that has survived bureaucratic reduction must be regarded as highly significant evidence for the rhetorical register of the original dialogue.[42] In addition to assessing the dynamics of these hearings and the identity of legal practitioners captured in them, I offer solutions to issues of legal procedure and textual problems that have impeded accurate interpretation of these texts.

1. A Lowly Creditor Pursues an Eminent Debtor: An Unequal Confrontation between Orators before the Prefect of Egypt

The first example is a hearing that took place before the Roman governor of Egypt (*praefectus Aegypti*) in the Flavian period.[43] A man named Isidoros *alias* Phibion was attempting to recall a large loan of grain made many years earlier by his late father to a debtor who was himself deceased. After encountering resistance from the debtor's son, Phibion did not file a petition and serve it on his opponent (ll. 14–18) but took the initiative of seizing him and his wife and hauling them to the governor's assize (ll. 6–11). News of this reached the prefect, who agreed to hear the case. The setting was a public audience at which the prefect listened to the presentation of claims (*postulationes*) that he would either reject, approve and delegate, or choose to adjudicate himself.[44] To be included in the governor's list of *postulationes*, it was customary to submit a petition and receive written

from the main centres of culture, and are concerned with affairs at a relatively humble social level, at which we should expect to find less elaborate and sophisticated advocacy"; 77: "these men are not orators at the pinnacle of the profession."

[41] The abbreviation of Roman judicial records is described by Philo, *In Flacc.* 16.131 and Lucian, *Apol.* 12. See the discussion of Coles, *Reports of Proceedings* (1966) 19–24.

[42] A good test case is provided by the Syrian inscription documenting proceedings before the emperor Caracalla featuring two of the most celebrated orators of the age (*SEG* XVII 759, 216 CE, discussed further below). In the record, their statements appear brief and straightforward, but specific words and phrases give a sense of the rhetoric that characterized the original proceedings. See also the analysis in Babusiaux and Bubb, below, p. 235.

[43] See *P.Flor.* I 61 = *M.Chr.* 80, ll. 44–48 (Arsinoite? 85 CE) and my emended text of the papyrus in Dolganov, 'Rich vs. poor in Roman courts' (2023) no. 1. For discussions of this document, see Mitteis, 'Ägyptischer Schuldprozess' (1906); Wilcken, 'Zu den Florentiner und den Leipziger Papyri' (1907) 444–449; Arangio-Ruiz, 'Commento giuridico' (1937) 208; Schmidt, 'Einfluss der Rhetorik' (1950) 171–173; Purpura, '*Katholikon diatagma*' (1982) 515–516; Katzoff, 'Law as katholikos' (1986) 123; Crook, *Legal Advocacy* (1995) 70–72; Chapman and Schnabel, *The Trial and Crucifixion of Jesus* (2015) 258–262; Dolganov, 'Rich vs. poor in Roman courts' (2023).

[44] On *postulationes*, see the rubric *de postulando* in D. 3.1. The distinction between *postulationes* and other types of hearings is spelled out by Ulpian, who states that a governor did not leave time for the presentation of petitions before his tribunal (*postulationes pro tribunali*) if his schedule was already full with military matters (*rebus militaribus*), capital crimes (*custodiis*), and judicial proceedings (*cognitionibus*); see Ulp. (49 *ad ed.*) D. 38.15.2.1–2.

acceptance, then serve the petition on one's adversary with summons to the assize, then submit a second petition *in situ* to the assize court.[45] Phibion, however, had failed to file a petition (ll. 14-18) and seems to have simply showed up with his debtors. That Phibion's case was heard by the prefect without a written petition constituted a notable exception to the regular procedure.

The hearing begins in an unusually brusque fashion, with the prefect castigating Phibion and threatening him with corporal punishment:

> (ll. 9–11) Septimius Vegetus [pronounced to(?)] Phibion:
>
> "Having produced [your opponent(?)] claiming that he is indebted to you [and having seized him(?)] by your own means [you deserve to be(?)] flogged immediately."
>
> (ll. 11–12) Phibion:
>
> "I concede the case to him, so that I may remain unscathed."
>
> (l. 13) Septimius Vegetus:
>
> "What are you prosecuting him about?"

Then follows the introductory speech of Phibion's advocate Kephalon, who obsequiously addresses the prefect with an apology for Phibion's failure to submit a written petition:

> (ll. 14–23) Kephalon, advocate:
>
> "Needful of your beneficence, this man petitions you while first and foremost asking your forgiveness, since he was misled regarding the procedure of petitioning. For he should have submitted a written petition to you, in accordance with your wishes, so we beg you not to have him flogged. The subject of the lawsuit is as follows: the father of our opponent took a loan of 100 artabae of wheat from the father of my client. This claim is heritable, for I believe that it is compulsory for heirs not only to inherit the legal personhood of testators but also to return any debts owed by them."

To bolster his rather simple point about the heritability of debt claims, Kephalon makes reference to the notion of universal succession in Roman testamentary law.[46] After he presents the details of the case and reads out Phibion's documentary proof of the loan, the proceedings are dominated by Aristonikos, the advocate of the defendant, who speaks to the prefect in a tone of remarkable familiarity (ll. 24–58):

[45] On the procedures of petitioning and summons, see Foti Talamanca, *Ricerche sul processo II* (1984): 1–66; Haensch, 'Die Bearbeitungsweise' (1994); and Kelly, *Petitions* (2011) 94–103. The names of litigants who were granted hearings were entered into a register and posted in public, see *P.Oxy.* XXXVI (Oxyrhynchus, 111 CE) l. 10.

[46] See Buckland and McNair, *Roman Law and Common Law* (1952) 143–195.

(l. 24) Aristonikos, advocate:

"Let him read out under what circumstances he owes these debts."

(ll. 25–34) After Kephalon read the pay order issued by Archias *alias* Polydeukes dated to the 11th year of the Divine Claudius (50–51 CE), Aristonikos (said):

"This loan-shark, as those with long-standing loans are [typically(?)] called here, is fit for amphitheater spectacles, since he is... whereas my client is an eminent man [and an officeholder(?)] in [the city of] Arsinoe(?)...

(l. 35) Phibion:

"I do not know."

(ll. 35–36) Septimius Vegetus:

"What even you do not know we could not possibly say."

(ll. 37–40) Kephalon:

"This is a pay order from this man's father. The slave, being his administrator, signed that he would measure out the grain but did not measure it out at any point after the order was issued."

(ll. 40–43) Septimius Vegetus:

"The first point of inquiry is whether this is indeed the writing of this man's father and secondly why you have not sued for the return of the loan until now? For it is possible that he (the slave) measured out the grain and confirmed it in writing."

(ll. 44–48) Aristonikos:

"You are right to ask this, and I will give you the general policy on this issue: prefects of Egypt have established five years as a time-limit for filing long-standing claims, while those who have established ten years did not do so for places where governors and judicial assizes occur. Ask him: for how many years did his father survive (after issuing the pay order)?"

(ll. 49–51) Phibion:

"This man refused the inheritance of his father and I that of my own father, since both were collectors of grain taxes (*sitologoi*) and indebted to the *fiscus*."

(ll. 52–53) Aristonikos:

"Particularly if grain was owed to the *fiscus*, why did he not sue for its return back then?"

(ll. 53–55) Septimius Vegetus:

"Suffering hunger during a famine, would you not sue for the return of grain if it were owed to you?"

(ll. 55–56) Phibion:

"He invited me to take four minae."

(ll. 56–58) Aristonikos:

> "If he is allowed to go this far, thousands more will bring documents issued by the father of my client, claiming that he has left them destitute."

In contrast to Kephalon's plain and deferential rhetoric, which employs stock-phrases commonly attested in petitions, Aristonikos pleads in a confident manner, instructing the prefect on statutes of limitations and employing an array of rhetorical devices.[47] By casting aspersions on Phibion's modest status and the time elapsed between the loan and the lawsuit (ll. 27–34), Aristonikos employs what ancient rhetorical manuals call argumentation from conjecture (*coniectura* = *στοχασμός*), described by Quintilian as a rhetorical strategy for interpreting past events with reference to character, capacity, and intent (*personae, causae, consilia*), considering what an individual "intended to do, was able to do, and actually did."[48] The goal of Aristonikos is to persuade the prefect that Phibion has both the character, the motive, and the capacity to present the court with a false claim. His character-assassination of Phibion as a malevolent "loan-shark... fit for amphitheater spectacles" receives no response from Phibion's advocate. The prefect picks up the conjectural argument and proceeds to question the authenticity and probative value of the pay order, suggesting that the slave's signature could indicate that the grain had already been returned (ll. 40–43). Quick to react, Aristonikos deploys the device of procedural objection, arguing that Phibion's claim should be regarded as expired and therefore inadmissible (ll. 44–48).[49] He concludes with another well-known tactic in ancient oratory, insisting that to condone Phibion's claim would set a dangerous precedent and open the door to a flood of similar claimants in the future (ll. 56–58).[50] The prefect ends the hearing in the same harsh tone as it began (ll. 59–66):

[47] For Kephalon's stock phrases, see e.g. l. 14: *τῆς σῆς εὐεργεσίας δεόμενος* and l. 15: *πρῶτον καὶ ἀναγκαιότατον*.

[48] See Quint. *Inst.* 7.2.27: *nam is ordo est, ut facere voluerit potuerit fecerit*. On conjecture, see Quint. *Inst.* 7.2 and Hermog. *Stas.* 46.8–47.7 with Heath, *On Issues* (1995) 81–83 and 156–159. At 7.2.50 Quintilian mentions loans and deposits as a category of conjectural cases where arguments arise from capacity (whether there was any money to lend) and character (whether the plaintiff could plausibly have made a loan to the defendant or was accusing him unjustly), as well as basic questions of fact (was the money delivered? had it been it repaid?). All of these elements are present in the argument of Aristonikos—as well as Palamedes in *P.Mil.Vogl.* I 25, discussed below.

[49] On objection, see Quint. *Inst.* 7.5 and Hermog. *Stas.* 42–44 and 80–81 with Heath, *On Issues* (1995) 80–81 and 136. Heath deduces that practical use of objection as a forensic tactic made the category more prominent in Greek rhetorical theory, see Heath, 'Practical advocacy' (2004) 78–79.

[50] This form of argumentation was a favorite of Cicero, see for example *Verr.* II 2.27: *nam si hanc defensionem probabitis, "Non accepit ipse", licet omnia de pecuniis repetundis iudicia tollatis* ("For if you accept the defense, 'He did not receive the money himself,' then you might as well abolish all corruption trials").

> (ll. 59–66) Septimius Vegetus to Phibion:
>
> "You deserve to be flogged for seizing an eminent man and his wife by your own means. But I shall concede your case to the crowd and be more humane to you. You present a pay order after forty years; I concede you half that time: in twenty years, you may return to my court." And he ordered the document to be torn up.

Evidently, the assize court was being attended by a large gathering of spectators who were loudly reacting to the proceedings.

The boldness and rhetorical skill of Aristonikos, which is apparent even from this abridged record, suggest that unlike his opponent Kephalon he was an orator of high social standing. Circumstantial details indicate that Kephalon was engaged by Phibion *in situ* at the assize.[51] How the defendant, who found himself in custody, came to have legal assistance is less clear. It is documented in Roman legal literature that defendants without access to an advocate could have one granted by the court.[52] It is possible, in this context, that Aristonikos was a high-profile orator appointed by the prefect's staff. His confidence in addressing the prefect suggests a further possibility: that Aristonikos belonged to a group of legal practitioners from Alexandria who travelled with the prefect's assize court.[53] Aristonikos has a potent effect on the course of the proceedings: in addition to virtually silencing his opponent, he exercises a clear influence on the prefect, who agrees with him and even reiterates his statements (Aristonikos: "... whereas my client is an eminent man ..." l. 30 ... Septimius Vegetus: "you deserve to be flogged for seizing an eminent man and his wife by your own means," ll. 60–61). Even though some of the arguments advanced by Aristonikos are manifestly tendentious, they are upheld in the prefect's ruling.[54] It would seem that Aristonikos' status and skill had a decisive impact on the prefect's judgment.

Upon closer scrutiny, however, the proceedings emerge in a distinctly orchestrated light. The prefect's initial threats (ll. 9–12) show that he had, from the outset, a hostile disposition toward the plaintiff Phibion. This is confirmed by the inquisitorial tone of the hearing, where the prefect and Arstonikos take turns interrogating Phibion, including overtly sarcastic remarks (Phibion: "I do not know," Septimius Vegetus: "What even you do not know we could not possibly

[51] Phibion's failure to submit a petition, for which Kephalon apologizes, speaks against Kephalon's involvement earlier in the dispute. The deferential tone of Kephalon accords with a local advocate, rather than an orator from the prefect's Alexandrian entourage (discussed further below).

[52] There was a corresponding clause in the Roman praetor's edict, which, according to Ulpian, applied to individuals who were, for a variety of reasons, hindered in their access to an advocate (see Ulp. (6 *ad ed.*) D. 3.1.1.4) or had an advocate of low status who stood no chance against his opponent (see Ulp. (1 *de off. procons.*) D. 1.16.9.5).

[53] The appearance of an orator named Aristonikos in another, fragmentary court transcript, where he dominates the dialogue, supports this argument, see *SB* XX 15148 (unknown location, late 1c. CE?).

[54] For example, Aristonikos' insistence that Phibion is a man of low status attacking a prominent person was clearly somewhat contrived, since the fathers of both litigants had held the same civic liturgy and died insolvent, as Phibion points out in ll. 49–52.

say," ll. 35–36). Additional sarcasm is employed in rejecting Phibion's claim and destroying his documentation of the loan, while restating threats of corporal punishment. The prefect's unrelenting hostility and ostensible collaboration with Aristonikos suggest that the hearing was not an ordinary *postulatio* but a carefully calibrated performance. It is relevant that Phibion's seizure of his opponent without summons or a written petition introduced an element of private violence that made him liable to coercive sanctions.[55] One strongly suspects that this occasion was exploited to turn Phibion's case into a punitive spectacle. Replete with transgressive elements (breach of legal procedure, use of violence, affront to an individual of high status, and so on), the legal narrative proferred by Aristonikos and upheld by the prefect turns Phibion into a paragon of deviance demanding punishment. The brutal measures announced by the prefect at the start of the hearing create dramatic suspense, causing Phibion to cower in fear (ll. 10–12) and crowds of spectators to plead for his release (ll. 61–62). This permits the prefect to withhold his prerogative of official violence and display the benevolent side of his judicial authority. At the same time, physical destruction of the pay order serves as a symbolic reminder of the coercive apparatus of Roman criminal justice.[56]

For a distinguished figure like Aristonikos—likely an orator from Alexandria, as suggested above—the stakes of forensic performance clearly transcended the outcome of this particular hearing. It seems unlikely that an easy victory over an inferior opponent in a financial dispute in the Egyptian hinterland was of consequence to him. More significant for his reputation and career was his facilitation of the prefect's public judicial activity, which in cases like this could be effectively dramatized to function as a theater of Roman power. Reception of this judicial spectacle was not confined to the spectators witnessing the hearing: the papyrus on which this court transcript is preserved is written in a calligraphic, semi-uncial script with indentations marking each speaker, suggesting that the case was

[55] Although forcible conveyance of opponents to court was permitted by the Twelve Tables (Crawford, *Roman Statutes* II no. 40 I.1: *si in ius vocat, ito. ni it, antestamino. igitur em capito* ("If the plaintiff summons him to court, he shall go. If he does not go, the plaintiff is to call to witness. Then, the plaintiff is to take him") and is occasionally mentioned in republican sources (see Hor. *Serm.* 1.9.75–78; Plaut. *Curc.* 5.2), this practice recedes from the evidence under the Principate (although see Luke 12:58). In Roman legal literature, we find a citation of the Hadrianic jurist Salvius Iulianus to the effect that a creditor who employed violence to extract what was owed to him automatically forfeited his claim and was liable for *vis* under the *lex Iulia de vi* (D 4.2.12.2, Ulpianus *libro 11 ad edictum*). The same policy is articulated in a judicial hearing before Marcus Aurelius in D 48.7.7 (Callistratus *5 de cognitionibus*). Our Flavian-era papyrus appears to be the earliest known documentary instance of this Roman policy, which may stem from the Augustan *lex Iulia de vi* itself. This question is explored by me in a separate paper.

[56] If I am right that this case was selected to serve as a punitive *exemplum*, it is noteworthy that it was still staged as an examination of a civil claim, where effort was taken to demonstrate that the claim itself was illegitimate.

anthologized and became part of a lawyer's collection.[57] In this way, the spectacle of Phibion's castigation would serve as a monitory *exemplum* for future audiences.

2. A Lowly Creditor Pursues an Eminent Debtor: Another Unequal Confrontation, in a Case Delegated by the Prefect of Egypt to a Local Official

A legal dispute of a similar nature came before the prefect Flavius Titianus in the 120s CE.[58] This time, a freedman named Demetrios, a former estate-manager of a wealthy landowning family, was attempting to reclaim a mortgage and a deposit of 2,000 drachmas from Paulinus, the brother of his recently deceased debtor Geminus. Both brothers had held the office of the gymnasiarchy, the pinnacle of a municipal career, which placed them in the top tier of the local civic elite.[59] Demetrios outlined his two claims in a petition to the prefect and was apparently granted a hearing to present his petition.[60] While adjudication of the first claim concerning the mortgage was postponed pending investigation, the second claim involving 2,000 drachmas was delegated by the prefect to a local administrator, the *stratēgos* Andromachos, who examined the case at his assize in the Arsinoite village of Tebtynis.[61] The heading of the record introduces it as a lawsuit of "Demetrios the freedman against Paulinus the former gymnasiarch," underscoring the discrepancy in wealth and status between the two litigants.

In line with standard practice in Roman courts, both parties were assisted by advocates. Since this seems to have been a case of private litigation according to regular procedure, with a petition served by the plaintiff on his adversary, the advocates had presumably been engaged in advance by their respective clients.

[57] That this case was anthologized is further suggested by its thematic heading in ll. 6–7: ὑ̣πόθεσι̣ς̣ [περὶ(?)] etc. For another example of a calligraphic case-collection, see *P.Oxy.* XVII 2111 (after 135 CE).

[58] See *P.Mil.Vogl.* I 25 (Tebtynis, 27 December 126 CE–25 January 127 CE) and my emended text of the papyrus in Dolganov, 'Rich vs. poor in Roman courts' (2023) no. 2. For discussions of this text, see the *editio princeps* with Arangio-Ruiz, 'Commento giuridico' (1937); Crook, *Legal Advocacy* (1995) 75–77; Heath, 'Practical advocacy' (2004) 65–70; Dolganov, 'Rich vs. poor in Roman courts' (2023).

[59] On the family of Paulinus, see Smolders, 'Patron's descendants' (2005) and Dolganov and Rebillard, 'Not a Roman trial of Christians' (2021) 202–204.

[60] An in-person hearing seems to be implied by Palamedes' allegation that Demetrios has "deceived the prefect" (col. ii l. 39–col. iii l. 2). Paulinus was apparently not present at this hearing, since he and Palamedes are not familiar with all the details of the case. Perhaps Demetrios had traveled ahead to Alexandria or another assize center to file the complaint, then served the prefect's response on Paulinus through the local *stratēgos*. For a similar strategy of anticipating one's opponent in advance of a local assize, see *P.Wisc.* I 33 (Arsinoite, *ca.* 147 CE) with Dolganov, 'A *stratēgos* on trial' (2021) 363–365.

[61] On postponement pending investigation: the technical expression is ὑπερτίθεται εἰς διάκρισιν (col. i l. 10 and ii l. 30); for a parallel, see *SB* 1 5240 (Arsinoite, after 17 CE). This meaning is missed in the translation of Heath, 'Practical advocacy' (2004) 65–66. It appears that Demetrios asked the prefect to order a local investigation of his urban property holdings (col. ii l. 30) before the case was adjudicated again. Palamedes casts aspersions on this as a delay tactic (col. ii ll. 29–33).

The hearing begins with the introductory speech (*narratio*) of Demetrios' advocate Ammonios, who states his client's claims in rather plain and direct terms:

> (ll. 4–19) Ammonios, advocate (said) on behalf of Demetrios:
>
> "By means of the petition brought by my client he has defined two charges against his opponent: one regarding a mortgage of houses, the other regarding 2,000 drachmas that he deposited with Geminus, the brother of Paulinus. . . . By what means Geminus came by the money I will now relate. My client, being a member of Geminus' household and occasionally employed as an estate manager, made a deposit of 2,000 drachmas and had a deed of deposit drawn up in the name of his friend, a certain Hatres. Accordingly, he presents the deed written by Geminus to Hatres and asks to receive the money back."

Ammonios' speech ostensibly summarizes the information contained in Demetrios' petition, which Ammonios proceeds to recite. It is possible but not certain that Ammonios was the petition's author. He does not appear to offer any arguments beyond the content of the petition. Like Phibion's advocate Kephalon, Ammonios introduces the case and falls silent for the rest of the hearing.

Then enters Palamedes, the advocate of Paulinus, whose diction is skilled and elaborate, employing elegant language and a number of rhetorical devices, conveyed even by this abbreviated record:

> (ll. 20–33) After the petition brought by Demetrios was read out, Palamedes, advocate (said) on behalf of Paulinus:
>
> "My client could have repelled the claim of the 2,000 drachmas, since he is not the guardian of his brother's children. However, just so that you learn of the evildoings of our opponent, my client is prepared to defend himself on both charges in the petition. The first charge, as this man has defined it, is as follows: he has alleged that his case against Paulinus concerning the mortage of houses was adjudicated by the former *stratēgos* Claudius Dionysius, adding that the judgment was for Paulinus to restore him the mortgaged property. But now he begs for an investigation into this matter because he knows that he will be defeated, since Paulinus can prove that the case of the mortgage was not adjudicated against him at all, but against other persons."
>
> (l. 33) Demetrios:
>
> "[I am not arguing] this case right now."
>
> (ll. 34–36) Palamedes:
>
> "He has 'defined this charge by means of his petition'; if he does not wish to speak about it, he must at least answer me this: was the case of the houses really adjudicated against Paulinus?"

(ll. 36–37) The stratēgos to Demetrios:

"What is your response to Paulinus?"

(ll. 37–39) Demetrios:

"The case of the houses was not adjudicated against Paulinus. As I said earlier, I am not arguing this case right now but asking to get back the money."

(l. 39) Palamedes:

"Demetrios has confessed to deceiving the most illustrious prefect already in his first charge,

col. iii

(ll. 1–18) but you will be even more inclined to condemn him in the charge concerning the money. But first, as regards the persons involved, it is necessary to say this much: Geminus was a most eminent man (εὐσχημονέστατος), while our opponent is indigent (ἄπορος) and has no means of demonstrating where he could have gotten the money in the first place. His confession to being a 'member of Geminus' household and occasionally employed as an estate manager' is especially relevant to the present lawsuit, since through this he is revealed to be working for wages and the fact of his lacking in necessities makes him suspicious. Perhaps, while spending time in the household of my client, he stole the deed?—which he tellingly never brought to court while Geminus was alive and could demonstrate precisely how it was mislaid. But now that Geminus is dead he pursues the money..."

Palamedes begins his speech with a gesture at procedural objection ("my client could have repelled the claim..."), a strategy outlined in rhetorical handbooks.[62] Although rejection of the claim was evidently not possible in practice, this assertion had the rhetorical effect of casting doubt on the claim's legitimacy. Since Ammonios had mentioned the postponed lawsuit concerning the mortgage (col. ii ll. 6–7), Palamedes reacts by denouncing Demetrios' presentation of that claim as factually misleading (col. ii ll. 26–col. iii l. 2); this serves to undermine the credibility of Demetrios, which is central to Palamedes' rhetorical strategy. Curiously, Ammonios does not assist Demetrios in responding to these allegations. It is noteworthy that the *stratēgos* treats Palamedes' words as if they had been spoken by Paulinus himself (the *stratēgos* to Demetrios: "What is your response to Paulinus?" col. ii ll. 36–37). A similar phenomenon is observable in other court records, where orators often assume the first-person perspective of their clients.[63]

[62] See the analysis of Heath, 'Practical advocacy' (2004) 65–68. On objection and quasi-objection in ancient rhetorical manuals, see n. 49.

[63] See the other documents in the Appendix, discussed below.

Like Aristonikos, Palamedes employs the techniques of conjectural argument to reinterpret the circumstances of the case toward a narrative that favors his client. He lays emphasis on Paulinus' high rank and Demetrios' low status as a sign of the latter's venal and vicious character ("...he is revealed to be working for wages and the fact of his lacking in necessities makes him suspicious" col. iii ll. 9–10); in line with the tactics of Aristonikos, Palamedes infers suspicious motives from the timing of the lawsuit ("but now that Geminus is dead he pursues the money"). These aspersions are employed to argue that Demetrius had the character, motive, and capacity to steal a document that had been misplaced ("perhaps, while spending time in the household of my client, he *stole* the deed?" col. iii ll. 11–12). Palamedes thus reframes the case into a counteraccusation against the plaintiff, a strategy that corresponds to precepts from ancient rhetorical manuals.[64]

The hearing encounters an unexpected obstacle when it turns out that Ammonios has given the wrong name for Demetrios' friend and titulary of the deposit. Consequently, Palamedes has employed the incorrect name as well:

> Palamedes:
>
> "...To this I add the gravest matter of all, which is most revealing of Demetrios' evildoing: for I declare that he never knew Hatres, in whose name he says the deed was drawn up, nor is he able to answer who he is or where he is from."
>
> Demetrios:
>
> "It is not Hatres but Deios, son of Hatres, a friend of mine in whose name I had the deed drawn up."
>
> Palamedes:
>
> "Neither does he know who Deios is nor where he is from. Nor is this sufficient, since he also needs to bring a written statement by Deios confirming that it is his (Demetrios') money that he gave by means of the deed."
>
> (ll. 24–25) Demetrios:
>
> "I have his written statement as well!"[65]

Palamedes is quick on his feet, correcting himself as he speaks. Ammonios' error may have been due to inadequate briefing by Demetrios or insufficient time to

[64] On the so-called incident conjecture, see Hermog. *Stas.* 56.25–57.11 with the remarks of Heath, 'Practical advocacy' (2004) 67.

[65] The rhetorical punchline of Palamedes—that Demetrios has no connection to Deios—appears to be based on his assumption that Demetrios has only the contract of deposit and no other documents. It seems to come as a surprise when Demetrios suddenly produces a written statement by Deios confirming the deposit. Heath, 'Practical advocacy' (2004) 68–69 supposes that Demetrios did not previously mention this document because he believed its date to be deficient, but it seems likely that he kept it as "insurance" in case the judge was inclined to doubt his claim. On the withholding of evidence as a legal strategy, see e.g. *PSI* IX 1033 (Oxyrhynchus 166) ll. 7–8, where a litigant pressed for details states: "I have not come to argue the case but merely to deliver summons."

prepare for the hearing.[66] It is telling that his mistake concerns information that was not included in Demetrios' written petition, which seems to reflect the extent of Ammonios' knowledge of the details of the case. The error inflicts further damage on Demetrios' credibility and facilitates the effort of Paulinus to question the authenticity of Deios' statement, his identity and even his existence:

> Paulinus:
>
> "... Indeed, he may be presenting a document written on this very day by anyone whatsoever in the name of a certain Deios. But let him explain where this Deios comes from."
>
> Demetrios:
>
> "He is a merchant, a friend of mine, from the Herakleopolite nome."
>
> Paulinus:
>
> "Let him produce (Deios)!"
>
> The *stratēgos* (said) to Demetrios:
>
> "In how many days will you produce Deios?"
>
> Demetrios:
>
> "In fifteen days."

The names of the two advocates are revealing: an orator named Ammonios, a name of Demotic origin, is attested in a number of lawsuits in Tebtynis and other locations in the Arsinoite nome in this period. He appears to have been a local Arsinoite lawyer who provided legal services to local families.[67] Palamedes, on the other hand, bears a lofty Homeric name, which together with his confident demeanor and manifest rhetorical skill suggests that, like Aristonikos, he was an elite orator—possibly an orator from Alexandria who had been sought out by his wealthy client. If so, Palademes may have had the same social provenance as Andromachos, the *stratēgos* adjudicating the case.[68]

After his initial speech presenting Demetrios' claims, Ammonios is not heard from again and leaves Demetrios to defend himself alone. Palamedes, by contrast, participates in the dialogue and aggressively pushes his client's interests, thereby facilitating Paulinus' interventions on his own behalf in the second half of the hearing. Since Demetrios is described as a man of slender means, it is possible that

[66] See Crook, *Legal Advocacy* (1995) 66 and 76–77. For another badly briefed advocate, who is engaged spontaneously in the last minute and requests an adjournment to acquaint himself with his client's paperwork, see *M.Chr.* 93 (Arsinoite, ca. 250 CE) with Crook ibid. 96–98.

[67] See *P.Fam.Tebt.* 19 = *SB* VI 9252 (Arsinoite, April 6, 118 CE) and *P.Fam.Tebt.* 24 ll. 22–40 (Arsinoite nome, 124 CE).

[68] On the Roman use of the Alexandrian elite to govern the hinterland, see Bowman and Rathbone, 'Cities and Administration' (1992) 125–127.

Ammonios was providing a minimal legal service as per his client's modest budget. There is plainly a huge gulf in skill between the two orators: Ammonios lacks invention, primarily restating his client's petition, and exhibits a defective memory for detail—characteristics that Roman rhetoricians regarded as paradigmatic for bad orators.[69] By contrast, Palamedes is quick and inventive, employs rhetorical strategy and deftly exploits weaknesses in his opponent's arguments. When Palamedes mockingly cites Ammonios' own words ("he has 'defined this charge by means of his petition'..." col. ii l. 34; "his confession to being a 'member of Geminus' household and occasionally employed as an estate manager' is particulary relevant to the present lawsuit..." col. iii ll. 6–8) the latter offers no counterargument and engages in no altercation. As one suspects in the confrontation between Kephalon and Aristonikos, Ammonios may have been intimidated into silence by his more eminent and expert adversary.

The conclusion of the proceedings contrasts with the brutal denouement of Phibion's hearing, but not without some notable similarities:

> (ll. 9–17) Andromachos the *stratēgos* (said) to Demetrios:
>
> "The statements have been entered into the minutes. Instead of the fifteen days you have asked for, I give you a whole thirty in which to produce Deios, whose handwritten deed you claim to present. In the meantime this deed—which you will certify with your signature has been handwritten by Deios, who you claim is from the Herakleopolite nome—will be affixed with seals by you and Paulinus and remain with Theon the assistant. Whenever Deios happens to be present, we shall see what he himself has to say about it."

Demetrios is given thirty days to produce Deios and authenticate his deed of deposit or, implicitly, face consequences for bringing false charges or failing to pursue the matter. The sardonic tone of the *stratēgos* in granting Demetrios twice as much time as he requests conveys his skepticism concerning the claim. This recalls the prefect's specious generosity in allowing Phibion to return to court in "only" twenty years. Sarcasm appears to have been a common rhetorical device of officials in formulating demeaning or latently hostile judicial sentences.[70]

Unlike the highly public and visible setting of the governor's assize court, a local tribunal in an Arsinoite village was less conducive to rhetorical display for the sake of public performance. One would imagine that the orator Palamedes was

[69] See for example Pliny the Younger's critique of the orator Regulus as deficient, among other things, in speed, memory and creativity, and relying on written speeches in *Ep.* 4.7 and 6.11.

[70] For another example, see *P.Oxy.* I 40 (Oxyrhynchus, 2c. CE), where a prefect responds to a doctor complaining of a liturgical appointment by individuals whom he had treated: "your treatment must have been bad." On invective and humiliation as integral to the Roman cultural practice of power, and by extension Roman imperial administration, see Peachin, 'Attacken und Erniedrigungen' (2007), esp. 121–124 on humiliation in judicial settings.

primarily concerned with securing a legal victory for his client, who belonged to a wealthy and influential Arsinoite family. It is clear from the dialogue that Palamedes elicits respect from the *stratēgos*, who reiterates his questions and demands to the plaintiff. Ammonios, by contrast, appears to do very little to achieve a favorable outcome for Demetrios. As in the case of Phibion, the presiding official has a clear affinity toward the wealthier litigant represented by the superior advocate. In this respect, both cases appear to show differences in socioeconomic status translating into discrepancies in quality of legal assistance and prospects for success.

But this is where the similarity ends. While the circumstances of Phibion's hearing suggest, as I have argued, that his case was *a priori* deemed illegitimate and staged as a punitive spectacle, the claims of Demetrios had been taken seriously by the prefect and delegated for adjudication.[71] In spite of Paulinus' expert defence and Demetrios' inferior status and inept advocate, the case continued into the next stage. What happened if Demetrios managed to produce his friend Deios who was able to confirm his deposit? The dossier of Paulinus' papers in which this judicial record appears is prefaced by the phrases "with good fortune" and "for a favorable outcome," which suggests that the final outcome was not a foregone conclusion.

3. *Patria potestas* and Marriage: A Public Rhetorical Contest before the Prefect of Egypt

In line with evidence for forensic oratory as a field of elite competition in the Roman Empire, a number of papyri attest to agonistic confrontations between elite orators in the courtroom of the governor. One such case from 128 CE involved an accusation of violence (*βία* = *vis*) by a certain Sempronius against his son-in-law Antonius, residents of the Egyptian hinterland who despite their Roman names were provincials of peregrine status.[72] The prefect Flavius Titianus granted Sempronius a preliminary hearing and issued a letter summoning all

[71] From a legal perspective, the prefect's delegation constituted substantive approval of the claim pending its factual verification, not unlike the granting of a legal action in Roman praetorian law.

[72] See *P.Oxy.* II 237 col. vii ll. 19–29 = *Sel. Pap.* II 258 (Alexandria, 2 June 128 CE) and the new readings published online by K. Balamoshev at http://www.dionysia.wpia.uw.edu.pl/ (accessed on January 24, 2023). For previous discussions and translations of this text, see the extensive commentary of the *editio princeps*; Katzoff, 'Precedents' (1972) 259; Lewis, *Life in Egypt* (1983), 191–192; Rowlandson, *Women and Society* (1998) 186–187; Kreuzsaler and Urbanik, 'Humanity and inhumanity of law' (2008) 138–141; Platschek, 'Nochmals zur Petition der Dionysia' (2015) 161–163; Dolganov, 'Reichsrecht and Volksrecht' (2019) 54–55. On charges of violence in Roman Egypt corresponding to the Roman legal categories of *vis* and *iniuria*, see Mascellari, 'La descrizione di atti criminosi' (2016). The peregrine status of Antonius is indicated by his patronym "son of Apollonios." The Egyptian status of Sempronius is specified by the forensic orators who cite this case as a judicial precedent in *P.Oxy.* II 237 col. vii l. 34.

parties for judicial proceedings at Alexandria.[73] To receive this level of attention, Sempronius' report of violence was presumably quite dramatic.[74] He may have benefited from the jurisdictional priority accorded by governors to complaints of parents against offenses by their children.[75]

The judicial record, as we have it, only briefly summarizes the orators' arguments. These were clearly elaborate and highly rhetorical: first, the orator Isidoros the Younger told a colorful tale about Sempronius being instigated by his wife or mother to provoke a conflict with his son-in-law and forcibly remove his daughter from her husband's house.[76] The daughter fell so "ill with suffering" that the regional procurator (*epistratēgos*) struggled to maintain his composure and ruled that the happily married couple should not be forcibly separated.[77] But Sempronius hushed up the ruling and submitted a petition to the prefect accusing Antonius of violence. In what appears to be the peroration of his speech, Isidoros articulated Antonius' plea "not to be unyoked from a wife who felt affection toward him," employing a rare technical expression for divorce and appealing to the Roman principle of conjugal affection (*affectio maritalis*) as the legally relevant element of intent defining the state of marriage.[78] In response, the orator Didymos employed the rhetorical tactic Greek theorists call non-documentary objection (ἄγραφος παραγραφή), conceding Sempronius' actions but insisting that these were justified by the circumstances, since Antonius had threatened to denounce Sempronius for incest (criminalized in Roman law).[79] Unable to bear this outrage (ὕβρις = *iniuria*), Sempronius had exercised his legal power (ἐξουσία = *potestas*)

[73] The verb ἐκπέμπω (col. vii l. 25), which signifies litigants being "sent out" to another location, here refers to the prefect's permanent tribunal in the provincial capital; for parallels, see e.g. *M.Chr.* 91 (Alexandria, *ca.* 157–159 CE) col. iii l. 15 and *P.Mil.Vogl.* I 27 (Arsinoite, 129 CE) col. i l. 22 and col. iii ll. 7 and 13.

[74] On narratives of violence in petitions from Roman Egypt, see Bryen, *Violence in Roman Egypt* (2013) 89–125 and 203–207. Bryen envisions the development of Roman provincial law through a "flood of individual narratives" (207) and sees the normative claims formulated in petitions as constitutive of the provincial legal order. For a different perspective, laying emphasis on the Roman state's implementation of a substantive legal order in its provinces, see Dolganov, *The Administration of Justice* (forthcoming).

[75] Such cases fell under the governor's *ex officio* jurisdiction, probably as a result of Augustan legislation, see *SB* XII 10929 (133–137 CE) col. iii ll. 14–16 and Ulp. (1 *de off. procons.*) D. 1.16.9.3 with my discussion in Dolganov, 'Reichsrecht and Volksrecht' (2019) 39–41 and 43–44 and Dolganov, 'Imperialism and social engineering' (2022) 681.

[76] It is noteworthy that the record of proceedings has Antonius making these statements "through" his advocate, who functions as a borrowed voice.

[77] This appears to be the sense of μετριοπαθῶς ἀναστραφέντα, which refers to the *epistratēgos* controlling his emotions. The advocate underscores that the ruling is rational and in keeping with the law.

[78] In papyri, the poetic term ἀποζευχθῆναι is attested in only one other document, with reference to the divorce of a Roman soldier: *P.Diog.* 3 = *P.Turner* 30, Antinoupolis, 209 CE. It may have been a Greek rendition of the Latin *seiungere*. On *affectio maritalis*, see Treggiari, *Roman Marriage* (1991) 54–57. On the key rhetorical function of perorations, see Winterbottom, 'Perorations' (2004).

[79] On non-documentary objection, see Hermogen. *Stas.* 42.7–43.9 with Heath, *On Issues* (1995) 72–73, 78–79, and 130–139.

to reclaim his daughter from her husband. Didymus also sought to generate indignation concerning the moral damage inflicted by Antonius' "inappropriate" accusations of incest. A final intervention was made on behalf of Antonius by the orator Procleianus, who pointed out that if the marriage was understood to be intact (ἀπερίλυτος) the father had no legal power over his married daughter or her dowry. The prefect followed this reasoning and ruled, in line with the Roman notion of *affectio maritalis*, that the integrity of the marriage depended on the wishes of the married woman.

Although the legal process had been initiated by Sempronius, the order of the proceedings shows Antonius acting as the plaintiff and Sempronius as the defendant.[80] Evidently, as the full history of the dispute was revealed prior to the hearing, likely through the submission of a counterpetition by Antonius, the legal substance of the case was modified accordingly.[81] Ultimately, the proceedings were not configured around Sempronius' accusation of violence but concerned Antonius' effort to reclaim his wife from her father.

The monumental setting of the governor's tribunal, which was set up in the forum of Augustus at Alexandria in the vicinity of the Caesareum, meant that the judicial session received maximal public visibility.[82] Even our minimalistic record exhibits clear signs that the forensic orators delivered a dynamic performance, incorporating technical legal arguments as well as rhetorical elements reminiscent of Roman declamation, such as the figure of the manipulative matriarch and the proverbial rivalry between father and son-in-law, sensationalized through allegations of incest.[83] On one side of the story there were lovers suffering from the machinations of a jealous father acting in bad faith. On the other side an outraged parent trying to reclaim his daughter from a violent son-in-law who was disparaging his reputation. At the same time, both sides of the debate addressed the question whether, and under what circumstances, a father had the legal power to end his daughter's marriage.

Both the context of the proceedings and what it is possible to glean from their content suggest that the orators pleading the case were prominent figures from the forensic sphere at Alexandria. The Latin *cognomen* of Procleianus implies Roman citizenship, while his authority with the prefect suggests a man of high status. Orators named Isidoros and Didymos appear in a number of hearings at the prefect's assizes in this period, in the Arsinoite nome and in several locations in

[80] On the order and length of trials, see Bablitz, *Actors and Audience* (2007) 170–182.

[81] The petition of Dionysia (*P.Oxy.* II 237, *ca.* 186 CE) in which this judicial record is cited probably had this function as well.

[82] On the location, see Pfeiffer, 'The imperial cult in Egypt' (2012) 86–87 and Capponi, 'Spaces of justice in Roman Egypt' (2010) 271–272.

[83] The legal arguments are reflected by the presence of juridical terminology, noted above. On the relevant declamatory motifs, see Krapinger, 'The stepmother' (2015) and Breij, 'Incest in Roman declamation' (2009).

the Nile Delta, suggesting orators who traveled with the assize court.[84] By what mechanisms were these orators engaged to participate in the proceedings? According to Pliny the Younger, compelling reasons for an eminent orator to take on a case included: (1) to oblige one's friends; (2) to showcase one's moral fiber, if no other orator wished to handle the case; (3) to ensure that justice was done, if a case constituted an important precedent (*exemplum*); (4) to pursue fame and glory in a *cause célèbre*; (5) additionally, an orator could be appointed to plead by the state on behalf of a province or provincial community.[85] A further reason not mentioned by Pliny, but arguably implicit in his reference to *causae clarae et illustres* ("famous and illustrious cases"), was the prospect of remuneration by wealthy clients. In a family conflict of Egyptian provincials summoned to Alexandria from the hinterland, it seems unlikely that personal connections or remuneration played a significant role. Instead, it seems probable that the forensic orators took on the case by virtue of the prestige of the prefect's tribunal or were appointed to plead by the court. For elite orators in the provincial capital, the governor's tribunal offered an illustrious venue for rhetorical display and possibilities for career advancement, such as the coveted *advocatio fisci* established in this period.[86] Through their artful debate on both sides of the question of *patria potestas* and marriage, the court reached a consequential judgment on a substantive legal issue while at the same time providing performative entertainment for a mass of provincial spectators. As in Phibion's case, the impact of the hearing was amplified by the judicial record being anthologized and cited as an authoritative precedent, as illustrated by the late second-century petition in which this record has survived.[87]

4. A Surety Confronts a Rapacious Creditor: A Sportsmanlike Debate before the Prefect of Egypt

A record of proceedings before the renowned jurist Lucius Volusius Maecianus as prefect of Egypt vividly conveys the dynamics of courtroom interactions between

[84] Isidoros: *P.Oxy.* II 237 col. vii l. 31 (assize at Xois, 133 CE); *SB* XIV 12139 col. ii l. 17 (assize at Xois, 146 CE); *SB* XX 15147 (unknown location, after 138 CE); Didymos: *BGU* II 592 (Arsinoite assize, mid-2c.); *BGU* III 969 (Arsinoite assize, *ca.* 139 CE). Some of these cases are adjudicated by *iudices dati* of the prefect in the presence of the prefect's administrative representatives.

[85] See Plin. *Ep.* 6.29 and 2.11 with Tempest, 'Oratorical performance' (2017).

[86] On the *advocatio fisci* and its place in provincial careers, see de Ruggiero, *Dizionario epigrafico* (1895) 1.125–131; Pflaum, *Les procurateurs* (1950) 89; Jones, *The Later Roman Empire* (1964) 509–511; and Dolganov, '*Nutricula causidicorum*' (2020) 382–386 and 407–411.

[87] On the petition of Dionysia (*P.Oxy.* II 237, *ca.* 186 CE), see Dolganov, 'Reichsrecht and Volksrecht' (2019) 42–60 with references to earlier literature. The petition includes a dossier in which the judgment of Titianus determines the outcome of another case four years later (*P.Oxy.* II 237 col. vii ll. 30–38); both judicial records were then apparently anthologized together.

forensic orators and the provincial governor.[88] The proceedings took place in the coastal city of Paraetonium in 160 CE. The case concerned a group of debtors who were unable to repay a number of loans, forcing their surety (ἔγγυος = *fideiussor*) Iulius Voltimus to step in and organize the transfer of real securities. To accomplish this, Voltimus transferred his own property in the vicinity of Alexandria into the possession of Sempronius Orestinus, one of the creditors, so that the profits would gradually offset the loan.[89] When the interest had exceeded the capital sum and Orestinus refused to release the property, Voltimus petitioned the prefect, who granted a hearing at his next assize in the area.[90]

The hearing begins with the introductory arguments of the advocates Crispinus on behalf of the plaintiff and Isidoros on behalf of the defendant, who present their respective accounts of the case and read out relevant evidence (ll. 3–18). These arguments are punctuated by interventions from Maecianus, who queries individual points. The dialogue culminates in an altercation between Maecianus and Isidoros, the advocate of Orestinus, who refuses to back down from his aggressive defence of his client's position:

> (ll. 18–20)... After Orestinus stated that he was claiming his rightful due, Maecianus said:
>
> "Surely the rightful due of creditors is normally without profit. It is told to you: as far as the loan is concerned, the decision of the tribune stands firm... but the interest is far greater than the loan. Receive the loan and give back the mortgaged property."
>
> (ll. 20–22) Isidoros said:
>
> "... we obtained all of his landed estates. This is justly said against us. Then, when others petitioned saying that these people also owed money to the colony and were debtors of Fidus, Honoratus ordered for the estates to be sold."
>
> (ll. 22–23) Maecianus said:
>
> "You take the loan and do not worry about the rest."
>
> (l. 23) Isidoros said:
>
> "Let him also pay back the interest!"
>
> (ll. 23–24) Maecianus said:

[88] See *P.Oxy.* III 653b (Oxyrhynchite, after 160 CE), published as a *descriptum* with only a partial transcription by Grenfell and Hunt in 1903. Crook, *Legal Advocacy* (1995) 111 briefly mentions the papyrus as "complicated and obscure." In the Appendix, I include several lines of the unpublished half of the text; a full transcription and interpretation of the document will be published by me in a separate article.

[89] All of this is revealed by my new readings of the unpublished portions of the papyrus in a separate article.

[90] The prefect will have traveled to Paraetonium by sea. This papyrus does not seem to be mentioned in studies of the Roman assize system in Egypt, cited in nn. 7 and 45.

"You are enjoying it as we speak!"

(ll. 24–26) After Isidoros stated that he had never enjoyed (the interest), Maecianus said:

"You entered into possession of his landed property. Whether or not the opponents are present, they will receive a judge who, in accordance with the decision of Honoratus, will investigate the Canopos district, so that neither the debtor nor the creditor will lose or profit from the situation."

In line with a rhetorical convention often attested in court records from Roman Egypt, Isidoros employs the first-person voice on behalf of his client and Maecianus responds to him as if Orestinus himself were speaking. After Maecianus states that he has no intention of allowing the interest to exceed the capital, Isidoros retorts with the familiar rhetorical tactic of conceding the act while reframing it with reference to mitigating circumstances—in this case, other debts owed by the defendants and an earlier judgment that the property should be auctioned off.[91] This elicits a firm reaction from Maecianus. And yet, Isidoros persists with his client's demands and continues to deny that Orestinus has collected any interest. This result is an irate reaction from the prefect:

(ll. 26–27) After Orestinus stated again that he did not have the property in his possession, Maecianus said:

"You will give it back to him whether you want to or not—and if you do not, you will not only be sentenced but also flogged. In the exceptional case that other individuals believe that money is due to them from the mortgages, they will see to it themselves."

By threatening corporal punishment, Maecianus signals the limit of what he is willing to tolerate from Isidoros and his client.[92] Despite this apparent escalation, the hearing ends in a conciliatory tone:

(ll. 28–29) After he asked whom they wished to receive as a judge and Crispinus stated "whomever you give us" Maecianus said:

"(Honoratus) the tribune, whom I deem right to summon."

[91] On the device of non-documentary objection, see n. 79.

[92] One wonders, in this context, whether the threat of corporal punishment is an expression of arbitrary power or a concrete measure warranted by Orestinus' refusal to obey the governor's orders. This is illustrated, for example, by Pliny's punishment of those who persisted in identifying themselves as Christians, see Plin. *Ep.* 10.96: *confitentes iterum ac tertio interrogavi supplicium minatus; perseverantes duci iussi. neque enim dubitabam, qualecumque esset quod faterentur, pertinaciam certe et inflexibilem obstinationem debere puniri* ("Those who confessed (to being Christian) I asked a second and a third time, threatening them with execution. Those who would not recant I had executed. Nor did I much doubt that, whatever it was that they were confessing to, their impertinence and inflexible stubbornness surely deserved to be punished"), with Corke-Webster, 'Trouble in Pontus' (2017) 381–382. It appears that Maecianus, too, adhered to a three-strikes rule in questioning Orestinus.

The pugnacious rhetoric of Isidoros identifies him as an experienced orator of high social standing. An orator named Isidoros is found in a number of hearings at assizes in the period between 128 and 146 CE.[93] It is possible that the same orator was still active in 160 CE, or (obviously) this could be a different man. An orator named Crispinus, clearly a Roman citizen, appears in a contemporary hearing at an unknown location, where he boldly instructs the prefect about the liturgical immunity of Romans and Alexandrians.[94] The name Iulius Crispinus is attested fifteen years later at an Arsinoite assize in the prefect's judicial *consilium*, which features a legionary tribune and an Alexandrian *dioiketēs* with the same Roman nomenclature.[95]

The businesslike conclusion of the proceedings conveys a sense that the animated forensic debate was conducted in a spirit of sportsmanship, with calculated provocations on the part of the advocates, who remained on favorable terms with the prefect. This performative roleplay furnishes additional evidence for the elevated status of the advocates in question. From the perspective of elite orators, who regularly pleaded at the governor's tribunal and for whom forensic activity typically went hand in hand with the pursuit of public careers, the interests of clients had to be balanced against interpersonal relations with governors, as well as a developing institutional role within the Roman judicial system, to which we now turn.

5. Elite Orators Plead Cases by Virtue of their Affiliation with Courts

Two final examples shed light on the institutional relationship between elite orators and imperial courts and its ramifications for the performativity of the legal process. The first example is a hearing before a regional procurator (*epistratēgos*) at an assize in the late third century.[96] The case involved the widow and minor children of a deceased shepherd whose flock had been seized by a local tax official (*dekaprōtos*) named Syrion, whom the widow accused of withholding receipts for grain taxes paid by her husband in order to fabricate his

[93] See n. 84.

[94] See *BGU* XI 2058 (unknown location, 164 CE) ll. 15–16: "both you and the prefects before you have granted to those immune from liturgies. . . ."

[95] See *P.Daris* 2 = *SB* XVI 12749 = *P.Strasb.* IV 179 ll. 5–6 (Arsinoite, 176–179 CE).

[96] See *P.Sakaon* 31 = *P.Thead.* 15 (Arsinoite, 280–281 CE) with Crook, *Legal Advocacy* (1995) 101–102. The case is briefly mentioned by Kelly, *Petitions and Litigation* (2011) 194 but incorrectly classified as an inheritance dispute. On the family archive of Aurelius Sakaon, whose grandmother Artemis was the widow in question, see the commentary of Parássoglou, *The Archive of Aurelius Sakaon* (1978) and the overview and family tree in Geens, 'Aurelius Sakaon' (2013).

indebtedness to the *fiscus*.[97] The widow had submitted a petition to the prefect, who instructed the *epistratēgos* to hear the case.[98]

The widow's grievances are presented by a forensic orator named Isidoros with the epithet *ἀπὸ συνηγοριῶν*, which signifies a statutory *advocatus* (*συνηγορία* = *advocatio*) attached to a specific court.[99] This reflects an administrative trend that begins to be documented in the late second century, whereby legal practitioners began to acquire institutional ties with imperial tribunals that eventually developed into a hierarchical system of salaried officials in the late empire.[100] The *συνηγορία* of Isidoros may refer to his serving as an *advocatus fisci* or as an *advocatus fori* of the *epistratēgos*. An orator with the latter affiliation is attested in another third-century case, where it is claimed that his status as an "orator of the *epistratēgos*" makes it impossible to plead against him in that court.[101] Isidoros was presumably in a similarly authoritative position, and might thus influence the handling of cases at the court of the *epistratēgos*.

The speech of Isidoros, although abridged in the judicial record, attests to his rhetorical skill, employing long hypotactic periods alongside paratactic elements for rhetorical effect ("... her children, who are minors, approach your court. They approach it on orders from the prefect... to curb the exercise of violence. This violence we have on multiple occasions placed on record..."). In summarizing the case history, Isidoros embeds the *epistratēgos* himself in the story, recounting how "being violently incensed" he gave orders for Syrion to produce other shepherds as witnesses and attributing to him the belief that Syrion is guilty ("so that in this way (Syrion) would return the sheep to the children without legal controversy"). Similarly manipulative is Isidoros' insistence that the prefect has defined the case as official violence (*βία* = *vis*), since this remained to be demonstrated, and given that the prefect's response to the widow's petition merely states that the *epistratēgos* will assess "in the most just fashion" what is "expedient for imperial revenues."[102] Syrion is not present at the hearing, where he is represented

[97] A similar context of abuse by local officials, who are accused of appropriating undocumented grain dues and confiscating flocks as compensation for supposed debts to the *fiscus*, is reported in the sixth-century archive of Dioskoros of Aphrodito: *P.Cair.Masp.* I 67021, *P.Lond.* V 1674, and *P.Lond.* V 1677 with Stern, 'Der Pagarch' (2015). Undocumented dues were apparently a notorious problem, targeted in imperial legislation stipulating the exact content of tax receipts, see Iust. *Nov.* 17.8 (535 CE). On the office of *dekaprōtos*, see Thomas, 'The introduction of dekaprōtoi' (1975).

[98] For the petition of the widow Artemis, see *P.Sakaon* 36 = *P.Ryl.* II 114 = *Sel. Pap.* II 293 (Arsinoite, ca. 280 CE). This petition is translated but not discussed in Bryen, *Violence in Roman Egypt* (2013) 251–252.

[99] For *ἀπό* signifying a former official, see *ἀπὸ στρατηγιῶν* in *PSI* III 201 (Oxyrhynchus, 327 CE) and *ἀπὸ συνηγοριῶν ταμίου* (*IG* II^2 3704, Marathon 3c. CE, l. 13, cited by Crook, *Legal Advocacy* (1995) 101 n. 179). Another possibility would be to understand *ἀπό* as signifying one of a group of *advocati* (see e.g. *CPR* I 244 (Arsinoite, 2–3c. CE) l. 2: *ἀπὸ οὐητρανῶν*) which would mean that Isidoros currently held the position of *advocatus fori*. There may have been a rotating position of primacy within a broader circle of orators affiliated with a particular court.

[100] See n. 39.

[101] See *SB* I 5676 (Hermoupolis Magna, 232 CE).

[102] See *P.Sakaon* 36 = *P.Ryl.* II 114 = *Sel. Pap.* II 293 (Arsinoite, ca. 280 CE) ll. 34–36: *πρὸς τὸ τοῖς φόροις χρήσιμον* | [- ca. 11 -] *κατὰ τὸ δικαιότατον δοκιμάσει ὁ κράτιστος* | [*ἐπιστράτηγο*]*ς*.

by a fiscal procurator (*epitropos*) who, in a supercilious tone, excuses his absence "on more urgent matters of import to the *fiscus*." Isidoros concludes with a rhetorical question: what is to be done if Syrion evades justice? The *epistratēgos* declares that he will give judgement even if Syrion fails to attend the next hearing.

That the prefect had singled out this case for adjudication by the *epistratēgos* was likely due to a number of criteria that received privileged attention from Roman provincial authorities. On the one hand, women and minors were vulnerable groups to whom the Roman state extended its protection.[103] On the other hand, the case involved charges of official corruption, a category of offenses that the Roman state energetically pursued at all levels of imperial administration.[104] The presence of a fiscal procurator on the side of the *dekaprōtos* suggests, in turn, that the fiscal administration sought to protect its agents against accusations of this sort.

The involvement of Isidoros in representing an impecunious widow and her children is most plausibly explained as a function of his affiliation with the court of the *epistratēgos*.[105] In contrast to private litigation, where advocates promoted the interests of individual litigants, the role of Isidoros seems to have been similar to that of a public prosecutor, to assist the court in pursuing what the Roman state defined as a matter of public importance. His forceful rhetoric likely facilitated the task of the *epistratēgos* of holding the *dekaprōtos* accountable for his actions—and perhaps exercised pressure on an administrator who, being confronted by a fiscal procurator, may have been slow or reluctant to act.[106]

The second example is a petition presented to the prefect at an assize in the Nile Delta in the mid-third century CE.[107] The petitioner was an elderly landowner and cultivator of imperial properties, whose status was sufficient for him to address not only a petition but also a personal letter to the prefect.[108] He complained of a violent seizure of crops by a group of named individuals on his leasehold of imperial land. After he reported this to a local official, the men allegedly took revenge by seizing his flocks and cattle as well (ll. 12–16). As in the case of the shepherd's widow, the petitioner likely gained admission to the prefect's audience by fulfilling a number of criteria prioritized by the Roman state. His advanced age

[103] On the supposed weakness of women and children and their need for special protection, see the sources collected in Evans-Grubbs, *Women and the Law* (2002) 47–55.

[104] See Dolganov, 'A strategos on trial' (2021) 366–374.

[105] It is relevant that the legal protection accorded to women and children by governors included the appointment of advocates, see Ulp. (1 *de off. procos.*) D.1.16.9.5.

[106] One may detect a dynamic whereby Isidoros exerts pressure, reminding the *epistratēgos* that the case has been handled before, instructing him about his opinion of the case and calling for immediate action.

[107] See *P.Stras.* I 5 ll. 7–19 (Hermopolis Parva, 14 August 262 CE); Crook, *Legal Advocacy* (1995) 99–100; my new edition of the papyrus in Dolganov, 'Rich vs. poor in Roman courts' (2023) no. 3.

[108] See *P.Stras.* I 5 l. 6. To compose *epistulae* to officials was a mark of high social standing, exemplified by a former gymnasiarch from Oxyrhynchus who addressed a letter to the prefect and received a hearing, see *P.Oxy.* II 237 col. vi ll. 12–15 (Oxyrhynchus, *c.*186 CE).

and status as a cultivator of imperial properties placed him in a category of individuals whose grievances received privileged consideration.[109] The crime of armed robbery ostensibly described by the petitioner was a capital offense that fell under the governor's jurisdiction.[110] If the accused men were administrative or fiscal functionaries, the case fell under the prefect's jurisdictional oversight of corruption and abuse by officials.

In court, the petitioner is assisted by an advocate named Hermon, who is revealed to be a high-ranking official from Alexandria (*archidikastēs*).[111] In an elegant speech that begins with a *captatio benevolentiae* praising the prefect for "the peace you maintain for us all" (l. 8) Hermon presents the petitioner's grievances with pathos, dramatizing his advanced age and laying emphasis on the losses his stolen harvest represents for the *fiscus*. Through Hermon's rhetorical slant, it appears as if the landowner were cultivating imperial properties altruistically, eliding any financial incentives. The petition is successful and the prefect grants the petitioner's request for local officials to be ordered to arrest the culprits and force them to restore the property.

Why was the *archidikastēs* of Alexandria tasked with presenting the petition of a landowner from a village in the Egyptian hinterland? It seems improbable that Hermon had a personal relationship with the petitioner or was in any sense hired by him as an advocate. Instead, his involvement was probably due to his connection to the governor's court. Hermon's rank indicates that he belonged to the prefect's administrative inner circle (φιλοί = *amici*), whose members are routinely attested serving as the prefect's judicial advisors and delegated judges.[112] Evidently, the prefect could also call upon his closest associates to present petitions and plead cases in his presence. One may think of various reasons for doing so: a governor who heard numerous *postulationes* in a single session may have preferred concise summaries of petitions to be delivered by trusted members of his entourage; in the public setting of Roman assizes, a governor may have relied on the rhetorical skill of his *amici* to dramatize petitions for performative effect. Either way, Hermon's participation means that the orator presenting the case had a weak connection to the litigant and strong personal ties to the court, factors that favored the legal process unfolding in a controlled manner that facilitated the

[109] The special attention given to cultivators of imperial properties is illustrated by petitions to the emperor from *coloni* of imperial estates, see e.g. *CIL* VIII 10570 = *CIL* VIII 14464 = *ILS* 06870 = *ILTun* 01237 (Africa Proconsularis, 181–182 CE) with Hauken, *Petition and Response* (1998) 2–28.

[110] See D. 43.16 and *SB* XII 10929 (133–137 CE) col. ii ll. 7–8 with Jördens, 'Eine kaiserliche Konstitution' (2011).

[111] On the office, see Calabi, 'L'ἀρχιδικαστής' (1952).

[112] On the governor's φιλοί serving as advisors and judges, see e.g. *P.Oxy*. XXXVI (Oxyrhynchus, 111 CE), *M.Chr*. 372 = *P.Catt*. (Arsinoite case collection, case dated to 115 CE) col. iv ll. 12–13 and *SB* XVI 12749 = *P.Daris* 2 = *P.Strasb*. IV 179 (Arsinoe, 176–179 CE). On the prosopography of the governor's entourage, see Kantor, '*Qui in consilio estis*' (2017) and Pittia, 'La cohorte du gouverneur Verrès' (2007).

governor's public self-fashioning and ability to orchestrate his judicial role in the context of his copiously attended tribunal.

This dynamic is strongly reminiscent of two court cases brought before the emperor Caracalla during his tour of the eastern provinces in the early third century, records of which have been fortuitously preserved in a Syrian inscription and two Egyptian papyri.[113] One hearing took place at Antioch and the other at an assize in Egypt, in both instances involving peasants from hinterland villages who were complaining of oppression by rapacious tax-officials. In each case, the villagers were represented by an advocate named L. Egnatius Victor Lollianus, known to us from other sources as one of the preeminent orators of his day, who attained an illustrious senatorial career.[114] More challenging than describing the plight of the villagers was to speak with equal persuasiveness and skill in defence of the tax collectors. In the Syrian case, this intricate task was entrusted by Caracalla to C. Sallius Aristaenetus, another supereminent orator with a dazzling imperial career.[115] The hearings convey a distinct sense of the legal process as an orchestrated performance by orators from the emperor's circle, whose rhetorical display and competitive debate served to promote their standing in the eyes of the emperor and others in his entourage, as well as to impress and entertain a large audience of spectators, including the emperor himself. At the same time, the orators participated in the enactment of judicial narratives in which the emperor was manifestly intended to appear to his best advantage as a magnanimous benefactor and protector of the humble and meek against abuses by the wealthy and powerful. Like the excoriation of Phibion the loan-shark and Syrion the corrupt tax-official, these were *par excellence* public spectacles of Roman justice.

Conclusions

In this chapter I have sought to show how, in important ways, high imperial forensic culture may be linked to the legal tradition of the Roman Republic, in which the courts were the stomping ground of the political elite, for whom the forum was synonymous with the public sphere and whose social role it was to

[113] For the Syrian inscription, see *SEG* XVII 759 (Dmeir, after May 216 CE) with Crook, *Legal Advocacy* (1995) 91–95; Stolte, 'Jurisdiction and representation of power' (2003); and Tuori, *Emperor of Law* (2016) 248–252 with references to earlier literature. For the hearing in Egypt, see *P.Mich.* IX 529 ll. 25–38 = *SB* XIV 11875 (Arsinoite, after July 237 CE) and *P.Berol.* inv. 7216 = *SB* XIV 11876 (Arsinoite, after fall 215, before April, 217 CE) with Lewis, 'The Michigan-Berlin Apokrima' (1976). My textual emendations and interpretations of these documents will be published in a separate article.

[114] On Lollianus, see Puech, *Orateurs et sophistes* (2002) no. 35 and Haensch, 'L. Egnatius Victor Lollianus' (2006).

[115] On Aristaenetus, honored as *orator maximus* at Rome, see Philostr. *VS* 2.11 and *CIL* VI 1511 = *ILS* 2934 = *AE* 2003, +182 (Rome, mid-3c.).

provide legal advocacy and advice to their clients and friends. In the age of Cicero, Roman political patronage was extending its reach beyond Rome and Italy to the provinces. At the same time, the traditional role of patronage in legal practice was giving way to a process of professionalization (involving the rise of technical training and expertise in the fields of oratory and jurisprudence) in conjunction with the growing importance of forensic activity as a sphere of elite competition and means of political advancement.[116] As I have argued, this development was likewise mirrored in the provinces. At the same time as Cicero and other upwardly mobile Roman politicians were making their names pleading high-profile cases at Rome, similarly performative forms of legal practice were being implemented at the assizes of Roman governors by a small circle of businessmen who constituted a Roman colonial elite. Under the Principate, the forms of Roman forensic culture came to be embraced by enchoric provincial elites throughout the empire as part of their broader self-integration within the imperial order.

This cultural process took place within an evolving institutional landscape, where Roman judicial administration gradually became the most important public interface between the imperial state and provincial populations. Already in the age of Cicero, the provision of justice was regarded as essential for provincial acceptance of the legitimacy of Roman rule.[117] In the high empire, the Roman assize system served a legal order of oecumenical ambition that was notionally available to the entire imperial population.[118] Legal and documentary sources show that the tribunals of Roman governors repeatedly heard the grievances of women seeking legal protection, parents complaining of insolence from their children, lowly creditors recalling loans from wealthy debtors, and rural villagers reporting abuse by tax collectors. The recurrence of such court cases in the evidence, including the examples examined here, suggests distinct patterns in the selection of cases for adjudication and in the legal narratives enacted in grand public settings in the highest courts of the empire. In this respect, it appears that the composition of the highly selective rosters of the governor's assize sessions was, to a significant extent, influenced by the ideological claims of the Roman judicial system and the need for performative communication generated by these claims. To hear the woes of the widow Artemis and her defrauded children, regardless whether these would ultimately be substantiated and result in the conviction of Syrion the tax collector, was a judicial spectacle that projected a strong public message of transgression of legal and social norms incurring just punishment from Roman provincial authorities.

Such spectacles were by definition orchestrated events, and it is relevant that the public judicial activity of governors tended to be mediated by legal practitioners

[116] See n. 4.

[117] See e.g. Cic. *QFr.* 1.7.20–22, referring to the administration of Asia as being "predominantly sustained by jurisdiction" (*sed ea tota iurisdictione maxime sustineri*).

[118] See Bryen, 'Judging empire' (2012).

from their administrative entourage, whose participation enhanced the governor's ability to stage-manage his own judicial performance. This seems already apparent at the court of Verres in Sicily, where the Syracusan *negotiator* Minucius defies expectations by refusing to participate in the orchestrated condemnation of his Sicilian client, with punitive consequences for his business affairs. In imperial Egypt, prefects touring the province were accompanied by an itinerant circle of orators and legal experts from the officeholding class of the provincial capital. Then, over the course of the Principate, as legal practice became subject to institutional regulation and integration within the imperial system of civil service through specialized career paths, elite legal practitioners acquired formal ties with imperial courts.[119] In the late empire, forensic activity became firmly established as the principal avenue into administrative careers and the beating heart of civic culture and public life throughout the empire.[120]

In contrast to the republican tradition of legal patronage, where a *patronus* defending his client brought his own person and social authority into play, the high imperial *advocati* documented in Roman Egypt generated rhetorical arguments on behalf of their clients without directly interposing their person, and on occasion while notionally inhabiting their clients' identity. Whoever Aristonikos or Palamedes may have been in sociopolitical terms (and the evidence suggests that one or both were members of the Alexandrian elite) this identity temporarily recedes from view in favor of their institutional role as forensic orators. If not for a chance remark in the heading of a judicial record, we would never know that Hermon the advocate was, in fact, Hermon the *archidikastēs* of Alexandria, who was climbing the ladder of the imperial civil service.

In general terms, the arc from the late Republic to the high empire appears to illustrate the institutional demands of the imperial judicial system asserting themselves over the traditional socially performative function of legal practice. Accordingly, alongside personal ties with litigants and the prestige of cases, Pliny the Younger emphasizes the importance of pleading cases that would set judicial precedents, taking on abandoned cases, and being appointed to cases from the provinces.[121] If the *negotiator* Minucius was deterred from assisting a Sicilian litigant who was destined to lose, elite orators in the entourage of governors in the high empire appear to have been routinely involved in pleading both sides of disputes between ordinary provincials and even appear to have welcomed the rhetorical challenge of defending the flawed or indefensible positions of their clients.[122] This intellectual distance highlights the

[119] See nn. 39 and 86. [120] See n. 9. [121] See n. 85.

[122] See e.g. Isidoros at the court of Maecianus and Aristaenetus at the court of Caracalla, discussed above. That Aristaenetus was skilfully arguing an indefensible position is a point developed by me in a separate article on the hearings before Caracalla.

professionalization that took place in the forensic sphere of the empire under the Principate, eventually culminating in the *militia officialis* of late antiquity.[123]

In the end, one might say that the public-facing nature of judicial administration in the Roman Empire and the immensely important performative function of Roman assizes in conveying imperial ideology through communicative action strongly favored a coextensive relationship between the legal profession and the administrative class.[124]

I have, here, only skimmed the surface of the ways in which the legal process in Roman courts was affected and shaped by the performative dynamics of legal practice. This remains a subject for further inquiry and discussion.

Appendix

1. Proceedings before the prefect Septimius Vegetus regarding the return of a loan[125]
P.Flor. I 61 = *M.Chr.* 80
location and date of the hearing: assize in the Arsinoite(?) nome, 8 February 85 CE
presiding official: Roman governor of Egypt (*praefectus Aegypti*) Septimius Vegetus
plaintiff: Isidoros *alias* Phibion
plaintiff's advocate: Kephalon
defendant: Achillion, son of Archias *alias* Polydeukes
defendant's advocate: Aristonikos

col. i

ἀ̣ν̣τίγραφο̣ν̣ [ἐξ ὑπομνημα]τισμῶν
ἔτους δ̄ Α̣ [ὐτοκράτο]ρ̣ο̣ς̣ Καίσαρος Δομιτιανοῦ
Σ̣ε̣β̣αστο̣ῦ̣ Γ̣ε̣ρ̣[μανικοῦ] Μ̣εχεὶρ ιδ̄
Ἰ̣σ̣ίδωρο̣ς̣ ὁ̣ κ̣α̣ὶ̣ [Φιβίων π]ρ̣ὸ̣ς Ἀχιλλε̣ίω̣ν̣α̣ Ἀρχ̣[ίοῦ τοῦ]
Ἀ̣ρ̣χίπ̣π̣ο̣υ̣ [ca. 10 πρὸ βήμ]ατ̣ο̣ς̣ ἐν τῷ̣ ca. 9.
ὑ̣πόθεσι̣ς̣ [περὶ(?) ca. 9] κ̣α̣τα̣σ̣χεῖν [ca. 9]
ε̣ἴσ̣π̣ρα[ξ]ι̣ν̣... [ca.?]... vac.
Σεπτίμιος Οὐέ[γετος κελεύσας προσα]χ̣θ̣ῆν̣α̣ι τ̣ὸ̣ν Φιβίωνα ἔ̣φη̣·
π̣αραστή̣[σας τὸν ἀντίδικον(?) φ]ά̣μενο̣ς [ὀ]φ̣ε̣ίλειν σ̣οι
διὰ σαυτο̣ῦ̣ ca. 9 [..] ca. 8 ε̣ὐ̣θέως
μαστιγω̣θ̣ῆν̣α̣ι̣. [Φι]β̣ί̣ω̣ν̣ [εἶ]π̣ε̣ν· τ̣ὸ̣ π̣ρ̣ᾶ̣[γ]μ̣α χαρίζομαι
αὐτῶι, ἵν' ἀμελῶ[ς ἔχ]ω̣.
Σεπτίμιος Ο̣ὐ̣έ̣γετος· [π]ε̣ρ̣[ὶ ποίο]υ̣ ἐ̣γκαλεῖς αὐτῶι;
Κεφάλων ῥήτωρ· τῆ̣ς̣ σῆ̣ς̣ εὐε̣ρ̣γε̣σίας δεόμενος ἐντυγ-

[123] See Jones, *The Later Roman Empire* (1964) I 101 and II 566 and n. 39 above.

[124] The concepts of communicative action and consensus-oriented communication are developed by Habermas, *Theorie des Kommunikativen Handels* (1981). For productive application of these concepts to public interactions between the Roman state and provincial populations, see Ando, *Imperial Ideology* (2000) 73–205.

[125] For my new edition of this papyrus, see Dolganov, 'Rich vs. poor in Roman courts' (2023) no. 1.

χάνει σοι τὸ πρῶτοṿ κ[α]ὶ ἀναγκαιότατον συ[γ]γνώμην
αἰτούμενος, ἐπεὶ ἐ̣π̣λ̣ανήθη περὶ τὴν ἔντευξιν· ἔ-
δει γὰρ ἀναφόριόν σο̣[ι] δοῦναι, ὡς καὶ σὺ ἠ̣θέλησας. δε̣[ό-]
μεθα οὖν μὴ μαστιγωθῆναι αὐτόν. τὸ δὲ ζή̣τημα [νῦν(?)]
ἐστι τοιοῦτο. ὁ πατὴρ τοῦ ἀντιδίκου ἐδανε̣ίσατο [παρὰ]
τοῦ πατρὸς τοῦ ἡμετέρου ἑκατὸν ἀρτάβας πυροῦ. κ[λη-]
ρονομικὸν δὲ τὸ δίκ[α]ιον. δοκῶ δὲ ὅτι οὐ τῶν χαρα[κτή-]
ρων μόνων κληρο[ν]όμους δεῖ εἶναι, ἀλλὰ καὶ τὰ ὀφ[ειλό-]
μενα ὑπὸ τῶν κληρονομηθέντων ἀποδ[ιδ]όναι.
[Ἀρ]ιστόνικος ῥήτωρ· ἀναγνώτω πῶς ὀφείλετα[ι ταῦτα.]
[Κε]φάλωνος ἀναγνόντος ἐπίσταλμα Ἀρχ̣ίου τοῦ [καὶ Πολυ-]
δεύκους ἐπὶ τοῦ ια̅ (ἔτους) θ̣εοῦ Κλαυδίου
Ἀριστόνικος· τὸν μὲν δ[ανειο]κόπον τοῦτο[ν ὡς συνήθως(?)]
ἐνθάδε καλοῦνται ο[ἱ δεδ]αν<εικότ>ες ἐκ πολλ[ῶν ἤδη χρο-]
ṿω[ν] ἄνθρωπον στα[τέον] εἰς τὰ θέατρ[α ca. 4-7]
[.]ο̣[..]ṿτα, ὁ δὲ ἡμ[έτερός ἐστι]ν ε̣ὐσχήμο̣ṿ [ca. 5-8]
[....]ων ἐν Νε[ίλου πόλει(?)..]ν τοῦ μεν̣[ca. 5-8]
[...]... π̣οτε δ̣[ca. 12] ἄ̣γραφοṿ ὀ̣φ[είλημα]
[..... γ]εγραπ̣[τ ca.11] τ̣ῶι ἐ̣π̣[ιστάλματι]
[.....]νου τ[ca. 18]. [ca. 11]

col. ii

Φιβίων· ο̣ὐκ̣ ο̣ἶδα. Σ̣επτίμιος Οὐέγετος· ὅ γε σὺ οὐ-
κ οἶδας οὐδὲ ἡμεῖ[ς] ἐ̣ρῶμεν.
Κεφάλων· τ̣ὸ̣ μὲν ἐπίσταλμα τοῦ π̣α̣τ̣ρ̣ὸ̣ς τούτου
ἐστ̣ίν· προστάτης δὲ ὢν ὁ δοῦλος ὑπέγραψεν ὅτι
μετρήσε̣ι̣, ο̣ὐ̣δ̣ὲ̣ν̣ δ̣ὲ̣ μεμέτρηκεν ἅπ̣α̣ξ̣ ἀ̣πὸ τοῦ ἐπι-
στά̣λ̣μ̣α̣τ̣ο̣ς. Σεπ̣τ̣ί̣μ̣ι̣ο̣ς Οὐέγετος· π̣ρ̣ῶ̣τον μὲν
ζητεῖται, ε̣ἰ̣ τοῦ πα̣τ̣ρ̣ὸ̣ς̣ τούτου γράμμα̣τ̣ά ἐστιν, δεύ-
τερον διὰ τ̣ί̣ ἕως σήμερον οὐκ ἀπήτη̣σ̣α̣ς̣· δ̣ύναται
γὰρ καὶ γεγραφένα̣ι̣ ἐκ̣[εῖ]ṿος καὶ μεμετ̣ρ̣ηκέναι.
Ἀριστόνικος· σ̣ὺ̣ μὲν ζητ̣[εῖ]ς ὀρθῶς ταῦτ̣α̣, ἐ̣γὼ δέ σοι τὸ
καθ̣ο̣λικὸν λέγω· ἡγημ̣ό̣ν̣ες πεν[τ]α̣ε̣τίαν ὥρισαν
περὶ τῶν πολυχρονίων· ἀλλ' οἱ δεκ̣α̣ετίαν, οὐχ ὅπου
διαλογισμοὶ καὶ ἡγεμόνες παραγενό̣μενοι. πυθο̣ῦ̣
αὐτοῦ πόσα ἔτη ὁ πατὴρ αὐτοῦ ἐπέζησεν.
Φιβίων· ἠρνήσατο οὗτος [τὴ]ν κλη[ρ]ονομίαν τοῦ πατρὸς
⟦και εγω την⟧ καὶ ἐγὼ τὴν τοῦ ἰδίου π̣α̣τρός, ἐπεὶ σιτο-
λόγοι ἦσαν καὶ ἀπητο[ῦ]ντο εἰς τὸν Κ[α]ίσαρος λόγον.
Ἀριστόνικος· εἰ οὖν καὶ ὠφείλετο εἰς τὸν Κ[α]ίσαρος λόγον,
διὰ τί οὐκ ἀπ̣ῄτει τότε̣; Σεπτίμιος Οὐέγετος·
λειμοῦ γεν[ομ]ένου πε[ι]νῶν οὐκ ἀπῄ[τ]εις τ̣ὸ̣ν̣ πυρόν,
εἰ ὠφείλετό σοι; Φιβίων· π̣α̣ρεκάλει με τέσσαρας

μνᾶς λαβεῖν. Ἀριστόνικος· ἐὰν τού̣τ̣ῳ προχωρήσῃ, ἐποίσουσιν μυρίοι χειρόγ̣ρ̣α̣φα τοῦ̣ π̣α̣τρὸς τούτου· ἐν ὀρφανείᾳ γὰρ κατε[λί]π̣η ο̣ὗ̣τος.

Σεπτίμιος Οὐέγετος τῶι Φ̣ι̣βίωνι· ἄξιος μ̣ὲ̣ν ἦς μαστιγωθῆναι, διὰ σεαυτοῦ κ̣α̣τ̣α̣σχὼν ἄ̣ν̣θ̣ρωπον εὐσχήμονα καὶ γυν[αῖ]καν· χαρίζο̣μαι δέ σε τοῖς ὄχλοις καὶ φιλαν̣θρω̣π[ότ]ερ[ό]ς̣ σ̣ο̣ι̣ ἔ̣σ̣ο̣μ̣αι. διὰ̣ τεσσ̣εράκοντα ἐτῶν ἐπι̣φέ[ρε]ι̣ς ἐ̣π̣ί̣σ̣ταλ[μ]α̣· τὸ ἥμισ[ύ] σοι τοῦ χρόν̣ο̣υ χαρίζομαι· [μ]ετὰ εἴκοσι ἔτη ἐπανελεύσῃ πρὸς ἐμέ. καὶ ἐκ[έ]λ̣ευσε τὸ χειρ[ό]γ̣ραφον χιασθῆναι.

Translation:

Copy from judicial records (*commentarii*).
Year 4 of the emperor Domitian Caesar Augustus Germanicus, Mecheir 14.
Isidoros *alias* Phibion against Achillion, son of Archias, son of Archippos, before the tribunal [in the Arsinoite nome(?)] in the…A case [concerning(?)]…to seize…exaction…

(ll. 9–11) Septimius Vegetus, [having ordered] Phibion to be brought forward, said:
"Having produced [your opponent(?)] claiming that he is indebted to you [and having seized him(?)] by your own means [you deserve to be(?)] flogged immediately."

(ll. 11–12) Phibion said:
"I concede the case to him, so that I may remain unscathed."

(l. 13) Septimius Vegetus:
"What are you prosecuting him about?"

(ll. 14–23) Kephalon, advocate:
"Needful of your beneficence, this man petitions you while first and foremost asking your forgiveness, since he was misled regarding the procedure of petitioning. For he should have submitted a written petition to you, in accordance with your wishes, so we beg you not to have him flogged. The subject of the lawsuit is as follows: the father of our opponent took a loan of 100 artabae of wheat from the father of my client. This claim is heritable, for I believe it is compulsory for heirs not only to inherit the legal personhood of testators but also to return any debts owed by them."

(l. 24) Aristonikos, advocate:
"Let him read out under what circumstances he owes these debts."
(ll. 25–34) After Kephalon read the pay order issued by Archias *alias* Polydeukes dated to the 11th year of the Divine Claudius (50–51 CE), Aristonikos (said):

"This loan-shark, as those with long-standing loans are [typically(?)] called here, is fit for amphitheater spectacles, since he…whereas my client is an eminent man [and a landowner(?)] in Nilopolis(?)…undocumented debt…was written…in the pay order…

(l. 35) Phibion:
"I do not know."

(ll. 35–36) Septimius Vegetus:
"What even you do not know we could not possibly say."

(ll. 37–40) Kephalon:
"This is a pay order from this man's father. The slave, being his administrator, signed that he would measure out the grain but did not measure it out at any point after the order was issued."

(ll. 40–43) Septimius Vegetus:
"The first point of inquiry is whether this is indeed the writing of this man's father and secondly why you have not sued for the return of the loan until now? For it is possible that he (the slave) measured out the grain and confirmed it in writing.

(ll. 44–48) Aristonikos:
"You are right to ask this, and I will give you the general policy on this issue: governors have established five years as a time-limit for filing long-standing claims, while those who have established ten years did not do so for places where governors and judicial assizes occur. Ask him: for how many years did his father survive (after issuing the pay order)?"

(ll. 49–51) Phibion:
"This man refused the inheritance of his father and I that of my own father, since both were collectors of grain taxes (*sitologoi*) and indebted to the *fiscus*."

(ll. 52–53) Aristonikos:
"Particularly if grain was owed to the *fiscus*, why did he not sue for its return back then?"

(ll. 53–55) Septimius Vegetus:
"Suffering hunger during a famine, would you not sue for the return of grain if it were owed to you?"

(ll. 55–56) Phibion:
"He invited me to take four minae."

(ll. 56–58) Aristonikos:
"If he is allowed to go this far, thousands more will bring documents issued by the father of my client, claiming that he has left them destitute."

(ll. 59–66) Septimius Vegetus to Phibion:
"You deserve to be flogged for seizing an eminent man and his wife by your own means. But I shall concede your case to the crowd and be more humane to you. You present a pay order after forty years; I concede you half that time: in twenty years, you may return to my court." And he ordered the document to be torn up.

2. Proceedings before a local official (*stratēgos*) on delegation by the governor regarding the return of a deposit[126]

P.Mil.Vogl. 1 25 col. i–col. iv l. 17
location and date of the hearing: Tebtynis, Arsinoite nome, ca. 27 December 126 CE–25 January 127 CE
presiding official: Andromachos, local official (*stratēgos*)
plaintiff: Demetrios, freedman of Herakleides
plaintiff's advocate: Ammonios
defendant: Paulinus son of Patron, landowner in the Arsinoite nome
defendant's advocate: Palamedes

col. i

ἀγαθῆι τύχηι
κερδῶν Ἑρμῆς Ἀφροδείτη
ἐπ' ἀγαθῷ
vac. (ca. 14 lines)

[126] For my new edition of this papyrus, see Dolganov, 'Rich vs. poor in Roman courts' (2023) no. 2.

[ἀ]ντίγ[ρα]φ̣[ο]ν ὑπομ̣ν̣ημ̣[α]τισμ(οῦ)

vac. (ca. 2 lines)

ἐ̣ν Τ̣ε̣βτ̣ύ̣νι Π̣ο̣λέ[μ]ω̣νος μ̣ε̣ρίδος [ca.?]

vac.

\- - - - - - - - - -

col. ii

Ἀνδρομ[ά]χου στρατηγοῦ Ἀρσι(νοΐτου) Πολ(έμωνος) μερίδ(ος) (ἔτους) ια Τῦβ[ι X]

ἐξ ἀναφορίου Φλαυίου Τιτιανοῦ τοῦ κρατίστου ἡγεμ[όνο]ς̣ Δημητρίου ἀπελευθέρου Ἡρακλείδου πρὸς Παυλεῖνο[ν] Πάτρωνος τῶν γεγυμνασιαρχηκότων. Ἀμμώνιο̣[ς] ῥήτωρ ὑπὲρ Δημητρίου· δεῖ οὗ παρ[ε]κόμισε̣ν̣ ὁ συνηγο[ρού-]μενος ἀναφορίου ἐνκλήματα δύο ὥρισεν κατὰ τοῦ ἀ[ν-]τιδίκου, ἓν μὲν περὶ πίστεως οἰκοπέδων, τὸ δ' ἕτερο̣ν̣ περὶ δραχμῶν δισχιλίων, ἃς παρέ[θ]ετο ⟦τῷ̣⟧ Γεμείνῳ̣ ἀδελφῷ τοῦ Παυλείνου. τὸ μὲν οὖν περὶ τῶν οἰκοπέδων τὸ παρὸν ὑπερτίθεται, τὰς δὲ δισχιλίας δραχμὰς τοῦ Γεμείνου τελευτήσαντος ἀξιοῖ παρὰ τοῦ Παυλείνου, φροντίζοντος τῶν ὑπ' ἐκείνου ἀπολιφθέντων, ἀπολαβεῖν. πῶς δὲ ὁ Γέμεινος ἔσχεν τὸ ἀργύριον λέγω. ὁ συνηγορούμενο[ς], οἰκιακὸς ὢν ἐ̣κείνο[υ], ἐνίοτε δὲ καὶ φροντιστής, παραθέμενος αὐτῷ τὰ[ς] δισχιλίας δραχμάς, ἐποίησεν τ[ὸ] τῆς παραθέ[σ]ε̣ω̣ς̣ γράμμα ε̣[ἰ]ς ὄνομα [φ]ί̣λο̣υ ἑ̣αυτ̣ο̣ῦ Ἀ[τρ]ή̣ο̣υ̣ς̣ τινος γραφ[ῆ]ναι. ἀ̣ξι̣[ο]ῖ οὖν, ἐπιφέρων τὰ τοῦ Γεμείνο[υ] εἰς τὸν Ἀτρῆ̣ν̣ γ[ρ]ά̣μματα, τὸ ἀργύριο̣[ν] [ἀ]πο[λα]βεῖν. ἀ̣ν̣α̣[γ]νω[σθ]έντ̣ο̣ς̣ οὗ π̣αρ[ε]κ̣όμ[ι]σε[ν] ὁ Δημήτρ[ι]ος [ἀ]ναφορίου vac. Παλαμήδης ῥήτωρ ὑπὲρ [Π]αυλε[ί]νου· [ἐ]δ̣ύν̣ετο μὲν ὁ̣ σ̣υ̣ν̣[ηγ]ορ̣ο̣ύ̣μενο̣ς τ̣ὸ̣ περὶ τ[ῶ]ν̣ δ̣ισχι̣λ̣ίων [δρ]α̣χ̣μ̣ῶ̣ν ζή[τ]ημ[α] διακρ̣ο̣ύ̣σασθαι· ο̣ὐ̣ γά[ρ] ἐ[στι]ν ἐπ[ί]τροπος [τ]ῶν [τοῦ] ἀδελφ[ο]ῦ [υἱ]ῶν. [ἵ]ν̣α δὲ ἐπιγνῶς τὴν [τ]οῦ ἀντιδίκου [κ]ακοπραγμοσύνην [ἑ]το̣ί̣μως ἔχ̣ει̣ π̣ρ̣[ὸ]ς ἀμφότερα τὰ διὰ τ[οῦ] ἀναφορίου ἐνκλήματα ἀπολογήσασθαι. ἐ̣στὶν δὲ τὸ πρῶτον ἔνκλημα ὡς αὐτὸς ὥρισεν τοιοῦτον· ἐπὶ τοῦ προστρατηγήσαντος Κλαυδίου Διονυσίου κεκρῖσθαι π̣ρ̣ὸς τ̣ὸν Π̣[αυ]λ̣εῖνον περὶ πείστεω[ς οἰ]κοπέδων ἐνκ[έ]κληκεν καὶ προσέθη[κεν] κεκρῖσθαι ἀποκατ[ασ]τῆσαι αὐτῷ τὸν Παυλεῖνον τὴν π̣ε̣ί̣στ[ιν]. νῦν δὲ τὴν περ[ὶ τ]ούτου διάκρισιν ε̣ἰ̣δὼ̣ς ὅτι καταγνωσθήσεται παραιτεῖται. [ὁ] γὰρ Παυλεῖνος διαβεβαιοῦται μηδ' ὅλως κεκρῖσθαι πρὸς αὐτὸν ἐπὶ τοῦ Διονυσίου περὶ πίστ̣ε̣ως οἰκοπέδων, ἀ̣λ̣λ̣ὰ πρὸς ἕτερα πρόσ[ωπα.] Δημήτριος· περὶ τ̣ο̣ύ̣[του ἐγὼ(?)] ν̣ῦν [οὐ λέγω. vac. (?)] Παλ̣α̣μήδης· διὰ τοῦ ἀναφορεί[ου] τὸ ἔνκλημα [ὥρισεν· εἰ μ]ὲν περὶ τούτοu μὴ βούλεται λέγειν, αὐτὸ τοῦ[τό γ]ε ἀποκρει[θῆναι μ]οὶ δ̣ε̣ῖ̣. ἆρα μ̣ὲν ἐκρίθ[η] π̣[ρ]ὸς τὸν Π̣αυλεῖνον περὶ οἰκοπέδων; ὁ στρα[τηγ]ὸς Δημητρίῳ· τί πρ[ὸς] τ̣[ὸν] Π[αυ]λεῖ[ν]ον; Δημήτρειος· πρὸς μ[ὲ]ν τὸν Παυλεῖνον ο̣ὐ̣κ ἐκρίθην περὶ τῶν οἰκοπέδων· ὡς δὲ προε[ῖ]πον, νῦν πε[ρ]ὶ τούτ[ου] οὐ λέγω. τὸ δὲ ἀργύριον ἀξιῶ ἀπολαβεῖν. Παλαμή[δης· ἤ]δη μὲ̣ν ἐν τῷ̣ [πρ]ώτῳ ὁ Δημήτριος ὡμολόγησεν παραλελογ[ί]σθαι τὸν κράτιστον

col. iii

ἡγεμ̣ό̣να, ἀλλὰ κ̣α̣[ὶ] ἐ̣ν τῷ περὶ [το]ῦ̣ ἀ̣ργυ[ρ]ίου ἔτι μᾶλλον αὐτ̣[οῦ] κ̣αταγν<ώ>ση. ἀνανκαῖον δ̣ὲ̣ [κα]ὶ περὶ τῶν προσώπων̣ [τ]οσοῦτον προειπεῖν ὅτι ὁ μ[ὲν Γέ]μ̣εινος ε̣ὐ̣σχημονέ[στ]ατος ἦν ἄνθρωπος, ὁ δὲ ἀντίδικος ἄπορός ἐστιν οὐδεμ[ία]ν ἀφορμὴν ἔξων ἀποδεῖξα[ι, ἀφ]ʼ ἧς τὸ ἀργύριον δύνατ̣[αι ἐ]σ̣χηκέναι. καὶ [τ]ὸ ὡμολογηκ̣έν̣α̣ι δὲ αὐτὸν οἰκιακὸν γεγονέναι, ἐν[ί]ο̣τε δὲ καὶ φροντιστὴν τοῦ Γεμε[ί]νο[υ] μάλιστα σ̣υ̣ν̣κ̣α̣τ̣α̣βάλλεται πρὸς τὸ παρὸν ζήτημα· ἐκ τούτου γὰρ ἐλένχεται ὀψονίου μὲν ὑπηρετῶν, ἐνδείᾳ τῶν ἀνανκαίων ὕποπτος δʼ ἐστ̣[ὶ]ν̣. μὴ ἄρα ἐν τῇ τοῦ ἡμετέρου οἰκίᾳ διατρείβων τ̣ὸ̣ χιρόγραφον ἔκλεψεν, ὅπερ, ζῶντος μὲν αὐτοῦ δυναμένου ἀκρειβέστερον διδάξαι πῶ̣ς παρέπεσεν, οὐκ ἐπήνεγκεν. ἡνίκα δὲ ἐκεῖνος ἐτελεύτησεν τὸ ἀργύριον μετέρχεται. τούτοις προστίθημ̣ι̣ τ[ὸ] πάντων μεῖζον καὶ σ̣υ̣ν̣ε̣λέγχον τ̣[ὴ]ν τοῦ Δημ̣ητ[ρ]είου [κα]κουρ̣γείαν· [φη]μὶ γὰρ αὐτ̣ὸ̣ν μ[η]δ[ὲ] τὸν Ἀτρῆν οὗ εἰς ὄνομα ε̣[ἶ]π̣ε συντε̣τ̣ά̣χθαι τὸ χειρόγ̣ραφον εἰδέναι, μη[δ]ὲ δύ̣ν̣α̣σθαι ἀ̣ποκρειθ̣ῆναι τίς ἐστι[ν] ἢ ἀπὸ π[όθεν.] Δημήτριος· [ο]ὔκ ἐστ[ιν] Ἀ̣τ̣[ρ]ῆ̣ς ἀ[λ]λ̣ὰ̣ Δ̣ε̣ῖ̣ος Ἀτρήου̣ς, φίλ[ος μου,] [εἰ]ς̣ ὃν ἐποίησα τὸ χε[ι]ρ[ό]γραφον [γ]ρ̣α̣φῆναι. vac. Π[α]λαμ[ή]δης· οὐδὲ ὁ Δ[ε]ῖος τίς ἐστ[ιν] ἐπίστατ̣αι ἢ οὔτε ὁ̣πό̣θ̣εν ἐστίν. καίτοι οὐκ ἀπαρκε̣ῖ̣ τοῦτ[ο, ἀ]λλὰ κα[ὶ] γράμμα[τ]α τ[ο]ῦ Δ̣[ε]ίου̣ [ἐ]π̣ενενκ̣ε[ῖ]ν̣ [ὀ]φείλει ὁμολ[ογ]ο̣ῦ̣ντο[ς] τούτου̣ [δοῦ]να̣ι τὸ δ̣ιὰ τοῦ χιρογ̣[ρ]ά[φο]υ [ἀ]ργύριον. Δημήτριος· κ[αὶ γρ]ά̣μ̣[μα]τα αὐτοῦ ἔχω. ὁ στρατηγός· ἀνάγνωθι τά τε το[ῦ] Γεμείνου καὶ τὰ τοῦ Δείου γράμματα. ἀναγνωσθέντος τοῦ μὲν̣ Γ̣εμ̣είν̣ου̣ χιρογράφου κεχρονισμένου εἰς τὸ ὄγδοον ἔτος Ἁδρ[ια]νοῦ Καίσαρος τοῦ κυρίου, ὧν δὲ [λέγει ὁ] Δημήτριος εἰληφέναι παρὰ τοῦ Δείου γραμμάτων κεχρονισμένων εἰς τὸ δ̣έκατον ἔτος Θῶθ τρειακάδα. ὁ στρατηγὸς Δημητρείῳ̣· διὰ τί οὐχ ἅμα [τ]ο̣ῖς τοῦ̣ [Γ]εμείνου γράμμ̣ασιν καὶ παρὰ τοῦ Δείου ἐξομολογουμένου τὴν πίστιν τὸ χιρόγραφον ε̣ἴ̣λ̣ηφας; Δημήτριος· ἐφʼ ὅσον ὁ Γέμεινος περιῆν ὑπεισχ̣ν̣εῖτο ἀποδώσε[ιν], μετὰ δὲ τελευτὴν ἐκείνο̣υ ἀ[γ]νωμονούντων τῶν ἀντι[δίκω]ν ἐδέη̣σε με καὶ γράμματ[α] τοῦ

Δείου [λ]αβεῖν. Π[αυλ]ε[ῖνο]ς̣· καὶ ἐ[κ τῶ]ν χειρογ[ράφ]ων το[ύτ]ων ἡ κακουρ[γεία συν]ελέγχετα[ι]. τοῦ μὲ̣ν γὰρ [ἀδ]ελφοῦ μου παραθέσ̣[εώς ἐ]στιν χιρόγραφον·

col. iv

ὃ δὲ λέ[γει] μετὰ τελευτὴν αὐτοῦ εἰληφέναι παρὰ τοῦ Δείου ὡ̣ς περὶ δ̣α̣νείου ἐγράφη καὶ κεχρόνισται μὲν εἰς Θῶθ τριακάδα τοῦ δεκάτ̣ου ἔτους, ὁ δὲ Γέμεινος ἐτελεύτησεν δωδεκάτῃ τοῦ Φαῶφι. δ[ύ]ναται δὲ κα̣ὶ σήμερον ὑφ' ὅτου δήποτε γραφ<έ>ν ἐξ ὀνόματος Δείου τινὸς [ἐ]νφέρεσθα̣ι· πλὴν λεγέτω πόθεν ἐστὶν Δεῖος.

Δημήτριο̣ς· ἔνπορός ἐστιν, φίλος μου, ἀπὸ νομοῦ Ἡρακλεοπολίτου.

Παυλεῖνος· π̣αραστησάτω αὐτόν. ὁ στρατηγὸς Δημητρίῳ̣· ἐν πόσαι̣ς ἡ̣μ̣έραις τὸν Δεῖον παραστήσεις; Δημήτριος· ἐν ἡμέραις δεκαπέντε. Ἀνδρόμαχος ὁ στρατηγὸς Δημητρίῳ̣· τὰ μὲν εἰρημένα ὑπεμ[νη]ματίσθη, ἀν[τ]ὶ̣ δ̣ὲ ὧν ᾐτήσω ἡμ̣ε̣ρῶν δεκαπέντε, δίδω[μ]ί σοι ὅλας τριάκοντα ἐν αἷς παρα̣σ̣τ̣ή̣[σ]ειν τὸν Δῖον, οὗ λέγεις εἶναι ὃ ἐπιφέρεις χιρόγραφον. ἐν τοσούτ[ῳ̣] δὲ αὐτὸ τὸ χιρόγραφον [ὑ]π[ο]γραφὲν ὑπό σου ὅτι ἐστὶν ἰδιόγραφον τοῦ Δίου, ὃν [λέγει]ς ἀπὸ [νομ]οῦ Ἡρακλεοπολίτου, καὶ σφρα[γι]σ̣[θὲ]ν ὑπό τέ σου καὶ τ̣οῦ Παυ[λε]ίνου μενῖ παρὰ Θέωνι ὑπη[ρ]έτ̣ῃ̣· [ὅτ]α̣ν̣ γ̣ὰρ ὁ Δεῖος παρατύχῃ, ὀ[ψόμ]εθα τί καὶ αὐτὸς περὶ τούτου λ[έγει.] καὶ ἐπέτρεψεν τῷ Θέωνι τ[ὸ ἀ]κόλουθον ποιῆσαι. vac. *ἀ̣ν̣έ̣[γνων.]*

Translation:

col. i

With good fortune, Hermes the profit-bringer and Aphrodite, for a favorable outcome.
Copy of a judicial record (*commentarius*).
In Tebtynis of the district of Polemon . . .

col. ii

(Judicial record) of Andromachos, *stratēgos* of the Arsinoite nome, district of Polemon, year 11 Tybi X.

From a petition submitted to Flavius Titianus, most illustrious prefect. (A lawsuit) of Demetrios, freedman of Herakleides, against Paulinus, son of Patron, former gymnasiarch.

(ll. 4–19) Ammonios, advocate (said) on behalf of Demetrios:
"By means of the petition brought by my client he has defined two charges against his opponent: one regarding a mortgage of some houses, the other regarding 2,000 drachmas that he deposited with Geminus, the brother of Paulinus. While the charge regarding the houses has presently been postponed, the 2,000 drachmas he asks to receive back from Paulinus, since Geminus has died and Paulinus is the one managing the property left by him. By what means Geminus came by the money I will now relate. My client, being a member of Geminus' household and occasionally employed as an estate manager, made a deposit of 2,000 drachmas and had a deed of deposit drawn up in the name of his friend, a certain Hatres. Accordingly, he presents the deed written by Geminus to Hatres and asks to receive the money back."

(ll. 20–33) After the petition brought by Demetrios was read out, Palamedes, advocate (said) on behalf of Paulinus:

"My client could have repelled the claim of the 2,000 drachmas, since he is not the guardian of his brother's children. However, just so that you learn of the evildoings of our opponent, my client is prepared to defend himself on both charges in the petition. The first charge, as this man has defined it, is as follows: he has alleged that his case against Paulinus concerning the mortgage of houses was adjudicated by the former *stratēgos* Claudius Dionysius, adding that the judgment was for Paulinus to restore him the mortgaged property. But now he begs for an investigation into this matter because he knows that he will be defeated, since Paulinus can prove that the case of the mortgage was not adjudicated against him at all, but against other persons."

(l. 33) Demetrios:
"[I am not arguing] this case right now."

(ll. 34–36) Palamedes:
"He has 'defined this charge by means of his petition'; if he does not wish to speak about it, he must at least answer me this: was the case of the houses really adjudicated against Paulinus?"

(ll. 36–37) The *stratēgos* to Demetrios:
"What is your response to Paulinus?"

(ll. 37–39) Demetrios:
"The case of the houses was not adjudicated against Paulinus. As I said earlier, I am not arguing this case right now but asking to get back the money."

(l. 39) Palamedes:
"Demetrios has confessed to deceiving the most illustrious prefect already in his first charge,

col. iii

(ll. 1–18) but you will be even more inclined to condemn him in the charge concerning the money. But first, as regards the persons involved, it is necessary to say this much: Geminus was a most eminent man (εὐσχημονέστατος), while our opponent is indigent (ἄπορος) and has no means of demonstrating where he could have gotten the money in the first place. His confession to being a 'member of Geminus' household and occasionally employed as an estate manager' is especially relevant to the present lawsuit, since through this he is revealed to be working for wages and the fact of his lacking in necessities makes him suspicious. Perhaps, while spending time in the household of my client, he *stole* the deed?—which he tellingly never brought to court while Geminus was alive and could demonstrate precisely how it was mislaid. But now that Geminus is dead he pursues the money. To this I add the gravest matter of all, which is most revealing of Demetrios' evildoing: for I declare that he never knew Hatres, in whose name he says the deed was drawn up, nor is he able to answer who he is or where he is from."

(ll. 19–20) Demetrios:
"It is not Hatres but Deios, son of Hatres, a friend of mine, in whose name I had the deed drawn up."

(ll. 21–24) Palamedes:
"Neither does he know who Deios is nor where he is from. Nor is this sufficient, since he also needs to bring a written statement by Deios confirming that it is *his* (Demetrios') money that he gave by means of the deed."

(ll. 24–25) Demetrios:
"I have his written statement as well!"

(ll. 25–33) The *stratēgos*:
"Read the documents of Geminus and Deios."
After the deed of Geminus, dated to the eighth year of Hadrian our lord (123/124 CE) and the document Demetrios [claims] to have obtained from Deios, dated to the 30th of Thoth of the tenth year (27 September 125 CE), were read out, the *stratēgos* (said) to Demetrios: "Why did you not receive the document from Deios confirming the deposit at the same time as the deed of Geminus?!"

(ll. 33–36) Demetrios:
"As long as Geminus was alive, he was able to return (the deposit), but after his death since my opponents were ignoring my claim it became necessary for me to obtain a written statement from Deios as well."

(ll. 36–38) Paulinus:
"Through these documents too his evildoing is revealed, for this is a handwritten deed of a deposit made by my brother,

col. iv

(ll. 1–5) while the document he says he obtained from Deios after my brother's death was written about a loan and dated to the thirtieth of Thoth of the tenth year (27 September 125 CE). Geminus, however, died on the twelfth of Phaophi (9 October 125 CE). Indeed, he may be presenting a document written on this very day by anyone whatsoever in the name of a certain Deios. But let him explain where this Deios comes from!"

(l. 6) Demetrios:
"He is a merchant, a friend of mine, from the Herakleopolite nome."

(l. 7) Paulinus:
"Let him produce (Deios)!"

(ll. 7–8) The *stratēgos* (said) to Demetrios:
"In how many days will you produce Deios?"

(ll. 8–9) Demetrios:
"In fifteen days."

(ll. 9–17) Andromachos the *stratēgos* (said) to Demetrios:
"The statements have been entered into the minutes. Instead of the fifteen days you have asked for, I give you a whole thirty in which to produce Deios, whose handwritten deed you claim to present. In the meantime this deed—which you will certify with your signature has been handwritten by Deios, who you claim is from the Herakleopolite nome—will be affixed with seals by you and Paulinus and remain with Theon the assistant. Whenever Deios happens to be present, we shall see what he himself has to say about it." And he instructed Theon to act accordingly. "I have read (the minutes)."

3. Proceedings before the prefect Flavius Titianus regarding the interference of a father in his daughter's marriage[127]
P.Oxy. II 237 col. vii ll. 19–29
location and date of the hearing: Alexandria, 2 June 128 CE
presiding official: Roman governor of Egypt (*praefectus Aegypti*) Flavius Titianus

[127] This text incorporates several new readings made by K. Balamoshev, published online at http://www.dionysia.wpia.uw.edu.pl/ (accessed on January 24, 2023). The reading περὶ ὧ̣ν̣ π̣[οίει ἀπ]ρ̣ε̣π̣ές (compare περ̣ι̣[.......]π̣ε̣ς̣ Balamoshev; περὶ [.......]π̣ε̣ς̣ ed. pr.) is my own.

plaintiff: Antonius, son of Apollonios
plaintiff's advocates: Isidoros the Younger and Procleianus
defendant: Sempronius, father-in-law of Antonius
defendant's advocate: Didymos

ἐξ ὑπομνη-
ματισμῶν Φλαυίου Τειτιανοῦ τοῦ ἡγεμονεύσαντος. (ἔτους) ιβ̄ θεοῦ Ἁδριανοῦ, Παῦνι η̄, ἐπὶ τοῦ ἐν τῇ ἀγορᾷ βήματος. Ἀντωνίου
τοῦ Ἀπολλωνίου προσελθόντος λέγοντός τε διὰ Ἰσιδώρου νεωτέρου ῥήτορος Σεμπρώνιον πενθερὸν ἑαυτο[ῦ] ἐκ μη[τ]ρὸς ἀφορ-
μῆς εἰς διαμάχην ἐλθ[όν]τ̣α̣ ἄκουσαν τὴν θυγατέρα ἀπεσπακέναι, νοσησάσης δὲ ἐκείνης ὑπολοίπης τὸν ἐπιστράτηγον Β̣άσσον
μετρ̣ι̣ο̣παθῶς ἀναστρ̣α̣φ̣έ̣ντα ἀποφαίνεται ὅτι οὐ δεῖ αὐτὸν κωλύεσθαι εἰ συνοικεῖν ἀλλήλοις θέλοιεν, ἀλλὰ μηδὲν ἠνυκέναι·
τὸν γὰρ Σεμπρώνιον ἀποσι̣[ω]π̣ήσαντα τοῦτο καὶ τῷ ἡγεμόνι περὶ βίας ἐντυχόντα ἐπιστολὴν παρακεκομικέναι ἵνα οἱ ἀντίδι-
κοι ἐκπεμφθῶσι· αἰτ̣ε̣ῖσθα̣ι̣ ο̣ὖ̣ν̣ ἐὰν δοκῇ μὴ ἀποζευχθῆναι γυναικὸς οἰκείως πρὸς αὐτὸν ἐχούσης. Δίδυμος ῥήτωρ ἀπεκρεί-
νατο μὴ χωρὶς λόγου τὸν Σεμπρώνιον κεκεινῆσθαι· τοῦ γὰρ Ἀντων[ί]ου προσενεγκαμένου θυγατρομειξίας ἐγκαλεῖν, μὴ ἐνεγκαν-
τος τὴν ὕβριν τῇ κατὰ τοὺς νόμους συνκεχωρημένῃ ἐξουσίᾳ κεχρῆσθαι, ἠτιᾶσθαι δ' αὐτὸν καὶ περὶ ὧ̣ν̣ π̣[οίει ἀπ]ρ̣ε̣π̣ές ἐ̣[νκ]λ̣ημάτων.
Προκ̣λ̣ηιανὸς ὑπὲρ Ἀντωνίου προσέθηκεν, ἐὰν ἀπερίλυτος ἦν ὁ γάμος, τὸν πατέρα μήτε τῆς προικὸς μηδὲ τῆς παιδὸς τῆς ἐκδεδο-
μένης ἐξουσίας ἔχειν. Τιτιανός· διαφέρει παρὰ τίνι βούλεται εἶναι ἡ γεγαμημένη. ἀνέγνων. σεσημ(είωμαι).

Translation:
From the judicial records (*commentarii*) of Flavius Titianus, former prefect. Year 12 of the deified Hadrian, Pauni 8 (2 June 128 CE), at the tribunal in the *agora.*

(ll. 20–25) Antonius, son of Apollonios, came forward and stated through his advocate Isidoros the Younger that Sempronius, his father-in-law, on instigation by the mother, came to quarrel with him and took his (Sempronius') daughter away against her will, and that, when the abandoned daughter fell ill with suffering, the *epistratēgos* Bassus conducted himself with composure and pronounced that Antonius must not be impeded if the couple wished to live together. But this was of no avail, because Sempronius, keeping quiet about this pronouncement, submitted a charge of violence to the prefect and brought back a letter summoning his opponents (to Alexandria).[128] Accordingly, Antonius asked, if it pleased the prefect, not to be unyoked from a wife who felt affection toward him.

[128] The verb ἐκπέμπω refers to the prefect's permanent tribunal at Alexandria, see e.g. *M.Chr.* 91 (Alexandria, *ca.* 157–159 CE) col. iii l. 15 and *P.Mil.Vogl.* I 27 (Arsinoite, 129 CE) col. i l. 22 and col. iii ll. 7 and 13.

(ll. 25–27) The advocate Didymos responded that it was not without reason that Sempronius was moved to take action, since Antonius had threatened to accuse him of incest and he could not bear this insult (ὕβρις = *iniuria*) and had used the power conferred on him by the laws. Sempronius further denounced Antonius for the inappropriate accusations he was making.

(ll. 28–29) Procleianus added on behalf of Antonius that, if the marriage was deemed legally intact, the father had no power over the dowry or the daughter whom he had given in marriage.

(l. 29) Titianus (said): "What matters is with whom the married woman wishes to live." "I have read and signed the record."

4. Proceedings before the prefect Volusius Maecianus regarding property mortgaged to compensate a large loan[129]

P.Oxy. III 653b
location and date of the hearing: Paraetonium, 6 December 160 CE
presiding official: Roman governor of Egypt (*praefectus Aegypti*) Volusius Maecianus
plaintiff: Iulius Voltimus, surety (ἔγγυος = *fideiussor*) of unnamed debtors
plaintiff's advocate: Crispinus
defendant: Sempronius Orestinus, a creditor to whom Voltimus has had to mortgage some of his property
defendant's advocate: Isidoros
other defendants: unnamed debtors, absent from court

1 ἐ̣ξ̣ ὑπομνημ(ατισμῶν) Λουκίου Οὐολουσίου Μαι̣[κι]α̣ν̣ο̣ῦ̣ (ἔτους) κ̣δ̄ [Ἀντω]νίνο̣υ̣ Καί[σαρο]ς τοῦ̣ [κ]υ̣ρ̣ίου Χ̣[οι]ὰκ̣ ῑ. [ε]ἰ̣σ̣ενε̣[γ]κ̣α̣μ̣έ̣ν̣ο̣υ̣ [Γα]ί̣ο̣υ Ἰουλίο̣υ Οὐ̣ο̣λ̣τίμ̣ο̣υ̣ [ἐν(?)]

2 Π̣αραιτονίῳ̣ τοῦ καὶ ὑπακούσαντος, παρ̣[ό]ν̣τος Σεμπ̣ρ̣[ωνί]ου Ὀρεστίνου [τ]οῦ Σεμπρωνίου [Τ]αραντιανοῦ, [Κ]ρ̣[ησπίνος ῥ]ή̣τ̣ωρ̣ π̣α̣ρ̣ε̣[σ]τ̣ὼ̣[ς τῷ]

3 [Οὐ]ο̣λτίμῳ̣ ε̣ἶ̣π̣εν· τῶν ἀντιδίκων̣ [τὰ ἐνεχ]υ̣ρ̣ασίων̣ [γράμματα(?) ἔγγ]υος ἐτελ̣είω̣σ̣ε̣ν κ̣αὶ̣.. [ca. 9 κολ]ω̣ν̣ε̣ί̣αν [ca. 10].. ν α̣ὐ̣τῷ̣ ἐ̣π̣ι-

4 δ̣ιδόμεν[ος] τὰ ὑ̣πάρχοντ̣α…

9 …Ἰσιδ̣ώ̣[ρου ῥή]τ̣ορος ὑπὲρ Σεμπ̣ρ̣ω̣[νίου Ὀρεστίνου ἀπο]κ̣ριναμένου

10 ἐπὶ Σεμπρωνίου Ὁνοράτου χιλιάρχ̣ο̣υ̣ ἠ̣ρῆσθαι τ̣ὸ̣ πρᾶγμα καὶ κατακεκρίσθαι τὸ̣ν̣ Ο̣ὐ̣όλτιμον…

18 …Ὀρεστίνου λ̣έ̣γοντος νομίμ̣ο[ι]ς̣ κ̣εχρῆσθαι, Μαικιανὸς εἶπεν· τ̣ὰ ν[όμιμα]

19 [χρεώσταις χωρὶς κ]έρδου[ς οὖν] φιλεῖ γε̣ίνεσθαι. λέγεταί σοι, περὶ μὲν τοῦ δα̣νίο̣υ συνέστηκε̣ν ὡς ἔκρινεν ὁ χιλία̣ρχο[ς̣..]

20 [..]…[..οἱ δὲ τόκο]ι̣ πολλῷ πλε̣ο̣νές εἰσιν ἢ τὸ δάνειον· ἀπόλαβε τὸ δάνειον καὶ ἀ̣πόδος τὰς ὑποθήκας. Ἰσίδωρος εἶπε̣ν· [..]

[....]ν ἡμ̣[ca. 6]υ̣σι ἀπ̣ηνεγκάμεθα πάντα τὰ του̣ῦτ̣ο̣υ̣ χωρία· δικαίως τοῦτο πρὸς ἡμᾶς λ̣έ̣γεται. ἐντυχόντων δέ τινω̣ν

[129] A complete transcription and new edition of this text will be published by me in a separate article.

[και λε]γόντων [καὶ τῇ] κ̣ολω̣ν̣είᾳ̣ ὀφείλ̣[ε]σθαι καὶ Φί̣δ̣ου [δ]α̣νιστὰς εἶναι, Ὀνορᾶτος ἐκέλευσεν αὐτὰ πραθῆναι. Μαικιανὸ[ς]

[εἶπε]ν· σὺ τὸ δ̣[άνειον λ]αβὲ κ̣αὶ περὶ τῶν λοιπῶν μὴ φρόντιζε. Ἰσίδωρος εἶπεν· καὶ τοὺς τόκους ἀποδότω. Μαικιανὸς εἰπεν·

[σὺ τ]ο̣ύτο̣υ̣ς καρπ[οί. Ἰ]σ̣ιδώρου λέγοντος μὴ κεκαρπῶσθαι, Μαικιανὸς εἶπεν· σὺ ἐνεβάδευσας. εἴτε οὖν πάρεισιν οἱ ἀντί-

δ̣ι̣κ̣[οι] ε̣ἴτ̣ε̣ μὴ πάρε̣ι̣σ̣ι̣, δικαστὴν λήμψονται ὃς παρακολουθῶν τῆι Ὀνοράτου κρίσει τὴν Κανωπῖτιν ἐξετάσει ἵνα̣ μ̣ήτ̣ε̣ ὁ δανιστὴ[ς]

[ἐλατ]τ̣ωθῇ μ̣ήτε ὁ χρε̣ώστης, μηδέτερος δὲ ἐν κέρδει γένηται. Ὀ̣ρεστίνου πάλιν λέγοντος μὴ εἶναι πα̣ρ' ἑ̣α̣υτῷ̣ τὰ ὑπάρχοντ[α,]

Μαικι̣ανὸς εἶπ̣εν· θέ[λ]ων καὶ μὴ θέλων ἀποκαταστήσεις αὐτῷ̣. ὅπε̣ρ ἐὰν μὴ ποιήσῃς οὐ μόνον κατακριθήσει ἀλλὰ̣ καὶ δαρήσ[ε]ι̣.̣

μόν̣[ο]ν εἴ τινες δὲ ἄλλοι ἐνόχους ἑαυτοῖς νομίζουσιν εἶναι τὰς ὑποθήκας αὐτοὶ ὄψονται. [ἐπ]ε̣ὶ̣ ἐπύθ̣ετο̣ τ̣ί̣ν̣α̣ [ἐ]β̣ο̣ύ̣λ̣[οντο δι-]

καστὴν λαβεῖν, Κρηπείνου λέγοντος ὃν ἐὰν σὺ δῷς Μαικιανὸς εἶπεν· ὁ χιλίαρχος ὃν μ̣ε̣τα̣π̣έμπειν̣ δικα̣[ιο]ῦ̣μεν.

Translation:

From the judicial records (*commentarii*) of Lucius Volusius Maecianus, year 24 of Antoninus Caesar our lord, Choiak 10 (6 December 160 CE). When Julius Voltimus as plaintiff [in] Paraetonium was called and came forward in the presence of Sempronius Orestinus, son of Sempronius Tarantianus,

(ll. 2–4) Crispinus, the advocate assisting Voltimus, said:
"As surety (*fideiussor*) of the opponents, he has executed their deeds of security, both(?) ... [to] the colony [and(?)] ... delivering to him the property ..."

(ll. 9–10) ... Isidoros the advocate answered on behalf of Sempronius Orestinus that the case had already been taken up by the tribune Sempronius Honoratus and that Voltimus was condemned ...

(ll. 18–20) ... After Orestinus stated that he was claiming his rightful due, Maecianus said: "Surely the rightful due of creditors is normally without profit. It is told to you: as far as the loan is concerned, the decision of the tribune stands firm ... but the interest is far greater than the loan. Receive the loan and give back the mortgaged property!"

(ll. 20–22) Isidoros said:
"... we obtained all of his landed estates. This is justly said against us. Then, when others petitioned saying that these people also owed money to the colony and were debtors of Fidus, Honoratus ordered for these estates to be sold."

(ll. 22–23) Maecianus said:
"You take the loan and do not worry about the rest."

(l. 23) Isidoros said:
"Let him also pay back the interest!"

(ll. 23–24) Maecianus said:
"You are enjoying it as we speak!"

(ll. 24–26) After Isidoros stated that he had never enjoyed (the interest), Maecianus said:

"You entered into possession of his landed property. Whether or not the opponents are present, they will receive a judge who, in accordance with the decision of Honoratus, will investigate the Canopos district, so that neither the debtor nor the creditor will lose or profit from the situation."

(ll. 26–27) After Orestinus stated again that he did not have the property in his possession, Maecianus said:

"You will give it back to him whether you want to or not—and if you do not, you will not only be sentenced but also flogged! In the exceptional case that other persons believe that money is due to them from the mortgages, they will see to it themselves."

(ll. 28–29) After he asked whom they wished to receive as a judge and Crispinus stated "whomever you give us" Maecianus said:

"(Honoratus) the tribune, whom I deem right to summon."

5. Proceedings before a procurator (*epistratēgos*) concerning sheep sequestered from the orphaned children of a shepherd

P.Sakaon 31 = *P.Thead.* 15

location and date of the hearing: Arsinoe, 29 August 280 CE–28 August 281 CE

presiding official: Roman procurator (*epistratēgos*) Aurelius Herakleides

plaintiff: orphaned minor children of Aurelia Artemis, wife of a deceased shepherd

plaintiff's advocate: Isidoros, a former(?) *advocatus fisci* or *advocatus fori* of the *epistratēgos*

defendant (absent): Syrion, a grain tax official (*dekaprōtos*, see *P.Sakaon* 36, 280 CE)

other: an unnamed procurator, speaking on behalf of Syrion

ἔτ[ο]υς ϛ τοῦ κῠ̣[ρίο]υ ἡμῶν Μάρκ[ο]υ Αὐρηλίο[υ Π]ρόβου Σεβα[στοῦ, ἐν τῷ Ἀρσι-]

vac. νοΐτῃ, πρὸ βήματος. vac.

Ἰσίδωρος ἀπὸ συνηγοριῶν εἶ(πεν)· Ἄρτεμις ἐντυγχάνει δύο μηνῶν χ̣[ηρουμέ]ν̣η καὶ οἱ παῖδες οἱ ἀφήλικες προσεδρεύουσίν σου τῷ δικαστηρίῳ̣. προ[σ]εδρεύουσιν δὲ ἐκ κελεύσεως τοῦ διασημοτάτο[υ] ἡγεμόνος, ἀναπέμψαντος τὸ πρᾶγμα ἐπὶ σέ, ἵνα τὴν βίαν κωλύσῃς. τὴν δὲ βίαν πολλάκις παρεθέμεθα διὰ τῶν σῶν ὑπομνημάτων. Συρίων γὰρ μετὰ θάνατον τοῦ πατρὸς τῶν παίδων ἐποφθαλμιάσας τοῖς θρέμμασιν τοῖς ὑπὸ τοῦ πατρὸς αὐτῶν καταλιφθεῖσιν, ποιμὴν γὰρ ἐτύγχανεν, ἑξήκοντα ὄντα τὸν ἀριθμὸν ἥρπασεν. καὶ σὺ ἀγανακτήσας ἐκέλευσας αὐτῷ τῷ Συρίωνι παραστῆσαι τοὺς ποιμένας μεθ' [ὧ]ν ἐποίμαινεν ὁ τῶν παίδων πατὴρ καὶ Αὐνῆν καὶ τὸν ἀδελφὸν αὐτοῦ, ἵ[ν'] οὕτως μηδεμιᾶς ἀμφισβητήσεως οὔσης ἀποκατασταθῇ τοῖς παιδίοις τὰ πρόβατα. ἀλλ' ὅρα τί διαπράττεται Συρίων· ἀντιπράττει τοῖς ὑπὸ σου̣ κελευσθει̣σιν καὶ τοῖς ὑπὸ τῆς ἡγεμονίας. καὶ διὰ τοῦτο καὶ νῦν μαρτυρόμεθα ὅπως ἤδη ποτὲ κελεύσῃς αὐτὸν ἀχθῆναι καὶ ἀποδοῦναι τοῖς παιδίοις ἃ ἥρπασεν. / ὁ ἐπίτροπος εἶ(πεν)· ἐπειδὴ Συρίων εἰς τὰ ἀναγκαιότερα τὰ τῷ ταμείῳ̣ διαφέροντα ἀπέσταλται, ὁσονουδέπω ἐπανελθὼν ἀποκριθήσεται πρὸς τὰ ἐπιφερόμενα αὐτῷ̣. Ἰσίδωρος ἀπὸ συνηγοριῶν εἶ(πεν)· ἐὰν οὖν φυγοδικήσῃ; / Αὐρήλιος Ἡρακλείδη[ς ὁ] κρά(τιστος) ἐπιστρά(τηγος) εἶ(πεν)· ἐντευχθεὶς ὅρον δώσω.

Translation:

Year 6 of Marcus Aurelius Probus Augustus, our lord, in the Arsinoite nome before the tribunal.
Isidoros, former(?) *advocatus*, said:
"Artemis, who has been widowed for two months, petitions you and her children, who are minors, approach your court. They approach it on orders from the prefect, *vir clarissimus*, who has delegated the case to you to curb the exercise of violence. This violence we have on multiple occasions placed on record in your *commentarii*. For, after the death of the children's father, Syrion cast his eye on the flocks of sheep that the father had left them (since he was a shepherd). He seized the sheep, being 60 in number, and you, being violently incensed, ordered Syrion to produce the shepherds with whom the children's father had tended the flocks—both Aunes and his brother—so that in this way (Syrion) would return the sheep to the children without legal controversy. But now what does Syrion do? He counters your orders and those of the prefect. Hence we now call upon you once again to immediately order him to be summoned and return to the children what he has seized."

The procurator said:
"Since Syrion has been sent away on more urgent matters of import to the *fiscus*, as soon as he returns he will answer the charges against him."

Isidoros, former(?) *advocatus* said:
"And if he evades summons?"
Aurelius Heraklides the *epistratēgos*, *vir egregius*, said:
"When petitioned I will give judgment."

6. Petition citing a record of proceedings before the prefect Aurelius Theodotos, concerning the violent seizure of crops from an elderly cultivator of imperial land[130]
petition: *P.Stras.* I 5 ll. 5–20 (Hermopolis Magna, 7 September, 262 CE)
record of proceedings: *P.Stras.* I 5 ll. 7–19
location and date of the hearing: Hermopolis Parva, 14 August 262 CE
presiding official: Roman governor (*praefectus Aegypti*) Aurelius Theodotos
plaintiff: an elderly landowner from the village of Alabastrine
plaintiff's advocate: Hermon, the *archidikastēs* of Alexandria
defendants (absent): Canopos, son of Anoubis; Hargothes, son of Silvanus; Peiomis and Hasies, sons of Pachymis

(hand 2) [N. N. στρατηγὸς Ἑρμο]π̣ολίτου δι' Αὐρηλίου [Κ]α̣λλιστράτου δια[δόχ]ου̣ / [Νεμ]ε̣σίνῳ̣ ὑπηρέτ[η] /

[ca. ? N. N. ἀπὸ κώμης] Ἀλαβαστρίνη[ς] ἐν̣[γεγραμμέ]νου ἀντιγράφου ἐ̣[νκελεύ]σ̣ε̣ω̣ς̣ τοῦ λ[α]μπροτ[άτου ἡ]γ̣ε̣μ̣ό̣νος Αὐρηλίου Θεοδ̣ότ[ο]υ /

ἐπιστέλλετα[ί] σ̣οι ἀγαγεῖν τ̣οὺς ἐνγεγρ̣αμμένους εἰς τὸ το
[ca. 51 ἀπ]οπληρωθῆναι. —

[(ἔτους) ι̅ Αὐτοκράτορος Καίσαρος Πουβλίου Λικιννίου Γαλλιηνοῦ Γερμα]νικοῦ Μεγίστου [Εὐσε]βοῦς Εὐτυχοῦς Σ̣ε[βαστο]ῦ̣ — [Θὼ]θ ι̅. —

[130] For my new edition of this papyrus, see Dolganov, 'Rich vs. poor in Roman courts' (2023) no. 3.

(hand 1) [N. N. στρατηγῷ Ἑρμοπολίτου διὰ Αὐρηλίου Καλλιστρ]ạ́του διαδόχου. [παρὰ N. N. γεουχοῦντος ἐν κώμῃ Ἀλαβαστρείνῃ(?) ca. ? φ]θάσας κατέφυγον ἐπὶ τὸ μέγεθος τοῦ λαμπροτάτου Θεοδότου ἡγεμόνος. ἐνέτυχον δι᾽ ὑπομνημάτων οὐ μόνον ἀλλὰ [κ]αὶ δι᾽ ἐπιστολῆς κεχρ[ο]νισμένης εἰς τὸ $\overline{θ}$ (ἔτος) // τ̣οῦ κυρίου [Γαλλιηνοῦ Σεβαστοῦ Μεσορὴ(?) ca. 14 ἔστιν τὸ ἀντίγραφον] δὲ τοῦ ὑπομνήματος· (ἔτους) $\overline{θ}$ / τοῦ κυρίου ἡμῶ[ν] Γαλλιηνοῦ Σεβαστοῦ Μεσορὴ $\overline{κα}$. ἐν Ἑρμουπόλει μεικρᾷ πρὸ βήματος. Ἕρμων ἔ̣ναρχος ἀρχιδικαστὴς ῥήτωρ εἶπεν·

[κέλευσον κληθῆναι(?) N. N. γεουχοῦντα(?) ἐν κώμῃ Ἀλαβασ]τρείνῃ τοῦ Ἑρμοπολείτου ν̣[ο]μοῦ. κληθέντος καὶ ὑπακ̣[ο]ύ̣σαντος εἶπ̣εν· ἀνάξια [τ]ῆ̣ς ὑπὸ σοῦ πᾶσιν ἡμῖν πρυτανευομένη̣ς εἰρή[ν]ης ὁ πρεσβύτης παθὼν ἐπὶ τὸ σὸν [μέγεθος καταφεύγει(?) ca. 36]α̣ι εἰς τοῦτ[ο] ἡλικίας ἥκω̣ν πέπονθεν βίαν πα[ρ]ὰ̣ πάντας τοὺς νόμου̣ς, γῆν μὲν γὰρ γεωργεῖν οὐσιακήν, ἀλλὰ καὶ ἀπὸ τῆς δ[ι]οικήσεως ἑτέραν ἐπρίατο καὶ ὁ ἀν-

[ca. 53] πολλάκις τῆς γῆς ταύτης [πο]ταμοφορήτου γενομέν[ης] ὅμως αὐτός, ἐπειδήπερ ἐκ παλαιοῦ χρόνου τὴν γεωργίαν ἐνπιστευθεὶς ἐτύνχανεν, τοὺς φόρους καταβέβλη̣κεν καὶ

[ca. 50 ταβ]ουλαρίῳ ἔσχε̣ν ἐπι̣[κοιν]ω̣νεῖν(?) παρ᾽ ἕκαστα ἐ̣πανη̣ρημένος, καὶ δὴ τού̣του ἐνστάντος τοῦ καιρο̣ῦ̣ πάλιν κατὰ τὸ ἔθος τ̣ὸ̣ ἑαυτο̣ῦ τῆς γῆς ἐπιμέλειαν πεποίηται καὶ

[ca. 53] καρπούς, ἀλ̣λ̣ὰ̣ ἔφοδον α̣ὐ̣τ̣ῷ πεποίηνται καταφρο̣νήσαντες τῆ[ς] ἡλικίας τοῦ ἀνδρὸς Κά̣νωπος Ἀνουβᾶτος καὶ Ἀργώθης Σιλβανοῦ καὶ Πειῶμις καὶ Ἀσιῆς Παχύ-

[μιος ca. 44 κατασ]τάσεις ἐνσυνλαβόμενο[ι] τοὺς καρποὺ[ς] ἥρπασα̣ν τ[ο]ὺ̣ς μέλλοντας τῷ ἱερωτάτῳ ταμείῳ· ἀπὸ τῶν καρπῶν καὶ τοὺς φόρο̣υ̣ς τελεῖσθαι καὶ τῇ ἐπιτροπῇ καὶ τῶν

[ca. 51 πά]ντα χρόνον γεωργεῖ̣ν. ἀ[λ]λὰ οὐχ ἡσυχά̣σαμεν, βιβ̣λ̣ία ἐπιδεδώκαμεν τῷ [σ]τρατηγῷ αὐτὰ ταῦτα μαρτυρόμενοι, οἱ δ[ὲ] ἐ̣δεήθησα̣ν̣ ἴ̣σ̣α ποιήσασθαι, ὥ̣σ̣τε καὶ ἡμῶν παραγ-

[γειλάντων ca. 40 ἀπολ]ο̣γησομένους πρὸ̣ς τὰ [ἀ]εὶ α̣[ἰ]ρόμενα αὐτοῖς καὶ τὴν ἁρ[π]α̣γὴν τὴν τῶν καρπῶν. οἱ δὲ μετὰ ταῦτα καὶ τὰ θρέμματα καὶ τὰ τετ̣ρ̣άπο̣δ̣α τὰ ἡμέτερα ἀφήρπα̣σ[α]ν, ὅσα εἴχομεν

[ca. 53]η τί δεῖ λ̣έ̣γ̣ε̣ι̣ν ἀνά̣σ̣τ̣ατο̣ν τ̣ὸν πρ̣[ε]σβύτην π̣ε̣π̣οίηνται̣. διὰ τοῦτο ἐπὶ σὲ καταφεύγει καὶ το̣ὺ̣ς νόμους, καὶ ὃ δεῖται τοῦτό ἐστιν· ὥστε ἐπιστεῖλαί σε τοῖς εἰρηνάρχαις

[ca. 51 τῷ] π̣ρε[σ]βύτῃ κ̣[α]ὶ τῷ ο[ὐσια]κ̣ῷ λόγῳ ἢ ε̣[ἰ] ἐπιμ̣έ̣ν̣ο̣ιε̣ν̣ ἐκεῖνοι ἀπ[ο]νοίᾳ̣ χρώμεν̣ο̣ι εἰς τὸ σὸν δικαστήριον παραπέμψαι, ὧν παρὰ τοὺς νόμους ἔπραξαν καὶ ὧν

[ca. 50 Θεό]δοτος ἔ[παρχος] Αἰγύπτ̣[ο]υ εἶπεν· [ἐ]π̣ιστ̣ελῶ τῷ στρατη[γ]ῷ κ̣α̣ὶ τοῖς ε̣ἰ̣ρηνάρχ[αι]ς, ὥστε, εἴ τι πρὸ[ς] βίαν ἐλήμφθη, το̣ῦτο ἀποκατασταθῇ τὴν ταχίστην

[ca. 50 *πρᾶ]γμα ἀναπ[έμπῃ ὁ ἐπίτρο]πος ἐπὶ τὸ ἐ[μὸν] δ[ι]κασ̣τήριον.* vac. *ὅ̣θ[ε]ν φανερά σοι ἐ̣πο[ί]ησα εἰς τὸ τὰ ἀκ̣ο̣λου̣θα πραχθῆνα̣ι κα̣ὶ ἐπιστεῖλαί σε τ̣οῖς τοῦ νομοῦ εἰρη-*

[*νάρχαις* ca. 35 *κατὰ τὸ κελευ]σθὲν τὰ δ̣[ίκαια ἀπ]ολαβεῖν. δ̣ι̣[ευ]τύχει. (ἔτους) ῑ Αὐτοκράτορος [Κ]αίσαρος Πουβλίου Λικιννίο̣[υ Γ]αλλιηνοῦ Γερμανικοῦ̣ Μ̣εγίστου Εὐσεβοῦς Ε̣ὐτυχοῦς Σεβαστοῦ*

Translation:

(ll. 1–4) (hand 2) [N. N. *stratēgos*] of the Hermopolite nome via his deputy Aurelius Kallistratos to [Nem]esinus the assistant ... of the inscribed copy of the order of the prefect Aurelius Theodotos, *vir illustris* ... [N. N.] from the village of Alabastrine. You are instructed to convey the inscribed persons for ... orders(?) to be fulfilled.
Year 10 of the emperor Caesar Publius Licinius Gallienus Germanicus Maximus Pius Felix Augustus, Thoth 10 (7 September 262 CE).

(ll. 5–7) (hand 1) ["To N. N. *stratēgos* of the Hermopolite nome] via his deputy Aurelius Kallistratos.
[From N. N. landowner in the village of Alabastrine(?) ...] I have already sought refuge with his greatness the prefect Theodotos, *vir illustris*. I petitioned him not only on record in his *commentarii* but also by means of a letter dated to year 9 of our lord [Gallienus Augustus, Mesorē(?) ... and here is the copy] of the judicial record:

(ll. 7–8) 'Year 9 of our lord Gallienus Augustus, Mesorē 21 (14 August 262 CE). In Hermopolis Parva before the tribunal. Hermon the *archidikastēs* in office, acting as advocate, said: "[Order to call forward N. N. landowner(?)] in the village of Alabastrine of the Hermopolite nome."

(ll. 8–18) After he was called and came forward, (Hermon) said:
"Having suffered things unworthy of the peace you maintain for us all, this old man [seeks refuge with(?)] your [greatness(?)] ... having reached such an advanced age he has suffered violence contrary to all the laws. For he cultivates imperial land, as well as other land that he purchased from the *fiscus*, and the ... although his harvest was often swept away by the river, he nevertheless paid the taxes because he had been entrusted with cultivation of this land for many years ... he was obliged to share with(?) the *tabularius/tabularium*, having taken this on beyond everything else. And when it was time he tended to the land as was his custom, and ... the fruits, but Canopos, son of Anoubis, Hargothes, son of Silvanus, and Peiomis and Hasies, sons of Pachymis, attacked him in contempt of his age ... taking advantage of the circumstances they carried off the fruits that were intended for the imperial *fiscus*. From the fruits ... to pay taxes both to the procurator's office and ... to cultivate [the land] throughout this time. But we did not stay silent, we submitted petitions to the *stratēgos* calling him to witness these events. But (the opponents) failed to do the same, with the consequence that even after we filed a formal accusation (*παραγγελία*) [it was not possible for us to bring them to court(?)] to account for what they have presently seized for themselves and for the robbery of the fruits. But after this they carried off our flocks and cattle as well, all that we had ... what is there to say: they ruined the old man. For this reason he seeks refuge with you and with the laws, and what he asks is this: for you to send written orders to the *eirēnarchai* ... to the old man and to the imperial estate treasury, or, if these men persist in their lunacy, to send them to your tribunal to ... of their illegal deeds and ..."

(ll. 18–19) Theodotos, prefect of Egypt, said:
"I will send written orders to the *stratēgos* and the *eirēnarchai* that, if anything has been taken through violence, it should be restored as quickly as possible... the procurator should refer the matter to my court."'

(ll. 19–20) For this reason I have reported these things to you, so that you act accordingly and send orders to the *eirēnarchai* of the nome... [for me] to receive my rightful due in accordance with the (prefect's) orders. Farewell.
Year 10 of the emperor Caesar Publius Licinius Gallienus Germanicus Maximus Pius Felix Augustus."

Bibliography

Abbott, *System of Professions* (1988) = A. Abbott, *System of Professions: An Essay on the Division of Expert Labour* (Chicago: University of Chicago Press, 1988).

Ando, *Imperial Ideology* (2000) = C. Ando, *Imperial Ideology and Provincial Loyalty in the Roman Empire* (Berkeley: University of California Press, 2000).

Arangio-Ruiz, 'Commento giuridico' (1937) = V. Arangio-Ruiz, 'Commento giuridico a P.Mil.Vogl. I 25' in A. Vogliano, ed., *Papiri della R. Università di Milano (P.Mil. Vogl. I)*, (Milano: Istituto editoriale Cisalpino, 1937) 207–213.

Bablitz, *Actors and Audience* (2007) = L. E. Bablitz, *Actors and Audience in the Roman Courtroom* (London: Routledge, 2007).

Balbo, 'Roman oratory and power' (2017) = A. Balbo, 'Roman oratory and power under the Flavians,' in F. Bessone and M. Fucecchi, eds., *The Literary Genres in the Flavian Age: Canons, Transformations, Reception* (Berlin/Boston: De Gruyter, 2017) 83–99.

Bowman and Rathbone 'Cities and Administration' (1992) = A. K. Bowman and D. Rathbone 'Cities and Administration in Roman Egypt,' *Journal of Roman Studies* 82 (1992) 107–127.

Breij, 'Incest in Roman declamation' (2009) = B. Breij, 'Incest in Roman declamation,' in L. Pernot, ed., *New Chapters in the History of Rhetoric* (Leiden: Brill, 2009) 197–214.

Brunt, 'Patronage and politics' (1980) = P. A. Brunt, 'Patronage and politics in the Verrines,' *Chiron* 10 (1980) 273–289.

Bryen, 'Judging empire' (2012) = A. Z. Bryen, 'Judging empire: courts and culture in Rome's eastern provinces,' *Law and History Review* 30 (2021) 771–811.

Bryen, *Violence in Roman Egypt* (2013) = A. Z. Bryen, *Violence in Roman Egypt: An Interpretation* (Philadelphia: University of Pennsylvania Press, 2013).

Buckland and McNair, *Roman Law and Common Law* (1952) = W. W. Buckland and A. D. McNair, *Roman Law and Common Law* (Cambridge: Cambridge University Press, 1952).

Burnand, 'The advocate as a professional' (2004) = C. Burnand, 'The advocate as a professional: the role of the *patronus* in Cicero's *pro Cluentio*,' in Powell and Patterson, *Cicero the Advocate* (2004) 277–289.

Burton, 'Proconsuls, assizes' (1975) = G. P. Burton, 'Proconsuls, assizes and the administration of justice under the empire,' *Journal of Roman Studies* 65 (1975) 92–106.

Calabi, 'L'ἀρχιδικαστής' (1952) = A. Calabi, 'L'ἀρχιδικαστής nei primi tre secoli della dominazione romana,' *Aegyptus* 32 (1952) 406–424.

Capponi, 'Spaces of justice in Roman Egypt' (2010) = L. Capponi, 'Spaces of justice in Roman Egypt,' in F. De Angelis, ed., *Spaces of Justice in the Roman world* (Leiden: Brill, 2010) 251–276.

Chapman and Schnabel, *The Trial and Crucifixion of Jesus* (2015) = D. W. Chapman and E. J. Schnabel, *The Trial and Crucifixion of Jesus: Texts and Commentary* (Tübingen: Mohr Siebeck, 2015).

Coleman, 'Fatal charades' (1990) = K. M. Coleman, 'Fatal charades: Roman executions staged as mythological enactments,' *Journal of Roman Studies* 80 (1990) 44–73.

Coles, *Reports of Proceedings* (1966) = R. A. Coles, *Reports of Proceedings in Papyri* (Brussels: Fondation égyptologique Reine Élisabeth, 1966).

Corke-Webster, 'Trouble in Pontus' (2017) = J. Corke-Webster, 'Trouble in Pontus: the Pliny-Trajan correspondence on the Christians reconsidered,' *Transactions of the American Philological Association* 147 (2017) 371–411.

Crook, *Legal Advocacy* (1995) = J. A. Crook, *Legal Advocacy in the Roman World* (Ithaca: Cornell University Press, 1995).

David, *Le patronat judiciaire* (1992) = J.-M. David, *Le patronat judiciaire au dernier siècle de la République romaine* (Paris: De Boccard, 1992).

Dionisotti, 'From Ausonius' schooldays' (1982) = A. C. Dionisotti, 'From Ausonius' schooldays? A schoolbook and its relatives,' *Journal of Roman Studies* 72 (1982) 83–125.

Dolganov, 'Reichsrecht and Volksrecht' (2019) = A. Dolganov, 'Reichsrecht and Volksrecht in theory and practice: Roman justice in the province of Egypt,' *Tyche* 34 (2019) 27–60.

Dolganov, '*Nutricula causidicorum*' (2020) = A. Dolganov, '*Nutricula causidicorum*: legal practitioners in Roman North Africa,' in K. Czajkowski and B. Eckhardt, eds., *Law in the Roman Provinces* (Oxford: Oxford University Press 2020) 358–416.

Dolganov, 'A strategos on trial' (2021) = A. Dolganov, 'A strategos on trial before the provincial governor: a new look at a petition to the Roman prefect of Egypt (P.Wisc. I 33),' *Archiv für Papyrusforschung* 67 (2001) 354–391.

Dolganov, 'Imperialism and social engineering' (2022) = A. Dolganov, 'Imperialism and social engineering: Augustan social legislation in the Gnomon of the Idios Logos,' *Klio* 104 (2022) 656–692.

Dolganov, 'Rich vs. poor in Roman courts' (2023) = A. Dolganov, 'Rich vs. poor in Roman courts: a new text and interpretation of three judicial records from Roman Egypt,' *Tyche* 37 (2023) in press.

Dolganov, *Administration of Justice* (forthcoming) = A. Dolganov, *The Administration of Justice in the Roman Empire: Sociology and Institutions* (Cambridge: Cambridge University Press, forthcoming).

Dolganov and Rebillard, 'Not a Roman trial of Christians' (2021) = A. Dolganov and É. Rebillard, 'Not a Roman trial of Christians: a reassessment of P. Mil. Vogl. VI 287,' *Journal of Late Antiquity* 14 (2021) 177–212.

Dominik, 'Tacitus and Pliny' (2007) = W. Dominik, 'Tacitus and Pliny on oratory,' in Dominik and Hall, *A Companion to Roman Rhetoric* (2007) 323–338.

Dominik and Hall, *A Companion to Roman Rhetoric* (2007) = W. Dominik and J. Hall, eds., *A Companion to Roman Rhetoric* (Oxford: Blackwell, 2007).

Ermann, 'Ius Gladii' (2001) = J. Ermann, '*Ius Gladii*—Gedanken zu seiner rechtshistorischen Entwicklung,' *Zeitschrift der Savigny-Stiftung für Rechtsgeschichte. Romanistische Abteilung* 118 (2001) 365–377.

Evans-Grubbs, *Women and the Law* (2002) = J. Evans-Grubbs, *Women and the Law in the Roman Empire: A Sourcebook on Marriage, Divorce and Widowhood* (London: Routledge, 2002).

Foti Talamanca, *Ricerche sul processo II* (1984) = G. Foti Talamanca, *Ricerche sul processo nell'Egitto greco-romano, II: L'introduzione del giudizio* (Naples: Jovene, 1984).

Foucault, *Surveiller et punir* (1975) = M. Foucault, *Surveiller et punir: naissance de la prison* (Paris: Gallimard, 1975).

Frier, *The Rise of the Roman Jurists* (1985) = B. W. Frier, *The Rise of the Roman Jurists. Studies in Cicero's* Pro Caecina (Princeton: Princeton University Press 1985).

Frier, 'Review of David' (1994) = B. W. Frier, 'Review of David, *Le patronat judiciaire* (1992),' *Classical Philology* 89 (1994) 290–293.

Geens, 'Aurelius Sakaon' (2013) = K. Geens, 'Aurelius Sakaon' TM Arch id: 206. www.trismegistos.org/archive/206.

Gildenhard, *Cicero,* Against Verres (2011) = I. Gildenhard, *Cicero,* Against Verres, *2.1.53–86: Latin Text with Introduction, Study Questions, Commentary and English Translation* (Cambridge: Open Book Publishers, 2011).

Grig, 'Torture and truth' (2002) = L. Grig, 'Torture and truth in late antique martyrology,' *Early Medieval Europe* 11 (2002) 321–136.

Habermas, *Theorie des kommunikativen Handels* (1981) = J. Habermas, *Theorie des kommunikativen Handels* (Frankfurt: Suhrkamp, 1981).

Haensch, 'Die Bearbeitungsweisen' (1994) = R. Haensch, 'Die Bearbeitungsweisen von Petitionen in der Provinz Aegyptus,' *ZPE* 100 (1994) 487–546.

Haensch, 'Zur Konventsordnung' (1997) = R. Haensch, 'Zur Konventsordnung in der Provinz Aegyptus und den übrigen Provinzen des römischen Reiches,' in B. Kramer, W. Luppe, H. Maehler, and G. Poethke, eds., *Akten des 21. Internationalen Papyrologenkongresses, Berlin, 13.–19.8.1995* (Stuttgart/Berlin: Teubner, 1997) 320–391.

Haensch, 'L. Egnatius Victor Lollianus' (2006) = R. Haensch, 'L. Egnatius Victor Lollianus,' in A. Vigourt, X. Loriot, A. Berenger-Badel, and B. Klein, eds., *Pouvoir et religion dans le monde romain, en hommage à Jean-Pierre Martin* (Paris: Presses de l'Université de Paris-Sorbonne, 2006) 289–302.

Hall, 'Roman judges' (2017) = J. Hall, 'Roman judges and their participation in the "theatre of justice",' in Papoiannou et al., *The Theatre of Justice* (2017) 243–262.

Harris, *War and Imperialism* (1979) = W. V. Harris, *War and Imperialism in Republican Rome, 327–70 B.C.* (Oxford: Clarendon Press, 1979).

Hauken, *Petition and Response* (1998) = T. Hauken, *Petition and Response: An Epigraphic Study of Petitions to Roman Emperors, 181–249* (Bergen: Norwegian Institute at Athens, 1998).

Heath, *On Issues* (1995) = M. Heath, *On Issues: Strategies of Argument in Later Greek Rhetoric* (Oxford: Oxford University Press, 1995).

Heath, *Menander* (2004) = M. Heath, *Menander: A Rhetor in Context* (Oxford: Oxford University Press, 2004).

Heath, 'Practical advocacy' (2004) = M. Heath, 'Practical advocacy in Roman Egypt,' in M. J. Edwards and C. Reid, eds., *Oratory in Action* (Manchester: Manchester University Press, 2004) 62–82.

Humfress, *Orthodoxy and the Courts* (2007) = C. Humfress, *Orthodoxy and the Courts in Late Antiquity* (Oxford: Oxford University Press, 2007).

Jones, *The Later Roman Empire* (1964) = A. H. M. Jones, *The Later Roman Empire, 284–602. A Social Economic and Administrative Survey* (Oxford: Oxford University Press, 1964).

Jones, 'Juristes romains' (2007) = C. Jones, 'Juristes romains dans l'orient grec,' *Comptes Rendus de l'Académie des Inscriptions* 151 (2007) 1331–1359.

Jördens, 'Eine kaiserliche Konstitution' (2011) = A. Jördens, "Eine kaiserliche Konstitution zu den Rechtsprechungskompetenzen der Statthalter," *Chiron* 41 (2011) 327–356.

Kantor, '*Qui in consilio estis*' (2017) = G. Kantor, '*Qui in consilio estis*: the governor and his advisers in the Early Empire,' *Istoricheskij vestnik* 19 (2017) 50–87.

Katzoff, 'Precedents' (1972) = R. Katzoff, 'Precedents in the courts of Roman Egypt,' *Zeitschrift der Savigny-Stiftung für Rechtsgeschichte. Romanistische Abteilung* 89 (1972) 256–282.

Katzoff, 'Law as katholikos' (1986) = R. Katzoff, 'Law as katholikos,' in R. S. Bagnall and W. V. Harris, eds., *Studies in Roman law in memory of A. Arthur Schiller* (Leiden: Brill, 1986) 119-126

Kelly, *Petitions* (2011) = B. Kelly, *Petitions, Litigation and Social Control in Roman Egypt.* (Oxford: Oxford University Press, 2011).

Krapinger, 'The stepmother' (2015) = G. Krapinger, 'The stepmother, the foisted poison and the changed will. Some preliminaries for pseudo-Quintilian, Decl. 2 and pseudo-Libanius, Decl. 49,' in M. Dinter, Ch. Guérin, and M. Martinho, eds., *Reading Roman Declamation. The Declamations Ascribed to Quintilian* (Berlin/Boston: De Gruyter, 2015) 237–252.

Kreuzsaler and Urbanik, 'Humanity and inhumanity of law' (2008) = C. Kreuzsaler and J. Urbanik, 'Humanity and inhumanity of law: the case of Dionysia,' *Journal of Juristic Papyrology* 38 (2008) 119–155.

Laffi, *In greco per I greci* (2013) = U. Laffi, *In greco per i Greci. Ricerche sul lessico greco del processo civile e criminale romano nelle attestazioni di fonti documentarie romane* (Pavia: Pavia University Press, 2013).

Lehne-Gstreinthaler, Iurisperiti et oratores (2019) = C. Lehne-Gstreinthaler, Iurisperiti et oratores. *Eine Studie zu den römischen Juristen der Republik* (Vienna, Cologne, Weimar: Böhlau Verlag, 2019).

Lendon, *That Tyrant, Persuasion* (2022) = J. E. Lendon, *That Tyrant, Persuasion: How Rhetoric Shaped the Roman World* (Princeton: Princeton University Press, 2022).

Lewis, 'The Michigan-Berlin Apokrima' (1976) = N. Lewis, 'The Michigan-Berlin Apokrima,' *Chronique d'Égypte* 51 (1976) 320–330.

Lewis, *Life in Egypt* (1983) = N. Lewis, *Life in Egypt under Roman Rule* (Oxford: Clarendon Press, 1983).

Liebs, *Vor den Richtern Roms* (2007) = D. Liebs, *Vor den Richtern Roms: berühmte Prozesse der Antike* (Munich: Beck, 2007).

Lintott, 'Legal procedure' (2004) = A. W. Lintott, 'Legal procedure in Cicero's time,' in Powell and Patterson, *Cicero the Advocate* (2004) 61–78.

Mascellari, 'La descrizione di atti criminosi' = R. Mascellari, 'La descrizione di atti criminosi e violazioni nei papiri: ὕβρις, αἰκία, πληγαί, βία,' in R. Haensch, ed., *Recht haben und Recht bekommen im Imperium Romanum. Das Gerichtswesen der Römischen Kaiserzeit und seine dokumentarische Evidenz* (Warsaw: University of Warsaw Press, 2016) 483–522.

Mitteis, 'Ägyptischer Schuldprozess' (1906) = L. Mitteis, 'Ägyptischer Schuldprozess v. J. 84/86 p. Chr,' *Zeitschrift der Savigny-Stiftung für Rechtsgeschichte. Romanistische Abteilung* 27 (1906) 220–228.

Morrell, *Pompey, Cato* (2017) = K. Morrell, *Pompey, Cato and the Governance of the Roman Empire* (Oxford: Oxford University Press, 2017).

Neuhauser, *Patronus und Orator* (1958) = W. Neuhauser, *Patronus und Orator: Eine Geschichte der Begriffe von ihren Anfängen bis in die augusteische Zeit* (Innsbruck: Wagner, 1958).

Palme, 'Roman litigation' (2014) = B. Palme, 'Roman litigation—reports of court proceedings,' in J. G. Keenan, J. G. Manning, and U. Yiftach-Firanko, eds., *Law and Society in Egypt from Alexander to the Arab Conquest* (Cambridge: Cambridge University Press, 2014) 482–502.

Papaioannou et al., *The Theatre of Justice* (2017) = S. Papaioannou, A. Serafim, and B. de Vela, eds., *The Theatre of Justice: Aspects of Performance in Greco-Roman Oratory and Rhetoric* (Leiden/Boston: Brill, 2017).

Parássoglou, *The Archive of Aurelius Sakaon* (1978) = G. M. Parássoglou, *The Archive of Aurelius Sakaon. Papers of an Egyptian Farmer in the Last Century of Theadelpheia (P.Sakaon)* (Bonn: Habelt, 1978).

Peachin, 'Attacken und Erniedrigungen' (2007) = M. Peachin, 'Attacken und Erniedrigungen als alltägliche Elemente der kaiserzeitlichen Regierungspraxis,' in R. Haensch and J. Heinrichs, eds., *Herrschen und Verwalten: der Alltag der römischen Administration in der Hohen Kaiserzeit* (Cologne/Vienna: Böhlau Verlag, 2007) 117–125.

Pfeiffer, 'The imperial cult in Egypt' (2012) = S. Pfeiffer, 'The imperial cult in Egypt,' in C. Riggs, ed., *The Oxford Handbook of Roman Egypt* (Oxford: Oxford University Press, 2012) 83–100.

Pflaum, *Les procurateurs* (1950) = H.-G. Pflaum, *Les procurateurs équestres sous le Haut-Empire romain* (Paris: Maisonneuve, 1950).

Pittia, 'La cohorte du gouverneur Verrès' (2007) = S. Pittia, 'La cohorte du gouverneur Verrès,' in J. Dubouloz and S. Pittia, eds., *La Sicile de Cicéron: Lectures des Verrines* (Besançon: Presses universitaires de Franche-Comté, 2007) 57–87.

Platschek, 'Nochmals zur Petition der Dionysia' (2015) = J. Platschek, 'Nochmals zur Petition der Dionysia (P.Oxy. II 237),' *Journal of Juristic Papyrology* 45 (2015) 145–163.

Powell and Patterson, *Cicero the Advocate* (2004) = J. G. F. Powell and J. Patterson, eds., *Cicero the Advocate* (Oxford: Oxford University Press, 2004).

Prag, 'Provincials, patrons' (2013) = J. R. W. Prag, 'Provincials, patrons, and the rhetoric of repetundae,' in Steel and van der Blom, eds., *Community and Communication* (2013) 267–283.

Puech, *Orateurs et sophistes* (2002) = B. Puech *Orateurs et sophistes grecs dans les inscriptions d'époche impériale* (Paris: Vrin, 2002).

Purpura, '*Katholikon diatagma*' (1982) = G. Purpura, '*Katholikon diatagma*. Sulla denominazione dell'editto provinciale egizio,' in *Studi in onore di Arnaldo Biscardi* vol. 2 (Milano: Istituto editoriale Cisalpino, 1982) 507–522.

de Ruggiero, *Dizionario epigrafico* (1895) = E. de Ruggiero, *Dizionario epigrafico di antichità romane* (Rome: Pasqualucci, 1895).

Rutledge, 'Oratory and politics in the empire' (2007) = S. H. Rutledge, 'Oratory and politics in the empire,' in Dominik and Hall, eds., *A Companion to Roman Rhetoric* (2007) 109–121.

Schmidt, 'Einfluss der Rhetorik' (1950) = H. Schmidt, 'Einfluss der Rhetorik auf die Gestaltung der richterlichen Entscheidungen in den Papyri,' *Journal of Juristic Papyrology* 4 (1950) 165–177.

Schmitz, 'Professionals of *paideia*?' (2017) = T. A. Schmitz, 'Professionals of *paideia*?: the sophists as performers,' in D. S. Richter and W. A. Johnston, eds., *The Oxford Handbook of the Second Sophistic* (New York: Oxford University Press, 2017) 169–180.

Schwameis, *Cicero, De praetura Siciliensi* (2019) = C. Schwameis, *Cicero, De praetura Siciliensi (Verr. 2,2). Einleitung und Kommentar* (Berlin: De Gruyter, 2019).

Shaw, 'Judicial nightmares' (2003) = B. D. Shaw, 'Judicial nightmares and Christian Memory,' *Journal of Early Christian Studies* 11 (2003) 533–563.

Smolders, 'Patron's descendants' (2005) = R. Smolders, 'Patron's descendants,' TM Arch id: 66. www.trismegistos.org/archive/66

Steel, 'Being economical with the truth' (2004) = C. Steel, 'Being economical with the truth: what really happened at Lampsacus?' in Powell and Patterson, eds., *Cicero the Advocate* (2004) 234–252.

Steel and van der Blom, *Community and Communication* (2013) = C. Steel and H. van der Blom, eds., *Community and Communication: Oratory and Politics in Republican Rome* (Oxford: Oxford University Press, 2004).

Stern, 'Der Pagarch' (2015) = M. Stern, 'Der Pagarch und die Organisation des öffentlichen Sicherheitswesens im byzantinischen Ägypten,' *Tyche* 30 (2015) 119–144.

Stolte 'Jurisdiction and representation of power' (2003) = B. Stolte, 'Jurisdiction and representation of power, or, the emperor on circuit,' in L. de Blois, P. Erdkamp, and O. Hekster, eds., *Representation and Perception of Roman Imperial Power. Proceedings of the Third Workshop of the International Network Impact of Empire (Roman Empire, c. 200 B.C.–A.D. 476)* (Amsterdam: Gieben, 2003) 261–268.

Stone, 'Gaius Verres troubleshooter' (2018) = M. Stone, 'Gaius Verres troubleshooter,' in H. van der Blom, G. Gray, and C. Steel, eds., *Institutions and Ideology in Republican Rome: Speech, Audience and Decision* (Cambridge, Cambridge University Press, 2018) 299–313.

Tempest, 'Oratorical performance' (2017) = K. Tempest, 'Oratorical performance in Pliny's *Letters*,' in Papaioannou et al., eds., *The Theatre of Justice* (2017) 175–197.

Thomas, 'The introduction of dekaprotoi' (1975) = J. D. Thomas, 'The introduction of dekaprotoi and comarchs into Egypt in the third century A.D.,' *Zeitschrift für Papyrologie und Epigraphik* 19 (1975) 111–119.

Treggiari, *Roman Marriage* (1991) = S. Treggiari, *Roman Marriage:* Iusti Coniuges *from the Time of Cicero to the Time of Ulpian* (Oxford: Oxford University Press, 1991).

Tuori, *Emperor of Law* (2016) = K. Tuori, *Emperor of Law. The Emergence of Roman Imperial Adjudication* (Oxford: Oxford University Press, 2016).

Webley, 'The sociology of legal professions' (2020) = L. Webley, 'The sociology of legal professions' in J. Přibáň, ed., *Research Handbook on the Sociology of Law* (Cheltenham: Edward Elgar Publishing, 2020) 215–229.

Wilcken, 'Zu den Florentiner und den Leipziger Papyri' (1907) = U. Wilcken, 'Zu den Florentiner und den Leipziger Papyri,' *Archiv für Papyrusforschung* 4 (1907) 423–486.

Winterbottom, 'Perorations' (2004) = M. Winterbottom, 'Perorations,' in Powell and Patterson, eds., *Cicero the Advocate* (2004) 215–232.

Medicine as Competitive Performance

Eristic and Erudition—Galen on Erasistratus and the Arteries

Luis Alejandro Salas

This chapter explores the place of polemical anecdote in the narrative of Galen's *Anatomical Procedures*. It examines Galen's use of tropes from other—more traditionally "literary"—genres of Greek writing, such as classical oratory and New Comedy, in an effort to illustrate important points of discontinuity between Galen's writing on technical subjects and contemporary expectations of technical writing, broadly construed. It argues that Galen's references to the Greek literary past in these contexts should be understood as part of a strategy of polemical engagement with rivals, characteristic of a second-century Greek intellectual (*pepaideumenos*).

Anatomical Procedures is a treatise on anatomical performance—not simply an anatomical handbook. The social and professional consequences of these live performances could be significant in Rome of the second century. Galen writes, for example, that in 157 CE a public demonstration of his surgical skill—and a display of his rivals' incompetence—gained him the post of gladiatorial physician in Pergamum.[1] After his arrival at Rome in 163 CE, a public demonstration on the function of the recurrent laryngeal nerve drew him and his work to the attention of the upper echelons of Roman society, including Marcus Aurelius.[2] Later in his life Galen would become a physician in the imperial court. In Book 7 of *Anatomical Procedures*, Galen turns to the question of arterial content and function. The book culminates in an experiment on the femoral artery of a living animal.[3] The account is a longer version of a demonstration that Galen reports in *Whether Blood Is Naturally Contained in the Arteries*, from which it differs in a few significant respects.[4] In *Anatomical Procedures*, Galen reports the experiment

This chapter appears, in slightly expanded form, as Salas, *Cutting Words* (2020) 169–195.

[1] See *Opt.Med.Cogn.* 9.6–7 (*CMG Suppl.Or.* IV 105.4–15).

[2] See *Praen.* 2 (XIV.612–613K = *CMG* V 8,1 80.25–82.7) and 5 (XIV.627–630K = *CMG* V 8,1 96.5–100.6).

[3] *AA* 7.1 (II.589–590K = 620–622 G).

[4] *AA* 7.16 (II.645–648K = 698–704 G) and *Art.Sang.* 8 (IV.733–734K = 178–180 F-W), respectively.

Luis Alejandro Salas, *Medicine as Competitive Performance: Eristic and Erudition—Galen on Erasistratus and the Arteries* In: *Medicine and the Law under the Roman Empire.* Edited by: Claire Bubb and Michael Peachin, Oxford University Press.
 DOI: 10.1093/oso/9780192898616.003.0004

as evidence in support of a feature of arterial function fundamental to his system of physiology. However, he also deploys it against Erasistratus (third century BCE) and second-century Erasistrateans for their view that the arteries are passageways for a substance called "pneuma" and normally contain no blood. This question was highly contested among Galen, his Erasistratean contemporaries, and Erasistratus' accounts from which they drew authority. Galen offers the demonstration and four brief but vivid anecdotes to illustrate the theoretical and technical failings of contemporary Erasistrateans and, by extension, to underwrite his medical authority.

The pattern of criticism that Galen lays out for the reader in the four vignettes is consistent: contemporary Erasistrateans make claims that contradict observational results because they are anatomically ignorant; they do not perform the experiments whose results they claim to know; and, finally, they attempt to deceive lay people with their fraudulent claims in order to conceal their ignorance. Galen's charge of deception against rival theorists, especially contemporaries at Rome, is a recurring theme in his work. The accusation binds his opponents' theoretical positions to their alleged ethical failures. The added moral overtones of his criticisms thereby allow Galen to position his targets as exempla for the reader to avoid. A spirited example of this phenomenon is found in *On the Natural Faculties*:[5]

> *ταῦτ' οὖν ἅπαντα συνιδὼν ὁ Ἐρασίστρατος ἀποριῶν μεστὰ καὶ μίαν μόνην δόξαν εὔπορον εὑρὼν ἐν ἅπασι τὴν τῆς ὁλκῆς, οὔτ' ἀπορεῖσθαι βουλόμενος οὔτε τὴν [πρὸς] Ἱπποκράτους ἐθέλων λέγειν ἄμεινον ὑπέλαβε σιωπητέον εἶναι περὶ τοῦ τρόπου τῆς διακρίσεως. ἀλλ' εἰ κἀκεῖνος ἐσίγησεν, ἡμεῖς οὐ σιωπήσομεν· ἴσμεν γάρ, ὡς οὐκ ἐνδέχεται παρελθόντα τὴν Ἱπποκράτειον δόξαν, εἶθ' ἕτερόν τι περὶ νεφρῶν ἐνεργείας εἰπόντα μὴ οὐ καταγέλαστον εἶναι παντάπασι. διὰ τοῦτ' Ἐρασίστρατος μὲν ἐσιώπησεν, Ἀσκληπιάδης δ' ἐψεύσατο παραπλησίως οἰκέταις λάλοις μὲν τὰ πρόσθεν τοῦ βίου καὶ πολλὰ πολλάκις ἐγκλήματα διαλυσαμένοις ὑπὸ περιττῆς πανουργίας, ἐπ' αὐτοφώρῳ δέ ποτε κατειλημμένοις, εἶτ' οὐδὲν ἐξευρίσκουσι σόφισμα κἄπειτ' ἐνταῦθα τοῦ μὲν αἰδημονεστέρου σιωπῶντος, οἷον ἀποπληξίᾳ τινὶ κατειλημμένου, τοῦ δ' ἀναισχυντοτέρου κρύπτοντος μὲν ἔθ' ὑπὸ μάλης τὸ ζητούμενον, ἐξομνυμένου δὲ καὶ μηδ' ἑωρακέναι πώποτε φάσκοντος... οὗτοι μὲν οὖν τοῖς ἐπ' αὐτοφώρῳ κατειλημμένοις οἰκέταις ὁμοίως ἐκπλαγέντες ὁ μὲν ἐσιώπησεν, ὁ δ' ἀναισχύντως ψεύδεται.*
>
> So since Erasistratus understood all of these beliefs were full of problems and he found that belief in a faculty of attraction was the only solution to all of them, but neither wanted to face these difficulties nor was willing to say that Hippocrates' belief was better, he figured that he had to keep quiet about the way in which the separation [of urine happened]. But even if *he* stayed quiet, I will not! For I know

[5] *Nat.Fac.* 1.16 (II.66–67K = *SM* 149–150).

> that it is impossible to ignore the Hippocratic view and claim something else about kidney function without being utterly ridiculous. And it is for this reason that Erasistratus kept quiet and Asclepiades lied, like slaves who earlier in life talked non-stop and often dodged many accusations through their excessive fraudulence but when caught in the act find no alibi. Then while the more modest one keeps quiet, as though he has been gripped by paralysis, the more shameless one still hides what one is looking for in his armpit, swearing and saying over and over that he has never even seen it.... And so, these two panic like slaves caught in the act, the one keeps quiet and the other lies shamelessly.

It is a cornerstone of Galen's physiological theory that organs possess basic capacities that are responsible for their self-maintenance (e.g., the capacity selectively to attract materials suitable for their sustenance, to retain this material, and then expel other materials). There is no evidence for such a view in the Hippocratic Corpus, although features of Galen's systematic theory of natural capacities have Aristotelian antecedents. Galen's attribution of his own view to Hippocrates allows him to assume the mantle of Hippocratic authority, which has the ancillary benefit of undermining his rivals' views with its ancient pedigree.[6] To the extent that Galen can retroject his view onto Hippocrates, he is able to demand that Erasistratus respond to a theory that post-dated him by over four centuries and to find ethical fault in him for not doing so. The terms in which Galen frames his accusations against Erasistratus position him as Hippocrates' moral and social inferior and, by extension, Galen's. Galen extends the comparison to Erasistrateans of his own day, who not only inherit the moral failure and social subordination of their intellectual forbearer but also add to it:[7]

> *τῶν δὲ νεωτέρων ὅσοι τοῖς τούτων ὀνόμασιν ἑαυτοὺς ἐσέμνυναν Ἐρασιστρατείους τε καὶ Ἀσκληπιαδείους ἐπονομάσαντες, ὁμοίως τοῖς ὑπὸ τοῦ βελτίστου Μενάνδρου κατὰ τὰς κωμῳδίας εἰσαγομένοις οἰκέταις, Δάοις τέ τισι καὶ Γέταις, οὐδὲν ἡγουμένοις σφίσι πεπρᾶχθαι γενναῖον, εἰ μὴ τρὶς ἐξαπατήσειαν τὸν δεσπότην, οὕτω καὶ αὐτοὶ κατὰ πολλὴν σχολὴν ἀναίσχυντα σοφίσματα συνέθεσαν, οἱ μέν, ἵνα μηδ' ὅλως ἐξελεγχθείη ποτ' Ἀσκληπιάδης ψευδόμενος, οἱ δ', ἵνα κακῶς εἴπωσιν, ἃ καλῶς ἐσιώπησεν Ἐρασίστρατος.*
>
> And the moderns, however many puff themselves up with the names of these men, calling themselves "Erasistrateans" and "Asclepiadeans," are like the Daoi and the Getae, the slaves introduced by the most excellent Menander into his comedies, who thought that they had done nothing good unless they had swindled their master three times. So also these [moderns] at great leisure cobble together shameless frauds, some [the Asclepiadeans] in order that Asclepiades

[6] For more on Galen's deployment of Hippocrates, see Bubb, this volume.
[7] *Nat.Fac.* 1.17 (II.67–68K = *SM* 150.10–20).

> may never be refuted when he lies and the others [the Erasistrateans] in order that they may do badly in asserting what Erasistratus did well in keeping quiet.

Daoi and Getae were stock slave characters in Menandrean comedy. In what remains of Menander's work, these characters are frequently incompetent and inveterate schemers.[8] And, while Galen may be making a more specific association between the two characters and his rivals, it appears more likely that he is gesturing toward slaves in comedy as a generic social type. In either case, Galen's comparison does double duty. It reinforces the identification of his rivals with a socially subaltern group, marked by a lack of *paideia* as much as of moral character. Simultaneously, it puts Galen's status as a *pepaideumenos* on display in a learned reference to the Greek literary past, a rhetorical maneuver that has the added benefit of drawing the reader who understands his allusion into Galen's circle of *pepaideumenoi*, framed as both culturally elite and morally upright.[9] It is of course difficult to tell how closely Galen intended to draw the analogy between these rivals and Menander's stock characters. However, it is worth observing that amidst accusations of Erasistratean and Asclepiadean bluster, ignorance, and stupidity, Galen implies that their attempts at fraud will prove unsuccessful much in the way that the comic plot progresses in Menander's work.

Galen frequently argues that he is compelled to condemn his rivals in order to right their intellectual and moral wrongs. For the frauds of Erasistrateans and Asclepiadeans to fail, someone, perhaps Galen, has to catch them out. Galen thus places himself squarely in a satirical tradition, in which a lone figure is forced to stand against a degenerate present as a champion of an earlier age.[10] He invokes this rhetoric of didactic compulsion to great effect in the close of Book 7 of *Anatomical Procedures*. There are four elements in this narrative on which I would like to focus.[11] First, anatomical training and blind adherence to theoretical commitments. Second, ridicule. Third, a dichotomy between antiquity and modernity. Finally, training and the character to pursue it.

[8] According to MacCary, 'Menander's Slaves' (1969) 285–286 unsuccessful or pointless scheming is characteristic of Daoi in Menander's extant work. The association is not so clear-cut, however. For some examples of this behavior, see, e.g., Men. *Epit.* 218–375; *Per.* 1–16; *Pk.* 267–396.

[9] See Rosen, 'Galen on Poetic Testimony' (2013) 188 on Galen's use of poetry as an invocation of cultural authority in the context of his technical writing. For the similarities between Galen's patterns of reference to Greek comedy and that of self-identified sophistical authors of the second century CE, see Coker, 'Galen and the Language of Old Comedy' (2019), especially 84–85. Cf. Rosen's 'Galen, Satire and the Compulsion to Instruct' (2010) 329 discussion of the function of this Galenic trope as a *captatio benevolentiae*.

[10] See Rosen, 'Galen, Satire and the Compulsion to Instruct' (2010) 326–327. Rosen (331) argues that Galen's stance in these passages, especially his rhetoric of compulsion, should be understood against the backdrop of Greco-Roman satirical authors from Juvenal, through Hellenistic authors, Old Comedy, Hipponax, ultimately stretching back to Archilochus. While he is cautious not to assert that Juvenal and the Roman satirical tradition were direct influences on Galen's writing, he (339–340) raises the possibility as a plausible one.

[11] *AA* 7.10 (II.620–621K = 664–668 G).

Maryllus the Mime-Writer and the Value of Anatomical Experience

Shortly after a discussion of the coronary arteries, Galen segues to an explanation of how to conduct demonstrations on the respiratory organs of living animals. One need not be overly anxious about keeping alive an animal whose heart has been exposed, Galen writes. He offers a case history as an explanation of his claim: the slave of a mime-writer named Maryllus suffered an injury while wrestling at the palaestra.[12] About four months later his chest began to suppurate. A physician was called to treat the injury but ultimately failed to do so successfully. Consequently, Maryllus summoned a crowd of physicians that included Galen for a group consultation. While all of the gathered physicians agreed that the suppurating bone should be removed, Galen writes that none of the others could bring themselves to do so from fear of accidentally perforating the thoracic cavity and killing the patient:[13]

> *οὐδεὶς ἐκκόπτειν ἐτόλμα τὸ πεπονθὸς ὀστοῦν· ᾤοντο γὰρ, ἐξ ἀνάγκης ἐπ' αὐτῷ σύντρησιν ἔσεσθαι τοῦ θώρακος. ἐγὼ δ' ἐκκόψειν μὲν ἔφην αὐτὸ χωρὶς τοῦ τὴν καλουμένην ἰδίως ὑπὸ τῶν ἰατρῶν σύντρησιν ἐργάσασθαι· περὶ μέντοι τῆς παντελοῦς ἰάσεως οὐδὲν ἐπηγγελλόμην, ἀδήλου ὄντος, εἰ πέπονθε καὶ μέχρι πόσου πέπονθε τῶν ὑποκειμένων τι τῷ στέρνῳ.*
>
> None of them dared to excise the affected bone; for they supposed that a perforation of the thorax at the spot of the bone would be inevitable. But I said that I would excise it, without causing a perforation, as it is technically called by physicians. However, I promised nothing regarding his complete recovery, since it was unclear if anything situated underneath the sternum was affected and, if so, how much it was affected.

It is important to note Galen's language of promise and prognosis. The other physicians mistakenly believe that it is impossible to excise the bone safely; it is simply impossible *for them*. It is indeed possible to excise the bone safely, as Galen goes on to show; the excision merely requires a high degree of technical skill. In part, the episode is an advertisement of Galen's surgical acumen. While his colleagues fail to understand the limits of the profession, Galen is educated enough to know that the procedure is medically possible, skilled enough to perform it, and sufficiently experienced to realize what he cannot promise or predict. In the remainder of the episode, Galen reports details that affect both his prognosis and his confidence in it. At first, he finds that the affected area had not spread beyond the sternum. Consequently, he grows more sanguine over the

[12] The case history runs through *AA* 7.13 (II.632–634K = 680–684 G).
[13] *AA* 7.13 (II.632–633K = 682 G).

possibility of the patient's recovery. After he safely excises the bone and exposes the heart, he finds that the pericardium in that area had decayed or putrefied (*ἐσέσηπτο*).[14] In the end, Galen has very little hope that the patient will survive. The patient does survive of course, which Galen writes, "would not have happened if no one had dared to excise the affected bone. And no one *would have dared* without previous training in anatomical procedures."[15] Had they dared, the consequences would have been equally dire, as Galen illustrates in the short case history that follows. Another physician recognizes the need for surgical intervention in a septic arm, but he lacks the proper anatomical training. This one severs an artery. Then he panics when the artery hemorrhages. Finally, he manages to get the bleeding under control, only to kill the patient during recovery. The moral of these two histories, according to Galen, is that proper anatomical training, as exemplified in *Anatomical Procedures*, is necessary for the practicing physician and useful even to the educated reader.[16] Galen's digression on his successful treatment of Maryllus' slave sets the stage for a series of cardio-arterial experiments, in which he serially refutes his rivals and reveals them as charlatans. Galen says explicitly that one of the aims of vivisectory experiments on the heart is to expose rival theorists as liars (*ὡς ἂν ψευδομένους δείξωμεν*); and, as we will see, this aim comes to dominate the remainder of Galen's narrative in Book 7.[17]

Compulsion of the Truth and the Anatomy of Deception

In the case of Maryllus' slave, the physicians around Galen did not dare to treat the patient because they lacked the experience to excise the bone from his chest and the training to recognize that it could be done. Galen's opponents in *Anatomical Procedures* suffer from a distinct but related professional malady. They too lack the anatomical expertise to expose the heart without perforating the pericardium. However, his rivals offer inexperience as an excuse for their failure to demonstrate their broader theoretical claims in public. Galen writes:[18]

[14] *AA* 7.13 (II.633K = 682 G).

[15] *AA* 7.13 (II.633K = 682–684 G): *ὅπερ οὐκ ἂν ἐγένετο, μηδενὸς τολμήσαντος ἐκκόψαι τὸ πεπονθὸς ὀστοῦν· ἐτόλμησε δ' ἂν οὐδεὶς ἄνευ τοῦ προγεγυμνάσθαι κατὰ τὰς ἀνατομικὰς ἐγχειρήσεις*. Cf. Celsus' anecdote (*Med.* 1.*pr*.49–50) about the emergence of a new disease that the most elite physicians (*nobilissimi medici*) were unable to treat. He writes that none attempted diagnosis and treatment because they were afraid to be accused of killing the patient if she died. Something may have saved the patient, writes Celsus, if only one of the physicians had been more courageous. In *Anatomical Procedures,* Galen reframes an ethical question about the point at which a physician must intervene into a question of competence, one about whether physicians have the training to intervene.

[16] *AA* 7.13 (II.634K = 684 G): "Let these few things I have mentioned as a digression (apart from many others) serve as a demonstration of the usefulness of my present treatise to any who are intelligent" (*ταυτὶ μὲν οὖν ἀπὸ πολλῶν ὀλίγα κατὰ πάρεργον εἰρήσθω, τοῖς νοῦν ἔχουσιν ἐνδεικνύμενα τῆς προκειμένης πραγματείας τὴν χρείαν*).

[17] *AA* 7.14 (II.636K = 686 G).

[18] *AA* 7.14 (II.636K = 686–688 G).

λεγόντων δ' ἐπειράθην ἀεὶ ταῦτα τῶν μηδὲ γυμνῶσαι καρδίαν δυναμένων ἄνευ συντρήσεως, ἀλλ' εἰ καὶ βιάσαιτό τις αὐτούς, εὐθέως συντρησάντων τὸν θώρακα, φασκόντων χαλεπὸν εἶναι τυχεῖν τούτου, καὶ διὰ τοῦτ' ἀναβαλλομένων τὴν χειρουργίαν εἰς αὖθις, ὡς, εἴ γ' εὐτυχηθείη γυμνωθῆναι, περιβάλλοντες ἂν τὸν βρόχον ἐπιδεῖξαι σαφῶς, ἅπερ ἐπηγγείλαντο.

I have made trial of those who are always saying these things; they cannot expose the heart without perforation and even if someone compels (*βιάσαιτο*) them, they immediately perforate the thorax. They say that it was difficult to get it right and postpone the practical demonstration to another time for this reason. [They say] that if they *had* managed to expose it, they would have clearly demonstrated what they promised after tying the ligature [around the pulmonary vein].

Galen's opponents make a series of claims about the putative results of ligating the pulmonary artery or vein in a living animal subject. Some, who can be identified as Erasistrateans, argue that when the pulmonary vein is ligated the arterial system becomes motionless and the lungs no longer contract.

The passage is striking for a number of reasons. First, Galen once again introduces a moral dimension to his critique of rival physicians. Not only do they lack the technical skill to perform the demonstrations about whose results they make false promises, they exploit their anatomical incompetence to escape being caught out. Second, the language of compulsion (*βιάσαιτο*) becomes prominent. Since Galen's opponents are unwilling to perform the demonstrations on which their claims depend, it is only possible to disprove their claims by forcing them to perform:[19]

τούτοις οὖν ἡμεῖς ἔμπαλιν ἐπαγγελλόμεθά τε καὶ πράττομεν. γυμνώσαντες γὰρ τὴν καρδίαν ῥᾳδίως ἄνευ τοῦ τρῶσαί τινα τῶν διαφραττόντων ὑμένων τὸ κύτος τοῦ θώρακος, ἀξιοῦμεν αὐτοὺς περιβαλεῖν τὸν βρόχον τοῖς τῆς καρδίας ἐκφυομένοις ἀγγείοις. οἱ δ' ἄχρι τοσούτου βιάζονται μέν, ἀνύουσι δ' οὐδέν, ἄχρι τοῦ διασπάσαι τινὰ τῶν ὑμένων σύντρησίν τε ἐργάσασθαι· τηνικαῦτα γὰρ οὐδ' ἐπιχειρεῖν ἔτι χρῆναί φασιν. ἀλλ' ἡμεῖς τε ἐν τάχει πάλιν ἐφ' ἑτέρου ζῴου γυμνώσαντες αὐτοῖς τὴν καρδίαν παρέχομεν, ἀναγκάζομέν τε πάλιν ἐγχειρεῖν, ἄχρι περ ἂν ἀσχημονήσωσιν ἐφ' οἷς ἠλαζονεύσαντο.

Contrary to these people, I promise *and* I deliver (*ἐπαγγελλόμεθά τε καὶ πράττομεν*). For after exposing the heart easily [for them] without damaging any of the membranes dividing the thoracic cavity, I ask them to tie the ligature around the vessels growing out of the heart. Although they are compelled (*βιάζονται*) to such a degree, they manage to accomplish nothing up until they

[19] *AA* 7.14 (II.636–637K = 688 G).

> tear apart some of the membranes and cause a perforation. Then they say that they should try their hands at it no further. But I quickly expose the heart again in another animal. I present it to them. And, I force them to try again until they disgrace themselves (ἀσχημονήσωσιν) because of the boasts they have made (ἐφ' οἷς ἠλαζονεύσαντο).

In order to compel his opponents to conduct the experiment, Galen removes all of the practical obstacles standing in their way. In doing so, he draws attention to the gulf between his anatomical training and his opponents' limitations. Galen's assertion that he demonstrates whatever anatomical claims he makes is a straightforward and pithy self-promotion of his technical acumen. The contrast Galen draws between his behavior and the Erasistrateans' also positions him and his practice opposite to their alleged intellectual dishonesty.

There are elenchic features of Galen's engagement with his opponents. They, or at least we as readers, must come to recognize openly that their claims to knowledge are false. First, his rivals demur from performance on the grounds that exposing the heart in public is too difficult for them. He exposes the heart for them easily, without incident. Then they hesitate further, until they are pressured to attempt to ligate the pulmonary vessels, which Galen has claimed cannot be done without perforating the membranes surrounding them. After the procedure is botched, they throw up their hands in an attempt to withdraw from public debate. Galen produces another animal and then another. The production of animal subjects in quick succession and in seemingly endless supply, in order to prevent his opponents from escaping refutation, is a stock feature of these experimental narratives. He easily prepares the animal for the Erasistrateans to resume where they had left off in the demonstration. Galen continues the process until his rivals are compelled at last to face their false claims (ἐφ' οἷς ἠλαζονεύσαντο) and, in doing so, disgrace themselves before a public audience (ἀσχημονήσωσιν).

The language of coercion plays multiple roles in these episodes. Galen's opponents will not reveal themselves as frauds unless compelled. The need for this external compulsion to engage sincerely marks them as morally subordinate to Galen, a subordination that is at least partly a natural result of their lack of cultural and intellectual education (*paideia*). The servile analogies that he deploys against them are evidence of the added social dimension of Galen's polemic. Galen's claim that Erasistrateans can only be truthful under compulsion also perhaps plays on a trope of classical Greek oratory, in which the testimony of slaves was said to be reliable only if they had been interrogated under torture—the so-called *basanos* (βάσανος). The servile terms in which Galen casts Erasistrateans elsewhere strengthens the association. Maud Gleason has made a similar observation about the echoes of criminal trials in Galen's language of compulsion, although for her the juridical setting that Galen's language evokes is a distinctly

Roman one.[20] On her view, "[f]or Galen's spectators public vivisection may have resonated with their memories of another sort of agonistic performance, violent but banal, familiar to all who frequented the assize cities of the Roman Empire: the criminal interrogation."[21] Gleason focuses on the forced testimony of animal bodies as a form of lurid display that perhaps will have been familiar to a Roman audience for whom "[t]he excitement of these performances was visceral as well as cerebral. However controlled or stylised the violence, killing and maiming were part of the show."[22] Anatomical demonstrations and criminal interrogations share in both gore and spectacle. Moreover, Gleason is right to draw attention to the visceral register of their persuasive force. I think that more can be said about this point of resemblance, however. There is certainly a sense in which Galen compels his animal subjects to produce a form of testimony, a metaphor most apt in the case of his experiments on the voice. He does so not only to reveal the goal-oriented structure of body, but also to testify against his opponents' views. In these passages, however, Galen's language of compulsion does not center around his animal subjects; rather, it is his Erasistratean rivals whom he forces to testify—against themselves. To the extent that Galen associates Erasistrateans with the sorts of people who can be coerced to testify and, indeed, can only testify truthfully under coercion, he reinforces the image of the Erasistratean as a subaltern figure. Whether, as Gagarin has argued, the practice of testimony by interrogation under torture (*βάσανος*) was a legal fiction or not, its close cultural association with slaves rather than free Athenian citizens meant that *βάσανος* had a powerful social function as a tool of marginalization.[23] However, Galen also uses the language of compulsion to describe his own behavior in these debates. While only coercion can motivate the Erasistrateans in *Anatomical Procedures* (and *On the Natural Faculties*) to be truthful, Galen reports that only the great weight of moral compulsion can motivate him to engage in these public debates at all. The enormity of his opponents' fraudulence compels him to enter the fray.[24]

[20] Gleason, 'Shock and Awe' (2009) 105–108.

[21] Gleason, 'Shock and Awe' (2009) 106.

[22] Gleason, 'Shock and Awe' (2009) 106. Cf. Petit, *Galien de Pergame ou la rhétorique de la Providence* (2018) 153–161. Petit distinguishes between the violence and gore of Galen's anatomical procedures and Galen's dispassionate and detached written accounts of them. Galen's procedural writing aids in establishing his intellectual authority. It allows him to present himself as a disinterested observer of the body and participant in dissection. To the degree that an audience's interest was piqued by the blood and spectacle of the procedures themselves, all the better. Galen's instructions to the reader suggest he was sensitive to both concerns.

[23] Gagarin, 'The Torture of Slaves in Athenian Law' (1996) 17. Cf. Finley, *Ancient Slavery and Modern Ideology* (1980) 94–95 and du Bois, *Torture and Truth* (1991) 35–62. In this vein, it is also worth considering the ways in which the staged and competitive aspects of Athenian trials align with Galen's public experiments. Indeed, both were explicitly called "*ἀγῶνες*" whose outcomes were determined by the acclaim of a public audience who adjudicated between their competing *λόγοι*. See Gagarin, 'The Torture of Slaves in Athenian Law' (1996) 2. Also, for the torture of slaves in Roman judicial contexts, see Schumacher, Servus index (1982).

[24] See, e.g., *AA* 7.14 (II.637–638K = 688 G): "So great is the fraud and audacity about things of which they have no knowledge that some people use against people who are ignorant" (*τοσαύτῃ τινὲς ἀλαζονείᾳ τε ἅμα καὶ τόλμῃ περὶ ὧν οὐκ ἴσασι πρὸς τοὺς οὐκ εἰδότας χρῶνται . . .*). The close collocation

A Polemic in Four Parts

Book 7 ends with a sustained polemic against the Erasistratean view that the arteries are devoid of blood under non-pathological circumstances. Discussion of this point, Galen says, is superfluous to the primary aims of *Anatomical Procedures*. And, while the subject matter does not merit continued discussion, the effrontery and deceit of his opponents compel him to write further (*δι᾽ ἐκείνους δεήσει καὶ ἡμᾶς ἔτι διατρίψαι περὶ τὸν τόπον*). His Erasistratean rivals falsify (*καταψευδόμενοι*) the results of their demonstrations, then brazenly insist that the falsified results are true (*ἀναισχύντως φλυαροῦσιν*). Since he is compelled to argue against his rivals for the public good, Galen's justification allows him to engage in debates that he decries as manifestly absurd, while he remains unsullied by the engagement. The four vignettes all exhibit the same cluster of criticisms: Erasistrateans argue in bad faith, making false claims that are intentionally difficult or impossible to test. Their fraudulent claims are motivated by the need to conceal their medical ignorance and their lack of intellectual rigor. Each of the vignettes underscores the high professional stakes of live public medical debates. As Galen progresses from one episode to the next, however, the context in which the public debates he describes are conducted shifts from a live arena to a literary one.

In the first episode, an Erasistratean continually promises to show that the aorta is empty of blood, but never does so. The claim is about a point of long-standing debate, in this case Erasistratus' belief that the arteries contain pneuma rather than blood. A band of young people associated with Galen challenges the Erasistratean to deliver, at last, on his promises. They arrive on the scene with subjects for vivisection in tow: "... when some young people, hungry for distinction, brought him some animals and challenged him to a demonstration, he began to say that he would not perform a demonstration without payment."[25] This agonistic strategy has a powerful effect. It can be seen, for example, in Galen's confrontation with

of *ἀλαζονεία* and *τόλμη* is relatively infrequent in Greek before Galen, twice, fittingly, in Isoc. *Orat.* 13, *Against the Sophists*; once in Polemo *Ep.* 2, once in a fragment of Menander, and finally in Philo of Judea. Verbal forms of each word occur close to one another twice in Isoc. *Orat.* 13, which contains a number of close thematic parallels with the end of Book 7 of *Anatomical Procedures*. In section 1, where Isocrates accuses sophists of promising more than they can hope to deliver, failing to respect serious study, and being disputation, he describes them in these terms (*οἱ τολμῶντες λίαν ἀπερισκέπτως ἀλαζονεύεσθαι*). Sections 3–8 are an extended invective against accepting payment for education. In section 10, which contains the second instance of such a phrase (*κακῶς εἰδότες ὅτι μεγάλας ποιοῦσι τᾶς τέχνας οὐχ οἱ τολμῶντες ἀλαζονεύεσθαι περὶ αὐτῶν, ἀλλ᾽ οἵτινες ἄν, ὅσον ἔνεστιν ἐν ἑκάστῃ, τοῦτ᾽ ἐξευρεῖν δυνηθῶσιν*), Isocrates decries that sophists have no regard for experience, training, or native ability and insist that they can teach their subject as though they would teach students their letters. I am not arguing that Galen has Isocrates' speech specifically in mind when writing the end of Book 7, although it is tempting to think so. My point, rather, is that Galen frames these episodes in terms that are recognizably oratorical and performative.

25 *AA* 7.16 (II.642K = 696 G): *κομισάντων αὐτῷ τῶν φιλοτιμοτέρων νεανίσκων ζῷα καὶ προκαλεσαμένων ἐπὶ τὴν δεῖξιν, οὐκ ἄνευ μισθοῦ δείξειν ἔφασκεν*. Cf. *AA* 7.14 (II.636–637K = 688 G).

Pergamene doctors for the post of gladiatorial physician, which launched his early career.[26] The number of animal subjects is sufficient to forestall the opponents' potential evasion of Galen's challenges on the grounds that meeting them would be pragmatically difficult or impossible. The tactic adds to the spectacular nature of these anatomical contests. And, while Galen offers us few specifics about just how many animal subjects he (or his surrogates) bring to ambush their adversaries, the practice reminds the reader of the wealth and status required of such a display.[27] After the man refuses to perform publicly *without a suitable fee*, the challenge takes dramatic shape:[28]

> *αὐτίκα δ' ὑπ' ἐκείνων εἰς μέσον κατατεθεισῶν δραχμῶν χιλίων, ἵν', εἰ δείξειε, κομίσαιτο, πολλὰς μὲν ἀπορῶν ἐστρέφετο στροφάς· ἀναγκαζόμενος δ' ὑπὸ πάντων τῶν παρόντων, ἐτόλμησε λαβὼν σμίλην τέμνειν κατὰ τὸ ἀριστερὸν μέρος τοῦ θώρακος, ἔνθα μάλιστ' ᾤετο, τῆς συντρήσεως γενομένης, ἐναργῶς αὐτῷ φαίνεσθαι τὴν μεγάλην ἀρτηρίαν. εὑρέθη δ' οὕτως γεγυμνασμένος ἐν ταῖς ἀνατομαῖς, ὥστε κατ' ὀστοῦ ποιήσασθαι τὴν τομήν. ἄλλος δ' ἐκ τούτου χοροῦ κατὰ μὲν τὸ μεσοπλεύριον ἔτεμεν, ἀλλ' εὐθὺς ἅμα τῇ πρώτῃ τομῇ τήν τ' ἀρτηρίαν διέκοψε καὶ τὴν φλέβα.*
>
> Right away, they laid down a thousand drachmae on the spot for him to carry off should he perform the demonstration. He turned every which way, finding no way out. Forced by everyone present, he picked up a lancet and dared to cut along the right side of the thorax at the point where he most believed that the aorta would be plainly visible to him. He was found out to be *so practiced* in anatomy that he cut all the way to the bone! And another member of this troupe cut between the ribs; but with the very first cut he immediately severed the artery along with the vein.

This vignette maps closely on to the case of the Erasistratean in our earlier discussion, who insisted on the results of ligating the pulmonary vessels but would not—then could not—do so. Galen's charge of technical incompetence against this Erasistratean, and as we will see, against a series of Erasistrateans in these vignettes, is a common strategy in his writing. In these instances, however, Galen's critique cuts especially deep. Erasistratus himself had condemned practitioners who did not engage in rigorous training:[29]

> *οἱ μὲν γὰρ ἀσυνήθεις τὸ παράπαν τοῦ ζητῆσαι ἐν ταῖς πρώταις κινήσεσι τὴν διάνοιαν τυφλοῦνται καὶ ἀποσκοτοῦνται καὶ εὐθέως ἀφίστανται τοῦ ζητεῖν*

[26] See *Opt.Med.Cogn.* 9.4–7 (*CMG Suppl.Or.* IV 103.10–105.19).
[27] See, e.g., *Praen.* 5 (XIV.627–630K = *CMG* V 8,1 96–100).
[28] *AA* 7.16 (II.642–643K = 696 G).
[29] Fr. 247.22–30 Garofalo = Galen *Cons.* 1 (*CMG Suppl.* III 12.28–14.7).

κοπιῶντες τῇ διανοίᾳ καὶ ἐξαδυνατοῦντες οὐκ ἧττον ἢ ὅσοι πρὸς δρόμους ἀσυνήθεις ὄντες προσέρχονται· ὁ δὲ συνήθης τοῦ ζητεῖν πάντη διαδυόμενός τε καὶ ζητῶν τῇ διανοίᾳ καὶ μεταφερόμενος ἐπὶ πολλοὺς τόπους οὐκ ἀφίσταται τῆς ζητήσεως, οὐχ ὅτι ἐν μέρει ἡμέρας ἀλλ' οὐδὲ ἐν παντὶ βίῳ ἀναπαύων τὴν ζήτησιν· καὶ μεταφέρων ἐπ' ἄλλας ἐννοίας τὴν διάνοιαν, οὐκ ἀλλοτρίας μὴν τοῦ ζητουμένου, προβαίνει ἐπὶ τὸ προκείμενον ἐλθεῖν.

Those who are altogether unaccustomed to research are made blind in the initial movements of their minds and become baffled. And becoming mentally exhausted, they immediately shrink away from doing research—quite incapable, no less than those people who enter races unaccustomed to them. But the person practiced at doing research slips through any opening, does research, and turns to many places with his mind. He does not shrink away from doing research, not resting at it in any part of a day, nor in the whole of his life. And turning his mind to other thoughts, relevant to what is under investigation, he advances to meet what lies before him.

Galen does not merely criticize second-century Erasistrateans for their lack of training and their incompetence. In depicting them as the sorts of thinkers whom Erasistratus would scorn, Galen turns Erasistratus' ethical and intellectual advice against his *epigones*.

Although this dispute is the kind in which Galen might himself engage, here it arises between an Erasistratean and some young associates who stand in for him, another recurring feature of his polemical digressions.[30] This relationship allows Galen to distance himself from the acute agonism of the debate. Their effective surrogacy adds to the Erasistratean's public humiliation; after all, Galen describes them merely as young people hungry for distinction (τῶν φιλοτιμοτέρων νεανίσκων) and, later, as engaged members of the audience to Galen's previous anatomical performances.[31] The authority of the Erasistratean is undercut by the youth of Galen's surrogates, and by the implication that their training comes primarily from observing Galen at work, rather than from professional experience. The fee that the Erasistratean demands and that the young men offer is also noteworthy. Galen shares a common elite Greek and Roman disdain toward accepting money as a fee, an attitude that he further embraces as a Platonic inheritance.[32] The

[30] Cf. *AA* 7.10 (II.620K = 664 G), 7.13 (II.637K = 688 G), 7.15 (II.642–643K = 696–698 G); *Sem.* 2.1 (IV.595K = *CMG* V 3,1 146.11–13).

[31] The *philotimia* of Galen's associates here does not appear to bear a negative connotation. On some of its more positive uses in Greek science writing, see Berrey, *Hellenistic Science at Court* (2017) 94, 99. Galen often, however, uses "*philotimia*" pejoratively, to criticize the character of his rivals. It is a use shared with other similar terms, such as *philoneikia*. Lloyd, 'Galen on Hellenistics and Hippocrateans' (1991) 400, n. 8 contains a range of instructive examples.

[32] On Galen's professed disdain for the acquisition of money and its corrupting influence, see, e.g., *Opt.Med.* 2 (1.57K = *SM* 2, 4.13–21) and 3 (I.61K = *SM* 2, 7); *PHP* 9.5 (V.751–752K = *CMG* V 4,1,2 564.19–30); *Cris.* 2.2 (IX.645K = 129.10–15 Alex.); *HVA* 1.16 (XV.450K = *CMG* V 9,1 132.20–23); *Praen.* 4 (XV.623K = *CMG* V 8,1 92.11–20); *CP* 1.2 (70.7–10 H). Although Ecca, 'The *Μισθάριον* in the

Erasistratean's demand of payment for intellectual production associates him with historical sophists, a further Platonic echo; it also associates him with the vice of Roman *luxuria* that Galen so frequently bemoans.[33] The money that the young people lay down as a deposit on his performance, one thousand drachmae, is a substantial sum.[34] Their display of wealth, like the ready supply of animal subjects they bear with them, draws attention to their status as elite members of Roman society. It is worth lingering on this point. The status of the young people challenging the Erasistratean—and their success in doing so—is a powerful advertisement to Galen's readership, which encourages his contemporary elite readers to consider that they too could learn to perform publicly in anatomical contests like these with Galen's instruction. Galen's opponent finds himself cornered and coerced to demonstrate his claims, a demonstration that reveals his inexperience with dissection and undercuts his claims to anatomical knowledge:[35]

> καταγελάσαντες οὖν αὐτῶν οἱ θέντες τὰς χιλίας νεανίσκοι τοῖς ἠθροισμένοις ἐπὶ τὴν θέαν, αὐτοὶ τὴν ἐκείνου ἐπαγγελίαν ἐποιήσαντο, τεμόντες μὲν, ὡς ἑωράκεισαν παρ' ἐμοί, τὸ μεσοπλεύριον ἄνευ τοῦ τρῶσαί τι τῶν ἀγγείων, περιβαλόντες δὲ διὰ ταχέων δύο βρόχους, ἕνα μὲν μετὰ τὴν ἔκφυσιν εὐθέως ἐκ τῆς καρδίας, ἕτερον δ' ἐπιβαίνειν μελλούσης τῇ ῥάχει τῆς ἀρτηρίας, ἵν', ὡς οἱ θρασεῖς ἐπηγγείλαντο, μετὰ τὸν τοῦ ζῴου θάνατον, ὅσον ἐν τῷ μεταξὺ τῶν βρόχων ἐστὶ τῆς ἀρτηρίας, ἐπιδειχθῇ κενὸν αἵματος.
>
> Laughing at them, the young people who had given the thousand drachmae to the crowd gathered there for safekeeping, *they* fulfilled the Erasistrateans' promise. They cut between the ribs without damaging any of the vessels, as they had seen [done] at my side, and they applied two ligatures quickly, one right past the point where the aorta grows out of the heart and the other where it meets the spine, so that after the death of the animal the section of the artery that is between the ligatures might be shown to be devoid of blood, as these blowhards claimed.

In the compass of one sentence, Galen evokes the Erasistrateans' humiliation and its public context (καταγελάσαντες οὖν αὐτὸν ... τοῖς ἠθροισμένοις ἐπὶ τὴν θέαν ...); he reminds the reader of the hefty stakes involved in the demonstration (οἱ θέντες

Praecepta' (2016) focuses on the late Hippocratic text *Precepts*, its discussion of the sometimes fraught relationship between the physician and payment in the Roman period offers helpful context for this attitude.

[33] See, e.g., *Praen.* 1 (XIV.603–605K = *CMG* V 8,1 72.13–74.11). Cf. Sen. *Ep.* 76.1–7; Juv. *Sat.* 3; 11.1–55; Lucian *Nig.*; and Max. Tyr. 4. For the many evils of urban life, especially in the city of Rome, as a spur to authorship see, e.g., Juv. *Sat.* 3; Plin. *Ep.* 1.9; Mart. *Ep.* 3.38; Tac. *Dial.* 11ff; Dio Chrys. *Or.* 7; and Lucian *Nig.*

[34] There is some inscriptional evidence for payments of this size to medical practitioners. See, e.g., Samama, *Les médecins dans le monde grec* (2003) no. 341. Cf. also (and placing doctors' salaries in a broader context), Szaivert and Wolters, *Löhne* (2005) 48, 324.

[35] *AA* 7.16 (II.642–643K = 696 G).

τὰς χιλίας νεανίσκοι); and he shows that, where his opponents fail, his surrogates succeed (αὐτοὶ τὴν ἐκείνων ἐπαγγελίαν ἐποιήσαντο . . .). Naturally, they owe their success to Galen's expertise and the time they have spent by his side watching him at work (ὡς ἑωράκεισαν παρ' ἐμοί).

After the young men partition a section of the artery from the arterial system, they dissect it. They then reveal that, contrary to the Erasistratean's claims, it contains blood. Galen's Erasistratean cannot recognize that he has been beaten. He alleges that the young men have merely demonstrated that there is blood in the artery because of the damage caused to it by the initial ligatures. Their placement caused an irruption of blood into the arteries drawn through invisible pathways connecting the arterial system to the venous system, which Erasistratus called anastomōses (ἀναστομώσεις).[36] The Erasistratean's appeal to irruption is a final and amateurish attempt to avoid refutation, a characterization that Galen explicitly compares to the behavior of untrained wrestlers, a long-standing metaphor of Greek argumentation. Even though they have been soundly beaten and are lying on their backs, they continue to grasp at the necks of their opponents in a vain attempt to avoid a loss.[37] The narrative of the public debate shifts abruptly to a more private context, although one disseminated to a broader public through Galen's written account. Galen reports that another Erasistratean designed a special ax, whose blade was square-shaped, to prove that the arteries were devoid of blood:[38]

> τοιοῦτος δὲ καὶ ὁ τὸν τετράστομον πέλεκυν ἐπινοήσας, εἶτα μήτε κατασκευάσας ποτ' αὐτὸν, μήτε πειραθείς, ὅμως οὐκ ᾐδεῖτο δι' αὐτοῦ τούτου δείξειν ἐπαγγελλόμενος ἀρτηρίαν κενὴν αἵματος. ἦν δ' οὖν αὐτοῦ τοιόνδε τι τὸ ἐνύπνιον.
>
> And a man of this sort even thought up a four-bladed ax, although he never made it nor even tried to! Nevertheless, he was not ashamed (οὐκ ᾐδεῖτο) to promise that he would show an artery devoid of blood with it. His dream went something like this.

[36] See, e.g., *Art.Sang.* 2 (IV.709K = 50 F-W); *Ven.Sect.Er.* 3 (XI.153–154K) See also Furley and Wilkie, *Galen on Respiration and the Arteries* (1984) 36–37 and Garofalo, Erasistrati Fragmenta (1988) 33–35. The term "anastomosis" continues to be used in contemporary medical discourse. In ancient Greek medical writing, *anastomōseis* are junctures between the arterial and venous systems that are a typical feature of vascular anatomy. They share limited functional similarities with modern capillary beds. Galen uses the term to refer to connections at the terminal points of vessels. These include connections between some arteries and the pores of the skin. See, e.g., *SMT* 1.12 (XI.402K).

[37] See, e.g., *Art.Sang.* 5 (IV.717K = 160.25–35 F-W). Cf. Galen's allegation of their evasion and his colorful contempt for it in *Art.Sang.* 7 (IV.727K = 172.1–4 F-W), where he accuses Erasistrateans of running off to an altar of Podunk Pyrrhonism for sanctuary (ἐπί τινα βωμὸν ἐλέου καταφεύγουσι τὴν Πυρρωνείαν ἀγροικίαν . . .).

[38] The episode occurs at *AA* 7.16 (II.643–644K = 698 G). It is worth noting that there is not, so far as I know, any surviving evidence for a tool of this sort and there is no reference to a πέλεκυς in Bliquez, *The Tools of Asclepius* (2015). Indeed, the satirical force of this episode depends partly on the fantastical nature of the device and its construction.

Like the other Erasistrateans in these episodes, the inventor of the improbable ax remains unnamed. It is not possible to say who the anonymous Erasistratean may have been or whether indeed Galen is referring to a historical figure at all. It is not uncommon for ancient medical authors to omit the names of their contemporaries when referring to them. The anonymity of his Erasistratean targets, however, also permits Galen to paint his rivals with a broad critical brush more easily and encourages the reader to envision them as a comic type.

The four blades of the ax would form a square. On striking a pronated animal on the back, the inventor hoped the blade would make a cut that included a section of the aorta. The shape of the blade would allow the experimenter to remove a section of the artery so quickly that it could control for the possible irruption of blood into the artery. It was structured:[39]

> ... *ἵνα μιᾷ πληγῇ τετράγωνόν τι σχῆμα τῆς ῥάχεως ἐκκοπῇ κατὰ περιγραφὴν ἰδίαν, ἐν ᾧ τὸ περιλαμβανόμενον τῆς μεγάλης ἀρτηρίας εὑρεθήσεσθαι κενὸν αἵματος ἔφασκε. τοῦτο μὲν οὖν εἰς γελωτοποιΐαν τοῖς γράφουσι τοὺς μίμους τῶν γελοίων ἀφείσθω.*
>
> ... in order that it would cut out a square section of its back with one blow in the shape of its peculiar outline, in which he kept on saying the part of the aorta enclosed [in the ax head] would be found to be devoid of blood. But let this thing be left to people who write mimes of absurd subjects for laughs.

Galen's account of the Erasistratean's ax is interesting in part because his opponent explicitly did not perform the experiment, despite making strong claims about its experimental results. Indeed, far from just failing to construct the ax, the Erasistratean never even attempted to have it made. Consequently, the public context for the Erasistratean's humiliation is a wholly written one. In the earlier cases I have discussed, Galen presents his opponent as making theoretical claims without the technical skills to support them, strongly implying that these claims are not founded or tested against empirical observations. Galen's critique of his adversaries is thematic: they are charlatans who are prone to assertion, although they lack either the ability to provide adequate proofs for what they claim or the scruple to engage in debate honestly. In this instance, Galen's criticism is more pointed. Like the others he has mentioned, this Erasistratean makes medical claims that he does not, and indeed cannot, support with anatomical demonstrations. He cannot even make a pretense of a performance at a later time, however. The device is so far removed from reality that it belongs in a dream, a comic prop.

The third vignette tells the story of an older Erasistratean, who had devised a demonstration of arterial content. The experiment that Galen describes is

[39] *AA* 7.16 (II.644K = 698 G).

elaborate; its description alone constitutes most of the episode. The experiment is so elaborate because it aims to control for the possible irruption of blood into the arteries from their *anastomōseis*, a consequence that was the basis for the Erasistratean's final objection to this sort of demonstration in the first episode Galen describes. I have mentioned one challenge to the Erasistratean view that the arteries contain only pneuma under normal circumstances, namely that whenever their contents can be observed directly the arteries can be seen to contain blood. One response to the challenge is to argue that the contents of the arteries can never be observed directly without injury to the vessels. Since injury to the vessel allows their pneumatic contents to escape very quickly and with tremendous force, the potential vacuum left in the wake of their departure pulls blood into the arteries from the veins through minute connections (*anastomōseis*) between the arterial and venous systems. The Erasistratean's experiment attempts to circumvent the observational challenges posed by injury to the vessel:[40]

> μνημονεύσωμεν δ᾽ ἡμεῖς ἑτέρας ἐγχειρήσεως, ἐφ᾽ ἧς δείξειν ἔφασκε γέρων τις ἑβδομηκοντούτης πάνυ σεμνὸς ἀρτηρίαν κενὴν αἵματος. ἠξίου γὰρ εἶναι μὲν τὸ ζῷον ἕν τι τῶν δαρτῶν ὀνομαζομένων, οἷον ἢ πρόβατον, ἢ βοῦν, ἢ αἶγα, διαιρεθῆναι δὲ κατά τι μόριον, ἔνθα μεγάλη μετὰ τὸ δέρμα εὐθύς ἐστιν ἀρτηρία, περιδαρῆναι δ᾽ ἐκείνην καὶ γυμνωθῆναι τῶν πέριξ σωμάτων, ὡς προσηρτῆσθαι μηδενὶ, κᾄπειτα φυλαττομένης τῆς κατὰ τὸ δέρμα τομῆς μεθ᾽ ἡμέρας ἓξ ἢ ἑπτὰ, διαστήσαντας τὰ χείλη τοῦ ἕλκους, περιβάλλειν βρόχους δύο περὶ τὴν ἀρτηρίαν, καθόσον οἷόν τε πλεῖστον, ἀλλήλων διεστῶτας, εἶτ᾽ ἐκκόπτειν τὸ μέσον αὐτῶν, εὑρεθήσεσθαι γὰρ κενόν. ἐκεῖνος μὲν οὖν, ἑβδομήκοντα γεγονὼς ἐτῶν, τὴν ἐγχείρησιν ταύτην οὐδέποτ᾽ ἐτόλμησεν ἔργῳ βασανίσαι. πρὸς ἡμῶν δ᾽ εὐθέως ἐβασανίσθη μετὰ τὸ πρῶτον ἀκοῦσαι, καὶ ὡς ἐπειράθημεν αὐτῆς, αἶγα καὶ πρόβατον οὕτω προπαρασκευάσαντες, ἐκομίσαμεν τῷ γέροντι παρακαλοῦντες αὐτὸν ἐξεγερθέντα θεάσασθαί ποτε κᾂν ἅπαξ παρελεγχόμενος τὰ κατὰ τὸν ὕπνον αὐτῷ φαντασθέντα.

> Let me recall another procedure, in which some senescent septuagenarian used to say that he would demonstrate an artery devoid of blood. He required that the animal be one of those called "skinnable," such as sheep, oxen, or goats. Then [he required] that a cut be made in some place where there is a large artery right under the skin, then that the artery be stripped of skin and that it be laid bare from the material all around it, so as to be attached to nothing. Then after six or seven days in which the incision is kept safe, having separated the edges of the wound, apply two ligatures around the artery separate from one another as much as possible. Then excise the section between the ligatures, for it would be found to be empty. So, while that 70-year-old man never dared to test this procedure in action, I tested it right after I first heard about it. And when I tested it, I prepared

[40] *AA* 7.16 (II.644–645K = 698–700 G).

> a goat and a sheep in advance. Then I took them to the old man, calling to him to wake up and see me refute, once and for all, the things that appeared to him in a dream.

After the artery is stripped of its surrounding material, the wound is allowed time to heal. During the healing process, the artery will have cleared itself of any blood that may have entered it due to the initial incisions made around it. Only then are ligatures applied to a segment of the artery. Consequently, the experimenter can be more certain that the experiment itself has not introduced blood into the artery under observation when an incision is finally made into the isolated section of the vessel. The structure of the demonstration is clear and the attempt at controlling for irruption is clever. Galen underscores the complexity of the procedure to satirical effect, however. As we have seen in the first episode, the Erasistratean notion of irruption was a source of some ridicule for Galen, since the mechanism under which it operates could neither be seen nor tested. Although the Erasistratean's underlying concern to control for arterial irruption explains the complexity of the experiment, the force of Galen's closing remark draws a sharp contrast between mere assertion of empirical outcomes and the actual observation of them: the old man's experiment is all plan and no action. Galen's depiction of him is of a piece with the other Erasistrateans in these narratives. The older man has had a lifetime to perform the demonstration but has never dared to do so (*τὴν ἐγχείρησιν ταύτην οὐδέποτ᾽ ἐτόλμησεν ἔργῳ βασανίσαι*). Galen, on the other hand, tests the procedure immediately upon learning of it: What he promises, he delivers.

In one sense, this test takes emphatically public form. Galen arrives at what one imagines is the Erasistratean's home with experimental subjects in train. Once there he summons the old man out into the open and into the waking world, where he is to be a witness to his own refutation. As in the case of the Erasistratean who devised the four-bladed ax, Galen here uses the language of dreams and dreaming to emphasize how little the Erasistrateans ground their views in empirical observations. It is not merely the case that their arterial theory lacks an observational basis; its basis in dreams stands at one further remove from reality.[41] The demonstration implicitly occurs in some local space, the house out of which the man is called. Likewise, Galen only implies the audience that bears witness to the Erasistratean's refutation, effectively creating a place in which the reader can be incorporated into the written performance of his experiment. Like the young men who challenged the earlier Erasistratean to prove that the arteries were devoid of blood—before an audience and under its compulsion—Galen's experimental narrative coopts his reading audience to participate in a reenactment of his refutation.

[41] Galen's references to the dreaming life of his opponents to signal their disconnection from reality are a recurring theme in his work. Cf. *Art.Sang.* 7 (IV.729K = 174.5–8 F-W).

The episodes grow progressively less moored to a time and place. In the first episode, Galen describes a richly detailed scene that includes an audience of onlookers. By adding that they acted as guarantors for the hefty sum at stake in the dispute, he reinforces their role as referees of the debate. Not one but two Erasistrateans fail to carry out the demonstrations that they profess will bear out their theoretical claims. Their failure is exacerbated by the many opportunities Galen affords them to perform on a series of animal subjects that he provides. Galen reminds the reader that his rivals fail because they lack the requisite training, which the young people who shame them possess, in virtue of their association with Galen himself. The second and the third episodes lack much of the performative detail of the first. Neither episode contains an internal audience to adjudicate Galen's performance or to shame the two Erasistrateans for their failure to perform, although experimental incompetence continues as a theme. The Erasistratean of the second episode is unwilling or unable even to commission the device that he offers as evidence for his theoretical claim, a figment of his dreaming life that Galen dismisses as prop comedy. The septuagenarian of Galen's third anecdote is a comic figure, whose engagement in these abstract debates also takes place in a dream-world. The length of his long life, a point on which Galen fixates, underscores the many opportunities he has had to undertake his own experiment and the enormity of his failure to do so.

In the fourth and final episode of the series, Galen introduces writing explicitly into the narrative of his debates with Erasistrateans. In this instance, an Erasistratean has publicly contradicted the results of an experiment on the femoral artery about which Galen had written in an earlier work: "then, not long ago, someone else gave an account of the experiment written by me in my book titled, *Whether Blood Is Naturally Contained in the Arteries*, contrary to the truth of the matter."[42] While it is not uncommon for Galen to refer to his other treatises, this reference foregrounds textual engagement. The experiment is a written procedure (*γεγραμμένην ἐγχείρησιν*), contained in one of his books (*ὑπ' ἐμοῦ κατὰ τὸ βιβλίον*), whose title he is careful to identify *as a book-title* (*οὗ τοὐπίγραμμά ἐστιν*). As in the first of these episodes, a group of people who had observed Galen conduct the experiment previously are present at the occasion:[43]

> *θαυμάζοντες οὖν αὐτοῦ τὴν τόλμαν οἱ τεθεαμένοι παρ' ἐμοὶ τὴν ἐγχείρησιν ἠρώτων, εἴποτ' αὐτὸς ἐποίησεν αὐτήν, ἢ διηγουμένου τινὸς ἀκούσας ἐπίστευσεν. ὁ δὲ καὶ πάνυ πολλάκις ἔφη πεποιηκέναι. κομίσαντες οὖν αἶγα αὐτῷ δεικνύειν ἠνάγκαζον.*

[42] *AA* 7.16 (II.645K = 700 G): *καὶ τοίνυν καὶ ἄλλος τις οὐ πρὸ πολλοῦ γεγραμμένην ἐγχείρησιν ὑπ' ἐμοῦ κατὰ τὸ βιβλίον, οὗ τοὐπίγραμμά ἐστιν, εἰ κατὰ φύσιν ἐν ἀρτηρίαις αἷμα, διηγεῖτο πρὸς τοὐναντίον, ἢ κατὰ ἀλήθειαν ἔχει.* The experiment is found in *Art.Sang.* 8 (IV.733–734K = 178.12–180.2 F-W).

[43] *AA* 7.16 (II.645–646K = 700 G).

> *ὡς δ᾽ οὐκ ἐβούλετο, διότι μηδ᾽ ἠπίστατο, δείξαντες τοῖς παροῦσιν ἐναντίως ἔχον τὸ φαινόμενον, ἔπαυσαν οὕτως τῆς εἰς τὸ λοιπὸν ἀλαζονείας.*
>
> Then, marveling at his audacity (*τόλμαν*), those who had witnessed the experiment at my elbow began to ask him if he had conducted the experiment himself or if he held this belief because he had heard someone explain it to him. He said that he had conducted it very often. So, after bringing out a goat for him they attempted to force (*ἠνάγκαζον*) him to demonstrate. And when he was unwilling (because he did not know how to do it), they demonstrated to those present that the facts of the matter contradicted [him], putting an end to his charlatanry (*ἀλαζονείας*) once and for all.

The Erasistratean responds to Galen by explaining (*διηγεῖτο*) this written procedure in the context of a live performance. The narrative setting appears to be a public *epideixis* of the sort Galen describes in *My Own Books*, where Galen and Martialius (also, it turns out, an Erasistratean) interpret and argue over a passage of Erasistratus', as a *problēma* or proposed topic of intellectual debate.[44] In this case, however, the text under public discussion is Galen's own, a feature of this narrative that positions Galen's work alongside more ancient authorities, as an object for analysis and discussion. It is a matter of pointed irony that Galen's Erasistratean engages with this Galenic account of the experiment since the procedure was originally devised by Erasistratus.

This passage shares a number of features with earlier sections of *Anatomical Procedures* that I have already discussed. Galen's references to his opponent's audacity (*τόλμα*) and charlatanry (*ἀλαζονεία*) echo his justification for engaging with Erasistrateans on the question of arterial content in the first place, a question which he dismisses as absurd. He is drawn into debate with them, he says, to prevent the truth from being distorted and laypeople from being defrauded: "So great is the fraud (*ἀλαζονείᾳ*) and audacity (*τόλμῃ*) about things of which they have no knowledge that some people use against people who are ignorant."[45] His opponents must be compelled (*ἠνάγκαζον*) to demonstrate the truth of their claims—in this case the Erasistratean does not perform, even under compulsion. The language is wrought. It has oratorical associations and closes a ring composition with Galen's introduction of Erasistrateans as opponents who, in contrast with him, cannot perform what they promise.[46] This theme, which Galen has maintained throughout the first three episodes, also dominates the last. The audience-members had previously witnessed Galen conduct the procedure, here an experiment on the femoral artery. They stand in as surrogates for him, like the

[44] *Lib.Prop.* 1 (XIX.14K = 138–139 B-M).

[45] *AA* 7.14 (II.637–638K = 688 G): *τοσαύτῃ τινὲς ἀλαζονείᾳ τε ἅμα καὶ τόλμῃ περὶ ὧν οὐκ ἴσασι πρὸς τοὺς οὐκ εἰδότας χρῶνται . . . .*

[46] See *AA* 7.14 (II.636–637K = 686–688 G).

young men in the first episode who had learned from Galen how to isolate an arterial segment in order to demonstrate that the arteries contain blood even under healthy conditions. The Erasistratean here refuses to perform the experiment for the same reasons as his counterparts have: he lacks technical know-how (διότι μηδ' ἠπίστατο), a pretense of which he must maintain as far as he is able. Galen's surrogates again produce an animal subject, with which they attempt to compel the Erasistratean to reveal his ignorance. His refusal to perform the demonstration incriminates him, and it affords Galen's surrogates an opportunity to demonstrate both the truth of Galen's experiment and the efficacy of his instruction.

Furthermore, one recalls that Galen's surrogates ask the Erasistratean if he held his belief about the emptiness of the arteries on the basis of first-hand experience conducting the experiment or through having learned about it second-hand. In isolation, Galen's language suggests that the distinction here is between practical experience (εἴποτ' αὐτὸς ἐποίησεν αὐτήν) and some kind of verbal instruction, a belief acquired after having "heard someone articulating it" (διηγουμένου τινὸς ἀκούσας). The Greek accommodates a more expansive reading of this passage, however. As a consequence of the historic aural dimensions of Greco-Roman reading, one can "hear" written accounts.[47] The textual dimension to this last episode is worth exploring further, especially in light of Galen's careful introduction of himself as an author and his writing as an object for public interpretation and debate. It is possible that Galen's criticism of his Erasistratean opponent is not *limited* to his lack of first-hand knowledge but extends to his uncritical reading of texts. On this more expansive reading, Galen's critique of the Erasistratean includes the theme he has maintained throughout these four episodes. This opponent, like his counterparts, certainly lacks the anatomical and philosophical training, in short, the education, to support his claims. Indeed, his lack of education is in part explanatory of his uncritical reliance on Erasistratus' written account of the experiment. As Galen hastens to observe, this report is not only contrary to the facts of the matter; it is of course contrary to Galen's actual observations:[48]

> τὸ μὲν οὖν ἀληθῶς φαινόμενον οὕτως ἔχει. διηγεῖτό γε μὴν ἐναντίως ὁ Ἐρασίστρατος ὑπὲρ αὐτοῦ, φαίνεσθαι λέγων κινούμενον τὸ κάτω τοῦ καλάμου. τοσαύτη τίς ἐστιν ἐνίων τόλμα, προπετεῖς ἀποφάσεις ποιουμένων ὑπὲρ ὧν οὐδέποτ' ἐθεάσαντο.
>
> The real observational result is so [i.e., in agreement with Galen's view]. And yet, on this point Erasistratus reports the opposite result, saying that the segment distal to the reed clearly moves. This is how great the audacity (τόλμα) is of some

[47] Cf. Polyb. *Hist.* 1.13.6 and 2.59.5.

[48] *AA* 7.16 (II.648K = 704 G).

> people who make reckless claims about things which they have never seen for themselves!

While Erasistratus may have been mistaken about the results of the experiment, Galen clearly believes that he performed it.[49] The great vice of Galen's contemporary opponents is to possess the audacity to make public assertions merely on the basis of written authorities without recourse to first-hand observations or the skill to conduct them.

Galen offers the reader very little in the way of an argument against the theoretical positions held by his Erasistratean opponents throughout the close of Book 7. Galen is perfectly capable of engaging with their arguments directly. The persuasive force of Galen's digression on the question of arterial content in *Anatomical Procedures*, however, depends entirely on the satirical portrait he draws of contemporary Erasistrateans. They are, as a group, bad intellectual actors. They lack the requisite training—anatomical and intellectual—to make informed medical claims or to test them empirically. What is worse, their educational failures align closely with moral ones. Galen's Erasistrateans are desperate to hide their ignorance, and so they habitually deceive a lesser-informed public with misdirection. His rivals' moral shortcomings contribute to their intellectual ones, and vice versa. The pattern of Galen's criticisms is highly socially coded. The servile terms in which he frequently describes Erasistrateans reinforce the image of them as morally and intellectually subaltern. The same pithy and engaging indictments of his rivals, imitative of tropes drawn from literature of the classical Greek past and steeped in references to it, advertise Galen's culturally elite status. To the extent that his rhetoric encourages the reader to align moral and intellectual virtue with social status, the sophistication of Galen's invective against Erasistrateans of his day affirms the quality of his mind and character as it undercuts the quality of theirs.

Galen's narrative throughout Book 7 in *Anatomical Procedures* shifts away from the live performances upon which he often hangs his professional success. As the episodes progress, Galen's engagement with Erasistrateans occurs purely in a world of text. His written engagement, however, belongs to the same competitive and agonistic matrix as its live counterparts.[50] These anecdotes, highly wrought as they are, sit comfortably among procedural discussions of the other respiratory organs. Textuality and texts traditionally understood as literary play an integral role in Galen's four-part polemic against Erasistrateans of his day. There is no hint that the technical subject matter or generic constraints of *Anatomical Procedures* preclude Galen from including learned echoes of fifth-century Athenian forensic

[49] Cf. *Art.Sang.* 8 (IV.735, 736K = 180.28–182.4, 182.9–10 F-W).

[50] For Galen's use of writing and written demonstrations to perform some of the social functions of live demonstrations, see Salas (2020) 16–55.

oratory, making pointed use of tropes drawn from pages of New Comedy—in short, from signaling his status as a second-century Greek *pepaideumenos* at Rome to the reader through displays of his *paideia*.

Bibliography

Berrey, *Hellenistic Science at Court* (2017) = M. Berrey, *Hellenistic Science at Court* (Berlin: De Gruyter, 2017).

Bliquez, *The Tools of Asclepius* (2015) = L. Bliquez, *The Tools of Asclepius: Surgical Instruments in Greek and Roman Times* (Leiden: Brill, 2015).

Coker, 'Galen and the Language of Old Comedy' (2019) = A. Coker, 'Galen and the Language of Old Comedy: Glimpses of a Lost Treatise at *Ind.* 23b–28,' in C. Petit, ed., *Galen's Treatise Περὶ Ἀλυπίας (De Indolentia) in Context: A Tale of Resilience* (Leiden: Brill, 2019) 63–90.

DuBois, *Torture and Truth* (1991) = P. DuBois, *Torture and Truth* (New York: Routledge, 1991).

Ecca, 'The *Μισθάριον* in the *Praecepta*' (2016) = G. Ecca, 'The *Μισθάριον* in the *Praecepta*: The Medical Fee and its Impact on the Patient,' in G. Petridou and C. Thumiger, eds., *Homo Patiens: Approaches to the Patient in the Ancient World* (Leiden: Brill, 2016) 323–344.

Finley, *Ancient Slavery and Modern Ideology* (1980) = M. Finley, *Ancient Slavery and Modern Ideology* (New York: The Viking Press, 1980).

Furley and Wilkie, *Galen on Respiration and the Arteries* (1984) = D. J. Furley and J. S. Wilkie, *Galen on Respiration and the Arteries* (Princeton: Princeton University Press, 1984).

Gagarin, 'The Torture of Slaves in Athenian Law' (1996) = M. Gagarin, 'The Torture of Slaves in Athenian Law,' *Classical Philology* 91.1 (1996) 1–18.

Garofalo, Erasistrati Fragmenta (1988) = I. Garofalo, Erasistrati Fragmenta: *Collegit et digessit* (Pisa: Giardini, 1988).

Gleason, 'Shock and Awe' (2009) = M. Gleason 'Shock and Awe: The Performance Dimension of Galen's Anatomy Demonstrations,' in C. Gill, T. Whitmarsh, and J. Wilkins, eds., *Galen and the World of Knowledge.* (Cambridge: Cambridge University Press, 2009) 85–114.

Lloyd, 'Galen on Hellenistics and Hippocrateans' (1991) = G. E. R. Lloyd, 'Galen on Hellenistics and Hippocrateans: Contemporary Battles and Past Authorities,' in id., *Methods and Problems in Greek Science: Selected Papers* (Cambridge: Cambridge University Press, 1991) 398–416.

MacCary, 'Menander's Slaves' (1969) = W. T. MacCary, 'Menander's Slaves: Their Names, Roles, and Masks,' *Transactions and Proceedings of the American Philological Association* 100 (1969) 277–294.

Petit, *Galien de Pergame ou la rhétorique de la Providence* (2018) = C. Petit, *Galien de Pergame ou la rhétorique de la Providence: Médecine, littérature et pouvoir à Rome* (Leiden: Brill, 2018).

Rosen, 'Galen, Satire and the Compulsion to Instruct' (2010) = R. Rosen, 'Galen, Satire and the Compulsion to Instruct,' in H. F. J. Horstmanshoff, ed., *Hippocrates and Medical Education. Selected Papers Presented at the XIIth International Hippocrates Colloquium, Universiteit Leiden, 24–26 August 2005.* (Leiden: Brill, 2010) 325–342.

Rosen, 'Galen on Poetic Testimony' (2013) = R. Rosen, 'Galen on Poetic Testimony,' in M. Asper, ed., *Writing Science: Medical and Mathematical Authority in Ancient Greece* (Berlin: De Gruyter, 2013) 177–189.

Salas, *Cutting Words* (2020) = L. A. Salas, *Cutting Words: Polemical Dimensions of Galen's Anatomical Experiments* (Leiden: Brill, 2020).

Samama, *Les médecins dans le monde grec* (2003) = É. Samama, *Les médecins dans le monde grec: Sources épigraphique sur la naissance d'un corps médical* (Geneva: Librairie Droz, 2003).

Schumacher, Servus index (1982) = L. Schumacher, Servus index. *Sklavenverhör und Sklavenanzeige im republikanischen und kaiserzeitlichen Rom* (Wiesbaden: Franz Steiner Verlag, 1982).

Szaivert and Wolters, *Löhne* (2005) = W. Szaivert and R. Wolters, *Löhne, Preise, Werte. Quellen zur römischen Geldwirtschaft* (Darmstadt: Wissenschaftliche Buchgesellschaft, 2005).

Response

Does the Performance Undercut the Substance?

Kendra Eshleman

Not being a specialist in either law or medicine, in my response to these two papers, I will focus on the element of performance and the social construction of expertise and authority, both collaborative and competitive. I will zero in on a theme that percolates under the surface of the episodes discussed in both papers: the role of other people in the performances they describe—not only in the crucial roles of audience member and reader, but also as witnesses and participants in the protagonists' display of self, and as players with their own goals and perspectives.[1] In these public contests to establish hidden truths—the guilt or innocence of a defendant, the nature of an invisible anatomical structure—the outcomes depend not only (or even mainly) on empirical fact, but on creating visible consensus among those whose approbation counts.[2] Again and again in these episodes, the presence or absence of the right other people is manipulated as a tool to demonstrate, amplify, or obstruct the principals' claims about rank, class, education, and hence truthfulness and authority. To borrow from Matt Roller, this is one of the ways in which "competitors seek to define or configure an arena of competition to their own advantage."[3] At the same time, there are often multiple performances going on, not just by the protagonists, and where possible I am interested in uncovering the goals and strategies of the other actors as well.

This pattern intersects with and reinforces a theme that is explicit in both papers, namely, that the contests under consideration are conducted across disparities of power, arising from often interlocking asymmetries of political status, ethnicity, citizenship, class, and education. In late republican Sicily, the gap is between wealthy, reputable Roman citizens and non-citizen Sicilian Greeks; in the

I am grateful to Claire Bubb and Michael Peachin for their invitation to participate in this conference, and for their helpful suggestions on this essay.

[1] On the active relationship between performer and audience, Korenjak, *Publikum und Redner* (2000) is fundamental. For audiences in the Roman courtroom, see Bablitz, *Actors and Audience* (2007) 120–140.

[2] In similar vein, Lendon, *Empire of Honour* (1997) 37, observes that aristocratic "honour was mediated through the perceptions of others, and even a superfluity of worthy qualities was of no use unless these qualities were publicly known, *and approved by other aristocrats*" (emphasis added).

[3] Roller, this volume, p. 56.

Kendra Eshleman, *Response: Does the Performance Undercut the Substance?* In: *Medicine and the Law under the Roman Empire.* Edited by: Claire Bubb and Michael Peachin, Oxford University Press.
DOI: 10.1093/oso/9780192898616.003.0005

eastern provinces of the imperial era, non-citizen litigants and their small-time local lawyers are pitted against more educated, skilled citizen lawyers who may be traveling in the entourage of the Roman governor. Dolganov brings out the ways in which the more privileged parties subtly (and not so subtly) exploit those disparities to their advantage. Salas, meanwhile, shows Galen working to magnify, if not manufacture, the gap between himself and his professional rivals, portraying them as uneducated and socially sub-altern, while he depicts himself and his surrogates as elite *pepaideumenoi* with extensive resources and access to performance venues, itself a form of authorization.[4] These men inhabit a world in which the trustworthiness (*fides*) of witness testimony was assessed based, in no small part, on the status (*condicio*, *dignitas*, *existimatio*, *auctoritas*) of the witness—a status which laboriously acquired *paideia* made to appear innate and deserved.[5] In both arenas, truth is being sought, but truthfulness—or the ability to be perceived as truthful—is always a function of class.

Authority has different bases in the two arenas: the Roman judges and some of the lawyers Dolganov profiles derive authority from official positions, while Galen has to conjure his authority into being by speaking, performing, and writing. This is a real, but also somewhat false dichotomy, for even people who hold elected or appointed office or academic professorships nonetheless have to go on proving themselves, to show that they are worthy of respect, belief, honor, funding, and so on. And the socio-political standing that Galen, like the doctor Herakleitos and the jurist Julian, acquired through intellectual achievement and manifested through medical practice, public displays, and voluminous written output transcends the public posts he held as official doctor to the gladiators of Pergamum and as imperial physician under Marcus Aurelius, although they are necessarily entwined.[6]

In the scenes analysed by Salas, Galen consistently portrays his Erasistratean opponents as socially and professionally isolated. Galen himself, by contrast, always seems to be in the company of or acting through others, whether in person or virtually present.[7] These scenes are not among those where Galen performs for a star-studded crowd of Second Sophistic intellectuals and high Roman officials, but nonetheless he comes across as a well-connected impresario. In the umbrella narrative in *Anatomical Procedures*, Galen describes what he suggests is a habitual practice of cornering Erasistratean physicians and forcing them to perform

[4] Galen *MM* 1.2.3 (X.10K); von Staden, 'Galen and the "Second Sophistic"' (1997) 44–47.

[5] See, e.g., *D.* 22.5.3.pr-2; *CTh.* 11.39.3 The classic study of *paideia*'s naturalization of social and political status is Schmitz, *Bildung und Macht* (1997). Atherton, 'Children, Animals, Slaves and Grammar' (1998) and Gleason, 'Truth Contests' (1999) esp. 297–303, among others, connect the harsh physical methods of ancient education to its role in socializing privileged children for adult social dominance, including the right to exert coercive force against inferiors.

[6] On the place of Galen's official posts in his career, see Mattern, *Prince of Medicine* (2013) 81–97, 195–198, 204–208, 212–223.

[7] Mattern, *Prince of Medicine* (2013) 160 points out that Galen is never alone.

dissections: the passage quickly switches from a simple past tense ("I have made trial" (ἐπειράσθην)) to the present ("I ask them" (ἀξιοῦμεν), "I compel them" (ἀναγκάζομεν), "they disgrace themselves" (ἀσχημονήσωσιν)), as if this is a repeated event.[8] Here, as in several other scenes, Galen is the one taking the fight to obviously reluctant opponents. The main point is to show that they are unable to perform the experiments that would provide evidence for their position that undamaged arteries contain only *pneuma*, not blood. But implicit in the scenario itself is that Galen knows these men and where to find them, and that he has the upper hand in this relationship. Meanwhile, he is mugging both for the invisible in-person audience, before whom his rivals are humiliated, and even more for the audience of his readers, all of whom are implicitly drawn onto Team Galen.[9] In this episode, as usual, Galen appears surrounded by a crowd of supportive witnesses, both literal and virtual, with a professional reach that includes even his rivals. They, by contrast, seem almost entirely alone, except for each other, in the anonymous third-person plural—for Galen has lured the whole audience away from them.

That is even more true in the story in which Galen apparently goes to the home of an elderly Erasistratean to confront him with an experiment that the other doctor had described theoretically but never tried and to "rouse him from his dream."[10] Here Galen's access to experimental materials and performance venues extends to even his target's own home. He tells the entire story in the first-person plural, which can be a way of blunting the competitive edge of the narrative, but could also mean, or give the impression, that he is acting in a group.[11] The target, meanwhile, seems entirely alone, without companions or students, isolated even from reality in his intellectual dream-state. Even more isolated is the target in the second episode, the doctor who had designed a four-sided tool for taking an arterial core, but never made, much less tried it.[12] This man has never done anything for anyone, at least as far as Galen lets us see. In a sense, he and his unrealized invention exist only as fodder for possible mime writers to ridicule.

In the two framing episodes, Galen acts through surrogates—students (ἑταῖροι) who, just by observing dissections "at my side" (παρ' ἐμοί), have acquired more expertise than supposed experts.[13] Being trounced by young sub-experts adds to the Erasistrateans' humiliation, as Salas points out, but it also makes Galen himself look more powerful. He is a person around whom others flock, to watch and learn from his dissections. As a result, he has numerous stand-ins who vicariously

[8] Galen *AA* 7.14 (II.634-638K).

[9] Mattern, *Rhetoric of Healing* (2008) 16–19, 80–92 surveys the live and textual audiences for Galen's cures, for whose approbation he competes.

[10] Galen *AA* 7.16 (II.644–645K).

[11] König, 'Self-Promotion and Self-Effacement' (2011) 185–187; Mattern, *Rhetoric of Healing* (2008) 138–140.

[12] Galen *AA* 7.16 (II.643–644K).

[13] Galen *AA* 7.16 (II.642–643, 645–646K).

multiply his presence; as he remarks in *On Seed*, if he died, all his students could go on performing a certain demonstration in his stead.[14] He also claims to be motivated by a desire to protect ignorant laypeople against deception—deftly insinuating that his opponents' main adherents are untrained non-experts (i.e., not professional peers, and thus not worth counting), while also positioning himself as a benevolent patron of ordinary people, widening his network further.[15] In both cases, a pack of Galenites teams up on a single opponent in the presence of an audience that is quickly brought over to their side, if they did not start out there. The disparity Galen sketches between his well-connected, well-approved supporters and the pathetically isolated Erasistrateans dovetails with the purported disparity in their class and educational levels. That impression is deliberately cultivated; these are not simply realistic records of who was present at these performances. If nothing else, Galen elides the presence of attendants who must have been assisting both him or his surrogates and their rivals in dissecting live animals, a necessity he acknowledges elsewhere in the *Anatomical Procedures*.[16] Clearing the stage of extraneous persons, especially those attached to his opponents, declutters the narrative and sharpens the polemic. The first episode begins with multiple Galenites and a supportive crowd of "all those present" (*πάντων τῶν παρόντων*) ganging up on a lone doctor in the third-person singular (*αὐτῷ*) to force him to perform. But midway through the man turns out not to be alone after all: when he has flubbed the dissection, "another member of this chorus" (*ἄλλος…ἐκ τούτου χοροῦ*) steps up (or is compelled) to try his hand, too. One wonders how many other colleagues and supporters of these two have been invisibly written out of the story.

In the final episode, where an Erasistratean is misinterpreting an experiment published by Galen in one of his own books, the doctor has evidently gathered a crowd of potentially supportive listeners. But he is again portrayed as a lone third-person actor (*αὐτοῦ*) cornered by a group of incredulous Galenites. They give him the chance to say that he has heard someone else explain the experiment, but he insists that he has performed it himself. When that claim turns out to be false, the doctor is deprived of both grounds of authority: personal experience and a relationship to a mentor. As the audience turns against him, this doctor, too, is left personally and professionally isolated.

The role of the students and their derisive laughter—"a key weapon in the intellectual's armory"[17]—is evocative of another incident from the *Anatomical Procedures* that Salas has written about elsewhere, the story of the elephant heart

[14] Galen *Sem.* 2.1 (IV.595K = *CMG* V 3,1 146).

[15] For the status of the untrained non-expert, see Eshleman, *Social World* (2012) 70–77.

[16] Galen *AA* 7.12 (II.627K).

[17] Gleason, 'Shock and Awe' (2010) 95. For laughter as a feature of Galen's agonistic healing narratives, cf. Mattern, *Rhetoric of Healing* (2008) 76 with n. 18.

bone, which is too irresistible to pass up.[18] In this episode, Galen claims that he was present at Rome when an unusually large elephant died, and doctors crowded around to witness the dissection of its heart, to see whether it contained a bone or not. Galen had confidently predicted that it would, on analogy to other "air-breathing animals," and lo and behold, he and his students were able to thrust their hands into the heart and easily put their fingers on the bone—but they laughingly persuade him not to show it to the "untrained" (ἀγύμναστοι) doubters. Later, he sends an assistant to ask Caesar's butcher to extract the bone for him. He claims to have the bone in his possession even now, and to show it off to visitors who are unfailingly stunned that any doctor could have missed something so massive.

Three details of this narrative stand out. First, that Galen and his chums exclude his rivals even from the community of witness; this is a story about seeing that is also about not allowing the wrong people to see. (No wonder! As Salas explains, elephants have no bones in their hearts, so whatever Galen put his finger on—if there even was an elephant—it was not an elephant's heart bone.)[19] As often, exclusion is a power move, drawing tight the boundary around those who deserve access to knowledge.[20] In this case, that division is created in real time, by circular means. Those who deserve knowledge are those who assent to it *a priori*: the scene begins with an undifferentiated group of doctors (πολλοὶ τῶν ἰατρῶν) peering at the dead elephant, but those who do not share Galen's starting assumption are immediately relabeled "untrained" and hence unworthy of learning what they do not already believe. Meanwhile Galen, his students, and we readers are privy to empirical visual proof withheld from those incompetent rivals, confirming and perpetuating their (supposed) ignorance. Of course, we cannot actually see Galen's evidence any more than his opponents can. Either we take Galen at his word, trusting and validating his authority, and remain within the circle of those in the know, or we doubt him, staking our authority against his at the risk of exclusion.[21] Second, Galen's reach extends even into the kitchens of the emperor. Finally, we are given an image of Galen in the present in his well-attended office, inviting viewers (real or imaginary) of this (non-existent?) artifact to join him in community-building laughter at his benighted adversaries, a community to which we readers are invited as well. Whether these are real visitors being shown something other than an elephant heart bone—say, the bone from the heart of a

[18] Galen *AA* 7.10 (II.618–620K); Salas, *Cutting Words* (2020) 144–168.

[19] Salas, *Cutting Words* (2020) 144–168.

[20] Elsewhere, Galen is eager for stories about his exploits to be shared, but only with "someone worthy of participation in such debates" (τινι τῶν ἀξίων κοινωνίας τοιούτων λόγων) (*Praen.* 5.7 (XIV.626K = *CMG* V 8,1 94)). For this move in second-century intellectual culture more broadly, see Eshleman, *Social World* (2012) 38–49.

[21] Galen has stronger cards to play when he can invoke his addressee as an authenticating eyewitness, although that strategy is confined to a few works; see Lehoux, 'The Authority of Galen's Witnesses' (2017).

large ox—or the visitors are as imaginary as the artifact, the effect of the remark is to place Galen at the heart of an outward-spreading network, real and virtual—students, visitors, readers—while his opponents are again left intellectually, professionally, and personally isolated. Ultimately, the actual existence of the bone is immaterial; what matters is that the right people *agree* that it exists. This tactic, I suggest, is of a piece with and reinforces his other techniques for casting his rivals as uneducated, unqualified, sub-altern.

In the trials in Dolganov's paper, the stakes are obviously different: the presence or absence and attitude of lawyers, judges, advisors, and other participants materially affects the outcome of a case. Nonetheless, an unavoidable element of social networking and self-presentation bubbles through the case studies Dolganov examines. She highlights the clubbiness of Roman judges and the well-educated prosecutors who seem to travel in their train and close ranks with them against non-citizen defendants and their small-time local lawyers. Here too, the isolation of the defendants compared to the well-connected forces arrayed against them is conspicuous: in two cases, the defendants are essentially deserted by their attorneys, who fall silent after their opening statements.

Those dynamics are illustrated in greater detail in the trial of Sopater from *Verrine* 2. Verres' *consilium* is made up of "the usual people" (*idem qui solebant*), and Sopater's defense strategy counts on their turning up in large numbers—on the *frequentia et dignitas* of the *consilium*.[22] Unfortunately for him, Verres contrives to have the entire *consilium* diverted to assist with another trial, which he assigns a *consilium* member with many *amici* in the group to hear at the same time. One gets the impression that these men, members of the local *conventus*, bound by ties of mutual *amicitia*, are showing up mainly for each other. They are certainly not attached to Verres himself, but to the office of governor and their own role: Verres has been in Sicily only a year, and they had also served on the *consilium* of his predecessor. Nor is their commitment to the litigants, either the plaintiffs, against whom they had ruled the year before and who never appear in Cicero's narrative, or the hapless Sopater, whom they abandon in order to honor the obligations they feel to each other, which are plainly more pressing than the ones they feel to the principals in this trial. Sopater's own lawyer is himself one of this group. Being a distinguished Roman *eques* mindful of his rights and *dignitas*, he refuses to be stranded with his client and maneuvered into a humiliating loss.[23] He quits the trial, pleading obligations to the *iudex* of the other trial, and the remaining Roman citizens go with him. For Cicero and us, this is a story about Verres' abuse of provincial justice, but these men have their own agendas, and their own relationships and status to maintain and display.

[22] Cic. *Verr.* 2.2.71. [23] Cic. *Verr.* 2.2.69, 73.

What stands out further is the way that Verres himself comes to be isolated and shamed—at the level of Cicero's narrative, if not in real life. At the point where the defendant Sopater has been stripped of effective defenders and his fate is sealed, the tables also turn for Verres, because he has overplayed his hand and isolated himself as well as his victim. He panics, realizing that going ahead with an obvious sham trial will be a PR disaster, but that he also cannot afford a delay that would allow the usual *consilium* to re-form. Dolganov remarks that once the *honesti homines* are gone from Verres' *consilium*, all that remain are his cronies. That is surely correct, but as Cicero portrays it, no doubt exaggerating, those cronies amount to only four people: Verres' freedman agent Timarchides, and the scribe, doctor, and haruspex on whose ruling he ends up convicting Sopater (*de sententia scribae, medici, haruspicisque*).[24] It falls to Timarchides to pull Verres out of his terrified indecision, repeatedly whispering instructions in his ear while a large crowd (*maximus conventus*) watches in shocked silence. To be seen taking direction from low-status subordinates would shame a more self-respecting expert. It is fine to make use of the labor of underlings, as Galen does, but not to rely on their knowledge. As Frontinus puts it, they should serve "as the hands and tool of the principal actor" (*ut manus quaedam et instrumentum agentis*), not the brains; to act on the instructions of assistants (*ex adiutorum agere praeceptis*) is unseemly (*indecorum*) for a decent person, because it betrays lack of expertise (*imperitia*).[25] In a legal setting, Quintilian considers it professionally disqualifying if an advocate needs to draw on a subordinate's knowledge for crucial parts of his case, and particularly disgraceful (*deformiter*) to have to consult junior counsel to handle an unexpected problem in court; an advocate who leans on prompters (*monitores*) because he has not mastered the facts of his case may embarrass himself (*erubescamus*) by mouthing stupid arguments on their advice.[26] In the final tableau that Cicero paints for the judges at Rome, then, it is Verres who looks marginal and sub-altern, reduced to relying on a freedman and three anonymous advisors of risibly low status.

The end of Dolganov's paper brings us to the court of Caracalla, hearing cases argued by eminent orators, including one mentioned in Philostratus' *Lives of the Sophists* (Aristaenetus), apparently more for the emperor's entertainment than in pursuit of justice.[27] I will conclude, therefore, with another case, again featuring Caracalla, that both does and does not conform to the patterns Dolganov has set out. Another lawyer from the eastern provinces, in this case an 'Arabian' named Heliodorus, appears before the bored emperor Caracalla, this time on a tour of western, Celtic provinces.[28] In this story from Philostratus' *Lives of Sophists*, the lines between legal advocacy and sophistic entertainment are explicitly blurred, to the great displeasure of Philostratus himself, who consistently relegates forensic

[24] Cic. *Verr.* 2.2.75. [25] Frontin. *Aq.* 1.2. [26] Quint. *Inst.* 12.3.1–3; 6.4.8–9.
[27] Philostr. *VS* 591. [28] Philostr. *VS* 625–627.

oratory to the margins of sophistic rhetoric.[29] Heliodorus has been sent on an embassy to the emperor, but when his fellow ambassador falls ill, he is forced against his will to plead his case alone. Caracalla reacts in a way that could appear sarcastic: "I've never seen a man like this! A new discovery of our time!" Indeed, that is how the *pepaideumenoi* in the audience take it, and they start laughing, thinking that they are in on a joke with the emperor at the expense of this low-status provincial. The joke is on them, though: either the capricious Caracalla is genuinely charmed by the Arabian ambassador, or he decides to use him to humiliate the educated Greeks in his entourage, because he promptly grants equestrian status to Heliodorus and his whole family. He then allows Heliodorus to give a proper sophistic declamation, chooses the theme himself, and forces his entourage to applaud it. The scene ends with Heliodorus being named *advocatus fisci*—an atypical entry into a typical equestrian career. Philostratus, who was in the audience, resents all of this, as is evident from his sniffy introduction of Heliodorus as one who "should not be considered unworthy of the circle of sophists" (*μηδὲ Ἡλιόδωρος ἀπαξιούσθω σοφιστῶν κύκλου*) and his studiously tepid conclusion that, with his imperial patron dead, this accidental sophist is living out his life at Rome, neither admired nor neglected. In these events, diplomatic and legal advocacy are converted to pure performance, while the lines of ethnicity, class, and access are briefly redrawn for the sake of entertainment—before being reasserted in the pages of Philostratus, our only witness to this man's existence.

This response has sought to draw out a common thread running through these two papers: that ancient performances, both medical and legal, were socially situated; that in a society profoundly oriented toward the public gaze, that measured status, honor, and even truth by public approbation, the actions, reactions, and even mere presence or absence (real or imagined) of other people were vital to the persuasive and self-presentational work of those performances; and that those other participants had goals and perspectives of their own that can sometimes be glimpsed between the lines of the protagonists' accounts. In important ways, performance *becomes* substance.

Bibliography

Atherton, 'Children, Animals, Slaves, and Grammar' (1998) = C. Atherton, 'Children, Animals, Slaves and Grammar,' in Y. L. Too and N. Livingstone, eds., *Pedagogy and Power: Rhetorics of Classical Learning* (Cambridge: Cambridge University Press, 1998) 214–244.

[29] Eshleman, 'Sophists' (2020) 337–338.

Bablitz, *Actors and Audience* (2007) = L. Bablitz, *Actors and Audience in the Roman Courtroom* (New York: Routledge, 2007).

Eshleman, *Social World* (2012) = K. Eshleman, *The Social World of Intellectuals in the Roman Empire: Sophists, Philosophers, and Christians* (Cambridge: Cambridge University Press, 2012).

Eshleman, 'Sophists' (2020) = K. Eshleman, 'Sophists,' in K. de Temmerman, ed., *Oxford Handbook of Ancient Biography* (Oxford: Oxford University Press, 2020) 335–348.

Gleason, 'Truth Contests' (1999) = M. Gleason, 'Truth Contests and Talking Corpses,' in J. I. Porter, ed., *Constructions of the Classical Body* (Ann Arbor: University of Michigan Press, 1999) 287–313.

Gleason, 'Shock and Awe' (2010) = M. Gleason, 'Shock and Awe: The Performance Dimension of Galen's Anatomy Demonstrations,' in C. Gill, T. Whitmarsh, and J. Wilkins, eds., *Galen and the World of Knowledge* (Cambridge: Cambridge University Press, 2010) 85–114.

König, 'Self-Promotion and Self-Effacement' (2011) = J. König, 'Self-Promotion and Self-Effacement in Plutarch's *Table Talk*,' in F. Klotz and K. Oikonomopoulou, eds., *The Philosopher's Banquet: Plutarch's* Table Talk *in the Intellectual Culture of the Roman Empire* (Oxford: Oxford University Press, 2011) 179–203.

Korenjak, *Publikum und Redner* (2000) = M. Korenjak, *Publikum und Redner: Ihre Interaktion in der sophistichen Rhetorik der Kaiserzeit* (Munich: C. H. Beck, 2000).

Lehoux, 'The Authority of Galen's Witnesses' (2017) = D. Lehoux, 'The Authority of Galen's Witnesses,' in J. König and G. Woolf, eds., *Authority and Expertise in Ancient Scientific Culture* (Cambridge: Cambridge University Press, 2017) 260–282.

Lendon, *Empire of Honour* (1997) = J. E. Lendon, *Empire of Honour: The Art of Government in the Roman World* (Oxford: Clarendon Press, 1997).

Mattern, *Rhetoric of Healing* (2008) = S. P. Mattern, *Galen and the Rhetoric of Healing* (Baltimore: Johns Hopkins University Press, 2008).

Mattern, *Prince of Medicine* (2013) = S. P. Mattern, *The Prince of Medicine: Galen in the Roman Empire* (Oxford: Oxford University Press, 2013).

Salas, *Cutting Words* (2020) = L. A. Salas, *Cutting Words: Polemical Dimensions of Galen's Anatomical Experiments* (Leiden and Boston: Brill, 2020).

Schmitz, *Bildung und Macht* (1997) = T. Schmitz, *Bildung und Macht: zur sozialen und politischen Funktion der zweiten Sophistik in der griechischen Welt der Kaiserzeit* (Munich: C. H. Beck, 1997).

von Staden, 'Galen and the "Second Sophistic"' (1997) = H. von Staden, 'Galen and the "Second Sophistic,"' in R. Sorabji, ed., *Aristotle and After* (London: Institute of Classical Studies, 1997) 33–54.

PART III

OVER-SHOOTING THE SUBJECT-MATTER

When Pragmatism and Expertise Collide

Introduction

What Makes the Expert, and His Expertise?

Alice König and Michael Peachin

Medicine and law, two fields of endeavor which ought to have been, on the face of it, practically and pragmatically oriented. At the very least, these were territories lorded over by highly specialized experts. But, what if the ace doctor or lawyer, when he sat himself down to write about his métier, allowed concerns beyond the pure science to lean, in one way or another, and to one degree or another, upon the stuff of his text? Bruce Frier and Claire Bubb will momentarily give some thought to this; and James Uden will push the discussion further. However, before we consider how different authors encumbered the boundaries of their specialist self-presentation, it is worth getting a sure-footed understanding of just what we are talking about here. How was specialized expertise altogether construed in the Roman context? And how was a figure of authority in an area of specialization marked out as such? How was his proficiency to be demonstrated? And are we talking of a stature for such people that is in any way, or ways, similar to modern professionalism? To ask such questions will only return us to a puzzle just alluded to, namely: when an authority on medicine or law took to writing about his bailiwick, how much leeway did he have to wander at will, and how did that affect—even enhance—his 'expert' status? These are far-reaching issues, and there will not be space here to tackle them comprehensively. Luckily, however, there is now quite a bit of excellent literature on much of this; and that work will allow the present contribution to meander in its own particular fashion.[1]

Instead of attempting to offer a comprehensive overview of specialized expertise in the Roman world, the present essay is structured around some particular texts, which can provide us with illustrative case studies: Vitruvius'

The ideas in this essay were contributed by König, but their publication was facilitated by Peachin, who took time (while König was hard-pressed with pandemic-related home-schooling) to help re-constitute the original lecture to fit the format of the volume. König notes sincere thanks to both Peachin and Bubb for their kindness and collaborative spirit during this time.

[1] On the range issues involved here, see especially Lloyd, *Adversaries and Authorities* (1996); Barton, *Power and Knowledge* (2002); Cuomo, *Technology and Culture* (2007); König and Whitmarsh, *Ordering Knowledge in the Roman Empire* (2007); Lloyd, *Disciplines in the Making* (2009); Asper, *Writing Science* (2013); König and Woolf, *Authority and Expertise* (2017); Riggsby, *Mosaics of Knowledge* (2019).

Alice König and Michael Peachin, *Introduction: What Makes the Expert, and His Expertise?* In: *Medicine and the Law under the Roman Empire.* Edited by: Claire Bubb and Michael Peachin, Oxford University Press. © Claire Bubb and Michael Peachin 2023. DOI: 10.1093/oso/9780192898616.003.0006

De architectura; Balbus and the *Corpus Agrimensorum*; Frontinus' *De aquis*; the tenth book of Pliny's *Epistulae*. Underlying this modus operandi is a keen awareness of the variety of attitudes to, and manifestations of, expertise and specialization in the Roman cultural sphere—and, hence, a range of case studies will be offered, flagging up several particular aspects of this whole, rather than a more flattening 'general trends' survey.[2] It is crucial to recognize that this approach derives from an understanding of expertise as something that is socially constructed in a way that specialization is not. To illustrate, Alice König might easily, and persuasively, declare the following: "I am a specialist in Latin literature, fact; I have focused my studies on it, I know more about it than I know about most things, it is truly what I specialize in. But am I an *expert* on Latin literature? Well, the point is: that is not for *me* to say." There is much theorizing about expertise, by psychologists, philosophers, business scholars, and social scientists, among others.[3] Arguably, the most stimulating work in this field is the scholarship that urges us to see expertise as a performance, as well as a property; something that is *enacted* and endlessly "negotiated between aspiring experts and potential audiences; a status that individuals and organizations struggle to have attributed to them by others and which they must work to retain."[4] On that basis, studying expertise must involve studying how people talked about, or represented, or negotiated it, and ought not simply identify types of expertise, or (say) the function of expertise in society. That explains why this essay focuses particularly on *texts*, to look at Roman *discourses* of expertise, as well as actual examples of specialization. Of course, we cannot hope to excavate very much more than elite discourses of expertise from our surviving texts. Nonetheless, it can be hoped that the passages selected here will provide a reasonably diverse picture, with a few glimpses here and there of how specialist knowledge sometimes migrated across social boundaries, as different kinds of expertise were constructed in dialogue with other forms of authority.

[2] It is a leitmotif of Lloyd's work that generalization is problematic, given how much variety we see in ancient constructions of wisdom, expertise, and authority (e.g., Lloyd, *Adversaries and Authorities* (1996) 209). Cuomo also stresses this, drawing attention to diachronic, cross- and intra-cultural differences, and the equally complex range of disciplinary and personal standpoints: see esp. *Technology and Culture* (2007) 7–40: e.g. "the answer to the question 'What is techne?', even limited to classical Greece, especially Athens, to a specific period and to the case of medicine, ought probably to be 'It depends on whom you ask.'"

[3] Some of it sees expertise as a tangible phenomenon, something we can come up with a universal definition for and that individuals can aspire to acquire (e.g., through study or practice); other theories view it less straightforwardly, as a status that is granted (or not) by others rather than (simply) achieved by ourselves. For a sample of views, see, e.g., Ericsson, *Towards a General Theory of Expertise* (1991); Ericsson and Pool, *Peak* (2016); Montero, *Thought in Action* (2016); Ericsson, Hoffman, Kozbelt, and Williams, *The Cambridge Handbook of Experts and Expert Performance* (2018).

[4] Collins and Evans, 'A Sociological/Philosophical Perspective on Expertise' (2018) 21; also Hartelius, *The Rhetoric of Expertise* (2011). See also Collins and Evans, *Rethinking Expertise* (2007); Summerson Carr, 'Enactments of Expertise' (2010).

We will now work through the texts mentioned just above, so as to raise a series of questions which we would do well to think about as we home in on law and medicine. For example, how was trust in experts generated, or eroded? Could limited, or functional, or temporary expertise carry as much weight in some contexts as lifelong vocational learning? How important was knowing-how relative to knowing-that? Did methodological approaches matter as much as depth of knowledge? How important was the concept of progress (i.e., developments in understanding, or new discoveries) in representations of specialist knowledge and expertise? And what did first-hand research, personal discovery, or innovation count for? How were learning, talent, and virtue thought to relate to each other in the person of 'the expert'? What role did literary interactions play in shaping discourses of expertise?[5] How collaboratively did some communities of specialists construct their areas of expertise? Who else (from powerful patrons to the general public) had a say on the identification/authentication of 'expertise'? And what relationships were fashioned between specialist knowledge, expertise, and the state? These, of course, are only some of the questions we might ask, but they will be at the forefront in the discussion that follows.

One further point that must inform our answers to questions like these is that expertise was often fashioned opportunistically; however, this was accomplished while using a recurring set of tropes and manoeuvres (or intertexts, even, in the broadest sense of that word). Expertise could also be attacked or questioned opportunistically (again, often with resort to recurring tropes); and this might occur in ways that did not necessarily reflect pervasive views or values at the time, yet could end up shaping them, or shaping later perceptions of experts and expertise. Therefore, the constitution (or denigration) of expertise certainly played by some common rules. That said, this was also a very dynamic phenomenon, and was closely related to contemporary social, cultural, and political trends. In short, the rules could, at any given moment, shift or mutate rather speedily—often in connection with wider political or cultural developments.[6] That observation is as relevant to the study of expertise in the twenty-first century as it is for the study of ancient constructions of expertise; but our focus is the latter, so now we proceed to some Roman examples.[7]

[5] See, e.g., König, 'Reading Frontinus in Martial's *Epigrams*' (2018) and Harries, 'Saturninus the Helmsman' (2018), on the role played by literary interactions in different constructions of expertise; also König. 'Discourses of Authority in Pliny *Epistles* 10' (forthcoming).

[6] Below, for instance, we discuss several examples of Roman 'experts' adapting their self-presentation to shifting models of Roman imperial power/activity; König, 'Tactical Interactions' (2020) also discusses how two Greek authors adapted their construction of Greek military expertise to the conditions of Roman military hegemony.

[7] Lately, a good deal of attention has been paid to some radical changes in the construction and currency of different kinds of expertise, with some celebrating a growing 'democritization' of knowledge and others bemoaning a perceived 'crisis of expertise.' For a sample of views, see, e.g.: Maasen and Weingart, *Democritization of Expertise?* (2005); Hartelius, 'Wikipedia and the Emergence of Dialogic Expertise' (2010); Pfister, 'Networked Expertise in the Era of Many-to-Many Communication' (2011);

Vitruvius' *De architectura* is obviously a very rich starting point for thinking about the function and currency of specialist knowledge.[8] Written by a practicing architect (who clearly designed buildings, and also worked as a military engineer), it transmits much distinctly specialized knowledge about a very wide range of things—the properties of different kinds of stone, types of temple design, the ins and outs of stucco work, how to source water, the construction of pulleys, water screws, siege engines, and so on. Yet, for all that this book promotes the vital importance of specialist knowledge in many different respects, it also offers us glimpses of some alternative attitudes—for example, the architect who needs only 'functional' expertise in some areas of practice (*De arch.* 1.1.18), and property owners who decide to get along without employing specialists because there are so many unskilled architects out there that they might as well have a go themselves:[9]

> *Cum autem animadverto ab indoctis et inperitis tantae disciplinae magnitudinem iactari et ab is, qui non modo architecturae sed omnimo ne fabricae quidem notitiam habent, non possum non laudare patres familiarum eos, qui litteraturae fiducia confirmati per se aedificantes ita iudicant: si inperitis sit committendum, ipsos potius digniores esse ad suam voluntatem quam ad alienam pecuniae consumere summam.*
>
> But when I observe that this great and noble discipline is being bandied about by people without training or skill (*indoctis et inperitis*), by those who are ignorant not only of architecture but of all knowledge of building, I cannot blame home-owners, who, strengthened by confidence in their own learning, decide to build for themselves, judging that if inexperienced people are to be employed, they themselves would prefer to spend their own capital to their own liking rather than to that of anyone else. [trans. Granger (1931), adapted]

Collins, *Are We All Scientific Experts Now?* (2014); Millgram, *The Great Endarkenment* (2015); Nichols, *The Death of Expertise* (2017); Moore, *Critical Elitism* (2017); Hordern, 'Higher Expertise, Pedagogic Rights and the Post-Truth Society' (2019).

[8] This is so, not least, because Vitruvius himself straddled social boundaries (on which, see the opening chapters of Nichols, *Author and Audience in Vitruvius' De architectura* (2017)). He also takes his reader to many different contexts, in which different kinds of knowledge (philosophical as well as technical, historical as well as mechanical, medical as well as astronomical) had value. On Vitruvius' 'construction of expertise,' see esp. Oksanish, *Vitruvian Man* (2019) 20; Harris-McCoy, 'Making and Defending Claims to Authority in Vitruvius' *De architectura*' (2017); König, 'From Architect to *Imperator*' (2009).

[9] Vitr. *De arch.* 6.pr.6. Note also Vitr. *De arch.* 10.pr., where unskilled architects lead to extra expense for property owners. As for doing it oneself, cf. Cuomo, *Technology and Culture* (2007) 131, on a story told by Cassius Dio about Hadrian's altercation with an architect (Apollodorus) who sneered at Hadrian's lack of architectural knowledge. Hadrian's response was to design a temple, and send the plans to Apollodorus, to prove that a great work could be accomplished without his aid. When Apollodorus wrote back with criticisms, Hadrian had him executed (although, or because, the architect was clearly right).

Vitruvius' various complaints about people not valuing architectural skill enough, and about bad (unskilled or unscrupulous) architects, were presumably motivated in part by professional competitiveness; indeed, one of the things which the *De architectura* does is to advertise to prospective employers a claim that the architect Vitruvius is worth his weight in gold.[10] But complaints such as these are also part of a bigger story that Vitruvius tells across the ten books of the treatise; a story that transforms a technical profession into an elite kind of science.

As it turns out, there is an incredibly ambitious skill set which girds a true (i.e., a genuinely expert) architect. The full requisite ability rests upon both practical, hands-on work (*fabrica*), and on the kind of reasoning ability (*ratiocinatio*) which can only result from a sound grounding in a range of, let us say, academic disciplines:[11]

> *Itaque architecti, qui sine litteris contenderant, ut manibus essent exercitati, non potuerunt efficere, ut haberent pro laboribus auctoritatem; qui autem ratiocinationibus et litteris solis confisi fuerunt, umbram non rem persecuti videntur. at qui utrumque perdidicerunt, uti omnibus armis ornati citius cum auctoritate, quod fuit propositum, sunt adsecuti.*
>
> And so, those architects who contended without a proper intellectual background (*sine litteris*), relying rather upon the fact that they possessed significant hands-on skills, were not able to achieve ascendency (*auctoritas*) on account of their efforts. On the other hand, those who leaned exclusively upon theory and academic training, seemed to have been chasing a shadow, and not the thing itself. However, those who have dedicated themselves to both areas, so that they are girded in full panoply, these men have accomplished what was aimed at more quickly, and with authority (*cum auctoritate*).

What, then, are the *litterae* which the architect must have lapped up? He is to be grounded in draftsmanship, geometry, optics, arithmetic, history, philosophy, physiology, music, mathematics, medicine, law, and astronomy.[12] Vitruvius draws a conclusion thus:[13]

> *Cum ergo tanta haec disciplina sit, condecorata et abundans eruditionibus variis ac pluribus, non puto posse iuste repente profiteri architectos, nisi qui ab aetate puerili his gradibus disciplinarum scandendo scientia plerarumque litterarum et artium nutriti pervenerint ad summum templum architecturae.*

[10] Cf. the disclaimer at Vitr. *De arch.* 6.pr.5, where Vitruvius stresses his modesty and desire to 'be sought' out, rather than to advertise.

[11] Vitr. *De arch.* 1.1.2.

[12] Vitr. *De arch.* 1.1.4–10. Compare this list with the other catalogues of what might be called 'a gentleman's appropriate range of knowledge,' pointed to by Bubb and Peachin above (pp. 9, 19).

[13] Vitr. *De arch.* 1.1.11.

> Therefore, since this is such a great discipline, adorned by and abundant in so many and such various types of erudition, I do not believe that architects can simply announce themselves as such, unless they have climbed step by step, nurtured from an early age by education (*scientia*)—above all, in letters and the arts—to reach the loftiest sanctuary of Architecture. [trans. Rowland and Howe, *Vitruvius* (1999), adapted]

This can all be put in a nutshell: simply specializing in architecture is not enough—the truly expert architect must also be something of an all-rounder.[14] Thus, in a sense, expertise is precisely not equivalent to specialization. And let us note: if we put the matter into precise Roman terms, then the ultimate goal of amassing this variegated skill set is the establishment of one's architectural *auctoritas*. This word, this concept, this value, is key (n.b.) whenever expertise, specialization, professionalism—in sum, whenever one's credentials, and hence, one's potential influence—come into play in a Roman context.

Before moving on, let us make one final point about how expertise is constructed in the *De architectura*. From time to time, Vitruvius allows us glimpses of great innovations in his field: for instance, discoveries by Archimedes, Pythagoras, and Eratosthenes.[15] The preface to book seven then opens with a lengthy celebration of the contributions that many *authors* have made by passing down knowledge over time, enabling wisdom to accumulate and be developed by successive generations. Vitruvius offers a fantastic simile for this, visualising streams of learning all pooling together, like water from different fountains—the source on which he now draws to establish a new set of teachings himself.[16] However, the tight structure and apparently definitive nature of Vitruvius' text (*De arch.* 1.pr.3) imply that further innovation—i.e., the development or addition of new

[14] In fact, two more ingredients ultimately complete the recipe: innate talent and virtue must be added to the mix. Talent: *De arch.* 1.1.3: an architect should be ingenious (*ingeniosum*), and apt in the acquisition of knowledge (*ad disciplinam docilem*). Deficient in either of these qualities, he cannot be a perfect master (*perfectum artificem*). Virtue: *De arch.* 1.1.7: moral philosophy will teach the architect to be above meanness in his dealings. It will make him just, compliant and faithful to his employer; and what is of the highest importance, it will prevent avarice gaining an ascendancy over him. Others engaged in the construction of expertise similarly highlight both talent and virtue, for example Quint. *Inst.* 1.pr.9–12 and *Inst.* 1.pr.26.

[15] Vitr. *De arch.* 9.pr.4–14; note also the gradual evolution of architectural know-how sketched at *De arch.* 2.1–7.

[16] Vitr. *De arch.* 7.pr.1, 10: (1) "Our predecessors, wisely and with advantage, proceeded by written records to hand down their ideas to after times, so that they should not perish, but being augmented from age to age and published in book form, they should come step by step in the course of time to the highest refinement of learning (*ut… gradatim pervenirent… ad summam doctrinarum subtilitatem*)… (10) I owe great gratitude to all those who with an ocean of intellectual services which they gathered from all time, each in his department provided stores from which we, like those who draw water from a spring (*unde nos uti fontibus haurientes aquam*) and use it for their own purposes, have gained the means of writing with more eloquence and readiness; and trusting in such authorities we venture to put together a new manual of architecture (*institutiones novas comparare*)" [trans. Granger (1931), minimally adapted]. On how this gets picked up in Book 8, Vitruvius' water book, see König, 'Tracing the Ebb and Flow of *de Architectura* 8' (2016).

knowledge—has now become unlikely. The impression that the *De architectura* gives, overall, is that an architectural expert is someone who can master all the knowledge that Vitruvius has meticulously, and decisively, set down here—and not someone who will innovate further. Put bluntly, Vitruvius plainly means to have the last word on the subject. He is, in effect, depending upon the *auctoritas* he claims to have amassed to undercut any effort by any potential future (as well as past and present) competitors in the field. And so, one might even wish to pose a provocative question: At some most fundamental level, is *this* what the expertise achieved by a member of the Roman elite was all (or very largely) about? Was having the last word (by writing the definitive, say, manual) the ultimate goal of any given striving for specialized expertise?

We now turn away from architecture to consider another (related) terrain trod by experts: land surveying. The first thing that strikes anyone who dips into the *Corpus Agrimensorum* is surely the hyper-technical, hyper-specialized material which marks its various texts.[17] There are diagrams, statistics, complex instructions, and much more, all of this apparently set out for the benefit of one particular, and seemingly unmistakable, audience: practicing surveyors. That said, the reader also discovers, for example, etymologies and histories, which suggest not just pure pragmatism, but the elevation of *techne* into an intellectually oriented science.

Along these lines, Courtney Roby has shown that, while these texts incorporate a great deal of complex mathematical (especially geometric) *learning* (among other things), they also engage closely with Greek mathematic *literature*, appropriating it and refashioning some of its rhetorical moves—and doing so in ways that helped to enhance the cultural status of surveying, as well as outsiders' impressions of its complexity. She likewise points to the fact that some of these treatises offered complex etymologies of technical terms, or sketched mini histories of land surveying—again, elevating gromatic practice above what we would perceive as the merely practical, giving readers something more than how-to instructions to get their teeth into, and anchoring land surveying firmly in the broad seabed of Roman culture.[18] Serafina Cuomo has also written about similar trends in the *Corpus*, discussing particularly the ways in which some of their exacting mathematical discourse enabled surveyors to claim a distinct set of virtues for their art. Thus, the attention paid to numbers allowed the *agrimensores* to present their work as impartial, just, fair, disinterested, as a brand of discourse consumed with finding the 'truth' of a place.[19] All of this will have served practical

[17] The most accessible edition of the *Corpus* is Campbell, *The Writings of the Roman Land Surveyors* (2000).

[18] Roby, 'Experiencing Geometry' (2014) 29.

[19] Cuomo, *Technology and Culture* (2007) 111–113. Also Cuomo, 'Divide and Rule' (2000) 198: "On the one hand, mathematics guaranteed the possibility and reliability of calculations, and made cataloguing and recording easier, so it was 'directly' useful. On the other hand, it was the values associated with mathematics—fairness, accountability, order, stability, justice—that bolstered the propaganda, or,

purposes, of course. For land surveyors adjudicated in disputes, just as they worked to divide up land in the first place; and, hence, the association of their craft with justice, integrity, and so on must have been helpful on the ground. But such claims went further, helping to transform specialist gromatic knowledge into a much broader kind of expertise, investing it with characteristics and qualities that carried significant cultural, social, and political weight.

As a specific example, we might consider a text which stands at the forefront of a contemporary re-imagining and re-positioning of gromatic expertise: Balbus' *Expositio et ratio omnium formarum* (ch. 1):

> *Notum est omnibus, Celse, penes te studiorum nostrorum manere summam, ideoque primum sedulitatis meae inpendium iudiciis tuis offerre proposui. nam cum sibi inter aequales quendam locum deposcat aemulatio, neminem magis conatibus nostris profuturum credidi quam qui inter eos in hac parte plurimum possit. itaque quo cultior in quorundam notitiam ueniat, omnia tibi nota perlaturus ad te primum liber iste festinet, apud te tirocinii rudimenta deponat, tecum conferat quidquid a me inter ipsas armorum exercitationes accipere potuit. et si meretur publica conuersatione sufferre uniuersorum oculos, a te potissimum incipiat: quod si illi parum diligentem adhibitam curam esse credideris et in aliqua cessasse uidebimur parte, non exiguum laboris mei consequar fructum, quod te monente malignorum lucri fecerim existimationem. quaeso itaque, si non est inprobum, habeat apud te quandam excusationem, quod non potuerit eo tempore consummari, quo genus hoc instrumenti feruentibus studiis nostris disputatum est.*
>
> It is known to everyone, Celsus, that you represent the high point of our science, and consequently I decided to offer to your judgement the first product of my industry. For, although rivalry demands some place for itself among people of the same age, I thought that no one would promote my efforts more effectively than the one who, among his coevals, has the greatest capacity in this activity. So, this book should hurry to you first, bringing material all of which is already known to you, in order that it should come to the attention of certain people in a more polished condition; it should deposit with you the rudiments of my apprenticeship, and discuss with you whatever it was able to receive from me in the midst of my military service. And if it deserves to go before everyone's eyes in public intercourse, it can most appropriately start from you. But if you think that too little care and attention have been applied to the book, and if I seem to have failed in some respect, I shall obtain no insignificant reward for my labour, if through your advice I get the better of the attitude of unfriendly critics. If it is not improper, I beg that you should excuse the book, in that it could not be

if you like, that mediated the relationship between land-surveyor, land and occupiers... between administrators and the administered." On the general principle, see also Lloyd, *Adversaries and Authorities* (1996) 71–72, 207–208.

completed at the time when this type of work was under discussion, when our studies were thriving. [trans. Campbell, 2000, p. 205, L 91.1]

So, the preface is staged as a letter; and in his address to Celsus, Balbus conjures up a close-knit community of gromatic experts, all studying away, but with Celsus as particularly expert and authoritative. Clearly, there is some hierarchical jostling within this community; nonetheless, we also see the surveyors corresponding with each other, to share expertise, so as collaboratively to hone a gromatic treatise for the edification of others (rather as Pliny the Younger corresponds with a select circle of *literati* in his *Epistles*, asking for advice on forthcoming publications).[20] Why the collaboration? Does this perhaps involve a form of protectionism, i.e., the construction of an exclusive and esoteric body of knowledge checked and controlled by the insiders, which is not easily available to others, and which then affords the surveyors a palpable ascendancy, based on their closely guarded skill set? Perhaps.[21] Be that as it may, what we are most certainly confronted with here is a group of men who were not merely dreary technicians; they were equally scholars. And again, these scholars work collaboratively to develop, elevate, and communicate their expertise, thus establishing a distinct sense of progress. But perhaps first and foremost, land surveying is imagined not simply as a specialist *techne*, but as an intellectual and literary endeavor.[22]

The construction of expertise, then, is not simply about elevating specialist knowledge to a higher status: it is sometimes about marrying high-status forms of authority (like social status, and elite education) with technical know-how.[23] To exemplify this further, we also see specialist surveyors borrowing the language and ideology of imperial administration to enhance their authority and expertise. Balbus, for instance, writing under either Domitian or Trajan,[24] takes care to stress the importance of land surveying to the business of Roman *imperium*. In recounting his own military service, he notes that it temporarily interrupted the composition of his treatise: "the famous expedition of our most revered emperor

[20] Pliny's *Letters* are cited here in part to challenge assumptions about what we count as 'literature,' and how we relate more technical kinds of writing—and their audiences—to texts we more comfortably read *as texts*.

[21] This issue of community and its effects, though among the jurists, is also raised by Frier below.

[22] It is worth noting that Frontinus and Balbus are amongst the earliest known writers on Roman land surveying, and thus at the forefront of efforts to elevate this functional, technical activity into something more refined. On their relative dates (sometime under Domitian and/or Trajan) and the administrative/imperial context for their elevation of their 'science,' see e.g. Dilke, 'The Roman Surveyors' (1962) 171; Campbell, 'Shaping the Rural Environment' (1996) 76–77; Campbell, *The Writings of the Roman Surveyors* (2000) xxxix–xl; Guillaumin, 'Le livre gromatique du Haut-Empire' (2010) 161; Roby, 'Experiencing Geometry' (2014) 13–15, with further references in the notes.

[23] On the marriage of different kinds of knowledge and authority, see e.g. Cuomo, *Technology and Culture* (2007) 69–73, discussing the conscious sharing of traits in the construction of military leaders, or 'technician-warriors'.

[24] Balbus mentions the emperor's recent 'victory' in Dacia, suggesting a composition date in the late 80s/early 90s, or (more likely) sometime after Trajan's Dacian Wars in 101–106 CE.

intervened, which lured me from speedy writing. While I was more occupied by military service, I laid aside this entire business, virtually forgetting it, and I thought about nothing but military glory." However, "after we entered enemy territory for the first time, the operations of our emperor immediately began to require surveying skill (*mensurarum rationem*)."[25] He then details a number of ways in which surveying proved instrumental to the mission's success, from the establishment of fortifications and the safeguarding of supply routes to the calculation of river widths and mountain heights on the battlefield, explaining that this inspired him "to cultivate it with even more fervour, as if it were worshipped in every temple, and to hurry to complete this book."[26] Balbus thus performs a similar rhetorical manoeuvre to Vitruvius (*De arch.* 1.pr.), in claiming that the emperor's expansionist activities initially delayed his publication, before allying his science firmly to the imperial project.

Indeed, in Balbus' text (as in Vitruvius') both practicing and *writing about* land surveying (or architecture) are vigorously promoted, as being of huge relevance to contemporary political and administrative activities.[27] As we noted above, the construction of expertise can be understood as a dialogic phenomenon, with would-be-experts constantly requiring others to grant them that status. In this particular case, the dialogic negotiation of expertise and authority is constructed without direct input from other parties, as Balbus co-opts the needs of the state and implicit endorsement of the emperor to establish the social and political value of his discipline and text. Writing about land surveying, then, is not simply concerned with measurements and boundary disputes on the ground; it is also an exercise in some metaphorical boundary *pushing*, indeed a *crossing* of social, political, intellectual, and literary boundaries in the (sometimes pseudo-)dialogic construction of a matrix of different kinds of expertise.

Now, with Frontinus as our guide, let us move from land to water—in this rapid tour of Latin 'technical' (or not-simply-technical) writing. This man's booklet *De aquis* is a striking example of what might be called hyperspecialization—and it is unparalleled, to boot.[28] At the outset of this text, the author claims to have researched everything set down by himself, and to have done this for his own guidance—he is a pure autodidact (*Aq.* 1–3). In other words, neither cumulative scholarship nor collaboration with learned colleagues plays a role in getting this

[25] Trans. Campbell, *The Writings of the Roman Surveyors* (2000) p. 205, L91.1: *interuenit clara sacratissimi imperatoris nostri expeditio, quae me ab ipsa scribendi festinatione seduceret. nam dum armorum magis exerceor cura, totum hoc negotium uelut oblitus intermiseram, nec quicquam aliud quam belli gloriam cogitabam. at postquam primum hosticam terram intrauimus, statim, Celse, Caesaris nostri opera mensurarum rationem exigere coeperunt.*

[26] Cf. Vitr. *De arch.* 10.16, where Vitruvius draws parallels between architects and *imperatores* (commanders or emperors) in the context of sieges: König, 'From Architect to *Imperator*' (2009).

[27] In a forthcoming article, König offers a more detailed reading of the preface of Balbus' land surveying treatise which elaborates on this point.

[28] On its contours and agenda, see esp. DeLaine, '"*De Aquis Suis*"?' (1996); Peachin, *Frontinus* (2004); König, 'Knowledge and Power in Frontinus' *On Aqueducts*' (2007).

expert up to speed. Why? This is presumably due to the simple fact that the only experts available were individuals of significantly lesser status, fellows who might be grilled for information, but who most certainly were not to be parsed as colleagues, with whom one might decorously consult. And obviously, there was no tradition of a scholarly literature on water supply to be had from such folk—or indeed, to be had at all. Be that as it may, Frontinus turned himself into *the* expert par excellence on Rome's hydraulic system, a fact substantiated laboriously and incontrovertibly in the pages of the *De aquis*. This *commentarius* establishes its author's unqualified *auctoritas* firstly by its punctilious examination of every conceivable facet of Rome's water supply.[29] Every last drop of water—precisely where it is and exactly how it got there—is intimately known by this *curator aquarum*. And the *De aquis* itself appears to have aimed at a position as the be-all and end-all of writing on the topic. What Frontinus did not manage to achieve, however, was the establishment of a new field for research and composition (in contrast to his gromatic peers); his foray into a written world of water would remain, throughout antiquity, one of a kind.

That said, Frontinus makes moves that might have served to fit this *formula administrationis* quite nicely into the ambit of humane discourse—or at the very least, his thoughts are couched in such terms. So, one reads that everything in the booklet stems from a great new emperor's solicitous concern for the health and safety of the empire's core, Rome herself (*Aq.* 1). And of course, the whole business must be settled into its proper and venerable historical context (*Aq.* 4–15). Frontinus' parade through the past then culminates with a description of the Anio Novus conduit, whose arches are the very highest of all the aqueducts, in some places more than 109 feet—*hi sunt arcus altissimi* (*Aq.* 15.7). One last bit of all-encompassing contextualization was surely apposite, before getting down to the dull drudgery of facts and figures (*Aq.* 16):[30]

> *Tot aquarum tam multis necessariis molibus pyramidas videlicet otiosas conpares aut cetera inertia sed fama celebrate opera Graecorum.*
>
> Perhaps you might like to compare those good-for-nothing pyramids, or all those feeble (even if they are famous) Greek constructions, with so many indispensable colossal structures carrying such a flood of water.

[29] His *methodical* methods are as important here as the knowledge he amasses. Note, however, Frontinus' own formulation. He says that in making his rounds of the water lines, he will not need lictors to elicit obeisance. Rather, he will depend upon his own *fides*, along with the *auctoritas* devolved upon him by the emperor (*Aq.* 101.4). In other words, his level of expertise appears to be subsumed in the quality *fides* (on which, see also *Aq.* 1, where the word means more flatly a sense of duty), whereas *auctoritas* now expresses a level of formal power deputized to him by the Princeps. As we saw above with architects and land surveyors, different aspects of expertise and authority meet and merge on a complex matrix made up of different intellectual, social, and political values/strands.

[30] Rather astonishingly, Frontinus says, straight out, that much of what he writes is deathly dull (*Aq.* 77).

Nor is this matchup, pitting Rome against impotent Greeks and frivolous Egyptians, the sum total of the *aemulatio* floating about in this document. Having listed all of his predecessors in the post as *curator aquarum* (*Aq.* 102), Frontinus straightaway shows his reader what these men ought to have been doing, but clearly were not doing; and that is what he, now, will correct. Indeed, he flat out derides his predecessors, growling that, in their sloth and indolence (*inertia et segnitia*), they disdained lowering themselves to fulfilling the necessary duties of the position they had been lucky enough to receive (*Aq.* 101.2).

We might summarize Frontinus' stance about his own hydraulic expertise as follows; and in drawing up this tally, it will be noticed that various issues of concern to Vitruvius or the *agrimensores* surface here, too. Firstly, those who perhaps knew something concrete about the business Frontinus needed to learn, that is, the humble functionaries in the bureau, were allegedly, and to a man, corrupt. The individuals in charge, i.e., all of the previous gentlemen who had held the post as *curator aquarum*, turned out to be benighted loafers. The result: Frontinus taught himself, thus becoming not only the greatest expert on Rome's water, but the *only* one among the elite—and a man of integrity to boot. (Virtue rears its head again.) In this, the man appears to have acted in a rather singular fashion; moreover, the book he produced was similarly idiosyncratic. And of course, his own *fides*, along with the *auctoritas* lent him by Nerva, will have served to buttress the whole effort. Ultimately, however, the level of this curator's expertise looks not to have been challenged; nor has it been, really, down to the present. That is to say, Frontinus, especially by writing the *De aquis* in the way that he did, established himself in perpetuity as Rome's resident expert on water supply.

However, despite all of the exceptionality on display here, the essential tools with which Frontinus fashioned his claim to prowess were those we have already seen deployed elsewhere: a carefully crafted piece of writing, involving aesthetic devices of several sorts, which serve to spruce up, and undergird, the highly technical material on offer. Thus, the elevation of a *techne* into an intellectually oriented science, and the *technites* into a *pepaideumenos*; the marriage of high-status forms of authority with technical know-how (like Vitruvius and Balbus, Frontinus borrows a good deal of rhetoric and *auctoritas* from the emperor and the wider Roman imperial project); competitive denigration of any possible rival (though here, as it turns out, there is little or no interest in cooperation with colleagues, which we did notice among the land surveyors, and will notice below among the lawyers); appeal to the particular grandeur of the business at hand; a sense that there might be progress made in the science at hand, but, also, that the work of the speaker or writer might be offered up as the alpha and omega to that progress. One might encapsulate this all by asserting the following: with these self-same tools, Frontinus might likewise have shaped for himself (had he opted for yet another field in which to excel, in addition to his forays into land surveying and military science), a renowned place among the doctors or the lawyers.

Not all senators, however, felt the need to go as far as did Frontinus in forging himself as Rome's water guru—and this is where Pliny the Younger merits another mention. In a longer piece, König has suggested that Pliny constructs his authority as an imperial administrator, across Book 10 of his *Epistles*, in dialogue with the influential model that his one-time patron Frontinus had set.[31] But (she argues), while Pliny at times makes capital out of sounding like Frontinus (especially at *Ep.* 10.37, where he starts spouting aqueduct facts and figures), on the whole he *rejects* the Frontinian model of hyper-specialization. In fact, *Epistles* 10 largely sketches Pliny's gradual and diverse learning journey, displaying how he becomes increasingly adept at governing Bithynia by amassing (limited) knowledge of many different areas of governance. We observe him acquiring financial, legal, hydraulic, architectural, and other kinds of specialist knowledge, all of this, though, on the job. We are not so much in the presence of Pliny the fully formed pro, but we watch as the student progresses through his studies, as it were. That said, such technical skills as Pliny gradually masters combine with other assets (his political position as a representative of the emperor, his social status, his ethics, along with his willingness to research, reflect, and learn) so as ultimately to reveal him as an exemplary, and expert, administrator. What is more, Pliny constructs his administrative expertise, throughout this book of his *Epistles*, dialogically with his interlocutor, the emperor Trajan, whose wisdom and expertise are always greater than Pliny's (though the balance shifts somewhat over the course of the book).[32] Trajan's own expertise at governing is again founded partly on some (limited) command of specialist knowledge, but also on other qualities: virtues, like foresight, justice, and so on.[33] Also key here are the epistemological approaches evinced by the emperor: the careful weighing up of evidence, consideration of multiple angles, astute judgement in complex cases. Thus, while both Trajan and Pliny display some specialist know-how, it is plain that neither of them feels the need to dig as deep as did Frontinus: indeed, they both favor delegation, recommending specialist advisors at times (land surveyors, architects, engineers, and so on) even as they display some limited literacy in those fields.

[31] König, 'Discourses of Authority in Pliny *Epistles* 10' (forthcoming 2023).

[32] The most influential studies of Pliny's 'dialogue' with Trajan in Book 10 remain Woolf, 'Pliny's Province' (2006); Stadter, 'Pliny and the Ideology of Empire' (2006); and Noreña, 'The Social Economy of Pliny's Correspondence with Trajan' (2007); Lavan, 'Pliny Epistles 10 and Imperial Correspondence' (2018) offers some important counter-arguments.

[33] A little like Frontinus' *fides* in the *De aquis*, 'foresight' (*providentia*, or *pronoia*) was often conceived of as a mix between a virtue and a technical kind of know-how, e.g., in Frontinus' *Strategemata* and a range of Hellenistic military manuals (Cuomo, *Technology and Culture* (2007) 69–70).

Harry Collins and Robert Evans might describe the expertise that Pliny depicts himself acquiring over the course of *Epistles* 10 as 'functional' or 'interactional expertise': that is to say, he knows *about* things (though plainly to a lesser degree than does Frontinus), yet not enough about those things so as to be able adeptly to *do* them (i.e., 'contributory expertise').[34] In some ways, though, the construction of the expert governor (and the ideal emperor) in *Epistles* 10 is much more about doing than about knowing—or rather, it is about a kind of wisdom that consists of significantly more than mere knowledge: it is the embedding of some (limited) 'interactional expertise' into a wider set of qualities and processes, like critical analysis and good judgement: intellectual and ethical *activities* which make appropriate use of technical know-how (among other things). This is the kind of 'expertise' upon which administrative and political power—leadership—is *really* founded, a kind of expertise that does not require an emperor or administrator to *know everything*.

Let us now formulate a few takeaways from all of the above. First, it must be realized that this has inevitably been a very partial picture, focused very much on the kinds of circles that upper-crust doctors and lawyers mixed in, and ignoring many lower-status or less visible forms of specialist knowledge and expertise. Even within elite culture, though, we have seen that the value of specialist knowledge was situationally variable, with limited/functional/temporary and doxic (common) knowledge sometimes carrying as much weight as highly technical, esoteric, specialist knowledge did with different audiences, in different settings. Then, it should be plain that expertise was constructed dialogically, interdiscursively, even intertextually, and (for all that) often quite opportunistically—very much in response to contemporary social, cultural and political pressures or trends, as well as personal circumstances. That all said, if we were to tender one generalization about expertise in the Roman world, it might well be that this was quite a hybrid phenomenon, comprising talent, values and methods, as well as unvarnished specialist knowledge. Furthermore, we have seen expertise imagined as a 'summit,' or something almost divine—but above all, the models of expertise that we have looked at tend to mould 'experts' (as opposed to specialists) in the image of the ruling elite.[35] That could lead to a degree of social mobility for experts (if they were recognized, or fought for recognition, as such). However, there was also a conservative, protectionist tendency which bonded knowledge to power in ways that disempowered others who were 'simply' knowledgeable. The construction (or ongoing re-imagination) of expertise was thus a dynamic social force (for it could lead to some power re-structures). Yet, on the whole, ancient constructions of

[34] Collins and Evans, 'A Sociological/Philosophical Perspective on Expertise' (2018).

[35] Another example (just one of many) can be seen in the preface to Aelianus Tacticus' *Tactical Theory*, where Trajan and Alexander the Great function as co-ordinates against which the military expert can define his credentials: König, 'Tactical Interactions' (2020).

expertise tended principally to conserve power in traditional places—with people who were part of (or who looked like, or who could communicate successfully with) the elite benefiting most. With all of this now before us, let us turn to the issue of what happens when a medical or legal expert, writing about his area of specialty, arguably moves beyond the purely pragmatic aspects of his discipline.

Bibliography

Asper, *Writing Science* (2013) = M. Asper, ed., *Writing Science: Medical and Mathematical Authorship in Ancient Greece* (Berlin: De Gruyter, 2013).

Barton, *Power and Knowledge* (2002) = T. Barton, *Power and Knowledge. Astrology, Physiognomics, and Medicine under the Roman Empire* (Ann Arbor: University of Michigan Press, 2002).

Campbell, 'Shaping the Rural Environment' (1996) = J. B. Campbell, 'Shaping the Rural Environment: Surveyors in Ancient Rome,' *Journal of Roman Studies* 86 (1996) 74–99.

Campbell, *The Writings of the Roman Land Surveyors* (2000) = J. B. Campbell, *The Writings of the Roman Land Surveyors: Introduction, Text, Translation and Commentary* (London: The Society for the Promotion of Roman Studies, 2000).

Collins, *Are We All Scientific Experts Now?* (2014) = H. Collins, *Are We All Scientific Experts Now?* (Cambridge: Polity Press, 2014).

Collins and Evans, 'A Sociological/Philosophical Perspective on Expertise' (2018) = H. Collins and R. Evans, 'A Sociological/Philosophical Perspective on Expertise: The Acquisition of Expertise through Socialization,' in Ericsson, Hoffman, Kozbelt, and Williams, eds., *The Cambridge Handbook of Expertise and Expert Performance* (2018) 21–32.

Collins and Evans, *Rethinking Expertise* (2007) = H. Collins and R. Evans, *Rethinking Expertise* (Chicago: University of Chicago Press, 2007).

Cuomo, 'Divide and Rule' (2000) = S. Cuomo, 'Divide and Rule: Frontinus and Roman Land-Surveying,' *Studies in History and Philosophy of Science* 31.2 (2000) 189–202.

Cuomo, *Technology and Culture* (2007) = S. Cuomo, *Technology and Culture in Greek and Roman Antiquity* (Cambridge: Cambridge University Press, 2007).

DeLaine, '"*De Aquis Suis*"?' (1996) = J. DeLaine, '"*De Aquis Suis*"? The "commentarius" of Frontinus,' in C. Nicolet, ed., *Les littératures techniques dans l'antiquité romaine: Statut, public et destination, tradition* (Geneva: Fondation Hardt, 1996) 117–145.

Dilke, 'The Roman Surveyors' (1962) = O. A. W. Dilke, 'The Roman Surveyors,' *Greece & Rome* 9.2 (1962) 170–180.

Ericsson, *Towards a General Theory of Expertise* (1991) = K. A. Ericsson, *Towards a General Theory of Expertise: Prospects and Limits* (Cambridge: Cambridge University Press, 1991).

Ericsson, Hoffman, Kozbelt, and Williams, *The Cambridge Handbook of Experts and Expert Performance* (2018) = K. A. Ericsson, R. R. Hoffman, A. Kozbelt, A. M. Williams, eds., *The Cambridge Handbook of Experts and Expert Performance*, 2nd ed. (Cambridge: Cambridge University Press, 2018).

Ericsson and Pool, *Peak* (2016) = K. A. Ericsson and R. Pool, *Peak: Secrets from the New Science of Expertise* (Boston: Houghton Mifflin Harcourt, 2016).

Granger (1931) = Vitruvius: *De architectura*, trans. Frank Granger (Cambridge, MA: Harvard University Press, 1931).

Guillaumin, 'Le livre gromatique du Haut-Empire' (2010) = J.-Y. Guillaumin, 'Le livre gromatique du Haut-Empire,' in Y. Perrin, ed., *Neronia VIII: Bibliothèques, livres et culture écrite dans l'empire romain de César à Hadrian. Actes du VIII*[e] *Colloque international de la SIEN (Paris, 2–4 octobre 2008)* (Brussels: Éditions Latomus, 2010) 156–164.

Harries, 'Saturninus the Helmsman' (2018) = J. Harries, 'Saturninus the Helmsman, Pliny and Friends: Legal and Literary Letter Collections,' in A. König and C. Whitton, eds., *Roman Literature under Nerva, Trajan and Hadrian: Literary Interactions, AD 96–138* (Cambridge: Cambridge University Press, 2018) 260–279.

Harris-McCoy, 'Making and Defending Claims to Authority in Vitruvius' *De architectura*' (2017) = D. Harris-McCoy, 'Making and Defending Claims to Authority in Vitruvius' *De architectura*,' in J. König and G. Woolf, eds., *Authority and Expertise* (Cambridge: Cambridge University Press, 2017) 107–128.

Hartelius, *The Rhetoric of Expertise* (2011) = E. J. Hartelius, *The Rhetoric of Expertise* (Lanham, MD: Lexington Books, 2011).

Hartelius, 'Wikipedia and the Emergence of Dialogic Expertise' (2010) = E. J. Hartelius, 'Wikipedia and the Emergence of Dialogic Expertise,' *Southern Communication Journal* 75.5 (2010) 505–526.

Hordern, 'Higher Expertise, Pedagogic Rights and the Post-Truth Society' (2019) = J. Hordern, 'Higher Expertise, Pedagogic Rights and the Post-Truth Society,' *Teaching in Higher Education: Critical Perspectives* 24 (2019) 288–301.

König, 'Knowledge and Power in Frontinus' *On Aqueducts*' (2007) = A. R. König, 'Knowledge and Power in Frontinus' *On Aqueducts*,' in J. König and T. Whitmarsh, eds., *Ordering Knowledge in the Roman Empire* (Cambridge: Cambridge University Press, 2007) 177–205.

König, 'From Architect to *Imperator*' (2009) = A. R. König, 'From Architect to *Imperator*: Vitruvius and his Addressee in the *De Architectura*,' in L. Taub and A. Doody, eds., *Authorial Voices in Greco-Roman Technical Writing* (Trier: WVT Wissenschaftlicher Verlag, 2009) 31–52.

König, 'Tracing the Ebb and Flow of *de Architectura* 8' (2016) = A. R. König, 'Tracing the Ebb and Flow of *de Architectura* 8,' *Arethusa* 49.2 (2016) 161–181.

König, 'Reading Frontinus in Martial's *Epigrams*' (2018) = A. R. König, 'Reading Frontinus in Martial's *Epigrams*,' in A. König and C. Whitton, eds., *Roman*

Literature under Nerva, Trajan and Hadrian: Literary Interactions, AD 96–138 (Cambridge: Cambridge University Press, 2018) 233–259.

König, 'Tactical Interactions' (2020) = A. R. König, 'Tactical Interactions: Dialogues between Greece and Rome in the Military Manuals of Aelian and Arrian,' in A. R. König, R. Langlands, and J. Uden, eds., *Literature and Culture in the Roman Empire, 96–235 CE:Cross-Cultural Interactions* (Cambridge: Cambridge University Press, 2020) 134–158.

König, 'Discourses of Authority in Pliny *Epistles* 10' (forthcoming 2023) = A. R. König, 'Discourses of Authority in Pliny *Epistles* 10,' in M. Neger and S. Tzounakas, eds., *Absorbing Genres: Intertextual Studies in Pliny's Epistles* (forthcoming 2023).

König and Whitmarsh, *Ordering Knowledge* (2007) = J. König and T. Whitmarsh, eds., *Ordering Knowledge in the Roman Empire* (Cambridge: Cambridge University Press, 2007).

König and Woolf, *Authority and Expertise* (2017) = J. König and G. Woolf, eds., *Authority and Expertise in Ancient Scientific Culture* (Cambridge: Cambridge University Press, 2017).

Lavan, 'Pliny Epistles 10 and Imperial Correspondence' (2018) = M. Lavan, 'Pliny *Epistles* 10 and Imperial Correspondence: The Empire of Letters,' in A. König and C. Whitton, eds., *Roman Literature under Nerva, Trajan and Hadrian: Literary Interactions,* AD *96–138* (Cambridge: Cambridge University Press, 2018) 280–301.

Lloyd, *Adversaries and Authorities* (1996) = G. E. R. Lloyd, *Adversaries and Authorities. Investigations into Ancient Greek and Chinese Science* (Cambridge: Cambridge University Press, 1996).

Lloyd, *Disciplines in the Making* (2009) = G. E. R. Lloyd, *Disciplines in the Making. Cross-Cultural Perspectives on Elites, Learning, and Innovation* (Oxford and New York: Oxford University Press, 2009).

Maasen and Weingart, *Democritization of Expertise?* (2005) = S. Maasen and P. Weingart, eds., *Democritization of Expertise? Exploring Novel Forms of Scientific Advice and Political Decision-Making* (Dordrech: Springer, 2005).

Millgram, *The Great Endarkenment* (2015) = E. Millgram, *The Great Endarkenment: Philosophy for an Age of Hyperspecialisation* (Oxford: Oxford University Press, 2015).

Montero, *Thought in Action* (2016) = B. Montero, *Thought in Action: Expertise and the Conscious Mind* (Oxford: Oxford Scholarship Online, 2016).

Moore, *Critical Elitism* (2017) = A. Moore, *Critical Elitism: Deliberation, Democracy and the Problem of Expertise* (Cambridge: Cambridge University Press, 2017).

Nichols, *Author and Audience in Vitruvius' De architectura* (2017) = M. F. Nichols, *Author and Audience in Vitruvius' De architectura* (Cambridge: Cambridge University Press, 2017).

Nichols, *The Death of Expertise* (2017) = T. Nichols, *The Death of Expertise: the Campaign against Established Knowledge and Why It Matters* (Oxford: Oxford University Press, 2017).

Noreña, 'The Social Economy of Pliny's Correspondence with Trajan' (2007) = C. F. Noreña, 'The Social Economy of Pliny's Correspondence with Trajan,' *American Journal of Philology* 128.2 (2007) 239–277.

Oksanish, *Vitruvian Man* (2019) = J. Oksanish, *Vitruvian Man: Rome under Construction* (Oxford: Oxford University Press, 2019).

Peachin, *Frontinus* (2004) = M. Peachin, *Frontinus and the Curae of the Curator Aquarum* (Stuttgart: Franz Steiner Verlag, 2004).

Pfister 'Networked Expertise in the Era of Many-to-Many Communication: On Wikipedia and Invention' (2011) = D. Pfister, 'Networked Expertise in the Era of Many-to-Many Communication: On Wikipedia and Invention,' *Social Epistemology: A Journal of Knowledge, Culture and Policy* 25.3 (2011) 217–231.

Riggsby, *Mosaics of Knowledge* (2019) = A. M. Riggsby, *Mosaics of Knowledge. Representing Information in the Roman World* (Oxford and New York: Oxford University Press, 2019).

Roby, 'Experiencing Geometry' (2014) = C. Roby, 'Experiencing Geometry in Roman Surveyors' Texts,' *Nuncius* (2014) 9–52.

Rowland and Howe, *Vitruvius* (1999) = I. D. Rowland and T. N. Howe, *Vitruvius: Ten Books on Architecture* (Cambridge: Cambridge University Press, 1999).

Stadter, 'Pliny and the Ideology of Empire' (2006) = P. A. Stadter, 'Pliny and the Ideology of Empire. The Correspondence with Trajan,' *Prometheus* 32 (2006) 61–76.

Summerson Carr, 'Enactments of Expertise' (2010) = E. Summerson Carr, 'Enactments of Expertise,' *Annual Review of Anthropology* 39 (2010) 17–32.

Woolf, 'Pliny's Province' (2006) = G. Woolf, 'Pliny's Province,' in T. Bekker-Nielsen, ed., *Rome and the Black Sea Region; Domination, Romanisation, Resistance* (Aarhus: Aarhus University Press, 2006) 93–108.

Juristic Literature and the Law

Competition and Cooperation

Bruce W. Frier

In this paper, I explore an aspect of legal culture among the Roman jurists in the Early and High Classical periods, roughly 100 BCE to 150 CE. During these two and one-half centuries, the Roman jurists, a relatively small community of legal experts, enunciated and developed the legal norms to be applied in private litigation in Roman courts, even though they had no direct control of the process of adjudication. The question I want to ask is this: to what extent is it likely that the jurists, in their rule-finding, may in some instances have been motivated less by purely legal considerations than by an "extra-legal" desire to establish their individual superiority over their peers?

On the basis of surviving evidence (as preserved mostly in the collected excerpts of Justinian's *Digest*), it is impossible to answer this question decisively. But the question can be put obliquely: were individual jurists ever led by their 'juristic ambition' to take unreasonable legal positions, simply in order to demonstrate their superior intelligence and wit? In this paper, I only raise the question and try to examine it on the basis of one famous juristic controversy.

The starting point is a paradox. It is well known that early imperial jurists were usually members of the upper classes and that, indeed, a good many were senators who attained the consulate, the highest Republican magistracy.[1] They lived in a demanding and intensely competitive political milieu that is well known from Pliny's letters, for instance.[2] Those who pursued public careers, such as Javolenus, Neratius, Celsus, and Julian in the High Classical period, held offices that

The author would like to thank Caroline Humfress and Tom McGinn for their close reading of a draft, as well as the editors of this volume for useful dialogue.

[1] Kunkel, *Herkunft*[2] (1967) 272–290; Wieacker, *Rechtsgeschichte* II (2006) 29–31.

[2] For some remarks on Pliny and the jurists, see James Uden's response paper below. Senators could often be astonishingly rude toward one another, almost as if such conduct was expected; see Peachin, 'Friendship and Abuse' (2001) and 'Attacken und Erniederigungen' (2007). Compare the jurist Javolenus' disruptive behavior in a non-legal setting: Plin. *Epist.* 6.15. As Barbara Levick observed, 'Politics of the Early Principate' (1985) 64, the decline in the Principate of many traditional roads to elite fame and fortune "gave greater prominence to the contest for place and dignity that had always been important in Roman politics."

Bruce W. Frier, *Juristic Literature and the Law: Competition and Cooperation* In: *Medicine and the Law under the Roman Empire.* Edited by: Claire Bubb and Michael Peachin, Oxford University Press. © Claire Bubb and Michael Peachin 2023. DOI: 10.1093/oso/9780192898616.003.0007

frequently carried them into administrative positions across the vast empire;[3] and even a jurist like Titius Aristo, who eschewed a public career, could find himself overwhelmed with ordinary legal business at Rome (Pliny, *Epist.* 1.22.2, 6).

Roman law was not a full-time occupation for the jurists, nothing remotely like law is for most lawyers today. The pursuit of private law blended complexly with their lives as powerful, gifted, and highly experienced statesmen. And yet they found time to write, voluminously: in Julian's case, for instance, ninety books of *Digesta*, plus ten more of commentaries on two prior jurists, works filled with intricate analysis of legal problems. Anyone who has spent weeks on end untying the knots in Julian's analogies will come away with an appreciation of his extraordinary ease in handling legal materials. But despite the obvious devotion of the Roman jurists to their craft, they received no direct compensation for their work (luckily, most came from wealthy families to begin with), and their practice of law resembled, to speak in modern terms, less a vocation than an avocation.

Puzzlingly, however, when we turn to what survives of their writing, this competitive drive seems almost to evanesce. Here a brilliant monograph by Mario Bretone, building on an earlier study by Andreas Schwarz, has elucidated the ostensible working methods of the jurists to the extent these emerge from their surviving opinions.[4] As Romanists now generally recognize, the jurists often disagreed with one another, the frequency of such disagreement being only thinly disguised, in the *Digest*, by the eagerness of Justinian's compilers to resolve juristic disputes whenever feasible. Of course, such disagreement among legal professionals is not unusual from an historical perspective. What is more extraordinary is the willingness of the jurists to let such disagreements carry on over centuries without coming to a clear resolution.

Moreover, this high level of juristic disagreement was maintained within a conventional structure of argument that is, certainly by the standards of modern legal scholarship, remarkably polite, almost mannerly. When a disagreement arises, jurists commonly refer to it as a *quaestio*, "inquiry," or *dubitatio*, "uncertainty"; the corresponding Latin verbs are *quaeritur*, "question has arisen," and *dubitat*, "it is uncertain." For subsequent juristic discussion, the mild word *disputatio* is occasionally used.[5] Avoided, by contrast, are a wide range of more forceful Latin words for "disagreement," such as *altercatio*, *discrepatio* or *discrepantia*, *discidium*, *discordia*, *dissensio* or *dissensus*, *iurgium*, *rixa*, and especially

[3] This is evident in inscriptions listing the offices of Javolenus (*ILS* 1015, provincial offices only; compare Plin. *Epist.* 6.15.3) and Julian (*ILS* 8973); see also Pactumeius Clemens (*ILS* 1067).

[4] Bretone, *Ius Controversum* (2008); Schwarz, 'Das Strittige Recht' (1951).

[5] Gaius *Inst.* 1.188 (*longa erat disputatio*); and compare the *Disputationes* of Ulpian and Tryphoninus. Cf. Schulz, *History* (1946) 225. Compare Cic. *Top.* 56 (*in respondendo disputationes*), 66 (*de consultationibus suis disputare*), 72; also Paul (1 *ad Vitellium*) D. 28.2.19 (*Scaevola respondit non videri, et in disputando adiciebat* . . .). On *disputatio fori* in Pomponius (*libro singulari enchiridii*) D. 1.2.2.5, see below. *Disputatio* is more often used of private disputes: Julian (54 *digestorum*) D. 50.17.65 (= Ulpian, D. 50.16.177), Ulpian (13 *ad edictum*) D. 4.8.21.6.

controversia.[6] Roman jurisprudence thus allows for legal uncertainty, but not for *ius controversum*.[7]

In many passages, when a *quaestio* is mentioned, there follows a brief and usually rather neutral description of the disagreement, usually without report of extensive argumentation. The initial query remains open until the jurists ultimately reach a degree of consensus as to the correct answer, at which point, most commonly, the verb often used is *constat*, "it is agreed," or *satis constat*, "it is sufficiently agreed." Other formulations are, for instance, *fere convenit*, "the general view is"; *magis placuit* or *plerisque placuit*, "most jurists have held"; or *maxime placuit*, "there is widespread agreement," and so on.[8] This is "the law we use" (*ius quo utimur*). What such wording suggests is a process whereby juristic opinions might gradually converge on the one answer deemed preferable.

There is, however, no evidence for any recognized mechanism, such as organized open discussion or voting, in order to obtain, or at least to facilitate, juristic consensus on such an answer. In the absence of these mechanisms, one might anticipate that the jurists would have informally relied on the relative authority of those advocating a contested position. But although authority is doubtless tacitly invoked when a Celsus or a Julian is cited, express use of argument from a previous jurist's *auctoritas* apparently occurs only in republican jurisprudence.[9] Likewise, although the preference of *iudices*, judges in actual lawsuits, for one position over another may have had greater weight than Romanists once supposed, no reliable external means for settling juristic disagreements existed before the emperors began forcefully legislating for private law especially after the mid-second century CE.

Nor is it totally clear what criteria the jurists themselves use in preferring one answer to another. In some passages, a jurist praises a rule as preferable on grounds of its greater fairness (*aequius*) or liberality (*benignius*) or practicality (*utilius*); but no clear scheme for choosing can be discerned.[10]

[6] *Dissentio* of jurists only at Gaius *Inst.* 1.7, 3.141. On *controversia*: it appears once in Scaevola (8 *quaestionum*) D. 29.7.14 pr., on which Bretone, *Ius Controversum* (2008) 802–804. Far more frequently this word is used for litigation: *VIR* (1903–87) s.v. "controversia," cols. 1008–1010.

[7] *Ius controversum* is a rhetorical concept that allows for conflicting "valid" rules within a single legal system, with a judicial choice between them then made on a fact-specific basis that accords trial advocates maximum room for maneuver: Frier, *Rise* (1985) 127–128; also Schwarz, 'Das Strittige Recht' (1951) 204–207, noting passages like Cic. *De or.* 1.241–242 and *Off.* 3.91, in which juristic disagreements are offhandedly described by the orator as *controversiae*. Juristic avoidance of the term and the concept is surely deliberate.

[8] Bretone, *Ius Controversum* (2008) 843–848.

[9] Schiller, 'Jurists' Law' (1958) 1232–1233; *Mechanisms* (1978) 284–291. In the late Republic, the students of Servius often appear to treat him as a definitive authority (e.g., Alfenus, 2 *Dig. a Paulo Epit.*, D. 28.5.46); see Bremer, *Iurisprudentia* I (1896) 152.

[10] See also Wieacker, *Rechtsgeschichte* II (2006) 44–51.

But here Bretone is particularly helpful in isolating one frequently repeated phrase, that a particular answer to a legal question is considered "truer" (*verius*) than others.[11] Pomponius gives a nice example:[12]

> *Si supra tuum parietem vicinus aedificaverit, proprium eius id quod aedificaverit fieri Labeo et Sabinus aiunt: sed Proculus tuum proprium, quemadmodum tuum fieret, quod in solo tuo alius aedificasset: quod verius est.*
>
> If a neighbor builds atop your wall, Labeo and Sabinus say that what he builds becomes his property; but Proculus, that it is your property, just as what a third party had built on your land becomes yours. This position is truer (*verius*).

In translating the Latin, the temptation is irresistible to render *verius* as "more correct" (so the Watson *Digest*) or "most correct" (the Dutch translation: "meest juiste"). But Pomponius appears to go even further, beyond correctness to a standard of actual truthfulness.

Still more startling are texts such as this one from Javolenus:[13]

> *Si debitor mulieris dotem sponso promiserit, posse mulierem ante nuptias a debitore eam pecuniam petere neque eo nomine postea debitorem viro obligatum futurum ait Labeo. falsum est, quia ea promissio in pendenti esset, donec obligatio in ea causa est.*
>
> If a woman's debtor promises a dowry to her fiancé, Labeo says that before the marriage the woman can (nonetheless) sue for this money from the debtor, nor will the debtor thereafter be liable to the man on this account. This position is false (*falsum*), since the promise remains in suspense so long as the obligation is in this situation.

[11] Bretone, *Ius Controversum* (2008) 834–843, with further bibliography. This usage is clearly Classical; see Gaius *Inst.* 3.64a, 183, 193–194; perhaps also 4.60. If Pomponius (5 *ad Quintum Mucium*) D. 24.1.51 is to be believed, the usage was already late republican.

[12] Pomponius (33 *ad Sabinum*) D. 41.1.28.

[13] Iavolenus (6 *ex posterioribus Labeonis*) D. 23.3.80 (cf. D. 23.3.83). See Bretone, *Ius Controversum* (2008) 825–826. Compare, for instance, Iavolenus (2 *ex posterioribus Labeonis*) D. 35.1.40.2 (Labeo demonstrates that Ofilius' position is *falsum*); Celsus (6 *Digestorum*) D. 15.1.6 (Labeo's criticism of Tubero is *falsum*); Gaius *Inst.* 3.64 (an opinion of Pegasus is *aperte falsa*); Pomponius (11 *ad Sabinum*) D. 21.2.29 pr. (Celsus described Nerva's view as *falsum*); Pomponius (9 *ad Quintum Mucium*) D. 34.2.34 (a view of Q. Mucius is partly *verum* and partly *falsum*); Ulpian (18 *ad edictum*), *Collatio* 12.7.10 (Celsus described Proculus' opinion as *falsum*); Ulpian (20 *ad Sabinum*) D. 33.7.12.42 (Papinian's holding on craftsmen is *falsum*); Paul (5 *ad legem Iuliam et Papiam*) D. 31.49.2 (Fulcinius deservedly called a Trebatius holding *falsum*); Paul (54 *ad edictum*) D. 41.2.3.14 (an unascribed holding is *falsum*), and (74 *ad edictum*) D. 46.7.11 (the view of some jurists is *falsum*); Paul, in Labeo (1 *pithanon a Paulo epitomatorum*) D. 8.5.21 (Labeo's holding is *falsum*), and in Labeo (6 *pithanon a Paulo epitomatorum*) D. 41.1.65.2 (Labeo's position is *falsum* in some situations); and in Labeo (4 *pithanon a Paulo epitomatorum*) D. 50.16.244 (each of Labeo's two propositions is *falsum*). Likewise, a previous jurist's *sententia* can be held "untrue," *non vera*; Iavolenus (7 *epistularum*) D. 50.16.116 (of Labeo); Ulpian (5 *ad edictum*) D. 5.1.16 (of Julian).

Labeo had held that a woman's debtor, who had promised her future husband that he would provide her with a dowry, is no longer liable to the promisee if the woman herself sues the debtor on this debt; but Javolenus describes Labeo's position as "false" (*falsum*).

The precise meaning of "truth" (*veritas*) or "falsehood" (*falsitas*) in relation to a contested legal rule is, of course, difficult to decipher; but it may seem, at first sight, to accord ill with the relaxed mode of "disputation" that the jurists favored. As Bretone observes, apparently a rule's "truth" is related, in the jurists' minds, to its intellectual coherence within a larger legal framework, the *ratio iuris*.[14] As he remarks, a jurist's "modern colleague would say that 'there is no need to associate the idea of reason with that of truth' and that a juridical decision is reasonable not because it is true, but [because] 'it can be justified by the best reasons.'"[15] The jurists, however, appear to have seen the matter otherwise. They thought of their law as possessing an inherent, almost scientific truth, against which suspect legal propositions could be tested. The plain inference is that, despite their astonishing tolerance for disagreements, the jurists believed that legal questions had only one correct answer; and hence, there is *ius dubitatum*, but no *ius controversum*.

And so we come to a central question. Why is it that the outsized egos of the great Classical jurists appear so domesticated in their specialist writings, as these are known to us from the *Digest* of Justinian and other sources? Such a phenomenon can scarcely be duplicated in all later eras of the Western legal tradition, where the great scholars of law strut the public stage like so many self-aggrandizing, quarrelsome aristocrats. What held Roman law together?[16]

The dangers of unleashed personality are well represented by the quarrel between two leading jurists under Augustus, Antistius Labeo and Ateius Capito. Our sources trace the quarrel to methodological, political, and personal causes, but whatever the explanation, the consequences were serious: an actual rupture, as

[14] This may be confirmed by passages describing a rule as *rationabilis*, "reasonable," or *magis rationale* or *rationibilius*: Ulpian (3 *ad edictum*) D. 5.1.2.3 (citing Celsus); Pomponius (2 *ad Urseium Ferocem*) D. 45.3.37, (8 *ad Quintum Mucium*) D. 50.16.122; Paul (*libro singulari de concurrentibus actionibus*) D. 44.7.34 pr. See generally Bretone, *Ius Controversum* (2008) 799–808. But there are exceptions, as Julian (86 *digestorum*) D. 9.2.51.2, observes: *multa autem iure civili contra rationem disputandi pro utilitate communi recepta esse innumerabilibus rebus probari potest* ("For it can be proved by countless examples that many rules which have been received in the Civil Law are contrary to legal logic (*ratio disputandi*) but benefit the common good (*utilitas communis*)"). This famous maxim is discussed below.

[15] Bretone, *Ius Controversum* (2008) 756 (English abstract); at 802 the quotation is ascribed to Chaim Perelman. As it seems, this mode of juristic thinking is very old, found already in Quintus Mucius as quoted in Pomponius (5 *ad Quintum Mucium*) D. 24.1.51; see also Alfenus (2 *digestorum a Paulo epitomatorum*) D. 33.7.16 pr.-1. But see also Bix, 'Truth in Law' (2020).

[16] While I have no entirely convincing answer to this question, I believe that the likeliest answer may lie through the sociological theories of Niklas Luhmann as to discipline within semi-autonomous subsystems such as law, see esp. Luhmann, *Social System* (2004), and *Sociological Theory*^{2} (2013). And see now, on Roman law as a "semi-autonomous social subsystem," Verhagen, *Security and Credit* (2022) 8–61. The problem of self-assertion is ubiquitous within ancient social subsystems; see the essays in König and Woolf, *Authority and Experience* (2017), esp. Harries, '*Iurisperiti*,' 83–106.

subsequent jurists divided their juristic community into two opposed camps, the Proculians and the Sabinians, with differences on a range of legal issues that today are difficult to treat systematically.[17] It took more than a century before this divide was finally bridged. In general, however, the jurists observed an admirable level of self-restraint, with only a few exceptions during the High Classical period.[18] Juristic outbreaks of outright contempt are exceedingly rare, at least in preserved sources.

In the remainder of this paper, I consider a famous problem exemplifying the difficulties I have discussed.[19] The problem is this: in many instances, a wrongful act (in our law, typically a tort or a crime) has, as its predictable and likely consequence, harm to another person; but a subsequent, more or less independent act or event may interrupt the chain of causation, with a legal result limiting the original offender's liability for the harm. Such an act or event is called, in modern terminology, an intervening cause.[20]

In Roman law, liability for damage to another person's property was governed by the Lex Aquilia, a statute from the early third century BCE concerning wrongful infliction of loss (*damnum iniuria datum*). The Lex Aquilia was ancient and written in crabbed, rather murky language, so the jurists often struggled with how to apply it correctly.[21] In Classical law, the word "wrongfully" (*iniuriā*) is regularly interpreted to mean "with fault" (*culpā*), a more sophisticated concept loosely akin to our "negligence."[22] The first section of the statute prescribed liability for wrongfully "killing" (*occidere*) another's slave or four-footed herd animal; the third section, all other wrongful infliction of loss (*damnum*).[23]

A handful of Roman sources deal with the legal effect of intervening causes after such a wrongful act.[24] Roman law scholars have discussed these texts for centuries,

[17] On the quarrel between Labeo and Capito, and its uncertain relation to the growth of the two schools, the major sources are Tac. *Ann.* 3.75; Gell. *NA* 13.12.1–4; Pomponius (*libro singulari enchiridii*) D. 1.2.2.47–48. A standard account is Wieacker, *Rechtsgeschichte* II (2006) 52–59.

[18] The notoriously irascible Celsus, for instance, is reported as having "adroitly mocked" (*eleganter deridet*) a view of Proculus: Ulpian (10 *ad Edictum*) D. 3.5.9.1. Celsus may also be responsible for the derision heaped on Nerva for a misguided opinion: Paul (*libro singulari de officio praefecti vigilum*) D. 20.2.9.

[19] For a summary of the dispute, see Lawson and Markesinis, *Tortious Liability*, vol. I (1982) 30–33.

[20] See Hart and Honoré, *Causation* (1985) 239–245; Moore, *Causation* (2009) 145–154. On the law: Keeton et al., *Law of Torts* (1984) 301–319. Surviving Roman sources deal with only small aspects of this extremely complex set of issues; no general Roman doctrine is discernible.

[21] The commonly accepted date (ca. 287 BCE) is little more than an educated guess based on Ulpian (18 *ad edictum*) D. 9.2.1.1, that the law was a plebiscite. In general on the statute, see now Desanti, *Legge Aquilia* (2015).

[22] E.g., Gaius, *Inst.* 3.211; Ulp. (8 *ad edictum*) D. 9.2.5.1. See generally Zimmermann, *Obligations* (1996) 1004–1013.

[23] The crucial statutory language is quoted by Gaius (7 *ad edictum provinciale*) D. 9.2.2 pr., and Ulp. (18 *ad edictum*) D. 9.2.27.5, respectively. See Crawford, *Roman Statutes* (1996) II 723–726.

[24] The limits on their discussion deserve stress. As Danuta Mendelson, 'Aspects' (2002) 69, notes, comparing Roman legal and medical writings on causation, "Roman jurists did not develop jurisprudence relating to direct and indirect causation in a multifactorial setting, even when they provided examples of it, as in" Ulpian (18 *ad edictum*) D. 9.2.11 pr. (ball, struck by ballplayer, hits barber's hand

with sharply divided opinions; but since the Renaissance, Romanists have generally agreed with the distinguished French humanist Jacques Cujas (1522–1590) that the sources indicate a substantial disagreement between two paragons of early second-century jurisprudence: Juventius Celsus (*cos.* 115, *cos. II* 129) and Salvius Julianus (*cos.* 148).[25] For the most part, their disagreement is modulated through the Late Classical jurist Ulpian writing two generations later, and Ulpian's references, although not always easily interpreted (possibly due in part to subsequent abbreviation by the *Digest* compilers), can with some effort be reconciled. But these sources appear to stand in sharp contrast to a long and famous fragment of Julian (D. 9.2.51), a fragment that, in fact, is the subject of an entire recent monograph by Prof. Wolfgang Ernst.[26]

Ernst's book offers an exhaustive historical account of the controversies surrounding this fragment, which stretch back to the thirteenth century. He then argues at length for the minority view that there is no underlying disagreement in the Roman sources: "In no way do our cases betray a radical dispute between Julian and other lawyers regarding the fundamental structure of the statutory requirements for Aquilian liability."[27]

Although I adopt the majority view, Ernst's book certainly illustrates how challenging it can be to establish with complete conviction the existence and nature of juristic disagreement. In what follows, I give my own view as to the most probable interpretation of the sources, without directly engaging Ernst's arguments.[28] My interest is rather in considering, on the assumption that Celsus and Julian did in fact disagree, how they (and especially Julian) went about the process of disagreeing against the background of prevailing juristic culture.

The opening salvo came with the jurists' interpretation of the statute's first section, which set damages for a slain slave at his or her highest value during the previous year (*quanti is homo in eo anno plurimi fuisset*).[29] But suppose that a slave was mortally wounded and subsequently died of this wound after an

and causes him to slit throat of slave being shaved; ballplayer's potential liability is ignored). The jurists scarcely distinguish, if at all, between deliberate, negligent, and accidental intervening causes; between foreseeable and unforeseeable ones; and so on. See Dobbs et al., *Hornbook*[2] (2000) 361–375.

[25] On the contribution of Cujas, see Ernst, *Digest 9.2.51* (2019) 26–27, citing Cujas, *Opera* III (1758/2012) column 716. Of recent scholarship on the question, see esp. Schindler, 'Streit' (1957); Dallo, 'Giuliano' (1974); Rastätter, *Marcelli Notae* (1981) 116–123; Nörr, *Causa Mortis* (1986) 181–190; Wallinga, 'Actio' (2009); Sirks, 'Delictual Origin' (2009); Desanti, *Legge Aquilia* (2015) 47–53. Further bibliography is reviewed by Ernst, *Digest 9.2.51* (2019) 39–102. The scholarship is extensive and (owing to the paucity of sources) necessarily somewhat repetitious.

[26] Ernst, *Digest 9.2.51* (2019).

[27] Ernst, *Digest 9.2.51* (2019) 140. Ernst reaches this position by arguing that the texts are concerned less with causation as we understand it now, than with the rules of statutory liability under the Lex Aquilia. There is something to be said for this view (foreshadowed among British scholars: Johnston, 'Causation' (2018) 214–217), and Ernst's argument is impressively learned and ingenious; however, it tends to downplay other, much more significant issues that also inform these texts.

[28] By and large, I have tried to adhere to normal Latin meanings of contested vocabulary.

[29] Zimmermann, *Obligations* (1996) 961–962.

extended interval: say, more than a year later.[30] According to Ulpian, Celsus (as it appears) had calculated the highest value by reckoning backward from the date of the slave's death, but Julian instead calculates backward from when the wound was inflicted, a view that Ulpian and later jurists also adopt.[31] Julian's reasoning is that the slave is effectively killed when mortally wounded, even if the homicide becomes known only retrospectively when the slave actually dies—reasoning that may seem sound enough, but that initiates what will emerge as a logical trap.

A significant interval between a wrongful act and an eventual harm considerably increases the probability that an intervening cause may alter the predictable course of events. For example, the wrongdoer's initial act may impose duties of care on other parties: if the wrongful wounding of a slave is not necessarily lethal but leads to death when the slave does not receive proper medical attention because either the slave owner carelessly fails to provide such care, or a doctor commits malpractice, the initial wrongdoer is liable only for wounding (under the statute's third section) and not for killing.[32]

These intervening causes are easy to deal with, but others are more problematic. What if one person inflicts a "mortal wound" on a slave, and subsequently an intervening cause (e.g., a blow from a second, apparently independent person) results in the slave dying more quickly than would have otherwise been the case? According to Celsus (whose view both Ulpian and Julian's pupil Marcellus approve), this question of law should be decided purely on a factual basis: the slave actually dies from the intervening cause, which thus makes it impossible for the first "mortal wound" to proceed to its predictable result.[33] Our criminal law takes a similar view.[34]

[30] *mortifere vulneratus*; *mortifere* means "mortally, fatally" (*OLD* s.v.). As Hart and Honoré, *Causation* (1985) 241–242, observes, "mortal wound" has three distinct meanings: a wound fatal to "a person of average constitution under ordinary circumstances"; one fatal to a particular person or a person in particular circumstances; or, one that is not necessarily fatal but leads to death when it is not properly treated. The second situation is usually presumed, it seems, also in Roman sources.

[31] Ulpian (18 *ad edictum*) D. 9.2.21.1: *annus autem retrorsus computatur, ex quo quis occisus est: quod si mortifere fuerit vulneratus et postea post longum intervallum mortuus sit, inde annum numerabimus secundum Julianum, ex quo vulneratus est, licet Celsus contra scribit* ("The year is reckoned back from when someone was killed. So if he was mortally wounded and later after a long time he died, according to Julian we number the year from when he was wounded, although Celsus writes the opposite"). See also Ulpian (18 *ad edictum*) D. 9.2.23.2, citing Julian. Celsus' view, though not stated expressly, can be inferred.

[32] Alfenus (2 *digestorum*) D. 9.2.52 pr.; Paul (22 *ad edictum*) D. 9.2.30.4 (generalizing the rule). See also Paul (10 *ad Sabinum*) D. 9.2.45.2 (action lies for wounding if injured slave recovers).

[33] Ulpian (18 *ad edictum*) D. 9.2.11.3: *Celsus scribit, si alius mortifero vulnere percusserit, alius postea exanimaverit, priorem quidem non teneri quasi occiderit, sed quasi vulneraverit, quia ex alio vulnere periit, posteriorem teneri, quia occidit. quod et Marcello videtur et est probabilius* ("Celsus writes that if one person strikes with a mortal wound, and subsequently a second person kills, the first person, indeed, is not liable as for killing, but as for wounding, since he [the victim] perishes from the other wound; the later person is liable because he killed. This both seems right to Marcellus and is more credible"). The final sentence indicates this view was controversial.

[34] See *State v. Phillips*, 74 Ohio St.3d 72, 656 N.E.2d 643 (1995) (evidence "clearly demonstrates that appellant hastened Sheila's death," and thus "appellant cannot escape criminal liability by arguing that

In another, considerably more difficult fragment, Ulpian reports Julian's view on the same question.[35] Although Julian's view is similar in result to Celsus', his reasoning is subtly but significantly different. In the text as preserved, the "second blow" (*alius ictus*) is associated with physical causes like a building's collapse or a shipwreck.[36] Whereas Celsus had emphasized the second wrongdoer as the "cause in fact" of the victim's quicker death, Julian instead points to uncertainty as to whether the earlier act would actually have resulted in the victim's death. (By contrast, since on Julian's view the slave who dies of a "mortal wound" is killed at the time of initial wounding, subsequent purely legal status changes such as manumission or alienation are of no consequence as causes of death; they are not intervening causes.)

Julian's position raises a potentially interesting line of argument. Suppose that we can be completely certain, far beyond a reasonable doubt, that the first act would indeed have led to the slave's death; the probability is not 0.95 or even 0.99, but 1.00. In the classic modern hypothetical (which Jerome Hall proposed in a criminal law context), an accused A throws a victim from the top of the Empire State Building and a second person B, acting independently, shoots the victim as he plunges past the forty-ninth floor. Here, "the second act is independent of the first except in the sense that the first actor provided the opportunity for the second

Sheila was going to die anyway"); *State v. McDonald*, 90 Wash.App. 604, 953 P.2d 470 (1998) (even though victim would have ultimately died from previously being shot by another, when defendant shot victim in head and that hastened death, defendant was the cause of death). See LaFave, *Criminal Law* (2017/2020) Part II Chapter 6.4(b) ("Cause in Fact"). So, too, in tort: Keeton et al., *Law of Torts*[5] (1984) 264–265. However, this outcome may be complicated by additional factors such as the relationship between the two causes. For instance, what if someone mortally wounds another person, who is then transported moribund to a hospital where he or she dies more quickly from a preventable staph infection? Except for the initial wound, after all, the victim would never have been exposed to the substantial risk of infection.

[35] Ulpian (18 *ad edictum*) D. 9.2.15.1: *si servus vulneratus mortifere postea ruina vel naufragio vel alio ictu maturius perierit, de occiso agi non posse, sed quasi de vulnerato, sed si manumissus vel alienatus ex vulnere periit, quasi de occiso agi posse Iulianus ait. haec ita tam varie, quia verum est eum a te occisum tunc cum vulnerabas, quod mortuo eo demum apparuit: at in superiore non est passa ruina apparere an sit occisus*... ("Julian says that if a slave was mortally wounded and subsequently dies more swiftly from a [building's] collapse or a shipwreck or by a second blow, Julian says that there can be no action for killing, but [only] as for wounding; but if he was manumitted or alienated and died from the wound, the action can be brought for killing. These outcomes differ in this way because in truth [in the second case] he [the victim] was killed then when you wounded, as finally became clear when he died; but in the earlier case the collapse did not allow it to be clear whether he was killed [by the initial blow]..."). Ankum, 'Problem' (1980), tries to bring this text into harmony with others by altering it; this view, which forces a meaning onto the fragment, should be rejected.

[36] This unexpected collocation has caused much difficulty for commentators and translators. In context, the Latin phrase cannot mean other than "or by a second blow" (after the first wound); and so most translators. But Ernst, *Digest 9.2.51* (2019) 9 and 135–136, renders it as "or by some other kind of blow," effectively connecting the "blow" to a collapsing building or a shipwreck as "a sweeper clause." Here Ernst follows a tradition in some scholarship on the passage (e.g., Behrends et al., *Corpus Iuris Civilis* II (1995) 741: "durch... irgendeinen anderen Unglücksfall"), in an evident attempt to dodge the interpretive difficulties; but this is very strained. Most probably, as often occurs in the *Digest*, Justinian's compilers collapsed two rulings into one; in Ulpian, Julian had originally dealt only with physical events and then gone on to extend the rule by analogy to a second blow.

to shoot."[37] More realistically, assume that a negligent driver hits a pedestrian who is certain to die from the injury, but who is then killed more quickly when a firetruck hits the ambulance as the victim is being transported to the hospital. Is this an intervening event that, although unforeseen, somehow lessens the culpability of the original wrongdoer, or is it not? Tens of thousands of first-year law students tear their hair out over such problems in their Torts and Crime Law classes.

This brings me to *Digest* 9.2.51, among the most celebrated texts in the entire *Digest*: Julian's extended reflections on the problems I have been discussing. It is not at all clear why Justinian's compilers admitted this fragment, since, as it seems, it directly contradicts several other *Digest* texts; but they may simply have been overwhelmed by the force of the passage. The text is so long that I have had to abbreviate it, but I have included the entirety of the argument as to the main problem (Julian (86 *digestorum*) D. 9.2.51):

> **pr.** *Ita vulneratus est servus, ut eo ictu certum esset moriturum: medio deinde tempore heres institutus est et postea ab alio ictus decessit: quaero, an cum utroque de occiso lege Aquilia agi possit. respondit:... rursus Aquilia lege teneri existimati sunt non solum qui ita vulnerassent, ut confestim vita privarent, sed etiam hi, quorum ex vulnere certum esset aliquem vita excessurum. igitur si quis servo mortiferum vulnus inflixerit eundemque alius ex intervallo ita percusserit, ut maturius interficeretur, quam ex priore vulnere moriturus fuerat, statuendum est utrumque eorum lege Aquilia teneri...*
>
> **2.** *Aestimatio autem perempti non eadem in utriusque persona fiet: nam qui prior vulneravit, tantum praestabit, quanto in anno proximo homo plurimi fuerit repetitis ex die vulneris trecentum sexaginta quinque diebus, posterior in id tenebitur, quanti homo plurimi venire poterit in anno proximo, quo vita excessit, in quo pretium quoque hereditatis erit. eiusdem ergo servi occisi nomine alius maiorem, alius minorem aestimationem praestabit, nec mirum, cum uterque eorum ex diversa causa et diversis temporibus occidisse hominem intellegatur.*
>
> *Quod si quis absurde a nobis haec constitui putaverit, cogitet longe absurdius constitui neutrum lege Aquilia teneri aut alterum potius, cum neque impunita maleficia esse oporteat nec facile constitui possit, uter potius lege teneatur. multa autem iure civili contra rationem disputandi pro utilitate communi recepta esse innumerabilibus rebus probari potest: unum interim posuisse contentus ero....*
>
> **pr.** A slave was so seriously wounded that it was certain he would die from this blow; then, in the meantime, he was instituted heir, and afterwards he was struck by another person and died. I ask whether an action under the Lex Aquilia can lie against both men for the slaying.... On the other hand, persons are held liable

[37] Hall, *Principles* (1947) 262; the quotation is from Hart and Honoré, *Causation* (1985) 243.

under the Lex Aquilia not only when they wound so seriously that they take life immediately, but also when, because of their wound, it is certain that someone will lose life. Therefore if someone inflicts a mortal wound on a slave, and after an interval a second person so strikes him that he dies sooner than he would have died from the earlier wound, it must be determined that both of them are liable under the Lex Aquilia....

2. But the evaluation of the dead slave will not be the same for both persons. For the one who first wounded him will owe as much as the man's maximum value in the past year, counting back three hundred and sixty-five days from the date of the wound. But the second person will be liable for the maximum value of the man in the year preceding his death; and the value of the inheritance will be included. Therefore, on account of the same slain slave, one person will owe a larger evaluation and the other a smaller; nor is this surprising, since each of them is understood to have slain the slave under different circumstances and at different times.

But if someone thinks my decision is preposterous, let him consider that it would be far more preposterous if neither was liable under the Lex Aquilia, or just one, since it ought not to be that misdeeds go unpunished and it cannot easily be determined which one is rather liable by statute. For it can be proved by countless examples that many rules which have been received in the Civil Law are contrary to legal logic (*ratio disputandi*) but benefit the common good (*utilitas communis*)....

Julian sets out the problem succinctly: "A slave was so seriously wounded that it was certain he would die from this blow; then, in the meantime, he was instituted heir, and afterwards he was struck by another person and died." Two points stick out. First, Julian emphasizes the certainty of the slave's death from the first injury, a stipulation he then repeats.[38] Second, he introduces the issue of the inheritance, which was left to the moribund slave between the first and second woundings but was never accepted; had it been accepted, this inheritance would have gone to the slave's master.[39] The lost inheritance has an effect on the calculation of damages, as Julian notes in the first part of section 2, where he repeats his own views on how to interpret the Lex Aquilia: you count backward one year from the infliction of the wound.[40] During the period when the slave was moribund but named as heir, he was, of course, potentially worth a great deal because of the inheritance.

[38] Julian assumes that the two blows are independent and sequential; and he does not consider the possibility that they might be interrelated if, e.g., the second blow would not have been fatal had not the first blow preceded it.

[39] Ulpian (23 *ad edictum*) D. 9.2.23.2 (citing Julian).

[40] In section 2, Julian seems to say that the reckoning of the second assailant's damages would be backward from the time of the slave's death (*in anno proximo, quo vita excessit*) and not from the time of the wound; but, since he does not mention subsequent acquisitions, Julian probably assumes that the second blow led to instantaneous death. Contra, Desanti, *Legge Aquilia* (2015) 50.

But the most startling and most important part of Julian's opinion is his insistence that both the first and the second defendant should be held independently liable as killers for the maximum value of the slave during the year prior to their respective acts. This holding is decidedly counterintuitive, so much so that even Julian concedes that someone might find it "preposterous" (*absurdum*).[41] It means rejecting the view that the most basic aim of Aquilian liability is to compensate the plaintiff for the loss; indeed, the plaintiff may well receive a substantial windfall from the two defendants. To modern lawyers this would doubtless seem objectionable in the case of a private lawsuit.[42]

At the end of this passage, however, Julian justifies his opinion by strongly asserting that the primary purpose of the Lex Aquilia is not compensatory (as one might have anticipated) but instead punitive, the punishment of wrongful conduct. He argues that under a different interpretation, possibly not just one but both culprits might escape: the first, by arguing that the slave did not in fact die from the first wound; the second, by arguing that since the slave was going to die anyway, the later wound did not materially alter the slave's condition. But the main point is that Julian considers the conduct of both culprits as equally reprehensible; even though their penalties are different, they must be treated equally. This is, essentially, a criminal law argument. When two people rob a bank, both are in principle subjected to the full rigor of the law.

Julian further justifies his position by suggesting that the common good (*utilitas communis*) often must dictate rulings that are contrary to what he calls the *ratio disputandi*, a strong inner logic of Roman law that the jurists (who usually call it the *ratio iuris*) frequently adopt as a standard for judging the correctness of their holdings.[43] Important here is Julian's implicit concession that his holding on supervening cause does not meet this usual standard.

So we are left to conjecture: is it possible that the great jurist Julian was led into an untenable position—a cul-de-sac, so to speak—by his competitive ambition to best Celsus? That is, could the driving motive of Julian's decision be personal rather than legal? The question is not an easy one to ask, and still harder to answer. Among Romanists, the dominant image of the jurists is one of cooperation in a common project, where the good faith of individuals is presumed. Here, for instance, is Karl von Savigny: "Even if [the jurists'] writings lay before us in their completeness we should find therein far fewer individualities than in any other literature; they all collaborate more or less in one and the same great work...."[44]

[41] See Ernst, *Digest 9.2.51* (2019) 90–91, with bibliography.

[42] The modern view is that tort damages essentially aim to restore the plaintiff to the status quo ante the tort. However, some important wrinkles in applying this rule result mainly from the availability of insurance. See Goldberg, 'Tort Theory' (2003), and 'Tort' (2021), with a critique.

[43] See Ankum, 'Utilitatis Causa' (1968) 8–9, 22.

[44] Savigny, *Vom Beruf*[3] (1840) 87, quoted by Schulz *Principles* (1936) 106. On the history of the concept, see Schiavone, 'Singularity and Impersonality' (2021) 6–9.

While there may be an element of truth to this view, it has long since been deemed simplistic at least as to the lack of individuality—albeit a muted individuality.[45]

But Romanists still have an ingrained tendency to assume that the jurists are operating aboveboard and that their disagreements are fundamentally honest differences of opinion within a collaborative legal culture.[46] This generosity of interpretative method is also, of course, characteristic of modern legal scholarship more generally: a reluctance to explain judicial opinions through personal attitudes or through social or political bias. It seems to me likely that a hermeneutic principle is involved here, one that is historically internal to the legal profession itself.

In recent years, especially as I worked closely with Roman texts for my *Casebook on the Roman Law of Contracts*, I have come upon various instances in which juristic holdings have initially struck me as at least strange if not outright incorrect.[47] (Needless to say, this is not normal with the *Digest*.) In many instances, further research into the social and economic background has enlightened me about what was going on in these texts.[48] However, for a small but significant remainder, no such explanation has seemed plausible. In many such instances, a more systemic elucidation seems preferable: for instance, the jurists may have encountered difficulties because of the paucity of forensic cases arising in a particular area (as looks to be true, for instance, in their scant treatment of wage labor); or they may have articulated a legal principle that they then carry too far in particular situations; or they may have overelaborated—in fact, over-legalized—certain areas of law, such as *fideicommissa* and real securities (*hypothecae*), that presented them with unusually intricate intellectual challenges. Difficulties such as these are, I believe, endemic to any professionalized legal culture that relies for its efficacy on simplified representations of a fact-rich environment.

In surviving legal sources, *Digest* 9.2.51 presents perhaps the clearest case where one might suppose juristic competition as a possible impulse for obtuse innovation. Julian's error can be diagnosed as over-reliance on a concept of punishment as the basic aim of Aquilian liability (*neque impunita maleficia esse oporteat*), when, in fact, this liability had rested, apparently from its origins onward, on a combination of giving compensation to aggrieved plaintiffs and punishing

[45] Recent research on this topic begins with Baldus, *Storia dei Dogmi* (2012), and continues in the series *Scriptores Iuris Romani: Texts and Thought* under the general direction of Aldo Schiavone at the Università degli Studi di Roma "La Sapienza": http://www.scriptores-iuris-romani.eu/it/content/pubblicazioni. See also Amarelli et al., 'Nascita' (2005); Nasti and Schiavone, *Jurists and Legal Science* (2021).

[46] Unsurprisingly, Ernst, *Digest 9.2.51* (2019) 133–141, defends a view of "Roman jurisprudence" as "a product of group intelligence." Contrast Brutti, "Stories of Legal Dogmas" (2021).

[47] Frier, *Casebook* (2021).

[48] This general problem is examined in more detail in Spagnolo and Sampson, *Principle and Pragmatism* (2022).

delinquent defendants—an antinomy that remains characteristic of much subsequent negligence law as well.[49] Still more fundamentally, Julian appears to confuse liability (Who should be held legally responsible for the harm the plaintiff has suffered?) with the extent of liability (What are the monetary limits on the plaintiff's recovery?), even when his maxim may lead to an unexpected, undeserved, and exorbitant windfall for the plaintiff. The example he gives in 51.1 to buttress his case (a slave is attacked by several persons, among whom the actual killer cannot be identified; each attacker is liable for the dead slave's full worth) perfectly illustrates Julian's inflexibility.[50]

Yet the text itself is obdurate. Although Julian's tone is plainly disputatious, and although few contemporary legally trained observers could have been in doubt about his target, Julian, as is his wont, does not mention Celsus by name, nor does he make more than limited engagement with Celsus' probable arguments; there is no trace of *ad hominem* attack, and indeed of rhetoric generally (except for those who confuse argument with the art of persuasion). Further, we have the broader reality—here, as elsewhere—that subsequent jurists do not feel obliged to choose between Celsus and Julian, but accept their views selectively: Julian as to when a mortally wounded slave is "killed," but Celsus as to the consequence of a supervening cause that hastens death. Cujas had already noticed that Julian disagrees with Celsus "in a great many other cases" (*in plerisque aliis causis*), but an inference of "enmity" is not necessarily warranted.[51]

And similarly with the early imperial split between the Proculians and the Sabinians: although ancient sources did indeed trace this division to private conflict between two leading Augustan jurists, the Wall of Impersonality separating us from them has prevented modern scholars from discerning much more than the apparition of an honest and lingering dogmatic difference of opinion that seems perhaps not altogether unlike the modern dispute between "plain meaning" and "purposive" interpreters of legal texts.[52] There is, needless to say, much persuasive force on either side of such debates.

[49] See the essays in Gamauf, *Ausgleich oder Buße* (2017), especially the essay by Finkenauer, 'Pönale Elemente' (2017), on Aquilian liability; also Zimmermann, *Obligations* (1990/1996) 969–975; Wallinga, 'Actio' (2009); Sirks, 'Delictual Origin' (2009). Could Julian be thinking of Aquilian liability mainly in terms of deliberate infliction of physical harm akin to criminal conduct? Julian speaks of punishment and not deterrence, but most scholars who defend Julian's view shift attention to deterrence: Ernst, *Digest 9.2.51* (2019) 84–90. On the distinction, see the classic article by Gibbs, 'Crime' (1968).

[50] This rule is given also by Ulpian (18 *ad edictum*) D. 9.2.11.2, 4. Parallel overcompensation rules when one person aids and abets another's infliction of wrongful harm, Ulpian, 11.1 (but an analogous action); or induces another, see esp. Iavolenus (14 *ex Cassio*) D. 9.2.37 pr., and Paul (2 *ad Plautium*) D. 50.17.169 pr. Julian's perspective makes more sense for obviously penal, quasi-criminal delicts like *furtum*, as in the example he gives at the end of 51.2.

[51] Cujas, *Opera* III (1758/2012) column 716.

[52] Stein, 'Two Schools' (1972). A far more anodyne account in Leesen, *Gaius Meets Cicero* (2010). On the modern debate, see Congressional Research Service, *Statutory Interpretation* (2018).

So let me conclude by addressing a question to the spirit of Julian. Suppose that Bertha, intent on killing Archie, gives him a slow-working but highly toxic poison for which there is no antidote and from which recovery is impossible. Then, dissatisfied because Archie lingers so long near death, Bertha sneaks into his hospital room, plunges a dagger through his heart, and kills him instantly. Julian, my very good friend, are you seriously contending that Bertha has murdered Archie twice? Really?[53]

Bibliography

Amarelli et al., 'Nascita' (2005) = Francesco Amarelli, Aldo Schiavone, and Emanuele Stolfi, 'Corpus Scriptorum Iuris Romani: Nascita di un Progetto,' *Studia et Documenta Historiae et Iuris* 71 (2005) 4–14.

Ankum, 'Utilitatis Causa' (1968) = Hans Ankum, '"Utilitatis Causa Receptum"—On the Paragmatical Methods of the Roman Lawyers,' in Hans Ankum et al., eds., *Symbolae Iuridicae et Historicae Martino David Dedicatae*, vol. I (Leiden: Brill, 1968) 1–31.

Ankum, 'Problem' (1980) = Ankum, Hans 'Das Problem der "Überholenden Kausalität" bei der Anwendung der Lex Aquilia im Klassischen Römischen Recht,' in *De Iustitia et Iure, Festgabe für Ulrich von Lübtow* (Berlin: Dunker & Humblot, 1980) 325–358.

Baldus, *Storia dei Dogmi* (2012) = Christian Baldus, ed., *Storia dei dogmi e individualità storica dei giuristi romani* (Trento: Università degli Studi di Trento, 2012).

Behrends et al., *Corpus Iuris Civilis* II (1995) = Okko Behrends, Rolf Knütel, Berthold Kupisch, and Hans Hermann Seller, *Corpus Iuris Civilis: Text und Übersetzung*, vol. II *Digesten 1–10* (Heidelberg: Müller, 1995).

Bix, 'Truth in Law' (2020) = Brian Bix, 'Reflections on Truth in Law,' *Cosmos + Taxis* 8 (2020) 35–43.

Bremer, *Iurisprudentia* I (1896) = F. P. Bremer, *Iurisprudentiae Antehadrianae Quae Supersunt*, vol. I (Leipzig: Teubner, 1896; reprinted 1985).

Bretone, *Ius Controversum* (2008) = Mario Bretone, *Ius Controversum nella Giurisprudenza Classica* (Rome: Bardi, 2009; = *Atti della Accademia Nazionale dei Lincei, Memorie* ser. 9, vol. 23 (2008) 755–881).

[53] Gaius (7 *ad edictum provinciale*) D. 9.2.32.1, gives the correct answer to this problem: "If the same person wounds the same slave and subsequently then slays him" (*si eundem servum vulneraverit, postea deinde etiam occiderit*), the assailant is liable only for slaying if the wounds are given in a single attack, but for both wounding and for slaying if the two acts are distinct. But the latter outcome might seem to be foreclosed for Julian if the first blow was mortal. Nonetheless, Julian (50 *ad Sabinum*) D. 9.2.47, limits total damage awards in the two Aquilian actions to the value for slaying the slave; he does not explore the potential contradiction further.

Brutti, 'Stories of Legal Dogmas' (2021) = Massimo Brutti, 'Stories of Legal Dogmas, Stories of Roman Jurists: An Uncompleted Transition,' in Nasti and Schiavone, *Jurists and Legal Science* (2021) 13–50.

Congressional Research Service, *Statutory Interpretation* (2018) = Congressional Research Service, *Statutory Interpretation: Theories, Tools, and Trends* (2018), available at https://www.everycrsreport.com/reports/R45153.html.

Crawford, *Roman Statutes* (1996) = M. H. Crawford, ed., *Roman Statutes*, 2 vols. (London: Institute of Classical Studies, 1996).

Cujas, *Opera* III (1758/2012) = Jacques Cujas (Jacobus Cuiacius), *Opera ad Parisiensem Fabrotianam Editionem Diligentissime Exacta in Tomos XI Distributa Avctiora atqve Emendatiora*, vol. III (Charles Annibal Fabrot, ed.; Venice: Storti, 1758; reprinted Charleston, SC: Nabu Press, 2012).

Dallo, 'Giuliano' (1974) = Danilo Dalla, 'Giuliano e il *Longum Intervallum* in Tema di Applicazione dell Aquilia,' *Archivio Giuridico* 187 (1974) 145–176.

Desanti, *Legge Aquilia* (2015) = Lucetta Desanti, *La Legge Aquilia: Tra Verba Legis e Interpretazione Giurisprudenziale* (Giappichelli: Turin, 2015).

Dobbs et al., *Hornbook* (2000) = Dan B. Dobbs, Paul T. Hayden, and Ellen M. Bublick, *Hornbook on Torts* (2nd ed.; St. Paul, MN; West, 2000).

Ernst, *Digest 9.2.51* (2019) = Wolfgang Ernst, *Justinian's Digest 9.2.51 in the Western Legal Canon: Roman Legal Thought and Modern Causality Concepts* (Cambridge, Antwerp, and Chicago: Intersentia, 2019).

Finkenauer, 'Pönale Elemente' (2017) = Thomas Finkenauer, 'Pönale Elemente der *Lex Aquilia*,' in Gamauf, *Ausgleich oder Buße* (2017) 35–71.

Frier, *Rise* (1985) = Bruce W. Frier, *The Rise of the Roman Jurists* (Princeton: Princeton University Press, 1985).

Frier, *Casebook* (2021) = Bruce W. Frier, *A Casebook on the Roman Law of Contracts* (New York: Oxford University Press, 2021).

Gamauf, *Ausgleich oder Buße* (2017) = Richard Gamauf, ed., *Ausgleich oder Buße als Grundproblem des Schadenersatzrechts von der* Lex Aquilia *bis zur Gegenwart* (Vienna: Manz, 2017).

Gibbs, 'Crime' (1968) = Jack P. Gibbs, 'Crime, Punishment, and Deterrence,' *The Southwestern Social Science Quarterly* 48 (1968) 515–530.

Goldberg, 'Tort Theory' (2003) = John C. P. Goldberg, 'Twentieth-Century Tort Theory,' *Georgetown Law Journal* 91 (2003) 513–583.

Goldberg, 'Torts' (2021) = John C. P. Goldberg, 'Torts,' in Andrew S. Gold, John C. P. Goldberg, Daniel B. Kelly, Emily Sherwin, and Henry E. Smith, eds., *The Oxford Handbook of the New Private Law* (Oxford: Oxford University Press, 2021) 261–275.

Hall, *Principles* (1947) = Jerome Hall, *General Principles of Criminal Law* (Indianapolis: Bobbs-Merrill, 1947).

Harries, '*Iurisperiti*' (2017) = Jill Harries, '*Iurisperiti*: Men Skilled in the Law,' in König and Woolf, *Authority and Expertise* (2017) 83–106.

Hart and Honoré, *Causation* (1985) = H. L. A. Hart and Tony Honoré, *Causation in the Law* (2nd ed.; Oxford: Oxford University Press, 1985).

Johnston, 'Causation' (2018) = David Johnston, 'Causation and Remoteness: British Steps on a Roman Path,' in Paul J. du Plessis, ed., *Wrongful Damage to Property in Roman Law: British Perspectives* (Edinburgh: Edinburgh University Press, 2018) 211–223.

Kaser, *Privatrecht*² I (1971) = Max Kaser, *Das Römische Privatrecht*, vol. I *Das Altrömische, das Vorklassische und Klassische Recht* (2nd ed.; Munich: Beck, 1971).

Keeton et al., *Law of Torts*⁵ (1984) = W. Page Keeton, Dan B. Dobbs, Robert E. Keeton, and David G. Owen, *Prosser and Keeton on the Law of Torts* (5th ed.; St. Paul, MN: West, 1984).

König and Woolf, *Authority and Expertise* (2017) = Jason König and Greg Woolf, eds., *Authority and Expertise in Ancient Scientific Culture* (Cambridge: Cambridge University Press, 2017).

Kunkel, *Herkunft*² (1967) = Wolfgang Kunkel, *Herkunft und Soziale Stellung der Römischen Juristen* (2nd ed.; Graz, Vienna, and Cologne: Böhlau, 1967).

LaFave, *Criminal Law*³ (2017/2020) = Wayne R. LaFave, *Substantive Criminal Law Part II* (3rd ed.; Eagan, MN: Thomson Reuters, 2017; October 2020 update).

Lawson, *Negligence* (1950) = F. H. Lawson, *Negligence in the Civil Law* (Oxford: Clarendon Press, 1950).

Lawson and Markesinis, *Tortious Liability* (1981) = F. H. Lawson and B. S. Markesinis, *Tortious Liability for Unintentional Harm in the Common Law and the Civil Law*, 2 vols. (Cambridge: Cambridge University Press, 1982). (The portions of this book pertaining to the Lex Aquilia largely reproduce Lawson's original text.)

Leesen, *Gaius Meets Cicero* (2010) = Tessa G. Leeson, *Gaius Meets Cicero: Law and Rhetoric in the School Controversies* (Leiden and Boston: Nijhoff, 2010).

Levick, 'Politics of the Early Principate' (1985) = Barbara Levick, 'The Politics of the Early Principate,' in T. P. Wiseman, ed., *Roman Political Life, 90 B.C.–A.D. 69* (Exeter: University of Exeter Press, 1985) 45–68.

Luhmann, *Social System* (2004) = Niklas Luhmann, *Law as a Social System*, trans. Klaus Ziegert (Oxford: Oxford University Press, 2004), from *Recht der Gesellschaft* (Berlin: Suhrkamp, 1993).

Luhmann, *Sociological Theory*² (2013) = *A Sociological Theory of Law*, trans. Elizabeth King and Martin Albrow (2nd ed.; Abingdon: Routledge, 2013), from *Rechtssoziologie* (4th ed.; Wiesbaden: VS Verlag für Sozialwissenschaften, 2008).

Mendelson, 'Aspects' (2002) = Danuta Mendelson, 'Aspects of Causation in Hippocratic Medicine and Roman Law of Delict,' in Ian Freckelton and Danuta Mendelson, eds., *Causation in Law and Medicine* (London: Taylor & Francis, 2002) 58–77.

Moore, *Causation* (2009) = Michael S. Moore, *Causation and Responsibility: An Essay in Law, Morals, and Metaphysics* (Oxford: Oxford University Press, 2009).

Nasti and Schiavone, *Jurists and Legal Science* (2021) = Fara Nasti and Aldo Schiavone, eds., *Jurists and Legal Science in the History of Roman Law* (London and New York: Routledge, 2021).

Nörr, *Causa Mortis* (1986) = Dieter Nörr, *Causa Mortis: Auf den Spuren einer Redewendung* (Munich: Beck, 1986).

Peachin, 'Friendship and Abuse' (2001) = Michael Peachin, 'Friendship and Abuse at the Dinner Table,' in Michael Peachin, ed., *Aspects of Friendship in the Graeco-Roman World* (*Journal of Roman Archaeology* Supp. 43; Portsmouth, 2001) 135–144.

Peachin, 'Attacken und Erniedrigungen' (2007) = Michael Peachin, 'Attacken und Erniederigungen als Alltägliche Elemente der Kaiserzeitlichen Regierungspraxis,' in Rudolf Haensch and Johannes Heinrichs, eds., *Herrschen und Verwalten: Der Alltag der Römischen Administration in der Hohen Kaiserzeit* (Cologne, Weimar, and Vienna: Böhlau, 2007) 117–125.

Rastätter, *Marcelli Notae* (1981) = Jürgen Rastätter, *Marcelli Notae ad Iuliani Digesta* (Diss. Universität Freiburg, 1981).

Savigny, *Vom Beruf*^{3} (1840) = Friedrich Carl von Savigny, *Vom Beruf Unsrer Zeit für Gesetzgebung und Rechtswissenschaft* (3rd ed.; Heidelberg: Mohr, 1840).

Schiavone, 'Singularity and Impersonality' (2021) = Aldo Schiavone, 'Singularity and Impersonality in the Thought of Roman Jurists,' in Nasti and Schiavone, *Jurists and Legal Science* (2021) 3–11.

Schiller, 'Jurists' Law' (1958) = A. Arthur Schiller, 'Jurists' Law,' *Columbia Law Review* 58 (The Hague, Paris, and New York: Mouton, 1958) 1226–1238.

Schiller, *Mechanisms* (1978) = A. Arthur Schiller, *Roman Law: Mechanisms of Development* (Berlin: De Gruyter, 1978).

Schindler, 'Streit' (1957) = Karl-Heinz Schindler, 'Ein Streit Zwischen Julian und Celsus: Zum Problem der Überholenden Kausalität,' *Zeitschrift der Savigny-Stiftung für Rechtsgeschichte, Rom. Abt.* 74 (1957) 201–233.

Schulz, *Principles* (1936) = Fritz Schulz, *Principles of Roman Law*, trans. Marguerite Wolff (Oxford: Clarendon Press, 1936).

Schulz, *History* (1946) = Fritz Schulz, *History of Roman Legal Science* (Oxford: Oxford University Press, 1946).

Schwarz, 'Das Strittige Recht' (1951) = Andreas B. Schwarz, 'Das Strittige Recht der Römischen Juristen,' in *Festschrift Fritz Schulz*, vol. II (Weimar: Bohlaus, 1951) 201–225.

Sirks, 'Delictual Origin' (2009) = Boudewijn Sirks, 'The Delictual Origin, Penal Nature, and Reipersecutory Object of the *Actio Damni Iniuriae Legis Aquiliae*,' *Tijdschrift voor Rechtsgeschiedenis* 77 (2009) 303–353.

Spagnolo and Sampson, *Principle and Pragmatism* (2022) = Benjamin Spagnolo and Joe Sampson, eds., *Principle and Pragmatism in Roman Law* (Oxford: Hart Publishing, 2022).

Stein, 'Two Schools' (1972) = Peter Stein, 'The Two Schools of Jurists in the Early Roman Principate,' *Cambridge Law Journal* 31 (1972) 8–31.

Verhagen, *Security and Credit* (2022) = Hendrik L. E. Verhagen, *Security and Credit in Roman Law: The Historical Evolution of* Pignus *and* Hypotheca (Oxford: Oxford University Press, 2022).

VIR (1903–1987) = *Vocabularium Iurisprudentiae Romanae*, vols. I–V (Berlin: Reimer, 1903–1987).

Wallinga, 'Actio' (2009) = Tammo Wallinga, 'Actio legis Aquiliae—Buße oder Schadensersatz?,' in Holger Altmappen, Ingo Reichard, and Martin Josef Schermaier, eds., *Festschrift für Rolf Knütel zum 70. Geburtstag* (Heidelberg: Müller, 2009) 1385–1399.

Wieacker, *Rechtsgeschichte* II (2006) = Franz Wieacker, *Römische Rechtsgeschichte*, vol. II *Die Jurisprudenz vom Frühen Prinzipat bis zum Ausgang der Antike* (Joseph Georg Wolf, ed.; Munich: Beck, 2006).

Zimmermann, *Obligations* (1990/1996) = Reinhard Zimmermann, *The Law of Obligations: Roman Foundations of the Civilian Tradition* (Oxford: Clarendon Press, 1996).

Medical Literature and Medicine

Going beyond the Practical

Claire Bubb

Greek medical literature was a source of practical wisdom for millennia. The elites of the ʿAbbasid dynasty of ninth century CE Baghdad recognized its utility and had an enormous number of medical texts translated into Syriac and Arabic.[1] The leading medical thinkers of the medieval West, too, centered their curricula on Greek authorities, largely in Latin and Arabo-Latin translations. In turn, the Humanists of the fifteenth and sixteenth centuries began to fear that the potency of Greek knowledge had been diluted by all this translation and championed a return to Greek manuscripts, in full confidence that lurking in the wisdom of the pristine texts were forgotten therapies, cures, and practical knowledge.[2] Even into the eighteenth and nineteenth centuries, as advances by Harvey, Snow, Darwin, and other luminaries of medical history began to erode all its theoretical credibility, confidence in Greek medicine's practical utility remained tenaciously rooted in medical education, with Carl Gottlieb Kühn publishing his edition and Latin translation of Galen's complete works expressly for the benefit of medical audiences as late as the 1830s.[3] Indeed, Galenism can still be found at the heart of Unani medicine, an alternative form of medicine actively taught and practiced in India and Pakistan.[4] The avowedly practical content and intent of ancient medical texts (regardless of the reliability of their practical effect) is perhaps their most undeniable and salient feature.

Galen himself would be the first to champion the idea that his writing and the writing of his predecessors and contemporaries—at least those he did not openly despise—was useful, practical, and contained technical wisdom. Two of his foundational books, indeed, are called the *Art of Medicine* and the *Method of*

[1] On the Arabic reception of Greek medicine, see Savage-Smith, 'Medicine' (1996); Pormann and Savage-Smith, *Medieval Islamic Medicine* (2007); and the articles in Part Two of Bouras-Vallianatos and Zipser, *Companion* (2019); as well as Gutas, *Greek Thought* (1998) for general background.

[2] For an overview of the situation, see Nutton, 'Fortunes of Galen' (2008) 366–379; for details on the new translators of the Greek and their translations, see Fortuna, 'Editions and Translations' (2019).

[3] Carl Gottlieb Kühn's *Claudii Galeni Opera Omnia* (Leipzig: Knobloch) was published bit by bit from 1821 to 1833; Kühn was an eminent professor of medicine at the University of Leipzig and his intended audience for the edition was a medical one; see Nutton, 'Kühn' (2002).

[4] Pormann and Savage-Smith, *Medieval Islamic Medicine* (2007) 173–175.

Claire Bubb, *Medical Literature and Medicine: Going beyond the Practical* In: *Medicine and the Law under the Roman Empire*. Edited by: Claire Bubb and Michael Peachin, Oxford University Press.
DOI: 10.1093/oso/9780192898616.003.0008

Medicine. He is teaching an art, with technical and pragmatic rules, practices, and information. And yet there is much more to the picture. Those who later sought medical wisdom from the Galenic texts in particular found themselves floundering in an ocean of words. Annotations in multiple medieval manuscripts bemoan his prolixity.[5] Galen's readers from late antiquity and the medieval Islamic world found it desirable to untangle, repackage, distill, and generally manhandle the material contained in the corpus into a state of tractable and practical digestibility.[6] Galen could—and often did—write in order to convey specific knowledge clearly to his audience, but that was often not his only, nor even his primary, objective in writing medical literature. It is some of these alternative motivations that this paper will explore.

The fluctuating ways in which Galen's work was received in the two millennia after his death, as briefly sketched above, have informed my approach here to thinking about the contours of Roman medical literature and the nuances to its role as a means of conveying technical or practical knowledge. I will therefore begin with a visual and long-historical approach to the exploration of the non-pragmatic elements of Galen's literary output: namely, mapping out what survived and what did not. Now, to be sure, this process will tell us mostly about the practical needs of the societies that were receiving and copying (or choosing not to copy) the texts in question, and not so much about the society in which the texts were actually written. But, in the case of the particular question to hand, this winnowing effect should work in our favor. The main goal of every society in seeking medicine is to achieve health. Texts that seem to later eyes not to translate directly to health, but to be primarily serving some other motivation, are likely to be deemed less worth the effort of preservation; they are also the ones most likely to be an artifact of their original context.

We are fortunate that Galen, at the end of his life, became concerned about the accurate preservation of his literary legacy. He wrote two works, *On the Order of My Own Books*, which briefly describes the sequence in which he thinks his books ought to be read, and *On My Own Books*, which is much longer and lists his entire literary output, organized at first chronologically, but then by topic. His

[5] See Nutton, 'Fortunes of Galen' (2008) 361.

[6] At some point in late antiquity, a medical canon of sorts was selected, the so-called Sixteen Books, containing only those books by Galen that were deemed most directly practical for the student of medicine; these in turn, were summarized and organized for scholastic use; see Garofalo, 'Galen's Legacy' (2019) for an up-to-date overview with bibliography. For the reception of Greek medical ideas in the Islamic world, see Savage-Smith, 'Medicine' (1996) 913–927 and Pormann and Savage-Smith, *Medieval Islamic Medicine* (2007) 41–76; Vagelpohl, 'User-friendly Galen' (2018), especially 123–124, considers the specific efforts of Hunayn ibn Ishaq in this direction. Interestingly, Mike Peachin has pointed out to me that the legal scholars of antiquity faced a similar battle against sheer mass of information. Thus, for example, Tacitus complains at *Ann*. 3.25 about "the infinite multitude and variety of the laws" (*multitudinem infinitam ac varietatem legum*), and then equates this directly with the level of society's corruption (*Ann*. 3.27); cf. Tert. *Apol*. 4.7. Similarly, Justinian grumbled that, in times gone by, the law was so vast that judges simply decided cases as they liked (Just., *De conf. Dig*. 17).

discussions in these two texts, supplemented by cross-references elsewhere, give us a very detailed picture of his literary output (Figure 1a).[7] He divided his attentions fairly equally across a wide number of sub-topics, identified here roughly according to his own divisions from *On My Own Books*. Zooming out a little (Figure 1b), it becomes clearer that only about 38% of his output covered topics that we would today categorize as "medical literature," that is, treatises discussing pharmacology,

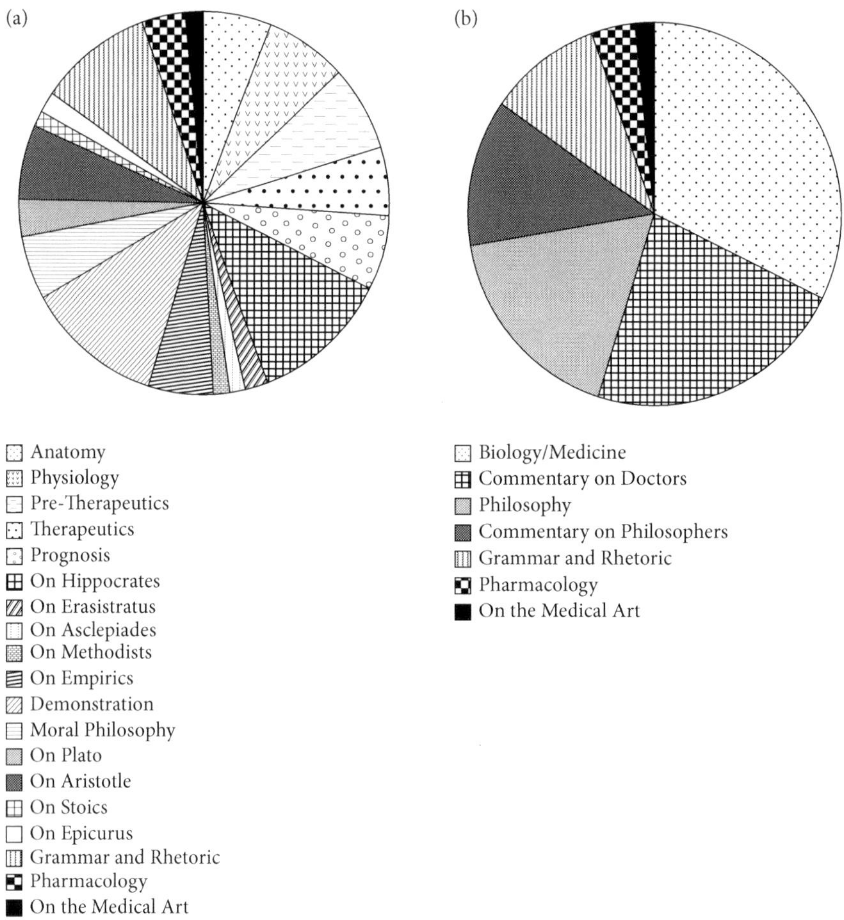

Figure 1a Specific Topics Addressed by Galen (Clockwise from the Top)
Figure 1b Categories of Topics Addressed by Galen (Clockwise from the Top)

[7] These figures derive from my own tabulation of the works of Galen, based on the works he himself names in *On My Own Books* and from the list collected from there and from references elsewhere by the ninth-century translator Hunayn ibn Ishaq in his *Risala* (edition and translation in Lamoreaux, *Hunayn* (2016)); in order to accurately reflect the proportional attention that he paid to each topic, the categories calculate the total number of books, rather than the total number of treatises (that is, *On the Usefulness of the Parts* counts as seventeen books, rather than one).

medical education, and medicine itself, with its underlying biology. The rest is divided between commentary, philosophy, and, of all things, grammar and rhetoric, including a sizable Attic dictionary and studies of vocabulary in ancient Comedy.

When we look at what survives today, the picture is entirely different (Figure 2b).[8] Overwhelmingly, it is the most "practical" texts that survive. The linguistic studies are gone, as is almost all of the philosophy; the medical commentaries, which previously were nearly equal in proportion to the original medical output, have shrunk to about a third of its size. Looking at a finer grain (Figure 2a), in the medical commentaries, where previously Hippocratic commentary accounted for about half of the category, it has now almost entirely

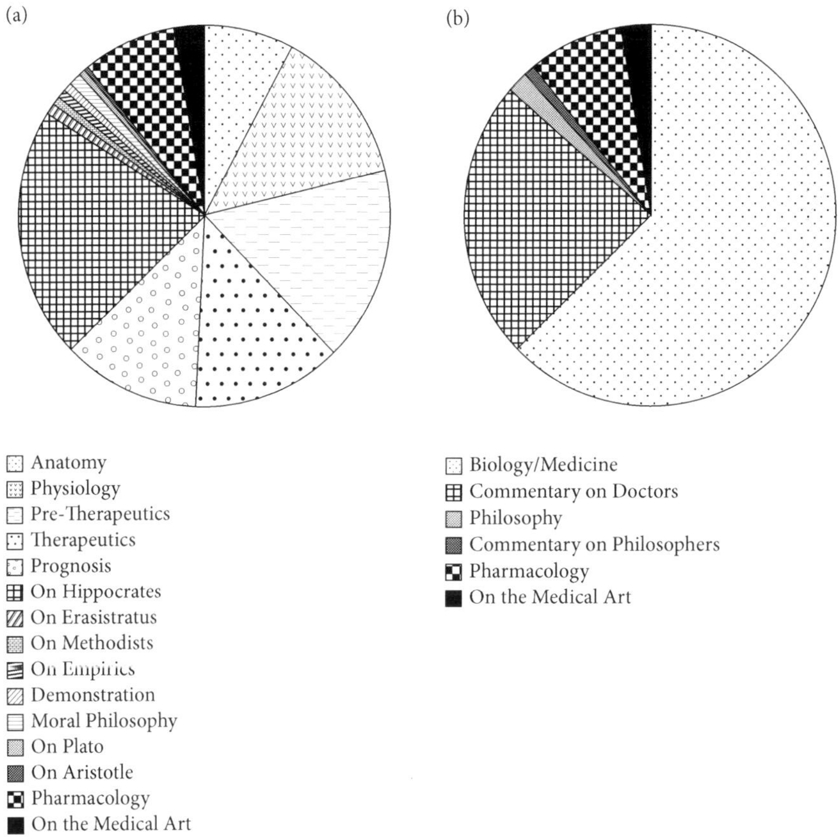

Figure 2a Specific Topics in the Extant Works (Clockwise from the Top)
Figure 2b Categories of Topics in the Extant Works (Clockwise from the Top)

[8] This figure includes texts extant in any language, not just in Greek. When the picture is limited only to surviving Greek texts, the changes are further exaggerated.

overwhelmed it. Less drastically, but also notably, within the five sub-categories of works on directly medical topics, anatomy, which originally constituted an equal fifth, has now shrunk to be half the size of the others. These trends point to two aspects of medical literary output in the Roman period that, to readers outside of that world and that time, appeared to offer limited practical utility in a medical context: (1) detailed textual exegesis and commentary on a range of authors and (2) therapeutically irrelevant anatomy.

Before I begin on these topics, however, a word of caution is due. As Caroline Petit and Luis Salas have explored elsewhere in this volume, it is impossible to extricate Galen's literary motivations from Galen's own personality and self-presentation. Vast portions of Galen's corpus are devoted to rhetoric and polemic: with every addition to a corpus of knowledge, he is also actively positioning himself within his wider social world, both that of doctors and that of the Roman intellectual elite more broadly. This very fact is, of course, intrinsically interesting and essential to my subject of inquiry here. It highlights the fact that literature was a socio-intellectual vehicle as much for doctors as it was for any other members of the educated elite of the time, be they poets, historians, or, indeed, jurists. However, the aggression of Galen's self-presentation and self-promotion have left us in a somewhat difficult position with respect to evaluating medical literature of the Roman period as a whole. He wrote so voluminously and proselytized for his own worth so effectively that he all but entirely eclipsed his peers: an overwhelmingly vast proportion of the surviving medical literature from this period is by Galen. Thus, when talking about medical writing in Rome, one must be careful not to overgeneralize from the idiosyncrasies of the one individual who has come to dominate what survives. That said, while we are probably justified in dismissing his penchant for Aristophanes as a personal quirk, the diversity of the rest of his writings was not unique to him. In the two fields that I am going to consider, he indicates that he was in dialogue with a good number of other contemporaries and near contemporaries: that is, these apparently non-pragmatic topics captured the attention of a variety of doctors in this period.

Textual exegesis—now the purview of philologists—was an important element of Galen's persona as an intellectual and a doctor. By Galen's day, the study of medicine, at least at its most elite level, had taken a decidedly academic turn. Established names and established texts were central to certain strains of medical discourse. Whether or not a name or a text was "established," however, was a somewhat moving target.[9] While Hippocrates, for example, was widely accepted as an authoritative voice, there was not consensus as to what counted as genuine Hippocratic texts. Thus, the act of textual exegesis, for a doctor, was at its heart one of interpretive self-presentation. A doctor of the Roman period, with its

[9] von Staden, 'Caelius Aurelianus' (1999) explores the example of how the Methodists, a medical sect with a very different approach from Galen, deployed different ancient sources in different ways.

heavily antiquarian intellectual culture, was well served by creating a Hippocrates or an Erasistratus in his own image and then trusting that phantasm to be a venerable mouthpiece for his own ideas.[10]

Hippocrates was a particularly protean figure because of the wide range of texts attributed to him. Already by the Hellenistic period more than sixty texts by a diversity of authors were collected under the name of the venerable doctor, containing different—at times even directly contradictory—doctrine.[11] Complicating this situation was the fact that Hippocrates, also beginning in the Hellenistic period, was established as a quasi-divine founding figure for the medical profession.[12] Thus doctors from differing sects of medical thought were keen to claim him as an intellectual antecedent, and the diversity of the corpus allowed them all simultaneously to succeed in doing this to one degree or another.[13] This textual landscape meant that the editorial and exegetical skills required to convincingly support one's reading of a text, as well as to convincingly attribute a text to a specific author (or convincingly rebut such an attribution by someone else) became an important, if seemingly incongruous, set of tools for writers of medical literature.

Galen takes considerable pain to establish his credentials as an editor. He describes the time-consuming and physically uncomfortable lengths that he is willing to go to in order to acquire a venerable text. He scours libraries, reporting that he unearthed previously unknown treatises by Aristotle and others, and seeks out numerous exemplars of the texts that he edits.[14] He takes the time to go through papyri rotting in an ill-placed collection in order to examine and preserve their contents, evocatively complaining that "they caused [him] no little pain as [he] was copying them ... for the place is marshy and depressed in the extreme and stifling in the summer."[15] He demonstrates an acute understanding of paleographical dilemmas, noting, for example, that thetas are liable to be misread as

[10] Though it would be easy to attribute a level of cynical self-awareness to this practice (see Lloyd, 'Scholarship' (1988) for examples of patently opportunistic cherry-picking in Galen's use of Hippocrates and others), it seems most plausible that Galen himself was sincere in his belief that he was uncovering the "true" Hippocrates; Vallance, 'Galen, Proclus' (1999) offers a defense of his sincerity, while also highlighting that he, like any commentator, was susceptible to the intellectual trends of his moment.

[11] Smith, *Hippocratic Traditions* (1979) 199–215 offers a reconstruction of the Hellenistic collection and codification of the Hippocratic corpus; see also Nelson, 'Woozle' (2016).

[12] On the establishment of Hippocrates as the medical authority figure *par excellence*, see Smith, *Hippocratic Traditions* (1979) 204–222 and King, 'Origins' (2006), especially 250–258.

[13] On the diversity and malleability of the Hippocratic corpus and on Galen's own relationship to it, see Smith, *Hippocratic Tradition* (1979); Lloyd, 'Hellenistics and Hippocrateans' (1991); and Boudon-Millot, 'Galen's Hippocrates' (2018).

[14] Galen *Indol.* 17 (7 BJP). For Galen's thoroughness in consulting multiple different readings, see López Férez, 'Galeno, lector' (1992) and Totelin, 'Multiple Manuscript Copies' (2009). On the specifics of Galen's library visits, see Jones, 'Books and Libraries' (2009).

[15] Galen *Indol.* 19 (8 BJP) (*ταῦτ' ἄρα καὶ κάματον ἡμῖν παρέσχεν οὐ μικρὸν ἐγγραφομένοις αὐτά ... ἔστι γὰρ ἑλῶδές τε καὶ κοῖλον τὸ χωρίον ἐς τὰ μάλιστα, καὶ διὰ θέρους πνιγηρόν*). All Greek and Latin translations are my own; Arabic translations are drawn from the cited editions.

omicrons if the middle line is destroyed, which, he explains, might happen "if a thin fiber [of the papyrus] is lost... also if insects eat it, also if, straight from the beginning, it was written faintly, then it becomes faded over time."[16] Indeed, despite the fact that he almost certainly possessed slaves trained as scribes, Galen indicates that he does not entrust the scrutiny and copying of important manuscripts to anyone but himself.[17] He himself endured the sweaty, unpleasant conditions he describes above, just as he himself put in the time to compare manuscripts and produce new editions of texts "of all of the ancient doctors" and of many philosophers, each written out in fair copies in which he personally attended to the placing of each period and comma—an unusual degree of punctuation for an ancient book roll, indicative of a high level of close reading and editorial care.[18] All of this knowledge and activity would be expected and laudable in a philologist, but seems supremely non-pragmatic for a man of medicine.

These philological skills, however, allow Galen to claim complete control over Hippocrates' legacy and thus to fortify his own medical output. His efforts in the library ensure that he has the most venerable texts on which to base his claims.[19] Galen's editorial peers in other fields would have appreciated the value in this: a potent test of the reliability of a reading in second-century scholarship was its age—the older a manuscript, the thinking went, the closer it was to the original, and, therefore, the most reliable. Consequently, possession of or access to venerable manuscripts was considered grounds for both authority and some concomitant boasting. Lucian mocks the target of his *Ignorant Book Collector* for not being able to tell the difference between a valuable old book and a book that simply looks old by virtue of being in poor repair—he knows that it is desirable to possess old books without being sophisticated enough to quite evaluate why.[20] More seriously,

[16] Galen *Hipp.Epid.VI* pr. (XVIIa.795K = *CMG* V 10,2,2 4) (*δυνατὸν γὰρ δὴ οὕτως καὶ λεπτῆς ἰνὸς ἀπολωλυίας συναπολέσθαι τὴν γραμμὴν ταύτην, καὶ μυίας <γ'> αὐτὴν ἐκφαγούσης, καὶ κατ' ἀρχὰς εὐθὺς αὐτὴν ἀμυδρῶς γραφεῖσαν ἐξίτηλον [αὐτὴν] ὑπὸ τοῦ χρόνου γενέσθαι*).

[17] At *Aff.Pec.Dig.* 1.9 (V.48K) Galen chastises a friend for being too miserly to spend his wealth in what Galen considers to be the appropriate way, that is: "the buying and preparation of books, the training of scribes, either for speed-writing or for beautiful and exact writing, and also... [the training] of lectors who read correctly" (*εἰς βιβλίων ὠνὴν καὶ κατασκευὴν καὶ τῶν γραφόντων ἄσκησιν ἤτοι γ' εἰς τάχος διὰ σημείων ἢ εἰς κάλλος <καὶ> ἀκρίβειαν, ὥσπερ γε... τῶν ἀναγινωσκόντων ὀρθῶς*). He is similarly distrustful of outsourcing menial tasks in his more narrowly medical research; he says at *AA* 1.3 (II.233K) that he initially entrusted the skinning of his anatomical specimens to underlings, "believing the task to be beneath [him]" (*μικρότερον ἢ κατ' ἐμὲ νομίζοντι τοὖργον*), but took over the practice himself after discovering that their careless work was destroying subcutaneous muscles.

[18] Galen *Indol.* 14–15 (6 BJP) (*τῶν παλαιῶν ἰατρῶν πάντων*). On the punctuation he describes, see Boudon-Millot, Jouanna, and Pietrobelli, *Chagriner* (2010) 58–60; contrast to the punctuation typical of ancient book rolls, as described in Johnson, 'Ancient Book' (2009) 261–262.

[19] For the value Galen placed on old witnesses, see *Hipp.Epid.VI* pr., 2.47 (XVIIa.793–794, 1005K = *CMG* V 10,2,2 3, 121), as well von Staden, 'Staging the Past' (2009) 144–150, where he marshalls the huge number of instances in which Galen references and valorizes "old copies" (*παλαιαὶ ἀντίγραφαι*) and "old" or "ancient readings" (*παλαιαὶ* or *ἀρχαῖαι γραφαί*). For an introduction to Galen's exegetical principles, see Manuli, 'Stile del Commento' (1983) and Mansfeld, *Prolegomena* (1994) 131–168.

[20] Lucian *Ind.* 1. For this reliance on age as indicator of textual quality and the book connoisseur's ensuant vulnerability to fraud, see Howley, 'Book Forgery' (forthcoming).

Aulus Gellius reports several anecdotes concerning the value and prestige of old manuscripts.[21] In one, a certain Apollinaris says:[22]

> *Sed enim contentus inquit ego his non fui et, ut non turbidae fidei nec ambiguae, sed ut purae liquentisque esset, equusne an eques scriptum Ennius reliquisset, librum summae atque reuerendae uetustatis, quem fere constabat Lampadionis manu emendatum, studio pretioque multo unius uersus inspiciendi gratia conduxi et eques, non equus, scriptum in eo uersu inueni.*
>
> But, indeed, I was not content with these [examples] and, so that it might be a matter not of confused and ambiguous, but of pure and clear belief whether Ennius wrote '*equus*' or '*eques*,' I borrowed, with considerable outlay of effort and money, a book of great and venerable antiquity, which was generally agreed to have been edited by the hand of Lampadio, for the sake of looking at a single verse, and I found '*eques*' not '*equus*' written in that verse.

Devotion to the uncovering of genuine ancient readings was a thing to be bragged of, worthy of the time and cost that Apollinaris, with careful self-advertisement, attributes to it. Galen would have won both intellectual and social aplomb for his literary activities; there is, no doubt, a shade of braggadocio in his claim that he "deliberately choose[s] the ancient readings, even if they seem to be unlikely or to present greater difficulty."[23]

When an ancient reading alone is insufficient to solve a problematic point in a text, Galen flexes his editorial authority, taking recourse in his favorite pair of editorial principles: historicity and truth. In his commentary on the third book of the *Epidemics*, he includes a lengthy digression on the sins of poor exegetes, in which one of the major offenses consists of imposing post-Hippocratic thought on Hippocrates.[24] To do so is to take to an improper extreme the desire to adopt Hippocrates as the founder of any given idea: one can deploy him, to be sure, but one must first properly establish what one is deploying. Secondarily, an editor is remiss in ascribing to Hippocrates any idea that Galen does not consider to be true. In the course of his diatribe against such abuses, he says:[25]

> *ὅταν δὲ καὶ τὰ σφάλματ᾽ αὐτῶν οὐ μόνον ἀποχωρῇ τῆς Ἱπποκράτους γνώμης, ἀλλὰ καὶ τῆς ἐν τοῖς πράγμασιν ἀληθείας, διπλασίως ἄν τις αὐτοῖς μέμψαιτο. κάλλιστον μὲν γάρ ἐστιν ἀμφοτέρων ἔχεσθαι τῶν σκοπῶν τῶνδε τὸν [ἀκόλουθον] ἐξηγητήν,*

[21] See Gell. *NA* 1.7.1, 1.21.2, 2.14, 5.4.1, 9.14, 13.21.4, 18.5.11, 18.9.5–6.
[22] Gell. *NA* 18.5.11.
[23] Galen *Hipp.Epid.VI* 2.47 (XVIIa.1005K = *CMG* V 10,2,2 121) (*ἀλλ᾽ ἐγὼ τὰς παλαιὰς γραφὰς προαιροῦμαι, κἂν ἀπίθανοι δοκῶσιν εἶναι καὶ μείζονα τὴν ἀπορίαν ἔχειν*).
[24] Galen *Hipp.Epid.III* 1.4 (XVIIa.496–524K = *CMG* V 10,2,1 10–26); the material on anachronistic exegesis occurs at 506–507, 515K.
[25] Galen *Hipp.Epid.III* 1.4 (XVIIa.507K = *CMG* V 10,2,1 17).

> *ἀκόλουθά τε λέγοντα τῷ συγγραφεῖ καὶ ἀληθῆ. θάτερον δὲ μόνον φυλάττοντι μεμπτέον ὡς τοῦ ὅλου τὸ ἥμισυ διεφθαρκότι. τὸν δὲ μήτ' ἀληθῆ λέγοντα μήτ' ἀκόλουθα τῷ γεγραφότι τὸ βιβλίον ἐξηγητὴν ἐσχάτως ἁμαρτάνειν ὑποληπτέον.*
>
> when the errors of these men dissent not only from the opinion of Hippocrates, but also from the truth of the matter, then someone could blame them on two counts. For it is best for an exegete to hold himself to both of these goals: the words should be in accordance with the author and also true. Someone who only pays attention to one of these points should be blamed on the grounds that he has ruined half of the whole.

The problem with this, of course, is that it precludes the possibility that an ancient author might have made a mistake. Galen is not so blinded by his respect for the ancients that he does not acknowledge this. Several paragraphs later he resumes:[26]

> *τῆς μὲν γὰρ κατὰ διέξοδον σκοπός ἐστιν ἀληθείας εὕρεσις, ἐν δὲ ταῖς ἐξηγήσεσι πρόκειται γνῶναι τὴν δόξαν τοῦ παλαιοῦ. προμεμαθηκότα γοῦν ἀκριβῶς ἕκαστα μετὰ ταῦτα χρὴ πρὸς τὰς ἐξηγήσεις ἔρχεσθαι τῶν παλαιῶν συγγραμμάτων, τὸν μὲν πρῶτον ἔχοντα <σκοπὸν> εὑρεῖν τὴν γνώμην τοῦ παλαιοῦ, <τὸν> δεύτερον δ' ἐπ' αὐτῷ, πότερον ὀρθῶς ἢ οὐκ ὀρθῶς εἴρηται.*
>
> The goal of instruction given in detail is the discovery of truth, but in exegesis the matter at hand is to understand the opinion of the ancient. Therefore, having accurately learned in advance each of the pertinent matters one must broach the exegesis of ancient texts having as a first goal to discover the opinion of the ancient and as a second, after that, whether he spoke correctly or not.

Thus, it is possible, in the final instance, for an editor to produce a text of Hippocrates in which Hippocrates speaks falsely. Further, it is important to the credibility of the editor that he appear willing to do so. But in practice Galen has difficulty bringing himself to take this step.[27] Indeed, because of the highly constructed nature of Galen's Hippocrates, in which he only accepts as genuine those parts that agree with medical truth as he himself sees it, it is rare for these two criteria to be at odds with one another.

One of Galen's favorite Hippocratic texts—in fact, the one that he considers to be the touchstone of Hippocratic thought—is *On the Nature of Man*.[28] However,

[26] Galen *Hipp.Epid.III* 1.4 (XVIIa.516K = *CMG* V 10,2,1 22).

[27] See, for example, Galen *Ut.Diss.* 10 (II.905K = *CMG* V 2,1 54) where he prefers to reinterpret their definition of a word rather than admit that Hippocrates and his immediate followers were wrong, because "it is not just to think so about such men" (*οὐ θέμις ὑπὲρ ἀνδρῶν τηλικούτων οὕτω φρονεῖν*). On Galen's (and others') belief that Hippocrates epitomized true thinking, see Roselli, 'Hippocrates and the Truth' (2016).

[28] On Galen's relationship to and evaluation of this text, see Jouanna, '*Nature of Man*' (2012) and Curtis, 'Rhetorical Analysis' (2016).

like many texts in the Hippocratic corpus, it is unevenly composed. The end of the text seems quite unrelated to the beginning, and there is a truly anomalous anatomical section thrown in in the middle for no clear reason. As a result, this treatise, which lays out the humoral system of medicine—one that Galen would catapult into the medieval consciousness with long-lasting consequences—was a nexus of medical scholarly debate in antiquity. Some argued that it was a genuine work of Hippocrates; others that it was the work of his almost-as-good student and son-in-law Polybus; still others that it was entirely spurious.[29] Galen decides to pick and choose. He opines, at some length, that the first, humoral, section—which is squarely in line with his own medical theory—must be genuine Hippocrates; the last section, which he considers sound, if unimpressive and not clearly relevant, must be Polybus; while the middle section, which is completely incompatible with observable anatomy, is clearly the later insertion of whichever idiot or malfeasant decided to bridge the first two texts together.

Galen's creatively selective approach to deciding the authenticity of *Nature of Man* highlights the importance of textual exegesis in contemporary medical literature. It is important to Galen that Hippocrates expound a clearly articulated vision of humoral balance as central to health. This is the view that he himself argues for, and being able to make it a central tenant of Hippocrates bolsters his position. It is important to him also that Hippocrates be a masterful anatomist, since anatomically informed physiology was the foundation upon which Galen based his own therapeutic program. Therefore, he winnows through the various, often inchoate, attempts at anatomical discussion in the Hippocratic corpus and harvests as genuine only those texts and passages containing anatomical comments that he can somehow square with reality. He is thus able to craft a Hippocrates who is "one of the most skillful and proficient observers of what appears during dissection."[30] Textual commentary, in short, and the philological skills that support it, allow Galen to retroject his own brand of medical thinking onto a past authority and then turn around and call up that doctored authority as a witness to a centuries-long medical tradition of which he is the true heir.

But this does not really answer the question of why all this so important to Galen. Would anyone else have cared to the same degree? Would this sort of literary exercise really have garnered him any practical professional capital? The answer to both of these questions is quite clearly, 'yes.' Textual exegesis was a routine element of medical discourse in this period, at least among the upper tier

[29] For attribution of the whole text to Hippocrates, see Galen *HNH* pr. (XV.11K = *CMG* V 9,1 8) and *PHP* 6.3.29 (V.528K = *CMG* V 4,1,2 380); for attribution of the work to Polybus, see Galen *HNH* pr. (XV.11–12K = *CMG* V 9,1 8), as well as Anon. Lond. XIX.1–18 and Arist. *Hist. an.* 3.3, 512b12–513a8; for skepticism of the work as a whole, see Galen *Lib.Prop.* 9.12 (XIX.36K = 161 B-M).

[30] Galen *Hipp.Epid.II* 4.1 (*CMG Suppl.Or.* V 2 633); cf. 705, where he describes his "meticulous dissection of the nerves."

of medical practitioners.[31] Indeed, the medico-philological landscape held such potential for impact that Galen feels the need to caution and control his readers. In his *On the Order of My Own Books*, he tells them that it is only "with an understanding of my writings" that "one can broach the books of Hippocrates," though he then goes on to suggest that directly reading the books of the master is not even really necessary.[32] He hopes to live long enough to write commentaries on all the most important Hippocratic texts, but if he should die before he can accomplish this, he tells his readers:[33]

> *ἕξουσιν οἱ βουλόμενοι τὴν γνώμην <γνῶναι> αὐτοῦ καὶ τὰς ἡμετέρας μέν, ὡς εἴρηται, πραγματείας ἅμα τοῖς ἤδη γεγονόσιν ὑπομνήμασι καὶ τῶν ἐξηγησαμένων γὲ τὸν ἄνδρα τοῦ τε διδασκάλου Πέλοπος <καί> εἴ πού τι καὶ τῶν Νουμισιανοῦ ἔχοιεν—ἔστι δ' ὀλίγα τὰ διασῳζόμενα—καὶ πρὸς τούτοις τά τε Σαβίνου καὶ Ῥούφου τοῦ Ἐφεσίου. Κόϊντος δὲ καὶ οἱ Κοΐντου μαθηταὶ τὴν Ἱπποκράτους γνώμην οὐκ ἀκριβῶς ἐγνώκασι, διὸ καὶ πολλαχόθι τὰς ἐξηγήσεις οὐκ ὀρθῶς ποιοῦνται· Λύκος δ' ἐνίοτε καὶ προσεγκαλεῖ τῷ Ἱπποκράτει καί φησι ψεύδεσθαι τὸν ἄνδρα μὴ γιγνώσκων αὐτοῦ τὰ δόγματα· καίτοι τά γε τοῦ Λύκου βιβλία φανερῶς πάντα γέγονεν.*
>
> those who wish to understand his thought will have both my [general] writings, as has been said, together with [my] already extant commentaries, and [those] of those who have done exegetical work on him, both my teacher Pelops and Numisianus—if anyone can find [his writings]; few have survived—and in addition to these, those of Sabinus and Rufus of Ephesus. Quintus and the students of Quintus have not rightly understood the thought of Hippocrates, wherefore they have often not done their exegesis correctly; Lycus sometimes even accuses Hippocrates and, out of ignorance of his doctrines, says that the man spoke false. Nevertheless, Lycus's books all seem to be everywhere.

In short, Galen does not actually trust beginners to broach Hippocrates directly at all.[34] The material within is too volatile, too potentially malleable to be trusted in the hands of the unanointed masses. As he puts it elsewhere:[35]

[31] Flemming, 'Commentary' (2008) 336 concludes that Hippocratic commentary had basically become *de rigueur* in the medical community by Galen's time.

[32] Galen *Ord.Lib.Prop.* 3.3 (97 B-M) (*τινὰ μετὰ τὴν γνῶσιν τῶν ἡμετέρων ἐντυγχάνειν δύνασθαι τοῖς Ἱπποκράτους βιβλίοις*).

[33] Galen *Ord.Lib.Prop.* 3.6–8 (XIX.57K = 98 B-M).

[34] He makes a similar statement at *Nat.Fac.* 1.2 (II.6K): "[it is possible] for those who wish it to thoroughly learn the opinions of the ancients from the things which I personally have investigated about them" (*<ἐνὸν> τοῖς βουλομένοις τὰ τῶν παλαιῶν ἐκμανθάνειν κἀξ ὧν ἡμεῖς ἰδίᾳ περὶ αὐτῶν ἐπεσκέμμεθα*).

[35] Galen *MM* 7.2 (X.459K).

> *δεῖται δὲ καὶ τὰ [σπέρματα] Ἱπποκράτους αὐτοῦ γεωργῶν ἀγαθῶν, οἳ σπεροῦσί τε αὐτὰ καὶ αὐξήσουσι καὶ τελειώσουσι προσηκόντως. καὶ ὅτι πρὸ ἡμῶν οὐδεὶς τοῦτ᾽ ἔπραξεν, ἀλλ᾽ οἱ πλεῖστοί γε καὶ προσδιέφθειραν αὐτοῦ τὰ σπέρματα, νομίζω σαφῶς ἐπιδεδεῖχθαι τοῖς προσεσχηκόσι τὸν νοῦν.*
>
> even the seeds of Hippocrates himself require good husbandmen to sow them and grow them and bring them to their full potential. And, that no one before me has done this, but that the majority have actually spoiled his seeds, I think that I have clearly shown to those who have been paying attention.

Galen does not want anyone to fall prey to the alternative Hippocrateses that have been manufactured by his peers and immediate forebears along different molds—especially not that of Lycus, whose willingness to attribute incorrect statements to Hippocrates undermines the entire game that everyone else is playing.[36]

This textual game was intimately bound up in the educational and societal norms of the world within which these doctors operated. Bookish knowledge was a highly valued marker of elite identity.[37] Further, much of the intellectual activity of this period was of an antiquarian nature: education focused to an intense degree on Homer and the authors of the fifth and fourth centuries, the speeches of the famous contemporary sophists centered almost obsessively on Classical Athens, and the pages of Aulus Gellius are rife with discussion of old words and old customs. Indeed, almost any text you read from this period, whether philosophical, rhetorical, or technical, takes care to link itself to a distant authority. Paradigmatically, Philostratus, who coined the term "Second Sophistic" for the rhetorical movement that flourished in this century, rather tortuously takes Aeschines as its founder, even though he lived in the fourth century BCE, in the midst of the very "First Sophistic" against which Philostratus defines his term.[38] Juvenal satirizes this valuation of intimate familiarity with history and textual sources:[39]

> *Sed uos saeuas inponite leges, ut praeceptori uerborum regula constet, ut legat historias, auctores nouerit omnes tamquam ungues digitosque suos, ut forte rogatus, dum petit aut thermas aut Phoebi balnea, dicat nutricem Anchisae, nomen patriamque nouercae Anchemoli, dicat quot Acestes uixerit annis, quot Siculi Phrygibus uini donauerit urnas.*
>
> But you impose savage laws: that grammatical rules should be unbroken by a teacher, that he should read histories, that he should know all authors like he

[36] On the surprising diversity among the opinions of 'Hippocratics', see Smith, *Hippocratic Tradition* (1979) 62–77 and Nutton (2005).

[37] Johnson, *Readers* (2010) maps this readerly world and situates doctors, particularly Galen, squarely within it.

[38] Philostr. *VS* 481.

[39] Juv. 7.229–236.

> knows his own fingers and nails, that, should he happen to be asked, on his way to the warm baths or the baths of Phoebus, he should be able to tell you who Anchises' nurse was and the name and country of Anchemolus' stepmother and he should be able to say how many years Acestes lived and how many urns of Sicilian wine he gave to the Phrygians.

In this case, the ambusher is catechizing the prospective teacher on antiquarian knowledge related to the background of the relatively recent *Aeneid*, but equal facility with more ancient texts was also *de rigeur*. Consider the embarrassment heaped on the various unfortunates who, in the pages of Gellius, find themselves unable to adequately discuss word usage in ancient authors.[40] Or the pesky character at Athenaeus' overwhelmingly antiquarian dinner party, who is nicknamed *Keitoukeitos*, or Mr. Attested-Not-Attested, for his irritating habit of constantly querying "at every hour in streets, walkways, bookshops, and bathhouses" and before every meal whether various words are truly Attic and can be found somewhere in the corpus of the ancients.[41]

Doctors engaged with their own, medical, version of this same phenomenon. In one example, Galen finds himself in a very *Keitoukeitos* situation. A hapless fellow, whom Galen identifies simply as "one of the well-reputed doctors in Rome," is discussing diet and claims that Hippocrates would have prescribed groats—a sort of wheat-based version of oatmeal and this doctor's favorite cure-all—if it had been in current use in the fifth century; however, he claims, the dish was not yet attested at that period and that is why his own teaching differs from that of Hippocrates, who would, had he lived in modern, groat-filled times, have greatly approved of it.[42] Galen jumps in not only with a Hippocratic example of the word, but also with contemporaneous instances of its use in Old Comedy, which he triumphantly brings forth from his linguistic research. In another situation, the tables are turned. Much like Juvenal's beleaguered teacher, Galen finds himself accosted in the street by a rival physician who asks him, without any greeting or preamble, whether he had read the second book of the *Prorrhetics* of Hippocrates and if he is familiar with a particular sentence within it.[43] Though Galen clearly feels that this particular doctor's manners are lacking, he is not at all against this sort of quizzing in principle. Indeed, in his *On Recognizing the Best Physician*, he advises potential clients to ask just these sorts of questions:[44]

[40] For example, Gell. *NA* 1.18, 2.6, 10, 3.11, 11.7, 13.31, 15.9, 17.3, 18.4.

[41] Ath. *Deipn.* 1d–e (ἃς ἀνὰ πᾶσαν ὥραν ποιεῖται ἐν ταῖς ἀγυιαῖς, περιπάτοις, βιβλιοπωλείοις, βαλανείοις).

[42] Galen *Indol.* 25 (9-10 BJP) (<τινὸς> ἐν Ῥώμῃ τῶν εὐδοκιμούντων ἰατρῶν).

[43] Galen *Praen.* 4.2 (XIV.620K = *CMG* V 8,1 88).

[44] Galen *Opt.Med.Cogn.* 5.1–2 (*CMG Suppl.Or.* IV 69).

> If you wish primarily to examine the matter whether a physician knows or does not know about medicine, you should begin first by asking him questions on those things which I have described: "Where and how did Hippocrates mention them, and what evidence has he provided to prove them?"... You should further ask him: "Did Erasistratus approve or disapprove of Hippocrates' precepts about treatment of patients? Did he disapprove of one thing or many things or all of his precepts? Or did he give contradictory instructions?" Moreover, you should ask questions about the opinions of all other famous physicians; these are: Diocles, Pleistonicus, Phylotimus, Praxagoras, Dieuches, Herophilus, and Asclepiades.

As this passage indicates, though Hippocrates was the marquee name, he was not the only author subject to this scholarly and exegetical attention.

Other ancient authorities tended to be associated more with one sect or another, but all were fair game for any doctor in search of historical support. Indeed, one of Galen's favorite tools in his arsenal against one group of rivals, the Roman Erasistrateans, was to turn the very text of Erasistratus against them, claiming that he was more familiar with and in a better position to interpret and understand his texts than his own disciples were:[45]

> *θαυμάζουσι μὲν γὰρ τοὺς Ἐρασιστράτου λόγους καὶ τοὔνομα ἐπ᾽ αὐτοῖς ἀπ᾽ ἐκείνου τίθενται, προσαγορεύοντες Ἐρασιστρατείους, οὕτω δὲ αὐτῶν ἀμαθεῖς εἰσὶν ὥστε πάντα μᾶλλον ἢ τὴν ἐκείνου γνώμην ἐξηγοῦνται...εἶτ᾽ οὖν ἐμὲ βούλει προσέχειν ἀνθρώποις Ἐρασιστράτου φλυαροῦσιν, αὐτὰς ἔχοντα Ἐρασιστράτου φωνάς; οὐδενὶ τὸν τρόπον ἡγοῦμαι προσήκειν. ἀκούσωμεν οὖν αὐτοῦ τῶν φωνῶν....*
>
> they marvel at the words of Erasistratus and take his name for themselves, calling themselves Erasistrateans; yet, they are so lacking in understanding of his writings that they preach everything except for his own opinion.... So would you really like me to heed these men who speak nonsense in the name of Erasistratus, when I have the actual words of Erasistratus? I do not think that way of proceeding would seem appropriate to anyone. So, let us listen to his own words:....

Galen thus leverages his superior relationship to texts as a means of dominating his professional rivals. He describes another occasion when he delivered a lengthy anti-Erasistratean lecture with a text of Erasistratus before him, stylus pointing to the precise words against which he had been called upon to argue. From the context, it seems likely that this is his own book, brought for this purpose. His ownership of the text—enhanced by his reputation for scholarly rigor in the accumulation of his library—thus elevates him to be in a position to argue directly

[45] Galen *Ven.Sect.Er.* 7 (XI.175K).

with Erasistratus, bypassing his contemporary Erasistrateans, whom he is thereby deliberately setting out to "harass."[46]

Galen is tapping into contemporary mores here. Books themselves were a status symbol in certain intellectual circles of the second century. Lucian mocks his "ignorant book collector" for ostentatiously carrying about a book in his hand everywhere he goes: "you always have one in every situation."[47] However, Lucian's scorn is not directed at the fact that he parades his book-ownership, but rather that for him it is an empty prop—he is unable to discuss the book knowledgably when people, as seemingly invited, strike up a conversation about it. Indeed, in Gellius' circle, seeing a book in a friend's hand is an unremarkable catalyst for conversation, and happening to have and duly producing an apposite book was often the trump card in social situations.[48] Galen is adept at parlaying his carefully cultivated literary expertise and meticulously accumulated library of books into professional clout. In the most spectacular example, Galen has been accused by slanderous rivals of falsifying his anatomical texts to gain a reputation for having discovered things that are in fact not there. His friends urge him to respond publicly, and he pulls out all the stops. Rather than simply demonstrate his anatomical findings publicly, he:[49]

> *εἰς τὸ μέσον ἀνέθηκα* **τὰ τῶν ἀνατομικῶν ἁπάντων βιβλία** *τὴν ἐξουσίαν δοὺς ἑκάστῳ τῶν παρόντων ὃ βούλεται μόριον ἀνατμηθῆναι προβάλλειν ἐπαγγειλάμενος δείξειν, ὅσα διεφώνησαν τοῖς ἔμπροσθεν, ἀληθῶς ὑπ᾽ ἐμοῦ γεγραμμένα.*
>
> set[s] up in the middle [of the group] **the books of all the anatomists**, giving authority to each of those present who wished it to propose a part to be dissected, having announced that [he] would demonstrate that [he] wrote accurately in each area where [he] disagreed with those who came before.

He uses the texts that he has edited and collected to advertise that, not only is he confident that he can ably dissect any part of an animal on command, he also owns an enormous library of medical books and is so familiar with the contents of all of them that he will be able to find the relevant point in each of them instantaneously while lecturing before a large crowd. Suddenly, his detractors have taken on not just Galen, but all of written medical knowledge.

All of these passages underscore the fact that Galen did not limit the deployment of his exegetical credentials to Hippocratic texts alone, nor, as his denouncements of inferior exegetes remind us, was his the only voice in the fray. However,

[46] Galen *Lib.Prop.* 1.11 (XIX.14K = 138–139 B-M) (*λυπήσαιμι*).

[47] Lucian, *Ind.* 18 (*ἀεὶ δέ τι πάντως ἔχεις*).

[48] For seeing a book in-hand, see Gell. *NA* 3.1.1; for producing books to win arguments, see 13.31.2, 17.3.4, 19.1.14. For more discussion, see Johnson, *Readers* (2010) 98–136, especially 110–114.

[49] Galen *Lib.Prop.* 3.16 (XIX.22K = 144–145 B-M).

subsequent generations found only Galen's views on Hippocrates to be practically worthwhile—no doubt because of his relentless promoting of them—and, even then, their interest was lukewarm. While a decent fraction—though significantly less than all—of his Hippocratic commentaries have survived, only a tiny handful of the work he dedicated to other medical authors has come down to us (including none of the commentaries); further, despite his clear indication of interlocutors in both Hippocratic and non-Hippocratic exegesis, scarcely any trace of all this extra-Galenic activity survives.[50] In short, in the realms both of medical literature and of in-person medical interactions, literary analysis, textual study, and access to a serious library of historical texts allowed a Roman doctor to dialogue with and dominate his peers in a way that was particularly characteristic of his time and place.

I will end by turning briefly to my second topic, one that Galen himself derides as non-pragmatic: therapeutically irrelevant anatomy. That Galen, of all people, should hold the position that any aspect of the study of anatomy is a waste of time may come as a surprise. He views anatomy as foundational to the study of medicine, and it is an area in which he is particularly passionate.[51] However, even an anatomical devotee like himself, who finds it totally unremarkable to keep various monkey bones handy around the house for ease of reference and who happily dissects mice and fish and birds, draws a line somewhere. His main complaint is that doctors have become too trendy and superficial. He denounces the "daily" sight of:[52]

> *θεωροῦντας ὁσημέραι τῶν ἰατρῶν τοὺς ἐπισταμένους μὲν, ὁπόσοι τέ εἰσι καὶ ὁποῖοι κατὰ τὴν καρδίαν ὑμένες, ἢ τῆς γλώττης οἱ μύες, ὅσα τ᾽ ἄλλα τοιαῦτα, μὴ γινώσκοντας δὲ τὴν ἐκτὸς ἀνατομὴν, ἐν προγνώσει τε καὶ χειρουργίᾳ τῶν κατὰ ταῦτα τὰ μέρη γινομένων παθῶν μέγιστα σφαλλομένους, τοὺς δὲ ταύτην μὲν γινώσκοντας, ἀγνοοῦντας δ᾽ ἐκεῖνα, κατορθοῦντας ὁσημέραι.*
>
> doctors who are versed in how many and of what sort are the membranes in the heart or the muscles in the tongue and other such things, yet do not know the anatomy of the external parts, making the gravest errors in their prognosis and surgery of the diseases that affect those parts, while those doctors who know these things, though unversed in the others, daily proceed correctly.

[50] Of the seventy-seven books devoted to Hippocratic exegesis and analysis (those that Galen describes at *Lib.Prop.* 9 (XIX.33–37K = 159–162 B-M) and the three further titles that Hunayn mentions at *Risala* 93, 111, 113), only forty-seven survive in Greek (fifty-seven in any language); of the sixty-eight books he dedicated to the texts and ideas of Erasistratus, Asclepiades, the Empiricists, and the Methodists (*Lib.Prop.* 10–13 (XIX.37–38K = 162–163 B-M)), several of which he describes as commentaries, only five survive in Greek, wholly or partially (seven in any language).

[51] On the foundational importance of anatomy to Galen's thinking, see Bubb, *Dissection* (2022) 304–315.

[52] Galen *AA* 3.1 (II.346K). Compare *AA* 4.1 (II.419–420K) for the ignorant damage inflicted by doctors who spend all their time enquiring into the cartilage of the pineal gland and the bones of the heart rather than learning basic anatomy; cf. 3.1 (II.341K).

His favorite example of this kind of "useless" anatomy is the muscles of the tongue, but he gives a variety of other examples as well. Interestingly, he himself has much to say in this very text on many of the topics he lists. His point of grievance is not that there is no place for these discussions, but that physicians are eclipsing the more pragmatically important basics—a familiarity with the arrangement of the muscles in the arms or an understanding of which areas have nerves or arteries that, when cut, can cause paralysis or death—in order to engage in animated theoretical discussions and aggressive anatomical one-upmanship, heatedly debating the internal structures of the heart and the embryo, areas that no second-century doctor could ever hope to operate on. He bemoans that people are increasingly enthusiastic about the parts of anatomy that are least pragmatic and "more suitable for sophists."[53]

Indeed, the flashy, almost rhetorical nature of these topics was a large part of their charm. While the prosaic arrangement of arm muscles might serve a practicing doctor better from day to day, much more social mileage could be got out of a heated and erudite debate about aspects of anatomy so small and difficult to access that any discussion of them was little short of hypothetical. Much as Bruce Frier has explored for the jurists in the companion to this essay, it is in the hypothetical aspects of a pragmatic art that there is room for personalities—and reputations—to blossom. Further, as Luis Salas' contribution to this volume elaborates, this particular intellectual arena opened the door to real-time, live-action events, with actual dissection and vivisection playing a role as proof even in the more hypothetical debates.

Later generations, unfortunately, conformed to what Galen thought he wanted, but it was something of a Pyrrhic victory. Those receiving Galen's texts in the millennium after his death agreed that the intricacies of internal anatomy were essentially non-pragmatic for the day-to-day practitioner and, accordingly, spared little interest for Galen's own detailed anatomical work. They were content to focus only on Galen's introductory works on the subject, with the result that nearly two-thirds of his anatomical writing has been lost in Greek. Even if we include the fortunate preservation of more material in Arabic, almost half of his anatomical output is gone. As in the case of his prolific textual exegesis, later doctors, in their later social contexts, saw little value in these non-pragmatic topics.[54] Both are features of the socio-intellectual milieu in which they were born: while philology tapped into the erudite, archaizing, and "gotcha" side of the culture of the Roman imperial period, obscure anatomy appealed to its equal love of competition, spectatorship, argument, and good old-fashioned gore. The

[53] Galen *AA* 4.1 (II.416K) (τὸ σοφιστικώτερον).

[54] Of course, like historical textual study, the minutiae of internal anatomy once again became a central focus of medical study in the Renaissance and—unlike textual study—they have remained so to this day; in the intervening centuries, however, detailed, personal familiarity with the minutiae of internal anatomy was not emphasized as a pragmatic necessity for the practicing doctor.

authors of Roman medical literature would be well served by both, regardless of whether they ever informed a single practical cure.

Bibliography

Boudon-Millot, 'Galen's Hippocrates' (2018) = V. Boudon-Millot, 'Galen's Hippocrates,' in P. E. Pormann, ed., *The Cambridge Companion to Hippocrates* (Cambridge: Cambridge University Press, 2018) 292–314.

Boudon-Millot, Jouanna, and Pietrobelli, *Chagriner* (2010) = V. Boudon-Millot, J. Jouanna, and A. Pietrobelli, *Galien. Tome IV. Ne pas se chagriner* (Paris: Belles Lettres, 2010).

Bouras-Vallianatos and Zipser, *Companion* (2019) = P. Bouras-Vallianatos and B. Zipser, eds., *Brill's Companion to the Reception of Galen* (Leiden: Brill, 2019).

Bubb, *Dissection* (2022) = C. Bubb, *Dissection in Classical Antiquity: A Social and Medical History* (Cambridge: Cambridge University Press, 2022).

Curtis, 'Rhetorical Analysis' (2016) = T. Curtis, 'Author, Argument and Exegesis: A Rhetorical Analysis of Galen's *In Hippocratis de natura hominis commentaris tria*,' in L. Dean-Jones and R. Rosen, eds., *Ancient Concepts of the Hippocratic* (Leiden: Brill, 2016) 399–420.

Flemming, 'Commentary' (2008) = R. Flemming, 'Commentary,' in Hankinson, *Galen* (2008) 323–354.

Fortuna, 'Editions and Translations' (2019) = S. Fortuna, 'Editions and Translations of Galen from 1490 to 1540', in Bouras-Vallianatos and Zipser, *Companion* (2019) 437–452.

Garofalo, 'Galen's Legacy' (2019) = I. Garofalo, 'Galen's Legacy in Alexandrian Texts Written in Greek, Latin, and Arabic', in Bouras-Vallianatos and Zipser, *Companion* (2019) 62–85.

Gutas, *Greek Thought* (1998) = D. Gutas, *Greek Thought and Arabic Culture* (London: Routledge, 1998).

Hankinson, *Galen* (2008) = R. J. Hankinson, ed., *Cambridge Companion to Galen* (Cambridge: Cambridge University Press, 2008).

Howley, 'Book Forgery' (forthcoming) = J. Howley, 'Reading against the Grain: Book Forgery and Book Labor at Rome', in J. N. Hopkins and S. McGill, eds., *Forgery Beyond Deceit: Fabrication, Value, and the Desire for Ancient Rome* (Oxford: Oxford University Press, forthcoming).

Johnson, 'Ancient Book' (2009) = W. A. Johnson, 'The Ancient Book', in R. Bagnall, ed., *The Oxford Handbook of Papyrology* (Oxford: Oxford University Press, 2009) 256–281.

Johnson, *Readers* (2010) = W. A. Johnson, *Readers and Reading Culture in the High Roman Empire* (Oxford: Oxford University Press, 2010).

Jones, 'Books and Libraries' (2009) = C. P. Jones, 'Books and Libraries in a Newly-Discovered Treatise of Galen,' *Journal of Roman Archaeology* 22 (1): 390–397.

Jouanna, '*Nature of Man*' (2012) = J. Jouanna, 'Galen's Reading of the Hippocratic Treatise *The Nature of Man*: The Foundations of Hippocratism in Galen', in id., *Greek Medicine from Hippocrates to Galen* (Leiden and Boston: Brill, 2012) 313–333.

King, 'Origins' (2006) = H. King, 'The Origins of Medicine in the Second Century AD', in S. Goldhill and R. Osborne, eds., *Rethinking Revolutions through Ancient Greece* (Cambridge: Cambridge University Press, 2006).

Lamoreaux, *Hunayn* (2016) = J. C. Lamoreaux, *Hunayn ibn Ishaq on his Galen Translations: A Parallel English-Arabic Text* (Provo, UT: Bringham Young University Press, 2016).

Lloyd, 'Scholarship' (1988) = G. E. R. Lloyd, 'Scholarship, Authority, and Argument in Galen's *Quod Animi Mores*', in P. Manuli and M. Vegetti, eds., *Le Opere Psicologiche di Galeno* (Naples: Bibliopolis, 1988) 11–42.

Lloyd, 'Hellenistics and Hippocrateans' (1991) = G. E. R. Lloyd, 'Galen on Hellenistics and Hippocrateans: Contemporary Battles and Past Authorities', in id., *Methods and Problems in Greek Science* (Cambridge: Cambridge University Press, 1991) 398–416.

López Férez, 'Galeno, lector' (1992) = J. A. López Férez, 'Galeno, lector y critico de manuscritos,' in A. Garzya, ed., *Tradizione e ecdotica dei testi medici tardoantichi e bizantini* (Naples: d'Auria, 1992) 197–209.

Mansfeld, *Prolegomena* (1994) = J. Mansfeld, *Prolegomena: Questions to Be Settled before the Study of an Author, or a Text* (Leiden and New York: Brill, 1994).

Manuli, 'Stile del Commento' (1983) = P. Manuli, 'Lo Stile del Commento. Galeno e la Tradizione Ippocratica', in F. Lasserre and P. Mudry, eds., *Formes de Pensée dans la Collection Hippocratique* (Geneva: Librairie Droz S.A., 1983) 471–482.

Nelson, 'Woozle' (2016) = E. Nelson, 'Tracking the Hippocratic Woozle: Pseudepigrapha and the Formation of the Corpus', in L. Dean-Jones and R. Rosen, eds., *Ancient Concepts of the Hippocratic* (Leiden: Brill, 2016) 117–140.

Nutton, 'Kühn' (2002) = V. Nutton, 'In Defense of Kühn', in id., ed., *The Unknown Galen, Bulletin of the Institute of Classical Studies*, Supplement 77 (2002) 1–7.

Nutton, 'The Fatal Embrace' (2005) = V. Nutton, 'The Fatal Embrace: Galen and the History of Ancient Medicine,' *Science in Context* 18.1 (2005) 111–121.

Nutton, 'Fortunes of Galen' (2008) = V. Nutton, 'Fortunes of Galen,' in R. J. Hankinson, ed., *Cambridge Companion to Galen* (Cambridge: Cambridge University Press, 2008) 355–390.

Pormann and Savage-Smith, *Medieval Islamic Medicine* (2007) = P. E. Pormann and E. Savage-Smith, *Medieval Islamic Medicine* (Washington, D.C.: Georgetown University Press, 2007).

Roselli, 'Hippocrates and the Truth' (2016) = A. Roselli, '"According to both Hippocrates and the Truth": Hippocrates as Witness to the Truth, from Apollonius of Citium to Galen,' in Dean-Jones, L. and Rosen, R., eds., *Ancient Concepts of the Hippocratic* (Leiden: Brill, 2016) 331–344.

Savage-Smith, 'Medicine' (1996) = E. Savage-Smith, 'Medicine', in R. Rashed and R. Morelon, eds., *Encyclopedia of the History of Arabic Science* (London and New York: Routledge, 1996) 903–962.

Smith, *Hippocratic Tradition* (1979) = W. D. Smith, *The Hippocratic Tradition* (Ithaca: Cornell University Press, 1979).

von Staden, 'Caelius Aurelianus' (1999) = H. von Staden, 'Caelius Aurelianus and the Hellenistic epoch: Erasistratus, the Empiricists, and Herophilus', in P. Mudry, ed., *Le Traité des Maladies Aigües et des Maladies Chroniques de Caelius Aurelianus* (Nantes: Université de Nantes, 1999) 85–119.

von Staden, 'Staging the Past' (2009) = H. von Staden, 'Staging the Past, Staging Oneself: Galen on Hellenistic Exegetical Traditions,' in C. Gill, T. Whitmarsh, and J. Wilkins, eds., *Galen and the World of Knowledge* (Cambridge: Cambridge University Press, 2009) 132–156.

Totelin, 'Multiple Manuscript Copies' (2009) = L. M. V. Totelin, 'Galen's Use of Multiple Manuscript Copies in his Pharmacological Treatises', in L. Taub and A. Doody, eds., *Authorial Voices in Greco-Roman Technical Writing* (Trier: Wissenschaftlicher Verlag, 2009) 81–92.

Vagelpohl, 'User-Friendly Galen' (2018) = U. Vagelpohl, 'The User-Friendly Galen: Hunayn ibn Ishaq and the adaption of Greek Medicine for a New Audience,' in P. Bouras-Vallianatos and S. Xenophontos, eds., *Greek Medical Literature and Its Readers. From Hippocrates to Islam and Byzantium* (New York and London: Routledge, 2018) 113–130.

Vallance, 'Galen, Proclus' (1999) = J. T. Vallance, 'Galen, Proclus, and the Non-submissive Commentary,' in G. W. Most, ed., *Commentaries/Kommentare* (Göttingen: Vandenhoeck und Ruprecht, 1999) 223–244.

Response

Expert or Intellectual? Other Views of Legal and Medical Expertise

James Uden

Success as a jurist or physician in the Roman Empire, as Bruce Frier and Claire Bubb demonstrate in the two preceding chapters, depended on more than technical knowledge or skill. Frier explores the possibility of competition, as well as collaboration, in the responses of jurists to legal questions in the Empire. In the celebrated *D.* 9.2.51, the curious swerve in the thinking of the author Salvius Julianus may be explained, Frier argues, by Julian's desire to refute the opinion of his rival and predecessor, Juventius Celsus, even though any trace of *ad hominem* attack is of course missing from the excerpt preserved in the *Digest.* Bubb's chapter illustrates the extraordinary range of skills that Galen and other doctors displayed in the hothouse intellectual environment of medicine in the imperial age. Galen's work as editor and investigator of ancient medical texts is by no means separate from his work as a doctor: he fashions his own *persona* as a supremely competent physician in part by creating a vision of medical history that leads inexorably up to him. In both cases, doctors and lawyers address the past as much as the present, preserving older texts and traditions while challenging and transforming them to suit their own objectives. The vision of intellectual life we see from these chapters is also fundamentally public and social. It was not enough to be a master in one's field; one had to be recognized as such.

Both chapters invite further questions, though, about how the dynamics within disciplines were seen by audiences outside of them, and how the perception of expertise could shift in different contexts and among different audiences. Expertise is, as the sociologist Steve Fuller has put it, a 'constitutively social phenomenon.' He identifies four attributes that characterize expertise in contemporary society.[1] First, expertise is the product of specialized training; the knowledge of an expert goes far

Thank you to Claire Bubb and Michael Peachin for inviting me to write this response paper, and for their very helpful comments on a draft.

[1] Fuller, 'The Constitutively Social Character of Expertise' (2006) 342–357 [article originally published in 1994].

James Uden, *Response: Expert or Intellectual? Other Views of Legal and Medical Expertise* In: *Medicine and the Law under the Roman Empire.* Edited by: Claire Bubb and Michael Peachin, Oxford University Press.
© Claire Bubb and Michael Peachin 2023. DOI: 10.1093/oso/9780192898616.003.0009

beyond what one could normally gather in everyday life. Second, its relevance is limited to a particular area. The cultural authority of expertise comes from its being well fitted to a particular aspect of human experience, not from its claim to answer questions of universal scope or significance. Third, public respect for expertise depends in part on the perceived degree of agreement between experts in a particular area. If experts are constantly battling with each other, these disagreements will erode confidence in the authority and usefulness of their field. Fourth, there can be too many experts. Expertise becomes devalued if mastery of a particular area becomes widely shared; its "value is directly tied to other people not having it."[2] For Fuller, the unifying bond between these four characteristics is a desire to ensure the continuing social legitimacy of expertise by setting limits and boundaries around it. This drive, he suggests, is a legacy of the nineteenth-century separation of the 'expert' from the 'intellectual.' The modern conception of the expert arose from the drive towards specialized skills and training in an age of industrialization. The intellectual, by contrast, is not limited to a particular area, taking instead "the entire world as fair game for his judgment."[3] Moreover, whereas the persuasive power of expertise is weakened by disagreement (think of the use of rival expert witnesses in a legal case), intellectuals court controversy. Their standing is not diminished by disagreement, but enhanced by it.[4]

In antiquity, by contrast, the two roles of 'expert' and 'intellectual' are fundamentally intertwined. In a world without institutional accreditation or formalized training, proving one's authority involved a far greater degree of persuasive rhetoric and self-fashioning, so the skills one needed for success ranged well beyond those of any single discipline.[5] The legitimacy of doctors' and jurists' opinions emerged from a public world of contest and competition, and so disagreements were a regular and important part of the emergence of 'truth' (a term used by jurists to describe the object of their inquiries, as Frier shows). In a pre-industrial society, the narrow specialization associated with contemporary forms of expertise simply did not exist, and indeed 'law' and 'medicine' were themselves highly heterogeneous fields, with different sorts of practitioners wielding different forms of authority. Yet the contemporary division between 'expert' and 'intellectual' is, nonetheless, foreshadowed in an ongoing tension in our ancient sources between competing claims of narrowness and breadth. Certain groups charge others (grammarians, jurists, doctors) with having a circumscribed

[2] Fuller, 'The Constitutively Social Character of Expertise' (2006) 352.

[3] Fuller, 'The Constitutively Social Character of Expertise' (2006) 342, who refers to Williams, *Keywords* (1983) 129. The earliest example of 'expert' as a noun in the *OED* is 1825, although of course the word's roots lie in antiquity (cf. *experto credite*, Verg. *Aen.* 11.283).

[4] Said, *Representations of the Intellectual* (1994) 65–83.

[5] See [J.] König, 'Self-Assertion and Its Alternatives in Ancient Scientific Writing' (2017) 7–8. As he notes, open expressions of rivalry and competition were only one form of self-authorization in antiquity; in other cases it was precisely an effacement of personal reference that was key to self-assertion as an authority.

set of skills, while claiming a more elevated, often philosophical sort of erudition for themselves.[6] In the Roman Empire, there was no absolute or objective distinction between 'technical' practitioners and the cultured elite—although social status was often a significant factor—and the appraisal between these two depended upon audience and context. Shift the social frame just slightly, and intense competition seems like internecine squabbling. Spectacular demonstrations of learning could seem like pompous display. An intellectual giant might merely be expert in a skill.

In this brief response paper to the chapters of Frier and Bubb, I re-examine some of the cultural dynamics they have observed among jurists and doctors, but from the perspective of outsiders to each field. Within the space of medical and juristic literature, authors could conjure a world with its own history, its own conventions, its own hierarchies—a world in which the author's skills really mattered. Outside that textual space, their authority and esteem could not simply be assumed. In the literary texts I sample here, we see the embodied performance of knowledge by jurists or doctors through the gaze of critical outsiders—outsiders who nonetheless appropriated aspects of juristic or medical discourse for themselves, so as to judge the insiders. These passages also shed light on differences, as well as similarities, between the cultural dynamics of law and medicine in the Roman Empire. If expertise was embodied as well as socially constituted in the Roman world, then it mattered all the more *who* was embodying that knowledge. Elite authors of Roman texts could be condescending towards jurists because knowledge of the law was a vital part of their preparation for public life. To return again to Steve Fuller's contemporary conception of expertise, jurists faced a problem in bounding and delimiting a field of knowledge in which too many people had a share. If Roman writers were skeptical about doctors, however, it was in part because the practice of medicine remained, even in the Empire, something that other people did. The rise in esteem of Greek doctors in Rome in the imperial period has been well documented by epigraphic evidence, as well as by legal evidence regarding the various immunities and other benefits won by successful physicians.[7] But the emphasis on translation in the passages I examine in this chapter is a reminder that medicine was persistently associated with Greek learning, and so the authority of medicine was enmeshed with the politics of cultural difference to a far greater extent than was law.[8]

My first outsider is Pliny the Younger, whose views on jurists in his letters have recently been analyzed by Jill Harries.[9] Pliny's best-known letter about a jurist

[6] Roby, *Technical Ekphrasis* (2016) 82–86.

[7] See e.g. Nutton, 'Two Notes on Immunities' (1971); Israelowich, *Patients and Healers in the High Roman Empire* (2015) 11–44.

[8] On the rise and place of an emphatically Greek medical tradition in the Roman context, see Rawson, *Intellectual Life* (1985) 170–184.

[9] Harries, 'Saturninus the Helsman' (2018) 272–275.

describes L. Javolenus Priscus, an older man who had been suffect consul in 86 CE and later a governor, and an influential jurist frequently cited in the *Digest*. This is a fish-out-of-water tale: Priscus has come to hear poetry. Pliny picks up the story as Passennus Paulus, an imitator (and allegedly, descendant) of Propertius, is about to begin:[10]

> *Is cum recitaret, ita coepit dicere: "Prisce, iubes . . .". Ad hoc Iavolenus Priscus (aderat enim ut Paulo amicissimus): "Ego vero non iubeo." Cogita qui risus hominum, qui ioci.*
>
> When Paulus started to recite, he began to say: "Priscus, you bid me . . .". At that point, Javolenus Priscus—he was there because he was very friendly towards Paulus—said: "Indeed I do *not* bid you!" Just think of the smiling and joking in response!

But Pliny disapproves. Here is a man highly respected as an expert in civil law, and yet his untimely interjection—an act "absurd and worthy of censure" (*ridiculum et notabile, Ep.* 6.15.3)—has ruined Paulus' event. Pliny goes so far as to say that Priscus is "of doubtful soundness of mind" (*dubiae sanitatis*), and he ends the letter by stating that anyone planning a recitation should ensure that "not only they themselves are sound, but that the people they invite are sound too" (*providendum est, non solum ut sint ipsi sani verum etiam ut sanos adhibeant*). Pliny may well be misreading (or willfully misinterpreting) the situation. After all, the jurist was there because he was very fond of Paulus (*ut Paulo amicissimus*). Rather than being an expression of impatience or a literalistic misunderstanding of poetic convention, his remark could just as easily have been a good-natured jest: upon hearing his own, very common cognomen as the first word of Passus' new poem, he thought it funny to act as if the line were being addressed to him.[11] But that sort of attention-stealing witticism violates the elaborate protocols of the *recitatio* as Pliny describes them in his *Epistulae*. The crowd should offer constructive, tactful criticism, and certainly not attract attention to themselves.[12]

To invoke again a more contemporary division, Pliny mocks Priscus by reducing him from the status of 'intellectual' to 'expert.' The clear implication is that his specialized skills in civil law have not outfitted him with the general refinement necessary for him to participate in the aristocratic ritual of the poetry reading.

[10] Plin. *Ep.* 6.15.2 [cited from Mynors, *C. Plini Caecili Secundi Epistularum Libri Decem*, 1963].

[11] Priscus was an "extremely common cognomen," per Moreno Soldevila et al., 'A Prosopography to Martial's Epigrams' (2019) 506. Pliny's *Epistulae* contain at least seven Prisci, plus three cases in which the identification is unclear: Birley, *Onomasticon to the Younger Pliny* (2000) 83. For a review of scholars' varied interpretations of Priscus' outburst, see Beck, '*Pro captu lectoris habent sua fata . . .*' (2013) 297–298.

[12] For the rules of the *recitatio* as represented by Pliny, see Johnson, *Readers and Reading Culture* (2010) 42–56; Uden, *The Invisible Satirist* (2015) 94–104; Roller, 'Amicable and Hostile Exchange in the Culture of Recitation' (2018) (with discussion of *Ep.* 6.15 at pages 201–205).

Indeed, it is precisely Priscus' formidable reputation as a jurist that makes his quip so concerning, and worthy of being recorded and censured in Pliny's published correspondence. After relating the incident at the *recitatio*, Pliny identifies Priscus as someone who plays an important role in public life, who is "called upon for advice" (*adhibetur consiliis*) and who "gives official responses on the *ius civile*" (*ius civile publice respondet*). These somewhat general phrases nonetheless suggest a person with influence at the highest levels of government. If *consiliis* alludes obliquely to the emperor's *consilium*, then Priscus could be giving judicial advice to Trajan himself, and the wording of *ius... respondet* may similarly indicate that the jurist had received the specific privilege of the *ius respondendi* ("right of giving responses") from the emperor.[13] When Pliny depicts Priscus responding to the first words of the poem with such a deficit of social grace, and then goes on to remind us that making 'responses' is what Priscus has been entrusted to do, he draws attention to the gulf between this man's cultural sophistication and the power and influence of his public persona.[14] Pliny's letter valuably articulates the assumption that a man like Priscus *should* be broadly cultivated and refined. If he cannot appreciate the importance of listening to elegant poetry, that is a concerning failure. Expertise is not enough.

Ep. 6.15 is positioned very deliberately within the epistolary *libellus*. It is followed by a letter addressed to a consular gentleman who was indeed broadly cultivated (Tacitus). Whereas Pliny admits freely that Priscus' *faux pas* was a "tale" (*fabula*) to which he was not witness (6.15.1), 6.16 begins the narration of the last days of Pliny the Elder in the eruption of Vesuvius, an event about which Pliny can indeed offer important, first-hand information. As Gibson and Morello have observed, "petty squabbles" among "Rome's elite" are thus immediately cast in shadow by the arrangement of Pliny's book.[15] Before that point, though, there had been one more run-in with a famous jurist in book 6. In *Ep.* 6.5, dissension re-emerges over the prosecution of Rufius Varenus, for whom Pliny had won the irregular privilege of calling witnesses in his own defense (cf. *Ep.* 5.20). Licinius Nepos, represented in earlier letters as a stern praetor insistent on enforcing regulations, raises the issue of the legal abnormality, arguing that the law should be changed. Then P. Juventius Celsus—a figure familiar from Frier's chapter, the notoriously irascible jurist whose opinion Julian challenged in *D.* 9.2.51—is aghast at this non-expert's attempt to become "some kind of reformer" (*tamquam emendatorem*, 6.5.4).[16] Their disagreement escalates into a fiery showdown.

[13] The exact nature of the *ius respondendi* is an object of longstanding debate: see Tuori, 'The *ius respondendi* and the Freedom of Roman Jurisprudence' (2004). On the imperial *consilium* in the second century, see Eck, 'The Emperor and His Advisers' (2000) 199–201.

[14] There is another pointed verbal correspondence in the letter: Priscus may be 'called upon' (*adhibetur*, 6.15.3) for legal advice, but Pliny's readers should be careful about whom they 'invite' (*adhibeant*, 6.15.4) to a literary recitation; cf. Bubb and Howley this volume, p. 310.

[15] Gibson and Morello, *Reading the* Letters *of Pliny the Younger* (2012) 66.

[16] On Celsus, see Hausmaninger, 'Publius Iuventius Celsus' (1976).

Senators rush from one man to the other, alternately stoking and quenching the flames of argument. Pliny, predictably, disapproves. His letter shows us the disputatiousness of a famous jurist, albeit in the public setting of the Senate house rather than on the page. Removed from the authoritative calm of the legal text, Celsus' wrangling looks to Pliny like some degrading theatrical show (*ut in ludicro aliquo*, 6.5.5).

Pliny's letters do contain images of 'good' jurists, friends such as Titius Aristo who share his interests, but also memorable character sketches of their opposite: the "narrow specialist, the man who lacked the broad culture of the truly civilized individual, liable to turn awkward in senatorial debates or to disrupt literary occasions with inappropriately thuggish behaviour."[17] This stereotype is hardly new. It is familiar, above all, from Cicero's acerbic description of the formulas and processes of the jurisprudent in his attack on Servius Sulpicius Rufus in the *Pro Murena*. Nobody can achieve renown by becoming expert, Cicero asserted, in a field that any politician should already know.[18] Quintilian, too, treats knowledge of the law as an essential prerequisite of the orator's training. For someone to specialize *only* in the law without also being an orator would be a sort of failure.[19] In each case, the attack on others' narrow expertise is inevitably attended by the implicit claim that the speaker himself has a broader mode of cultivation and erudition. Pliny, for his part, seems to take pleasure throughout the *Epistulae* in consulting legal experts and then dismissing their advice as ungenerous and aridly correct. It is typical of the "diligence" (*diligentia*) of his legal agent Annius, he says, to remind him of a technicality: "yet I have made it a certain law of my own, to guard the desires of the deceased as valid, even if they are not binding at law."[20] Passages like this, deliberately placed in the published correspondence, advertise Pliny's own beneficence while also implying that jurisprudence is a limited sort of expertise. He knows the law, but this knowledge is only part of a broader set of cultural attainments.

My second outsider to expertise is Aulus Gellius, who writes in a series of chapters in the *Attic Nights* about his reading of medical texts and his interactions with doctors.[21] In one of these chapters (*NA* 18.10), Gellius lies ill with a stomach ailment and fever at the home of Herodes Atticus. When his philosophical teacher L. Calvenus Taurus and a group of his students (*sectatores*) arrive from Athens to

[17] Harries, 'Saturninus the Helsman' (2018) 275.

[18] Cic. *Mur.* 28. See Benferhat, 'Cicero and the Small World of Roman Jurists' (2016); Harries, '*Iurisperiti*' (2017) 88.

[19] Quint. *Inst.* 12.3.8–10; Whitton, *The Arts of Imitation in Latin Prose* (2019) 83. On the cultural changes that led to the rising esteem of jurists as intellectuals in the Severan period, see Secord, *Christian Intellectuals and the Roman Empire* (2020) 123–128.

[20] *Ep.* 2.16.2: *sed ego propriam quondam legem mihi dixi, ut defunctorum voluntates, etiamsi iure deficerentur, quasi perfectas tuerer.* Cf. similarly *Ep.* 4.10, *Ep.* 5.7.

[21] On medicine in the *NA*, see Neuburger, 'Die Medizin in den 'Noctes Atticae' des Aulus Gellius' (1925); Heusch, *Die Macht der memoria* (2011) 352–355; Holford-Strevens, *Aulus Gellius* (2003) 301–305.

visit the patient, Taurus begins to chat with Gellius' doctor. The physician has good news: Gellius is on the road to recovery. You can see for yourself, he says:[22]

> *Tum in eo sermone, cum iam me sinceriore corpusculo factum diceret, "potes," inquit Tauro "tu quoque id ipsum comprehendere, ἐὰν ἅψῃς αὐτοῦ τῆς φλεβός," quod nostris verbis profecto ita dicitur, "si attigeris venam illius."*
>
> Then, amid that conversation, when he was saying that my poor body was already becoming healthier, he told Taurus: "You yourself can understand his recovery *if you touch his blood vessel,*" which is our language's way of saying: "if you touch his vein."

Taurus is shocked not by the diagnosis, but by the doctor's carelessness with words. How could this ostensible expert translate φλέψ as *vena* ("vein"), when surely he knows that it is the arteries that "show the condition and degree of fever by their movement and pulsation" (*motu atque pulsu suo habitum et modum febrium demonstrent*, 5)? Taurus chides him for his inaccuracy, quite unfairly, since he admits that the physician was probably just speaking "colloquially rather than ignorantly" (*pervulgate magis quam inscite*, 6). In Gellius' chapter, medical knowledge thus becomes an opportunity for the social performance of expertise—but not, in this case, the expertise of the doctor. The physician remains anonymous. He is the victim in one of Gellius' customary scenes of intellectual exposure, while the philosopher Taurus vindicates the *Attic Nights*' signature virtues of broad but selective erudition and verbal precision. Meanwhile, when Gellius reports the doctor's prognosis (*me sinceriore corpusculo factum*), his own phrasing seems deliberate, if not quite precise. Fronto similarly uses *corpusculum* to describe his own body while sick ("my poor body").[23] But the diminutive is also prominently connected to a Roman history of translating Greek scientific ideas: it is a translation for Democritean "atoms" in Lucretius and earlier Epicurean writings, and it is A. Cornelius Celsus' rendering for Asclepiades' disease-causing "particles."[24] In a chapter squarely about translation, it is a resonant choice of words.

In the second half of *NA* 18.10, Gellius explains how this experience of illness—and his mentor's rebuke of the doctor—spurred his own curiosity to delve into medical literature. Gellius' discussions of Greek medical texts are mostly clustered in the later books of the *Attic Nights*, as if medicine were a late development in his interests. Yet only in *NA* 18.10, when he describes his own illness, is this interest

[22] Gell. *NA* 18.10.4. Gellius is cited from the new *OCT* [= Holford-Strevens, *Auli Gelli Noctes Atticae*, 2020].

[23] Fronto *Ep. Ad M. Caes.* 5.62.1; 5.70.2 [= van den Hout, *M. Cornelii Frontonis Epistulae* (1988) 83–84].

[24] Cic. *Acad.* 1.6 (Amafinius); Lucr. 2.153; Cels. *Med.* pr. 16.

retrospectively explained.[25] Gellius says that he was inspired to devote "as much spare time as I had to dipping into books of the medical field, too," and he goes on to deliver his own concise explanation of the difference between veins and arteries. He writes:[26]

> *Vena est conceptaculum sanguinis, quod* ἀγγεῖον *medici vocant, mixti confusique cum spiritu naturali, in quo plus sanguinis est, minus spiritus; arteria est conceptaculum spiritus naturalis mixti confusique cum sanguine, in quo plus spiritus est, minus sanguinis;* σφυγμός *autem est intentio motus et remissio in corde et in arteria naturalis, non arbitraria. a medicis autem veteribus oratione Graeca ita definitus est:* σφυγμός ἐστιν διαστολή τε καὶ συστολὴ ἀπροαίρετος ἀρτηρίας καὶ καρδίας.
>
> The *vena* is a small receptacle, which doctors call an ἀγγεῖον, for blood mixed and infused with natural spirit, in which there is more blood, less spirit; *arteria* is a small receptacle of natural spirit mixed and infused with blood, in which there is more spirit, less blood; σφυγμός is the natural and unwilled movement of stretching and relaxing in the heart and artery. But by the ancient doctors it is defined in this way in Greek: "Pulsation is the involuntary dilation and contraction of the vessels and heart."

Taken as a whole, Gellius' chapter shows important parallels with the medical world elucidated by Claire Bubb in her chapter in this volume. Here, too, we see a contest of medical knowledge, which involves invoking authorities from the past to support one's case. Yet one striking difference between Gellius' medical chapters and the writings of Galen is the comparative invisibility of contemporary doctors themselves. In *NA* 18.10, the doctor remains nameless, and his words are quoted only to be criticized. Presumably he was successful in healing Gellius, but the story of Gellius' illness is never resolved, nor is the success or failure of the doctor in healing the patient the climax of this narrative. Similarly, in *NA* 16.3, Gellius learns about Erasistratus' views on the anatomy of the stomach, and yet that information is recounted by the philosopher and orator Favorinus, not by a doctor. Since the pair were visiting an ill friend at the time, there were physicians in the crowd for Favorinus' lecture, but in Gellius' vision of contemporary life, they do not talk; they just "happened to be there then" (*tum forte istic erant,*

[25] Cf. *NA* 16.3 (Erasistratus' view of the stomach); *NA* 18.18 (*synkrisis* of different anatomical views of the epiglottis and trachea). The exception is *NA* 3.16, in which Gellius cites Hippocrates among other authorities on the duration of a baby's gestation. For disruptions of narrative order in the *NA* as an invitation to readers to create their own maps through the text, see Howley, *Aulus Gellius and Roman Reading Culture* (2018) 38–52; and more broadly on active reading in the *NA*, DiGiulio, 'Gellius' Strategies of Reading (Gellius)' (2020). On verbal correctness as a means of distinguishing between insiders and outsiders in second-century Rome, see Uden, 'The Noise-Lovers' (2020).

[26] *NA* 18.10.9–11. On this passage as evidence of the popular diffusion of medical ideas, see Le Blay, 'Quelle place pour la médecine?' (2009) 89–92.

16.3.2). If Galen had been in the same situation, he presumably would not have kept quiet. But where is he? The celebrity doctor is nowhere to be seen in the *Attic Nights*, although the two authors were contemporaries, and characters from these medical chapters (Herodes Atticus, Favorinus) also appear in Galen's oeuvre. In fact, for all Galen's bravado in claiming to have won the attention of influential Romans, he is mentioned only four times in non-medical Latin texts from antiquity, and all four mentions are in Jerome, two centuries after Galen's death.[27] Like Galen, Gellius mines the texts of the past to solve a medical question in the present, demonstrating that the expert skills of the doctor-philologist are also available to the broadly cultivated intellectual. In the *Attic Nights*, though, the element of public spectacle in Galen's demonstrations has given way entirely to the quieter task of sifting through texts, and the genius of contemporary doctors does not occupy center stage.

Gellius ends the account of his own illness at *NA* 18.10 by saying that he finds it shameful (*turpe*) not only for doctors but for *every* educated individual to lack some understanding of medicine. The passage has often been cited as evidence that, by the second century CE, medicine's position as a discipline had risen to the point that it was accepted as part of the essential cultural learning of an educated Roman. Once read in context, though, Gellius' declaration means something rather less. First, Gellius expressly states the amount of medical knowledge that is desirable: not "of things that are recondite, deep and hidden, but of those things that nature has wished to lie ready and in the open, so that we can guard our own health."[28] Stated this way, the ideal is not terribly different from what a Roman could have read in Celsus a century earlier, or even in Pliny the Elder. At its core is the Roman conception of individual self-sufficiency: we should not have to depend on others to understand our own bodies. Second, Gellius' interest is in historical rather than contemporary doctors (*a medicis... veteribus*, *NA* 18.10.11), and in the theory of medicine rather than its practice. As demonstrated in the *Attic Nights*, the sort of medical knowledge that Gellius finds desirable is a knowledge of words, concepts, texts, ideas. Actually practicing medicine is well outside of that purview. There are class implications here, too: the perusal of medical books is a secondary sort of activity for one's leisure hours, the time that the elite Roman has partitioned off (*quantum habui temporis subsicivi*, 18.10.8) from more pressing tasks in his life. It is not a singular and divine calling, as Galen

[27] Four times: Mazzini, 'References to Medical Authors in Non-Medical Latin Literature' (2014) 82. Jerome and Galen: Courcelle, *Late Latin Writers and Their Greek Sources* (1969) 86–87. For contrasting accounts of Galen's prestige among his contemporaries, compare Bowersock, *Greek Sophists in the Roman Empire* (1969) 66 ("Galen was a lion of his time") with Nutton, *Ancient Medicine* (2004) 233, who notes Galen's absence from Gellius, Philostratus, and Marcus Aurelius, and urges caution in relying too much upon Galen's own writings when constructing a picture of his career.

[28] *NA* 18.10.8: *non altius occultiusque remota sunt et quae natura nobis tuendae valitudinis causa et in promptu esse et in propatulo voluerit.*

presented it, nor is it an occupation to win the respect and patronage of others.[29] Aulus Gellius does not explicitly criticize medicine as a narrow sort of expertise, then, but he does accord contemporary doctors a notably limited place in his *Attic Nights*. He never awards them the mantle of broad-minded intellectual that a doctor like Galen so confidently claimed.

In contemporary society, expertise has sometimes seemed suspicious precisely because its cognitive authority over our own lives and experience is so great. Jürgen Habermas, in particular, warned of the threat of "expert cultures" dominating our modern sense of ourselves and our possibilities, making it harder for alternative modes of knowledge and tradition to thrive.[30] In antiquity, without the same opportunity for any one voice or idea to dominate popular consciousness to the same extent, views of expertise were far more variegated, and estimations of their value and importance shifted greatly according to social context. If professionalization as we know it was absent, there was nonetheless a constant contest in worlds of knowledge between claims of narrowness and breadth—between, in our sense, the expert and the intellectual. Was it impossible, then, for a person to be both master of a particular body of knowledge or skill, and broadly cultivated as well? To be both expert *and* intellectual? For Galen and others in antiquity, that was certainly the goal. Whether any particular individual achieved those heights, though, depended upon whom you asked.

Bibliography

Beck, 'Pro captu lectoris habent sua fata...' (2013) = J.-W. Beck, 'Pro captu lectoris habent sua fata...—Plinius und der Eklat epist. 6, 15,' *Hermes* 141 (2013) 294–308.

Benferhat, 'Cicero and the Small World of the Roman Jurists' (2016) = Y. Benferhat, 'Cicero and the Small World of the Roman Jurists,' in P. J. du Plessis, ed., *Cicero's Law: Rethinking Roman Law of the Late Republic* (Edinburgh: Edinburgh University Press, 2016) 71–87.

Birley, *Onomasticon to the Younger Pliny* (2000) = A. R. Birley, *Onomasticon to the Younger Pliny: Letters and Panegyric* (Leipzig: K. G. Saur, 2000).

Bowersock, *Greek Sophists in the Roman Empire* (1969) = G. W. Bowersock, *Greek Sophists in the Roman Emipre* (Oxford: Clarendon Press, 1969).

[29] Gellius' phrase describing the left-over time he gives to medicine (*quantum... temporis subsicivi*, 18.10) is an intratextual echo of the preface of the *Attic Nights*, in which Gellius says that he will devote as much time to collecting useful knowledge as he has left-over and spare (*subsiciva et subsecundaria tempora*, *NA* pr. 23). The tension between theory and practice is an omnipresent one in antiquity; see e.g. the essays in Formisano and van der Eijk, *Knowledge, Text and Practice in Ancient Technical Writing* (2017); König, 'Tactical Interactions' (2020) 139–143.

[30] Habermas (1987) 297. See Turner, *The Politics of Expertise* (2004) 17–40 for an overview of this and related political and philosophical approaches to expertise.

Courcelle, *Late Latin Writers and Their Greek Sources* (1969) = P. Courcelle, *Late Latin Writers and their Greek Sources*, trans. H. E. Wedeck (Cambridge, MA: Harvard University Press, 1969).

DiGiulio, 'Gellius' Strategies of Reading (Gellius)' (2020) = S. J. DiGiulio, 'Gellius' Strategies of Reading (Gellius): Miscellany and the Active Reader in Noctes Atticae Book 2,' *Classical Philology* 115 (2020) 242–264.

Formisano and van der Eijk, *Knowledge, Text and Practice in Ancient Technical Writing* (2017) = M. Formisano and P. van der Eijk, eds., *Knowledge, Text and Practice in Ancient Technical Writing* (Cambridge: Cambridge University Press, 2017).

Fuller, 'The Constitutively Social Character of Expertise' (2006) = S. Fuller, 'The Constitutively Social Character of Expertise,' in E. Selinger and R. Crease, eds., *The Philosophy of Expertise* (New York: Columbia University Press, 2006) 342–357.

Gibson and Morello, *Reading the Letters of Pliny the Younger* (2012) = R. K. Gibson and R. Morello, eds., *Reading the Letters of Pliny the Younger: An Introduction* (Cambridge: Cambridge University Press, 2012).

Habermas, *The Theory of Communicative Action*, vol. 2 (1987) = J. Habermas, *The Theory of Communicative Action*, vol. 2, trans. T. McCarthy (Boston: Beacon Press, 1987).

Harries, 'Iurisperiti' (2017) = J. Harries, 'Iurisperiti: "Men Skilled at Law",' in J. König and G. Woolf, eds., *Authority and Expertise in Ancient Scientific Culture* (Cambridge: Cambridge University Press, 2017) 83–106.

Harries, 'Saturninus the Helsman' (2018) = J. Harries, 'Saturninus the Helmsman, Pliny and Friends: Legal and Literary Letter Collections,' in A. König and C. Whitton, eds., *Roman Literature under Nerva, Trajan and Hadrian: Literary Interactions, AD 96–138* (Cambridge: Cambridge University Press, 2018) 208–232.

Hausmaninger, 'Publius Iuventius Celsus' (1976) = H. Hausmaninger, 'Publius Iuventius Celsus: Persönlichkeit und juristiche Argumentation,' *Aufstieg und Niedergang der Römischen Welt* II.15 (Leiden: Brill, 1976) 382–407.

Heusch, *Die Macht der memoria* (2011) = C. Heusch, *Die Macht der memoria: Die "Noctes Atticae" des Aulus Gellius im Licht der Erinnerungskultur des 2. Jahrhunderts n. Chr.* (Berlin: de Gruyter, 2011).

Holford-Strevens, *Aulus Gellius* (2003) = L. Holford-Strevens, *Aulus Gellius: An Antonine Scholar and His Achievement*, 2nd ed. (Oxford: Oxford University Press, 2003).

Holford-Strevens, *Auli Gelli Noctes Atticae* (2020) = L. Holford-Strevens, *Auli Gelli Noctes Atticae*, 2 vols. (Oxford: Oxford University Press, 2020).

van den Hout, *M. Cornelii Frontonis Epistulae* (1988) = M. P. J. van den Hout, *M. Cornelii Frontonis Epistulae* (Leipzig: Teubner, 1988).

Howley, *Aulus Gellius and Roman Reading Culture* (2018) = J. A. Howley, *Aulus Gellius and Roman Reading Culture: Text, Presence, and Imperial Knowledge in the* Noctes Atticae (Cambridge: Cambridge University Press, 2018).

Israelowich, *Patients and Healers in the High Roman Empire* (2015) = I. Israelowich, *Patients and Healers in the High Roman Empire* (Baltimore: Johns Hopkins University Press, 2015).

Johnson, *Readers and Reading Culture* (2010) = W. A. Johnson, *Readers and Reading Culture in the High Roman Empire: A Study of Elite Communities* (New York: Oxford University Press, 2010).

König, 'Self-Assertion and Its Alternatives in Ancient Scientific and Technical Writing' (2017) = J. König, 'Introduction: Self-Assertion and Its Alternatives in Ancient Scientific and Technical Writing,' in J. König and G. Woolf, eds., *Authority and Expertise in Ancient Scientific Culture* (Cambridge: Cambridge University Press, 2017) 1–26.

König, 'Tactical Interactions' (2020) = A. König, 'Tactical Interactions: Dialogues between Greece and Rome in the Military Manuals of Aelian and Arrian,' in A. König, R. Langlands, and J. Uden, eds., *Literature and Culture in the Roman Empire, 96–235: Cross-Cultural Interactions* (Cambridge: Cambridge University Press, 2020) 134–156.

Le Blay, 'Quelle place pour la médecine?'(2009) = F. Le Blay, 'Quelle place pour la médecine? Étude d'un exemple de vulgarization scientifique,' in F. Le Blay, ed., *Transmettre les savoirs dans les mondes hellénistique et romain* (Rennes: Presses Universitaires de Rennes, 2009) 79–92.

Mazzini, 'References to Medical Authors in Non-Medical Latin Literature' (2014) = I. Mazzini, 'References to Medical Authors in Non-Medical Latin Literature,' in B. Maire, ed., *'Greek' and 'Roman' in Latin Medical Tetxs: Studies in Cultural Change and Exchange in Ancient Medicine* (Leiden: Brill, 2014) 77–91.

Moreno Soldevila, *A Prosopography to Martial's Epigrams* (2019) = R. Moreno Soldevila, A. Marina Castillo, and J. Fernández Valverde, *A Prosopography to Martial's Epigrams* (Berlin: De Gruyter, 2019).

Mynors, *C. Plini Caecili Secundi Epistularum libri decem* (1963) = R. A. B. Mynors, ed. *C. Plini Caecili Secundi Epistularum libri decem* (Oxford: Oxford University Press, 1963).

Neuburger, 'Die Medizin in den "Noctes Atticae" des Aulus Gellius' (1925) = M. Neuburger, 'Die Medizin in den "Noctes Atticae" des Aulus Gellius,' *Archivio di storia della scienza* 6 (1925) 1–17.

Nutton, 'Two Notes on Immunities' (1971) = V. Nutton, 'Two Notes on Immunities: Digest 27, 1, 6, 19,' *Journal of Roman Studies* 61 (1971) 52–63.

Nutton, *Ancient Medicine* (2012) = V. Nutton, *Ancient Medicine* (London: Routledge, 2012).

Rawson, *Intellectual Life* (1985) = E. Rawson, *Intellectual Life in the Late Roman Republic* (London: Duckworth, 1985).

Roby, *Technical Ekphrasis* (2016) = C. Roby, *Technical Ekphrasis in Greek and Roman Science and Literature: The Written Machine between Alexandria and Rome* (Cambridge: Cambridge University Press, 2016).

Roller, 'Amicable and Hostile Exchange in the Culture of Recitation' (2018) = M. Roller, 'Amicable and Hostile Exchange in the Culture of Recitation,' in A. König and C. Whitton, eds., *Roman Literature under Nerva, Trajan and Hadrian: Literary Interactions, AD 96–138* (Cambridge: Cambridge University Press, 2018) 183–207.

Said, *Representations of the Intellectual* (1994) = E. W. Said, *Representations of the Intellectual* (New York: Vintage Books, 1994).

Secord, *Christian Intellectuals and the Roman Empire* (2020) = J. Secord, *Christian Intellectuals and the Roman Empire: From Justin Martyr to Origen* (University Park, PA: University of Pennsylvania Press, 2020).

Tuori, 'The ius respondendi and the Freedom of Roman Jurisprudence' (2004) = K. Tuori, 'The ius respondendi and the Freedom of Roman Jurisprudence,' *Revue Internationale des droits de l'Antiquité* 51 (2014) 295–337.

Turner, *The Politics of Expertise* (2004) = S. Turner, *The Politics of Expertise* (London: Routledge, 2004).

Uden, *The Invisible Satirist* (2015) = J. Uden, *The Invisible Satirist: Juvenal and Second-Century Rome* (New York: Oxford University Press, 2015).

Uden, 'The Noise-Lovers' (2020) = J. Uden, 'The Noise-Lovers: Cultures of Speech and Sound in Second-Century Rome,' in A. König, R. Langlands, and J. Uden, eds., *Literature and Culture in the Roman Empire, 96–235: Cross-Cultural Interactions* (Cambridge: Cambridge University Press, 2020) 58–74.

Whitton, *The Arts of Imitation in Latin Prose* (2019) = C. Whitton, *The Arts of Imitation in Latin Prose: Pliny's Epistles/Quintilian in Brief* (Cambridge: Cambridge University Press, 2019).

Williams, *Keywords* (1983) = R. Williams, *Keywords: A Vocabulary of Culture and Society*, 2nd ed. (Oxford: Oxford University Press 1983).

PART IV
POSITIONING THE SUBJECT-MATTER
When Rhetoric and Science Converge

Introduction

The Ubiquity of Rhetoric

Ulrike Babusiaux and Claire Bubb

Rhetoric was at the heart of ancient education. In both the East and the West, elite children generally began their studies with the basics of literacy and numeracy, then moved on to the study of language and the elements of rhetoric under a *grammaticus*, before graduating to the study of eloquence with a rhetor.[1] Under the rhetor, their focus was performance. Faced with an array of tried-and-true hypotheticals—some mythological, some historical, some downright melodramatic—the boys (and, by this point, they were all boys) performed before and in competition with each other.[2] There were two main types of exercise: the *suasoria*, in which the speaker aims to persuade a hypothetical addressee to take a certain course, and the *controversia*, in which the speaker takes one side of an imaginary court-case carefully designed to allow an equal chance of success on either side. In each instance, the boys were being taught to persuade: to leverage an array of practiced techniques that would allow them to convince their audience that they were in the right, regardless of the knowability (or reality) of all the facts. Particularly in the *controversiae*, they were pitted directly against each other, imbibing the lesson that rhetorical skill was the path to success and the domination of one's rivals. As J. E. Lendon has put it in his new study of rhetoric's effects on the Roman world, "declamation was taught at so profound a level that it was often impossible to leave declamation behind. It haunted the minds of its students through all their lives, as the relentless appearance of rhetorical habits in the Latin literature of the Empire abundantly proves."[3]

This section of the book seeks to highlight the relationship between law and medicine on the one hand, and rhetoric on the other. We query here to what degree and in what ways their participation in this profoundly rhetorical culture

[1] For more details, see Cribiore, *Gymnastics* (2001); Wolff, *Éducation* (2015); Bloomer, *Companion* (2015); and Lendon, *Tyrant, Persuasion* (2022) 3–13; see also Hömke, 'Ludus impudentiae!' (2018) on the rocky introduction of rhetorical education to Rome.

[2] On the more truncated course of female education, see Cribiore, *Gymnastics* (2001) 74–101 and, for Rome specifically, Hemelrijk, 'Education of Women' (2015) and Wolff, *Éducation* (2015), 131–137.

[3] Lendon, *Tyrant, Persuasion* (2022) 23. Our thanks to the author for allowing us to consult the advanced proofs of this text, as well as for his excellent contribution to the conference that preceded this volume.

Ulrike Babusiaux and Claire Bubb, *Introduction: The Ubiquity of Rhetoric* In: *Medicine and the Law under the Roman Empire.* Edited by: Claire Bubb and Michael Peachin, Oxford University Press. © Claire Bubb and Michael Peachin 2023.
DOI: 10.1093/oso/9780192898616.003.0010

shaped the literature and activities of imperial Rome's legal and medical minds. Our focus is by necessity somewhat circumscribed. First, we have refrained from engaging here with the distinct field of philosophy, despite its close ties to both rhetoric and elite education.[4] Second, as already discussed in the general introduction to the book, we only profess to consider the elite manifestations of these two fields. In short, we are deliberately limiting ourselves to those actors who had indeed received some amount of rhetorical education before training more extensively in their chosen field. In the legal sphere, this requirement is not much of a limiting factor: legal training generally presupposed some rhetorical education.[5] The need for advocates in the court to train in rhetoric is self-evident, while even jurists—whose aim was not rhetorically charged advocacy, but rather the explanation and development of the law—seem to have generally been drawn from rhetorically educated backgrounds: all of the jurists whose writings are known from the Republic and the Principate show evidence of rhetorical training, and there is good reason to believe that their humbler counterparts shared in it too.[6] On the medical side of things, the educational spectrum is broader.[7] Particularly for the less wealthy, medical apprenticeship likely replaced much or all of the later stages of education as sketched above. Indeed, epigraphic evidence indicates that some young men had already embarked on full-fledged medical practice while their peers were still declaiming about murderous stepmothers.[8] Nevertheless, an elite fraction of the empire's medical community—largely the same subset, no doubt, who would have undertaken to write substantial treatises—had some

[4] On Roman law and philosophy, cf. Vander Waerdt, 'Philosophical Influence' (1994); Winkel, 'Droit romain' (1997); Thomas, 'Institution juridique' (2011); Mantovani, *Juristes écrivains* (2018) 79–128; Brouwer, *Law* (2021); on the relationship between medicine and philosophy, see van der Eijk, *Medicine* (2005) and Crignon and Lefebvre, *Médecins et philosophes* (2019). On philosophy's relationship to both, see Trapp, this volume.

[5] For legal training, see Liebs, 'Rechtsschulen' (1976), Ducos, 'Enseignement' (2008), Riggsby 'Legal Education' (2015), and Wolff, *Éducation* (2015) 74–75, as well as Liebs, 'Juristenausbildung' (2008) for the better-attested situation in late antiquity.

[6] In fact, the degree of *legal* education that advocates received is an interesting question: Quint. *Inst.* 12.3.1 underlines the importance of the knowledge of the law for an advocate, but it can be assumed that most forensic rhetors did not have a thorough understanding of the law but were mainly trained in rhetoric. For the differences and overlaps between orators and jurists, see Nörr, 'pragmaticus' (1965); David, *Patronat judiciaire* (1992); Lehne-Gstreinthaler, Iurisperiti et oratores (2019). On the situation of provincial jurists, see Fournier, 'Syndikoi' (2007) and Kolb, 'Rechtspflege in der Provinz' (2011).

[7] For the variable social and educational levels of doctors, see Nutton, *Ancient Medicine* (2013) 254–278; nevertheless, Galen feels confident at *Protr.* 14 (I.39 K = 117 B) in putting medicine on par with rhetoric and jurisprudence as three of the nine "high arts" suitable to right-thinking young men in search of a career, though the fact that he feels the need to write such an exhortation at all perhaps suggests a bit of special pleading.

[8] See, for example, *CIL* VIII.12923 (= Gummerus, *Ärztestand* (1932), ins. 309) (epitaph of a young man who was already an established doctor when he died at age seventeen); Alonso Alonso, *Médicos* (2018), ins. 82 (= Gummerus, *Ärztestand* (1932), ins. 169) and ins. 237 (both also seventeen); *CIL* V.89 (= Alonso Alonso, *Médicos* (2018), ins. 278 = Gummerus, *Ärztestand* (1932), ins. 261) and VI.08905 (= Alonso Alonso, *Médicos* (2018), ins. 132 = Gummerus, *Ärztestand* (1932), ins. 53) and Alonso Alonso, *Médicos* (2018), ins. 97 (all eighteen); and *SEG* XVIII.519 (= *I.Smyrna* 442.b) and *CIL* VI.8905 (= Alonso Alonso, *Médicos* (2018), ins. 132 = Gummerus, *Ärztestand* (1932), ins. 53) (both nineteen).

degree of rhetorical training: Galen, though unique in many ways, was hardly alone in having been well educated.[9]

Medicine and the law are two fields (but by no means the only two) where rhetoric's claim to universal relevance might seem dubious; while their more performative elements sit squarely in the realm of rhetoric—indeed, trial in the courts is at its very heart—their written outputs are less obviously or uniformly rhetorical. Juristic treatises and medical handbooks are just the types of texts where rhetorical flourish might be least expected.[10] Accordingly, we will begin by briefly addressing the performative, declamatory situation in each field, before turning to the more nuanced role of rhetoric in the literatures.

First of all, it is worth noting that rhetorical performance was not merely the pastime of schoolboys. Romans of all ages considered declamation to be a skill held in high esteem. Professional sophists, whose job it was to astound their audience with elocutionary gymnastics and to skillfully draw their emotions and reactions along a carefully curated trajectory, were wildly popular performers and enjoyed elite social and even political cachet across the empire.[11] The ability to perform rhetorically was, in fact, an important marker of elite Roman manhood, and this was lost on neither the advocates in the court nor the doctors on the street.[12] Indeed, Galen himself views rhetoric as a common thread that binds together the practices of law and medicine, for better and for worse. On the one hand, the ability to clearly and cogently guide one's listeners through an argument is an unambiguous advantage of a rhetorical education, whether one deploys it in the courtroom or in a medical dispute: Galen admires both the rhetors from the time of Lysias and Demosthenes and "those who speak in the law courts of today" for their ability to clearly articulate the essences of their subjects, a task he finds dispiriting in the convoluted world of medical nomenclature.[13] On the other hand, rhetoric can be put to more sinister use. Galen complains that some of his medical

[9] On Galen's own rhetorical education, see Petit, *Rhetorique* (2018) 8–12, 23–27. On the broader prevalence of elite education among doctors, see Lougovaya, '*Medici Docti*' (2019); cf. Ieraci Bio, 'Medico Pepaideuménos' (1991) and Marasco, 'Curriculum' (2010), though their non-Galenic evidence is mostly from late antiquity. On the relationship between medicine and rhetoric more broadly, see Pearcy, 'Medicine and Rhetoric' (1993).

[10] On the status of medical and legal texts as "literature," see the general introduction above, pp. 8–14, and the contribution of Petit in this volume. On the incorrect idea that the influence of rhetoric on legal writing is limited to stylistic embellishments, see Babusiaux in this volume.

[11] On the rhetorical culture of this period—the so-called Second Sophistic—and both its social and political elements, see Bowersock, *Greek Sophists* (1969); Swain, *Hellenism* (1996); Schmitz, *Bildung und Macht* (1997); Anderson, *Second Sophistic* (1993); Eshleman, *Social World* (2012); and the collected voices in Goldhill, *Being Greek* (2001) and Richter and Johnson, *Handbook* (2017).

[12] On rhetoric's defining role in Roman manhood, see Gleason, *Making Men* (1995).

[13] Galen *Diff.Puls.* 4.2 (VIII.718K) (*οἱ νῦν ἐν τοῖς δικαστηρίοις λέγοντες*); see also *Inst.Log.* 14.4 (33 Kalbfleisch), where he points out that a specific type of syllogism is "useful in many aspects of daily life, including the courtroom too" (*εἰς πολλὰς τῶν καθ' ὅλον τὸν βίον ἀποδείξ(εις ε)ἶν(α)ι χρήσιμον ἄχρι καὶ τῶν δικαστηρίων*).

peers knowingly use rhetoric to twist the opinions of their innocent audience, just like:[14]

> *τοῖς κατὰ τὰ δικαστήρια ῥήτορσιν, οἳ τοὺς φανερῶς ἤτοι φόνον ἐργασαμένους ἤ τι τοιοῦτον κακὸν ἐρρύσαντο τῆς προσηκούσης κολάσεως ἐξαπατήσαντές τε καὶ παρακρουσάμενοι τοὺς δικαστάς, ὅταν ἰδιῶται λόγων ὦσιν καὶ τὰς ἐν αὐτοῖς πανουργίας ἀγνοῶσιν.*
>
> rhetors in the courts, who, by deceiving and misleading the jurors, when they are unversed in rhetoric and ignorant of its wiles, spring men from appropriate punishment, despite their having obviously committed murder or some other such crime.

As Galen insinuates, proceedings in Roman courts of law were unabashedly rhetorical, and their medical counterparts scarcely less so.

The importance of rhetoric in forensic practice is already evident in the fact that a separate *genus dicendi* had been articulated for this purpose, the *genus iudiciale*, which came to dominate its counterparts, the *genus deliberativum* and the *genus demonstrativum*.[15] The regular reference to fictitious lawsuits in the collections of declamations for school-use, such as the lesser and major declamations attributed to Quintilian, also underscores rhetoric's direct relevance to republican and imperial Roman courts.[16] Further, the forensic speeches of Cicero and the *Apology* of Apuleius offer first-hand evidence of this influence of declamatory training on speech in the courtroom; indeed, Cicero's influence on Roman jurists on the one hand, and Apuleius' precise knowledge of legal terms and juristic doctrine on the other, demonstrate the strong connection between the two fields.[17] While the publication of these speeches removes them from the courts themselves and puts them more on the boundary between practice and literature, epigraphic and papyrological evidence, as well as realia transmitted through the Justinianic *Digest*, allow us a less filtered view of the use of rhetoric in the courts.[18] The

[14] Galen *Hipp.Prorrh.* 2.57 (XVI.689K = *CMG* V 9,2 98); see also *Dig.Puls.* 4.3 (VIII.954–955K), where he compares the inappropriate deployment of ancient sources in a medical argument to the false use of witnesses in court.

[15] Cf. Hohmann, 'Gerichtsrede' (1996).

[16] On the connections between the literary tradition of declamations and (certain kinds) of legal writing, cf. contributions in Tellegen-Couperus, *Quintilian* (2003); Mantovani, 'Giuristi' (2008); for a more general overview, cf. Wycisk, *Quidquid in foro fieri potest* (2008).

[17] Fuhrmann, 'Mündlichkeit' (1990); on the close connection between legal argument and rhetorical embellishment, cf. Kalivoda, 'Juristische Rhetorik' (2005). On Cicero and the Roman jurists, cf. Nörr, 'Cicero-Zitate' (1978); Tellegen-Couperus and Tellegen, 'Nihil Hoc ad Ius, ad Ciceronem' (2006); Frazel, *In Verrem* (2009); the contributions in du Plessis, *Cicero's Law* (2016); Keeline, *Reception of Cicero* (2018). On the rhetorical and legal aspects of Apuleius' *Apology*, cf. Pellecchi, 'Accusa contro Apuleio' (2010); Pellecchi, *Innocentia* (2012); Tischer, 'Sophist' (2019).

[18] On the influence of rhetoric on Latin literature, cf. Håkanson, 'Literarische Vorbilder' (2014). On papyrological documentation, see Dolganov in this volume, and cf. Jörs, 'Erzrichter' (1915); Crook, *Legal Advocacy* (1995) 58–171; Coles, *Reports of Proceedings* (1966); Haensch, 'Typisch römisch' (2008); Haensch, 'Protokolle' (2016); and for a view of social history, cf. Kelly, *Petitions* (2011).

documentary sources, through their summaries, or minutes, of the arguments put forward by the orators, show the importance of rhetoric in the structuring of the procedures and in the organization of the arguments presented by the advocates for their respective parties.[19] Relatedly, the trial records transmitted in the Justinianic *Digest*—often referred to, in abbreviated or condensed form, by the jurists or the compilers—offer similar insights.[20] One famous example is a decision of the imperial court under Marcus Aurelius, cited by the jurist Marcellus, where the structure of the speech and counter-speech is still clearly visible.[21] Despite Marcellus' rather concise and even truncated rendition of the proceedings, it is readily apparent that the various representatives of the different interests involved not only argue legally, but also use rhetorical amplification, especially arguments of equity, to convince the emperor in charge of the adjudication.[22] Indeed, the role of rhetoric as a common language, as it were, of the Roman elite is all the more observable in the imperial chancery and the imperial court, since the emperor's entourage included not only lawyers but also rhetors and representatives of other disciplines.[23] One could thus argue that rhetorical amplification, as evident, for example, in Papinian's legal writing, was an attempt to address all members of the emperor's circle and to open the discourse among legal experts to other disciplines present in the emperor's entourage.[24] The most striking example of the emperor's use of rhetoric in legal proceedings is the inscription at Dmeir, containing the so-called *cognitio Gohariensis* of Caracalla.[25] Here, not only do the advocates—mostly imperial "friends" (*amici*), several of whom are well-known rhetoricians of the Second Sophistic—make use of rhetorically inspired argumentation, but the emperor himself does too, thereby taking over the case.[26]

[19] The influence of rhetoric on these documents has not yet been fully analyzed; a first step is Wankerl, *Appello* (2009); cf. also Bürge, 'Typisches' (2016).

[20] For a comparison of appellate procedures, cf. Wankerl, *Appello* (2009).

[21] Marcell. (29 *dig.*) D. 28.4.3.

[22] Numerous scholars have analyzed the text in this respect, cf. Müller-Eiselt, *Divus Pius* (1982) 188–198; Palazzolo, *Potere imperiale* (1974) 63–69; Wankerl, *Appello* (2009) 68–94; Avenarius, 'Marc Aurel' (2012); Rizzi, *Imperator cognoscens decrevit* (2012) 151–174; Hendel, 'D. 28,4,3, Marcellus libro 29 digestorum' (2013); Coriat, 'L'empereur juge' (2016) 52–60; Stagl, 'Glanz' (2014).

[23] For example, one thinks of P. Messius Saturninus, who served Septimius Severus as *a studiis*, and later as *a declamationibus Latinis* (*ILTun* 250). This is surely the very Messius who participated in a legal debate during a meeting of Severus' *consilium*. Papinian and Tryphoninus were likewise involved in that discussion, and we even read that, "Papinian and Messius introduced a new opinion (*sententia*)" on the matter under consideration. Paul (*3 decret.*) D. 49.14.50. On this (surely one) man, see most recently *PIR*^{2} M 514 and 527, where he is taken, without reserve, to be a legal expert—albeit, one who evidently did not produce any writing.

[24] Babusiaux, 'Kommentare' (2009).

[25] *SEG* XVII 759; cf. Roussel and de Visscher, 'Inscriptions du temple de Dmeir' (1942/3); Wenger, 'Prozess von Caracalla' (1951); Kunkel, 'Prozess der Gohariener' (1953); Oliver, 'Minutes' (1974).

[26] At Col. II, 32–34 Caracalla uses a commonplace (the argument that he has nothing better to do) and a rhetorical question to redirect the defense's gambit to dismiss the case; cf. Oliver, 'Minutes' (1974) 292f. and Wankerl, *Appello* (2009) 203–226, with a thorough discussion. On the identity of the pleading advocates, cf. Puech, *Orateurs* (2002) 132f. It is still under debate how the prominent orators came to be the representatives of the village and the opposing priest; on the question, cf. Williams, 'Caracalla' (1974) 665–666.

In the field of medicine, the opportunities for rhetorical performance are slightly less self-evident, but, as Galen, indicates, they were nevertheless rife. Indeed, almost from the very beginning of medicine as an independently established field, suspicious patients identified its vulnerability to rhetorical malpractice. Plato influentially evoked the powerful potential of rhetoric in medical situations, depicting a rhetor as far more able to manipulate patient behavior than an actual doctor.[27] Pliny goes so far as to claim that Asclepiades, the famous and influential Roman doctor of the first century BCE, had no medical training at all, but was just a disgruntled teacher of oratory who decided to put his rhetorical skills to a more lucrative use.[28] Dio Chrysostom accordingly worries that the popular doctors of the imperial period have fully replaced competence with hot air, protesting that medical skill should lie in actions rather than words.[29] While these fears are no doubt overblown (to their own rhetorical ends), epigraphic evidence confirms that speech-giving could indeed be a prominent part of a successful doctor's public persona.[30] Galen, too, frequently depicts doctors, including himself, giving speeches to attract potential patients and to impress audiences of both colleagues and laymen, as well as publicly debating against each other in an effort to convince all participants of their superior understanding.[31] Indeed, there was even some professional fluidity between medicine and rhetoric: Timocrates—the teacher of no less a sophist that Polemo—began his career as a doctor before changing course towards declamation and, conversely, one of Galen's medical teachers, Satyrus, was reckoned equally sophist and doctor by Aelius Aristides.[32] Rhetorical speech, then, was a useful performative tool no less for a doctor than for an advocate. In fact, these two groups' audiences—comprised of the elite, rhetorically educated men who could best appreciate them—were likely overlapping and their speeches mutually evocative: the *auditorium* that housed a doctor's speech one day might host a trial the next or, indeed, the rhetorical performance of a sophist.[33]

[27] Pl. *Grg.* 456b–c. [28] Plin. *HN* XXVI.7.12. [29] Dio Chrys. *Or.* 33.6.

[30] See inscriptions nos. 51, 98, 341 in Samama, *Médecins* (2003), which include mention of doctors' speeches as proof of their professional skills.

[31] Examples of attracting patients: Galen *AA* 1.1 (II.217K), *SMT* 1.29 (XI.432–433K), *MM* 5.13 (X.369K); examples of impressing audiences: Galen *Ven.Sect.Er.Rom.* 1 (XI.191K), *Lib.Prop.* 1.12–15 (XIX.14–15K = 139 B-M), *Loc.Aff.* 3.3 (VIII.142–143K); examples of medical debates: Galen *Thras.* 2 (V.807K), *Nat.Fac.* 1.13 (II.34K), *Diff.Puls.* 1.1 (VIII.494–495K), *MM* 2.5 (X.109–114K), *Ven.Sect.Er. Rom.* 1 (XI.193K). See also the medical competitions at Ephesus, some fraction of which were no doubt based on delivered speeches (*I.Ephesos* IV. 1161–1169 and Bubb, 'Medical Competitions' (2022)). On the closely related subject of Galen's performative activities as related to the Second Sophistic, see Kollesch, 'Zweite Sophistik' (1987); von Staden, 'Second Sophistic' (1997); and Mattern, 'Galen' (2017) esp. 379–382.

[32] Timocratus: Philostr. *VS* 536; Satyrus: Aristid. *Or.* 49.8 (311 Jebb).

[33] On the overlap between doctors and jurists, cf. Herberger, *Dogmatik* (1981). The place of justice (*ius*) is indeed not linked to a special building or a precise location, but to the magistrate and the due procedure; cf. Paul. (14 *ad Sab.*) D. 1.1.11: "By a quite different usage the term 'ius' is applied to the place where the law is administered, the reference being carried over from what is done to the place

Though the rhetorical elements of public legal and medical activities are the more obvious and intuitive, those of their literatures arguably shed greater light on the similar roles that rhetoric played in these two fields. First, it is equally true in the texts as it was in the performances that rhetoric functions as a signaling device. Galen's scorn of the jurors who are too "unversed" in rhetoric to understand how they are being manipulated tips his hand: rhetorical competence is recognizable by the rhetorically competent, and its skillful use is consequently respected (even, perhaps, when it is being put to nefarious ends).[34] Similarly, within the fields themselves, rhetoric, as a shared educational norm, facilitates a certain degree of uniformity and, thus, accessibility to these more recondite genres. The example above of the emperor's council (*consilium*), where members from different disciplines had to communicate about and decide on legal advice (*responsa*) and lawsuits (*decreta*), highlights the need for this sort of accessibility, while Aulus Gellius' anecdote about an intellectual rebuking a doctor for imprecision in his language underscores the potential dangers of falling short.[35] Indeed, it is surely improbable, verging on impossible, that there was no dialogue between how legal and medical experts held forth in person and how they wrote—the norms by which they were evaluated in the former context must thus also have been operative for the latter.[36] In medical contexts, in fact, the line between the performative and the written can be blurred to the point of non-existent: many

where it is done. That place we can fix as follows: wherever the praetor has determined to exercise jurisdiction, having due regard to the majesty of his own imperium and to the customs of our ancestors, that place is correctly called 'ius'" (*alia significatione ius dicitur locus in quo ius redditur, appellatione collata ab eo quod fit in eo ubi fit. quem locum determinare hoc modo possumus: ubicumque praetor salva maiestate imperii sui salvoque more maiorum ius dicere constituit, is locus recte ius appellatur*); cf. Tamm, *Auditorium* (1963) 15–17 and Rea, 'Auditoria' (2014). On the location of trials, see Färber, *Römische Gerichtsorte* (2014) and Coriat, 'L'empereur juge' (2016), 44–51; in the imperial period, however, there was a tendency to restrict the audience from public discussions in the forum to the palace; cf. Kunkel, 'Funktion des Konsiliums' (1968); De Angelis, 'Emperor's Justice' (2010).

[34] See also his scornful dismissal at *Aff.Pecc.Dig.* 2.2 (V.64K) of ignorant audience members at his lectures who "received instruction neither from a rhetor nor from a *grammaticus* (and that is extremely attainable), but are unschooled in speech to such a degree that they cannot follow the things they hear me say" (οὐδὲ ῥήτορος οὐδὲ (τὸ προχειρότατον δὴ τοῦτο) γραμματικοῦ διδασκαλίας τυχόντες, ἀλλ' οὕτως ἀγύμναστοι περὶ λόγους ὄντες ὡς μὴ παρακολουθεῖν οἷς ἀκούουσιν ὑφ' ἡμῶν λεγομένοις).

[35] Gell. *NA* 18.10; see the more extensive discussion in Uden's essay in this volume. Another impressive example on the legal side of this important role for rhetoric can be found in Papinian's work *Quaestiones*, see Babusiaux, *Papinians Quaestiones* (2011); reviews: Manthe, 'Rez. Babusiaux' (2014); Wolf, 'Rez. Babusiaux' (2013); Peachin, 'Rev. Babusiaux' (2013); Simon, 'Rez. Babusiaux' (2011). Curiously, the Justinianic compilers took over long passages from the work and integrated the whole argumentation in their *Digest*, whereas for other jurists they often cite shorter passages; moreover, Papinian's style is known to be very elliptical and obscure. Both peculiarities can be explained, first, by recognizing the argumentative connection between different cases in a fragment from the *Quaestiones*. Secondly, it should be noted that Papinian often tries to make his argumentation acceptable to the opponent by masking its innovative character. The combination of these elements can be interpreted as a strategy to support the legal outcome in a rhetorical and dialectical way. It is precisely this rhetorical intensification of the legal argument that can be seen as one reason for the special esteem in which Papinian was held, and not only in late antiquity.

[36] On this question, see also Herberger, *Dogmatik* (1981).

texts seem to have derived more or less directly from oral performance.[37] Even in the legal sphere, where the advocates, who performed in the courts, were distinct from the jurists, who wrote on the law, the boundaries are not always clear-cut: some jurists did act as orators, and advocates did need some legal knowledge. Indeed, one could even question whether a separation between legal writing and forensic oratory ought to be maintained. Legal expertise had its own role in the courts, serving as inartificial proof; moreover, there are clearly argumentative and stylistic tendencies in legal writing that could be explained as stemming from the rules of procedure. Finally, one has to consider that there might be an overlap between some genres of legal writing (e.g. *libri quaestionum*) and the imperial *cognitio*, as both deal with the same questions of law—namely the law of succession and family law—and clearly use identical tools of persuasion.[38] The close connection between law and rhetoric was certainly salient to the Roman jurists themselves: consider Pomponius' etiology of law, where—at least in republican times—jurists and orators are not only one mixed group, but the application of the twelve tables is put under test on the *pro rostris* (the oratorical stage of the *forum*).[39] Indeed, the story of Servius Sulpicius, a famous republican jurist featured in Pomponius' genealogy, encapsulates this fluidity: he began his career as a forensic orator before immersing himself in the study of law.[40] Though he wrote many books and became a founding father of jurisprudence, on his death, he was memorialized equally as an orator.[41] In short, the role of rhetoric in legal writing

[37] In his *On My Own Books*, Galen explains that many of his treatises were the direct product of an in-person event, whether requested after one of his own lectures by an audience member as "a record of the things they heard" (*Lib.Prop.* pr.6 (ὧν ἤκουσαν … ὑπομνήματα), 1.12–13, 3.15 (XIX.10, 14–15, 22K = 135, 139, 144 B-M)), produced in reaction to someone else's lecture or to a quarrel (*Lib.Prop.* 1.7–10, 9.12 (XIX.13–14, 36K = 138, 161 B-M)), or directly transcribed from a live event (*Lib.Prop.* 2.2–4 (XIX.16–17K = 140–141 B-M)); conversely, others were used as the basis of performance (*Lib.Prop.* pr.6, 1.12, 2.5–6 (XIX.10, 14, 17K = 135, 139, 141 B-M)). Galen was not alone in this; Rufus of Ephesus' *On the Names of the Parts of the Body*, for example, is framed to mimic in-person instruction.

[38] Cf. Bürge,'Typisches' (2016) 578f., who argues that the *libri quaestionum* (written by Papinian, Paul, and Ulpian) were in close connection to the imperial *cognitio extra ordinem*. Thus, he assumes that the rhetorical structure and argumentation of these works could be directly linked to their use within the imperial courtroom.

[39] Pomp. (*l. sing. enchir.*) D. 1.2.2.4: "it was decided to appoint ten men with an official power conferred by the people, who were to ask for law from the Greek cities and to base the city ["state"] on laws. They wrote them down on ivory tablets and placed them in front of the oratorical stage of the forum so that they could be easily brought to attention" (*… placuit publica autoritate decem constitui viros, per quos peterentur leges a Graecis civitatibus et civitas fundaretur legibus: quas in tabulas eboreas perscriptas pro rostris composuerunt, ut possint leges apertius percipi …*).

[40] Pomp. (*l. sing. enchir.*) D. 1.2.2.43; further examples: Coelius Antipater: Pomp. (*l. sing. enchir.*) D. 1.2.2.40; Lucius Crassus: Pomp. (*l. sing. enchir.*) D. 1.2.2.4; Tubero: Pomp. (*l. sing. enchir.*) D. 1.2.2.46. A thorough analysis and more *testimonia* can be found in Lehne-Gstreinthaler, Iurisperiti et oratores (2019).

[41] As Peachin, 'Rev. Lehne-Gstreinthaler' (2021) 645 has put it: "There was no neatly-defined form of training which led to a singular and well-delineated type of expert in the law—The Jurist, par excellence. Nor were the various possibilities for putting legal knowledge to use coherently structured or defined. Thus, we face a variety of labels for those who had attained differing types and levels of skill in this area."

should be studied in tandem with that in forensic speech.[42] Since the legal writings collected in the Justinianic sources have mostly been amputated of the introductions, transitions, and dedications typical for artistic prose in the imperial era, the best way to test the importance of rhetoric for legal writing is a work transmitted outside the *Digest*. Fortunately, one—the *Institutes* of Gaius, the best-known textbook of Roman law, which probably dates to the mid-second century—allows us to examine an author's efforts to organize legal material. This examination shows that the juristic manual is clearly modeled after the rhetorical treaties from the late Republic to the Principate.[43] For other text genres of legal literature, rhetorical influences are in any case probable or can be assumed because of their title, the manner in which the cases are presented, or the persuasive means applied to convince the readership.[44]

This leads to the second, and more significant, role of rhetoric in our fields, namely its persuasive force. Ancient medicine and law both require a set of agreed-upon principles, yet most of these lack an empirical basis (or, in the case of ancient medicine, an incontestable and achievable method of empirical proof). In the realm of the law, it should first be noted that all catalogues of legal sources—in legal and in rhetorical writing—start with an empirical instance of law, the *ius naturale*.[45] Its rules are determined via the observation of "nature," which encompasses not only "wildlife" but also human nature and—in a further sense—the "nature of things," i.e., given features of a real object and even assumed features of a legal concept.[46] Thus, *ius naturale* covers a variety of empirically ascertained "rules" that serve as a starting point not only for the legislator, when formulating rules from conventions, but also for the magistrate, when applying the law, and for the jurist, whenever he gives his view on a particular case.[47] This diversity of uses

[42] Mantovani, *Juristes écrivains* (2018) 51–55 has recently argued that the degrees of style, ranging from *genus tenue* to *genus grande*, should not be applied to legal writing as such—that, in fact, the distinction is only legitimate for oratory itself, whereas technical literature needs to be categorized according to different criteria, such as the author's position and the standing of the discipline within the hierarchy of the different arts. He argues instead that the influence and importance of ancient rhetoric for Roman legal writing lies on another, no less significant, level: the structuring and presentation of the material, i.e., the technique of instruction (*docere*).

[43] The ground-breaking analysis is the one of Fuhrmann, *Lehrbuch* (1960); further development of the argument by Battaglia, 'Strutture espositive' (2020).

[44] For an attempt to classify the works of Roman jurists in accordance to these criteria, cf. Babusiaux, 'Legal Writing' (2016). In this respect, it is important to consider, as Mantovani, *Juristes écrivains* (2018) 30–37 argues, that the most important audience for any legal treatises, monograph, or commentary were other jurists, i.e., legal experts, willing to further develop the existing legal opinions and to overcome shortcomings of the ancestors, which meant convincing the legal community of their new and superior understanding of the law.

[45] On these catalogues, cf. Nörr, *Divisio* (1972); Ferrary, 'Droit naturel' (2007).

[46] The most famous example for "wildlife" is at Ulp. (1 *inst.*) D. 1.1.3. The inclusion of human nature is an important corrective to slave law rules (and participation of slaves in the *ius humanum*), cf. e.g. Iavolenus (2 *ex post. Lab.*) D. 35.1.40.3; Ulp. (26 *ad ed.*) D. 12.4.3.7; Paul. (35 *ad ed.*) D. 23.2.14.2. The best overview on all this is still Maschi, *Concezione naturalistica* (1937).

[47] On the function of *ius naturale* in contrast to *ius civile*, cf. Babusiaux, 'Rechtsschichten' (2023) nr. 217f.

explains why there is not only uncertainty about some of the rules and their extent, but also different understandings of the specifics of each *ius naturale* depending on the concrete context of its invocation. Other "layers of law" are less uncertain. The civil law (*ius civile*) is established in statutes, *plebiscita*, and *senatus consulta*; the jurists' work in this respect is, thus, less the research of applicable rules than the interpretation of existing ones. Since statutes, interpretations, and legal opinions can differ, the main point of legal advice lies in the reconciliation of different "layers of law" that might apply to one and the same case. There are no general rules of precedence of one layer over the other, so the reconciliation must be done within the framework of the case. To convince other legal experts of the validity of the result obtained, the advising jurist must have recourse to different rhetorical arguments, e.g.: the solution in similar cases (*exempla*, *illustrantia*, *argumentum a similibus*), the authority of the jurist whose opinion gave the decisive hint for the solution of the case (*auctoritas*), and, finally and more importantly, equity (*aequitas*), which embraces both the evaluation of the facts, persons, and particularities of the case and the appeal to higher standards and principles.[48]

Ancient medicine incorporated more opportunities for empirical proof than did ancient law, but it was nevertheless far from an exact science. Galen was immensely frustrated by this fact and strove to bring his arguments as close to geometrical demonstrations as possible—a form of proof that he considered to be the gold-standard, explicitly contrasting it with the inferior brand of "dialectical proofs of the sort that rhetors use."[49] But this was ultimately a doomed endeavor, as the very heterogeneity of ancient medical thought immediately attests. First, different schools of medical thinking accepted different thresholds of evidence: for example, two of Galen's most fundamental tools were observation via dissection and experiment via vivisection—both processes that resulted in facts that he considered observable, reproducible, and thus incontrovertible—but a healthy segment of his medical peers rejected the basic epistemic value of these approaches.[50] Second, even accepting these and other avenues of knowledge,

[48] On *exempla*, cf. Nörr, 'exempla' (2009); Kacprzak, *Logica* (2012). On *auctoritas*, cf. (most recently): Mantovani, 'Autorité' (2020). For equity, the principles appealed to vary from the prohibition of impunity (Iul. (86 *dig.*) D. 9.2.51.2), to the fair balancing of interests, which is considered to be the main characteristic of the praetorian law (cf. Gaius *Inst.* 2.119; 2.158–63; 2.135; 3.25–26, on this cf. 'Rechtsschichten' (2023) nr. 156–169), to the interdiction of unjust enrichment (cf. Stagl, 'Ausgleichung' (2007) 692–697).

[49] For his quest to make medicine adhere to geometrical-style proof, see *Lib.Prop.* 14.1–7 (XIX.39–41K = 164–165 B-M), *Ord.Lib.Prop.* 1.7–13 (XIX.51–53K = 89–91 B-M), and the discussions in Morison, 'Logic' (2008) 68–83 and Petit, *Rhetorique* (2018) 93–94. The comparison with rhetorical proof is at *Aff.Pecc.Dig.* 2.7 (V.102K) (*ἐξ ἐπιχειρημάτων . . . οἵοις οἱ ῥήτορες χρῶνται*).

[50] Neither the Empiricists nor the Methodists, two large and influential sects of ancient doctors, accepted the results of vivisection and dissection as valid data (see Celsus, *Med.* pr.41–42 on the Empiricists and Galen, *MM* 4.3, 6.4 (X.249, 422K) on the Methodists). This is but one example of the fundamentally different views on the general approach to medical knowledge held by the Empiricists, who rejected theoretical explanations of any kind, the Methodists, who are characterized by their

ancient methodologies were simply insufficient to address many medical questions: the ever-confident Galen himself is sometimes forced to speculate.[51] In both of these situations—faced with a set of theories which may or may not be true, or may or may not be accepted as true by his audience—the doctor must fall back on persuasion.[52] In both law and medicine, then, the path to consensus among experts rests to one degree or another on rhetoric and the expert's ability to sway his peers.[53]

Doctors and jurists thus both find themselves faced with the tricky proposition of deploying a rhetoric that is simultaneously clandestine and overt. Rhetorical polish is a desirable surface quality, signaling education and social status to readers; yet, as experts attempting to establish fundamental facts, the substance of their arguments is more effective the more its rhetorical underpinnings can operate unobtrusively. Rhetorical moments in the texts of these fields can therefore range from showy to subtle. In what follows, this section will provide two case-studies of rhetoric in action, one in the law, one in medicine. The first evaluates the rhetorical strategies at play in the writing of the jurists Ulpian, Paul, and Papinian, highlighting their subtle use of rhetorical argumentation, particularly the strategies of *ethos* and *pathos*, to bolster their jurisprudential authority. The second considers the deployment of rhetorical and stylistic strategies by diverse medical authors of the Roman period in order to situate their writing in the broader world of literary and artistic prose. Finally, by way of conclusion, the response highlights rhetors' and grammarians' parallel social position to doctors and to jurists as experts in their own field and explores some of the ramifications of rhetoric's standard educational role across fields of specialization.

Bibliography

Alonso Alonso, *Médicos* (2018) = M. Á. Alonso Alonso, *Los médicos en las inscripciones latinas de Italia (siglos II a.C.-III d.C.). Aspectos sociales y profesionales* (Santander: Ediciones Universidad Cantabria, 2018).

detractors, at any rate, as disinterested in engaging with models that did not fit their own basic framework, and the remaining "Rationalists," a diverse group who deployed diverse theoretical understandings.

[51] See, for example, at *Ut.Resp.* 5 (IV.498K = 116 F-W), where he says that "we have not discovered the sorts of things that would prove our theory **by necessity**; however, they are **the most persuasive** of all the other [options], especially since this theory is not refuted by any observable facts" (τὰ δὲ τὴν ἡμετέραν κατασκευάζοντα τοιαῦτα μὲν οὖν οὐχ εὕρομεν ὡς **ἐξ ἀνάγκης** περαίνειν, ἁπάντων μέντοι τῶν ἄλλων **πιθανώτατα** πρὸς τὸ μηδ' ἀνατρέπεσθαι πρός τινος τῶν φαινομένων ταύτην τὴν δόξαν).

[52] While Galen might be reluctant to admit that rhetorical persuasion has any place in medicine (as in the passages discussed at Pearcy, 'Medicine and Rhetoric' (1993) 452–453 and von Staden, 'Second Sophistic' (1997) 44 n. 44), Petit, *Rhetorique* (2018) has demonstrated that he uses it freely, including in places where his arguments need a lift (see especially 90–111).

[53] Lehoux, *What Did the Romans Know?* (2012) 13–14, 77–105 demonstrates that rhetoric, and that of the courtroom in particular, actively shaped Roman scientific discourse more broadly.

Anderson, *Second Sophistic* (1993) = G. Anderson, *The Second Sophistic. A Cultural Phenomenon in the Roman Empire* (London: Routledge, 1993).

De Angelis, 'Emperor's Justice' (2010) = F. de Angelis, 'The Emperor's Justice and Its Spaces in Rome and Italy,' in F. de Angelis, ed., *Spaces of Justice in the Roman World* (Boston: Brill, 2010) 127–159.

Avenarius, 'Marc Aurel' (2012) = M. Avenarius, 'Marc Aurel und die Dogmatik des römischen Privatrechts. Kaiserliche Rechtspflege im System der Rechtsquellen und die Ausfüllung von Gestaltungsspielräumen in einer Übergangszeit der Rechtsentwicklung,' in M. van Ackeren, ed., *Selbstbetrachtungen und Selbstdarstellungen. Der Philosoph und Kaiser Marc Aurel im interdisziplinären Licht* (Wiesbaden: Reichert Verlag, 2012) 203–282.

Babusiaux, 'Kommentare' (2009) = U. Babusiaux, 'Kommentare des Kaiserrechts in Papinians Quaestiones,' *Zeitschrift der Savigny-Stiftung für Rechtsgeschichte, romanistische Abteilung* 126 (2009) 156–186.

Babusiaux, *Papinians Quaestiones* (2011) = U. Babusiaux, *Papinians Quaestiones. Zur rhetorischen Methode eines spätklassischen Juristen* (Munich: C. H. Beck, 2011).

Babusiaux, 'Legal Writing' (2016) = U. Babusiaux, 'Legal Writing and Legal Reasoning,' in P. du Plessis, C. Ando, and K. Tuori, eds., *The Oxford Handbook of Roman Law and Society* (Oxford: Oxford University Press, 2016) 176–187.

Babusiaux, 'Rechtsschichten' (forthcoming 2023) = U. Babusiaux, '§ 6. Rechtsschichten,' in U. Babusiaux, Chr. Baldus, W. Ernst, F.-St. Meissel, J. Platschek, and Th.Rüfner, eds., *Handbuch des römischen Privatrechts* (Tübingen: Mohr Siebeck, forthcoming 2023).

Battaglia, 'Strutture espositive' (2020) = F. Battaglia, 'Strutture espositive in Gaio. Per una morfologia delle Institutiones,' in U. Babusiaux and D. Mantovani, eds., *Le Istituzioni di Gaio. Avventure di un bestseller. Trasmissione, uso e trasformazione del testo* (Pavia: IUSS Press, 2020) 205–278.

Bloomer, *Companion* (2015) = W. M. Bloomer, ed., *A Companion to Ancient Education* (Chichester: Wiley Blackwell, 2015).

Bowersock, *Greek Sophists* (1969) = G. W. Bowersock, *Greek Sophists in the Roman Empire* (Oxford: Clarendon Press, 1969).

Bubb, 'Medical Competitions' (2022) = C. Bubb, 'A New Interpretation of the Medical Competitions at Ephesus (I. Ephesos IV 1161-69),' *Zeitschrift für Papyrologie und Epigraphik* 221 (2022) 152–156.

Bürge, 'Typisches' (2016) = A. Bürge, 'Typisches und Untypisches bei der Urteilsfindung,' in Haensch, ed., *Recht haben* (2016) 561–579.

Brouwer, *Law* (2021) = R. Brouwer, *Law and Philosophy in the Late Roman Republic* (Cambridge: Cambridge University Press, 2021).

Coles, *Reports of Proceedings* (1966) = R. A. Coles, *Reports of Proceedings in Papyri* (Bruxelles: Fondation Égyptologique Reine Élisabeth, 1966).

Coriat, 'L'empereur juge' (2016) = J.-P. Coriat, 'L'empereur juge et son tribunal à la fin du Principat. Un essai de synthèse,' in Haensch, *Recht haben* (2016) 41–61.

Cribiore, *Gymnastics* (2001) = R. Cribiore, *Gymnastics of the Mind: Greek Education in Hellenistic and Roman Egypt* (Princeton: Princeton University Press, 2001).

Crignon and Lefebvre, *Médecins et philosophes* (2019) = C. Crignon and D. Lefebvre, eds., *Médecins et philosophes: une histoire* (Paris: CNRS Éditions, 2019).

Crook, *Legal Advocacy* (1995) = J. A. Crook, *Legal Advocacy in the Roman World* (London: Duckworth, 1995).

David, *Patronat judiciaire* (1992) = J.-M. David, *Le patronat judiciaire au dernier siècle de la république romaine* (Paris: École Française de Rome, 1992).

Ducos, 'Enseignement' (2008) = M. Ducos, 'L'enseignement du droit dans le monde romain,' in H. Hugonnard-Roche, ed., *L'enseignement supérieur dans les mondes antiques et médiévaux* (Paris: J. Vrin, 2008) 13–28.

van der Eijk, *Medicine* (2005) = P. J. van der Eijk, *Medicine and Philosophy in Classical Antiquity. Doctors and Philosophers on Nature, Soul, Health and Disease* (Cambridge: Cambridge University Press, 2005).

Eshleman, *Social World* (2012) = K. Eshleman, *The Social World of Intellectuals in the Roman Empire: Sophists, Philosophers and Christians* (Cambridge: Cambridge University Press, 2012).

Färber, *Römische Gerichtsorte* (2014) = R. Färber, *Römische Gerichtsorte. Räumliche Dynamiken von Jurisdiktion im Imperium Romanum* (Munich: C. H. Beck, 2014).

Ferrary, 'Droit naturel' (2007) = J.-L. Ferrary, 'Le droit naturel dans les exposés sur les parties du droit des traités de rhétorique,' in Mantovani and Schiavone, *Testi* (2007) 75–94.

Fournier, 'Syndikoi' (2007) = J. Fournier, 'Les 'syndikoi,' représentants juridiques des cités grecques sous le Haut-Empire romain,' *Cahiers Centre Glotz* 18 (2007) 7–36.

Frazel, *In Verrem* (2009) = T. D. Frazel, *The Rhetoric of Cicero's 'in Verrem'* (Göttingen: Vandenhoeck & Ruprecht, 2009).

Fuhrmann, *Lehrbuch* (1960) = M. Fuhrmann, *Das systematische Lehrbuch. Ein Beitrag zur Geschichte der Wissenschaften in der Antike* (Göttingen: Vandenhoeck & Ruprecht, 1960).

Fuhrmann, 'Mündlichkeit' (1990) = M. Fuhrmann, 'Mündlichkeit und fiktive Mündlichkeit in den von Cicero veröffentlichten Reden,' in G. Vogt-Spira, ed., *Strukturen der Mündlichkeit in der römischen Literatur* (Tübingen: Gunter Narr, 1990) 53–62.

Gleason, *Making Men* (1995) = M. Gleason, *Making Men: Sophists and Self-Presentation in Ancient Rome* (Princeton: Princeton University Press, 1995).

Goldhill, *Being Greek* (2001) = S. Goldhill, ed., *Being Greek under Rome: Cultural Identity, the Second Sophistic, and the Development of Empire* (Cambridge: Cambridge University Press, 2001).

Gummerus, *Ärztestand* (1932) = H. Gummerus, *Ärztestand im römischen Reiche nach den Inschriften* (Helsinki: Societas Scientarum Fennica, 1932).

Haensch, 'Typisch römisch' = R. Haensch, 'Typisch römisch? Die Gerichtsprotokolle der in Aegyptus und den übrigen östlichen Reichsprovinzen tätigen Vertreter Roms,' in H. Börm, N. Ehrhardt, and J. Wiesehöfer, eds., *Monumentum et instrumentum inscriptum. Beschriftete Objekte aus Kaiserzeit und Spätantike als historische Zeugnisse. Festschrift für Peter Weiß* (Stuttgart: Steiner Verlag, 2008) 117–127.

Haensch, *Recht haben* (2016) = R. Haensch, ed., *Recht haben und Recht bekommen im Imperium Romanum; das Gerichtswesen der Römischen Kaiserzeit und seine dokumentarische Evidenz* (Warsaw: Fundacja im. Rafała Taubenschlaga, 2016).

Haensch, 'Protokolle' (2016) = R. Haensch, 'Die Protokolle der Statthaltergerichte der spätantiken Provinzen Ägyptens,' in Haensch, *Recht haben* (2016) 299–324.

Håkanson, 'Literarische Vorbilder' (2014) = L. Håkanson, 'Zu den literarischen Vorbildern der Declamationes maiores: Cicero, Seneca, Declamationes minors,' in B. Santorelli, ed., *Lennart Håkanson, Unveröffentlichte Schriften* I (Berlin and New York: De Gruyter, 2014) 15–38.

Hemelrijk, 'Education of Women' (2015) = E. A. Hemelrijk, 'The Education of Women in Ancient Rome,' in Bloomer, *Companion* (2015) 292–304.

Hendel, 'D. 28,4,3, Marcellus libro 29 digestorum' (2013) = A. C. Hendel, 'D. 28,4,3, Marcellus libro 29 digestorum. Zum Sicherheitsgedanken bei der benignior interpretation,' *Zeitschrift der Savigny-Stiftung für Rechtsgeschichte, romanistische Abteilung* 130 (2013) 419–431.

Herberger, *Dogmatik* (1981) = M. Herberger, *Dogmatik. Zur Geschichte von Begriff und Methode in Medizin und Jurisprudenz* (Frankfurt a.M.: Vittorio Klostermann, 1981).

Hohmann, 'Gerichtsrede' (1996) = H. Hohmann, 'Gerichtsrede,' in G. Ueding, ed., *Historisches Wörterbuch der Rhetorik 3: Eup-Hör* (Darmstadt: Wissenschaftliche Buchgesellschaft, 1996) 770–815.

Hömke, 'Ludus impudentiae!' (2018) = N. Hömke, 'Ludus impudentiae! Der Streit um die "richtige" Wissensvermittlung an römische Schüler,' in N. Hömke and A. Forst, eds., *www.BrAnD2. Wissen. Zweites Brandenburger Antike-Denkwerk* (Potsdamer Lateintage, Bd. 10) (Potsdam, 2018) 49–74.

Ieraci Bio, 'Medico Pepaideuménos' (1991) = A. M. Ieraci Bio, 'Sulla Concezione del Medico Pepaideuménos in Galeno e nel Tardoantico,' in J. A. Lopéz Feréz, ed., *Galeno: Obra, Pensamiento e Influencia* (Madrid: Universidad Nacional de Educacion a Distancia) 133–151.

Jörs, 'Erzrichter' (1915) = P. Jörs, 'Erzrichter und Chrematisten. Untersuchungen zum Mahn- und Vollstreckungsverfahren im griechisch-römischen Ägypten,' *Zeitschrift der Savigny-Stiftung für Rechtsgeschichte, romanistische Abteilung* 36 (1915) 230–339.

Kacprzak, *Logica* (2012) = A. Kacprzak, *Tra logica e giurisprudenza. Argumentum a simili nei Topica di Cicerone* (Warsaw: JJP Suppl. XVII, 2012).

Kalivoda, 'Juristische Rhetorik' (2005) = G. Kalivoda, 'Juristische Rhetorik,' in K. D. Lerch, ed., *Recht verhandeln* (Berlin: Berlin-Brandenburgische Akademie der Wissenschaften, 2005) 321–342.

Keeline, *Reception of Cicero* (2018) = T. J. Keeline, *The Reception of Cicero in the Early Roman Empire. The Rhetorical Schoolroom and the Creation of a Cultural Legend* (Cambridge: Cambridge University Press, 2018).

Kelly, *Petitions* (2011) = B. Kelly, *Petitions, Litigation, and Social Control in Roman Egypt. Oxford Studies in Ancient Documents* (Oxford and New York: Oxford University Press, 2011).

Kolb, 'Rechtspflege in der Provinz' (2011) = A. Kolb, 'Rechtspflege in der Provinz. Ein causidicus am Rande der Alpen,' in Muscheler, *Festschrift Liebs* (2011) 331–345.

Kollesch, 'Zweite Sophistik' (1987) = J. Kollesch, 'Galen und die Zweite Sophistik,' in V. Nutton, ed., *Galen: Problems and Prospects* (London: Wellcome Institute for the History of Medicine) 1–11.

Kunkel, 'Prozess der Gohariener' (1953) = W. Kunkel, 'Der Prozess der Gohariener vor Caracalla,' in *Festschrift Hans Lewald* (Basel: Helbing & Lichtenhahn, 1953) 81–91.

Kunkel, 'Funktion des Konsiliums' (1968) = W. Kunkel, 'Die Funktion des Konsiliums in der magistratischen Strafjustiz und im Kaisergericht II,' *Zeitschrift der Savigny-Stiftung für Rechtsgeschichte, romanistische Abteilung* 85 (1968) 253–329.

Lehne-Gstreinthaler, Iurisperiti et oratores (2019) = C. Lehne-Gstreinthaler, Iurisperiti et oratores. *Eine Studie zu den römischen Juristen der Republik* (Cologne: Böhlau, 2019).

Lehoux, *What Did the Romans Know?* (2012) = D. Lehoux, *What Did the Romans Know? An Inquiry into Science and Worldmaking* (Chicago: University of Chicago Press, 2012).

Lendon, *Tyrant, Persuasion* (2022) = J. E. Lendon, *That Tyrant, Persuasion. How Rhetoric Shaped the Roman World* (Princeton: Princeton University Press, 2022).

Liebs, 'Rechtsschulen' (1976) = D. Liebs, 'Rechtsschulen und Rechtsunterricht im Prinzipat,' in H. Temporini, ed., *Aufstieg und Niedergang der römischen Welt*, II.15 (Berlin: De Gruyter, 1976) 197–286.

Liebs, 'Juristenausbildung' (2008) = D. Liebs, 'Juristenausbildung in der Spätantike,' in C. Baldus, Th. Finkenauer, and Th. Rüfner, eds., *Juristenausbildung in Europa zwischen Tradition und Reform* (Tübingen: Mohr Siebeck, 2008) 31–45.

Lougovaya, '*Medici Docti*' (2019) = J. Lougovaya, '*Medici Docti* in Verse Inscriptions,' *Archiv für Papyrusforschung* 40 (2019) 139–159.

Manthe, 'Rez. Babusiaux' (2014) = U. Manthe, 'Rezension zu U. Babusiaux, Papinians Quaestiones, München 2011,' *Zeitschrift der Savigny-Stiftung für Rechtsgeschichte, romanistische Abteilung* 131 (2014) 453–459.

Mantovani and Schiavone, *Testi* (2007) = D. Mantovani and A. Schiavone, eds., *Testi e problemi del giusnaturalismo romano* (Pavia: IUSS Press, 2007) 75–94.

Mantovani, 'Giuristi' (2007) = D. Mantovani, 'I giuristi, il retore e le api. Ius controversum e natura nella Declamatio maior XIII,' in Mantovani and Schiavone, *Testi* (2007) 323–385.

Mantovani, *Juristes écrivains* (2018) = D. Mantovani, *Les juristes écrivains. Les œuvres des juristes romains comme littérature* (Paris: Belles Lettres, 2018).

Mantovani, 'Autorité' (2020) = D. Mantovani, 'L'autorité des juristes romains mise en cause,' in J.-M. David and F. Hurlet, eds., *L'auctoritas à Rome. Une notion constitutive de la culture politique* (Bordeaux: Ausonius, 2020) 271–313.

Marasco, 'Curriculum' (2010) = G. Marasco, 'The Curriculum of Studies in the Roman Empire and the Cultural Role of Physicians,' in M. Horstmanshoff, ed., *Hippocrates and Medical Education* (Leiden and Boston: Brill, 2010) 205–219.

Maschi, *Concezione naturalistica* (1937) = C. A. Maschi, *La concezione naturalistica del diritto e degli istituti giuridic romani* (Milan: Vita e Pensiero, 1937).

Mattern, 'Galen' (2017) = S. Mattern, 'Galen,' in Richter and Johnson, *Handbook* (2017) 371–388.

Morison, 'Logic' (2008) = B. Morison, 'Logic,' in R. J. Hankinson, ed., *The Cambridge Companion to Galen* (Cambridge: Cambridge University Press) 66–115.

Müller-Eiselt, *Divus Pius* (1982) = K. P. Müller-Eiselt, *Divus Pius constituit. Kaiserliches Erbrecht* (Berlin: Duncker & Humblot, 1982).

Muscheler, *Festschrift Liebs* (2011) = K. Muscheler, ed., *Dogmatik, Überlieferung, Rezeption. Festschrift für Detlef Liebs zum 75. Geburtstag* (Berlin: Duncker & Humblot, 2011).

Nörr, 'pragmaticus' (1965) = D. Nörr, 'pragmaticus,' in *Paulys Realencyclopädie der classischen Altertumswissenschaft*, Suppl. X (Stuttgart: Metzler, 1965) 639–651.

Nörr, *Divisio* (1972) = D. Nörr, *Divisio und Partitio. Bemerkungen zur römischen Rechtsquellenlehre und antiken Wissenschaftstheorie* (Berlin: Schweitzer, 1972).

Nörr, 'Cicero-Zitate' (1978) = D. Nörr,'Cicero-Zitate bei den klassischen Juristen,' in *Atti del III Colloquium Tullianum* (Rome: Centro Studi Ciceroniani, 1978) 131–150.

Nörr, 'exempla' (2009) = D. Nörr, 'exempla nihil per se valent. Bemerkungen zu Paul. 15 quest. D. 46,3,98,8; 72 ad ed. D. 45,1,83,5,' *Zeitschrift der Savigny-Stiftung für Rechtsgeschichte, romanistische Abteilung* 126 (2009) 1–54.

Nutton, *Ancient Medicine* (2013) = V. Nutton, *Ancient Medicine*. 2nd ed. (London and New York: Routledge, 2013).

Oliver, 'Minutes' = J. H. Oliver, 'Minutes of a Trial Conducted by Caracalla at Antioch in A.D. 216,' in *Mélanges helléniques offerts à G. Daux* (Paris: De Boccard, 1974) 289–294.

Palazzolo, *Potere imperiale* (1974) = N. Palazzolo, *Potere imperiale ed organi giurisdizionali nel II secolo d.c.* (Naples: Giuffrè, 1974).

Peachin, 'Rev. Babusiaux' (2013) = M. Peachin, Review of U. Babusiaux, *Papinians Quaestiones*, Munich 2011, *Journal of Roman Studies* 103 (2013) 342–343.

Peachin, 'Rev. Lehne-Gstreinthaler' (2021) = M. Peachin, Review of C. Lehne-Gstreinthaler, *Iurisperiti et oratores*, Cologne 2019, *Zeitschrift der Savigny-Stiftung für Rechtsgeschichte, romanistische Abteilung* 138 (2021) 643–652.

Pearcy, 'Medicine and Rhetoric' (1993) = L. T. Pearcy, 'Medicine and Rhetoric in the Period of the Second Sophistic,' *Aufstieg und Niedergang der römischen Welt*, II.37.1 (Berlin and New York: De Gruyter, 1993) 445–456.

Pellecchi, 'Accusa contro Apuleio' (2010) = L. Pellecchi, 'L'accusa contro Apuleio: linee retoriche e giuridiche,' in D. Mantovani and L. Pellecchi, eds., *Eparcheia, autonomia e civitas Romana. Studi sulla giurisdizione criminale dei governatori di provincia (II sec.a.C.–II d.C.)* (Pavia: IUSS Press, 2010) 171–334.

Pellecchi, *Innocentia* = L. Pellecchi, *Innocentia eloquentia est. Analisi giuridica dell'Apologia di Apuleio* (Rome: Biblioteca di Athenaeum 57, New Press, 2012).

Petit, *Rhetorique* (2018) = C. Petit, *Galien de Pergame ou la rhétorique de la Providence: Médecine, littérature et pouvoir à Rome* (Leiden and Boston: Brill, 2018).

du Plessis, *Cicero's Law* (2016) = P. du Plessis, ed., *Cicero's Law. Rethinking Roman Law of the Late Republic* (Edinburgh: Edinburgh University Press, 2016).

Puech, *Orateurs* (2002) = B. Puech, *Orateurs et sophistes grecs dans les inscriptions d'époque impériale* (Paris: Vrin, 2002).

Rea, 'Auditoria' (2014) = R. Rea, 'Gli auditoria pubblici nel mondo romano,' in R. Meneghini and R. Rea, eds., *La Biblioteca Infinita. I Luoghi del Sapere nel Mondo Antico* (Milan: Electa, 2014) 133–154.

Richter and Johnson, *Handbook* (2017) = D. S. Richter and W. A. Johnson, eds., *The Oxford Handbook to the Second Sophistic* (Oxford: Oxford University Press, 2017).

Riggsby, 'Legal Education' (2015) = A. M. Riggsby, 'Roman Legal Education,' in Bloomer, *Companion* (2015) 444–451.

Rizzi, *Imperator cognoscens decrevit* (2012) = M. Rizzi, *Imperator cognoscens decrevit. Profili e contenuti dell'attività giudiziaria imperiale in età classica* (Milan: Giuffrè, 2012).

Roussel and de Visscher, 'Inscriptions du temple de Dmeir' (1942/3) = P. Roussel and F. de Visscher, 'Les Inscriptions du temple de Dmeir,' *Syria* 23 (1942/3) 173–200.

Samama, *Médecins* (2003) = É. Samama, *Les médecins dans le monde grec. Sources epigraphiques sur la naissance d'un corps medical* (Geneva: Librarie Droz, 2003).

Schmitz, *Bildung und Macht* (1997) = T. Schmitz, *Bildung und Macht: Zur sozialen und politischen Funktion der zweiten Sophistik in der griechischen Welt der Kaiserzeit* (Munich: C. H. Beck, 1997).

Simon, 'Rez. Babusiaux' (2011) = D. Simon, 'Rez. zu U. Babusiaux, Papinians Quaestiones, München 2011,' http://mops-block.de/index.php/16-babusiaux, 12.12.2011.

von Staden, 'Second Sophistic' (1997) = H. von Staden, 'Galen and the Second Sophistic,' in R. Sorabji, ed., *Aristotle and After* (London: Institute of Classical Studies, School of Advanced Study, University of London, 1997) 33–54.

Stagl, 'Glanz' (2014) = J. F. Stagl, 'Glanz der Rhetorik und Finsternis der Logik in einer Entscheidung Marc Aurels (Marcell. D. 28,4,3 pr.-1),' *Fundamina* 20 (2014) 871–880.

Stagl, 'Ausgleichung' (2007) = J. F. Stagl, 'Die Ausgleichung von Vorteil und Nachteil als Inhalt klassischer aequitas,' in Mantovani and Schiavone, *Testi* (2008) 675–713.

Swain, *Hellenism* (1996) = S. Swain, *Hellenism and Empire* (Oxford: Clarendon Press, 1996).

Tamm, *Auditorium* (1963) = B. Tamm, *Auditorium and Palatium. A Study on Assembly-Rooms in Roman Palaces during the 1st Century B.C. and the 1st Century A.D.* (Stockholm: Almquist & Wiksell, 1963).

Tellegen-Couperus, *Quintilian* (2003) = O. Tellegen-Couperus, *Quintilian and the Law. The Art of Persuasion in Law and Politics* (Leuven: Leuven University Press, 2003).

Tellegen-Couperus and Tellegen, 'Nihil Hoc ad Ius, ad Ciceronem' (2006) = O. Tellegen-Couperus and J. W. Tellegen, 'Nihil Hoc ad Ius, ad Ciceronem,' *Revue internationale des droits de l'antiquité* 53 (2006) 381–408.

Thomas, 'Institution juridique' (2011) = Y. Thomas, 'L'institution juridique de la nature. Remarques sur la casuistique du droit naturel à Rome,' in M.-A. Hermitte and P. Napoli, eds., *Les Opérations du droit* (Paris: Seuil, 2011) 21–40.

Tischer, 'Sophist' (2019) = U. Tischer, 'Der Sophist als Philologe. Inszenierung und Instrumentalisierung der grammatica in Apuleius' Rede Pro se de magia,' in G. Bitto and A. Ginestí Rosell, eds., *Philologie auf zweiter Stufe. Literarische Rezeptionen und Inszenierungen hellenistischer Gelehrsamkeit* (Stuttgart: Steiner, 2019) 231–255.

Vander Waerdt, 'Philosophical Influence' (1994) = P. A. Vander Waerdt, 'Philosophical Influence on Roman Jurisprudence? The Case of Stoicism and Natural Law,' in *Aufstieg und Niedergang der römischen Welt* II.36.7 (Berlin and New York: De Gruyter, 1994) 4851–4900.

Wankerl, *Appello* (2009) = Veronika Wankerl, *Appello ad principem. Urteilsstil und Urteilstechnik in kaiserlichen Berufungsentscheidungen (Augustus bis Caracalla)* (Munich: C. H. Beck, 2009).

Wenger, 'Prozess von Caracalla' (1951) = L. Wenger, 'Ein Prozess von Caracalla in Syrien. Zu einer neu bekannt gewordenen Inschrift,' in *Mélanges Henri Grégoire, Annuaire de l'Institut de Philologie et d'histoire orientales et slaves, Bruxelles* 11 (1951) 469–504.

Williams, 'Caracalla' (1974) = W. Williams, 'Caracalla and the Rhetoricians,' *Latomus* 33 (1974) 663–667.

Winkel, 'Droit romain' (1997) = L. Winkel, 'Le droit romain et la philosophie grecque, quelques problèmes de méthode,' *Tijdschrift voor rechtsgeschiedenis* 65 (1997) 373–384.

Wolf, 'Rez. Babusiaux' (2013) = J. G. Wolf, 'Rezension zu U. Babusiaux, Papinians Quaestiones, München 2011,' *Tijdschrift voor rechtsgeschiedenis* 81 (2013) 275–281.

Wolff, *Éducation* (2015) = C. Wolff, *L'éducation dans le monde romain: du début de la République à la mort de Commode* (Paris: Picard, 2015).

Wycisk, *Quidquid in foro fieri potest* (2008) = T. Wycisk, *Quidquid in foro fieri potest. Studien zum römischen Recht bei Quintilian* (Berlin: Duncker & Humblot, 2008).

Rhetoric in Legal Writing

The Ethos and Pathos of the Roman Jurists

Ulrike Babusiaux

I. Introduction: Roman Law and Rhetoric

The relationship between Roman law and rhetoric is a long-discussed and, still, very controversial topic. Some general considerations about the limitations observed and the methodology followed in this contribution thus seem to be necessary. The first limitation is obvious. The following analysis will not deal with the general question as to whether rhetoric had an influence on Roman legal writing, since, for one, the question seems wrongly posed.[1] Secondly, no consensus can be reached in the current state of the debate. The starting point will be that legal writing, in contrast to pleading in court, is not intended to entertain or to overwhelm the audience, but that the main aim of jurists' writing is the instruction of the reader on the content and the functioning of the law.[2] However, the construction of jurisprudence as *techne* or *ars* clearly depended on the teachings of rhetoric, also because the first technical literature (Fachliteratur) in the Latin language was that of rhetoric.[3] It is thus well known that the teaching of law was clearly structured according to rhetorical principles, which involved not only the organization and the presentation of legal thought, but also the juridical construction of definitions, divisions, and comparisons.[4]

For the relationship between law and philosophy, Mantovani has recently underlined the idea of "emprunts-transformation," literally "borrowing-transformation" already identified by Yan Thomas.[5] The term implies the idea that adapting philosophical teachings to legal writings transforms the meaning of

[1] In this I follow the very first critic of Johannes Stroux: Himmelschein, 'Studien zu der antiken Hermeneutica iuris' (1931) 392–393, who is often not considered, since Stroux's ideas of 1926 have principally been received via the re-publication in 1949, cf. Stroux, *Summum ius summa iniuria* (1926) = Stroux, *Römische Rechtswissenschaft* (1949).

[2] Mantovani, *Les juristes écrivains* (2018) 61.

[3] Mantovani, *Les juristes écrivains* (2018) 81 and 187.

[4] For a recent analysis of the *Institutes* of Gaius in this respect, cf. Battaglia, 'Strutture espositive in Gaio' (2020) 214–219.

[5] Mantovani, *Les juristes écrivains* (2018) 83; Thomas, 'L'institution juridique de la nature' (2011) 25: "…les juristes produisent une pensée autonome à partir de textes d'emprunt."

Ulrike Babusiaux, *Rhetoric in Legal Writing: The Ethos and Pathos of Roman Jurists* In: *Medicine and the Law under the Roman Empire.* Edited by: Claire Bubb and Michael Peachin, Oxford University Press. © Claire Bubb and Michael Peachin 2023. DOI: 10.1093/oso/9780192898616.003.0011

the philosophical concept for the sake of the legal argument. The role of philosophy is hence summarized as follows:[6]

> Philosophy helps the jurist to give a framework to problems, to name them, to put facts into categories, to make them manageable.... But the Roman jurists were not philosophers, neither in their outward attitude nor in their intellectual work. Their decisions were not built on philosophical dogmas, nor could they be, at the risk of betraying their mission. The use that jurists made of philosophy was mainly intended to transform facts into concepts, to reduce problems into such a form that they could be treated and decided according to legal values.

To my mind, one should ask if the same process of borrowing-transformation should not be used to describe and analyze the Roman jurists' use of rhetorical teachings and instructions for legal argumentation.

This hypothesis leads to two further limitations of the following sketch. The first involves the nature of the rhetorical argumentation examined; the second has to do with the timeframe that will be analyzed. As for the first concern, it is well known that rhetorical theory distinguishes three types of arguments: *logos*, *ethos*, and *pathos* according to Greek rhetorical writings from Aristotle onwards; *docere*, *delectare*, and *movere* are the equivalents in the Latin treatises on rhetoric, e.g., in Quintilian.[7] Whereas the use of *logos* or *docere* (logical and dialectical argumentation) has been accepted as a part of Roman legal reasoning since Schulz, the use of ethical and pathetic argumentation has been doubted to be adequate for juridical texts.[8] This seemed to contradict both the idea of "legal science" and the perception of the Roman jurists as prosaic and rather intuitive legal technicians.[9]

However, when reading the *Digest*, one can observe the use of ethical arguments, where the speaker (i.e., the legal writer) tries to show his *ethos*, i.e., his best manners, his sincere attitude, and his thorough understanding of the matter. Moreover, we even encounter pathetic argumentation in legal writings, i.e., the raising of lower emotions, such as hate, contempt, misery or pity. Very often,

[6] Mantovani, *Les juristes écrivains* (2018) 110, 128: "La philosophie aide le juriste à donner un cadre aux problems, à les nommer, à faire entrer les faits dans des categories, à les rendre maniables.... Mais les juristes romains n'étaient pas des philosophes, ni dans leur attitude extérieure, ni dans leur travail intellectuel. Leurs décisions n'étaient pas fondées sur des dogmes philosophiques, et elles ne pouvaient même pas l'être, au risque de trahir leur mission. L'usage que les juristes faisaient de la philosophie était principalement destiné à transformer les faits en concepts, à réduire les problèmes dans une forme telle qu'ils fussent susceptibles d'être traités et tranchés selon des valeurs juridiques."

[7] Arist. *Rh.* 1.2, 1356a2–4. Quint. *Inst.* 6.2.8 with discussion; cf. also Quint. *Inst.* 12.10.59.

[8] Schulz, *History of Roman Legal Science* (1946) esp. 62–69.

[9] On "legal science," see Pringsheim, 'Ius aequum und ius strictum' (1921); Albertario, 'La crisi del metodo interpolazionistico' (1930) 641–645; an overview of the background of these tendencies in Simon, 'Die animusbesessene Spätzeit' (1995). The consequences of the description of jurists as technicians are still visible in current scholarship, on which see Babusiaux, 'Les défauts de l'utilisation du "ius controversum"' (2020).

pathetic arguments are used rather selectively and, in any case, with subtlety and restraint. It is therefore necessary to analyze the context of the use and the legal background of the rhetorical device in question. To locate and present significant examples, a greater sample of texts for comparison is thus necessary. As Justinian's *Digest* mostly relies on Severan legal writing, it seems adequate to limit the present study to the analysis of the most influential jurists of this epoch, i.e., Ulpian, Paul, and Papinian.

II. Examples from Severan Legal Writing

The following texts are examples chosen to show the typical use of *ethos* and *pathos* in legal writing, which means that the logical and dialectic arguments are only touched upon as far as they are necessary for the understanding of the legal problem and the textual strategy. The *ethos*, the speaker's character, will be analyzed before turning to the use of ethical and pathetic amplification of cases. The last part deals with means of persuasion in the context of legal theory, i.e., discussions among legal experts about their legal concepts and argumentative techniques.

1. Self-Presentation of Jurists (*ethos*)

In his chapter on emotions (*affectus*), the imperial teacher of rhetoric Quintilian explains the speaker's *ethos* as follows:[10]

> ἦθος, *quod intellegimus quodque a dicentibus desideramus, id erit, quod ante omnia bonitate commendabitur, non solum mite ac placidum, sed plerumque blandum et humanum et audientibus amabile atque iucundum, in quo exprimendo summa virtus ea est, ut fluere omnia ex natura rerum hominumque videantur utque mores dicentis ex oratione perluceant et quodam modo agnoscantur.*
>
> The *ethos* which I mean, and which I want to see in a speaker, will be that, which is recommended primarily by goodness: not only mild and calm, but usually attractive and polite, and pleasing and delightful to the listeners. The great virtue in expressing lies in making it seem that everything flows from the nature of facts and the persons, so that the speaker's character shines through his speech and is somehow recognized. (trans. Russell)

[10] Quint. *Inst.* 6.2.13.

Thus, *ethos* is achieved if the speaker convinces the audience of his good character, his "ethics"; in the further course of his work, Quintilian stresses that the speaker will not bluntly proclaim this self-image, but will try to convey an ethical impression indirectly. For an orator in court, this means using the details of the case and the circumstances to present himself as an ethically flawless person.[11] Similarly, in legal writing, the jurist can use the presentation of his topic to portray himself as sincere. To show the manifold techniques of self-presentation and the differences in this regard between the three main Severan jurists, three examples will now be presented.

a. Establishing Common Ground with the Audience

A first example of self-presentation is provided in Ulpian's book *De censibus* ("on the census"). The monograph, presumably written under Caracalla, deals with the assessment of the poll tax and the property tax in the provinces.[12] In our transmission, the following fragment stands at the very beginning of Ulpian's exposition and explains the *ius Italicum*:[13]

> *Sciendum est esse quasdam colonias iuris Italici, ut est in Syria Phoenice splendidissima Tyriorum colonia, unde mihi origo est, nobilis regionibus, serie saeculorum antiquissima, armipotens, foederis quod cum Romanis percussit tenacissima: huic enim divus Severus et imperator noster ob egregiam in rem publicam imperiumque Romanum insignem fidem ius Italicum dedit.*
>
> One must realize that there are some colonies with *ius Italicum*, as, in Syria Phoenice, the most splendid colony of the Tyrians, which is my place of origin, outstanding in its territories, of very ancient foundation, powerful in war, always loyal to the treaty it made with the Romans. For the deified Severus and our emperor granted it *ius Italicum* because of its great and conspicuous faithfulness toward the Roman state and empire. (trans. Crawford, ap. Watson)

The text stresses the fact that *ius Italicum* does not depend on the geographical situation of the city. To prove his point, Ulpian gives the example of Tyre, a colony in Syria Phoenice, and mentions that this city is his place of origin (*origo*).[14] He narrates that it was the deified Septimius Severus who granted *ius Italicum* to the town because of its great and conspicuous faithfulness towards the Romans. Then follows a list of other cities, first from the same province and then from others, which had all received the benefit of the status of a colony with Italian rights. It is

[11] Cf. also Quint. *Inst.* 6.2.18–19.

[12] On the work, cf. Liebs, 'Domitius Ulpianius' (1997) 181.

[13] Ulpian (1 *de censibus*) D. 50.15.1pr., and Lenel, *Palingenesia iuris civilis II* (1889) nr. 19, col. 385; on the structure of Ulpian's book, cf. Watkins, '*Coloniae* and *Ius Italicum* in the Early Empire' (1983) 319.

[14] On the concept of *origo*, cf. Nörr, '*Origo*' (1963) esp. 569–571.

important to note that Tyre was a titular colony (though of non-citizens) with Italic right and hence—as Watkins has called it—a "bastard species violating more than five centuries of Roman practice."[15] Hence, it can be assumed that Septimius Severus' granting of *ius Italicum* to Tyre had been shocking for Ulpian's contemporaries.[16] As defender of the imperial decision, Ulpian finds himself in the situation labeled *genus admirabile*, i.e., a difficult position for the speaker, who has to overcome reservations among his audience.[17]

The first thing to say about this is that Ulpian, at the supposed time of writing (under Caracalla), is already one of, if not the leading jurist of the Empire; he has influence within the imperial council since—if we follow Honoré's chronology—he has by now published his extensive commentary on the praetorian edict.[18] Yet, Ulpian does not boast about his achievements; rather, he praises Tyre in highly laudatory terms, since he says that this city is "outstanding in its territories, of very ancient foundation, powerful in war, always loyal to the treaty it made with the Romans." This praise of the city corresponds to the indications given by Menander, a Greek rhetor of the third century, who distinguishes (a) the general praise of a city, (b) the praise of a city for its origin, (c) the praise of a city for its activities.[19] Ulpian's praise of Tyre for its origin (b) seems rather generic, since Menander advises to give praise for the founders or the legendary foundation of a city.[20] More similarities can be observed between Menander and Ulpian regarding the praise of the city for its achievements (c). In fact, Menander mentions that a city can be praised for courage, which in wartime means with respect to deeds in combat, and thus clearly corresponds to Ulpian's "powerful in war."[21] The second element of Ulpian's praise, loyalty to the treaty made with the Romans, can be subsumed under Menander's mention of "fair-dealing" (*dikaiopragia*), even if Menander explicitly mentions only the treatment of foreigners and fellow citizens.[22]

[15] Watkins, '*Coloniae* and *Ius Italicum* in the Early Empire' (1983) 321.

[16] Cf. Nollé, '*Colonia* und *Socia* der Römer' (1995) 357–360.

[17] Quint. *Inst.* 4.1.41; Cic. *Inv. rhet.* 1.15.20, on which see Bower, '*ΕΦΟΔΟΣ* and *insinuatio* in Greek and Latin Rhetoric' (1958) 224–230; Zinsmaier, 'insinuatio' (1998) 419.

[18] Honoré, *Ulpian* (2002) 190–191.

[19] General Praise: Men. Rhet. 346.26–351.19; further details in: Men. Rhet. 347.4–7, where a town's location is evaluated based on its situation "with respect to the heavens and seasons, or to terra firma or to the sea, or with regard to the territory in which it is situated, or as to the surrounding land and towns, or in consideration of its mountains or plains" (*ἢ πρὸς οὐρανὸν καὶ ὥρας, ἢ πρὸς ἤπειρον, ἢ πρὸς θάλατταν, ἢ πρὸς τὴν χώραν ἐν ᾗ κεῖται, ἢ πρὸς τὰς περιοίκους χώρας καὶ πόλεις, ἢ πρὸς ὄρη, ἢ πρὸς πεδία*). Origin: Men. Rhet. 353.4–359.15; cf. also Men. Rhet. 349.31–350.23. Activities: Men. Rhet. 359.16–367.8.

[20] Men. Rhet. 353.4–30.

[21] Men. Rhet. 364.20–23.

[22] This omission is due to the fact that for the rhetor, writing after the Constitutio Antoniniana, Roman law already applied within the *civitas*: Men. Rhet. 363.11–12, "but nowadays, the matter of local laws is irrelevant, since we all use in common the laws of the Romans" (*ἀλλὰ τὸ τῶν νόμων ἐν τοῖς νῦν χρόνοις ἄχρηστον· κατὰ γὰρ τοὺς κοινοὺς τῶν Ῥωμαίων νόμους πολιτευόμεθα*). On the loyalty to the treaty with the Romans, cf. Nörr, '*Origo*' (1963) 569.

The interesting aspect of this praise is that it reflects also on Ulpian as a writer, since he himself establishes the link between the city and his person by claiming Tyre as his hometown. The effect of this linking is double. On the one hand, he becomes an eye-witness of the extraordinary *ius Italicum* in Syria; on the other hand, he shares all the traits he previously attributed to the city, since—as also Menander says—cities are praised in accordance with the virtues applicable to individuals: courage, justice, moderation, and intelligence.[23] Hence, by praising Tyre as an ancient (experienced), courageous, and loyal city, Ulpian presents himself as endowed with the same virtues, i.e., as a writer with *ethos*. The strategy behind this (disguised) self-praise is clearly to smooth the audience's difficulties in accepting Septimius Severus' decision to create a new and hybrid type of colony. It is more delicate to object against somebody coming from such a colony and presenting such a high degree of credibility and strength of character. In this respect, one could say that Ulpian styles himself as a personification of the new kind of colony, so as to combat criticism and to move towards the actual treatment of the census. In this respect, the text is a very clear example of the technique of *insinuatio*, i.e., a subtle intrusion into the mind of the audience to convince it of the personal integrity of the speaker and the legitimacy of his topic. A similar strategy can be observed when jurists argue against an imperial decision.

b. Opposing an Unjust Decision

As seen above, *ethos* can be used as a tool to legitimate an uncommon or unpopular opinion, since the speaker puts his own ethical value in balance with the arguments of the opponent's side.[24] The ethical integrity of one's view is even more important to prove if the other side is a person of high authority, e.g., the emperor. It is interesting to read texts taken from Paul's *Libri decretorum* from this perspective. The *Libri decretorum vel imperialium sententiarum in cognitionibus prolatarum* are unique in the Roman legal writing, since they report the (otherwise secret) discussions among the members of the imperial council, and show the highly controversial and technical legal standard of these discussions.[25] The most important feature of Paul's work, however, is that the jurist rarely seems to agree with the emperor and often tries to present a dissenting opinion to the emperor's decision, e.g.:[26]

[23] Men. Rhet. 361.13–15: "now, as we have said, there are four essential virtues: courage, a sense of justice, sobriety, and prudence" (*οὐκοῦν ἀρεταὶ μέν, ὥσπερ ἔφαμεν, τέσσαρες· ἀνδρεία, δικαιοσύνη, σωφροσύνη, φρόνησις*). On eye-witnesses and *evidentia*, cf. below (pp. 260–264).

[24] Cf. Quint. *Inst.* 6.2.2, claiming that "oratory has no more important contribution to make than this" (trans. Russell) (*quoniam nihil adferre maius vis orandi potest*).

[25] On the peculiarities, cf. Daalder, *De rechtspraakverzamelingen van Julius Paulus* (2018) 9–187.

[26] Paul (3 *decretorum libri*) D. 29.2.97. On the text, cf. Daalder, *De rechtspraakverzamelingen van Julius Paulus* (2018) esp. 339–349; Babusiaux, 'Review of Daalder, De rechtspraakverzamelingen van Julius Paulus (2018)' (2021) 690–691.

> *Clodius Clodianus facto prius testamento postea eundem heredem in alio testamento inutiliter facto instituerat: scriptus heres cum posterius putaret valere, ex eo hereditatem adire voluit, sed postea hoc inutile repertum est. Papinianus putabat repudiasse eum ex priore hereditatem, ex posteriore autem non posse adire. dicebam non repudiare eum, qui putaret posterius valere. pronuntiavit Clodianum intestatum decessisse.*
>
> Clodius Clodianus, having made one will, had afterwards instituted the same person as heir in another will which was invalidly made; the appointed heir, when he thought that the later will was valid, wished to accept the inheritance under it, but afterwards this was found to be invalid. Papinian thought that he had repudiated the inheritance under the earlier one but could not accept under the later one. I held that he did not repudiate in that he thought that the later one was valid. He decided that Clodianus had died intestate. (trans. Gordon, ap. Watson)

The testator named Clodius Clodianus made two wills in both of which he instituted the same heir. A legal problem arose from the fact that the heir accepted the inheritance under the *second* will, which was later found to be invalid.[27] If the second will was invalid, the first will had never been revoked and could be enforced. However, taking over the inheritance under the second will could be interpreted in the sense that the heir had repudiated the appointment as heir in the first will. Paul tells us that Papinian actually took the view that the heir could not change his claim for the inheritance from the second to the first will, and that the emperor followed him by deciding that Clodius Clodianus had died intestate, which implies that he considered both wills as invalid.[28] Paul, however, states that the heir who did not know that the first will was still valid, had no intention to repudiate it: *dicebam non repudiare eum, qui putaret posterius valere* ("I held that he did not repudiate in that he thought that the later one was valid"). He would therefore consider that the repudiation was ineffective, and hence allow the heir to accept the inheritance on the grounds of the first will.

The value of Paul's argument has been debated in scholarship. Looking at Paul's arguments from a rhetorical perspective, one can argue that Paul's self-representation serves to defend a more equitable solution of the case. Equity is central for the *status qualitatis*, which deals with the qualification of the facts according to the law.[29] This implies, *inter alia*, the application of written, positive law and unwritten law, which is natural law, or *aequitas*, to the facts in question.

[27] On *revocatio testamenti* cf. Babusiaux, 'Coordination of Different Layers of Law in the Roman Empire and in the European Union' (2019) esp. 146–159.

[28] It must be noted that the will is equally considered invalid if the heir does not accept the inheritance. Hence, the first will had been repudiated, the second one was invalid.

[29] On *status qualitatis* and legal reasoning, cf. Horak, 'Die rhetorische Statuslehre und der moderne Aufbau des Verbrechensbegriffs' (1972).

It is important to note that both types of sources can be linked to equity. Natural law, on the one hand, derives from the virtues, e.g., *pietas* (piety), *fides* (good faith), *continentia* (temperance) (Quint. *Inst.* 7.4.5), and is from its origin in line with moral values; positive law, on the other hand, can at least partly correspond to natural law, and hence be consistent with equity.[30] More frequently, however, there will be a certain tension between the precepts of natural law and statutes (*leges*), mores (*mos*), customs (*consuetudo*), or judicial decisions (*iudicatum*).[31] This tension is also visible in Clodius Clodianus' case, since the traditional civil law (*ius civile*) clearly states that the repudiation of an inheritance cannot be revoked, which is exactly why the emperor and Papinian reached the result that the heir could not change his mind.

Paul does not challenge the existing law but relies upon an element of the case by stating that the heir did not repudiate the first will, since he thought that the will had been voided by the later one. Dogmatically speaking, the jurist claims that there was no intention to reject the first will. Thus, Paul does not contest the law itself, but the conditions of its application, and more precisely, the establishment of the facts. This argument belongs to the rhetorical category of *status coniecturae,* conjecture (*an fecerit* = "whether he did it"), which covers all obscure elements that cannot be proven by visual inspection, and thus, the suggestions of the mindset, such as the heir's intention in the present case.[32] At the same time, this argument is related to equity, in the sense that the "reality check" proper to the *status qualitatis* sets the facts against the existing law to obtain a fair-minded solution for the case in question.[33]

If this is correct, then Paul here reproaches the emperor (and Papinian) for having forgotten the circumstances of the case. By showing that he (Paul)—in contrast to Papinian—carefully considered the heir's intention, the jurist suggests a fairer solution—one that the emperor should have considered, or should consider for the future.[34] Thus, Paul is not only correcting Papinian, but also trying to convince the emperor of his (Paul's) better legal advice, i.e., of his personal integrity.

Despite Paul's efforts in this case, it is Papinian, not Paul, who even in modern scholarship is still widely considered to be the most concerned, of all the Roman jurists, with equity. Not only late antique and medieval writers praise him as the

[30] Cf. Babusiaux, '§ 6 Rechtsschichten' (2023) nr. 186–187 and 198.

[31] Cf. Babusiaux, '§ 6 Rechtsschichten' (2023) nr. 217–218.

[32] Quint. *Inst.* 7.2.1: *coniectura omnis aut de re aut de animo est* ("all conjecture involves either the matter at hand or the mindset"), on which see Lausberg, *Handbuch der literarischen Rhetorik* (1990) § 151. Quint. *Inst.* 7.2.4: . . . *ea vero, quae sunt praesentis temporis . . . oculis deprehendenda sunt, non egent coniectura* ("such things, indeed, as are of the present moment, if they are to be comprehended visually, require no guesswork"). For *Animi coniectura*, cf. Quint. *Inst.* 7.2.6.

[33] On *status qualitatis*, cf. Babusiaux, '§ 6 Rechtsschichten' (2023) nr. 205–218 with further references.

[34] Daalder underlines the important position of Clodius Clodianus within the imperial administration; one could suggest that his achievements were also a valid argument to show indulgence.

most "Christian" and "most equitable" of all Roman jurists.[35] Even current-day researchers think of Papinian as a particularly ethical person.[36]

c. Proving the Speaker's Integrity

Papinian's image is mainly due to his efficient use of ethical arguments, which not only demonstrate the equity of his legal opinions, but also sell the jurist's own integrity to the audience. A particularly telling example of his technique is the following well-known fragment:[37]

> *Filius, qui fuit in potestate, sub condicione scriptus heres, quam senatus aut princeps improbant, testamentum infirmet patris, ac si condicio non esset in eius potestate: nam quae facta laedunt pietatem existimationem verecundiam nostram et, ut generaliter dixerim, contra bonos mores fiunt, nec facere nos posse credendum est.*
>
> A son who was in parental power, appointed heir under a condition which the senate or the emperor disapproves, may upset his father's will, as if the condition were one not in his power [to fulfill]. For any acts which offend our sense of duty, our reputation, or our sense of shame, and, if I might speak generally, which are done against sound morals, it is not to be accepted that we are even able to do. (trans. Gordon, ap. Watson)

If we put Papinian's emphatic narrative in simpler terms, the facts are the following. In his will, a father appointed his son in power as heir. The appointment was under a condition, which violated imperial law (*senatus consulta, constitutiones principis*). According to the established legal opinion of his time, this would be without consequence for the father's will, since illegal and immoral conditions would be considered as "unwritten" and be set aside.[38] The will could thus be enforced.[39] Against this established view, Papinian states that asking the son to fulfill a condition that is against the pronounced intention of the senate or the prince means charging the son with something impossible. Thus, the son had no choice about fulfilling the condition, which leads Papinian to the conclusion that the whole will was invalid and that the father died intestate.

Before turning to the rhetorical side of Papinian's argument, let us take a brief look at the legal implications. First, it is important to note that the son instituted as

[35] On the praise of Papinian in late antique sources, cf. Babusiaux, 'Papinian's Late Antique Reception and His Myth' (forthcoming).

[36] Manthe, 'Ethische Argumente im Werk Papinians' (2005).

[37] Papinian (16 *quaestionum libri*) D. 28.7.15.

[38] Cf. Paul (45 *ad edictum*) D. 28.7.9; cf. also: Marcian (4 *institutionum*) D. 28.7.14.

[39] The same holds true for impossible conditions, cf. Ulpian (5 *ad Sabinum*) D. 28.7.1: *sub impossibili condicione vel alio mendo factam institutionem placet non vitiari* ("It is established that an appointment made under an impossible condition or through some other mistake, is not void/invalid", trans. Gordon, ap. Watson).

heir is still in power, and that this reduces the father's discretion in his will. In fact, a son in power can either be instituted or be disinherited; if the father passes him over (*praeterire*), the testament will be completely void. These principles determine also the validity of conditions, when appointing the son in power as heir: whereas, for other heirs, the testator is free to set all kinds of conditions, only potestative conditions can be used for the appointment of the son in power.[40] The reason behind this is that conditions bring about an element of uncertainty that—if the uncertain event was out of the hands of the son—would amount to a passing over (*praeterire*) leading to the invalidity of the father's will.[41] Hence, only conditions whose fulfillment is in the son's power are allowed, since they leave the fate of the institution as heir (or the disinheritance) in the son's hands. Against this background, Papinian's solution is brief, but precise: *testamentum infirmet patris, ac si condicio non esset in eius potestate* ("this may upset his father's will, as if the condition were one not in his power"). Thus, the father's will becomes invalid, as if the condition (set for the appointment of the son as heir) had not been a potestative condition.

In other words, Papinian considers that despite the theoretical possibility of choosing to do something in contravention of the wish or command of the senate or the prince, the son would in fact have to refrain from fulfilling any such condition. This argument is in principle not extraordinary, as we learn from other sources that the potestative nature of a condition should be considered in every single case, and with regard to the facts at hand.[42] The difference between the other jurists and Papinian lies in the consequences they attribute to the impossible condition. Whereas Ulpian's pupil Marcianus states that an impossible or an immoral condition should simply be set aside, and hence make the institution as heir unconditional, Papinian argues for the invalidity of the father's will.[43]

[40] Ulpian (4 *ad Sabinum*) D. 28.5.4pr.: *suus quoque heres sub condicione heres potest institui: sed excipiendus est filius, quia non sub omni condicione institui potest. et quidem sub ea condicione, quae est in potestate ipsius, potest: de hoc enim inter omnes constat* ("A *suus heres* also can be named as heir under a condition; however, a son must be considered separately, since he cannot be instituted under every sort of condition. Still, a son can be instituted under such a condition as it is in his power to carry out. In this regard there is general agreement", trans. Gordon, ap. Watson); cf. further Tryphoninus (20 *disputationum libri*) D. 28.2.28; Papinian (13 *quaestionum libri*) D. 28.7.28.

[41] The best analysis of this question is still Meinhart, 'Die bedingte Erbeinsetzung des Haussohnes' (1973).

[42] Similarly, Ulpian cites the example that the condition "if he comes to Alexandria" could be within the heir's power, if he is not far away from the city. The same condition can be impossible and thus out of his power, if he lives in another part of the Empire; cf. Ulpian (4 *ad Sabinum*) D. 28.5.4.1: *puto recte generaliter definiri: utrum in potestate fuerit condicio an non fuerit, facti potestas est: potest enim et haec "si Alexandriam pervenerit" non esse in arbitrio per hiemis condicionem: potest et esse, si ei, qui a primo miliario Alexandriae agit, fuit imposita* ("I think that this general definition is correct: whether the condition was in his power to fulfill, or not, is ruled over by fact. Indeed, the condition 'if he shall have come to Alexandria' might not be his to decide on account of winter weather. On the other hand, this could be in his power, if the condition were imposed on a person who was lingering at the first milestone from Alexandria", trans. Gordon, ap. Watson).

[43] Ulpian (*50 ad edictum*) D. 28.7.8pr.; Paul (*45 ad edictum*) D. 28.7.9; Marcian (4 *institutionum libri*) D. 28.7.14. Neither Ulpian nor Paul or Marcian clearly refer to the case of the son in power, but to general appointment of heirs (where any condition is allowed). In this respect, one should consider their argument for the removal of the condition: their intention is to grant the heir that has been

The argument used by Papinian to justify his view of the condition in question is explicitly based on equity. In fact, he explains that "any acts which offend our sense of duty, our reputation, or our sense of shame, . . . and which are done against sound morals" must be treated as if they were impossible acts. In other words, the jurist refuses to ask the son to fulfill a condition which would amount to a transgression of the legislator's intentions and to go against the commonly accepted welfare.

This argument justifies the invalidity of the father's will, which is a morally harsh sanction, since dying intestate is a social shame.[44] As jurists normally argue in favor of the validitiy of the will, Papinian has to demonstrate that his opposing view is not only legally but also morally defendable.[45] Appealing to the good manners (*boni mores*) of the Roman people is an effective way to find an argumentative basis.[46] In fact, Quintilian explains that proof of uncertain matters needs to be founded on certain matters, for which he cites objects that can be seen, generally accepted precepts such as "there are Gods" and "parents deserve piety," and finally laws and morals or customs (*mores*).[47] Considering Quintilian's statement, one could say that Papinian bases his argumentation on laws and morals that he considers to be applicable to all.

appointed under an illegal or immoral condition as heir anyway. For the son in power, the situation might be different, as he will be the natural heir according to the rules of intestacy and being the legitimate heir implies that he has not to fulfill the legacies and other charges of the testament. Besides, one could argue that the impossible condition might lead to uncertainty and thus to the forbidden *praeterire* of the son. Thus, a rescript of Alexander Severus from the year 224 states that the father who institutes his son in power as heir under a condition that was not in his power, and did not disinherit the son for some deficiency, had not made a valid will; cf. Alex. C. 6.25.4 (a. 224): *si pater filium quem in potestate habebat sub condicione, quae in ipsius potestate non erat, heredem scripsit nec in defectum eius exheredavit, iure testatus non videtur* ("If a father designated as heir a son whom he had in his power under a condition his son was unable to fulfill, and he did not disinherit him for a fault, he is not deemed to have made a valid will", trans. Frier et al., ap. Frier).

[44] On the social dimension of testamentary law, see Champlin, *Final Judgments* (1991) esp. 41–81.

[45] On *favor testamenti*, cf. Wieling, *Testamentsauslegung im römischen Recht* (1972) 115–118.

[46] In this part, Quintilian deals with artificial proofs; cf. Quint. *Inst.* 5.10.11: *nam probatio et fides efficitur non tantum per haec, quae sunt rationis, sed etiam per inartificialia . . . ergo, cum sit argumentum ratio probationem praestans, qua colligitur aliquid per aliud, et quae quod est dubium per id, quod dubium non est, confirmat, necesse est esse aliquid in causa, quod probatione non egeat* ("For proof and *fides* are effected not only by these rational means, but by non-technical ones also. . . . Therefore, since argument is proof-giving reasoning, by which one thing is inferred from another, and which confirms what is doubtful by means of what is not doubtful, there must be something in the cause which does not need proof," trans. Russell).

[47] On the precepts: Quint. *Inst.* 5.10.12: *alioqui nihil erit quo probemus, nisi fuerit quod aut sit verum aut videatur, ex quo dubiis fides fiat. pro certis autem habemus primum quae sensibus percipiuntur . . . deinde ea, in quae communi opinione consensum est, 'deos esse, praestandam pietatem parentibus'* ("For unless there is something which either is or seems to be true, and from which assurance may be given to what is doubtful, there will be nothing by which we can prove anything. Now we regard as certain things perceived by the senses, . . . then things about which common opinion is unanimous: the existence of the gods, the duty of respecting parents," trans. Russell). On laws, morals, and customs: Quint. *Inst.* 5.10.13: *praeterea, quae legibus cauta sunt, quae persuasione etiam si non omnium hominum, eius tamen civitatis aut gentis, in qua res agitur, in mores recepta sunt, ut pleraque in iure non legibus, sed moribus constant* ("furthermore, provisions of laws, what has been accepted as moral custom, if not in the belief of all mankind, at least in that of the city or nation where the case is being pleaded many matters of right, for example, involve custom rather than laws," trans. Russell).

This amplification of his legal argumentation also sheds a good light on him as a jurist. Stating that we cannot do what is not allowed, the jurist presents himself as a true moralist and highly ethical man. Thus, the audience is encouraged to follow his lead and to accept that the illegality of the condition means in this case that the father's will is void.

d. Conclusion

All three chosen Severan jurists provide evidence of self-presentation within their legal writing. As shown in three typical examples, looking at the devices of self-presentation in legal writing helps to get a deeper understanding of the texts. They can be read as proof for the solution of intricate legal problems, but they are also windows onto the self-representation of imperial legal counsellors, who had to sell their legal opinions to the emperor.[48] In my opinion, these two readings must be seen in conjunction with each other: persuasion, which is clearly an intention of legal writing, is not only based on technical arguments, but also on the personal authority of the jurist. One most important element of this authority stems from the speaker's *ethos*, the exemplary character visible also in speech and writing.

2. Prevailing in Controversies on Cases

It is generally acknowledged that Roman legal writing is full of legal controversies (*ius controversum*), and that in these constellations the Roman jurists fight with every means of persuasion to make their case and to assert their opinion.[49] This typically involves the ethical and pathetic amplification of the circumstances of the case. It is important to remember that the difference between *ethos* and *pathos* does not lie in their stylistic presentation, but in the emotions stirred in the audience. Taking over a simplification by Quintilian, one could say that *ethos* is linked to the positive emotions (and comedy), whereas *pathos* implies negative feelings (and is nearer to tragedy).[50] With regard to a legal case, rhetorically speaking a *narratio*, emotions can be caused through the exemplification and the envisioning produced by the orator, a means that is called *enargeia* in Greek or *evidentia* in Latin:[51]

[48] On the role of *auctoritas* (authority), cf. Mantovani, 'Iuris Scientia et Honores' (1997); Peachin, 'Exemplary Government in the Early Roman Empire' (2007).

[49] On *ius controversum*, cf. Bretone, 'Ius controversum' (2008) 750–852; Babusiaux, 'Les défauts de l'utilisation du "ius controversum"' (2020).

[50] Cf. Quint. *Inst.* 6.2.20.

[51] Quint. *Inst.* 6.2.29–32. On the qualification of cases as *narratio*, cf. Babusiaux, 'Legal Writing and Legal Reasoning' (2016) 177–178. On *evidentia*, cf. Calboli Montefusco, '*Ενάργεια* et *ἐνέργεια*' (2005) 43–58.

29 *At quo modo fiet, ut adficiamur? neque enim sunt motus in nostra potestate. temptabo etiam de hoc dicere. quas* φαντασίας *Graeci vocant (nos sane visiones appellemus), per quas imagines rerum absentium ita repraesentantur animo, ut eas cernere oculis ac praesentes habere videamur. . . .*

31 *Occisum queror: non omnia, quae in re praesenti accidisse credibile est, in oculis habebo? non percussor ille subitus erumpet? non expavescet circumventus, exclamabit vel rogabit vel fugiet? non ferientem, non concidentem videbo? non animo sanguis et pallor et gemitus, extremus denique expirantis hiatus insidet?*

32 *Insequitur* ἐνάργεια, *quae a Cicerone inlustratio et evidentia nominatur, quae non tam dicere videtur quam ostendere, et adfectus non aliter, quam si rebus ipsis intersimus, sequentur. an non ex his visionibus illa sunt: "excussi manibus radii revolutaque pensa"—"levique patens in pectore vulnus"—equus ille in funere Pallantis "positis insignibus"?*

29 But how can we come to be moved? Emotions, after all, are not in our own power. Well, I will try to explain this too. The person who will show the greatest power in the expression of emotions will be the person who has properly formed what the Greeks call *phantasiai* (let us call them "visions") by which the images of absent things are presented to the mind in such a way that we seem actually to see them with our eyes and have them physically present to us.

31 Suppose I am complaining that someone has been murdered. Am I not to have before my eyes all the circumstances which one can believe to have happened during the event? Will not the assassin burst out on a sudden, and the victim tremble, cry for help, and either plead for mercy or try to escape? Shall I not see one man striking the blow and the other man falling? Will not the blood, the pallor, the groans, the last gasp of the dying be imprinted on my mind?

32 The result will be *enargeia*, what Cicero calls illustration and *evidentia*, a quality, which makes us seem not so much to be talking about something as exhibiting it. Emotions will ensue just as if we were present at the event itself. It is not from such "visions" that we get: "The shuttle flew from her hand, the thread unravelled", and "On the smooth breast, the gaping wound", and the horse at Pallas' funeral "his trappings laid aside"? (trans. Russell)

Quintilian thus explains how to use the human imagination to create vivid pictures in the audience's mind, not only by talking about the fact in question, but also by exhibiting it (*evidentia*). The techniques mentioned by Quintilian involve the presentation of the accompanying facts, drawing the scene in detail, or evoking the reaction of bystanders. Again, due to its close connection to the content, the rhetorical device of *evidentia* can only be understood and analyzed within the context of a text. Then, among our three Severan jurists, and depending on the intention of the individual work, differences as to scale and intensity of this envisioning can be observed.

a. Ethical Amplification

One striking example is a case that is related by Papinian which was decided by the highest court for the city of Rome in the Severan time, the praetorian prefects:[52]

> *Cum Pollidius a propinqua sua heres institutus rogatus fuisset filiae mulieris quidquid ex bonis eius ad se pervenisset, cum certam aetatem puella complesset, restituere, idque sibi mater ideo placuisse testamento comprehendisset, ne filiae tutoribus, sed potius necessitudini res committerentur, eundemque Pollidium fundum retinere iussisset: praefectis praetorii suasi fructus, qui bona fide a Pollidio ex bonis defunctae percepti essent, restitui debere, sive quod fundum ei tantum praelegaverat sive quod lubrico tutelae fideicommissi remedium mater praetulerat.*
>
> Pollidius was made heir by a woman relative and asked to restore to the woman's daughter at a certain age whatever he obtained from the estate. The mother explained in her will that she did this in order to entrust her daughter's affairs to relatives rather than to tutors. She provided that Pollidius should retain certain land. I gave advice to the praetorian prefects that the fruits taken by Pollidius in good faith from the estate of the deceased should be handed over, either because only the land was prelegated to him or because the mother had chosen the remedy of *fideicommissum* to avoid the dangers of tutelage. (trans. Honoré, ap. Watson)

A certain Pollidius had been named heir by a woman who had asked him to restore everything he had obtained from her estate to her daughter, once the daughter should have reached a certain age. The mother had explained that she chose this *fideicommissum* in favor of her daughter because she did not want to trust the estate to tutors. In exchange for the restitution to the daughter, Pollidius had been given a preferential legacy (*praelegatum*) of a certain plot of land.[53] The question to be decided by the praetorian prefects was whether the heir (Pollidius) had also to restore the fruits of the plot of land to the daughter, or whether the legacy to him included the taking of the fruits. Papinian relates that he advised the praetorian prefects (*suasi*) to decide that Pollidius should restore the fruits of the land bestowed to him to the daughter. Papinian's arguments were that the preferential legacy only referred to the property of the land (not the advantages of its use before the transfer of the estate to the daughter) and that the mother's intention, when ordering the *fideicommissum*, had been to protect the daughter against the dangers of tutelage.

[52] Papinian (20 *quaestionum libri*) D. 22.1.3.3. On the social status of the praetorian prefects, cf. Mennen, 'Praetorian Prefects' Power and Senatorial Status in the Third Century' (2012).

[53] On the questions of *praelegatum*, cf. Wimmer, *Das Prälegat* (2004) esp. 190–231.

These arguments are legally completely valid: the preferential legacy applies, once the estate has been handed over to the daughter; in fact, *fundum retinere* ("to retain the plot of land") means that he can keep the ground, when restoring the estate. This formulation also implies that the land is part of the estate until then and, thus, falls under the *fideicommissum* in favour of the daughter. Moreover, the argument that the mother wanted to protect the daughter shows that Pollidius is a true fiduciary heir, who does not get the estate for his own sake, but out of altruistic motives for the beneficiary of the trust.[54]

However, and as has been discussed in legal scholarship for centuries, the proposed solution is new and contrasts with other legal advice given by Papinian himself.[55] Thus, one can argue that the exceptional grant of the fruits to the trustee (the daughter) is a consequence of the special circumstances of the case, namely, the mother's desperate attempt to ensure that the daughter gets the most complete enjoyment of the estate. Yet, the *evidentia* used by Papinian goes beyond this obvious appeal to elements of equity (protection of the weak; reliance on the trustworthiness of the heir).[56] In fact, despite the brevity of the description, some details of the case can be fleshed out. First, not only is the mother's will mentioned, but her deeper motivation is thoroughly explained; second, the name of one protagonist, Pollidius, is repeated several times; thirdly, Papinian alludes to the procedural situation by mentioning the praetorian prefects, which seems to imply an appellate procedure.[57] In contrast to this, some other facts remain strangely indistinct. Both mother's and daughter's names are left out. There is no information about the initial court decision or the identity of the appellant (Pollidius or the daughter?); and—most importantly—instead of relating the praetorian prefects' decision, Papinian swiftly states: "I gave the advice to the praetorian prefects that the fruits taken by Pollidius in good faith from the estate of the deceased should be handed over."[58] With this wording, he stresses his doing,

[54] On the *heres fideicommissarius* (*minister*) in the strict sense, cf. Coppola Bisazza, 'Osservazioni sul regime dei frutti nel fedecommesso de residuo' (1982) 212; in this sense also Babusiaux, 'D. 36.1.48 Iavolenus 11 epistularum' (2018); differently: Desanti, 'Di nuovo sul regime dei frutti nel fedecommesso de residuo e sul presunto contrasto tra D. 22.1.3.2 (Pap. 20 quaest.) e D. 36.1.60 (58).7 (Pap. 9 resp.)' (1999) 94.

[55] For further references, cf. Coppola Bisazza, 'Osservazioni sul regime dei frutti nel fedecommesso de residuo' (1982); Desanti, 'Di nuovo sul regime dei frutti nel fedecommesso de residuo e sul presunto contrasto tra D. 22.1.3.2 (Pap. 20 quaest.) e D. 36.1.60 (58).7 (Pap. 9 resp.)' (1999).

[56] On the typical elements of equity, cf. the overview in Stagl, 'Die Ausgleichung von Vorteil und Nachteil als Inhalt klassischer aequitas' (2007).

[57] On the competence of the praetorian prefect for appellate procedures in the third century, cf. Kaser and Hackl, *Römisches Zivilprozessrecht* (1996) § 75.I, 504; § 69.III.3, 464.

[58] *praefectis praetorii suasi fructus, qui bona fide a Pollidio ex bonis defunctae percepti essent, restitui debere*; a comparable formulation is used in Julian (42 *digestorum*) D. 40.2.5:... *exemplum eius secutus et in praetura et consulato meo quosdam ex servis meis vindicta liberavi et quibusdam praetoribus consulentibus me idem suasi* ("... I followed his example in my own praetorship and consulship and freed some of my own slaves *vindicta* and persuaded some of the praetors who asked my advice to do the same," trans. Brunt, ap. Watson).

the deliberation within the council of the praetorian prefects, but leaves aside the precise outcome of the case.

This seemingly arbitrary presentation of the case can be seen as a strategy to underline the practical wisdom (*φρόνησις* or *prudentia*) of the adviser, and to stress the justice of the decision taken.[59] In fact, practical wisdom is defined as "a virtue of reason, which enables men to deliberate well in regard to the good and evil things (. . .)."[60] Within the theory of virtues, *prudentia* is of the highest rank, since it allows one to reach morally sound goals.[61] A decision based on *prudentia* is thus a decision based on the practical implications of the case and its justification is not only rational. Rather, the audience must adopt the moral attitude of the speaker to grasp the foundation and the implications of the decision. The case description itself is designed to incite the audience to follow the speaker's moral example. Even more impressive than such ethical amplification, however, is the use of pathetic embellishment to convey the speaker's intention, i.e., the legal solution of the case.

b. Pathetic Embellishment

The following example stems from Ulpian's commentary on the praetorian edict on theft (*furtum*). Under Roman law, theft is a private delict, not a criminal offence, which implies that it is up to the aggrieved party to file a suit for theft (*actio furti*). The private nature of the delict might also explain the tendency to extend the notion of theft to detrimental financial transactions. Indeed, a great part of Ulpian's commentary deals with the application of the claim to cases of indirect "stealing." In this respect, the jurist addresses the recurrent problem, whether the *actio furti* may apply to "stealing" through a third party's involvement, or by simple non-disclosure of information.[62] Among all these cases of "high finance," the following case description seems completely out of the ordinary:[63]

> *Si quis asinum meum coegisset et in equas suas τῆς γονῆς dumtaxat χάριν admisisset, furti non tenetur, nisi furandi quoque animum habuit. quod et Herennio Modestino studioso meo de Dalmatia consulenti rescripsi circa equos, quibus eiusdem rei gratia subiecisse quis equas suas proponebatur, furti ita demum teneri, si furandi animo id fecisset, si minus, in factum agendum.*

[59] On the differences between both terms, cf. Aubert-Baillot, 'De la *φρόνησις* à la "prudentia"' (2015).

[60] Arist. *Rh.* 1.9, 1366b20–22 (trans. Freese, revised by Striker).

[61] Rapp, *Aristoteles Rhetorik. Kommentar* (2002) 410 with regard to the distinction between such practical wisdom and cunning (*panourgia*).

[62] Pal. 1042 = Ulpian (37 *ad edictum*) D. 47.2.52.7–24.

[63] Ulpian (37 *ad edictum*) D. 47.2.52.20. On the changing concept of *furtum*, cf. Pennitz, '§ 93 Diebstahlsklage (*actio furti*)' (2023) nr. 12–13 with further references.

> If someone drove off my male ass and set him loose among his own mares to impregnate them, he will not be guilty of theft unless he has a theftuous intent. I gave this reply to my pupil, Herennius Modestinus, who consulted me from Dalmatia concerning horses to which a man was alleged to have submitted his mares for the same purpose that he would be liable for theft if he had guilty intent, otherwise an *actio in factum* would lie. (trans. Thomas, ap. Watson)

Ulpian reports a request from his student Modestinus from Dalmatia. It concerns the removal of a donkey so as to mate the animal with the taker's own mares. Ulpian holds that the owner of the mares will only be held liable for theft if he acted with theftuous intent on the taking of the jackass.

The fact that the theft of the animal's seed is dressed up chastely with Greek words has led scholarship to attribute the wording of the case to Justinian's compilers.[64] Moreover, the seemingly absurd question whether taking away the seed of donkeys and horses could be called "theft," has been considered as unworthy of the attention of an imperial counsellor like Ulpian.[65] Even though the text is nowadays accepted as genuine, the riddle remains as to why Ulpian would cite a case from Dalmatia on agricultural problems within his legal commentary. Rhetorically speaking, however, Ulpian's presentation constitutes an application of *rusticitas*, rusticity, i.e., the deliberate referral to non-urban lifestyle.[66] This stylistic device is well known from non-legal writing, where demonstrating the rural or provincial world to the Roman elite was a way to remind them of simplicity and the humble life.[67] Depending on the context, the device stirs emotions of *pathos*, i.e., either shame (for the reader's own luxurious or unnatural lifestyle) or pity (for the poor uneducated people outside Rome).

The function of *rusticitas* in Ulpian's commentary emerges from the consequences that the Dalmatian case has for the definition of theft. In fact, Ulpian's reply to Modestinus conveys the clear message that a theft may be committed without direct interference of the wrongdoer—all the man did was to create the opportunity for the mares and the donkey to make physical contact.[68] Ulpian's capacious interpretation of theft contrasts with a traditional description that the jurist has cited in the foregoing parts of his commentary, summarizing the view of the republican jurist Mela: "No one commits theft by word or writing; our rule is

[64] I have argued elsewhere that the use of Greek words is authentic and a chaste way of presenting the breeding of the animals, cf. Babusiaux, 'Der Kommentar als Haupttext' (2014) 51–53.

[65] An overview of the former discussion in Watson, 'D. 47.2.52.20. The Jackass, the Mares and "furtum"' (1971); Guarino, 'Tra asini e cavalle' (1974) with further references.

[66] This imitation of *mores* can also be seen as *ethos* in a larger sense, cf. Quint. *Inst.* 6.2.17.

[67] On the different functions of *rusticitas* cf. Zinsmaier, 'rusticitas' (2007).

[68] Furthermore, the case shows that there may be theft without actual loss on the side of the victim, since there is no sign that the owner of the donkey or horse has suffered any damage.

that there can be no theft without wrongful physical interference (*contrectatio*)."[69] Mela held, in fact, that if a pledge had been taken away from a partnership (*societas*), only the partner who had the pledge in hand could sue for theft, but not the other, who had been without any physical contact with the stolen object.[70] Ulpian challenges this traditional view because, in his case, the stealing is committed without any physical contact on behalf of either the victim or the wrongdoer.

From this perspective, shifting the discussion to a case from the rural world can be interpreted as a clear rhetorical strategy. As Ulpian is arguing against the ancestral definition of the delict, he needs to prove that his new concept of theft is not an overly sophisticated and complicated idea of an elitist jurist distanced from reality, but rather offers a very down-to-earth approach to a quasi-natural problem. The down-to-earth character of the concept is indicated, first, by the fact that it is presented as a real case reported by his pupil Modestinus, who serves as an eyewitness; second, by the implantation in an agricultural setting (i.e., man's natural environment; humble life); and third, by the fact that the conflict arises out of procreation, i.e., a natural event without artifice.[71] With all these elements, Ulpian intends to show the sound sense of the concept and to insinuate its appropriateness. In other words, Ulpian's commentary uses *rusticitas* ("morals" per Quintilian) to disguise the innovative character of his interpretation and to gain acceptance for his thesis.[72] This reading of the text is supported by the fact that the following passage of his commentary turns back to stealing in financial affairs, for which Ulpian stresses the importance of the wrongdoer's larcenous intention, i.e., one main lesson to be taken from the Dalmatian case.[73]

Both examples for *evidentia* have shown that ethical and pathetic amplification cannot always be clearly distinguished. One might feel pity for the mother in the Pollidius case (2.a) and one might also be impressed by Ulpian's personal integrity in the Dalmatian case (2.b). An even stronger connection between *ethos* and *pathos* can be observed in a text from Papinian's *Quaestiones*.

[69] Ulpian (37 *ad edictum*) D. 47.2.52.19: *neque verbo neque scriptura quis furtum facit: hoc enim iure utimur, ut furtum sine contrectatione non fiat* ("No one commits theft by word or writing; our rule is that there can be no theft without wrongful physical interference," trans. Thomas, ap. Watson).

[70] Ulpian (37 *ad edictum*) D. 47.2.52.18: *si ex duobus sociis omnium bonorum unus rem pignori acceperit eaque subrepta sit, Mela scripsit eum solum furti habere actionem, qui pignori accepit, socium non habere* ("If there be two partners in a partnership of all assets and one receive a pledge, which is then stolen, Mela says that only the recipient, not the other partner, has the action for theft," trans. Thomas, ap. Watson).

[71] On the eye-witness as a clear sign of *evidentia*, cf. Quint. *Inst.* 6.2.32.

[72] Quint. *Inst.* 6.2.17.

[73] Ulpian (37 *ad edictum*) D. 47.2.52.21: *cum Titio honesto viro pecuniam credere vellem, subiecisti mihi alium Titium egenum, quasi ille esset locuples, et nummos acceptos cum eo divisisti: furti tenearis, quasi ope tua consilioque furtum factum sit: sed et Titius furti tenebitur* ("I wish to lend money to a respectable Titius and you present to me a penniless Titius, as if he were opulent, and then share the money with him; you will be liable for theft since theft is committed through your advice and assistance; Titius will also be liable for theft," trans. Thomas, ap. Watson).

c. Combining Ethical and Pathetic Argumentation

In the next example, the moral coloring of the facts stirs pathetic emotions within the audience, showing that the ethical representation of one side can lead to emotions of *pathos* towards the other side:[74]

> pr. *Cum tale legatum esset relictum Titiae "si a liberis non discesserit," negaverunt eam recte cavere, quia vel mortuis liberis legati condicio possit exsistere. sed displicuit sententia: non enim voto matris opponi tam ominosa non interponendae cautionis interpretatio debuit.* 1. *et cum patronus liberto certam pecuniam legasset, si a liberis eius non discessisset, permisit imperator velut Mucianam cautionem offerri: fuit enim periculosum ac triste libertum coniunctum patroni liberis eorundem mortem exspectare.*
>
> pr. Take the case of a legacy to Titia, formulated with the condition, "if she does not leave her children." Some jurists have argued that she could not legally provide a security, since the condition of the legacy could exist even after the death of the children. That view, however, did not commend itself; for so direful an interpretation of the illegality of her putting up a security should not have been set against the mother's wish. 1. For even when a patron left a sum of money to his freedman as a legacy, on the condition that the freedman not desert the patron's children, the emperor allowed that freedman to offer a sort of *cautio Muciana*; for it was both dangerous and sad that a freedman, who was so closely attached to the children of his patron, should anticipate their death. (trans. Thomas, ap. Watson, very significantly adjusted)

A father has left a legacy to his wife (and appointed a third person as heir). The legacy is under the condition *si a liberis non discesserit* ("if she does not leave her children"), meaning that the wife is to stay in the husband's family and take care of the common children, and not to go away to a new husband's home.[75] The

[74] Papinian (18 *Quaestionum libri*) D. 35.1.72 pr.-1. On this text, cf. Babusiaux, *Papinians Quaestiones* (2011) 106–108; Harke, 'Testamentsauslegung bei Papinian' (2013) 71–73, who interprets Papinian's decision as case of *coniectura voluntatis*. Cf. also Quint. *Inst.* 6.2.12: *quin illud adhuc adicio, πάθος atque ἦθος esse interim ex eadem natura ita ut illud maius sit, hoc minus, ut amor πάθος, caritas ἦθος, interdum diversa inter se* ("Indeed, I am prepared to add that *pathos* and *ethos* are sometimes of the same nature, and differ only in degree (for example, love is *pathos*, affection is *ethos*), but sometimes also incompatible," trans. Russell).

[75] This is close to the condition not to remarry, which would not be valid (due to the Augustan marital laws), cf. Gaius (3 *ad legem Iuliam et Papiam*) D. 35.1.63pr: *cum ita legatum sit "si Titio non nupserit" vel ita "si neque Titio neque Seio neque Maevio nupserit" et denique si plures personae comprehensae fuerint, magis placuit, cuilibet eorum si nupserit, amissuram legatum, nec videri tali condicione viduitatem iniunctam, cum alii cuilibet satis commode possit nubere* ("In the event of a legacy, "if she does not marry Titius" or "Titius, Seius, or Maevius," and, generally, if several persons be included, the rule has rather become settled that should she marry any of them, she would lose the legacy; this is not regarded as imposing a condition of widowhood; for she could make a quite satisfactory marriage with someone else," trans. Thomas, ap. Watson). The condition to stay with the children can, however, be held valid; the condition is only void if it has been set in fraud to the law,

problem is that this condition is a negative potestative condition, whose fulfillment is only ultimately certain once the woman is dead. This would imply that she cannot get the legacy during her lifetime. In principle, to help legatees to get their bequest under a negative potestative condition, the so-called *cautio Muciana*, a stipulation, had been designed. By means of this stipulation, the legatee promised to return the value of the bequest if he infringed upon the condition. This promise served as a security for the heir. Once the stipulation had been performed, the legatee would receive the legacy; but the heir would be able to claim its value if ever its condition were not respected by the legatee.[76]

As Papinian relates, this solution was denied by other jurists to the mother in our case: *negaverunt eam recte cavere* ("they argued that she could not legally provide a security"). Their logic was that the condition was not a purely potestative one, since it could also lapse if the children died before the mother.[77] Papinian opposes this view and explains that this interpretation of the father's will is direful (*ominosa*) and against the mother's wish (*votum*) (to stay with her children) and should therefore not be used to prevent her from giving the security.

Again, the morality of the jurist is at stake, and determines the interpretation of the father's will. According to Papinian, a jurist should not assume unethical facts, i.e., children dying before their mother, to solve a case. The ethical values of the case are *verecundia*, the parental devotion to children, and *pietas*, the parental wish to die before their children (i.e., in respect of the natural order of life and death).[78] This ethical amplification implies a pathetic argument against Papinian's legal opponents, who show no sympathy to the mother's sad fate: not only has she lost her husband, but excessively formalistic jurists are trying to withhold the legacy attributed to her by an interpretation of the father's will that is obviously in contrast to the parents' wishes. The audience will choose to follow Papinian, who helps the mother, whereas the anonymous jurists deserve the audience's contempt and scorn (*pathos*).

as explained by Terentius (5 *ad legem Iuliam et Papiam*) D. 35.1.64.1: *quod si ita scriptum esset "si Ariciae non nupserit," interesse, an fraus legi facta esset: nam si ea esset, quae aliubi nuptias non facile possit invenire, interpretandum ipso iure rescindi, quod fraudandae legis gratia esset adscriptum: legem enim utilem rei publicae, subolis scilicet procreandae causa latam, adiuvandam interpretatio* ("However, a legacy, 'if she does not marry at Aricia,' raises the point whether a fraud on the statute is perpetrated; for if her case be such that she would not find marriage easy elsewhere, the provision is to be regarded as automatically rescinded as having been introduced to evade the statute; an enactment for the common good, namely, the procreation of issue, is to be furthered by its interpretation," trans. Thomas, ap. Watson).

[76] On the *cautio Muciana*, cf. Galgano, 'Cautio Muciana e crisi di un'élite' (2016/17).

[77] The other jurists' view is clearly in line with the existing interpretation of the *cautio Muciana*, cf. Ulpian (18 *ad Sabinum*) D. 35.1.7pr.

[78] On both concepts (*verecundia* and *pietas*), cf. Manthe, 'Votum parentium' (2000); again, Papinian refers to a morally certain matter to prove incertain matter, see above; on *pietas*, cf. Cic. *Inv. rhet.* 2. 65 (innate and of normative value).

d. Conclusion

In all three examples of ethical or pathetic amplification, the Severan jurists use rhetorical devices, especially *evidentia*, to persuade the audience of an innovative or unconventional legal solution. The three texts just examined thus demonstrate that Roman legal reasoning cannot be restricted to logical or dialectical consistency. Rather, the Roman jurists aim to persuade the parties, the judges, and, of course, other jurists—and, indeed, the emperor himself.[79] That said, the use of a whole array of rhetorical devices is not limited to the discussion of individual cases. In fact, the Roman jurists use *ethos* and *pathos* also in the discussion of legal theories and concepts.

3. Rhetorically Oriented Challenges to Established Legal Concepts

The understanding of rhetoric as an analytical tool can be traced back to Aristotle.[80] The epistemological function of rhetoric is, i.a., explained in Aristotle's book "On the Heavens," where he deals with the limits of knowledge:[81]

> *καὶ γὰρ αὐτὸς ἐν αὑτῷ ζητεῖ μέχρι περ ἂν οὗ μηκέτι ἔχῃ ἀντιλέγειν αὐτὸς αὑτῷ. διὸ δεῖ τὸν μέλλοντα καλῶς ζητήσειν ἐνστατικὸν εἶναι διὰ τῶν οἰκείων ἐνστάσεων τῷ γένει, τοῦτο δ' ἐστὶν ἐκ τοῦ πάσας τεθεωρηκέναι τὰς διαφοράς.*
>
> A man will even pursue a question in his own mind no farther than the point at which he finds nothing to say against his own arguments. Therefore, to be a good investigator a man must be alive to the objections inherent in the genus of his subject, an awareness which is the result of having studied all its differentiae. (trans. Chambers Guthrie)

Aristotle opposes those who stop their inquiries too soon, mainly because they limit themselves to discussing the theories developed by others, instead of deepening the subject matter itself. To overcome these cognitive limitations, Aristotle introduces a third kind of inquiry apart from those open to scientific or empirical proof. He speaks of inquiries that can lead to *credible* results.[82] Credibility is established by means of logic, but also through "what is in general credible for

[79] On the persuasive nature of jurists' law see Giaro, *Römische Rechtswahrheiten* (2007) esp. 205–297.

[80] On the Aristotelian turn of rhetoric, see Rapp, 'Dialectic and Logic from a Rhetorical Point of View' (2016); on the aporetic use of dialectic, cf. Bolton, 'The Epistemological Basis of Aristotelian Dialectic' (1990) 188.

[81] Arist. *Cael.* 2.13, 294b9–14.

[82] Bolton, 'Two Standards for Inquiry in Aristotle's De caelo' (2009) 80, who stresses that credibility was a first significant advance, until better forms of proof (on a scientific level) were developed.

us," which aligns to something reasonable (εὔλογον).[83] Thus, in some respect, theories must be shared by the insiders of the respective field, i.e., they must be persuaded to recognize accredited beliefs, *endoxa*.[84] In this respect, rhetoric has an epistemological value, and there is a fluid transition between persuasion and epistemology.[85]

Although one can notice that Roman jurists follow a rather empirical approach to their law, notably in the concept of natural law, which is "found" in nature, legal writing is mainly concerned with the application and the challenging of accepted rules and accredited notions.[86] One important field in this respect involves the definitions that outline the meaning of legal terms and concepts. Definitions determine whether a legal rule (edict, law, jurists' rule) may be applied or not to a particular case.[87] As shown elsewhere, the epistemological connection between definition and case is not only deductive, in the sense that the definition determines the outcome of the case; rather, a particular case can also alter the meaning of a word by integrating a new connotation, and thus changing its sense in an inductive way. In ancient rhetorical theory, these two approaches to definition are named semasiology (starting with the wording and asking about its meaning) and onomasiology (starting with the meaning and asking about the wording).[88] The following sample of texts from Severan jurists focuses on ethical and pathetic amplification of semasiological or onomasiological challenging of existing definitions (*endoxa* in the dialectical sense).

a. Mocking Labeo: *definitio falsa est*

A vivid example of an onomasiological challenge of a definition is found in Paul's epitome on Labeo's book entitled "*pithana*" (probabilities):[89]

> *Si navem cum instrumento emisti, praestari tibi debet scapha navis. Paulus: immo contra. etenim scapha navis non est instrumentum navis: etenim mediocritate,*

[83] On the generally credible, see Bolton, 'Two Standards for Inquiry in Aristotle's De caelo' (2009) 67: "He means rather that what is needed is a proposal that is coherent or epistemically possible, one that fits well enough with what is in general credible for us." He also cites (p. 76) as devices for discovering that which is εὔλογον (reasonable): (1) appeal to tradition; (2) appeal to testimony of a recognized sage; (3) appeal to standard linguistic usage or etymology; (4) analogy from the known to the unknown; (5) appeal to what holds καθόλου (generally).

[84] On the qualification of legal opinions as *endoxa*, cf. Babusiaux, *Papinians Quaestiones* (2011) 63–65.

[85] Cf. Föllinger, 'Mündlichkeit in der Schriftlichkeit als Ausdruck wissenschaftlicher Methode bei Aristoteles' (1993).

[86] On the empirical understanding of natural law, cf. Babusiaux, '§ 6 Rechtsschichten' (2023) nr. 189–208.

[87] Lausberg, *Handbuch der literarischen Rhetorik* (1990) § 89a, 66.

[88] On these aspects of the *status finitionis*, see Babusiaux, 'Der Kommentar als Haupttext' (2014) 40–45.

[89] Labeo (1 *Pithanon a Paulo epitomatorum*) D. 33.7.29. On the text, cf. Formigoni, *ΠΙΘΑΝΩΝ a Paulo epitomatorum libri VIII* (1996) 43–46, with further references.

> *non genere ab ea differt, instrumentum autem cuiusque rei necesse est alterius generis esse atque ea quaequae sit: quod Pomponio libro septimo epistularum placuit.*
>
> If you bought a ship with its *instrumentum*, the ship's lifeboat should be delivered to you. Paul: On the contrary. For the ship's lifeboat is not *instrumentum* of the ship; for it differs from it in size, not in kind, whereas the *instrumentum* of a thing must be of a different kind from the thing, whatever it is. This is approved by Pomponius in his seventh book of his letters. (trans. Seager, ap. Watson)

The tersely framed question is as follows: If someone buys a ship (*navis*) with *instrumentum* (its equipment), is the lifeboat (*scapha*) also included in the sale? In other words, is the lifeboat an accessory (*instrumentum*) to the ship? The republican jurist Labeo seems to have accepted the lifeboat as accessory. Paul opposes Labeo's view by introducing a further distinction between the main object of the sale and the accessory. According to Pomponius, to whom Paul refers, there must be a difference in the kind of thing (*genus*) between the *instrumentum* and the object of sale. Thus, a lifeboat cannot be accessory to a ship, as they are objects of the same kind.[90]

The only explicit argument against Labeo comes from another authority, Pomponius; otherwise, the rather brusque refusal of Labeo's solution "*immo contra*" ("on the contrary") seems to lack a justification. It appears that the decisive argument is of methodological nature. In fact, definition is itself defined as "an accurate, lucid, and brief verbal expression of a fact," that "normally comprises . . . Genus, Species, Differentia, and Properties."[91] The choice of the defining differences and properties is essential, as Quintilian shows in the example of the definition of a horse:[92]

> *. . . ut si finias equum (noto enim maxime utar exemplo), genus est animal, species mortale, differens inrationale (nam et homo mortale erat), proprium hinniens.*
>
> For example, if you were to define a horse (I shall use a particularly familiar example), the Genus is 'animal', the Species 'mortal', the Differentia 'nonrational' (man too is 'mortal'!), the Property 'neighing' (trans. Russell).

Just as in the case of horse and man, which belong to the same genus and species, namely, animal and mortal, implying the need to find a further difference (viz.,

[90] Cf. also Alfenus (2 *Alfenus digestorum a Paulo epitomatorum*) D. 21.2.44, who states: "He replied that a little boat is not part of the ship and is not adjoined to it, for it is itself a sort of small ship; but all the fittings of the ship (for example, rudders, the mast, yards, and sails) are like limbs of the vessel" (trans. Thomas, ap. Watson).

[91] Quint. *Inst.* 7.3.3: *finitio igitur est rei propositae propria et dilucida et breviter comprensa verbis enuntiatio. constat maxime . . . genere specie differentibus proprii* (trans. Russell).

[92] Quint. *Inst.* 7.3.3.

nonrational), *navis* and *scapha* are both vessels. The only difference between *navis* and *scapha* might be—as Paul explains—their size; but, there are no properties that justify treating one of them an accessory to the other. Looking at Paul's disagreement with Labeo from this point of view, a significant difference between the two jurists emerges. While Labeo is dealing with the meaning of *instrumentum*, Paul's starting point is the distinction between *navis* and *scapha*. The crucial point for the Severan jurist is, therefore, that Labeo's definition does not account for reality. Following Paul's presentation, Labeo's definition is "wrong" (*falsa definitio*), since Paul's one counterexample has shown that the definition lacks specificity.[93]

As always, the argument against Labeo has a logical basis; but its presentation shows signs of pathetic amplification. First, the great Labeo is openly and very rudely contradicted; second, the common nature of *navis* and *scapha* as vessel is visible for anybody, which implies that Paul is mocking Labeo, who has overlooked something so blatantly obvious. Thus, Paul's treatment demonstrates contempt for his predecessor, i.e., a pathetic emotion.

b. Natural Equity of Definitions

An illustration for an ethical amplification of a definition can be found in Ulpian's edictal commentary. The jurist is dealing with the interdict *de fluminibus* ("on the rivers"), which states, "You are not to do anything in a public river or on its bank, nor put anything into a public river or onto its bank, which makes the landing or passage of a boat worse."[94] After citing the wording of the edict, Ulpian goes on to define the words of the edict by explaining the meaning of "river" and "public river." He then turns to "bank" (*ripa*) and states:[95]

> *Ripa autem ita recte definietur id, quod flumen continet naturalem rigorem cursus sui tenens: ceterum si quando vel imbribus vel mari vel qua alia ratione ad tempus excrevit, ripas non mutat: nemo denique dixit Nilum, qui incremento suo Aegyptum operit, ripas suas mutare vel ampliare. nam cum ad perpetuam sui mensuram redierit, ripae alvei eius muniendae sunt. si tamen naturaliter creverit, ut perpetuum incrementum nanctus sit, vel alio flumine admixto vel qua alia ratione, dubio procul dicendum est ripas quoque eum mutasse, quemadmodum si alveo mutato alia coepit currere.*
>
> A bank is rightly defined as that which contains a river when it is holding the line of its natural course. But when a river is sometimes temporarily swollen by rains

[93] A nice example in Quint. *Inst.* 7.3.26–27 regarding properties and differences.

[94] Ulpian (68 *ad edictum*) D. 43.12.1pr. (trans. Braun, ap. Watson), on which see Tomás, 'Limitations à la propriété riveraine et libre navigation fluviale' (2001).

[95] Ulpian (68 *ad edictum*) D. 43.12.1.5.

> or the sea or for any other reason, it does not change its banks. No one, after all, has said that the Nile, which covers Egypt with its flood, changes or enlarges its banks. For when it returns to its usual dimensions, the banks of its channel have to be built up. But if a river has grown naturally, so as to acquire a perpetual enlargement, either by admixture with another river or for some other reason, there is no doubt whatever that it has also changed its banks, just as if it had changed its bed and begun to run another course. (trans. Braun, ap. Watson)

The definition given by Ulpian for a bank (*ripa*) is rather plain. He defines it as the shore of a river that maintains the line of its natural course. The problem lies in the changing nature of banks due to rain and other swelling of the water. In fact, this could lead to a change in the course of the water, and therefore hinder the application of the interdict. Arguing that temporary high waters do not alter the banks, Ulpian states: "No one, after all, has said that the Nile, which covers Egypt with its flood, changes or enlarges its banks. For when it returns to its usual dimensions, the banks of its channel have to be built up." The floods of the Nile were known within and outside Egypt. Also, under Roman rule, the Egyptians worshipped the Nile as a God, with festivities and processions in his honor.[96] Ulpian's emphatic words allude to this natural spectacle, and raise the picture of the Nile flooding in the audience's mind.[97]

The impressive example of the Nile (*evidentia*) serves as proof for Ulpian's definition of *ripa*. The value of the proof lies in the conceptual (the Nile is not only a river but a God), and also in the ethical amplification of the definition. That the banks must be considered stationary, despite the changing nature of the river itself, is not only the jurist's opinion, but also due to the natural spectacle of the Nile in Egypt. Moreover, the example shows that this definition has its origin in nature and is thus in conformity with the requirements of equity.[98] This feeling is perhaps augmented by the fact that reverence for the Nile carried religious connotations for much of the populace.[99] With such support, it will be difficult for the audience to challenge Ulpian's view, and his definition will prevail.

[96] An overview by Blouin, 'Between Water and Sand' (2012) 22–37, with further references.

[97] Again, *evidentia* or *enargeia*, see Quint. *Inst.* 6.2.29.

[98] On the natural origin of law, cf. Cic. *Inv. rhet.* 2.65: *utrisque aut etiam omnibus, si plures ambigent, ius ex quibus rebus constet, considerandum est. initium eigo eius ab natura ductum videtur* ("Both parties (or all parties if there are more than two concerned in the litigation) must consider the sources from which law arises. Its origin seems to be in nature," trans. Hubbell, *Cicero. On Invention* (1949)).

[99] Cic. *Inv. rhet.* 2. 65–6: *ac naturae quidem ius esse, quod nobis non opinio, sed quaedam innata vis adferat, ut religionem, pietatem, gratiam, vindicationem, observantiam, veritatem. religionem eam quae in metu et caerimonia deorum sit appellant* ("And the law of nature is something which is implanted in us not by opinion, but by a kind of innate instinct; it includes religion, duty, gratitude, revenge, reverence, and truth. Religion is the term applied to the fear and worship of the gods," trans. Hubbell, *Cicero. On Invention* (1949)).

c. Challenging Established Rules and Sayings

Like definitions of concept, the Roman jurists produced rules and *sententiae* (opinions) that incorporated standards and principles.[100] However, a jurist can challenge these rules and test them on (real or fictitious) cases. When challenging accepted and long-established rules, rhetorically speaking, a jurist finds himself in the situation of *genus admirabile*, since he is defending a point of view to which his audience is hostile or reluctant.[101] To overcome this resistance, the speaker can use the means of insinuation and ethical or pathetic amplification as in the following text:[102]

> *Dolus tutorum puero neque nocere neque prodesse debet: quod autem vulgo dicitur tutoris dolum pupillo non nocere, tunc verum est, cum ex illius fraude locupletior pupillus factus non est. quare merito Sabinus tributoria actione pupillum conveniendum ex dolo tutoris existimavit, scilicet si per iniquam distributionem pupilli rationibus favit. quod in depositi quoque actione dicendum est, item hereditatis petitione, si modo, quod tutoris dolo desiit, pupilli rationibus illatum probetur.*
>
> Fraud on the part of the tutors ought neither to harm nor benefit a boy; but what is commonly said, that a tutor's fraud does not harm the *pupillus*, is true only when the *pupillus* does not become richer as a result of the tutor's fraud. Therefore, Sabinus justly thought that a *pupillus* could be sued in an action concerning payment as a result of his tutor's fraud, certainly if the tutor benefited the accounts of the *pupillus* by an unfair division of money. This must also be said in the case of an action on a deposit and also a claim for an inheritance; as long as it can be proved that what was lost through the tutor's fraud was transferred to the account of the *pupillus*. (trans. Honoré, ap. Watson)

Papinian cites a saying according to which fraud on the part of the tutor should neither harm nor benefit the child (*puer*). He then quotes a common saying (*vulgo dicitur*) that slightly differs from the first, as it states that the ward (*pupillus*) should not be harmed by the tutor's fraud. The jurist questions this second saying by stressing that it is only true if the ward has *not* become richer because of the tutor's fraud. Both sayings refer to the tutor's role as administrator of the ward's assets; depending on the age of the ward, all transactions that lead to an obligation of the ward need the tutor's consent (*auctoritas*), or can only be done by the tutor himself. If the tutor acts fraudulently, i.e., against the ward's best interests, the

[100] On *regulae* and *sententiae*, see Schmidlin, *Die römischen Rechtsregeln* (1970) 7–18; Nörr, 'Spruchregel und Generalisierung' (1972); Schmidlin, 'Horoi, pithana und regulae' (1976).

[101] Quint. *Inst.* 4.1.41: *admirabile autem vocant, quod est praeter opinionem hominum constitutum* ("They call a thing *admirabilis*, which is constituted outside of the the opinions of most men").

[102] Papinian (20 *quaestionum libri*) D. 26.9.3. On the text, cf. Knütel, 'Dolus tutoris pupillo non nocet' (1986) 105–106 with further references.

ward's assets will be considered undiminished. Thus, once the guardianship has ended, the guardian will have to compensate the ward for the losses caused by his fraud.[103] In other words, fraudulent actions of the tutor can only affect himself.

Papinian's modification of the saying, i.e., that the tutor's fraud should not benefit the ward, expands the view by looking also at the effects for third parties. In fact, the jurist claims that the ward is liable to third parties, if he has been enriched through the tutor's fraud. By doing so, Papinian implicitly refers to a reform issued by the emperor Antoninus Pius.[104] According to a rescript ascribed to this emperor, a ward had to reimburse all accrued benefits to a third party if these were still in the ward's property (liability for enrichment; liability for being *locupletior*).[105] Papinian's argument seems to be that due to the imperial enactment the existing maxim *tutoris dolus pupillo non nocere* ("the fraud of the guardian shall not harm the ward") can no more be maintained. To prove his opinion, however, he does not refer to the emperor, but to a case decided by Sabinus on an *actio tributoria*. This type of claim aims at the equitable distribution of a *peculium* (a sum of money given to the slave by the master) among the slave's creditors; Sabinus decided that if the division had been done in the ward's favor due to the tutor's fraud, the other creditors could reclaim their share directly from the ward.[106] Papinian extends this extraordinary solution to the *actio depositi* (claim for deposit) and the *hereditatis petitio* (claim for the inheritance) by stating that if the ward's estate has been enriched by the tutor's malice, the enrichment can directly be claimed from the ward.[107]

Looking at the text from a rhetorical perspective, Papinian's presentation begins with a sentence which not only serves as proof, but is also a typical prooemical element, as it catches the audience's attention.[108] On closer inspection, however, the two sayings cited in the text seem to contradict. Their comparison shows that Papinian's own saying has changed two elements compared to the usual sense (*vulgo dicitur*): first, instead of the general term "ward" (*pupillus*) he uses the term "child" (*puer*). Second, he adds another element to the usually accepted rule by prohibiting not only harm to the ward by the tutor, but also benefit.

[103] For other cases of succession see Paul (3 *ad edictum*) D. 2.14.17.6; Ulpian (3 *disputationum libri*) D. 44.3.5pr. and Ulpian (76 *ad edictum*) D. 44.4.4.23. To all these cases the maxim *neque nocere, neque prodesse* applies.

[104] The relevant passages are Ulpian (1 *ad Sabinum*) D. 26.8.1; Ulpian (40 *ad Sabinum*) D. 26.8.5pr.; Ulpian (10 *ad edictum*) D. 3.5.3.4, Marcian (4 *regularum libri V*) D. 46.3.47pr., on which see Labruna, *Rescriptum divi Pii* (1962) 10–76; Babusiaux, '§ 84 Klage aus Vormundschaft (*actio tutelae*)' (2023) nr. 72.

[105] The case referred to a female ward who had accepted a loan (*mutuum*) and undertaken a stipulation for the reimbursement (with the tutor's consent). The emperor allowed the creditor to claim back the money to the extent that the ward had been enriched.

[106] On the *actio tributoria*, cf. Gamauf, '§ 103 Klage wegen Verteilung (*actio tributoria*)' (2023).

[107] Cf. Knütel, 'Dolus tutoris pupillo non nocet' (1986) 106–107, who imagines rather difficult cases.

[108] Lausberg, *Handbuch der literarischen Rhetorik* (1990) § 876, 433.

A closer look reveals that this combination—*puer* for *pupillus* and *prodesse* plus *nocere*—creates an elaborate paradox that serves to hint at Papinian's new rule on the ward's liability. In fact, the term *puer* is ambiguous, as it can be used as a synonym for *pupillus*, but also for a child who is underage (*infans*), not yet in the torments of *adolescentia*.[109] This accentuation of the ward's age has its justification in the context of liability for being *locupletior*, as Antoninus Pius' rescript solely applies to the so-called *impubes infantia maiores*, i.e., elder wards, and not to small children who are underage, *infantes* or *infantes and infantes proximi*. If this were true, however, one would expect that precisely the *puer* not be mentioned in the new rule, but instead, the elder wards, *impubes infanti maiores*. Taken literally, Papinian's sentence seems to confound the two groups and to mix up their legal status.

This paradox, however, is clearly a rhetorical figure, which Quintilian describes as follows:[110]

> *Iam haec magis nova sententiarum genera: ex inopinato, ut dixit Vibius Crispus in eum, qui, cum loricatus in foro ambularet, praetendebat id se metu facere: "quis tibi sic timere permisit?" et insigniter Africanus apud Neronem de morte matris: "rogant te, Caesar, Galliae tuae, ut felicitatem tuam fortiter feras."*
>
> Here now are some more modern types of sententia: (1) Based on surprise: Vibius Crispus said to a man who was walking in the forum in body armor and claimed he was doing it because he was afraid, "Afraid? Who gave you permission?" Another distinguished example is Africanus' remark to Nero about his mother's death, "Caesar, your provinces of Gaul beg that you will bear your happiness like a man." (trans. Russell)

The examples show the nature of the *nova sententia* formed by the speaker: they work by their contradictory content, the obvious paradox, that surprises the audience and, by doing so, underlines the speaker's intention. Quintilian, of course, also emphasizes the risk of error entailed in such punch lines (Quint. *Inst.* 8.5.21). Papinian's sentence, however, cannot be critized, as it succeeds, first, in capturing the audience's attention; moreover, it is entertaining because it compels reflection; and finally, it serves a clear argumentative purpose because it hints at the criterion of differentiation introduced by Papinian, namely the age of the ward, which is decisive for liability of the ward because of his becoming *locupletior*, and thus steers the audience in the right direction.

[109] Paul (2 *Epitome Alfeni digestorum et Labeonis*) D. 50.16.204: *'pueri' appellatio tres significationes habet... tertiam, cum aetatem puerilem demonstraremus* ("The designation 'boy' has three meanings... a third when we indicate the age of childhood," trans. Crawford, ap. Watson).

[110] Quint. *Inst.* 8.5.15.

The fact that Papinian does not state his opinion more clearly—in particular, he neither mentions the imperial rescript nor explicates more precisely the distinction between *infantes* and *impubes infanti maiores*—can be explained by two considerations. On the one hand, the very purpose of the *libri quaestionum* is to challenge the audience and to make them think; on the other hand, Papinian's point of view is new and is directed against established legal opinion. This might be the reason why he chooses the subtle mechanism of *insinuatio*: indeed, before even realizing what is happening, the audience has accepted Papinian's legal opinion, which seems to be a simple reformulation of an existing legal rule.[111]

d. Conclusion

The examples of jurists challenging existing definitions and rules were intended to show that even the very core of legal argumentation can be rhetorically inspired, and can use every means of persuasion, not only dialectical proof. In fact, controversies about the correct definition or formulation of a rule or saying invariably result in the jurist addressing other juridical experts, i.e., his peers. By using rhetorical devices in his argumentation, the jurist tries to persuade the inner circle of experts of his exceptional ability, and of the superiority of his arguments. In short, he shows that his point of view is not only logically convincing, but is also the most ethical and the most compelling on an emotional level.

III. General Conclusions

Considering the functions of *ethos* and *pathos* in Roman legal writing, one can indeed observe a "borrowing-transformation" (see above pp. 249–250) from rhetorical theory to the jurists' work. Especially due to the controversial, or even agonistic, nature of the law, persuasion is a key element of legal discourse. Persuasion is obtained via authority, which comprises the *ethos* of the speaker or writer, and through the reasonableness of the solution presented, i.e., its conformity with existing statutes, traditional legal principles and accepted juristic interpretation, yet also depends upon persuasion at the more subtle level of *prudentia/phronesis*. At least in cases where a jurist wants to overcome the existing doctrine, ethical and

[111] Cic. *Inv. rhet.* 1.15.21: *in admirabili genere causae, si non omnino infesti auditores erunt, principio benivolentiam comparare licebit. sin erunt vehementer abalienati, confugere necesse erit ad insinuationem. nam ab iratis si perspicue pax et benivolentia petitur, non modo ea non invenitur, sed augetur atque inflammatur odium* ("In the difficult case, if the auditors are not completely hostile, it will be permissible to try to win their goodwill by an introduction; if they are violently opposed it will be necessary to have recourse to the insinuation. For if amity and good-will are sought from auditors who are in a rage, not only is the desired result not obtained, but their hatred is increased and fanned into a flame," trans. Hubbell); Quint. *Inst.* 4.1.42: *et eo quidam exordium in duas dividunt partis, principium et insinuationem, ut sit in principiis recta benivolentiae et attentionis postulatio*... ("Some therefore divide the Prooemium into two parts, the Introduction and the Insinuation, the former containing a direct appeal for goodwill and attention," trans. Russell).

pathetic amplifications are used to strengthen the technical legal argument. Thus, the circumstances of the case are presented in an arbitrary manner to serve the speaker's intention, or the discussion of the legal concept itself is amplified via ethical or pathetic *evidentia*.

In sum, the examples presented show that rhetorical theory, as part of the imperial elite's education, was not limited to forensic speech and epideictic presentation in didactic writing, but could be used as a toolbox for the solution and the presentation of legal problems. The transformation of rhetorical teachings, when applied to legal writing, lies less in the content and the essence of the rhetorical devices engaged (in contrast to philosophy) than in the addressees. Whereas forensic speech is intended to move the judge, a layman, and the public (mostly laymen), legal writing addresses, above all, the legal community of jurists, emperors, and other high officials present in the emperor's entourage. In this sense, the rhetorical amplification of legal reasoning is also a means of creating common understanding between the different disciplines engaged in the administration of justice.[112]

Bibliography

Albertario, 'La crisi del metodo interpolazionistico' (1930) = E. Albertario, 'La crisi del metodo interpolazionistico,' in *Studi in onore di Pietro Bonfante nel XL anno d'insegnamento I* (Milan: Treves, 1930) 609–672.

Aubert-Baillot, 'De la *φρόνησις* à la "prudentia"' (2015) = S. Aubert-Baillot, 'De la *φρόνησις* à la "prudentia",' *Mnemosyne. A Journal of Classical Studies* 68 (2015) 68–90.

Babusiaux, '§ 6 Rechtsschichten' (2023) = U. Babusiaux, '§ 6 Rechtsschichten,' in U. Babusiaux, C. Baldus, W. Ernst, F.-S. Meissel, J. Platschek, and Th. Rüfner, eds., *Handbuch des römischen Privatrechts* (Tübingen: Mohr, 2023).

Babusiaux, '§ 84 Klage aus Vormundschaft (*actio tutelae*)' (2023) = U. Babusiaux, '§ 84 Klage aus Vormundschaft (*actio tutelae*),' in U. Babusiaux, C. Baldus, W. Ernst, F.-S. Meissel, J. Platschek, and Th. Rüfner, eds., *Handbuch des römischen Privatrechts* (Tübingen: Mohr, 2023).

Babusiaux, 'Coordination of Different Layers of Law in the Roman Empire and in the European Union' (2019) = U. Babusiaux, 'Coordination of Different Layers of Law in the Roman Empire and in the European Union,' in U. Babusiaux and M. Igimi, eds., *Messages from the Antiquity. Roman Law and Current Legal Debates* (Vienna and Cologne: Böhlau 2019) 131–167.

[112] On rhetorical education as prerequisite for participation in the emperor's council, cf. Millar, *The Emperor in the Roman World* (1977) 88–101.

Babusiaux, 'D. 36.1.48 Iavolenus 11 epistularum' (2018) = U. Babusiaux, 'D. 36.1.48 Iavolenus 11 epistularum. Römischrechtliche Bemerkungen zum textlichen Ausgangspunkt der französischen fiducie à cause de mort,' in *Mélanges en l'honneur du Professeur Claude Witz* (Paris: LexisNexis, 2018) 41–59.

Babusiaux, 'Der Kommentar als Haupttext' (2014) = U. Babusiaux, 'Der Kommentar als Haupttext. Zur Gattung der libri ad edictum Ulpians,' in D. Kästle and N. Jansen, eds., *Kommentare in Recht und Religion* (Tübingen: Mohr, 2014) 15–55.

Babusiaux, 'Legal Writing and Legal Reasoning' (2016) = U. Babusiaux, 'Legal Writing and Legal Reasoning,' in P. du Plessis, C. Ando, and K. Tuori, eds., *Oxford Handbook of Roman Law and Society* (Oxford: Oxford University Press, 2016) 176–187.

Babusiaux, 'Les défauts de l'utilisation du "ius controversum"' (2020) = U. Babusiaux, 'Les défauts de l'utilisation du "ius controversum" en tant que concept herméneutique de droit romain,' in N. Cornu Thénard, A. Mergey, and S. Soleil, eds., *La controverse: étude d'histoire de l'argumentation juridique. Actes des journées internationales de la Société d'histoire du droit, Rennes 2015* (Paris: Société de Législation Comparée, 2020) 19–48.

Babusiaux, 'Papinian's Late Antique Reception and His Myth' (forthcoming) = U. Babusiaux, 'Papinian's Late Antique Reception and His Myth,' in D. Mantovani and M. Wibier, eds., *The Circulation, Use, and Reception of Classical Juristic Literature in Late Antiquity* (Oxford: Oxford University Press, forthcoming).

Babusiaux, 'Review of Daalder, De rechtspraakverzamelingen van Julius Paulus (2018)' (2021) = U. Babusiaux, 'Review of Daalder, De rechtspraakverzamelingen van Julius Paulus (2018),' *Zeitschrift der Savigny-Stiftung für Rechtsgeschichte, romanistische Abteilung* 138 (2021) 674–691.

Babusiaux, *Papinians Quaestiones* (2011) = U. Babusiaux, *Papinians Quaestiones. Zur rhetorischen Methode eines spätklassischen Juristen* (Munich: Beck, 2011).

Battaglia, 'Strutture espositive in Gaio' (2020) = F. Battaglia, 'Strutture espositive in Gaio: per una morfologia delle Institutiones,' in U. Babusiaux and D. Mantovani, eds., *Le Istituzioni di Gaio: avventure di un bestseller. Trasmissione, uso e trasformazione del testo* (Pavia: Pavia University Press, 2020) 205–277.

Blouin, 'Between Water and Sand' (2012) = K. Blouin, 'Between Water and Sand. Agriculture and Husbandry,' in Chr. Riggs, ed., *The Oxford Handbook of Roman Egypt* (Oxford: Oxford University Press, 2012) 22–37.

Bolton, 'The Epistemological Basis of Aristotelian Dialectic' (1990) = R. Bolton, 'The Epistemological Basis of Aristotelian Dialectic,' in D. Devereux and P. Pellegrin, eds., *Biologie, Logique et Métaphysique chez Aristote. Actes du séminaire C.N.R.S.-N. S.F. Oléron 28 juin–3 juillet 1987* (Paris: Editions CNRS, 1990) 185–236.

Bolton, 'Two Standards for Inquiry in Aristotle's De caelo' (2009) = R. Bolton, 'Two Standards for Inquiry in Aristotle's De caelo,' in A. Bowen and C. Wildberg, eds., *New Perspectives on Aristotle's De caelo* (Leiden: Brill, 2009) 51–82.

Bower, '*ΕΦΟΔΟΣ* and insinuatio in Greek and Latin Rhetoric' (1958) = E. W. Bower, '*ΕΦΟΔΟΣ* and insinuatio in Greek and Latin Rhetoric,' *The Classical Quarterly* 52 (1958) 224–230.

Bretone, 'Ius controversum' (2008) = M. Bretone, 'Ius controversum nella giurisprudenza classica,' in *Memorie. Accademia nazionale dei Lincei. Classe di scienze morali storiche e filologiche*, vol. 9 (Rome: Bardi Editore, 2008) 750–852.

Calboli Montefusco, '*Ενάργεια* et *ἐνέργεια*' (2005) = L. Calboli Montefusco, '*Ενάργεια* et *ἐνέργεια*: l'évidence d'une démonstration qui signifie les choses en acte (Rhet. Her. 4, 68),' *Pallas* 69 (2005) 43–58.

Champlin, *Final Judgments* (1991) = E. Champlin, *Final Judgments. Duty and Emotion in Roman Wills, 200* B.C.–A.D. *250* (Berkeley: University of California Press, 1991).

Coppola Bisazza, 'Osservazioni sul regime dei frutti nel fedecommesso de residuo' (1982) = G. Coppola Bisazza, 'Osservazioni sul regime dei frutti nel fedecommesso de residuo,' in *Studi per Lorenzo Campagna I* (Milan: Giuffrè, 1982) 185–222.

Daalder, *De rechtspraakverzamelingen van Julius Paulus* (2018) = E. Daalder, *De rechtspraakverzamelingen van Julius Paulus. Recht en rechtvaardigheid in de rechterlijke uitspraken van keizer Septimius Severus. Proefschrift Universiteit Leiden, 23 oktober 2018* (Den Haag: Boom Juridisch 2018).

Desanti, 'Di nuovo sul regime dei frutti nel fedecommesso de residuo e sul presunto contrasto tra D. 22.1.3.2 (Pap. 20 quaest.) e D. 36.1.60 (58).7 (Pap. 9 resp.)' (1999) = L. Desanti, 'Di nuovo sul regime dei frutti nel fedecommesso de residuo e sul presunto contrasto tra D. 22.1.3.2 (Pap. 20 quaest.) e D. 36.1.60 (58).7 (Pap. 9 resp.),' *Studia et documenta historiae et iuris* 65 (1999) 67–94.

Föllinger, 'Mündlichkeit in der Schriftlichkeit als Ausdruck wissenschaftlicher Methode bei Aristoteles' (1993) = S. Föllinger, 'Mündlichkeit in der Schriftlichkeit als Ausdruck wissenschaftlicher Methode bei Aristoteles,' in W. Kullmann and J. Althoff, eds., *Vermittlung und Tradierung von Wissen in der griechischen Kultur* (Tübingen: Gunter Narr, 1993) 263–280.

Formigoni, *ΠΙΘΑΝΩΝ a Paulo epitomatorum libri VIII* (1996) = W. Formigoni, *ΠΙΘΑΝΩΝ a Paulo epitomatorum libri VIII. Sulla funzione critica del commento del giurista Iulius Paulus* (Milan: Giuffrè, 1996) 43–46.

Galgano, 'Cautio Muciana e crisi di un'élite' (2016/17) = F. Galgano, 'Cautio Muciana e crisi di un'élite,' *Rivista di Diritto Romano* 16/17 (2016/17) 1–31.

Gamauf, '§ 103 Klage wegen Verteilung (*actio tributoria*)' (2023) = R. Gamauf, '§ 103 Klage wegen Verteilung (*actio tributoria*),' in U. Babusiaux, C. Baldus, W. Ernst, F.-S. Meissel, J. Platschek, and Th. Rüfner, eds., *Handbuch des römischen Privatrechts* (Tübingen: Mohr, 2023).

Giaro, *Römische Rechtswahrheiten* (2007) = T. Giaro, *Römische Rechtswahrheiten. Ein Gedankenexperiment* (Frankfurt a.M.: Klostermann, 2007).

Guarino, 'Tra asini e cavalle' (1974) = A. Guarino, 'Tra asini e cavalle,' in A. Watson, ed., *Daube noster. Essays in Legal History for David Daube* (Edinburgh: Scottish Academic Press, 1974) 119–121.

Harke, 'Testamentsauslegung bei Papinian' (2013) = J. D. Harke, 'Testamentsauslegung bei Papinian,' in J. D. Harke, ed., *Argumenta Papiniani. Studien zur Geschichte und Dogmatik des Privatrechts* (Berlin and Heidelberg: Springe, 2013) 59–78.

Himmelschein, 'Studien zu der antiken Hermeneutica iuris' (1931) = J. Himmelschein, 'Studien zu der antiken Hermeneutica iuris,' in *Symbolae friburgenses in honorem Ottonis Lenel* (Leipzig: Tauchnitz, 1931) 373–424.

Honoré, *Ulpian* (2002) = T. Honoré, *Ulpian. Pioneer of Human Rights*, 2nd ed. (Oxford: Oxford University Press, 2002).

Horak, 'Die rhetorische Statuslehre und der moderne Aufbau des Verbrechensbegriffs' (1972) = F. Horak, 'Die rhetorische Statuslehre und der moderne Aufbau des Verbrechensbegriffs,' in F. Horak and W. Waldstein, eds., *Festgabe für Arnold Herdlitczka zu seinem 75. Geburtstag* (Graz: Fink, 1972) 121–142.

Kaser and Hackl, *Römisches Zivilprozessrecht* (1996) = M. Kaser and K. Hackl, *Römisches Zivilprozessrecht*, 2nd ed. (Munich: Beck, 1997).

Knütel, 'Dolus tutoris pupillo non nocet' (1986) = R. Knütel, 'Dolus tutoris pupillo non nocet,' in H.-P. Benöhr, K. Hackl, R. Knütel, and A. Wacke, eds., *Iuris Professio. Festgabe für Max Kaser zum 80. Geburtstag* (Vienna, Cologne, and Graz: Böhlau, 1986) 101–126.

Labruna, *Rescriptum divi Pii* (1962) = L. Labruna, *Rescriptum divi Pii. Gli atti del pupillo sine tutoris auctoritate* (Naples: Jovene, 1962).

Lausberg, *Handbuch der literarischen Rhetorik* (1990) = H. Lausberg, *Handbuch der literarischen Rhetorik. Eine Grundlegung der Literaturwissenschaft*, 3rd ed. (Stuttgart: Steiner, 1990).

Lenel, *Palingenesia iuris civilis* (1889) = O. Lenel, *Palingenesia iuris civilis. Iuris consultorum reliquiae quae Iustiniani Digestis continentur ceteraque iurisprudentiae civilis fragmenta minora.* In 2 vols. Reprint of Leipzig 1889 (Scientia: Aalen 2000).

Liebs, 'Domitius Ulpianus' (1997) = D. Liebs, 'Domitius Ulpianius,' in K. Sallmann, ed., *Die Literatur des Umbruchs. Von der römischen zur christlichen Literatur 117 bis 284 n. Chr.* (Munich: Beck, 1997) § 424, 175–187.

Manthe, 'Ethische Argumente im Werk Papinians' (2005) = U. Manthe, 'Ethische Argumente im Werk Papinians,' *Orbis Iuris Romani* 10 (2005) 143–166.

Manthe, 'Votum parentium' (2000) = U. Manthe, 'Votum parentium: Pap. D. 29,4,26,' in U. Manthe and Chr. Krampe, eds., *Quaestiones Iuris. Festschrift für Joseph Georg Wolf zum 70. Geburtstag* (Berlin: Duncker & Humblot, 2000) 163–181.

Mantovani, 'Iuris Scientia et Honores' (1997) = D. Mantovani, 'Iuris Scientia et Honores. Contributo allo studio dei fattori sociali nella formazione giurisprudenziale del diritto romano (III-I sec. a. C.),' in *Nozione, formazione e interpretazione del diritto dall'età romana alle esperienze moderne. Ricerche dedicate al professor Filippo Gallo* (Naples: Jovene, 1997) 617–680.

Mantovani, *Les juristes écrivains* (2018) = D. Mantovani, *Les juristes écrivains de la Rome antique. Les oeuvres des juristes comme littérature* (Paris: Belles Lettres, 2018).

Meinhart, 'Die bedingte Erbeinsetzung des Haussohnes' (1973) = M. Meinhart, 'Die bedingte Erbeinsetzung des Haussohnes,' in D. Medicus and H. H. Seiler, eds., *Studien im römischen Recht. Max Kaser zum 65. Geburtstag* (Berlin: Duncker & Humbolt, 1973) 111–136.

Mennen, 'Praetorian Prefects' Power and Senatorial Status in the Third Century' (2012) = I. Mennen, 'Praetorian Prefects' Power and Senatorial Status in the Third Century: Re-evaluating Historia Augusta, Vita Alexandri 21.5,' *Mnemosyne. A Journal of Classical Studies* 65 (2012) 656–673.

Millar, *The Emperor in the Roman World* (1977) = F. Millar, *The Emperor in the Roman World (31 BC–AD 337)* (London: Duckworth, 1977).

Nollé, 'Colonia und Socia der Römer' (1995) = J. Nollé, 'Colonia und Socia der Römer. Ein neuer Vorschlag zur Auflösung der Buchstaben "SR" auf den Münzen von Antiocheia bei Pisidien,' in C. Schubert, K. Brodersen, and U. Huttner, eds., *Rom und der griechische Osten. Festschrift für Hatto H. Schmitt zum 65. Geburtstag* (Stuttgart: Steiner, 1995) 350–370.

Nörr, 'Origo' (1963) = D. Nörr, 'Origo. Studien zur Orts-, Stadt- und Reichszugehörigkeit in der Antike,' *Tijdschrift voor Rechtsgeschiedenis* 31 (1963) 525–600.

Nörr, 'Spruchregel und Generalisierung' (1972) = D. Nörr, 'Spruchregel und Generalisierung,' *Savigny-Zeitschrift für Rechtsgeschichte, romanistische Abteilung* 89 (1972) 18–93.

Peachin, 'Exemplary Government in the Early Roman Empire' (2007) = M. Peachin, 'Exemplary Government in the Early Roman Empire,' in O. Hekster, G. de Kleijn, and D. Slootjes, eds., *Crises and the Roman Empire. Proceedings of the Seventh Workshop of the International Network Impact of Empire (Nijmegen, June 20–24, 2006)* (Leiden and Boston: Brill, 2007) 75–95.

Pennitz, '§ 93 Diebstahlsklage (*actio furti*)' (2023) = M. Pennitz, '§ 93 Diebstahlsklage (*actio furti*),' in U. Babusiaux, C. Baldus, W. Ernst, F.-S. Meissel, J. Platschek, and Th. Rüfner, eds., *Handbuch des römischen Privatrechts* (Tübingen: Mohr, 2023).

Pringsheim, 'Ius aequum und ius strictum' (1921) = F. Pringsheim, 'Ius aequum und ius strictum,' *Savigny-Zeitschrift für Rechtsgeschichte, romanistische Abteilung* 42 (1921) 643–668.

Rapp, *Aristoteles, Rhetorik. Kommentar* (2002) = Chr. Rapp, *Aristoteles, Rhetorik. Übersetzt und erläutert*, 2. Halbband (Berlin: Akademie Verlag, 2002).

Rapp, 'Dialectic and Logic from a Rhetorical Point of View' (2016) = Chr. Rapp, 'Dialectic and Logic from a Rhetorical Point of View,' in J. Gourinat and J.-B. Lemaire, eds., *Logique et dialectique dans l'Antiquité* (Paris: Vrin, 2016) 161–191.

Schmidlin, 'Horoi, pithana und regulae' (1976) = B. Schmidlin, 'Horoi, pithana und regulae. Zum Einfluß der Rhetorik und Dialektik auf die juristische Regelbildung,' in H. Temporini, ed., *Aufstieg und Niedergang der römischen Welt 15.II: Recht (Methoden, Schulen, Einzelne Juristen)* (Berlin and New York: De Gruyter, 1976) 101–130.

Schmidlin, *Die römischen Rechtsregeln* (1970) = B. Schmidlin, *Die römischen Rechtsregeln. Versuch einer Typologie* (Cologne and Vienna: Böhlau, 1970).

Schulz, *History of Roman Legal Science* (1946) = F. Schulz, *History of Roman Legal Science* (Oxford: Clarendon Press, 1946).

Simon, 'Die animusbesessene Spätzeit' (1995) = D. Simon, 'Die animusbesessene Spätzeit,' *Rechtshistorisches Journal* 14 (1995) 253–283.

Stagl, 'Die Ausgleichung von Vorteil und Nachteil als Inhalt klassischer aequitas' (2007) = J. F. Stagl, 'Die Ausgleichung von Vorteil und Nachteil als Inhalt klassischer aequitas,' in D. Mantovani and A. Schiavone, eds., *Testi e problemi del giusnaturalismo romano* (Pavia: IUSS Press, 2007) 675–713.

Stroux, *Römische Rechtswissenschaft* (1949) = J. Stroux, *Römische Rechtswissenschaft und Rhetorik* (Potsdam: Stichnote, 1949).

Stroux, *Summum ius summa iniuria* (1926) = J. Stroux, *Summum ius summa iniuria. Ein Kapitel aus der Geschichte der interpretatio iuris* (Leipzig: Tauchnitz, 1926).

Thomas, 'L'institution juridique de la nature' (2011) = Y. Thomas, 'L'institution juridique de la nature. Remarques sur la casuistique du droit naturel à Rome' (1988), now published in M.-A. Hermitte and P. Napoli, eds., *Les Opérations du droit* (Paris: Gallimard/Seuil, 2011) 2–40.

Tomás, 'Limitations à la propriété riveraine et libre navigation fluviale' (2001) = G. Tomás, 'Limitations à la propriété riveraine et libre navigation fluviale,' *Revue international des droits antiques* 48 (2001) 361–372.

Watkins, 'Coloniae and Ius Italicum in the Early Empire' (1983) = T. W. Watkins, 'Coloniae and Ius Italicum in the Early Empire,' *Classical Journal* 78 (1983) 319–336.

Watson, 'D. 47.2.52.20. The Jackass, the Mares and "furtum"' (1971) = A. Watson, 'D. 47.2.52.20. The Jackass, the Mares and "furtum,"' in *Studi in onore di Edoardo Volterra II* (Milan: Giuffrè, 1971) 445–449.

Wieling, *Testamentsauslegung im römischen Recht* (1972) = H. J. Wieling, *Testamentsauslegung im römischen Recht* (Munich: Beck, 1972).

Wimmer, *Das Prälegat* (2004) = M. Wimmer, *Das Prälegat* (Vienna and Cologne: Böhlau, 2004).

Zinsmaier, 'insinuatio' (1998) = Th. Zinsmaier, 'insinuatio,' in G. Ueding, ed., *Historisches Wörterbuch der Rhetorik IV* (Tübingen: Niemeyer, 1998) 418–423.

Zinsmaier, 'rusticitas' (2007) = T. Zinsmaier, 'rusticitas,' in *Historisches Wörterbuch der Rhetorik VIII* (Tübingen: Niemeyer, 2007) 350–357.

Rhetoric in Medical Writing

Artistic Prose?

Caroline Petit

The rhetoric of ancient technical texts has been, to some extent, mapped out. Their features as well as the techniques used by medical and 'scientific' authors have been described in some detail, largely in relation with teaching. The practical and pedagogical value of those works (especially in antiquity and in other periods when the material to copy and transmit knowledge was expensive) was the main driving force in the transmission of such texts. This is true of many works of technical content in antiquity, especially medical works, many of which seem to focus on elementary knowledge: handbooks such as the pseudo-Galenic *Definitiones medicae* or *Introductio sive medicus*, collections of case-studies such as the Hippocratic *Epidemics*, compilations of short statements such as the Hippocratic *Aphorisms*, various works aimed at beginners and students, such as the four works on anatomy by Galen, collections of remedies (especially those 'easy to procure', *Euporista*), and so on.[1] The syntax of such works has been expertly described and corresponds to a basic level of rhetoric, one in which any extraneous developments, such as polemical digressions, narratives, or demonstrative passages, are excluded. Certain formats, such as the 'question and answer' pattern, proved popular.[2]

Another trend of scholarship has illuminated the complex argumentative aspects of medical prose—the art of making one's point. Defending a thesis is at the core of many a Hippocratic treatise, for example *On the Sacred Disease*; early medical texts thus share writing strategies with contemporary philosophical discourse on nature and invite comparisons on argumentative techniques, use of personal experience, refutation, and, later, syllogism. In Ian Lonie's words, Hippocratic texts are "rationalistic, bold in hypothesis, ingenious in argument,

[1] On the *Def.Med.*, see Kollesch, *Definitiones medicae* (1973) and her new edition (CMG V 13,2), as well as Cronier, 'Les manuscrits grecs des Definitiones medicae' (2021). On the *Euporista*, see Totelin, '*Euporista*' (2021). The latter has not received a critical edition yet. For an edition and detailed study of the *Introductio sive medicus*, see Petit, *Le médecin. Introduction* (2009).

[2] van der Eijk, 'Towards a Rhetoric of Ancient Scientific Discourse' (1997); Petit, 'Galien et le "discours de la méthode"' (2012). The literature on questions and answers is relatively abundant; see most recently the studies assembled in Meeusen, *Questions and Answers* (2020), with further references there.

Caroline Petit, *Rhetoric in Medical Writing: Artistic Prose?* In: *Medicine and the Law under the Roman Empire.* Edited by: Claire Bubb and Michael Peachin, Oxford University Press. © Claire Bubb and Michael Peachin 2023.
DOI: 10.1093/oso/9780192898616.003.0012

sceptical of received opinion, and they share the general commitment to intellectual analysis."[3] Persuasion, in all those contexts, serves the purposes of memorization and demonstration through clearness and the appearance of irrefutable truth. Of course, proof, in a medical context, partially relies on rhetoric rather than pure logic.[4]

This paper focuses on more literary and artistic aspects of ancient medical texts of the imperial period, which have received comparatively little attention.[5] Envisaging medical texts as literature is not entirely new—in this study, I will follow Heinrich von Staden in referring loosely to literary texts as "any body of textual compositions that display attentiveness to form and effect."[6] 'Form and effect' in medical texts will be the focus of my discussion, allowing me to occasionally go beyond the rhetoric of medical texts in a technical sense to consider their literary aspects. Defining criteria for artistic prose beyond this empirical approach is beyond the scope of this chapter.

The fact that medical texts, being labelled as 'technical', are seldom read by specialists of ancient literary texts is largely responsible for a relative lack of interest among mainstream or dare I say 'classic' classicists.[7] Yet for later periods, such as early modern times, the status of medical and scientific works as literature is not in question; several large projects currently taking place in Europe testify to this awareness, for example, 'Writing Doctors', led by Clark Lawlor at Northumbria University, or 'Nova Scientia', by Martin Korenjak at Innsbruck, as do a number of publications in the last couple of decades.[8]

It is therefore worth looking back to ancient texts labelled as 'medical' to probe their nature and qualities beyond conventional genre boundaries. As we will see,

[3] Lonie, 'Literacy' (1983) 149. Cf. Cross, *Hippocratic Oratory* (2018) 2.

[4] Cf. Petit, *Rhétorique de la Providence* (2018) 93–97.

[5] On ancient medical texts as literature see nonetheless Pigeaud and Pigeaud, *Les textes médicaux latins* (2000), especially the pieces by H. von Staden and J. Pigeaud; Fögen, *Antike Fachtexte* (2005) and *Wissen, Kommunikation und Selbstdarstellung* (2009); Taub and Doody, *Authorial Voices* (2009); Crombie, *Styles of Scientific Thinking* (1995). In more recent scholarship, see the comparative approach between medicine and mathematics attempted in Asper, *Writing Science* (2013); Gautherie, *Celse* (2017) on Celsus. Cf. Roby, *Technical Ekphrasis* (2016) on ekphrasis in ancient scientific texts (her study excludes medical texts).

[6] von Staden, 'Dangers of Literature' (2000) 356.

[7] This is changing, although fairly often 'the body' substitutes for medicine proper: see for example Kazantzidis, *Lucretius on Disease* (2021) on Lucretius; a number of papers in Bradley, Leonard, and Totelin, *Bodily Fluids in Antiquity* (2021); also a recent collection of papers on laughter and disease, which partially focuses on medical texts, in Kazantzidis and Tsoumpra, *Morbid Laughter* (2018) (see especially Thumiger on Aretaeus). Earlier book-length studies include Clarke-Kosak, *Heroic Measures* (2004) on Euripides.

[8] Among many excellent publications, see Charbonneau, *L'art d'écrire la science* (2005), an anthology of seventeenth- and eighteenth-century scientific and medical texts; the now classic collection of papers in Pender and Struever, *Rhetoric and Medicine* (2012). On the long history of medical texts envisaged from the perspective of rhetoric, see Coste, Jacquart, and Pigeaud, *Rhétorique Médicale* (2012). More recently, Moulinier-Bogi and Nicoud, *Ecritures médicales* (2019), with Coste discussing the findings of Pomata, 'Observation Rising' (2011) on medical narratives as an 'epistemic' genre. On figures in early modern texts, see Fahnestock, *Rhetorical Figures in Science* (1999).

detailed examination of medical works often leads to reassessing their classification as 'technical'.

Our earliest medical texts in Greek date back to fifth-century Athens, and they allow a preliminary sketch of artistic prose in the field of medicine, at a time of effervescent literary creation.

Rhetoric and Medicine in the Classical Period: Two Disciplines in Formation

It is now well known that a number of texts across the Hippocratic corpus share some rhetorical strategies with other works of the same period, ranging from the poetic to the philosophical. Powerful connections have been established, for example between Hippocrates and Herodotus.[9] Some Hippocratic works, as mentioned before, present a thesis and therefore adopt a strongly argumentative and, at times, polemical tone. Such is the case of *On the Sacred Disease*, where the first few chapters squarely attack the representatives of incantation-based medicine, called *goētai*, *alazones*, and other dismissive names. The author then turns to a demonstration of what he identified as the causes and nature of the so-called sacred disease (thought to be epilepsy). In other works, distinctive features of epideictic rhetoric have been recognized: such is the case of the treatise on *Winds*, displaying Gorgianic features.[10] A recent book-length study of five Hippocratic treatises (first categorized as 'essays' by Iain Lonie) by James Cross is providing a useful, if preliminary, overview of several strong rhetorical aspects of the corpus.[11] The fact, however, that rhetoric itself is, at this time, at an early stage of its long evolution invites caution in describing classical medical rhetoric. But let us note that Lonie thoughtfully set aside those five 'essays' as no different in form and nature from other examples of argumentative prose of the era. In other words, they are, in the eyes of a historian of medicine, literature.

Leaving aside those particularly rich texts for a while, we first ought to recognize that medical writing cannot always be mapped out against established shapes and canons: Jackie Pigeaud has rightly put special emphasis on the *Epidemics* (a work comprising seven books, written by three different authors) as a foundational genre of medical writing—focusing on the clinical picture of the disease.[12] As those seven/three works are essentially in the shape of brief notes, they seem to move away from any well-known type of extant writing from the classical period and they offer a rather singular type of (proto-?) 'ekphrasis'. But they also paved the way for medical interpretation and generated commentaries and imitations

[9] Thomas, *Herodotus in Context* (2000).

[10] Jouanna, 'Rhétorique et médecine' (1984); translated in Jouanna, *Greek Medicine* (2012) 39–53.

[11] Cross, *Hippocratic Oratory* (2018).

[12] Pigeaud, 'Le style d'Hippocrate' (1988).

through the centuries. Authentic imitations are not so numerous—but Pigeaud's interpretation of the Hippocratic *Epidemics* as 'foundational' or 'seminal' from the point of view of medical writing appears justified, when compared to the work of early modern Hippocratic doctor Guillaume de Baillou (Ballonius).[13] There is, therefore, something authentically creative in medical writing in the classical period, sometimes moving away from mainstream practices. Iain Lonie, too, insists on the creative and private nature and value of some of the notations in the *Epidemics*, namely *Epidemics* 6, to demonstrate their heuristic potential and their value for practitioners beyond the simple recording of cases. "The act of setting them down in writing," Lonie explains, "is an essential part of the whole painstaking process of groping one's way forward to the unknown and the unformulated."[14] They point to future development of thoughts, or elucidation of currently unclear facts, for the reference of the practitioner. The fact that their goal seems to point inwards, rather than towards an external audience, does not mean that they are exempt from any conscious rhetorical shaping. But it does set them apart from formally designed works such as *On the Sacred Disease*, *Breaths*, and other 'essays' in line with other contemporary writings besides medicine. The latter, as rightly hinted by Lonie and Jouanna and more recently explored by Cross, do indeed come close to 'literary' works of the same period. They use similar strategies, language, figures, and other devices demonstrating attention to form and to their audiences. The social context, of competition and need for performance in medicine, might be a key factor in this, although it cannot explain everything.[15] In a thoughtful enquiry on what a 'treatise' is, van der Eijk rightly cautions scholars against rash classifications of Hippocratic works, most of which offer a perceptible authorial voice (marked by the use of authorial *ego*), even when they are not "rhetorically crafted masterpieces such as *The Sacred Disease* or the *Regimen*."[16]

It is thus best to embrace the vast, diverse extant medical works as literature without applying partially arbitrary boundaries between them. Whatever the reason(s) explaining the flourishing of medical writings with recognizable rhetorical or literary features at this time, it is clear that, as Jackie Pigeaud would have put it, they *are* literature. Conversely, the increasingly recognized presence of medical language and thought in the literature of the time reinforces the need to consider medicine as part of classical literature: medical ideas and texts were known, and pondered, by the writers, the cultured, the thinkers.[17]

[13] Baillou was read and pondered through the early modern period. Cf. Coste 'Guillaume de Baillou' (2011) and Coste and Maggiori, *Les deux livres des Epidémies* (2021).

[14] Lonie, 'Literacy' (1983) 155–158, quotation from p. 157.

[15] The popular concept of 'medical market place' explains the competition among healers, not so much the rise of a medical literature.

[16] van der Eijk, 'Galen and the Scientific Treatise' (2013) 147.

[17] For a recent essay on interactions between medicine and classical texts, see Lane Fox, *The Invention of Medicine* (2020), especially 253–282 (with further literature in the notes).

In other words, classical medical writings seem to capture and echo (and, in turn, influence) some of the emerging patterns of contemporary prose through their composition, vocabulary, use of perspective, and argumentative techniques. In this perspective, it is tempting to study interactions appearing between medical literature and rhetoric. Both medicine and rhetoric are then *technai* in the making, and either of them bears witness to the development of the other.

In the Hellenistic period, however, technical writing more broadly is shaped up by new codes and modes of presentation, owed in a large part to the Aristotelian corpus. This, and the rise of commentary as a dominant form of scholarship in Hellenistic medicine, explain to an extent why medical texts have come to be seen as kind of systematic, technical, slightly unexciting. The real story of medical writing in the Hellenistic period is, of course, largely obfuscated by the considerable loss of texts of that period, which affects medicine, and other technical topics, as much as the rest of our sources. The surviving literature, mainly in the form of fragments, is illustrated by the cases of Herophilus and Erasistratus, both extremely important figures in medicine (way beyond their involvement in anatomical research) whose works have barely survived.[18] The commentary of Apollonius of Citium to the Hippocratic *Articulations* is the only of so many such works to have been preserved.[19] Enormous amounts of material are thus missing from, and dramatically affect our picture of, Hellenistic medical literature and medical rhetoric. But this is not the only limitation to our perspective; for we do have material, which often gets side-lined and forgotten in the well-known narrative of the loss of our sources. Does our evidence lie in lost medical treatises only? What we call medical literature here, once again, in fact expands beyond this label—for how can we distinguish appropriately between medical, and natural philosophical works when they deal with the same topics? In this respect, it would be fair to treat part of the Aristotelian corpus (including Theophrastus) as part of our enquiry, because the texts dealing with nature, animals, plants, stones, minerals, physiology, and so on overlap with medicine in very significant ways. As stated above, the new ways of writing on science, as illustrated by the Aristotelian corpus, have an enduring bearing on medical literature: Aristotelian language, and forms of argumentation, appear everywhere in Galen, in medieval texts, and ultimately in early modern medical and philosophical works.[20]

But the aim of this chapter is not so much to brush a comprehensive portrait of medical literature, as to highlight some of its most striking features and testimonies. Rather than looking for traces of rhetoric in Hellenistic sources, a relatively

[18] The fragments of Herophilus have been masterfully analysed and edited by H. von Staden (von Staden, *Herophilus* (1989)); the fragments of Erasistratus by I. Garofalo (Garofalo, *Erasistrati Fragmenta* (1988)). von Staden is working on a new edition of the fragments of Erasistratus.

[19] Kollesch, Kudlien, and Nickel, *Apollonii Citiensis* (1965) provides a critical edition.

[20] van der Eijk, 'Galen and the Scientific Treatise' (2013) 146–147, followed by a detailed study of Galen's *Mixtures* with discussion of Aristotelianism in the text (150–158).

vain pursuit, I will focus on the ways in which rhetoric, through its rise under the Roman Empire, helped shape medical writing. Rhetoric, as it became a fundamental training, as well as a comprehensive framework for thinking and writing, offered its followers deeper insights in their disciplines and better career prospects. Greek rhetorical training, then supplemented by its Latin counterpart in Rome, provided privileged physicians with a chance to shine in the competitive 'medical marketplace'. It provided them with a chance to raise medicine to the level of philosophy and literature: whatever the type of writing (a play, history, a speech, etc.), as a famous rhetor explained, the *progymnasmata* (or preliminary exercises) provided a near-universal framework for authors to thrive with infinite creativity.[21] In other words, rhetoric made ambition possible.

Such an ambition, as I have shown elsewhere, remains best exemplified by Galen of Pergamum in the second century of our era.[22] Of course, the context of Galen's rise to prominence as a medical writer is largely hidden from us: we have little literary evidence by comparable figures in imperial (or indeed ancient) medicine, although we do know of similarly successful individuals.[23] This means that we can easily, in this respect as in other aspects of Galen's legacy, overlook additional and alternative contributions to the field in terms of literary elaboration, and create a misleading impression of his 'uniqueness'. In the following, I would like to highlight Galen's artistic prose and examine how and why his writings remain *almost* unique among extant medical texts in their artistry and sophistication. I will then turn my attention to the backdrop to Galen's brilliance, by analysing near-contemporary medical and technical writings. Medical writings of the Antonine and Severan eras, I argue, show a slightly more diverse array of medical prose artists than is thought, even though many extant texts are in effect anonymous or dubious writings. Should we simply see those as foils to Galen's superlative achievements, or try and brush a more nuanced landscape of imperial medical literature?

Rhetoric and Medicine in Rome: Galen

It is not an overstatement to say that Galen embodies medical rhetoric. While much scholarship has focused on the performance aspect of his career and works, it is abundantly clear that rhetoric pervades the entirety of his extant production

[21] Aelius Theon, *Prog.* 70 Spengel. Cf. Penella, '*Progymnasmata* in Imperial Greek Education' (2011) and '*Progymnasmata* and Progymnasmatic theory' (2015).

[22] In the following, I will partially draw on Petit, *Rhétorique de la Providence* (2018). For more on Galen's competitive ambitions, see the contributions of Bubb and Salas in this volume.

[23] See, for example, the figure of Herakleitos presented in some detail in Bubb and Peachin, this volume, pp. 5–6.

in the wide array of argumentative, descriptive, and narrative texts that he has ventured into.[24]

Galen uses rhetoric in an extremely conscious way: proof of his interest in rhetorical, literary, and linguistic matters, he wrote many works aimed at rhetors, wrote about the many facets of language, logic and persuasion, and compiled lexicons for his contemporaries' use. His views on Hippocrates and other authors of the past (with no limits of form or topic) is informed and perceptive. He cites, quotes, and alludes to a myriad of ancient literary texts. Among those references, some are very well known, some less. His display of *paideia* is truly considerable (although we cannot tell how much of it is first-hand).[25] Much of the more literature-oriented material written by Galen is now lost, but the titles provided by his own catalogue of works are impressive.[26]

The pervasiveness of rhetoric in Galen's prose makes it difficult to offer a comprehensive picture of his artistry. Crafty rhetoric comes through everywhere—in sophisticated/heated arguments, often involving opponents he wishes to annihilate; in shorter or longer, usually colourful narratives; in descriptions (I will come back to *ekphrasis*); in many autobiographical pages, and so on. All are interwoven in such a way as to discourage a classification by text type. From a technical angle, providing a catalogue of figures and tropes would be tedious and pointless—but Galen provides a unique case for study due to the enormous quantity of works still extant; he also raises a number of questions as he escapes simple, clear-cut generic classifications.[27]

As far as argumentation technique and demonstration are concerned, the subtleties of Galen's writing in contradicting and challenging others' ideas has been highlighted many times—as for example in Teun Tieleman's detailed study of Galen's critique of Chrysippus.[28] Galen's ambivalence in handling dialectic, especially in his use of 'persuasive' or 'plausible' arguments (*pithanon*), has been explored convincingly by Riccardo Chiaradonna.[29] All the scholars reading Galen's philosophical works are very aware of Galen's sophisticated polemical style—indeed, refutation is an art where Galen truly excels and is sometimes even entertaining: his mastery of polemical discourse appears at every sentence in such works as *Against Lycus*, *Against Julian*, many famous passages of books I and II of

[24] On the performative aspect: Salas, *Cutting Words* (2020); Gleason, *Making Men* (1995) and 'Shock and Awe' (2009); von Staden, 'Galen and the "Second Sophistic"' (1997). On his rhetoric: Petit, *Rhétorique de la Providence* (2018); Curtis, 'Genre' (2014) (see also his 2009 doctoral thesis, not consulted).

[25] Petit, *Rhétorique de la Providence* (2018) 37–73; Nutton, 'Galen's Library' (2009).

[26] Petit, *Rhétorique de la Providence* (2018) 8–10. See Bubb, this volume pp. 198–199 for a visual breakdown of Galen's works, both originally and as now extant.

[27] Cf. the conclusions in van der Eijk, 'Galen and the Scientific Treatise' (2013).

[28] Tieleman, *Galen and Chrysippus on the Soul* (1996); on Galen and the Stoics, see also Tieleman, 'Galen and the Stoics' (2009); for a careful reconstitution of Chrysippus' *On Affections* (thanks to, and in spite of, Galen), see Tieleman, *Chrysippus' 'On Affections'* (2003).

[29] Chiaradonna, 'Galen on What Is Persuasive' (2014).

On the Method of Healing, and so on.[30] Here Galen's brilliance echoes that of many contemporary prose writers, including among Christian authors: Tertullian's acute sense of polemics, for example, or Sextus Empiricus's manipulation of logic.

Among the strikingly artistic features of Galen's prose however, his narratives stand out. Again, narration is not new in medical texts, and Galen himself comments on Hippocratic narratives with appreciation and flair, noticing how they contribute to the argument while entertaining the reader.[31] This unapologetically rhetorical take on narrative (to instruct, and to entertain at the same time) is central in his own use of this form. For, in Galen's works, narratives overlap, but do not coincide, with medical case histories. The latter are of course numerous.[32] Some of the most memorable stories told by Galen occur in his carefully crafted self-promotional work, *On Prognosis*: they do narrate case histories, but serve an additional purpose: to illustrate and memorialize Galen's most brilliant diagnoses and cast a retrospective look on his irresistible ascension to the role of physician to Marcus Aurelius. They serve Galen's autobiographical goal, support his particular theses and methodological points (for example, the idea that a 'love pulse' does not exist as such), and, almost incidentally, provide the usual details that will be useful to fellow practitioners. Although the latter are not exactly an afterthought, they come across as secondary in Galen's first-person narrative. In the details, those passages depict vivid scenes and portraits—not necessarily through many visual touches, but rather embracing characters and the sparkle of a conversation. At another level, of course, they emphatically stress Galen's deep knowledge and unique skills—chiselling the portrait of a physician with unparalleled experience; they also serve a demonstrative purpose, like the many case-stories scattered among his works. Finally, the stories Galen tells are not without echoings of previous or contemporary literary works—Galen is mindful to write within a literary tradition, which is not limited to the repertoire of classic Hippocratic case histories, but also includes a wealth of Hellenistic exempla.[33] There is an element of playfulness on Galen's part in such cases, which partially moves away from the strictly medical, sketching a lighter, more entertaining piece whenever he sees it fit: the lady in love with the dancer is a story in which Galen is especially attentive to entertain, creating and deceiving expectations in the reader's mind as he gets turned away at the patient's door and has to try several names whilst taking her pulse to identify the object of her secret affections. The progressive revelation of

[30] On Galen's polemical brio, see Petit, *Rhétorique de la Providence* (2018) 90–109.

[31] For example, Galen *Sem.* 1.4 (IV.525K = *CMG* V 3,1 76). On Galen's reflections on 'bad style' in Hippocratic works (as a criterion for authenticity), see now Börno and Coughlin, 'Galen on Bad Style' (2020).

[32] A convenient list can be found in Mattern, *Rhetoric of Healing* (2008), Appendix B.

[33] In the case of *Praen.* 6 (XIV.630–633K = *CMG* V 8,1 100–102) (the lady in love with the dancer), the background story is provided by a famous case solved by Erasistratus.

the Sicilian doctor's illness, and its calculated impact on the patient and his entourage, are a direct reflection of the effect they are aimed to produce on the reader.[34] Time, then, is an important element in some of Galen's narratives, demonstrating skilful practice of narration. Naturally, not all case histories are this elaborate; many are shorter, and sometimes seem to play a univocally demonstrative role in the context of an argument. More often than not, through arrangement of two or more narratives Galen is able to create a more complex argument, or picture, so that selecting a single story can be misleading as to his true intentions.[35] Galen's craft in narratives is therefore part of a broader architecture, which ought to be taken into account when interpreting his texts. This point, in itself, may suffice to set him apart from contemporary uses of case histories in other technical domains.[36] But as we will see, his narrative and descriptive technique appears at the same time accomplished and restrained when compared with Aretaeus of Cappadocia.

Galen's careful and clever use of the art of narration is supplemented by a similar ability to provide vivid descriptions, cultivating the same rhetorical virtue of *enargeia*. Galen often combines narrative and description, to highly expressive results, as (for example) in the detailed account of famines in Asia Minor that opens the work *On Good and Bad Humoral Fluid*.[37]

Galen's most treasured part of medicine, however, is anatomy—a domain of expertise that makes all the difference in a physician's capacity to describe the body, diagnose illnesses, and deal with wounds. Galen's special relationship with that sub-field results in some of his most elaborate pieces. His different anatomical works serve different purposes and audiences—from a students' use (the minor anatomical works) to more complex instructions for dissection (*Anatomical Procedures*). Those offer varying levels of interest from the point of view of rhetoric, from the more basic (indeed technical), to the more elaborate—especially in Galen's masterpiece, the *De usu partium* or *On the Usefulness of the Parts*. The latter work offers a detailed picture of the human body throughout, emphasizing at the same time the beauty and perfection of the creature. To say that Galen offers with the *De usu partium* a monumental *ekphrasis* would be fair—but it leaves aside the glorious celebration of the Creator responsible for its beauty. Galen sees the human body as a work of art, as demonstrated by his many references to the

[34] Galen *Loc.Aff.* 5.8 (VIII.361–366K). A new edition of *Loc.Aff.* Books 5–6 by W. Brunschön has just appeared in the *CMG* series. On this story, see Petit, *Rhétorique de la Providence* (2018) 81–84; Boudon-Millot 'Médecins et charlatans' (2003) 129.

[35] Reading the above-mentioned story of the lady in love with the dancer without continuing onto the next one, the case of a young man who was hiding food, leaves the reader liable to miss Galen's point, which is that pulse is an indication of emotional distress, but not of any particular emotion such as 'love.'

[36] By contrast, Rufus of Ephesus' case histories can appear quite crude, as do those in Artemidorus of Daldis, on which see Petit, 'Signes et présages' (2014).

[37] I discuss this passage in detail in Petit, *Rhétorique de la Providence* (2018) 140–145; on *enargeia* in technical descriptions, see also Roby, 'Technical Ekphrasis' (2016) 2–3.

great artists of Greek history, from Pheidias to Polycleitus, and to actual works of art or craft, such as an intricately designed golden signet ring. His own *logos* (which he describes as *hieros logos*, "sacred speech," using the same words as Aelius Aristides' *Sacred Tales*) emulates the beauty of the object in front of his eyes, the human body. Galen also presents himself as the privileged, chosen interpreter (*hermeneutēs*) of the divine—mimicking the posture of many a sophist of his time. Between praise, revelation, and demonstration, the magic of sophistic *paideia* operates here like in no other of his works.[38]

Finally, Galen offers a carefully crafted self-portrait throughout his works, especially those from his more mature age. In this aspect of his writing as in others, Galen plays on well-established rhetorical conventions. The art of painting oneself under favourable colours, which comes through in those passages about his character, his ancestry, his parents, his homeland and friends, his attitude in life in the face of distressing events (*On the Avoidance of Grief*), offers the portrait not only of an exceptional scholar but also of a moral and equanimous man, worthy of Marcus Aurelius' praise.[39] I have only highlighted a couple of aspects of Galen's prose that go beyond the technical and put his oeuvre among the more established literary works of his time. There is, of course, a lot more to be said, and it would be best to analyse passages taken from his works, but this is the matter of a book, or indeed many books.

In sum, Galen encapsulates the paradoxes of a highly rhetorical medical prose. To be taken seriously, he needs to 'demonstrate' (and claims to be doing so), but often ends up using the means of persuasion instead. Describing the human body proves such a challenge, a sacred mission, even, that he has recourse to hymnic prose to glorify its divine Creator. Art is therefore Galen's true aim and ambition. Galen, in turn, is not alone among other prose writers of the period—many parallels can be drawn between Galen and Lucian, Aelius Aristides, and Clement of Alexandria to name but a few. But he is alone in medicine. To some extent, the material of medicine, the flesh and blood of the human body, is beyond words—because of its complexity, because of its beauty, because of its extremely tiny parts, so difficult to see with the naked eye. Just like the body, medicine itself is a wonder to behold. It is therefore not surprising that its language ought to go beyond the standard means of expression.[40]

Galen's reasons to invest so much in style, are certainly complex. Writing with poise, with talent, was certainly helpful in establishing a career and, later, confirming superiority over his fellow physicians, notably in the imperial palace.[41] This is compounded by the continuing success of Second Sophistic authors. In the

[38] Cf. Petit, *Rhétorique de la Providence* (2018) 163–209.

[39] Petit, *Rhétorique de la Providence* (2018) 201–256; Raiola, *Nel tempo di una vita* (2015).

[40] Cf. Roby, *Technical Ekphrasis* (2016) 4–9 about the possibilities opened by *ekphrasis* broadly construed.

[41] Galen himself provides many examples of this competitive context, as is well known.

later part of his career, he seemed to be eager to justify and assert his own opinions, in part to prevent falsification or wrong interpretation.[42] His newly recovered treatise, *On the Avoidance of Grief* (*De indolentia*), has been read as an attempt to justify his role and escape criticism in the aftermath of Commodus' fall.[43] Finally, did he not desire to make his own supporters and friends (*hetairoi*) happy, by providing them with a good read? Ultimately, he left his mark on the field of medicine, leaving it changed forever. But Galen's case is extreme. To what extent is he representative of his time, and did he inform medical prose? Are there any other examples in the imperial period of similar authorial consciousness in medicine?

Beyond Galen: Artistic Prose in Imperial Medical Texts

While Galen overshadows much of medical literature, we can recover examples of medical writings that are contemporary to his oeuvre. To find 'Galenic' style, we sometimes need not look much further than some of the texts attributed to Galen but now thought to be inauthentic. The very controversy that arose from their authorship and date can be indicative of their organic links with Galenic thought and prose. Such is the case with the *Theriac to Piso*, a work once considered authentic and now again relegated to the nebula of spurious texts of the corpus.[44] As recently pointed out again by Vivian Nutton, the crafted prose of the author is reminiscent of Galen.[45] We know, through various elements inside the text, that it belongs to the Severan period, in the early third century CE. While some linguistic features set it apart from authentic works by Galen (such as the use of subjunctive following *εἰ* without *ἄν*, and other signs of relaxed syntax), the text is noticeably conceived and constructed as an homage to a powerful patron, with high-ranking charges: it starts with a long chapter of praise for the dedicatee's wide-ranging intellectual interests and natural abilities in medicine, and ends with a prayer that this remedy (theriac) will bring longevity to him. The dedicatee's taste for sophisticated discourse, both in writing and in deliberative contexts, is stressed both at the beginning at the end; on another occasion, the author also hopes that his account of the death of Cleopatra will have entertained him, thus stressing that he is definitely aiming at providing delight as well as instruction to the dedicatee.[46]

[42] Petit, 'Death, Posterity and the Vulnerable Self' (2019) 45–51.

[43] Nicholls, 'Galen and the Last Days of Commodus' (2019) 254–255.

[44] See Boudon-Millot, *Thériaque à Pison* (2016); Leigh, *Theriac to Piso* (2016). Cf. Nutton, 'Galen on Theriac' (1997), followed by Swain, *Hellenism and Empire* (1996) (Appendix D).

[45] Nutton, 'Three Pseudo-Galenic Texts' (2021) 7–8; see also Leigh, *Theriac to Piso* (2016) 10.

[46] Namely, *Ther.Pis.* 1.6 (XIV. 212 K = 3–4 B-M) and 19.14 (XIV.294K = 94–95 B-M) (*ἐπεὶ καὶ σὺ περὶ πάντας τοὺς λόγους φιλοτίμως ἔχεις*); Cleopatra at 8.14 (XIV.237K = 39–40 B-M) (*ἀλλὰ τοῦτο μὲν οὐκ ἀτερπῶς ἱστορείσθω, διὰ τὴν σὴν ἐν πᾶσι τοῖς λόγοις φιλοτιμίαν*)—this sentence is omitted in Arabic; note the use of *οὐκ* with the imperative, instead of *μή* (unless we read *οὖν* for *οὐκ*).

This is directly reminiscent of Galen's conception of narratives as aiming to delight and instruct, in line with the aims of rhetoric.[47] The work also contains literary and poetic allusions designed to please the reader or auditor (such as the allusion to the death of Polyxena, at 8.12). This piece, which is exactly contemporary with Galen's late years, is therefore undoubtedly conceived within the codes of epideictic rhetoric, not just a technical work on a famous remedy.

Other, similarly unloved works could be seen as artistic prose: the other work on theriac, addressed to Pamphilianus, is well written and its first chapter, again, shows awareness of epideictic rhetoric.[48] Just like the *Theriac to Piso*, it begins with high praise to the dedicatee of the work, Pamphilianus. Like the author of the *Theriac to Piso*, the author of the *Theriac to Pamphilianus* refers to a conversational or even rhetorical context as background to the written work (1.1–2). At the end of the first chapter (1.5), the author elegantly concludes his laudatory address with a clever pun on the traditional *nomen omen* word game: Fortune has given Pamphilianus a most appropriate name, for he was born to be loved (*phileisthai*) by all (*pantes*). Praise for the drug itself (along the lines of usefulness) occupies a large proportion of the opuscule, although the author cautions his dedicatee against any excess that would lead to believe theriac is a cure-all (4.24). Both works on theriac are built around the request or the needs of a powerful dedicatee, a practice which, of course, predated Galen and the authors of those two works: the commentary of Apollonius of Citium mentioned above, for example, addresses King Ptolemy at the beginning of each book. The work titled *On the Virtues of Centaurea* (*De virtutibus centaureae*), preserved only in Latin and quite popular in the Renaissance, is also a well-crafted piece, written by a Greek doctor to 'sell' a panacea.[49] Like both inauthentic works on theriac, it emerges from the world of educated Greek or Cretan doctors in Rome; to this group, one could yet attach the pseudo-Galenic *Doctor: Introduction* (*Introductio sive medicus*), which has been linked to an Egyptian background.[50] The latter is, however, more of a work for beginners, with more basic rhetorical strategies at play.[51] Other works in the corpus have been described as 'sophistic', for example the opuscule *Whether What Is in the Womb Is an Animal* (*An animal sit quod in utero est*), a work which resembles a declamation or at least the written version of a speech or lecture.[52] It concerns embryology, a medical and natural philosophical topic which was

[47] See above, p. 291.

[48] *Ther.Pamph.* 1.1–5 (XIV.295–297K = 2–3 B-M).

[49] For a comparative analysis in this text in relation with the two *Theriacs*, see Nutton, 'Three Pseudo-Galenic Texts' (2021).

[50] Boudon-Millot (in *Thériaque à Pison* (2016) xci–xciv and in *Thériaque à Pamphilianos* (2021) 21) has identified a number of parallels between the *Introductio* and the *Theriac to Piso*. On the Egyptian background in the *Introductio*, see Petit, *Le médecin. Introduction* (2009) l–li.

[51] For a discussion of the genre and style of the *Introductio*, in relation with similar ancient works, see Petit, *Le médecin. Introduction* (2009) xv–xxi; on introductory works more generally, see Asper, 'Struktur und Funktion' (1998).

[52] The editor of the text, H. Wagner, claims that it is the work of some sophist: Wagner, *Εἰ ζῷον* (1914) xiv–xv.

popular among the learned. The text, not unlike a number of Galenic works, draws on Plato and Hippocrates together.

In short, artistic prose is not confined to strictly Galenic works, even in Galen's own lifetime. Medical (artistic) writing was certainly part of practices and customs in the higher circles of the field, as it had an audience among literate patients as well as fellow practitioners, and Galen was not the only educated Greek carving his own career in Rome. We knew that already from his own account, referring to countless rivals and imposters. But Galen is easily accused of making up his own stories. Here, we encounter solid evidence. Taken separately, the works mentioned above, which consist mostly of short texts with a limited aim and audience, may seem irrelevant; but considered as a whole, they paint a diverse picture of medical prose at the turn of the third century. They ended up in the corpus of authentic works because they echoed very strongly Galenic ideas, preoccupations, and, possibly, style.

This complements the picture that arises from earlier imperial medicine, where the names of Celsus (in Latin) or Aretaeus of Cappadocia (in Greek) spring to mind.[53] Aretaeus of Cappadocia, of all ancient Greek doctors, wrote the most spectacular 'portraits' of diseases in his partially preserved works on acute and chronic diseases.[54] An emulator of Hippocrates in terms of language, Aretaeus has a knack for lending his topics the strongest visual traits. As remote from the Hippocratic note-taking style of the *Epidemics* as from the Galenic, objectivist gaze, Aretaeus seems to follow a full-on ekphrastic model of writing for each and every disease.[55] The vividness of his descriptions (called *enargeia* in rhetoric, as we have seen) has made his work an enduring object of fascination for early modern practitioners.[56] But, however inspirational in the modern era, the work of Aretaeus remained in splendid isolation among ancient medical works in spite of (or because of) its daring authorial quality. His brand of artistic prose, one may say, did not flourish beyond him; Galen's more calibrated writing, based on strict adherence to a form of plain language, eventually set standards of writing. Based on Galen's (often scathing) testimony, one may wonder how many such authorial voices were silenced with the wreck of ancient medical works that predated Galen. Archigenes, whom Galen blames for his over-flourishing language (which he deems unclear), was most likely a creative writer.[57] So was probably Erasistratus, who wrote a work on the usefulness of the parts long before Galen.

[53] On Celsus and rhetoric, see Gautherie, *Celse* (2017).

[54] Edition: Hude, *Aretaeus* (1958).

[55] See Gleason, 'Aretaeus' (2020); Petit, *Rhétorique de la Providence* (2018) 118–120.

[56] See the editions and translations of the Renaissance, as listed in Hude, *Aretaeus* (1958) vii–viii; the draft translation written by R. T. H. Laënnec (published by M. D. Grmek in 2000) bears witness to the inspirational nature of this text for the clinician.

[57] Galen, *Loc.Aff.* 2.9 (VIII.110–118K). The problem is exposed, with examples from Archigenes' own words, in Pigeaud, 'Rhétorique et médecine chez les Grecs' (1985) 40–41.

Has Galen, by his own power, wiped clean the slate of medical prose up to his time? As we have seen, some voices remain audible, almost silenced, but not quite. And it is fair to concede that Galen has a point when he criticizes the excessively idiosyncratic language that imbued some medical texts before him. Ambivalence created by form or choice of words, he is correct to say, is a problem in a domain like medicine, where absolute clarity ought to be the norm.[58] The normative, systematic effect that Galen's oeuvre has had on medical language and literature was probably desirable for 'scientific' minds. It may also have snuffed out creativity in some respects. Galen has, to an extent, planted the roots of classical rhetoric in medical writing, much more systematically than anyone before him; more adventurous attempts faded into irrelevance.

Galen's language and style, as we have seen, are more polished and sophisticated than most technical authors. The case of his contemporaries, Ptolemy and Artemidorus of Daldis, who both penned impressive works in their respective domains, comes in stark contrast to Galen's prose. Artemidorus deliberately turns away from a more discursive, ornate style.[59] Galen created a perfect 'sophistic' medical style, by contrast with contemporary authors who, consciously or not, decided to stick to the simple style required from technical works.[60]

Artistic Prose in Medicine: An Enduring Phenomenon?

In the Roman Empire, then, we saw medicine flourish in imperial literature, both in Greek and in Latin, in various texts, although Galen remains by far the most spectacular example of all. But was this due to last? Or was it simply a moment in history, linked, perhaps, to the Second Sophistic? Did it in any way shape up medical prose to come? The answer is not straightforward.

Galen was certainly not the first to combine medicine, performance genius, and celebrity. He is just our prominent example if we look for *texts* to evidence this type of medical 'sophist'. As we have seen, forms of artistic prose in medicine arise in contemporary or slightly later works, which were (for that reason?) attributed to him in manuscripts. A more difficult question is whether this trend continued long after Galen. At first glance, it is not the case: extant medical authors after Galen have left compilations, summaries, and commentaries. As mentioned in the beginning, a large part of this material had didactic purposes. They are carefully

[58] Pigeaud, 'Rhétorique et médecine chez les Grecs' (1985) 48 rightly notes however that Galen elsewhere condones and integrates certain metaphors and analogies in medical language, for example in the case of the epileptic boys describing the subjective symptom of seizure, 'aura', which means 'breeze' (*Loc.Aff.* 3.11 (VIII.198K)).

[59] Petit, 'Signes et présages' (2014) 167–168; Bowersock, 'Artemidorus' (2004).

[60] Demetrius, *On Style* 3 (pp. 55–57 Chiron). Cf. Petit, 'Galien et le "discours de la méthode"' (2012) 66–69.

written and meticulously composed; but do they qualify as artistic prose? Although this is not the place for a detailed assessment, it should be noted that late antique medical texts have attracted much more nuanced comments and analyses in recent years. Oribasius, to name but one, who as a physician was in a comparable position to Galen, since he attended to the emperor Julian, wrote extensive works which, although badly mutilated, display his expensive education and that of his distinguished readers (Eunapius, Julian himself).

Some physicians performed, spoke, and wrote like sophists—they were actually called 'iatrosophists', a category we know precisely thanks to the *Lives of the Sophists* by Eunapius. The author emphasizes the rhetorical skill of the famous physicians of his time, such as Zeno, his pupils Magnus (better known as Magnus of Nisibis), and, as well, Oribasius.[61] Including them in in an account of the Sophists of his time is, in itself, a significant step showing the importance of rhetorical education among high-profile physicians from the Greek East: it certainly moves away from Philostratus' *Lives of the Sophists*, which did not include physicians. Magnus, as a result of his 'sophistic' reputation, is later dismissed as "a doctor in word, clueless in practice" by Theophilus Protospatharius.[62]

In retrospect, Galen appears as a forerunner of those experts of rhetoric and medicine (or 'medical rhetoric', if I may use this phrase), who shone through their teaching. This tradition continued well after Oribasius; Gesius, a fifth-century doctor in Alexandria, is among the most famous, because, although a friend of many Christians, he is known to have been embroiled in the war between the many religious zealots of the city.[63] His fame was enormous, and, several decades later, he was still remembered fondly among physicians such as Stephanus of Alexandria (less so in Christian polemical sources such as the *Miracles of Cyrus and John* by Sophronius of Jerusalem).[64] New sources in Syriac have recently emerged about his *œuvre*, so that we may know more in the near future about his actual teaching (and his style).[65] Meanwhile, we can focus on the testimony of his contemporaries: Gesius was a renowned and appreciated intellectual, a friend of Damascius, Aeneas of Gaza, and Proclus. They exchanged letters, some of which have come down to us. In his sixteenth letter, for instance, Procopius praises the style of Gesius in no ambiguous terms.[66] In other words, Galen's legacy was not lost. A tradition of rhetoric combined with medicine did continue, at least in

[61] Eunap. *VS* 19–21 (Giangrande).

[62] Theophilus Protospatharius, *De urinis*, proem 5 (Ideler) (*ὁ Μάγνος, ἰατρὸς μὲν τῷ λόγῳ, ἄπειρος δὲ τῷ πράγματι*). There is a new edition by I. Grimm-Stadelmann, 2008.

[63] On Gesius as both a historical figure and literary character, see Watts, 'Gessius' (2009); on his role in medical and Christian polemics, see also Petit, 'Alexandrie' (2015) 292–293 and 306–7. I adopt the spelling Gesius, not Gessius.

[64] Watts, 'Gessius' (2009) 123–124 and Petit, 'Alexandrie' (2015).

[65] Cf. Kessel, 'Syriac Medicine' (2019), 447.

[66] Procopius *Ep.* 16, 3–7: *τοιοῦτος ἦν τις ἐγώ, πάντα θαυμάζων, τῶν ὀνομάτων τὴν ὥραν, τὴν πρὸς ἄλληλα τούτων ἁρμονίαν, τὸ διὰ πάντων κάλλος ἐπιφαινόμενον, καὶ τὸ δὴ μέγιστον, τοὺς ὑμετέρους τρόπους, ἐξ ὧν ἡμῖν προῆλθε τὰ γράμματα. καί σοι πολλὰ κἀγαθὰ γένοιτο τοιαύτην ἡμῖν*

Alexandria. It flourished until at least the time of Gesius, probably even later, considering that Gesius' memory lives on in the seventh century, just like the tradition of excellent medical teaching at Alexandria. Is this potentially a contribution to the debate around the Third Sophistic?[67]

It is well known that Islamic medicine built on the models of ancient medical literature, and narratives are no exception to this rule.[68] In fact, even scientific autobiography flourished in direct reference to Galen's autobiographical passages.[69] From there, Islamic scholars (not just physicians) took not only their love and reverence for Galen, but also a taste for clever rhetoric and artistic prose.[70] The flourishing of medical writings, the wide readership they conquered in the Islamic intellectual space, in conjunction with an extremely lively linguistic and rhetorical tradition, created a favourable context for the development of a 'medical rhetoric' in Arabic.

Conclusion

Galen's reception across the ages was contrasted and shows at times a lack of understanding for his crafted and deliberately complex style. Many have preferred dubious, but convenient summaries to his actual works; some have mutilated, recast, or rewritten them. Others, in turn, have been inspired, and the trend of a 'medical' or indeed 'scientific' rhetoric is a long-standing phenomenon in early modern literature and thought. Let us turn to the Renaissance, and towards the impressions of those who first rediscovered and brought to light ancient medical texts. It is maybe worth stressing that, to the humanists of around 1500, Galen and other physicians were no different from other ancient authors, nor unworthy of their interest. Of course, some, like Beatus Rhenanus, were not interested in medical texts.[71] Others were, especially in Italy and, soon after, France. It struck Symphorien Champier, inspired by his Italian colleagues and masters, that Galen's

ἀποδεδωκότι τὴν ἑορτήν. Watts, 'Gessius' (2009) 117 recognizes that "Procopius saw Gessius as both a social and cultural peer whose rhetorical skill and philosophical learning he could (and perhaps should) readily acknowledge."

[67] As a follow-up or revival movement of the Second Sophistic, the Third Sophistic showed a late antique flourishing of rhetoric among a wide range of scholars. Cf. Van Hoof, 'Greek Rhetoric and the Later Roman Empire' (2010); Pernot, 'The Second Sophistic' (2019) and 'Third Sophistic' (2021).

[68] Álvarez-Millán, 'Graeco-Roman Case Histories' (1999) and 'Practice vs. Theory' (2000).

[69] Menn, '*Discourse on the Method*' (2003).

[70] See the work of Al-Jâhiz, as analysed in Montgomery, *Al-Jâhiz* (2013), who draws parallels between Al-Biruni, Galen, and Hunayn in the respect of bio-bibliographical writing (p. 183) and stresses the paradigmatic value of Galen's *De usu partium* (pp. 294–295) as well as the lesser-known pseudo-Galenic commentary to Hippocrates' *Sevens* (pp. 285–296). In particular, he shows the filiation of Job of Edessa's *Book of Treasures* and of Al-Jâhiz's *Book of Living* with Galen's *De usu partium*. Among other influential works, deemed exemplary in their composition, was the Hippocratic *Aphorisms* (Montgomery, *Al-Jâhiz* (2013) 380).

[71] Magdelaine, 'Beatus Rhenanus' (2001).

style hovered somewhere between prose and poetry. He even wrote that words flowed from his mouth like honey, equating Galen to Homer's Nestor, the archetype of the great orator.[72]

Bibliography

Álvarez-Millán, 'Graeco-Roman Case Histories' (1999) = C. Álvarez-Millán, 'Graeco-Roman Case Histories and Their Influence on Medieval Islamic Clinical Accounts,' *The Society for Social History of Medicine* 12.1 (1999) 19–43.

Álvarez-Millán, 'Practice vs. Theory' (2000) = C. Álvarez-Millán, 'Practice versus Theory: 10th c. Case-Histories from the Middle-East,' *The Society for Social History of Medicine* 13.2 (2000) 293–306.

Anderson, *The Second Sophistic* (1993) = G. Anderson, *The Second Sophistic. A Cultural Phenomenon in the Roman Empire* (London: Routledge, 1993).

Asper, 'Struktur und Funktion' (1998) = M. Asper, 'Zur Struktur und Funktion eisagogischer Texte,' in W. Kullmann, J. Althoff, and M. Asper, eds., *Gattungen wissenschaftlicher Literatur in der Antike* (Tübingen: G. Narr, 1998) 309–340.

Asper, 'Un personnagio in cerca di lettore' (2006) = M. Asper, 'Un personnagio in cerca di lettore. Galens *Grösser Puls* und die "Erfindung" des Lesers,' in T. Fögen, ed., *Antike Fachtexte. Ancient Technical Texts* (Berlin: De Gruyter, 2006) 21–39.

Asper, *Writing Science* (2013) = M. Asper, ed., *Writing Science. Medical and Mathematical Authorship in Ancient Greece* (Berlin: De Gruyter, 2013).

Asper, *Thinking in Cases* (2019) = M. Asper, ed., *Thinking in Cases. Ancient Greek and Imperial Chinese Case Narratives* (Berlin: De Gruyter, 2019).

Barton, *Power and Knowledge* (1994) = T. Barton, *Power and Knowledge: Astrology, Physiognomics, and Medicine in the Roman Empire* (Ann Arbor, MI: University of Michigan Press, 1994).

Bompaire, 'Quatre styles d'autobiographie' (1993) = J. Bompaire, 'Quatre styles d'autobiographie au IIe s. de notre ère: Aelius Aristide, Lucien, Marc Aurèle, Galien,' in F. Baslez, P. Hoffmann, and L. Pernot, eds., *L'invention de l'autobiographie d'Hésiode à Saint Augustin* (Paris: Presses de l'École Normale Supérieure, 1993) 199–209.

Bowersock, 'Artimedorus' (2004) = G. W. Bowersock, 'Artimedorus and the Second Sophistic,' in B. Borg, ed., *Paideia: Die Welt der Zweiten Sophistik/The World of the Second Sophistic* (Berlin: De Gruyter, 2004) 53–63.

Börno and Coughlin, 'Galen on Bad Style' (2020) = M. Börno and S. Coughlin, 'Galen on Bad Style (*kakozelia*): Hippocratic Exegesis in Galen and Some Predecessors,' in V. Nutton and L. Totelin, eds., *Ancient Medicine, behind and beyond Hippocrates: Essays in Honour of Elizabeth Craik. Technai* 11 (2020) 145–175.

[72] Petit, 'Medical Humanism' (2021).

Boudon-Millot 'Médecins et charlatans' (2003) = V. Boudon-Millot, 'Aux marges de la médecine rationnelle: médecins et charlatans à Rome au temps de Galien (IIe s. de notre ère),' *Revue des Études Grecques* 116.1 (2003) 109–131.

Boudon-Millot, *Thériaque à Pison* (2016) = V. Boudon-Millot, *Galien. Tome VI. Thériaque à Pison* (Paris: Belles Lettres, 2016).

Boudon-Millot, *Thériaque à Pamphilianos* (2021) = V. Boudon-Millot, *Galien. Tome X. Thériaque à Pamphilianos* (Paris: Belles Lettres, 2021).

Bradley, Leonard, and Totelin, *Bodily Fluids in Antiquity* (2021) = M. Bradley, V. Leonard, and L. Totelin, eds., *Bodily Fluids in Antiquity* (London: Routledge, 2021).

Brunt, 'Bubble of the Second Sophistic' (1994) = P. Brunt, 'The Bubble of the Second Sophistic,' *Bulletin of the Institute of Classical Studies* 39 (1994) 25–52.

Camposampierro-Favaretti and Scribano, *Galen and the Early Moderns* (2022) = M. Camposampierro-Favaretti and E. Scribano, eds., *Galen and the Early Moderns* (Cham: Springer, 2022).

Charbonneau, *L'art d'écrire la science* (2005) = F. Charbonneau, *L'art d'écrire la science. Anthologie des textes savants du XVIIIe s. français* (Québec: Presses de l'université Laval, 2005).

Chiaradonna, 'Galen on What Is Persuasive' (2014) = R. Chiaradonna, 'Galen on What Is Persuasive (*pithanon*) and What Approximates to Truth,' in P. Adamson, R. Hansberger, and J. Wilberding, eds., *Philosophical Themes in Galen. Bulletin of the Institute of Classical Studies, Suppl.* 114 (2014) 61–88.

Clarke-Kosak, *Heroic Measures* (2004) = J. Clarke-Kosak, *Heroic Measures: Hippocratic Medicine in the Making of Euripidean Tragedy* (Leiden: Brill, 2004).

Coker, 'Galen and the Language of Old Comedy' (2019) = A. Coker, 'Galen and the Language of Old Comedy: Glimpses of a lost Treatise at *PA* 23b–28,' in C. Petit, ed., *A Tale of Resilience. Galen's De indolentia in Context* (Leiden: Brill, 2019) 63–90.

Coste 'Guillaume de Baillou' (2011) = J. Coste 'Guillaume de Baillou, Doctor Medicus Parisiensis', *Medicina e storia* 21–2 (2011) 95–111.

Coste, 'Genres littéraires médicaux' (2019) = J. Coste, 'Genres littéraires médicaux à l'époque moderne. Analyse conceptuelle et application aux recueils d'observations médicales du XVIe au milieu du XIXe siècle,' in L. Moulinier-Bogi and M. Nicoud, eds., *Écritures médicales. Discours et genres de la tradition antique à l'époque moderne* (Paris: De Boccard, 2019) 335–361.

Coste, Jacquart, and Pigeaud, *Rhétorique Médicale* (2012) = J. Coste, D. Jacquart, and J. Pigeaud, eds., *La rhétorique médicale à travers les siècles: actes du colloque international de Paris, 9 et 10 octobre 2008* (Geneva: Droz, 2012).

Coste and Maggiori, *Les deux livres des Epidémies* (2021) = J. Coste and H. Maggiori, eds., trans., *Les deux livres des Epidémies et Ephémérides de Guillaume de Baillou* (Paris: Belles Lettres, 2021).

Crombie, *Styles of Scientific Thinking* (1995) = A. Crombie, *Styles of Scientific Thinking in the European Tradition: The History of Argument and Explanation, Especially in the Mathematical and Biomedical Sciences and Arts* (London: Duckworth, 1995).

Cronier, 'Les manuscrits grecs des Definitiones medicae' (2021) = M. Cronier, 'Les manuscrits grecs des Definitiones medicae pseudo-galéniques,' in C. Petit, S. Swain, and K.-D. Fischer, eds., *Pseudo-Galenica. The Formation of the Galenic Corpus from Antiquity to the Renaissance* (London: Warburg Institute, 2021) 47–68.

Cross, *Hippocratic Oratory* (2018) = J. Cross, *Hippocratic Oratory: The Poetics of Early Greek Medical Prose* (London; New York: Routledge, 2018).

Curtis, 'Genre' (2014) = T. Curtis, 'Genre and Galen's Philosophical Discourses,' in P. Adamson, R. E. Hansberger, and J. Wilberding, eds., *Philosophical Themes in Galen* (London: Institute of Classical Studies, School of Advanced Study, University of London, 2014) 39–59.

van der Eijk, 'Galen and the Scientific Treatise' (2013) = P. J. van der Eijk, 'Galen and the Scientific Treatise: A Case Study of *Mixtures*,' in M. Asper, ed., *Writing Science. Medical and Mathematical Authorship in Ancient Greece* (Berlin: De Gruyter, 2013) 145–175.

van der Eijk, 'Towards a Rhetoric of Ancient Scientific Discourse' (1997) = P. J. van der Eijk, 'Towards a Rhetoric of Ancient Scientific Discourse: Some Formal Characteristics of Greek Medical and Philosophical Texts (Hippocratic Corpus, Aristotle),' in E. J. Bakker, ed., *Grammar as Interpretation. Greek Literature in Its Linguistic Contexts* (Leiden: Brill, 1997) 77–129.

Fahnestock, *Rhetorical Figures in Science* (1999) = J. Fahnestock, *Rhetorical Figures in Science* (Oxford: Oxford University Press, 1999).

Fögen, *Antike Fachtexte* (2005) = T. Fögen, ed., *Antike Fachtexte—Ancient Technical Texts* (Berlin and New York: De Gruyter, 2005).

Fögen, *Wissen, Kommunikation und Selbstdarstellung* (2009) = T. Fögen, *Wissen, Kommunikation und Selbstdarstellung. Zu Struktur und Charakteristik römischer Fachtexte der frühen Kaiserzeit* (Munich: Beck, 2009).

Garofalo, *Erasistrati Fragmenta* (1988) = I. Garofalo, *Erasistrati Fragmenta* (Pisa: Giardini Editori e Stampatori, 1988).

Gautherie, *Celse* (2017) = A. Gautherie, *Rhétorique et thérapeutique dans le 'De medicina' de Celse* (Turnhout: Brepols, 2017).

Gleason, *Making Men* (1995) = M. Gleason, *Making Men: Sophists and Self-Presentation in Ancient Rome* (Princeton: Princeton University Press, 1995).

Gleason, 'Shock and Awe' (2009) = M. Gleason, 'Shock and Awe: The Performance Dimension of Galen's Anatomy Demonstrations,' in C. Gill, T. G. J. Whitmarsh, and J. M. Wilkins, eds., *Galen and the World of Knowledge* (Cambridge: Cambridge University Press, 2009) 85–114.

Gleason, 'Aretaeus' (2020) = M. Gleason, 'Aretaeus and the Ekphrasis of Agony,' *Classical Antiquity* 39.2 (2020) 153–187.

Hude, *Aretaeus* (1958) = C. Hude, *Aretaeus. Corpus Medicorum Graecorum* II, 2nd ed. (Berlin: Akademie Verlag, 1958).

Jouanna, 'Rhétorique et médecine' (1984) = J. Jouanna, 'Rhétorique et médecine dans la Collection hippocratique. Contribution à l'histoire de la rhétorique au ve siècle,' *Revue des Études Grecques* 97 (1984) 26–44.

Jouanna, *Greek Medicine* (2012) = J. Jouanna with N. Allies (trans.) and P. van der Eijk (ed.), *Greek Medicine from Hippocrates to Galen. Selected Papers* (Leiden and Boston: Brill, 2012).

Kazantzidis, *Lucretius on Disease* (2021) = G. Kazantzidis, *Lucretius on Disease. The Poetics of Morbidity in De rerum natura* (Berlin: De Gruyter, 2021).

Kazantzidis and Tsoumpra, *Morbid Laughter* (2018) = G. Kazantzidis and N. Tsoumpra, eds., *Morbid Laughter: Exploring the Comic Dimensions of Disease in Classical Antiquity. Special issue of Illinois Classical Studies* 43.2 (2018).

Kessel, 'Syriac Medicine' (2019) = G. Kessel, 'Syriac Medicine,' in D. King, ed., *The Syriac World* (London: Routledge, 2019) 438–459.

Kollesch, 'Galen und die Zweite Sophistik' (1981) = J. Kollesch, 'Galen und die Zweite Sophistik,' in V. Nutton, ed., *Galen. Problems and Prospects* (London: The Wellcome Institute for the History of Medicine, 1981) 1–11.

Kollesch, *Definitiones medicae* (1973) = J. Kollesch, *Untersuchungen zu den pseudogalenischen Definitiones medicae* (Berlin: Akademie Verlag, 1973).

Kollesch, Kudlien, and Nickel, *Apollonii Citiensis* (1965) = J. Kollesch, F. Kudlien, and D. Nickel, *Apollonii Citiensis In Hippocratis De articulis commentarius. Corpus Medicorum Graecorum* XI 1,1 (Berlin: Akademie Verlag, 1965).

Lane Fox, *The Invention of Medicine* (2020) = R. Lane Fox, *The Invention of Medicine. From Homer to Hippocrates* (London: Allen Lane, 2020).

Leigh, *Theriac to Piso* (2016) = R. Leigh, *On Theriac to Piso, Attributed to Galen: A Critical Edition with Translation* (Leiden and Boston: Brill, 2016).

Lloyd, 'Galen's Un-Hippocratic Case-Histories' (2009) = G. E. R. Lloyd, 'Galen's Un-Hippocratic Case-Histories,' in C. Gill, T. G. J. Whitmarsh, and J. M. Wilkins, eds., *Galen and the World of Knowledge* (Cambridge: Cambridge University Press, 2009) 115–130.

Longo, 'La medicina nelle *Declamazioni maggiori*' (2016) = G. Longo, 'La medicina nelle *Declamazioni maggiori* pseudo-quintilianee,' in M. Dinter, C. Guérin and M. Martinho, eds., *Reading Roman Declamation: The Declamations Ascribed to Quintilian* (Berlin: De Gruyter, 2016) 167–187.

Lonie, 'Literacy' (1983) = I. Lonie, 'Literacy and the Development of Hippocratic Medicine,' in F. Lasserre and P. Mudry, eds., *Formes de pensée dans la Collection hippocratique. Actes du IVe Colloque International Hippocratique (Lausanne, 21–26 septembre 1981)* (Geneva: Droz, 1983).

Magdelaine, 'Beatus Rhenanus' (2001) = C. Magdelaine, 'Beatus Rhenanus et la médecine grecque,' in F. Heim and J. Hirstein, eds., *Beatus Rhenanus (1485–1547): lecteur et éditeur des textes anciens. Actes du Colloque International tenu à Strasbourg et à Sélestat du 13 au 15 novembre 1998* (Turnhout: Brepols, 2001) 129–150.

Mattern, *Rhetoric of Healing* (2008) = S. Mattern, *Galen and the Rhetoric of Healing* (Baltimore, MD: Johns Hopkins University Press, 2008).

Meeusen, *Questions and Answers* (2020) = M. Meeusen, *Ancient Greek Medicine in Questions and Answers: Diagnostics, Didactics, Dialectics* (Leiden and Boston: Brill, 2020).

Menn, '*Discourse on the Method*' (2003) = S. Menn, 'The *Discourse on the Method* and the Tradition of Intellectual Autobiography,' in J. Miller and B. Inwood, eds., *Hellenistic and Early Modern Philosophy* (Cambridge: Cambridge University Press, 2003) 141–191.

Montgomery, *Al-Jâhiz* (2013) = J. E. Montgomery, *Al-Jâhiz: In Praise of Books* (Edinburgh: Edinburgh University Press, 2013).

Moulinier-Bogi and Nicoud, *Ecritures médicales* (2019) = L. Moulinier-Bogi and M. Nicoud, eds., *Ecritures médicales. Discours et genres de la tradition antique à l'époque moderne* (Paris: De Boccard, 2019).

Nicholls, 'Galen and the Last Days of Commodus' (2019) = M. Nicholls, 'Galen and the Last Days of Commodus,' in C. Petit, ed., *Galen's Peri alupias (De indolentia) in Context. A Tale of Resilience* (Leiden: Brill, 2019) 245–262.

Nutton, *On Prognosis* (1979) = V. Nutton, *Galen. On Prognosis. CMG V, 8, 1* (Leipzig and Berlin: Akademie Verlag, 1979).

Nutton, 'Three Pseudo-Galenic Texts' (2021) = V. Nutton, 'Three Pseudo-Galenic Texts: Pharmacology and Society in Imperial Rome', in C. Petit, S. Swain, and K.-D. Fischer, eds., *PseudoGalenica: The Formation of the Galenic Corpus from Antiquity to the Renaissance* (London: The Warburg Institute, 2021) 1–11.

Nutton, 'Galen on Theriac' (1997) = V. Nutton, 'Galen on Theriac: Problems of Authenticity,' in A. Debru, ed., *Galen on Pharmacology: Philosophy, History, and Medicine* (Leiden: Brill, 1997) 133–151.

Nutton, 'Galen's Library' (2009) = V. Nutton, 'Galen's Library,' in C. Gill, J. M. Wilkins, and T. J. G. Whitmarsh, eds., *Galen and the World of Knowledge* (Cambridge: Cambridge University Press, 2009) 19–34.

Nutton, 'Galen and the Rhetoric of Certainty' (2012) = V. Nutton, 'Galen and the Rhetoric of Certainty,' in J. Coste, D. Jacquart, and J. Pigeaud, eds., *La rhétorique médicale à travers les siècles* (Geneva: Droz, 2012) 39–49.

Pender and Struever, *Rhetoric and Medicine* (2012) = S. Pender and N. Struever, eds., *Rhetoric and Medicine in Early Modern Europe* (Burlington, VT: Ashgate, 2012).

Penella, '*Progymnasmata* in Imperial Greek Education' (2011) = R. J. Penella, 'The *Progymnasmata* in Imperial Greek Education,' *Classical World* 105 (2011) 77–90.

Penella, '*Progymnasmata* and Progymnasmatic Theory' (2015) = R. J. Penella, 'The *Progymnasmata* and Progymnasmatic Theory in Imperial Greek Education,' in W. M. Bloomer, ed., *A Companion to Ancient Education* (Chichester: Wiley-Blackwell, 2015) 160–171.

Pernot, 'The Second Sophistic' (2019) = L. Pernot, 'The Second Sophistic: "Pointless Invention" or Operational Concept?,' *Eranos* 110 (2019) 75–87.

Pernot, 'Third Sophistic' (2021) = L. Pernot, 'The Concept of a Third Sophistic: Definitional and Methodological Issues,' *Rhetorica* 39.2 (2021) 177–187.

Petit, *Le médecin. Introduction* (2009) = C. Petit, *Galien. Tome III. Le médecin. Introduction* (Paris: Belles Lettres, 2009).

Petit, 'Galien et le "discours de la méthode"' (2012) = C. Petit, 'Galien et le "discours de la méthode": rhétorique(s) médicale(s) à l'époque romaine,' in Coste, Jacquart, and Pigeaud, *Rhétorique Médicale* (2012) 49–75.

Petit, 'Signes et présages' (2014) = C. Petit, 'Signes et presages: le discours prédictif et ses enjeux chez Galien, Artémidore et Ptolémée,' in C. Chandezon and J. Du Bouchet, eds., *Artémidore de Daldis et l'interprétation des rêves: quatorze études* (Paris: Belles Lettres, 2014) 161–190.

Petit, 'Alexandrie' (2015) = C. Petit, 'Alexandrie, carrefour des traditions médicales au VIIe s. Les témoignages de Sophrone de Jérusalem, Alexandre de Tralles, Paul d'Egine, Stéphane d'Alexandrie et Jean d'Alexandrie,' in J. P. Caillet, S. Destephen, B. Dumézil, and H. Inglebert, eds., *Des dieux civiques aux saints patrons* (Paris: Picard, 2015) 287–307.

Petit, 'Rhétorique et médecine' (2017) = C. Petit, 'Rhétorique et médecine: le *De elementis ex Hippocratis sententia* de Galien,' *Aitia. Regards sur la culture hellénistique au 21e s.* 7.2 (2017). https://doi.org/10.4000/aitia.1945.

Petit, *Rhétorique de la Providence* (2018) = C. Petit, *Galien de Pergame ou la rhétorique de la Providence. Médecine, littérature et pouvoir à Rome* (Leiden: Brill, 2018).

Petit, 'Death, Posterity and the Vulnerable Self' (2019) = C. Petit, 'Death, Posterity and the Vulnerable Self: περὶ ἀλυπίας in the context of Galen's later works,' in C. Petit, ed., *Galen's περὶ ἀλυπίας (De indolentia) in Context: A Tale of Resilience* (Leiden: Brill, 2019) 41–62.

Petit, 'Medical Humanism' (2021) = C. Petit, 'Medical Humanism in the Making: Symphorien Champier (1471–1539) and Galen,' *Arts et Savoirs* 15 (2021). https://doi.org/10.4000/aes.3753.

Pigeaud, 'Rhétorique et médecine chez les Grecs' (1985) = J. Pigeaud, 'Rhétorique et médecine chez les Grecs. Le cas d'Archigène,' *Helmántica* 36 (1985) 39–48.

Pigeaud, 'Le style d'Hippocrate' (1988) = J. Pigeaud, 'Le style d'Hippocrate ou l'écriture fondatrice de la médecine,' in M. Détienne, ed., *Les savoirs de l'écriture en Grèce ancienne* (Lille: Presses Universitaires de Lille, 1988) 306–329.

Pigeaud, 'La rhétorique d'Arétée' (2004) = J. Pigeaud, 'La rhétorique d'Arétée,' in J. Jouanna and J. Leclant, eds., *La médecine grecque antique. Actes du 14ème colloque de la Villa Kérylos à Beaulieu-sur-Mer les 10 & 11 octobre 2003* (Paris: De Boccard, 2004) 177–197.

Pigeaud and Pigeaud, *Les textes médicaux latins* (2000) = A. Pigeaud and J. Pigeaud, eds., *Les textes médicaux latins comme littérature: actes du VIe colloque international sur les textes médicaux latins du 1er au 3 septembre 1998 à Nantes* (Nantes: Institut universitaire de France, Université de Nantes, 2000).

Pomata, 'Observation Rising' (2011) = G. Pomata, 'Observation Rising: Birth of an Epistemic Genre, ca. 1500–1650,' in L. Daston and E. Lunbeck, eds., *Histories of Scientific Observation* (Chicago: University of Chicago Press, 2011) 45–80.

Raiola, *Nel tempo di una vita* (2015) = T. Raiola, *Nel tempo di una vita. Studi sull'autobiografia in Galeno* (Pisa: Fabrizio Serra, 2015).

Roby, *Technical Ekphrasis* (2016) = C. Roby, *Technical Ekphrasis in Greek and Roman Science and Literature: The Written Machine between Alexandria and Rome* (Cambridge: Cambridge University Press, 2016).

Salas, *Cutting Words* (2020) = L. Salas, *Cutting Words. Polemical Dimensions of Galen's Anatomical Experiments* (Leiden: Brill, 2020).

Schlange-Schöningen, *Die Römische Gesellschaft bei Galen* (2003) = H. Schlange-Schöningen, *Die Römische Gesellschaft bei Galen: Biographie und Sozialgeschichte* (Berlin and New York: De Gruyter, 2003).

Siraisi, 'Vesalius' (1997) = N. Siraisi, 'Vesalius and the Reading of Galen's Teleology,' *Renaissance Quarterly* 50.1 (1997) 1–37.

von Staden, *Herophilus* (1989) = H. von Staden, *Herophilus. The Art of Medicine in Early Alexandria* (Cambridge: Cambridge University Press, 1989).

von Staden, 'Anatomy as Rhetoric' (1995) = H. von Staden, 'Anatomy as Rhetoric: Galen on Dissection and Persuasion,' *Journal of the History of Medicine and Allied Sciences* 50.1 (1995) 47–66.

von Staden, 'Galen and the "Second Sophistic"' (1997) = H. von Staden, 'Galen and the "Second Sophistic,"' in R. Sorabji, ed., *Aristotle and After. Bulletin of the Institute of Classical Studies. Suppl.* 68 (1997) 33–54.

von Staden, 'Dangers of Literature' (2000) = H. von Staden, 'The Dangers of Literature and the Need for Literacy: A. Cornelius Celsus on Reading and Writing,' in Pigeaud and Pigeaud, *Les textes médicaux latins* (2000) 355–368.

Swain, *Hellenism and Empire* (1996) = S. C. R. Swain, *Hellenism and Empire. Language, Classicism and Power in the Greek World 50–250* A.D. (Oxford: Oxford University Press, 1996).

Taub and Doody, *Authorial Voices* (2009) = L. Taub and A. Doody, eds., *Authorial Voices in Greco-Roman Technical Writing* (Trier: Wissenschaftlicher Verlag, 2009).

Temkin, *Galenism* (1973) = O. Temkin, *Galenism. Rise and Decline of a Medical Philosophy* (Ithaca: Cornell University Press, 1973).

Thomas, *Herodotus in Context* (2000) = R. Thomas, *Herodotus in Context: Ethnography, Science, and the Art of Persuasion* (Cambridge: Cambridge University Press, 2000).

Thumiger, 'Aretaeus' "Stomachic" Patients' (2018) = C. Thumiger, 'Aretaeus' "Stomachic" Patients: Comic Features in a Medical Discussion?,' in Kazantzidis and Tsoumpra, *Morbid Laughter* (2018) 473–487.

Tieleman, *Galen and Chrysippus on the Soul* (1996) = T. Tieleman, *Galen and Chrysippus on the Soul: Argument and Refutation in the 'De placitis' Books II–III* (Leiden: Brill, 1996).

Tieleman, *Chrysippus' 'On Affections'* (2003) = T. Tieleman, *Chrysippus' 'On Affections': Reconstruction and Interpretation* (Leiden: Brill, 2003).

Tieleman, 'Galen and the Stoics' (2009) = T. Tieleman, 'Galen and the Stoics, or The Art of Not Naming,' in C. Gill, T. G. J. Whitmarsh, and J. M. Wilkins, eds., *Galen and the World of Knowledge* (Cambridge: Cambridge University Press, 2009).

Totelin, '*Euporista*' (2021) = L. Totelin, 'Easy Remedies—Difficult Texts: The Pseudo-Galenic *Euporista*,' in C. Petit, S. Swain, and K.-D. Fischer, eds., *PseudoGalenica: The Formation of the Galenic Corpus from Antiquity to the Renaissance* (London: The Warburg Institute, 2021) 31–45.

Van Hoof, 'Greek Rhetoric and the Later Roman Empire' (2010) = L. Van Hoof, 'Greek Rhetoric and the Later Roman Empire: The Bubble of the Third Sophistic,' *Antiquité tardive* 18 (2010) 211–224.

Wagner, *Eἰ ζῷον* (1914) = H. Wagner, *Galeni qui fertur libellus Eἰ ζῷον τὸ κατὰ γάστρος* (Borna and Leipzig: R. Noske, 1914).

Watts, 'Gessius' (2009) = E. J. Watts, 'The Enduring Legacy of the Iatrosophist Gessius,' *Greek, Roman, and Byzantine Studies* 49 (2009) 113–134.

Whitmarsh, *The Second Sophistic* (2005) = T. G. J. Whitmarsh, *The Second Sophistic* (Oxford: Oxford University Press, 2005).

Response

Experts of Rhetoric and the Rhetoric of Expertise

Claire Bubb and Joseph Howley

This section has tackled the ways in which rhetoric impacted the expert practice of law and of medicine. Ulrike Babusiaux demonstrated the jurists' subtle use of rhetorical devices to forward the authority of their interpretations, while Caroline Petit explored the doctors' various strategies of engaging their audiences and underscoring their theses. We propose, in response, to focus not on rhetoric itself but on the expert practitioners of rhetoric: the rhetors, sophists, and grammarians. These experts in many ways parallel the experts in law and medicine on whom this volume focuses, and their interactions with and parallels to their peers in other disciplines further develop many of the themes of this book.

In addition to its pervasive influence as an educationally embedded intellectual practice, rhetoric was a distinct field of expertise with specialists of its own. While some of its experts specialized in the performative practice of rhetoric, the very prominence of rhetoric as an educational cornerstone fed a proliferation of rhetorical experts who plied their skills to pedagogical ends. Sophists sat at the performative end of this spectrum, while rhetors and their humbler counterparts, grammarians, were more associated with teaching.[1] However, there was fluidity among these titles. Rhetors specialized in the final, exclusively rhetorical stage of education, and grammarians in the distinct and prior field of grammar; but grammarians did teach elements of rhetoric, too.[2] Meanwhile, the labels of rhetor and sophist overlap significantly: often the distinction seems to rely more on

[1] Cribiore, *Gymnastics* (2001) 53–73 describes these different figures and their roles, as well as the ambiguities among them.

[2] Suetonius, in his list of illustrious grammarians, claims that originally grammarians taught rhetoric fully as a discipline, but that they gradually came to offer only rhetorical training exercises (i.e., *progymnasmata*); though he protests that even these have now been given up, he describes a teacher from his own youth who alternated his days between declaiming and grammatical discussion (Suet. *Gram. et rhet.* 4) and several of his featured grammarians were involved with rhetoric one way or another (Suet. *Gram. et rhet.* 6, 7, 10, 22). Quintilian (*Inst.* 1.9) also addresses the rhetorical responsibilities of the grammarian. For more details on the types of exercises they oversaw, see Webb, '*Progymnasmata*' (2001) and Penella, '*Progymnasmata*' (2015).

Claire Bubb and Joseph Howley, *Response: Experts of Rhetoric and the Rhetoric of Expertise* In: *Medicine and the Law under the Roman Empire.* Edited by: Claire Bubb and Michael Peachin, Oxford University Press.
 DOI: 10.1093/oso/9780192898616.003.0013

degree of fame than on anything intrinsic to the job description.[3] Key for the present concerns, however, is the fact that all of these rhetorical experts were navigating the same social and intellectual world as the doctors and lawyers considered here.

In the general introduction to this volume, Bubb and Peachin formulated several criteria that seem to isolate medicine and the law as uniquely paralleled fields of study. Most essentially, both are fields with voluminous technical literature, but also with urgently pragmatic day-to-day operations. Further, both require the careful accumulation of specialized knowledge to practical ends, yet also support highly theoretical back-and-forth among experts. Each field requires public competition between their practitioners, and expertise in each—when cannily presented to its elite audience—can parlay into broad social recognition, which itself then enhances assessments of the practitioner's specialized expertise. Rhetoric, together with philosophy, seems to come closest of the other ancient intellectual pursuits to joining this pair on all of these fronts.[4] Experts of rhetoric—sophists, rhetors, and grammarians alike—certainly produced a robust literature, ranging from sample declamations to pedagogical guides and handbooks.[5] This literature collected specialized terms and skills and also fostered expert debate, while rhetoric's practical manifestations were some of the most competitive, spectacle-oriented, and reputation-building arenas to be found in the Roman world. The one area where rhetoric begins to part company from law and medicine is in its practical utility. Though it might occasionally seem so to a schoolboy, rarely was rhetoric actually a matter of life or death outside of the courtroom. Certainly, rhetorical education was of vital importance to the social and political careers of the elite, but rhetoric, as a field, simply does not achieve quite the same level of practical, sometimes even mortal, urgency as medicine or the law.

[3] Libanius indicates that in the formal school setting of the fourth century CE, rhetors were responsible for theory and sophists, who ranked higher, for the practice of declamation, but the terms are not so clear-cut elsewhere; see Cribiore, *Gymnastics* (2001) 56–57 and also Penella, '*Progymnasmata*' (2015) 160, which characterizes the distinction between rhetor and sophist as largely a geographic and linguistic one, the former being the term favored in the Latin West. Sophists routinely taught for fees in addition to declaiming, as Philostratus' *Lives of the Sophists* abundantly demonstrates.

[4] Michael Trapp explores the case of philosophy in the conclusion to this volume.

[5] Quintilian's *Institutio Oratoria* and the major and minor declamations attributed to him are prime examples, as are the surviving declamations of the sophist Polemo (for an edition of which, see Reader and Chvála-Smith, *Severed Hand* (1996)) and the various rhetorical handbooks and *progymnasmata* that survive; for an overview of theoretical writing on rhetoric in the imperial period, see Pernot, *Rhétorique dans l'Antiquité* (2000) 208–221. Suetonius also reveals a culture of book writing among rhetors and grammarians, notably exemplified by L. Aetius Philologus (*Gram. et rhet.* 10), "a rhetor among grammarians and grammarian among rhetors," who boasted a miscellany "in eight hundred books" (*inter grammaticos rhetorem, inter rhetores grammaticum . . . octingentos in libros*); cf. *Gram. et rhet.* 7, 9, 11. All translations of Greek and Latin are our own; translations of Arabic are drawn from the cited editions.

Still, in practice, these various experts of rhetoric found themselves in similar social positions to their peers in the medical and legal fields: they are experts to be called upon by the non-expert, and their claim to expertise is constantly queried on the public stage. Some of Aulus Gellius' anecdotes, for example, provide snapshots of these men's role in society. In addition to charging students for their instructional wisdom, rhetorical experts also marketed their expertise to a broader public: Gellius scorns two different men for boastful, self-advertising antics, "selling" themselves and their expert readings.[6] Yet, despite the pejorative framing here, part of an expert's role was indeed to be acquirable. Like a doctor, a rhetorical expert could be called onto a case. Gellius describes a bookshop scene in which a well-reputed grammarian has been "summoned (*adhibitus*) by a buyer in order to look at some books."[7] This is the very same word that Cicero uses to describe "summoning a doctor" to your bedside.[8] One should not imagine, however, that this was a completely preemptory process, in which the person summoned was little more than a convenient tool; to be summoned was also to receive a mark of distinction. Pliny proudly uses the same term for himself being "summoned to council by the prefect of the city."[9] As König and Peachin explore earlier in this volume, expert status materializes precisely by means of external recognition: thus, to be summoned was proof of expertise and, therefore, being "summonable" was an intrinsic part of being an expert of rhetoric or, for that matter, of anything else. Further, each such appearance that an expert made (whatever his area of specialization) inflected the trajectory of his perceived expertise. Indeed, Galen draws a direct parallel between the situations of the sophist and the doctor in this regard. He reports a conversation with the rhetorical super-star Herodes Atticus:[10]

> Herodes, the most able orator of his time, was once required to deliver a speech on a certain matter. His speech fell far short of his usual standard, something which he himself felt, for he informed us of its cause. He said that he had been busy during the previous three days, and consequently could not devote any time to reading or writing. I remember hearing another account from an orator who had delivered a bad speech, apologizing that he had been busy during the previous four days.

[6] Gell. *NA* 13.31 (*venditabat*), 18.4 (*venditatorem*).

[7] Gell. *NA* 5.4 (*ab emptore ad spectandos libros adhibitus*).

[8] Cic. *Fat.* 29 (*medicum adhibueris*).

[9] Plin. *Ep.* 6.11 (*adhibitus in consilium a praefecto urbis*). Cf. Pliny's letter concerning the jurist L. Javolenus Priscus (*Ep.* 6.15), in which the word *adhibere* is applied both to the audience invited to a private poetry recitation and to Priscus' being "called upon for advice" (*adhibetur consiliis*); on which see Uden above, pp. 219–220. Compare also Vitruvius' comment at *De arch.* 6 pr.5 that it is better for an architect "to be sought than seeking" (*rogatum, non rogantem*), on which see König and Peachin above, p. 163, n. 10.

[10] Galen *Opt.Med.Cogn.* 9.19–20 (*CMG Suppl.Or.* IV 113–115).

Galen deploys this anecdote as a lesson that expert skill requires constant practice: like these rhetorical experts, he warns, a medical expert who fails to properly practice his craft on a daily basis cannot possibly perform it at a high level. Expertise in any field must be continually cultivated—and any lapses duly excused.

In addition to the parallels that can be traced among these various experts' positions in society, the common rhetorical educational background that all of them draw upon allows for mutual feedback among law, medicine, and rhetoric itself, rather than just a unidirectional path from rhetoric outwards. Indeed, the elevated rhetoric of the specialized texts, as demonstrated above by Babusiaux and Petit, deliberately seeks to make them appear worthy of attention to the rhetorically educated more broadly. In the endlessly competitive world of Roman intellectuals, there was value to the specialist in making it clear to non-specialists, especially the powerful ones, that his work is both useful and erudite, both accessible and superior. To turn once again to Galen, he prided himself not just on the content of his medical writing but also on his style—and he views his style as worthy of elite connoisseurship. In the famous anecdote at the beginning of his *On My Own Books*, he describes an interesting scene: a group of men are browsing a bookshop and notice a book attributed to Galen, but with an unfamiliar title. Someone decides to buy it, but another bystander, whom Galen describes only as "some intellectual man," asks to take a look and, upon reading merely the first two lines, declares "this is not the style of Galen, and this book is falsely ascribed."[11] A gleeful, undercover Galen reports this anonymous validation of his intellectual worth. His work is both valued and valuable, and his high level of education makes itself felt in every sentence that he writes, at least to those who are themselves sufficiently well educated and discerning to recognize it.

Yet this anecdote also highlights the fact that the flow of familiarity went in both directions: on the one hand, Galen's writing is rhetorical enough to have a recognizable style, and, on the other, the most discerning of intellectuals have an educational breadth sufficient to recognize excellence in a range of fields.[12] This expectation that superlative education includes a broad range of study was a standard feature of contemporary educational ideals. Quintilian opines at length that the ideal rhetorical training includes at least basic familiarity with other disciplines.[13] Though his emphasis is on the benefits of learning music and geometry, he also requires "a knowledge of the civil law" and encourages reading

[11] Galen *Lib.Prop.* pr.2 (XIX.8–9K = 134 B-M) (*τις ἀνὴρ τῶν φιλολόγων... οὐκ ἔστιν ἡ λέξις αὕτη Γαληνοῦ καὶ ψευδῶς ἐπιγέγραπται τουτὶ τὸ βιβλίον*).

[12] Compare the instances in Gellius which witness similar activity in the very same booksellers' quarter on questions of history and poetry (e.g., *NA* 5.4, 13.31, 18.4).

[13] Quint. *Inst.* 1.10–12 and 12.17–30.

widely in "the other arts."[14] We learn here, too—though the precise details are a bit open to interpretation—that Celsus' encyclopedia of subjects fit for a gentleman may have included precisely our three fields: medicine, law, and rhetoric.[15] Legal authorities also recognized this affinity: Ulpian, for example, at one point lists rhetors and grammarians as practitioners of liberal arts deserving a public salary and adds that doctors have "perhaps even a better claim."[16] Doctors returned the compliment. Galen's *Exhortation to Study the Arts* urges well-born young men to give up their dreams of becoming star athletes and instead turn their attentions to the noble (and, incidentally, lucrative) arts, namely "**medicine, rhetoric**, music, geometry, arithmetic, logic, astronomy, grammar, and **jurisprudence**."[17] Thus, inasmuch as rhetoric was a baseline element of both legal and medical education, law and medicine were also implicated in the full education of a rhetor, as well as of a well-educated intellectual without any specific claim to expertise.[18]

Indeed, as Michael Peachin, Alice König, and James Uden explore elsewhere in this volume, the interface between expertise and intellectualism is a complex one. The claim to be educated in ancient Rome required enmeshing oneself in a web of knowledge that spanned disciplines. Aulus Gellius testifies eloquently to this ideal. He reveals in the preface to his *Attic Nights* that he views familiarity with topics from across disciplines—even "tricky and troublesome . . . [and] rather recondite" ones—to be an urgent social desideratum and that he has devoted himself to making sure that at least a presentable veneer be obtainable by even the busiest statesman:[19]

> *Ipse quidem volvendis transeundisque multis admodum voluminibus per omnia semper negotiorum intervalla in quibus furari otium potui exercitus defessusque sum, sed modica ex his eaque sola accepi quae aut ingenia prompta expeditaque ad honestae eruditionis cupidinem utiliumque artium contemplationem celeri facilique compendio ducerent aut homines aliis iam vitae negotiis occupatos a turpi certe agrestique rerum atque verborum imperitia vindicarent.*
>
> I busied and fatigued myself in unrolling and perusing many volumes in every single interval from business in which I was able to steal some leisure time, but

[14] Quint. *Inst.* 12.3.1 (*iuris quoque civilis . . . scientia*) (cf. 12.11.4, 9) and 12.11.20 (*ceterarumque artium*).

[15] Quint. *Inst.* 12.11.24; on the difficulties involved in pinning down the precise contents of Celsus' work—as well as the diversity of Roman views on the question of the ideal intellectual pursuits for a gentleman—see Bubb and Peachin, above, p. 9 nn. 23–24.

[16] Ulp. (8 *de omn. trib.*) *D* 50.13.1.pr-1 (*nisi quod iustior*); geometers form another member of this crowd. More broadly on the jurists and their vision of the liberal arts, see Visky, *Geistige Arbeit* (1977).

[17] Galen *Protr.* I.39K (117 B) (**ἰατρική τε καὶ ῥητορικὴ** *καὶ μουσική, γεωμετρία τε καὶ ἀριθμητικὴ καὶ λογιστική, καὶ ἀστρονομία καὶ γραμματικὴ καὶ* **νομική**).

[18] On the role of rhetoric in the elite education of these two fields, see Babusiaux and Bubb, above.

[19] Gell. *NA* praef. 12–13 (*scrupulosa et anxia . . . remotiora*).

> from these I took only a few things: only either those which would, by means of a quick and easy abridgement, lead ready and nimble minds to the desire for proper learning and the useful contemplation of the arts or those which would deliver men already occupied by the various businesses of life from truly shameful and rustic ignorance of facts and words.

The result of this catholic approach to intellectual culture, as Gellius also abundantly demonstrates, is that educated people felt comfortable challenging experts in their own fields.

Uden's essay already spotlighted the ease and confidence with which one of Gellius' companions shamed a doctor on a medical topic.[20] Rhetorical experts were no less susceptible to this behavior. Let us consider one such occasion in detail.[21] Gellius describes a visit that he paid to Cornelius Fronto, who was laid up with gout. At the time of the visit, though, the experts who surrounded Fronto were not doctors, as they well might have been, but architects and builders, who were displaying documents with various possible plans for a new bath that Fronto was constructing. In the course of the ensuing discussion, one of Fronto's friends uses the term *praeterpropter*, and Fronto queries the precise meaning of the word. The friend, eager to pass this hot potato, which he has inadvertently introduced, points out that there is a *grammaticus* "with no little reputation for teaching in Rome" sitting among them and that he is just the expert to answer the question.[22] The grammarian, alarmed at being put on the spot, deprecates the word and says, no doubt with an eye to the builders in the room, that it is "just too plebian and more familiar in the conversation of laborers than that of educated men."[23] Fronto takes exception at this response, pointing out that *praeterpropter* appears in both Cato and Marcus Varro, and a helpful friend remembers that it is also in Ennius, whereupon a copy of Ennius' *Iphigenia* is fetched and the relevant passage is read aloud. Faced with this turning of the tables, the grammarian, overcome by sweat and blushes, beats a hasty retreat, telling Fronto "I will talk to you alone about this later on, so that the uneducated might not hear and learn."[24] With this parting shot, aimed once again, no doubt, at the architect and builders, the grammarian attempts to preserve his dignity and establish his intellectual superiority over at least someone in the room.

This scene seethes with experts and intellectuals. Fronto has surrounded his sickbed with "many men renowned for their learning, birth, or wealth," including both specialists, like the famous grammarian, and non-specialists.[25] He has also

[20] Gell. *NA* 18.10; see Uden, this volume, pp. 221–225. [21] Gell. *NA* 19.10.

[22] *NA* 19.10.7 (*haud incelebri nomine Romae docentem*).

[23] *NA* 19.10.9 (*praenimis plebeium est et in opificum sermonibus quam in hominum doctorum notius*).

[24] *NA* 19.10.14 (*tibi... Fronto, postea uni dicam, ne inscitiores audiant ac discant*).

[25] *NA* 19.10.2 (*multis doctrina aut genere aut fortuna nobilibus viris*).

specifically "summoned" (*adhibiti*) an architect's team of experts to apply their specialized skills to a problem. Both the architects and the intellectuals are reinforced by the written work of their art: the architects wield parchment plans, while the intellectuals have a library of Latin literature at their fingertips, both literally and figuratively. The grammarian alone is lacking the written word. The intellectuals here allow the grammarian a chance to prove his expertise and, when he fails, shame him with their superior knowledge. This alleged expert, in turn, attempts to bolster his own expertise by diminishing the worth of others, but here, too, he fails. It is clear to us and to all present in the room that the architect is not the uneducated one, nor is his dignity or expertise in any way diminished by the grammarian's parting barb.

Galen describes a similar scene with a similar thrust, where (once again?) an architect emerges victorious. Here, the supposed experts under scrutiny are not grammarians but a group of philosophers. Galen, as the superlatively educated doctor-philosopher, leads a group of "lay" intellectuals in exposing their fraudulent expertise. His premise is that a grounding in logic is fundamental to a good education, whether one is an expert in one of the "logically based technical skills, namely mathematics, arithmetic, geometry, astronomy, architecture, **the law, rhetoric, grammar**, music," and, of course, medicine or whether one is simply one of the "men of letters, who are also educated in studies but do not practice an art since they have ample wealth."[26] The philosophers in question, it transpires, are not well educated and are able neither to present nor to follow logical demonstrations. Having embarked on an argument whether wood is heavier than water or vice versa, they each speak at length, arguing speciously for one answer or the other; an architect in the crowd then begins to laugh at them and is persuaded by the crowd to offer a scientific demonstration on the subject. He does so, "efficiently and clearly, so that all those present understood, except for the philosophers alone."[27] The architect here has turned the tables from the Gellian scene and mounts his own attack—a much more successful one than that aimed at his bath-building colleague—on the intellectual inferiority of an expert in a different field.

Thus, an interesting corollary of the entitlement that self-perceived educational superiority brings is that the urge to humiliate experts was not limited to non-specialized intellectuals alone. Experts in law, in medicine, in rhetoric, and even in architecture, by virtue of their own liberal educations, could themselves feel

[26] Galen *Aff.Pecc.Dig.* 2.7 (V.103K) (*τοὺς ἀπὸ τῶν λογικῶν τεχνῶν ἁπασῶν ἀριθμητικοὺς λογιστικοὺς γεωμέτρας ἀστρονόμους ἀρχιτέκτονας* **νομικοὺς ῥήτορας γραμματικοὺς** *μουσικούς*), 2.5 (V.93K) (*τινὲς τῶν φιλολόγων ἀνδρῶν καὶ πεπαιδευμένων ἐν τοῖς μαθήμασιν οὔτε δὴ τέχνην ἐργαζομένων δι' εὐπορίαν κτημάτων*); we have borrowed several turns of phrase from the translation in Singer, *Psychological Writings* (2013) 307–308, 313–314. Galen does not mention medicine specifically in his list here, but he is adamant elsewhere that it, too, is a logical art, as, e.g., *Protr.* 14 (I.39K = 117 B).

[27] *Aff.Pecc.Dig.* 2.7 (V.100K) (*ἐν τάχει τε καὶ σαφῶς, ὡς ἅπαντας τοὺς παρόντας νοῆσαι πλὴν μόνων τῶν φιλοσόφων*).

empowered to challenge experts in fields other than their own. Uden has argued in this volume that, from the perspective of the non-specialist, specialization led to a certain diminishment in the expert's status as a member of the intellectual elite and, indeed, to a narrowing of his cultural horizons. This view from the other side suggests that the specialists viewed themselves rather as augmented intellectuals: well-rounded polymaths, capable of assailing peers in all fields, but themselves particularly unassailable in one. It is thus a matter of perspective whether the specialist is, so to speak, an 'intellectual +' or an 'intellectual –'.

It would seem, then, that one result of the *lingua franca* of a universal rhetorical education was to allow for a fluidity of interests among both experts and non-experts and, accordingly, to promote non-expert pretensions to superiority in various fields, not just by generalist intellectuals but also by specialists in other areas. The experts in rhetoric, who have formed the backbone of this response, were no exception: their rhetorical work included dabbling in other fields. Juristic literature could serve as fodder for the debates of grammarians, as Gellius amply demonstrates.[28] J. E. Lendon has also shown the confidence with which the rhetorically educated translated their understanding of the fictitious laws that govern in the world of declamations into actual legal practice; sometimes the results were humiliating, but sometimes rhetorical conviction seems to have been enough to translate imaginary laws into real statute.[29] Similarly, rhetors and grammarians were not loathe to adopt medical themes when it suited them. The *Major Declamations* attributed to Quintilian display conversance with various medical ideas.[30] Most memorably, the declamation about a pair of ailing twins offers a blow-by-blow account of the vivisection of one twin by an opportunistic doctor who has offered to cure the other at the expense of his brother; the author waxes long on the methodologies of medical research and also includes a litany of symptoms and the cures appropriate to them, evidently drawing on contemporary medical practices.[31]

Medical and legal experts returned the favor. In addition to their deployment of rhetorical devices in their speeches and their literature, as highlighted by the preceding essays, they also felt empowered to speak on topics we would consider to be the purview of the rhetorical expert—not to mention on topics that fell within each other's jurisdiction. Thus, we learn that Galen dedicated a significant portion of his time to producing texts on topics that he labels as "subjects common to grammarians and rhetors," including, among others, a text entitled "*On Clarity and Obscurity*," another on "*Whether Reading Ancient Comedy is Useful for Students*," and yet another on "*Falsification of Atticisms*": all titles that would

[28] See the discussion in Howley, 'Why Read the Jurists?' (2013).

[29] Lendon, *Tyrant, Persuasion* (2022) 107–147.

[30] Longo, 'Medicina' (2015) provides a survey of these moments.

[31] Ps.-Quint. *Dec.Maj.* 8, with the list of symptoms and cures at 8.17; see Ferngren, 'Vivisection' (1982) 280–284 for the contemporary medical ideas on which the author was likely drawing.

seem more at home in the oeuvre of a rhetorical expert.[32] A few generations after him, one C. Calpurnius Collega Macedo is styled in his epitaph not only as *archiatros* and faithful follower of Hippocrates, but also as a "top-ten orator"; indeed, as Petit outlined in her essay, the roles of doctor and rhetor eventually merged under the mellifluous title of "iatrosophist."[33] Galen also undertook to write a treatise in one book "*On the Making of Wills*," the contents of which are lost, but which may have stepped on some juristic toes.[34] And, of course, there are the intriguing figures of C. Stertinius Xenophon, imperial physician also responsible for imperial (legal?) correspondence, and C. Calpurnius Asclaepiades, doctor and assessor, who appeared in the introduction to this volume, and who may have had a foot in both worlds.[35]

Legal experts, in turn, engaged in both rhetorical and medical discussions. There are numerous examples of jurists engaging in linguistic speculations of the sort that grammarians delighted in. Gellius tells us, for instance, that the renowned jurist Antistius Labeo:[36]

> *Altioresque penetrauerat Latinarumque uocum origines rationesque percalluerat eaque praecipue scientia ad enodandos plerosque iuris laqueos utebatur.*
>
> delved deeply into dialectic and older and more remote literature and became well versed in the origins and derivations of Latin words, and he applied this especially to the unknotting of many tough points of law.

Not satisfied with merely incorporating this linguistic research into his juridical writing, Labeo also left behind a plethora of posthumously published works, three volumes of which were "full of that kind of material that tends to explain and shed light on the Latin language."[37] As far as medical questions, when they occurred in the course of a legal case the norm was to consult rather than to supplant medical

[32] Galen *Lib.Prop.* 20 (XIX.48K = 173 B-M) (*Τὰ τοῖς γραμματικοῖς καὶ ῥήτορσι κοινά . . . εἰ χρήσιμον ἀνάγνωσμα τοῖς παιδευομένοις ἡ παλαιὰ κωμῳδία . . . Ἀττικῶν παράσημος . . . περὶ σαφηνείας καὶ ἀσαφείας*).

[33] Samama, *Les médecins* (2003), no. 334 (*ῥήτορα ἐν τοῖς δέκα Ἀθηναίων πρώτοις*). See Petit, *Artistic Prose?*, above, p. 298.

[34] *Lib.Prop.* 15.5 (XIX.46K = 170 B-M) (*περὶ διαθηκῶν ποιήσεως*). Interestingly, the only juristic writing which might be suspected to have paralleled this book (at least, given the titles transmitted) will likely have post-dated Galen's effort. We know of a *De forma testamenti liber singularis* by Iulius Paulus, and of a *De testamentis liber singularis* from the pen of Herennius Modestinus. On these (both will date to the Severan period), see respectively Liebs, 'Jurisprudenz' (1997) 165 and 196.

[35] See above, pp. 26–28.

[36] Gell. *NA* 13.10.1. For examples directly from the jurists, see Babusiaux, 'Funktionen der Etymologie' (2014), which explores the way that jurists participated in grammarians' dialogue around questions of etymology; cf. Babusiaux, '*Quod Graeci . . . vocant*' (2014).

[37] Gell. *NA* 13.10.2 (*pleni sunt id genus rerum ad enarrandam et inlustrandam linguam Latinam conducentium*).

experts.[38] Nevertheless, jurists had no qualms about wading into medical topics on their own steam in their writing.[39] Ulpian engages in an extensive consideration of the definition of disease, including the line between sanity and insanity; so confident is he of his judgement on medical subjects that he proffers his opinions even when he is admittedly a little shaky on the details:[40]

> *Si quis antiadas habeat, an redhiberi quasi vitiosus possit, quaeritur. et* ***si antiades hae sunt quas existimo****, id est inveteratas, et qui iam discuti non possint faucium tumores, qui antiadas habet vitiosus est.*
>
> There is a question whether, if [a slave] has tonsils, he may be rescinded on the grounds that he is diseased. And, **if tonsils are what I think they are**—that is, tumors of the throat that are long established and not now operable—one who has tonsils is diseased.

A discussion between Galen and Ulpian on the nature of disease would have been an event to behold—and one not lacking in rhetorical flair.

Experts of rhetoric, then, are intimately entangled with their peers in other fields of expertise, not least including law and medicine. On the one hand, their social position as experts puts them in comparable situations, with comparable goals and pitfalls. Their particular field, in turn, pervades just about all intellectual endeavors, allowing for both them and their peers to make creditable forays into multiple areas of expertise. It is in the context of this cross-pollinating intellectual world that the jurists and doctors considered by Babusiaux and Petit were deploying their rhetorical skill. And it is from this same world that various intellectually amphibious characters can emerge, like C. Calpurnius Asclaepiades, from above—doctor and assessor; or Timocrates—doctor turned declaimer—and his allegedly fraudulent counterpart Asclepiades—rhetor turned doctor; or M. Pomponius Marcellus—grammarian who moonlighted as an advocate—and L. Coelius Antipater—historian likewise skilled in jurisprudence.[41] In short, the educational and social system founded on rhetoric and the work of rhetorical experts was such that it was possible for these men to wear two hats with aplomb, and even those who did not could feel confident in their fluency across various styles of intellectual haberdashery.

[38] Israelowich, 'Physicians as Figures of Authority' (2014) 454–459 discusses the role of physicians and midwives as providers of expert evidence in legal contexts.

[39] See Ulp. (14 *ad Sab.*) D. 38.16.3.12 and Paul. (19 *Resp.*) D. 1.5.12 for instances of jurists engaging with medical literature; cf. Gellius, *NA* 3.16.12 and the discussion in Howley, 'Why Read the Jurists?' (2013) 25–26.

[40] Ulp. (1 *ad ed. aedil. curul.*) D. 21.1.14.8. On the disconnect between legal and medical definitions of sanity and insanity, see Israelowich, 'Physicians as Figures of Authority' (2014).

[41] Asclaepiades: see above, p. 316; Timocrates: Philostr. *VS* 536; Asclepiades: Plin. *HN* 26.7.12; Marcellus: Suet. *Gram. et rhet.* 22; Antipater: Cic. *Brut.* 102 and Pomponius (*lib. sing. enchir.*) D. 1.2.2.40.

Bibliography

Babusiaux, 'Funktionen der Etymologie' (2014) = U. Babusiaux, 'Funktionen der Etymologie in der juristischen Literatur,' *Fundamina* 20.1 (2014) 39–60.

Babusiaux, '*Quod Graeci*... *vocant*' (2014) = U. Babusiaux, '*Quod Graeci*... *vocant*—Emblematischer Codewechsel in den Juristenschriften,' in J. Hallebeek, M. Schermaier, R. Fiori, E. Metzger, and J.-P. Coriat, eds., *Inter cives necnon peregrinos. Essays in Honour of Boudewijn Sirks* (Göttingen: V&R Unipress) 35–59.

Cribiore, *Gymnastics* (2001) = R. Cribiore, *Gymnastics of the Mind: Greek Education in Hellenistic and Roman Egypt* (Princeton: Princeton University Press, 2001).

Ferngren, 'Vivisection' (1982) = G. B. Ferngren, 'A Roman Declamation on Vivisection,' *Transactions and Studies of the College of Physicians of Philadelphia* 5.4 (1982) 272–290.

Howley, 'Why Read the Jurists?' (2013) = J. Howley, 'Why Read the Jurists? Aulus Gellius on Reading across Disciplines,' in P. J. du Plessis, ed., *New Frontiers: Law and Society in Ancient Rome* (Edinburgh: Edinburgh University Press, 2013) 9–30.

Israelowich, 'Physicians as Figures of Authority' (2014) = I. Israelowich, 'Physicians as Figures of Authority in the Roman Courts and the Attitude towards Mental Diseases in the Roman Courts during the High Empire,' *Historia* 63.4 (2014) 445–462.

Lendon, *Tyrant, Persuasion* (2022) = J. E. Lendon, *That Tyrant, Persuasion. How Rhetoric Shaped the Roman World* (Princeton: Princeton University Press, 2022).

Liebs, 'Jurisprudenz' (1997) = D. Liebs, 'Jurisprudenz,' in K. Sallmann, ed., *Handbuch der lateinischen Literatur der Antike. Bd. 4. Die Literatur des Umbruchs: von der römischen zur christlichen Literatur; 117–284 n. Chr.* (Munich: Beck, 1997) 83–217.

Longo, 'Medicina' (2015) = G. Longo, 'La medicina nelle *Declamazioni maggiori* pseudo-quintilianee,' in M. T. Dinter, C. Guérin, and M. Martinho, eds., *Reading Roman Declamation: The Declamations Ascribed to Quintilian* (Berlin: De Gruyter, 2015) 167–187.

Penella, '*Progymnasmata*' (2015) = R. J. Penella, 'The *Progymnasmata* and Progymnasmatic Theory in Imperial Greek Education,' in W. M. Bloomer, ed., *A Companion to Ancient Education* (Chichester: Wiley-Blackwell, 2015) 160–171.

Pernot, *Rhétorique dans l'Antiquité* (2000) = L. Pernot, *La Rhétorique dans l'Antiquité* (Paris: Librairie Générale française, 2000). Translated into English in L. Pernot, *Rhetoric in Antiquity*, tr. W. E. Higgins (Washington, D.C.: Catholic University of America Press, 2005).

Reader and Chvála-Smith, *Severed Hand* (1996) = W. W. Reader and A. J. Chvála-Smith, *The Severed Hand and the Upright Corpse: The Declamations of Marcus Antonius Polemo* (Atlanta, GA: Scholars Press, 1996).

Samama, *Les médecins* (2003) = É. Samama, *Les médecins dans le monde grec. Sources épigraphiques sur la naissance d'un corps médical* (Geneva: Librairie Droz, 2003).

Singer, *Psychological Writings* (2013) = P. N. Singer, ed., *Galen. Psychological Writings* (Cambridge: Cambridge University Press, 2013).

Visky, *Geistige Arbeit* (1977) = K. Visky, *Geistige Arbeit und die "artes liberales" in den Quellen des römischen Rechts* (Budapest: Akadémiai Kiadó, 1977).

Webb, '*Progymnasmata*' (2001) = R. Webb, 'The *Progymnasmata* as Practice,' in Y. L. Too, ed., *Education in Greek and Roman Antiquity* (Leiden and Boston: Brill, 2001) 289–316.

PART V
EPILOGUE

How Does Philosophy Compare?

Michael Trapp

So, finally, how does philosophy compare? In a word, instructively. Philosophy as a practice, and philosophers as a category of specialists (practitioners able to distinguish themselves from mere ἰδιῶται, laymen), were every bit as much involved in the public, the spectacular, the competitive, and the rhetorical as medical and legal professionals. But their peculiar status—or at any rate, the peculiar status that they were committed to claiming on behalf of themselves and their calling—gave an edge to this involvement not characteristically experienced by doctors or lawyers. Like doctors and lawyers, philosophers had both a practical and a theoretical level to their activity; like them, they made use of the resources of rhetoric to display and communicate the subject-matter in which they claimed both theoretical expertise and practical efficacy; and like them, they competed visibly in public both with each other and with other kinds of professional for position and prestige, both inside and outside the confines of their own specialist area. Yet, fascinatingly, each of these levels of engagement in one way or another created a problem for them, in terms of their own ideals and values, or of the wider world's perception of them, or both. And the problems thus arising both do and do not correspond to those to which the other contributors to this volume have so incisively drawn attention.

We should not be surprised that philosophy stood out in this way. There was, after all, something odd quite in general about the social and ideological position of *philosophia* and *philosophoi*, suspended as they were—in a way that simply does not apply to either medicine or law—between marginality and centrality, between the vital and the utterly dispensable.[1] While it was always possible to say of any individual doctor or lawyer that he could be done without, it made no sense to say that doctors or lawyers as a class were of no use to the civic community, or to humanity at large. But this was precisely what could be and sometimes was said, categorically, about philosophers, even as they themselves claimed a centrality to human need and human self-understanding that went far beyond anything even the most ambitious doctor or lawyer might want to assert of their own vocations—and, what is more, articulated this claim in pointedly competitive terms, painting

[1] Here and in what follows, I draw shamelessly on my longer discussion in Trapp, *Philosophy* (2007) 226–257, cf. also Trapp, 'Authority' (2017).

Michael Trapp, *How Does Philosophy Compare?* In: *Medicine and the Law under the Roman Empire.*
Edited by: Claire Bubb and Michael Peachin, Oxford University Press.
 DOI: 10.1093/oso/9780192898616.003.0014

themselves metaphorically as doctors in a higher sense than any physician (doctors of the soul, not merely of the body), and legislators for the good life, rather than for the trivialities of everyday conduct.[2] It would be surprising if those committed to this self-understanding did not have both strong reasons for close engagement with the modes and procedures of the public arena and peculiar problems of their own in negotiating that engagement.

We should also bear in mind another important asymmetry between philosophy on the one hand, and medicine and law on the other, in the nature of their respective products and the corresponding ways in which they made them available to their immediate community and to the world at large. All three had an acknowledged good to offer, based on a body of specialist knowledge and expertise; but there was a categorical difference between what doctors and lawyers had, and what philosophers promised. Doctors, by their insight into the workings and malfunctionings of the human body, and their practical knowledge and skill in identifying and applying remedial measures, helped promote the manifest individual and collective good of physical health. Lawyers, by their knowledge of the meaning and workings of the regulations governing human interactions in a civic community, helped to secure the orderly resolution of disputes and the administration of justice. Philosophers, however, on their own account of things, dealt in Truth with a capital 'T'—insight into the fundamental realities and deep structures of the physical world, the human soul, rationality, and happiness—and thus offered not only knowledge at the deepest level, but also the most authoritative possible guide to fulfilled existence.[3]

A first asymmetry is immediately visible in the very magnitude of this claim. Precisely because what they offered was just on a different scale to the goods offered by any other body of experts, philosophers were more vulnerable to a sceptical reaction, or vulnerable to a more scathingly sceptical reaction, than any other body—with the scepticism centring either on the very availability of such fundamental (transcendent) truths, or (more usually) on the philosophers' claim that they were the ones with uniquely authoritative access to them.[4] But there were

[2] Doctors and medicine: e.g. Plut. *Mor.* 550a, 776d; Dio Chrys. *Or.* 27.7; Philo *Vit. Mos.* 1.42; Albinus *Didask.* 6; Arr. *Epict. diss.* 3.21.20, 3.23.30; Max. Tyr. 1.2, 3.6, 4.2–3. Legislators: e.g. Lucian *Pisc.* 30; Max. Tyr. 29.7, 37.2; Philo *Vit. Mos. passim.*

[3] E.g. Max. Tyr. 26.1, "How are we to understand philosophy if not as precise knowledge of things human and divine, the source of virtue and noble thoughts and a harmonious style of life and accomplished ways?" (*ταύτην* (*sc.* *τὴν φιλοσοφίαν*) *δὲ τί ἄλλο ὑποληψόμεθα ἢ ἐπιστήμην ἀκριβῆ θείων τε πέρι* <*καὶ*> *ἀνθρωπίνων, χορηγὸν ἀρετῆς καὶ λογισμῶν καλῶν καὶ ἁρμονίας βίου καὶ ἐπιτηδευμάτων δεξιῶν*), embroidering on the standard (originally Stoic) formula 'knowledge of things human and divine and their causes' (*SVF* 2.35; Cic. *Tusc.* 4.26.57; Alcin. *Didasc.* 1.1; Apul. *De dog. Plat.* 2.6.228). See further Frede, 'Philosopher' (2000) and Trapp, *Philosophy* (2007) 1–27.

[4] Satire at the expense of doctors and lawyers is of course anything but unknown—as witness for example the ass Lucius's scathing remarks about legal vultures and miscarriages of justice in Apul. *Met.* 10.33.1–4, or Gellius's story of the putting down of an ignorant doctor by Calvenus Taurus in *NA* 18.10—but it is noticeably less prominent in the surviving record than sallies against philosophers; see further Trapp, 'Plato' (2000) 357–360, *Philosophy* (2007) 253–254, and 'Due Respect' (2020).

divergences too in the kind of interaction with their lay fellows that flowed from these knowledge claims, and from the particular nature of philosophical expertise. Practicing doctors and lawyers provided (or attempted to provide) their proper goods primarily in action, tending the sick and pleading (or advising) in the run up to or during a legal procedure; anything they wrote or delivered out loud of a more generally reflective, theoretical, or educational nature, however voluminous, was formally ancillary to this practical contact between doctor and patient or lawyer and client, in which it was the expert who did the crucial work. Philosophers by contrast made their proper good available primarily by teaching, in written or spoken discourse. This discourse, to be sure, was intended to produce practical results, in the form of deepened insight, better characters and comportment, and happier lives. And certainly, philosophers were expected to embody these results manifestly in themselves, so as to recommend them by example as well as by precept. But for all their talk of being 'doctors' of the soul and 'legislators' for the good life, they could not operate directly and actively on their patients as literal doctors did; and they did not habitually play the role of active expert assistants in key encounters in their clients' lives, as lawyers did. Doctors and lawyers took the responsibility and did the work for you (indeed, in the case of doctors, on you) in a way philosophers did not.[5]

This leads neatly enough to one of this volume's leading areas of concern: the degree to which the practical disciplines of medicine and law could, in their written products, overshoot the practical, in the quest for (among other things) firmer theoretical foundations and greater intellectual respectability. Here it is immediately obvious that there cannot but be a marked contrast, amounting to a kind of inversion. As just noted, although asserting practical ends, philosophy in contrast to both medicine and law is a discipline that both *begins* with theory and remains rooted in it and validated by it throughout. Its problem is if anything the other way round: not whether it can usefully and successfully go beyond the practical into the theoretical, but whether it can ever get successfully as far as the practical from its theoretical starting-point.

And that is indeed notoriously an issue, both for philosophers themselves, and for their frequently sceptical lay observers. In its crudest version, most familiar probably from Lucian, it takes the form of the satirical perception of philosophers as comically and culpably unable either to bring about the good results in their

[5] I have deliberately drawn this contrast in fairly blunt terms; it does of course need some nuancing. On the legal side, it can fairly be urged that accumulating a body of written material and theoretical discussion was more important to that profession and status within it than it was for doctors. On the philosophical side, active practical intervention in the lives of others went on (ideally at least) in a number of different forms: think of the distinct models of the philosophical adviser or house philosopher, as exemplified by the unfortunate Stoic Thesmopolis in Lucian's *Merc. Cond.* (33–34); the philosophical 'flying doctor', as modelled by Dio Chrysostom (cf. Trapp, '*Philotimia*' (2012) 138–141); and the consultant visited by his 'patients', as represented in Arrian's *Epict. diss.* (e.g. 3.23.28–30, on which see further below).

pupils that they so loudly promise, or indeed even to practice what they preach in their own lives. So in the *Hermotimus* the philosophy tutor whose pupil has demonstrated his improved moral character by abducting and raping his poor neighbour's daughter continues to demand payment of his fees on the lame grounds that the boy would have been an even worse criminal had it not been for his philosophy lessons.[6] Or in the *Symposium* (significantly subtitled *The Lapiths*)—to give just one example out of many possible—the assembled philosophers, far from indulging in high-minded and sophisticated discussion, or even demonstrating normal social good manners, quarrel over the seating-plan, come to blows over their doctrinal differences, and generally abandon themselves to their gastric and sexual appetites.[7]

But proper management of the relationship between the theoretical and the practical was a talking-point also at a higher level, within the philosophical community, here too with a range of different possible emphases. Philosophers can be found debating both the relative merits of practical precepts as against systematic theoretical understanding (Seneca *Ep.* 94–95, looking back on a long history of discussion within Stoicism), and the rival claims of the practical and theoretical lives as the best philosophical ideal (Max. Tyr. 15–16, again drawing on a long tradition of discussion in the Platonic and Aristotelian tradition). To illustrate with just the one specific example, Maximus of Tyre in *Orations* 15 and 16 stages a debate between advocates of the rival virtues of practical action and theoretical contemplation. In *Oration* 15, the voice in favour of action urges that unless the philosopher sticks his head above the parapet and puts his hard-won wisdom and knowledge at the service of ordinary people in the real world (in *ἔργον καὶ πρᾶξις καὶ χρῆσις βίου πολιτική*, 15.7), he is frustrating its natural purpose:[8]

> *τίς ὄνησις τοῦ εἰδέναι <μὴ χρωμένῳ> εἰς ἅπερ συντελεῖ τὸ εἰδέναι; τίς χρεία ἰατρῷ τῆς τέχνης, μὴ ὑγιάζοντι κατὰ τὴν τέχνην; τίς χρεία Φειδίᾳ τῆς τέχνης, μὴ προστιθέντι τῷ ἐλέφαντι καὶ τῷ χρυσῷ;*
>
> [W]hat is the good of knowledge if it is not exercised towards the proper goals? What use is medical expertise to a doctor if he does not use it to cure people? What use is artistic genius to Phidias if he does not apply it to ivory and gold?

In the following oration the counter-plea is initially put into the mouth of Anaxagoras, who argues that in withdrawing from the political community in favour of solitary contemplation, he is in fact doing his proper job and, albeit invisibly, promoting the best interests of his fellow citizens; his specialism is the

[6] Lucian *Hermot.* 80–82.
[7] Lucian *Symp. passim*, but cf. also e.g. *Hermot.* 9 and 11–12, *Pisc.* 41–52.
[8] Max. Tyr. 15.6.

pursuit of knowledge through the exercise of reason, from which all else will follow provided only that he is allowed to devote himself to this mission undistracted:[9]

> *τὰ γὰρ κοινὰ σώζεσθαι φιλεῖ, οὐκ ἐὰν τὰ τείχη ὑμῖν ἀραρότα ᾖ... τὸ δὲ σῶζον τὰς πόλεις ἡ ἁρμονία καὶ ὁ τῆς πολιτείας κόσμος· ταῦτα δὲ ὑπὸ τῆς εὐνομίας γίγνεται, τὴν δὲ εὐνομίαν ἡ τῶν χρωμένων ἀρετὴ φυλάττει, τὴν δὲ ἀρετὴν διδόασιν οἱ λόγοι, τοὺς δὲ λόγους ἡ ἄσκησις, τὴν δὲ ἄσκησιν ἡ ἀλήθεια, τὴν δὲ ἀλήθεαιν ἡ περὶ αὐτὴν σχολή.... τοῦτο ἡ διατριβή, τοῦτο ἡ σχολή....*
>
> The preservation of the state does not depend on well-built walls... [but on] harmony and an ordered constitution; harmony and an ordered constitution are the product of a disposition to obey the laws; the disposition to obey the laws is secured by the virtue of those who live under them; virtue is the product of the exercise of reason; the exercise of reason is secured by practice, practice by truth, and truth by the leisure to pursue it.... That is how I use my time, this is my 'leisure'....[10]

But yet another voice—the orator's own—then intervenes, to urge that, however true this claim may be, it is still more interestingly true that the pursuit of rational insight in philosophical contemplation, whirling the intellect away from all mundane concerns, is an exalted and inspiring end in itself.[11]

It is indeed true that, in the case both of the active and contemplative lives and of the relative merits of precept and theory, the proposition that the ultimate purpose of any philosophical activity remains practical—bettering souls and promoting more truly fulfilled lives—is not called into question; the issue for argument is the right balance between the two—how firmly the proper business of philosophy lies with the theoretical understanding from which practical betterment can flow, rather than in active measures to ensure that the potential of philosophical understanding to secure practical results is actually realized. But this is quite enough to show both the commonality with medicine and law, and the degree of difference. Practice versus theory is an issue for both, but with strikingly different emphases.

What then of another of this volume's leading themes: the medium of communication, the encounter of technical writing with rhetoric and with aesthetic appeal? This too is a problem for philosophers with a directness and a complexity that doctors and lawyers are mercifully spared. Once more it is not hard to see why. Doctors and lawyers are specialists, who write with a range of purposes: to

[9] Max. Tyr. 16.3.

[10] A discussion indebted at some remove to Aristotle's attempted co-ordination of the theoretical and the practical (political) in *Pol.* 8.1–3.

[11] Max. Tyr. 16.6.

win position among fellow specialists; to teach trainee, future specialists; to spread at least some of their knowledge to a wider readership; and to win public recognition and status as experts, with the social and material benefits that follow. All of these aims can be felt as making aesthetic and persuasive demands beyond austere professional clarity and logical cogency. Other contributors to this volume have analysed some excellent examples of both doctors and lawyers deploying rhetorical resources to establish their professional superiority to rival specialists in writings principally for insiders to the trade. But it is equally obvious that a wider readership will shy away from technical writing if it does not come up to some level of accessibility and literary finish, and in the civic worlds of the Roman Empire recognition and high public honour are overwhelmingly more likely to be accorded to those who can match the depth of their knowledge with the formal and stylistic finish of the rhetorically cultivated.[12] It is not however the case for doctors or lawyers that rhetorical form and aesthetically pleasing stylistic finish raise a problem of principle, or arouse any anxiety that in co-opting the resources of rhetoric they may somehow be compromising themselves.[13] Which is precisely what does happen for philosophers.

There is of course a long back-history here. Plato's condemnation of rhetoric and all its works in the *Gorgias* as directly and multiply antithetical to philosophy, not just as a guide to structuring words but also as a value-scheme and a mode of interpersonal relationships, may not have been definitive—it was after all substantially nuanced by Plato himself in the *Phaedrus*, then directly challenged by Aristotle—but it put the issue of the properly philosophical way to communicate in words (whether written or spoken) on the agenda for keeps.[14] By the imperial period, generations of reflection, accompanied by practical experiment, on how best to convey the deep insights and saving truths of philosophy not just to fellow philosophers, but to the wider world, had generated a large and varied body of outreach materials, accompanied by sporadic incidents of theoretical reflection (generated both by didactically minded philosophers and by scholars and critics seeking to classify the forms of this growing body of writing), but also a set of recurrent scruples and anxieties about best practice.

On the one hand, the need for the truths of philosophy to be disseminated as widely as possible by some means or another was unchallengeable, because written into the understanding of what philosophy was that had been universally inherited from Socrates, Plato, and Aristotle. Achieving understanding of the reality of the world was not an end in itself; it was a means to fulfilled existence, not just for the specialist, but for any and every human being simply in virtue of their human

[12] Schmitz, *Bildung* (1997) 39–66; Lendon, *Empire* (1997) 36–47.

[13] See the contribution of Babusiaux and Bubb in this volume for more on doctors' and lawyers' relationship to rhetoric.

[14] Vickers, *Defence* (1989) 148–213; Trapp, 'Due Respect' (2020).

nature. There might therefore be room for discussion of who and how many the communicators should be (and correspondingly, how many could properly be freed from any obligation to communicate beyond the circle of their immediate pupils), but not of the need itself. But at the same time, communication had its pitfalls.

For it was also written into the self-understanding of philosophy that the insight it promoted, and the values and standards of conduct that flowed from this insight, ought to take its adherent in directions sharply at odds with the everyday and the conventional. The value of philosophy was precisely that it turned one away from unthinking adherence to social convention and towards a better founded and more deeply profitable outlook.[15] This naturally involved acknowledging the ultimate worthlessness of what the conventionally minded throng regarded as admirable and worthy of pursuit, and coming to see it as a mere diversion, or worse a seduction, from the proper business of enlightened living.[16]

Among the idols thus to be relinquished was rhetoric. In the ordinary world, as embodied in the structures and procedures of civic society as well as in individual life-plans, the acquisition, employment, and display of the skills of structured speaking was a key factor in the pursuit and distribution of status and respect.[17] But to the philosophical eye, status and respect are not valuable goals, and it is both an error and a distraction to suppose that they are: to value rhetoric and the ends it secures is to succumb to mistaken desire and the lures of harmful pleasure. And this in turn leads to a bind. On the one hand, how is the conscientious philosopher to communicate if not by employing the resources of rhetoric? Communication means adjusting to the tastes and expectations of the target audience, and the target audience likes and expects verbal structures shaped and styled as standard teaching dictates; this is how best to secure a hearing for the content of the message. But, on the other hand, that very shaping and styling embodies a false sense of what really matters, and thereby risks distracting the target audience, reinforcing their mistaken values, rather than enlightening them—and worse still, it risks seducing the philosophical teacher himself.

My touchstone text in this respect is one of Arrian's representations of the discourses of Epictetus: *πρὸς τοὺς ἀναγιγνώσκοντας καὶ διαλεγομένους ἐπιδεικτικῶς* ("A response to those who give readings and lectures for mere display," 3.23), where the acerbic Stoic is depicted laying into both speakers and audiences. Properly understood, the conscientious philosophical speaker should

[15] The Socrates of *Apol.* 29d–30a is a foundational and emblematic figure in this respect: "'Excellent friend,' I shall say; 'You are an Athenian. Your city is the most important and renowned for its wisdom and power; so are you not ashamed that, while you take care to acquire as much wealth as possible, with honour and glory as well, yet you take no care or thought for understanding and truth, or for the best possible state of your soul'" (tr. Waterfield)—as resumed in (e.g.) Dio Chrys. *Or.* 13.16–22.

[16] See for instance Sen. *Ep.* 7.2 and 94.52ff. and Arr. *Epict. diss.* 1.27 on the dangers of seduction by circumstances and habit (cf. Trapp, *Philosophy* (2007) 44–45).

[17] See Schmitz, *Bildung* (1997) 39–66.

summon his audience to hear that they are in a bad way, unfortunate and unhappy, because ignorant of what is really good and evil, and so taking care for everything but what they ought (3.23.28). And ideally, the audience member should go away saying to his companion, "That philosopher has well and truly seized hold of me: I must no longer behave as I do" (3.23.37). For the philosopher's lecture-hall is a moral surgery, in which the proper aim of the speaker should be to diagnose moral faults, and that of the audience to experience the salutary pain of their uncovering (3.23.30); it is not a place for displays of fine style and gratifying bursts of applause. But as things actually are, speakers ask anxiously after they have finished, "What did you think of me? . . . And how about my *ecphrasis* on Pan and the Nymphs?" (3.23.11). Audiences interject "bravo" at specially fine passages (3.23.32), and leave saying things to each other like, "That bit about Xerxes was neatly expressed" and "No, I thought the bit about Thermopylae was better" (3.23.38). "Is that really a philosophical lecture?" asks Epictetus, "Was anyone while listening to you reading or discoursing stricken with self-anguish, or turned back in on himself?"

This concern with what one might call the problem of aesthetic listening is anything but unique to Arrian's Epictetus; it is also confronted, in different versions (and perhaps differing degrees of honesty) by Seneca and Maximus, and it is there in the background to Plutarch's *De audiendo*.[18] The point I want to make by drawing attention to it is not that philosophers parted company with doctors and lawyers by not accompanying them into excursions into rhetoricizing form and fine style; of course they did venture onto the same ground, and for the good reasons that we have reviewed. It is rather that in this domain too, as with the question of the balance of the theoretical with the practical, philosophers saw a problem that called for theoretical reflection and debate in its own right; and they responded richly to the call, if sometimes with a vehemence that betrays a continuing unease.

Talking about philosophy's sometimes cautious, arm's-length relationship with rhetoric, fine style and aesthetic pleasure has in effect also moved us already towards the last of this volume's principal areas of concern, the issue of competition and competitiveness. Here there is certainly plenty to say about both inter- and intra-sectarian competitiveness within the philosophical family, and about how here once more philosophers had a particular problem of principle—if all philosophers alike pursue the truth, and truth must be one and unitary, how is the division of the philosophical landscape into warring sects (*haireseis*) to be regarded?[19] But for reasons of space, I shall concentrate instead on the

[18] Sen. *Ep.* 108.5–7; Max. Tyr. 1.7, 25.6–7; Plut. *De aud.* 9.42c–e.

[19] This is a concern that surfaces with a special visibility in the work of Maximus of Tyre (e.g. 1.10, 4.1–3, 26.2, 29.7), even if accompanied in his case with a bland confidence that it can be satisfactorily dealt with: Trapp, *Maximus* (1997) xxx–xxxii; cf. Kindstrand, 'Date' (1980). On intra-philosophical competitiveness more generally, see Trapp, 'Authority' (2017) 41–48.

outward-facing side of the issue: competition in engagement with public space, performance, and spectacle.

The same obligation to communicate—to spread the felicific truths of philosophy to humankind at large—that impelled philosophers into an engagement with rhetoric was also, to a degree at least, an incentive to assume some kind of visible, public presence. We should of course beware of overstating the power or the reach of this incentive, because there were in theory perfectly good reasons for some philosophers not to feel subject to it. Anyone who embraced a version of the theoretic ideal enunciated by Maximus's Anaxagoras could feel justified in leaving the downward and outward communication to others, while he himself thought his high thoughts in solitude; and an Epicurean would have to reflect carefully on the balance of the trade-off between the likely short-term upset, and the possible long-term enhancement of security and calm, that engagement with the everyday world would bring him. But overall, for the imperial period, public visibility is the norm rather than the exception.

The issue—once again both for philosophers and for their lay observers—was how to do it properly. Just what degree of involvement with the ordinary civic world and its manners and procedures was both effective and consistent with good philosophical values? Two examples, both from the late first or early second century CE and both involving small provincial towns, show reflective philosophers concluding that good results could flow from an intelligently qualified involvement. In the Carian town of Oenoanda, the affluent Epicurean Diogenes decided that the best way of getting the Epicurean message across to a larger number of fellow-citizens than he could buttonhole individually, and after his death as well as during his lifetime, was to finance the building of a stoa, where those gratefully enjoying its shade, or using its space to do business, could read it from a huge inscription all along the back wall.[20] Across the Aegean, building on his own experience in the local politics of Chaeronea, Plutarch in his *Precepts for Politics* paints a picture of the philosophically responsible politician participating actively and visibly in practical administrative activities (down to and including supervising the drains and the removal of night-soil, 811a–c), but relying on more unobtrusive persuasion and personal example to further his task of bettering his fellow citizens morally; he compares the enlightened statesman's influence to that of a fine wine, gradually seeping into the system of the drinker (799b).[21]

In both cases the course chosen or recommended involves a degree of engagement with the normal civic round, but a restricted one. Diogenes plays the civic euergete, but then leaves his benefaction to do its work by itself. Plutarch, more

[20] Diogenes of Oenoanda *fr.* 1–2. For the text of the Diogenes inscription, see Smith, *Diogenes* (1993) and *Supplement* (2003); for discussion, Smith, *Diogenes* (2003); Gordon, *Epicurus* (1996); and 'Epicureanism' (2017); Warren, 'Diogenes' (2000).

[21] On Plutarch's *Precepts* and their model of philosophical visibility, see further Trapp, 'Statesmanship' (2004).

strikingly, not only recommends the subtle approach, where engagement *qua* philosopher rather than *qua* administrator is involved, but also explicitly counsels against becoming sucked in to other aspects of standard civic practice. In particular, he warns the philosophically responsible statesman about the dangers of *philotimia*—ambition, competitiveness—and the pursuit of its standard physical embodiments:[22]

> ἡ δὲ φιλοτιμία, καίπερ οὖσα σοβαρωτέρα τῆς φιλοκερδείας, οὐκ ἐλάττονας ἔχει κῆρας ἐν πολιτείᾳ... ὥσπερ οὖν ὁ Πλάτων ἀκουστέον εἶναι τοῖς νέοις ἔλεγεν ἐκ παίδων εὐθύς, ὡς οὔτε περικεῖσθαι χρυσὸν αὐτοῖς ἔξωθεν οὔτε κεκτῆσθαι θέμις, οἰκεῖον ἐν τῇ ψυχῇ συμμεμιγμένον ἔχοντας... οὕτω παραμυθώμεθα τὴν φιλοτιμίαν, λέγοντες ἐν ἑαυτοῖς ἔχειν χρυσὸν ἀδιάφθορον καὶ ἀκήρατον καὶ ἄχραντον ὑπὸ φθόνου καὶ μώμου τιμήν, ἅμα λογισμῷ καὶ παραθεωρήσει τῶν πεπραγμένων ἡμῖν καὶ πεπολιτευμένων αὐξανόμενον. διὸ μὴ δεῖσθαι γραφομένων τιμῶν ἢ πλαττομένων ἢ χαλκοτυπουμένων, ἐν αἷς καὶ τὸ εὐδοκιμοῦν ἀλλότριόν ἐστιν.
>
> But ambition (*philotimia*), even though it is a more impressive word than 'acquisitiveness' (*philokerdia*), is no less pernicious for the civic community.... So just as Plato used to say that young people should be told from childhood that it isn't right for them to wear gold body-ornaments or own gold, because they have their own gold blended with their souls... let us talk down our ambitiousness in the same way, saying that we have within ourselves a worth like pure undefiled gold, which envy and criticism cannot stain and which grows with the exercise of reason and the contemplation of our deeds and public actions. We therefore have no need of status-markers that are painted or moulded or cast in bronze, in which the real object of admiration is somebody else's work.

In this angle of vision, philosophers, to be properly philosophical, should foreswear the normal competitiveness of the gubernatorial elite in public space, and take no interest in the manifest tokens of its success: honorific decrees and inscriptions, civic crowns, and statues.

But in propounding this high-minded view, however, Plutarch is self-consciously striking out against the current. For we know, from a gratifyingly rich and varied set of evidence, just how enmeshed philosophers, just as much as doctors and lawyers, were in this world of civic competition and honour. For a member of the privileged class, being a philosopher was something one could expect to be respected, congratulated, honoured, and even financially rewarded for.

There are again a number of strands of thought and practice in play. Philosophers were ornaments to their community in part because philosophy was a great Hellenic achievement, with a pantheon of past greats and a rich literary

[22] Plut. *Prae. ger. reip.* 819f–820a.

heritage. But they were also perceived as conferring a practical, educational benefit: from the Hellenistic period onwards in the civic imagination, the proper function of the philosopher was "associating with the young" (συνεῖναι τοῖς νέοις)—this is what their services were sought out for, and they could rightly be thanked and honoured for.[23] It was in this guise that they qualified under the Empire, for a while, along with doctors, teachers of oratory, and secondary-school teachers, for tax exemption (ἀτέλεια).[24] There were even such things as salaried posts—chairs—in philosophy as well as in oratory: on the grandest scale, the four chairs at Athens, endowed by Marcus Aurelius in 176 CE, on salaries of (it was said) 60,000 sesterces a year.[25] These were not only marks of public status and respect, but also prizes to be competed for. Notwithstanding Plutarch's principled disapproval, statues were set up not only of the greats of the past, but also of distinguished contemporaries: we possess a number of inscribed bases (one perhaps for a statue of Apuleius as *philosophus Platonicus*), and also inscriptions recording official decisions to dedicate them (as for instance that commissioned in honour of his father, also a philosopher, by the Peripatetic Alexander of Aphrodisias).[26] And besides the statues, there were other honorific inscriptions too.[27] Celebrated among these latter are the co-ordinated pair from the first century CE in Athens and Ephesus honouring the *theologos* Ofellius Laetus as a reincarnation of Plato.[28] The Ephesian item names him, identifies him as an expert in Platonism, and praises him for his "comprehensive excellence"; it then quotes a single elegiac couplet.

Ὀφέλλιον Λαῖτον Πλατωνικὸν φιλόσ[οφον]
ἐπιδειξάμενον λόγων καὶ ἠθῶν πᾶ[σαν]
ἀρετήν
εἰ κατὰ Πυθαγόραν ψυχὴ μεταβαίνει ἐς ἄλλον,
ἐν σοί, Λαῖτε, Πλάτων ζῇ πάλι σωζόμενος

In honour of Ofellius Laetus, Platonist philosopher, / who has demonstrated comprehensive excellence in his writings and his character: / "If indeed, as

[23] E.g. *SEG* 1.368; Lucian *Eun.* 3; Plut. *Cic.* 24.

[24] *Digest* 27.1.6.8. Bowersock, *Sophists* (1969) 33; Griffin, 'Rev. Bowersock' (1971) 279–280; Millar, *Emperor* (1977) 491–506; Trapp, *Philosophy* (2007) 19–20.

[25] Dio Cass. 71.21; Lucian *Eun.* 3; Philostr. *VS* 2.2.566; Tatian *Or.* 19. Millar, *Emperor* (1977) 502; Hahn, *Philosoph* (1989) 119–127.

[26] For Apuleius: *ILAlg* 1.2115 (Madauros); cf. *IK* 17,2, 4340 (Secundinus of Tralles, Platonist). For Alexander of Aphrodisias: Chaniotis, 'New inscriptions' (2004) 388–389; Sharples, 'Implications' (2005).

[27] On philosopher inscriptions and other forms of public honour, see Tod, 'Sidelights' (1957); Barnes, 'Ancient Philosophers' (2002); Scholz, 'Peripatetic Philosophers' (2004); Trapp, *Philosophy* (2007) 246–247; https://inscriptions.packhum.org/allregions (search for φιλοσοφ-).

[28] *IK* 17,2, 3901; *IG* 2^2 3816 (Athens). See Nollé, 'Ofellius' (1981); Bowersock, 'Plutarch' (1982); Runia, 'Heresiography' (1988) 242–243. One might add also the inscriptions honouring Arrian as *philosophos* noted in Bowersock, 'New Inscription' (1967) and Oliver, 'Arrian' (1970).

Pythagoras teaches, the soul migrates to another body, / then Plato lives in you, Laetus, restored to life."

The Athenian inscription consists of elegiacs alone: the same two, but preceded by another couplet:

θειολόγου Λαίτοιο μετάρσιον ὕμνον ἀκούσας
οὐρανὸν ἀνθρώποις εἶδον ἀνοιγόμενον·
εἰ κατὰ Πυθαγόραν ψυχὴ μεταβαίνει ἐς ἄλλον,
ἐν σοί, Λαῖτε, Πλάτων ζῇ πάλι σωζόμενος.

On hearing the lofty strains (*hymnos*) of Laetus the theologian, / I saw the heavens opened up to man. / If indeed, as Pythagoras teaches, the soul migrates to another body, / then Plato lives in you, Laetus, restored to life.

Philosophers, and the word 'philosopher' as a term of commendation, were thus drawn into the game and the vocabulary of public honour, and the opportunities for competition opened up were embraced by at least some. The situation could hardly have been otherwise, given that philosophers, besides being philosophers, were also members of the leisured gubernatorial elite, to whom competing for marks of distinction in some field or another came almost as naturally as breathing. In this respect at least, we find them once more on all fours with our lawyers and doctors. Yet in this domain too, there is a difference, specific to their peculiar, uneasily positioned calling. Both they and their lay observers have to negotiate with the feeling that they do not in fact entirely belong in this frame.

We have already seen Plutarch's principled reservations, from within the philosophical fold. But a corresponding perception was abroad outside it too. The obvious place to look first, as with the perceptions of philosophical hypocrisy I was discussing earlier, is once more Lucian's satire. In the *Life of Peregrinus* we find him castigating the tasteless, opportunistic showmanship both of the eponymous Peregrinus himself and of his Cynic supporters and PR men. In the *Eunuch* he turns his fire on the spectacle of two rival Peripatetics competing in public for the privilege of succeeding to the Athenian chair. But this sour perception of philosophers being out of place precisely when they compete for public position and respect crops up elsewhere too. One alternative instance comes in Aelius Aristides's first *Response to Plato*, the *In Defence of Oratory* (*Or.* 2). Here, reversing a Platonic taunt against oratory from the *Gorgias*, Aristides complains at the way that philosophers, though doing in effect no more for public morals than is effected everyday by humble nursemaids and pedagogues, loudly lay claim to superior public status:[29]

[29] Aristid. *Or.* 2.380.

> *σεμνύνονται καὶ γαυριῶσιν καὶ πρωτείων ἀντιποιοῦνται καὶ μεγάλους αὑτοὺς ἄγουσι καὶ ταὐτὰ λέγοντες ἐν αὑτοῖς, καὶ οὔτε τοῖς ῥήτορσιν ὑπείκουσιν οὔτε τοῖς παιδαγωγοῖς ἴσον οἴονται δεῖν φρονεῖν.*
>
> giv[ing] themselves airs and pranc[ing] about and claim[ing] first place (*prōteia*) and think[ing] themselves very grand for saying just the same things among themselves, neither yield[ing] to orators nor think[ing] that they should put themselves on a level with child-minders.

But I am still more taken by yet another piece of evidence, from an administrative rather than from a literary source.

As noted, there was a stretch of time under the Empire when philosophers qualified for tax immunity as valued contributors to public education and culture (along with doctors, though not lawyers). Yet here, too, it looks as if they were not felt to belong as securely as the other professional groups granted the privilege. For a start, it seems that they were not included in the first version of the relevant legislation, passed under Vespasian; they were added as a second thought, sometime between Vespasian and Trajan. More tellingly still, when under Antoninus Pius the time came to save imperial expenditure by limiting the numbers qualifying for immunities, it was the philosophers who lost out worst. In the words of the imperial rescript preserved in the *Digest*:[30]

> *φιλοσόφων δὲ οὐκ ἐτάχθη ἀριθμὸς διὰ τὸ σπανίους εἶναι τοὺς φιλοσοφοῦντας· οἶμαι δὲ ὅτι οἱ πλούτῳ ὑπερβάλλοντες ἐθελονταὶ παρέξουσι τὰς ἀπὸ τῶν χρημάτων ὠφελείας ταῖς πατρίσιν, εἰ δὲ ἀκριβολογοῖντο περὶ τὰς οὐσίας, αὐτόθεν ἤδη φανεροὶ γενήσονται μὴ φιλοσοφοῦντες.*
>
> No number was set for philosophers, because practitioners of *philosophia* are few and far between. I believe that the very wealthy will voluntarily provide financial support to their home towns; and if they quibble about their wealth, that very action will make it clear that they are not true philosophers.

That is to say, far from the refusal to set a number allowing cities to exempt as many philosophers as they liked, the enactment in fact encouraged them to exempt none at all, on grounds maliciously drawn from philosophy's own self-image (true philosophers are few, and philosophers are above mere wealth). In the eye of officialdom, it would seem, philosophers belonged to the crumbly periphery of the class of acknowledged contributors to the common good, not to its solid core.[31] But this official view chimed with a wider general uncertainty about just where philosophers belonged in relation to society and the political community at

[30] Modest. (2 *excusat.*) D. 27.1.6.7.

[31] Trapp, *Philosophy* (2007) 251–252.

large; and this was an uncertainty felt, even if in different ways, by philosophers themselves as well as by their more or less sympathetic lay observers.

Philosophers, then, to conclude, were interestingly comparable to doctors and lawyers in their negotiation of the balance between the theoretical and the practical, and in the degree and nature of their engagements with the values, procedures, and communicative forms of public life. They were interestingly unlike them in having particular problems of principle and perception arising from this engagement. These problems in their turn are connected to the distinctive, and curious nature of their calling. To pick up another thread from earlier in this volume, the difficulty can be spotlighted, among other ways, by asking about their professionalism. They can speak of themselves as standing out from the herd of laymen (ἰδιῶται), which implies that they have a distinctive *technē*. But what is that *technē*? When asked this question, they can only reply 'the art of life', *technē peri ton bion* (*ars vitae*)[32]—which is manifestly not a skill or a craft on all fours with those of doctors, or lawyers, or, come to that, architects. It is only metaphorically a *technē*, and its literal correlate is fuzzy. Philosophers cannot nail the challenge of explaining to themselves or to the outside world—in terms that the outside world would acknowledge as decisive—just what it is they do and why they matter. So, of course they had distinctive problems in engaging with the rest of their society, of a kind that doctors and lawyers in general did not have to worry about.

Bibliography

Barnes, 'Ancient Philosophers' (2002) = J. Barnes, 'Ancient Philosophers,' in G. Clark and T. Rajak, eds., *Philosophy and Power in the Greco-Roman World* (Oxford: Oxford University Press, 2002) 293–306.

Bowersock, 'New Inscription' (1967) = G. W. Bowersock, 'A New Inscription of Arrian,' *Greek Roman and Byzantine Studies* 8 (1967) 279–280.

Bowersock, *Greek Sophists* (1969) = G. W. Bowersock, *Greek Sophists in the Roman Empire* (Oxford: Oxford University Press 1969).

Bowersock, 'Plutarch' (1982) = G. W. Bowersock, 'Plutarch and the Sublime Hymn of Ofellius Laetus,' *Greek Roman and Byzantine Studies* 22 (1982) 275–279.

Chaniotis, 'New Inscriptions' (2004) = A. Chaniotis, 'New Inscriptions from Aphrodisias (1992–2001),' *American Journal of Archaeology* 108 (2004) 377–416.

Frede, 'Philosopher' (2000) = M. Frede, 'The Philosopher,' in J. Brunschwig and G. Lloyd, eds., *Greek Thought. A Guide to Classical Knowledge* (Cambridge, MA: Harvard University Press) 1–19.

[32] E.g. *SVF* 2.35, 3.598; Philo *Leg. all.* 1.57; Arr. *Epict.* 1.15.2; Plut. *Quaest. conv.* 613b; Clem. *Paed.* 2.25.3; Cic. *Acad.* 2.8.23; *Fin.* 3.4; Sen. fr. 17 Haase (Lact. *Div.* 3.15); Sellars, *Art* (2009) 5–6, 55–57.

Gordon, *Epicurus* (1996) = P. Gordon, *Epicurus in Lycia. The Second-Century World of Diogenes of Oenoanda* (Ann Arbor, MI: University of Michigan Press, 1996).

Gordon, 'Epicureanism' (2017) = P. Gordon, 'Epicureanism Writ Large: Diogenes of Oenoanda,' in D. Richter and W. Johnson, eds., *The Oxford Handbook of the Second Sophistic* (New York: Oxford University Press) 539–550.

Griffin, 'Rev. Bowersock' (1971) = M. Griffin, review of Bowersock, *Greek Sophists* (1969), *Journal of Roman Studies* 61 (1971) 279–280.

Hahn, *Philosoph* (1989) = J. Hahn, *Der Philosoph und die Gesellschaft* (Stuttgart: Steiner, 1989).

Kindstrand, 'Date' (1980) = J. Kindstrand, 'The Date and Character of Hermias' *Irrisio*,' *Vigiliae Christianae* 34 (1980) 341–357.

Lendon, *Empire* (1997) = J. E. Lendon, *Empire of Honour* (Oxford: Oxford University Press, 1997).

Millar, *Emperor* (1977) = F. G. B. Millar, *The Emperor in the Roman World* (London: Duckworth, 1977).

Oliver, 'Arrian' (1970) = J. H. Oliver, 'Arrian and the Gellii of Corinth,' *Greek Roman and Byzantine Studies* 11 (1970) 335–338.

Nollé, 'Ofellius' (1981) = J. Nollé, 'Ofellius Laetus, platonischer Philosoph,' *Zeitschrift für Papyrologie und Epigraphik* 41 (1981) 197–206.

Runia, 'Heresiography' (1988) = D. Runia, 'Philosophical Heresiography: Evidence in Two Ephesian Inscriptions,' *Zeitschrift für Papyrologie und Epigraphik* 72 (1988) 241–243.

Schmitz, *Bildung* (1997) = T. Schmitz, *Bildung und Macht. Zur sozialen und politischen Funktion der zweiten Sophistik in der griechischen Welt der Kaiserzeit* (Munich: Beck, 1997).

Sellars, *Art* (2009) = J. Sellars, *The Art of Living: The Stoics on the Nature and Function of Philosophy* (rev. ed., London: Bloomsbury, 2009).

Sharples, 'Implications' (2005) = R. W. Sharples, 'The Implications of the New Alexander of Aphrodisias Inscription,' *Bulletin of the Institute of Classical Studies* 48 (2005) 47–56.

Scholz, 'Peripatetic Philosophers' (2004) = P. Scholz, 'Peripatetic Philosophers as Wandering Scholars: Some Historical Remarks on the Socio-political Conditions of Philosophizing in the Third Century BCE,' in W. Fortenbaugh and S. White, eds., *Lyco of Troas and Hieronymus of Rhodes* (New Brunswick: Transaction, 2004) 315–353.

Smith, *Diogenes* (1993) = M. F. Smith, *Diogenes of Oenoanda, The Epicurean Inscription* (Naples: Bibliopolis, 1993).

Smith, *Supplement* (2003) = M. F. Smith, *Supplement to Diogenes of Oenoanda, The Epicurean Inscription* (Naples: Bibliopolis, 2003).

Tod, 'Sidelights' (1957) = M. N. Tod, 'Sidelights on Greek Philosophers,' *Journal of Hellenic Studies* 77 (1957) 132–141.

Trapp, *Maximus* (1997) = M. B. Trapp, *Maximus of Tyre. The Philosophical Orations* (Oxford: Oxford University Press, 1997).

Trapp, 'Plato' (2000) = M. B. Trapp, 'Plato in Athenaeus' *Deipnosophists*,' in D. Braund and J. Wilkins, eds., *Athenaeus and His World* (Exeter: Exeter University Press, 2000) 353–364.

Trapp, 'Statesmanship' (2004) = M. B. Trapp, 'Statesmanship in a Minor Key?' in L. de Blois, J. Bons, T. Kessels, and D. Schenkeveld, eds., *The Statesman in Plutarch's Works* (Leiden: Brill, 2004) 189–200.

Trapp, *Philosophy* (2007) = M. B. Trapp, *Philosophy in the Roman Empire* (Aldershot: Ashgate, 2007).

Trapp, '*Philotimia*' (2012) = M. B. Trapp, '*Philotimia* and Dio Chrysostom,' in G. Roskam, M. de Pourcq, and L Van der Stockt, eds, *The Lash of Ambition: Plutarch, Imperial Greek literature and the Dynamics of* philotimia (Louvain: Peeters, 2012) 119–141.

Trapp, 'Authority' (2017) = M. B. Trapp, 'Philosophical Authority,' in G. Woolf and J. König, eds., *Authority and Expertise in Ancient Scientific Culture* (Cambridge: Cambridge University Press, 2017) 27–57.

Trapp, 'Due Respect' (2020) = M. B. Trapp, 'With All Due Respect to Plato: The *Platonic Orations* of Aelius Aristides,' *Transactions of the American Philological Association* 150 (2020) 85–113.

Vickers, *Defence* (1989) = B. Vickers, *In Defence of Rhetoric* (Oxford: Oxford University Press, 1989).

Warren, 'Diogenes' (2000) = J. Warren, 'Diogenes *Epikourios*: Keep Taking the Tablets,' *Journal of Hellenic Studies* 120 (2000) 144–148.

Index of Subjects

For the benefit of digital users, indexed terms that span two pages (e.g., 52–53) may, on occasion, appear on only one of those pages.

Index Locorum

For the benefit of digital users, indexed terms that span two pages (e.g., 52–53) may, on occasion, appear on only one of those pages.

Made in the USA
Las Vegas, NV
19 September 2026

d3e3b296-6faf-4bea-a750-471490fcfc4eR01